Pablo Picasso

Carsten-Peter Warncke

Pablo Picasso
1881–1973

Edited by
Ingo F. Walther

PART I
The Works 1890–1936

TASCHEN

KÖLN LONDON LOS ANGELES MADRID PARIS TOKYO

Front cover:
Pablo Picasso. Photograph by Irving Penn
Cannes, France 1957
Copyright © 1960 Irving Penn, Courtesy *Vogue*

Endpapers:
The Crucifixion (after Grünewald)
Paris, Musée Picasso
(cf. p. 337)

Frontispiece:
Pablo Picasso, Photograph by Man Ray, c. 1931/32

This work was originally published
in 2 volumes.

To stay informed about upcoming TASCHEN titles,
please request our magazine at www.taschen.com or write to
TASCHEN America, 6671 Sunset Boulevard, Suite 1508, USA-Los Angeles, CA 90028,
Fax: +1-323-463.4442. We will be happy to send you a free copy of our magazine
which is filled with information about all of our books.

© 2002 TASCHEN GmbH
Hohenzollernring 53, D–50672 Köln
www.taschen.com
Original edition © 1992 Benedikt Taschen Verlag GmbH
© Succession Picasso/ VG Bild-Kunst, Bonn 2002
Edited and produced by Ingo F. Walther, Munich
Cover design: Angelika Taschen, Cologne;
Mark Thomson, London

Printed in Slovenia
ISBN 3–8228–1257–9

Contents

Self-portrait: "Yo Picasso"
Paris, spring 1901. Oil on canvas, 73.5 x 60.5 cm
Zervos XXI, 192; DB V, 2; Palau 570. Private collection

Editor's Preface

In spring 1980, for a highly regarded art publisher, I edited the German edition of the catalogue of the largest Picasso exhibition yet seen, the New York Museum of Modern Art's "Pablo Picasso. A Retrospective". In the process, I took the opportunity to deepen my familiarity with Picasso's work, which is of an extent unparalleled in the history of art, and to study his immense output and creative versatility. It is indeed the work of one of the century's great geniuses.

Some years later I had the good fortune to meet a collector and bookworm whose magnificent library included no less than fifty metres of shelves devoted to Picasso. When I asked if any one of the endless books on Picasso did justice to the universality of his creative genius – as painter and draughtsman, etcher and lithographer, sculptor and potter – he said no. Indeed, he went on, to this day no one has even managed to put an approximate number on the original works Picasso made. There must be over thirty thousand.

Ever since, I have been haunted by the wish to produce a book on Picasso that would be more than merely an addition to that endless shelfload. This book is the result of that wish. With luck it will have succeeded in conveying to the common reader and art lover something of the inventive wealth of Picasso's œuvre, of his seemingly infinite artistic imagination.

Carsten-Peter Warncke's text follows Picasso's evolution as an artist, from the academically trained student to the wild old man of the late work. He places special emphasis on recurring motifs and formal approaches in Picasso's work. His interpretation is on the hermeneutic side, giving less attention to Picasso's personality and private life; the well-illustrated biographical appendix covers this ground. Notes and a detailed bibliography also appear in the appendices.

In selecting the illustrations, I have tried to include both famous, "classical" works that belong in any book on Picasso and others that have been less often exhibited or reproduced. Picasso's late work is still rather too unfamiliar to a wider public, so I have paid particular attention to it. With only a few exceptions, the illustrations are arranged in chronological order. The French titles, and the numbers given in abbreviated form referring to the standard catalogues, are intended to help readers who consult the international literature on Picasso.

I wish to express my personal gratitude and that of the publisher to Pablo Picasso's son Claude for his interest in this project. I am indebted to the Picasso expert Gotthard Klewitz, who died far too soon, and his wife Lieselotte for productive ideas and for loans from their library. Georges Boudaille, the co-author of the œuvre catalogue dealing with the Blue and Rose Periods, was giving me valuable information until only a few weeks before his death.

This book would not have been possible without the support of the many museums and private collectors and the important galleries that made Picasso's work visible and established its importance. My thanks are addressed to all when I single out the two great public collections, the Musée Picasso in Paris and the Museu Picasso in Barcelona, and especially Margarita Ferrer, for special mention. Of the galleries that have so generously and unbureaucratically supported my labours I should particularly like to thank three that have rendered outstanding service to Picasso's work over the decades.

I thank the Galerie Louise Leiris in Paris, and the grand seigneur of Picasso studies, Maurice Jardot, together with Quentin Laurens. Through their good offices it proved possible to reproduce numerous works in the possession of Jacqueline Picasso's daughter Catherine Hutin-Blay, whom I also thank most warmly. I thank the Galerie Beyeler in Basle, which has done so much for Picasso's work through fine exhibitions and catalogues, and particularly Hildy and Ernst Beyeler and their assistant, Pascale Zoller. Without their help it would scarcely have been possible to present such excellent examples of Picasso's ceramic work. And I thank Angela Rosengart of Lucerne, who with her late father, Siegfried, has done so much on behalf of Picasso's work and to whom this book owes numerous invaluable enhancements.

In the final, somewhat pressured stage of production I was particularly assisted by Marianne Walther and by my tried and tested technical assistants, Uwe Steffen, Wolfgang Eibl, Klaus Hanitzsch and Wilhelm Vornehm, whose speed and grasp were exemplary. My father, Odo Walther, helped as always in researching the biographical material.

Ingo F. Walther

1 The Image of the Artist

Picasso was that rare thing in history, an artist of cultic presence, a secular manifestation of the spirit, a genuinely commanding phenomenon. Picasso's name and work are synonymous with 20th-century art. They are the very definition of our era's artistic endeavour. This was already the case in his own lifetime; and by now he has long since become a myth, a legend for the age of mass media. Because this is so, Picasso's image as artist is one of infinite diversity. Many were those who played a part in his life, and many were those who left records. The abundance of documents relating to his life and work, and above all Picasso's own statements, permit us access to his art.[1] And yet the vast quantity of biographical material is a mere drop compared with the ocean of analyses, critiques, studies and theses concerning his work that has been pouring steadily out for decades. As in the case of other artists, commentaries and exhibition notes accompanied his work from the outset. But as awareness of Picasso's distinctive importance grew, so too did the tidal wave of published statements on his work.[2]

Nowadays it is no longer unusual for an entire museum to be devoted to the work of a major artist. But three are devoted to Picasso's: in Antibes, in Barcelona, and in Paris. And the first two of these were created during the artist's lifetime. Picasso was not only significant and famous, he was also popular in the extreme – because his work seemed the very epitome of what people thought was modern in the visual arts. On the one hand, he turned his back on tradition and deconstructed images of natural form. On the other hand, he deliberately and randomly shifted the goalposts of visual creation. In a word, the bizarrely denatured forms that are characteristic of modern art are fully present in Picasso's work.

This has come to mean that Picasso's creations are not merely part of the sum total of 20th-century art, but rather are seen as its icons. "Guernica", for instance (pp. 400/401), is unquestionably the most famous modern painting, worldwide, matched as an art classic only by works such as Leonardo's "Mona Lisa" or Rembrandt's "Night Watch". The bombing of Guernica, thanks to Picasso, came to define the horror of modern war, the inhumanity of man to his fellow man. And, uniquely in modern art, "Guernica"

Self-portrait at the Age of 36
Autoportrait à l'âge de trente-six ans
Montrouge, 1917
Pencil on paper, 34 x 26.8 cm
Zervos III, 75
Maya Ruiz-Picasso Collection

Self-portrait (Head)
Autoportrait (Tête)
Mougins, 30 June 1972
Pencil and crayon on paper,
65.7 x 50.5 cm
Zervos XXXIII, 435
Tokyo, Fuji Television Gallery

has exerted a quite remarkable influence on younger artists such as the American pop artist Peter Saul or the political artists of the Spanish group "Equipo Crónica".[3] Their new versions and reworkings show how a single work can provide the matrix in which a sense of the "Zeitgeist" is popularly expressed. Thus in the early 1950s the portraits Picasso painted of a young girl, Sylvette David, transformed the innocent pony-tail, the teenage girl's hair-style of the day, into the very emblem of an epoch (cf. p. 519).

Not till Andy Warhol did his serigraphs of the famous (Marilyn Monroe, J. F. Kennedy, or Elvis Presley) were artworks again to make such an impact. No other 20th-century artist achieved Picasso's astounding omnipresence, not merely through his art but in his own right. The early painting "Child Holding a Dove" (p. 12) is a two-dimensional, stylized childish pose; but once the image was reproduced in millions it came to stand for naive grace and innocence. Indeed, it became so familiar that it (and its creator) entered the colourful world of comics.[4] And when the French film director François Truffaut made his classic "Jules et Jim" in 1961, it was Picasso's pictures he chose as aptest to signal the cultural habitat of the European intellectual before the Second World War. Significant sequences in the film show Picasso reproductions behind the protagonists.[5]

If Picasso's work acquired this kind of emblematic function, so too did the artist himself, as far as his contemporaries were concerned. It was only to be expected, then, that just a few years after his death he would be made the titular hero of a satirical film about artistic and political trends in the 20th century, "The Adventures of Picasso."[6] Precisely because Picasso was equated with modern art per se, all the extremes of public responses were unloaded upon him, at every stage in his career. When the National Gallery in London organized the first major post-war Picasso show in England, one newspaper described him as a great artist, a poet, a genius whose creations were inspired by the profoundest of dreams, while another damned his art as the work of the devil, dismissed piggynosed portraits as the imaginings of a schizophrenic, and declared that such work should not be publicly exhibited in England.[7]

Both extremes are the product of clichés and widely shared preconceptions. Inevitably the dismissal reminds us of the abuse the Nazis heaped on art they considered "degenerate". Equally, though, the praise is nothing but petty phrase-mongering, and tells us nothing of Picasso's success in realizing his intentions, or of his sheer skill. Though these views appear irreconcilable, there is less of a polarity than we might first think; in fact, they share a certain common ground. If the foes of modern art condemn it as the work of lunatics and would ban it if they had a say in the matter, its enthusiastic advocates emphasize what seems inspired and supposedly irrational, inaccessible to cool reason; and in both cases something beyond the everyday experience of the senses is taken to

The Tramp
Le chemineau
Madrid, 3 June 1901
Watercolour and pencil on paper,
20.4 x 12.4 cm
Zervos XXI, 240; DB V, 50; Palau 516
Reims, Musée des Beaux-Arts

Beggar in a Cap
L'homme à la casquette
Corunna, early 1895
Oil on canvas, 72.5 x 50 cm
Zervos I, 4; Palau 64; MPP$_1$
Paris, Musée Picasso

Child Holding a Dove
L'enfant au pigeon
Paris, autumn 1901
Oil on canvas, 73 x 54 cm
Zervos I, 83; DB VI, 14; Palau 669
London, National Gallery (anonymous loan)

be the final source of creativity. At a very early stage, Picasso haters and lovers alike saw his talent as something demonic. One American critic called him the "devil incarnate" in 1910; and the "New York Times", generally a restrained and proper paper, gnashed that he was the very devil and that his audacity was breathtaking, when his first American exhibition was held in Alfred Stieglitz's Photo Secession Gallery in New York in 1911. Not many years later, German critics (and not even the worst) were busy perpetuating the usual equation of visual deconstruction with insanity, viewing Picasso himself as a neurotic and pithily announcing: "People are no longer locked away in asylums. Nowadays they found Cubism."[8]

This is how legends are made; and, to this day, Picasso seems more the stuff of myth than a flesh-and-blood historical person. He himself, of course, must share the blame. Many who knew him in

The Gourmet (The White Child)
Le gourmet (Le gourmand)
Gósol or Paris, 1901
Oil on canvas, 92.8 x 68.3 cm
Zervos I, 51; DB V,53; Palau 617
Washington (DC), National Gallery of Art,
Chester Dale Collection

The Embrace
L'étreinte
Barcelona, 1903
Pastel on cardboard, 98 x 57 cm
Zervos I, 161; DB IX,12; Palau 856
Paris, Musée de l'Orangerie

the early days in Paris were quick to detect the artistic energy, creative depth and autonomous will of his art in the artist too. Picasso was a striking person, a stocky, robust Spaniard who invariably made an impression. He was all charisma and self-confidence. With his hair tumbling across his forehead and his intense gaze, his attitude became a pose. Everyone who photographed Picasso stressed his demonic side,[9] and in doing so, of course, merely repeated what he had proclaimed to be the case: for it was a demonic Picasso who appeared in a number of early self-portraits (cf. pp. 6, 80, 81, 147 and 152). From the outset, fellow-painters and critics and collectors saw Picasso in ways he himself dictated.

This has remained the case to the present day. Picasso's personal appearance, his style of life, his wilfulness, and his relations with women (attesting his vitality in the eyes of many), have provided

13 The Image of the Artist

Vase with Flowers
Fleurs sur une table
Paris, autumn 1907
Oil on canvas, 92.1 x 73 cm
Zervos II*, 30; DR 70
New York, The Museum of Modern Art

Exotic Flowers
Fleurs exotiques (Bouquet dans un vase)
Paris, summer 1907
Oil on canvas, 56 x 38 cm
Zervos II*, 37; DR 64
Monte Carlo, Private collection

irresistible media bait. In 1955, Georges Clouzot made a lengthy documentary of the artist at work, and the journalists had a field day celebrating Picasso as a kind of superman: "Summer 1955, and the cameras are rolling in the Victorine studios at Nice . . . Picasso, in shorts and bare to the waist, his torso tanned, his feet in slippers, strides into the bright daylight: a living bronze god come down off his pedestal, mighty, majestic, he belongs to all ages, to primitive cultures and to future times light years away. Depending on how the light falls on his head, his powerful chest or his sturdy legs, he can look like a witch doctor or a Roman emperor."[10] The unintentional humour of comparisons such as these nicely illustrates the image of Picasso that was then widely taken for granted. At a time when most people were glad if they could draw their pensions in peace and quiet, a Picasso rampant wearing a sporty turtle-neck jumper or beach clothes or in pugilist pose, stripped to the waist, was a conspicuous, dynamic exception to the rule.

But none of this would have happened without his art, which to this day resists easy access. The sheer size of his output is daunting. There are over ten thousand paintings alone. Then there are great numbers of sketches and drawings. There are printed graphics. There are ceramics and sculptures.[11] During his own lifetime, Picasso kept for himself a number of his works that he considered im-

portant, and some of these now constitute the core of the Musée Picasso's collection in Paris. Large quantities of work left at his death have been examined and classified; although no one yet has a full grasp of his entire œuvre, some help is to hand. The 34-volume catalogue of Picasso's work, compiled by Christian Zervos and published between 1942 and 1978, while far from complete reproduces over 16,000 works. Other catalogues document over 600 sculptures and 200-plus ceramic works;[12] they too are incomplete. For decades, major shows throughout the world have not only presented Picasso's work to an amazed public but have also laid the foundation of an understanding of his art.[13]

Born on 20 October 1881 in Málaga, the son of a painter and art teacher, Picasso started to draw and paint at the age of nine. His father guided him, and later he was professionally trained at Corunna, Barcelona and Madrid. At the age of fifteen he was already successfully taking part in exhibitions. In 1898, disappointed by academic teachings, he gave up his studies and set about making a name for himself in artistic circles in Barcelona, and then in Paris. By 1901 he had a Paris show in the Galerie Vollard almost to himself, sharing it with another Basque; he sold 15 of his 65 paintings and drawings before the exhibition had even opened.

The fact that a foreign newcomer could make so rapid an im-

Composition with a Skull (Sketch)
Composition à la tête de mort (Etude)
Paris, late spring 1908
Watercolour, gouache and pencil on paper,
32.5 x 24.2 cm
Zervos II*,49; DR 171
Moscow, Pushkin Museum

Composition with a Skull
Composition à la tête de mort
Paris, late spring 1908
Oil on canvas, 116 x 89 cm
Zervos II*, 50; DR 172
St. Petersburg, Hermitage

pression speaks volumes about the turn-of-the-century art market. But it also implies a great deal about the artist's energy and self-assurance. In both his early periods, Picasso was influenced by 19th-century academic approaches, and characteristically re-worked art that was currently in vogue or had come back into fashion. In 1901/02, three years after taking the plunge into the uncertain life of an artist, Picasso established not so much a style of his own as a style that was identifiably his and thus commercially useful. This marked the outset of the Blue and Rose Periods, which lasted till 1906 and have remained the public's favourites to this day. The year 1906 was both a caesura and a transition. Once again Picasso was trying out new forms; and, just as he was achieving recognition, he abandoned the path he had first chosen to take.

In the Blue and Rose Periods, form and content had seemed to harmonize. Now Picasso tackled form alone, at a radical level. In the Blue and Rose Periods, stylized forms had been given symbolic values fitting the portrayal of the old and lonely, of the poor and hungry, of beggars. In putting the earlier monochrome approach aside, the col-ourful world of circus artistes and harlequins in the Rose Period betrayed nothing of Picasso's creative emotion at that date. Melan-choly lay draped over the unmerry masquerade like a veil.

In 1906 warm reddish-brown tones continued to be emphasized, but now spatial forms became Picasso's dominant concern. The

Study for "Les Demoiselles d'Avignon"
Etude pour "Les Demoiselles d'Avignon"
Paris, May 1907
Pencil on paper, 10.5 x 13.6 cm
Zervos II**, 632; Palau 1526; MPP 1862
Paris, Musée Picasso

Study for "Les Demoiselles d'Avignon"
Etude pour "Les Demoiselles d'Avignon"
Paris, May 1907
Pencil on paper, 13.5 x 10.5 cm
Zervos II**, 633; Palau 1527; MPP 1862
Paris, Musée Picasso

Study for "Les Demoiselles d'Avignon"
Etude pour "Les Demoiselles d'Avignon"
Paris, May 1907
Charcoal on paper, 47.6 x 65 cm
Zervos II**, 644; Palau 1548
Basel, Öffentliche Kunstsammlung Basel,
Kupferstichkabinett, Gift of Douglas Cooper

The Image of the Artist **16**

Guitar, Sheet Music and Glass
Guitare, partition, verre
Paris, after 18 November 1912
Gouache, charcoal and papiers collés,
47.9 x 36.5 cm
Zervos II**, 423; DR 513
San Antonio (TX), Marion Koogler
McNay Art Institute

Head of a Man
Tête d'homme
Paris, 1912
Pencil on paper, 62.5 x 47 cm
Zervos II*, 327
Private collection

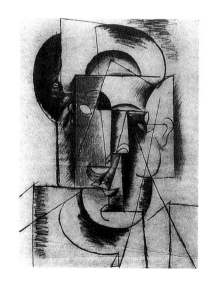

new work centred upon heavy objects rendered geometrically, and must be seen as a preliminary phase leading up to the great experiment of 1907. Picasso made his breakthrough in "Les Demoiselles d'Avignon" (p. 159), achieving a new formal idiom and pointing the way for much of Modernist art. Together with Georges Braque, a younger artist, he established Cubism, the first radically new artistic style of the 20th century. Initially they borrowed the convention of using simplified geometrical forms (hence the name Cubism), arranging them loosely on the surface of the composition without any attempt at unified spatial depth. Around 1910 they moved on to analytical Cubism, in which the spatial and line qualities of the subjects portrayed extend autonomously in parallel and counterpoint across the composition. Pictures thus created look like an agitated juxtaposition of interlocking forms.

In the third and final phase, post–1912, which was known as synthetic Cubism, Picasso and Braque achived compacted and au-

tonomous structures. Questions of a material or spatial nature became the subjects of their works: using materials that often lay ready to hand, such as newspaper, wood, sand and so forth, they established a new concept of the visual image. Cubism made Picasso internationally famous and lodged him in the history of art. Though he had changed modern art, Picasso himself did not remain in a rut, much to the admiration of his friends, patrons and advo-

The Image of the Artist **18**

cates; and in 1916 he surprised everyone by returning to conventional figural and spatial values, painting stylized, monumental, proportionally random figures that made a classical impression.

From about 1924 a lengthy period set in which can best be described as a synthesis of the two formal extremes of his œuvre to date. The Cubist fracturing of the image was married to clearer, more concentrated spatial zones and linear structures. This movement culminated in his most famous work, "Guernica", painted in 1937 for the rightful republican government in Spain, as a protest against totalitarian warmongering.

The formal idiom Picasso had now evolved was to remain at the core of his work till his death. In his later phases he reworked important works by earlier artists, to a greater or lesser extent. He further developed his own methods of three-dimensional work, and branched out into new areas, such as ceramics.

To review Picasso's evolution in this way is to present an essentially familiar view of an unarguably major artist. After the years spent learning the craft come the periods of experiment and of gradually locating a personal style. Following an authoritative period of mature mastery comes a late period which essentially plays variations on familiar themes. But if we look more closely at Picasso's case we begin to have our doubts. In his so-called classical period, Picasso rendered the human image in monumental fashion; but at the same time he was painting works that continued the line of synthetic Cubism, with all its deconstruction and indeed destruction of that selfsame human image. Surely this is an inconsistency?

These different works do still reveal an artist using his own artistic methods with complete assurance. They have that in common. In other cases, though, not even that common ground can be established. If we look at Picasso's early studies, done while he was being taught, they are clearly the work of a talented pupil. At the age of

Bowl of Fruit and Guitar
Compotier et guitare
9 September 1920
Gouache and watercolour on paper,
27.2 x 21 cm
Zervos XXX, 68
Private collection

The Open Book
Le livre ouvert
10 September 1920
Gouache and watercolour on paper,
26.7 x 21 cm
Zervos VI, 1383
Private collection

Candelabrum on Table
Le gueridon
Fontainebleau, 7 July 1920
Gouache and watercolour on paper,
26.7 x 21 cm
Zervos VI, 1384
Private collection

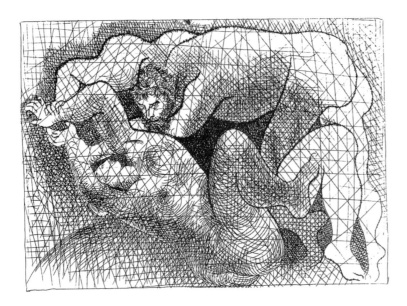

Man and Woman
Homme et femme
1927
Etching, 19.2 x 28 cm
Bloch 77; Geiser 118 b

Head
Tête
Boisgeloup (?), 1931
Coloured plaster, wood, iron and nails,
57 x 48 x 23.5 cm
Spies 79; MPP 268
Paris, Musée Picasso

The Image of the Artist 20

twelve or thirteen his drawings of plaster-cast figures strikingly had the contoured depth and volume that was required (cf. pp. 36 and 37). But the fourth of his sketches done on 1 May 1937 (p. 391) betrays none of this facility. Scrawled outlines sketch an irregular head, neck, rump and legs for the horse. There is little evidence for any well-planned distinction between the essential and unnecessary. All four legs and both eyes, though they would not be visible in a perspective rendering of a side view, are there to be seen. In other words, the drawing seems more a child's drawing than anything else. Yet it would be wrong to draw overhasty conclusions.

The Swallows
Les hirondelles
Paris, 14 May 1932
Oil on canvas, 41 x 41 cm
Zervos VII, 342
Paris, Courtesy Galerie Louise Leiris

Two Dressed Models and a Sculpture of a Head
("Suite Vollard", plate 42)
Deux modèles vêtus
Paris, 21 March 1933
Etching, 26.7 x 19.3 cm
Bloch 150; Geiser 302 II

Sculptor and Kneeling Model
("Suite Vollard", plate 69)
Sculpteur et modèle agenouillé
Paris, 8 April 1933
Etching, 36.7 x 29.8 cm
Bloch 178; Geiser 331 II c

Two Catalan Drinkers
("Suite Vollard", plate 12)
Deux buveurs catalans
Paris, 29 November 1934
Etching, 23.7 x 29.9 cm
Bloch 228; Geiser 442 II c

The Image of the Artist 22

Nine Heads
Neuf têtes
7 and 9 November 1934
Mixed media, 31.7 x 22.6 cm
Bloch 285; Geiser 438 Bb

Picasso, then aged 56, was not entering a premature second childhood: the sketch was one of many that served to prepare his great work "Guernica", done when he was at the height of his powers.

This poses a problem. Usual ways of examining an artist's creative characteristics do not allow for the fact that the urge to record a fleeting inspiration may lead him to forget the rules he has long since mastered and to relapse into a pre-training phase. In fact, people generally assume that mastery (and certainly genius) implies absolutely perfect technical command. In Picasso's case there is a discontinuity; indeed, his work is full of discontinuities. For it is far from simple to trace the meaning of his subjects, intentions, and aims.

Picasso's Cubist paintings and sculptures, and the late series of

23 The Image of the Artist

variations on Old Master paintings, alike show him aiming at absolute artistic autonomy of means. References to an objective world outside that of the artwork are subsidiary or indeed entirely immaterial. This, it would seem, is the very core of Picasso's art. It is this that made him so famous – and so controversial.

This may be true, but equally it is at variance with the facts; for Picasso's art was also, and to at least the same degree, an art of traditional pictorial concerns, from start to finish. We might instance his persistent, even stubborn adherence to the historical painting, a form considered superseded in 20th-century art. If the sixteen-year-old painted the allegorical "Science and Charity" (pp. 50/51) in 1897, we need only recall prevailing ideas on art in Spain at the time, and the training the young Picasso was receiving. And in 1903, in the most important painting of his Blue Period, "La Vie (Life)" (p. 105), Picasso transformed the suicide of his friend Carlos Casagemas into an allegorical scene: this, if we choose, we can view as a product of strong emotion, a late expression of his training. But "Guernica" too, much later, treats a real event in the form of a symbolic history painting. Similarly in "The Charnel House" (p. 457) and "Massacre in Korea" (pp. 500/501), specific wars in 1945 and 1951, not war as an abstract universal, prompt attempts to deal with exact historical subjects. And historical painting is by no means the only area in which Picasso pursued verifiable subject matter. His interest in formal games-playing was accompanied by an equally strong lifelong interest in certain subjects: painter and model, circus artistes and harlequins, lovers,

Reclining Woman on the Beach
Femme couchée sur la plage
Boisgeloup, 6 August 1932
Oil on canvas, 27 x 35 cm
Not in Zervos
Paris, Private collection

The Image of the Artist **24**

Two Figures
Deux personnages
Boisgeloup, 28 March 1934
Oil on canvas, 81.8 x 65.3 cm
Zervos VIII, 193
Private collection

Woman Writing
Femme écrivant
Paris (?), 1934
Oil on canvas, 162 x 130 cm
Zervos VIII, 183
New York, The Museum of Modern Art

Reclining Female Nude with Starry Sky
Femme nue couchée
Paris, 12 August and 2 October 1936
Oil on canvas, 130.5 x 162 cm
Zervos VIII, 310
Paris, Musée National d'Art Moderne,
Centre Georges Pompidou, Gift of Kahnweiler

25   The Image of the Artist

Faun Unveiling a Woman
("Suite Vollard", plate 27)
Faune dévoilant une femme
Paris, 12 June 1936
Etching and aquatint, 31.7 x 41.7 cm
Bloch 230; Baer 609

mother and child, bullfights. His treatment of these subjects persisted as late as the etchings from his final years.

But no single, unified, overall picture emerges. Does this imply that Picasso's art was exclusively centred upon himself? That it had no real concerns?[14] This must be disputed. What is true is that conventional methods of analysis cannot gain a purchase on his art. This explains the widely held and oft repeated claim that Picasso was basically a chameleon personality whose true distinguishing quality was that he had no true distinguishing quality – apart from

Curtain for "14 juillet" by Romain Rolland
Le rideau pour "14 juillet" de Romain Rolland
Made by Louis Fernandez from a design by Picasso
dated 28 May 1936 and titled "The Hide of the
Minotaur in Harlequin Costume" (cf. p. 378)
Paris, between 28 May and 14 July 1936
Tempera on cloth, approx. 11 x 18 m
Toulouse, Musée des Augustins,
on loan from the artist's estate

Bust of a Woman
Buste de femme
Paris (?), 1935
Oil on canvas, 65 x 54 cm
Not in Zervos
Basel, Private collection

a perfect grasp of artistic means, a childlike lack of conscious intent, an infinite curiosity and interest in experiment, together with a mulish persistence and unusual energy. Picasso's style, in this view, consists in his command of every available style.

This is too simple. In making Picasso both all and nothing, this interpretation capitulates before any challenge, substitutes anecdotes for analysis, and gives us statistics instead of evaluation.[15] The unusual lifelong devotion implied in Picasso's more-than-lifesize artistic output demands to be taken seriously. This means looking with a critical eye, seeing the weaknesses along with the strengths, and so making Picasso's real greatness comprehensible. Many works of criticism have been devoted to particular areas of Picasso's creative work, and have extended our understanding in important ways. Every age and every generation, however, will seek a new approach of its own to Picasso's art, will want a Picasso of its own. This book has been written for our own time. It is an attempt to trace a life lived in the service of art, to identify what is universal in the sheer copiousness of the unique.

2 The Making of a Genius 1890–1898

One of the earliest surviving drawings by Picasso dates from November 1890. The artist recalled that "Hercules with His Club" (see right) was copied from a painting in the parental home.[16] It is an awkward piece of drawing, of course. The proportions are wrong, the limbs out of scale, the left thigh far thicker than the right, the left arm anatomically incorrect; and the lines are uncertain, the repeated breaking off and resuming sure signs of inexperience. And yet it is also a remarkable drawing. After all, it was done by a nine-year-old. Most drawings by children of that age have the hallmarks of children's indifference to figural fidelity. This is a child's drawing; but it is not childish. It is no wonder that Picasso's painter father recognised his son's talent at an early stage and encouraged the boy accordingly. At eleven, the young Picasso was going to art school at Corunna. In 1895, aged just fourteen, he was admitted to the Academy of Art in Barcelona. A mere year later a large canvas by the young artist, titled "First Communion" (p. 38), was shown in a public exhibition.[17]

There is no need to follow the customary line of seeing Picasso as a miraculous infant prodigy.[18] Still, the sheer wealth and quality of his youthful output are staggering. No other artist has left us so much evidence relating to this early period of life – and of course it is a crucial period. One of the most fascinating sights 20th-century art can offer us is the spectacle of the young Picasso making his steady early advance.

His family realised that he was exceptionally gifted, and preserved the youngster's efforts carefully if they were even only slightly distinctive. The paintings, drawings and sketches Picasso did as a boy remained in his sister's home at Barcelona till the artist donated them to the Museu Picasso there in 1970. The collection is impressive for its sheer size: 213 oil paintings done on canvas, cardboard or other surfaces; 681 drawings, pastels and watercolours on paper; 17 sketchbooks and albums; four books with drawings in the margins; one etching; and various other artefacts. Fourteen of the paintings on wood or canvas, and a full 504 of the sheets with drawings, have been used on both sides (often for studies); and the sketchbooks contain 826 pages of drawings. The juvenilia

Hercules with His Club
Hercule avec sa massue
Málaga, November 1890
Pencil on paper, 49.6 x 32 cm
Not in Zervos; Palau I; MPB 110.842
Barcelona, Museu Picasso

Self-portrait with Uncombed Hair
Autoportrait mal coiffé
Barcelona, 1896
Oil on canvas, 32.7 x 23.6 cm
Not in Zervos; Palau 154; MPB 110.076
Barcelona, Museu Picasso

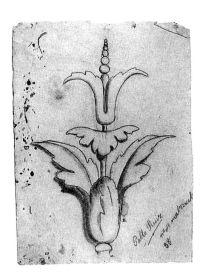

Acanthus Leaves (Academic drawing)
Feuilles d'acanthe (Dessin académique)
Corunna, 1892/93
Black chalk and charcoal on paper,
31.5 x 23.8 cm
Not in Zervos; Palau 12; MPB 110.859
Barcelona, Museu Picasso

Sketches in a Schoolbook
Etudes dans un livre d'école
Corunna, 1891
Pencil and ink on paper, 22.2 x 14.5 cm
Not in Zervos; Palau 7; MPB 110.930
Barcelona, Museu Picasso

Bullfight
Course de taureaux
Corunna, 1892
Pencil and gouache, 13 x 21 cm
Zervos XXI, 2
Estate of the artist

Doves and Rabbits
Pigeons et lapins
Corunna, 1892
Pencil on paper, 13 x 21 cm
Zervos XXI, 4; Palau 14
Estate of the artist

that has survived from the years 1890 to 1904, from the boy Picasso's first attempts to the Blue Period, runs to over 2,200 works in various formats and using various techniques.[19]

Different though the works are, they have the same quality, whatever one looks at. An impressive example is the pencil sketch of two cavalrymen done around 1891 to 1893 by the ten- or twelve-year-old Picasso in a schoolbook (p. 32). The horses and riders are done correctly, on the whole, and mistakes in detail do not detract from this. True, the horses' heads ought to be larger, and the officers' chests and arms could be improved; but the portrayal is not at all a child's, and the drawing shows signs of an increasing grasp of line. The boy's talent has noticeably amplified since "Hercules with His Club" and the way is clear to the art pupil's academic studies, done with full assurance. Those studies display the student's technical

prowess and his command of methods deliberately deployed; the essential visual approach remains the same.

The young Picasso's gift was a striking one, clearly different from normal children's artistic efforts. The artist himself felt as much: "It is quite remarkable that I never did childish drawings. Never. Not even as a very small boy."[20] What Picasso means is the kind of drawings children do unprompted, without any adult suggesting a subject; such drawings, free of influence, are nowadays considered the true sign of a child's creative impulses. The drawings the boy Picasso scribbled in his school books were doubtless the same kind of child's drawing; yet it is these that show us that he always drew like an adult.

But it would be wrong to take this as infallible proof of above-average maturity or even genius. A child's drawing derives its shape

31 The Making of a Genius 1890 – 1898

Double Study of a Bearded Man in Profile
Corunna, 1892/93
Pencil on paper, 23.7 x 31 cm
Zervos VI, 10; Palau 11
Private collection

Two Mounted Soldiers and the Tower of a Fortress
Dos soldados a caballo y un torreón
Corunna, 1894
Ink on paper, 27.1 x 18.5 cm
Not in Zervos; MPB 110.866
Barcelona, Museu Picasso

Double Study of the Left Eye
Corunna, 1892/93
Pencil on paper, 23.7 x 31.5 cm
Zervos VI, 9; Palau 9
Private collection

and imaginative form from a historical process, and bears witness to particular cultural influences.[21] Of course any child who draws is entering into a fundamental act of expression. But the nature of that expression is conditioned. It is only recently that such drawings have come to be valued in their own right, and so very few independently created drawings by children survive from earlier times.[22] And most of those that do betray the educational influence of adults. Just as children were once dressed and brought up as little adults, so too adults' visual preconceptions were once instilled into them. Children's drawings dating from pre–20th century times generally look like less successful adults' drawings. That is to say, they are not fundamentally different from those the young Picasso did. In the Bibliothèque Nationale in Paris, for instance, there is the diary of a 17th-century doctor by the name of Jean Héroard, which contains drawings by an eight-year-old boy. Some of them are on the same subjects as Picasso's schoolbook sketches. And the lad's touch is as sure as Picasso's. But this lad did not come from an artistic family; indeed, in later life he was better known as King Louis XIII.[23]

In a sense, this is typical of children's drawings, in historical terms: painting and drawing had not been part of the European educational curriculum since antiquity, and until the 18th century only two kinds of children were normally given any training in art – those who were meant to become professional artists, and those who were of aristocratic or well-to-do family. There was no such thing as universal drawing tuition.[24] Children were taught the professional rules of the craft. Nor did the introduction of drawing classes in schools change this. Even the great Swiss educational reformer Johann Heinrich Pestalozzi, the most progressive of his age, was concerned to make children adopt the adult method of pictorial representation as early and as completely as possible. Most educational systems in Europe and North America followed this example in the 19th century. It was not until the end of that century that children's own innate approach to drawing came to be valued and even encouraged; and not till our own day that it properly came into its own.[25]

The drawings done by the young Picasso are not those of a prodigy, then. But this is not to detract from his genius. Quite the contrary. Picasso the artist was moulded by the educational and academic ideas that then prevailed, as we can clearly see from his juvenilia: the education he was given was the making of a genius.

Picasso started school in Málaga in 1886, aged five. None of his drawings of that time survive. But we have a reliable witness to what they were like: Picasso himself. In conversation with Roland Penrose, he recalled drawing spirals at school in those days.[26] This suggests that art instruction at that Málaga primary school was

"La Coruña" (double page of a diary)
Corunna, 16 September 1894
Ink, India ink and pencil on paper, 21 x 26 cm
Zervos XXI, 10; Palau 31; MPP 402(r)
Paris, Musée Picasso

"La Coruña" (double page of a diary)
Corunna, 16 September 1894
Ink, India ink and pencil on paper, 21 x 26 cm
Zervos XXI, II; MPP 402(v)
Paris, Musée Picasso

"Azul y Blanco" (double page)
Corunna, 28 October 1894
Pencil on paper, 20.5 x 26.5 cm
Zervos XXI, 12; Palau 33; MPP 403(v)
Paris, Musée Picasso

"Azul y blanco" (double page)
Corunna, 28 October 1894
Ink, India ink and pencil on paper, 21 x 26 cm
Zervos XXI, 13; Palau 34; MPP 403(r)
Paris, Musée Picasso

Farmhouse
Maison de campagne
Corunna, 1893
Oil on canvas, 15.8 x 23 cm
Not in Zervos; Palau 20; MPB 110.103
Barcelona, Museu Picasso

designed along lines laid down by Pestalozzi, developed by Friedrich Fröbel, and subsequently adapted by teachers throughout the world. In essence the method was the same one everywhere. Linear drawing was the invariable point of departure: children were encouraged to think and create in geometrical terms. Then they were taught to abstract forms from the world about them. And only then did they move on to the representation of actual things. In this scheme of things, drawing straight or curved lines (such as spirals) was the first, basic step. The children copied lines and linear figures slavishly. Then they had to develop their own motifs by highlighting or omitting lines in what was shown them. Finally they practised free-hand drawing of geometrical figures such as circles, ovals or spirals. It was a way of making even tiny children see schematically. The irregularity and shakiness of children's representation was educated out of them.

Children (such as Picasso) who underwent this process were no longer able to draw in a truly childish way even if they wanted to.[27] In any case, children require something to follow, something they can grasp. Picasso's early drawings copied models; both the cavalrymen in the schoolbook and his numerous attempts to draw bullfights (cf. pp. 30 and 31) were versions done after the bright, colourful world of folksy prints and broadsheets.[28]

One of the ten-year-old Picasso's sheets is of special interest. It is a sheet he used twice, to draw a bullfight and to draw pigeons (p. 31). Plainly the task of depicting Spain's national sport was beyond him, even when he was copying a model. The bearing and movements of the protagonists, and the spatial realization of the overall scene, is most unsatisfactory. But the pigeons are another matter entirely; they are far more convincing. In drawing them, the boy's approach was a geometrical one, using linked ovals for the

The Barefoot Girl
La fillette aux pieds nus
Corunna, early 1895
Oil on canvas, 74.5 x 49.5 cm
Zervos I, 3; Palau 69; MPP 2
Paris, Musée Picasso

neck, crop and rump and then adding the other parts of the birds' bodies. His father's work prompted the boy to make these drawings,[29] but did not provide a model. What lies behind the frequent boyhood drawings of birds, and in particular pigeons, is drawing instruction at school, with its method of interposing geometrical schemata between the natural form and its representation. Birds were a popular subject because they could easily be seen in geometrical terms and were thus easy to draw.[30]

Other standard exercises included the perfecting of a leaf outline.[31] And so it was that children in the 19th century learnt to perceive a repertoire of stock shapes in all things, and to reduce individual forms to variations on geometrical themes. The drawbacks of this method are plain: individual characteristics are subordinated to unbending principles of representation. But we must not overlook a salient advantage. Anyone who had been schooled in this way, and (of course) had an amount of native talent, had the lifelong ability to register and reproduce objects and motifs quickly and precisely. Picasso benefitted from the training of his boyhood till he was an old man. It was that training that gave him his astounding assurance in his craft. His debt to his school training is

Arcadi Mas i Fontdevila:
Back Study. Oil on canvas
Barcelona, Museu d'Art Modern de Barcelona
(cf. p. 37 right)

Study of the Left Arm
(after a plaster cast)
Corunna, 1894
Charcoal and pencil on paper, 45 x 34 cm
Palau 25; MPB 110.843
Barcelona, Museu Picasso

Study of the Right Foot
(after a plaster cast)
Corunna, 1893/94
Charcoal and pencil on paper, 52.2 x 36.7 cm
Zervos VI, 7; Palau 21
Estate of the artist

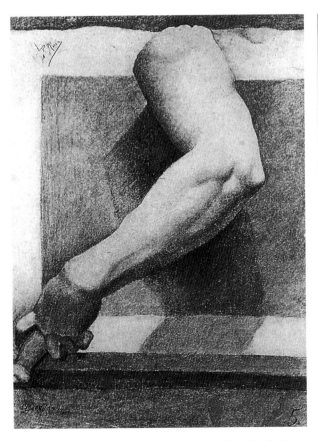

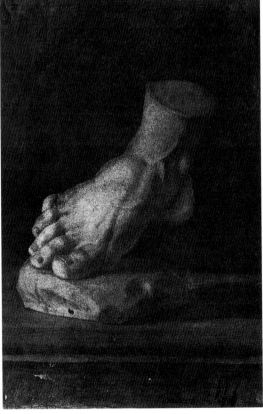

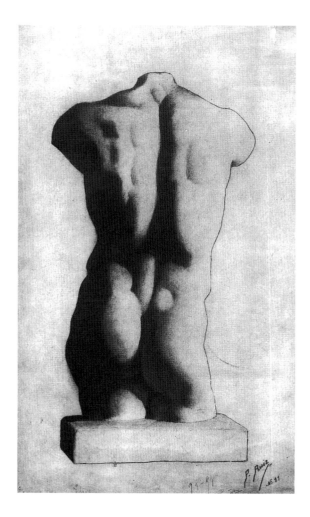

clearly visible in a drawing of boats (p. 46) in which a handful of lines rapidly establish the subject, in accordance with the principle he had learnt of calligraphic construction.[32]

It is small wonder that his school training remained so emphatically with Picasso, since professional tuition followed the same principles. After his family had moved to Corunna when his father took up a new position, the boy first attended general secondary school but then in September 1892 moved to La Guarda art school (where his father was teaching) at the beginning of the new school year. By 1895 he had taken courses in ornamental drawing, figure, copying plaster objects, copying plaster figures, and copying and painting from Nature. It was a strict academic education according to the Madrid Royal College of Art's guidelines.[33] This meant that he once again studied drawing and painting in terms of copying models. His study of an acanthus (p. 30), done in his first year at La Guarda, is a good example of this. It is essentially a line drawing with little interior work, of a kind taught in school art classes.[34]

Study of a Torso
(after a plaster cast)
Etude d'un plâtre (d'après l'antique)
Corunna, 1893/94
Charcoal and pencil on paper, 49 x 31.5 cm
Zervos VI,1; Palau 19; MPP 405
Paris, Musée Picasso

Female Nude from Behind
(after Arcadi Mas i Fontdevilla)
Barcelona, 1895
Oil on panel, 22.3 x 13.7 cm
Not in Zervos; Palau 122; MPB 110.212
Barcelona, Museu Picasso

Other basic representational tasks were set for the pupil. We still have a variable-profile study of the left eye which Picasso did at age twelve (p. 32). The drawing was copied from a plaster figure, according to time-honoured custom. The method was well established in 19th-century academies and dated back to the 15th century. Printed originals were used for the drawing of organs, then of larger parts of the body, and finally of whole figures.[35] Once the copying itself no longer posed a problem, the pupil moved on to copying from plaster models. This served a dual purpose: it developed the pupil's eye for a subject, and created the ability to produce three-dimensionally modelled plasticity by means of effective contouring and proper use of light and shadow. This dual purpose was achieved in as linear a manner as everything else in this system, progressing from basic geometrical figures to lightly-modelled line drawings to full three-dimensionality.[36]

Another Picasso study of the same date showing the head of a bearded man in two stages of profile (p. 32), one of them purely linear and the second lightly modelled, is thus not to be taken as proof of any unusual talent on his part where both realistic drawing and abstraction are concerned;[37] rather, it demonstrates that he was copying from one of the many exercise sources.[38] The educational drill was strictly followed in those days, and it was doubtless more of a soulless exercise than a fit encouragement of creative powers. Still, the constant repetition of the same task did provide the art student with an available repertoire of representational methods.

What was more, students were also taught the essentials of art history; the models they followed in their exercises were the masterpieces of ages past. So it was that in his early youth Picasso was familiar with the sculptures of antiquity. He had to copy them over and over, from figures on the frieze of the Parthenon to the Venus of Milo.[39] His lifelong engagement with the art of antiquity was thus as firmly rooted in his early training as his assured technique and his idiosyncratic manner of approaching a subject. In the same way that a pianist has to practise constantly, so Picasso too, throughout his life, kept his eye and hand in top form. His sketchbooks and his many studies contained endlessly repeated versions of the same motif (cf. p. 250), all executed with just a few lines and often with a single, assured stroke.

The single-line drawing was in fact a widely-used teaching method. It brings home the specific form of a subject better than any other technique; only if the drawer has looked very closely and has internalized the essentials of the form he will be able to reproduce it with a single line. A motif set down in this way remains in the artist's memory, always available. And because the technique was so basic, it was of central importance to Picasso. His whole life long, he created new visual worlds by means of representational copying.

The schematic nature of the academic approach to the appropri-

The Altar Boy
L'enfant de chœur
Barcelona, 1896
Oil on canvas, 76 x 50 cm
Zervos I, 2; Palau 140
Barcelona, Museu de Montserrat

First Communion
La première communion
Barcelona, 1896
Oil on canvas, 166 x 118 cm
Zervos XXI, 49; Palau 142; MPB 110.001
Barcelona, Museu Picasso

Portrait of José Ruiz Blasco (The Artist's Father)
Portrait du père de l'artiste
Barcelona, 1896
Watercolour, 18 x 11.8 cm
Not in Zervos; MPB 110.281
Barcelona, Museu Picasso

Portrait of the Artist's Father
Portrait du père de l'artiste
Barcelona, 1896
Oil on canvas on cardboard, 42.3 x 30.8 cm
Not in Zervos; Palau 143; MPB 110.027
Barcelona, Museu Picasso

ation of reality played a similar part in his development. First the subject was envisaged in geometrical terms, then it was rendered in outline, and then it was three-dimensionally modelled. This process was to remain the heart of Picasso's artistic method. For him, drawing always came first, irrespective of whether he was working in oil, printed graphics, sculpture or ceramics. This is why the seemingly rudimentary, often childlike sketches account for such a large body of his output. But the preliminary sketches for "Guernica" (cf. pp. 400/401) or the great sculpture "Man with Sheep" (p. 455) only look childlike at a first, cursory inspection. In fact they are skilful drawings with the precise task of recording the formal principles of new ideas. Only when a notion had acquired contour and recognisable form in this way did Picasso proceed. He worked in ways of such austerely rational, quasi-scientific logic that in this respect he must surely stand alone in modern art. It is only because his tireless labours produced such a superabundance of work that the popular image of his creative methods is a different and unclear one.

It need cause no surprise that Picasso's training struck such deep roots and influenced him for so long. After all, it was an intensive

schooling: he was exposed to it not only in extreme youth, but also repeatedly. The tuition he received at art college in Barcelona (1895 to 1897) was essentially the same again.[40] We do well to remember that the treadmill effect of such repetition must have been a more significant factor than Picasso's tender years.

In point of fact, beginning to study at an early age was by no means so very unusual. Ary Scheffer, famed internationally as a painter in the early 19th century, began systematic training at the age of eleven; and the French academic painter Jean-Jacques Henner, now totally forgotten, began professional training at twelve.[41] At Barcelona, the sculptor Damian Campeny began at fourteen, the earliest possible age there.[42] When Picasso was allowed to sit his entrance exam in advance of the regulation date, in September 1895, his fourteenth birthday was still a month away. For a prospective student only a month off formal entitlement, sterner treatment would have been small-minded.

Picasso's oils of that period treated relatively few subjects over and over, in a fairly uniform style. There are a striking number of human heads, of every age and walk of life and of both sexes. These studies are done in broad, expansive pastose, using monochrome

Portrait of the Artist's Mother
Portrait de la mère de l'artiste
Barcelona, 1896
Pastel on paper, 49.8 x 39 cm
Zervos XXI, 40; Palau 139; MPB 110.016
Barcelona, Museu Picasso

Portrait of the Artist's Mother
Portrait de la mère de l'artiste
Barcelona, 9 June 1896
Watercolour on paper, 19.5 x 12 cm
Not in Zervos; Palau 160; MPB 111.472
Barcelona, Museu Picasso

earthy browns or ochre yellows and sparing local colour to model the light and shadow on faces. Generous as Picasso's brushwork is, the contours remain precise, so that the overall impression tends to be one of draughtsmanlike clarity. We are reminded of great Spanish antecedents such as Diego Velázquez, Francisco de Zurbarán or Bartolomé Estéban Murillo.[43] Once again, however, the more immediate influence was of course Picasso's academic tuition.

Use of brush and paint followed preliminary training in drawing and priming. As with drawing, training proceeded in stages: first copying from existing designs, then from genuine objects, and finally the rendering of living models. In learning how to paint a face, students were also acquiring the basic principles of all painting from life: modelling of light effects, the establishment of a foundation tone using broad strokes, pale colours for the light areas and darker for the shade (with the hair constituting a distinct area in itself) – then a more specific distinction of light and dark through smaller brush strokes, working through to detailed toning. Every kind of painting, not only portraits but also (for example) landscapes, was done in accordance with this basic procedure.[44] Picasso's paintings, whether interiors, studies of heads, or landscapes, followed it precisely. That is to say, he was not yet betraying the influence of any contemporary movements in art – even if remote similarities can at times be identified.[45]

A rear view of a nude woman which he painted in 1895 (p. 37) is interesting in this connection. It is a copy of a work by the contemporary painter Arcadi Mas i Fontdevila.[46] The latter's painting also uses loose brushwork; but the brush strokes are not as patchy, schematic and indeed almost mosaic in effect as those in Picasso's Corunna head studies or the landscapes he painted on holiday at Málaga (p. 46). These works exemplify the next stage in his academic training. Light and shadow, and colour tonality, were established in contrastively juxtaposed brush strokes that conveyed a mosaic impression. This method was systematic, and well-nigh guaranteed strong impact; a painter who followed it would produce works of persuasive effect. Finally, the tuition programme culminated in the step-by-step rendering in oil studies of a live nude model. Picasso did good work of this kind as a youngster, much like that of any other 19th-century painter who underwent this kind of academic training (cf. p. 44).[47]

This training was rigorously formal and designed to drive out the spontaneity in an artist, and inevitably had considerable disadvantages. Autonomous values of colour, so important to new movements such as Impressionism, were played down. The expressive potential that is in the manner in which an artist applies the paint to the surface, important to great 17th-century artists and much later to Impressionists and Expressionists alike, was altogether out. Academic painting aimed to produce a final work in which the preliminaries were absorbed into a smooth overall finish.

Man with Sheep
(after a plaster cast)
L'homme au mouton (d'après l'antique)
Barcelona, 1895/96
Charcoal on paper, 63 x 47.5 cm
Not in Zervos; MPB 110.598
Barcelona, Museu Picasso

Academic Nude
Etude académique
Barcelona, about 1895–1897
Oil on canvas, 82 x 61 cm
Not in Zervos; Palau 180; MPB 110.047
Barcelona, Museu Picasso

Caricatures. Barcelona, 1898
Pencil on paper, 23.1 x 17 cm
Zervos VI, 153; Palau 328. Private collection

Head of a Boy (Academic Study)
Barcelona, 1896. Oil on canvas on cardboard,
29.8 x 26.1 cm. Palau 177; MPB 110.077
Barcelona, Museu Picasso

Bust of a Young Man (Academic Study)
Barcelona, 1895–1897. Oil on canvas,
43 x 39.3 cm. Palau 178; MPB 110.056
Barcelona, Museu Picasso

But the disadvantages were worth putting up with for a signal advantage. Colour established form, confirming the contour established by the drawn line. This sense of colour stayed with Picasso till the end of his career: colour was intimately connected with form, and could be used to intensify or defamiliarize it. Still, Picasso's academic training alone could never have made him what he became, much as he owed it in later life.

A schoolbook in which the ten-year-old Picasso scribbled sketches has survived from 1891. On one of the sheets he drew a frontal view of a cat (p. 30). The head is so outsize that at first we do not notice the few lines that indicate the body.[48] Those lines are randomly placed and uncertain, while the head, somewhat clumsy though it may be, shows a clear attempt to render the animal precisely. If the study were one done from nature, this would be remarkable, since it would signify an inconsistency; and it would be all the more remarkable if we bear in mind that the cat would have had to be caught in motion, a task that even professional artists are not necessarily equal to. But in fact if we take a look at the drawings in Picasso's schoolbooks we find that most of them were copies of other work, mainly of folksy graphic art; so probably the cat too was copied from someone else's model drawing, not from nature.

In point of fact, art-college textbooks were full of schematic nature studies for copying purposes, many of them showing cats. They looked much like Picasso's hasty sketch,[49] with the difference that the head and body, united in Picasso's drawing, were separate.

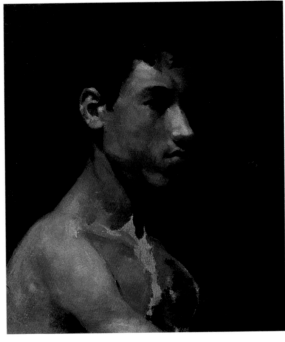

Portrait of Aunt Pepa
Portrait de la tante Pepa
Barcelona, summer 1896
Oil on canvas, 57.5 x 50.5 cm
Zervos XXI, 38; Palau 171; MPB 110.010
Barcelona, Museu Picasso

The inconsistency in his drawing resulted from an attempt to make a whole out of parts before he had the skill to do so. This is most instructive. It does not imply lack of ability; but it does point to a specific shortfall in his capacity at that stage. The boy will doubtless have known of these textbooks of model drawings through his father, who would have used them for teaching purposes himself. His father will have prompted the boy to copy the drawings in them.[50] Having seen his son's gift at work, he will have offered guidance – of a subtle and effective kind. If we look through the young Picasso's sketches, we see that his studies from academic originals were invariably done earlier than we might expect, given the stage he was at in his own training. At school he was already copying college work; at college he copied the next year's material in advance. His father enrolled the boy in courses ahead of normal schedules – though he also encouraged a free artistic imagination in the lad. The young Picasso's work includes not only studies of an academic nature but also an abundance of very different material, mostly caricatures and other studies of the home milieu, of parents and siblings, relations, friends. Caricatures were fun to do; but

A Quarry
Une carrière
Málaga, summer 1896
Oil on canvas, 60.7 x 82.5 cm
Not in Zervos; Palau 168; MPB 110.008
Barcelona, Museu Picasso

the pleasure Picasso presumably took in them must have afforded a safety valve for any irritation at his strict training, too. They also tell us that he had a sure hand at registering form with a constructive, creative imagination. No wonder he remained fond of caricature throughout his life.

Free work (of the student's own choice) was also a part of academic training. Students were encouraged to do their own studies outside studio requirements, to develop an ability to solve unusual problems. They were expected to have a sketchbook with them at all times, to record striking motifs.[51] Picasso's parents gave him his first album in early 1894, and that autumn gave him a second.[52] They were the first of a great many sketchbooks which served Picasso as his most direct and personal tool. The importance of these sketchbooks has only become evident in recent years.[53] Of course modern artists use sketchbooks; but to use them on Picasso's scale was more of a feature of art in older times. In this respect, again, Picasso was a creature of tradition.

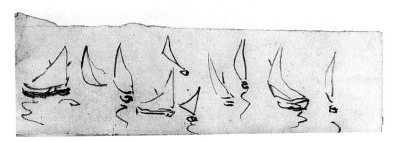

Sketches of Boats
Etudes des bateaux à voiles
Barcelona, 1896
Pencil on paper, 3.5 x 13 cm
Not in Zervos; Palau 172; MPB 111.373
Barcelona, Museu Picasso

The Making of a Genius 1890 – 1898 **46**

House in a Wheatfield
Maison dans un champ de blé
Horta de Ebro, summer 1898
Oil on canvas, 33 x 44 cm
Not in Zervos; Palau 254; MPB 110.936
Barcelona, Museu Picasso

Picasso's father was unremitting in moulding his son along his own lines. He wanted him to be the academic painter *par excellence*. He himself painted animal scenes and genre paintings, the kind of work traditionally considered of secondary value; and he wanted his son to paint figure and history paintings, which were then valued above all else.[54] And so Picasso's freely chosen studies turn out to be mainly figure and portrait studies. And his father's oppressive influence shows again in the fact that he himself was his talented son's preferred subject (cf. p. 40).

This process culminated in two paintings the father prompted the son to do in 1896 and 1897, "First Communion" (p. 38) and "Science and Charity" (pp. 50/51). Picasso's father sat for the doctor whose skill and knowledge will determine the patient's fate. And his father also influenced the reception of the pictures by using his contacts with newspaper critics.[55] He was omnipresent in the young Picasso's life. The boy's whole education took place in schools and colleges where his father was on the staff.

Deliberately though Picasso's training was steered by his father, and intelligent though it was, it was also outdated. Elsewhere in Europe, this academic method had been superseded. Compared with other countries, the art scene in Spain when Picasso was a youngster was decidedly on the conservative side. From 1860 to 1890 the history paintings of Eduardo Rosales, Mariano Fortuny and Francisco Pradilla dominated Spanish art; their work was comparable with that of a Thomas Couture in France, a Gustaaf Wapper in Belgium, or a Carl Friedrich Lessing in Germany – all of them artists clinging to a training acquired in the first half of the century, and to views on art that had peaked in mid-century.[56]

47   The Making of a Genius   1890 – 1898

Sketches in the Style of El Greco
Feuilles d'études à la Greco
Barcelona, 1898
Ink on paper, 31.8 x 21.6 cm
Zervos VI, 152; Palau 330

So a crisis was inevitable in Picasso's life. In 1897, when his father sent the sixteen-year-old to the Royal Academy in Madrid, it was a great mistake. The legend-makers have tended to claim that Picasso attended none of his courses at all[57] – but he did in fact go to those of Moreno Carbonero. Still, he was profoundly disappointed by studies at the Academy, and concentrated on copying the old masters in the Prado. In June 1898 he gave up his Madrid studies for good.[58]

It was the first evidence of his unusual personality. He could not learn anything new or better in Madrid because the tuition methods were the same as in Corunna or Barcelona. He could see all the shortcomings clearly, his own as well as the Academy's. It was not as if he no longer needed guidance. His copy of Velázquez's portrait of King Philip IV of Spain, for instance, is a decidedly mediocre piece of work. His whole life long he had certain fundamental weaknesses, such as a tendency to apply his concentration one-sidedly. If a subject made a variety of demands on him, Picasso would prefer to tackle the one he thought important. His early academic studies were accomplished enough, but often they were sloppy in one way or another; later, he would still often make crucial mistakes. For instance, in his portraits he often positions the eyes wrongly, a typical result of an inadequate grasp of the overall relation of parts to the whole.

A letter he wrote to a friend on 3 November 1897 shows how much he craved good instruction in Madrid. In it he complains

bitterly of the backwardness and incompetence of his teachers and says he would rather go to Paris or Munich, where the art tuition was the best in Europe. Munich would even be best, he said – although he was going to go to Paris – because in Munich people didn't bother with fashionable stuff such as pointillism![59] In other words, Picasso was longing for the kind of academic training a Franz von Stuck gave; but he was not interested in the methods and ideas that were currently considered avant-garde.

Though it may seem astonishing or paradoxical, the fact is that Picasso did not become Picasso under the influence of progressive ideas but because an old-fashioned milieu was imposing superannuated notions on him. He found it impossible to make do with routine and mediocrity. Fully aware that the decision to quit the Academy would seriously damage relations with his father, for whom Madrid still represented the gateway to desired success, Picasso made a radical break – despite the total uncertainty of his new future. Not yet seventeen, he set about achieving his independence in every respect. And from now on he went his own way.

Portrait of Philip IV (after Velázquez)
Portrait de Philippe IV (d'après Velázquez)
Madrid, about 1897/98
Oil on canvas, 54.2 x 46.7 cm
Not in Zervos; Palau 230; MPB 110.017
Barcelona, Museu Picasso

Self-portrait as an 18th-Century Gentleman
Autoportrait en gentilhomme du XVIIIe siècle
Barcelona, 1897
Oil on canvas, 55.8 x 46 cm
Zervos XXI, 48; Palau 149; MPB 110.053
Barcelona, Museu Picasso

Self-portrait with Close-Cropped Hair
Autoportrait aux cheveux courts
Barcelona, 1896
Oil on canvas, 46.5 x 31.5 cm
Not in Zervos; Palau 148; MPB 110.063
Barcelona, Museu Picasso

Head of a Man in the Style of El Greco
Tête d'homme à la Greco
Barcelona, 1899
Oil on canvas, 34.7 x 31.2 cm
Not in Zervos; Palau 332; MPB 110.034
Barcelona, Museu Picasso

Science and Charity
Science et charité
Barcelona, early 1897
Oil on canvas, 197 x 249.5 cm
Zervos XXI, 56; Palau 209; MPB 110.046
Barcelona, Museu Picasso

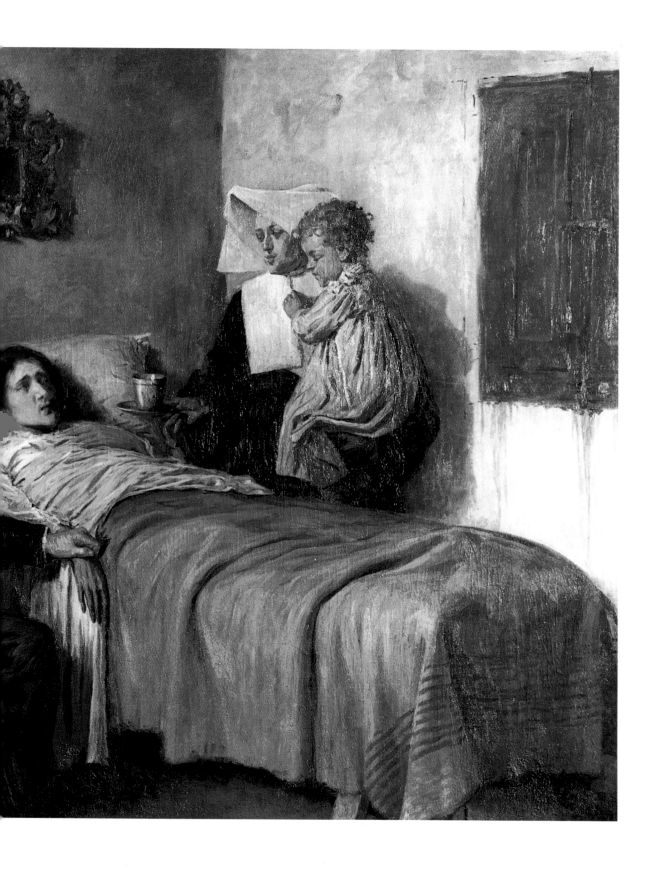

3 The Art of Youth
1898–1901

Picasso's decision to abandon his academic training was a decisive crisis in his youth. The upheaval of having to leave everything behind produced an immediate and visible result: he fell ill. In spring 1898 in Madrid he came down with scarlet fever, and was quarantined for forty days. We cannot say whether his psychological state was responsible for the illness, but his bad health hardened Picasso's resolve. He was scarcely recovered but he turned his back on Madrid. After spending a brief while in Barcelona, he went to Horta de Ebro with his friend Manuel Pallarès. He stayed for almost nine months in Pallarès's home village in the deserted hills of Catalonia, till February 1899. The two friends would go on long walks together, and painted and drew.

Picasso then returned to Barcelona and embarked on his independent career in art. The Catalan metropolis was his base till his definitive final move to France in 1904. They were restless years, and Picasso spent a number of longer periods in Paris as well as making a further five-month attempt to settle in Madrid in 1901[60]. And of course they were unsettled years of crisis for Spain, too. In 1898, through its colony Cuba, Spain became involved in a war with the USA. Defeat spelt the end of what remained of Spain's colonial empire and claims to be a world power.

It was a turning point, and brought profound political, social and cultural insecurity with it. People were torn between loyalty to a great past and new affiliation with Europe. Their ideas ran the entire gamut from liberal republicanism to anarchism. Castile and Andalusia lost their dominance, while the industrial north came into its own.[61]

In such a period, the seventeen-year-old Picasso had considerable capital, albeit not of a financial kind. He was confident, talented and young. He had contacts. And he had unlimited energy. His father's encouragement had married a natural talent that took demands easily in its stride, and the inevitable upshot was independence of character. It was helpful that his father indirectly cut the umbilical cord by renting a studio for his son during his studies in Barcelona.[62] More importantly, the father's strategies had already gained Picasso a certain professional recognition.

Angel Fernández de Soto at a Café
Angel Fernández de Soto au café
Barcelona, 1903
Ink, watercolour and crayon, 27 x 20 cm
Zervos XXI, 161; DB D IX, 9
Private collection

The Embrace in the Street
Les amants de la rue
Paris, 1900
Pastel on paper, 59 x 35 cm
Zervos I, 24; DB II, 12; Palau 498; MPB 4.263
Barcelona, Museu Picasso

In 1896 "First Communion" (p. 38) was exhibited in Barcelona. This was the third arts and crafts exhibition to be held there (after 1891 and 1894), a major event intended to showcase contemporary Catalan culture. Some thirteen hundred works were on show, by important artists of every aesthetic persuasion. The press response was also a major one. To be exhibited in that show was a triumph for a fifteen-year-old, even if his father's contacts had helped; to be praised in a leading newspaper, even if he won no prizes, was even better.[63]

A year later he painted the grand "Science and Charity" (pp. 50/51). Anecdotal realism was a popular variety of historical painting at the time. Picasso's picture had thematic links with various other paintings that had been successfully exhibited, some of them in the Barcelona show.[64] Again his father's prompting and influence were decisive. Picasso submitted the work to the Madrid General Art Exhibition, and it was taken by a jury that included the painter Antonio Muñoz Degrain, a friend and colleague of his

father's to whom the youth had already given a portrait study.[65] "Science and Charity" received an honourable mention at the exhibition, and subsequently a gold medal in Málaga.[66]

So Picasso was known to those who followed contemporary art when he set out on his own way. And Barcelona was a good place for it, a progressive city compared with traditionalist, academic Madrid. Spanish *art nouveau* was based in Barcelona, in the form of a group of artists known as the modernists, and in Barcelona too were their successors and antagonists, the post-modernists.[67] An architect of global importance, Antoni Gaudí, was changing the face of the city. The current aesthetic concerns of Europe were hotly debated, and adapted to local needs. Barcelona was the centre for avant-garde Spanish art, and at the nearby seaside resort of Sitges the Festa Modernista was held, an *art nouveau* event to which special trains were run.[68]

In June 1897 the Barcelona café "Els Quatre Gats" (The Four Cats) opened its doors. It was an artists' café and hosted changing

Portrait of Josep Cardona (by Lamplight)
Portrait de Josep Cardona (Homme à la lampe)
Barcelona, 1899
Oil on canvas, 100 x 63 cm
Zervos I, 6; Palau 320
Paris, Alex Maguy Collection

The Closed Window
La fenêtre fermée
Barcelona, 1899
Oil on panel, 21.8 x 13.7 cm
Not in Zervos; Palau 318; MPB 110.218
Barcelona, Museu Picasso

exhibitions in the spirit of "Le Chat Noir", the "Ambassadeur" or "Le Mirliton" in Paris. True, "Els Quatre Gats" survived only till 1903; but in its short life it was the hub of Catalonian artistic life. Leading "Modernistas" helped establish it: the painter Ramón Casas (who won an award at the exhibition of 1896), painter and writer Santiago Rusiñol, and the journalist Miguel Utrillo. And leading post-modernists were among its clientele, including Isidre Nonell, Joaquim Mir and Ricardo Canals.[69]

It cannot have been too difficult for Picasso to join these circles, since they would have heard his name; and belonging to them was a good start for his career. In the art world as in any other, talent and energy need personal contacts to help them on their way.

And it was contacts that helped decide Picasso for Paris. Though he was impressed by what he had heard about Munich, it was to Paris that he made his move. Munich art was seen in Barcelona, and indeed at the 1896 exhibition painters and sculptors from Munich constituted the largest foreign contingent.[70] But Paris was closer in various senses. It had an established Catalan community, including a number of artists temporarily living and working in the

Menu of "Els Quatre Gats"
Menu des "Quatre Gats"
Barcelona, 1899
Pencil and India ink, coloured,
22 x 16.5 cm
(cf. Zervos VI, 193; Palau 377)
Whereabouts unknown

Interior of "Els Quatre Gats"
Intérieur des "Quatre Gats"
Barcelona, 1900
Oil on canvas, 41 x 28 cm
Zervos I, 21; DB I, 9; Palau 375
New York, Simon M. Jaglom Collection

The Divan
Le divan
Barcelona, 1899
Pastel on paper, 26.2 x 29.7 cm
Zervos I, 23; DB I, 10; MPB 4.267
Barcelona, Museu Picasso

Woman Leaning on a Table. Three Female Profiles
Femme s'appuyant sur une table
et trois visages de profil
Paris, 1901
Coloured chalk on paper, 15 x 21 cm
Zervos XXI, 271

city. So Picasso did not have to conquer the great metropolis single-handed.

He first visited Paris in autumn 1900, for the World Fair, where his painting "Last Moments" had been chosen for the show of Spanish art.[71] Friends from "Els Quatre Gats" smoothed his way in Paris. He was able to use their studios when they were visiting Spain, and he was introduced to the industrialist and art dealer Pedro Mañach, who afforded him a first secure foothold. Mañach

Le Moulin de la Galette
Paris, autumn 1900
Oil on canvas, 90.2 x 117 cm
Zervos I, 41; DB II, 10; Palau 509
New York, The Solomon R. Guggenheim Museum,
Justin K. Thannhauser Foundation

signed a contract with Picasso guaranteeing to take his pictures for
two years and to pay 150 francs per month by way of fixed income.
He also floated the idea of a first Paris Picasso exhibition at the
Galerie Vollard in 1901[72].

To Picasso, this was no more than an entrée into the art market.
For the moment, Spain seemed the better territory for his ambitions. In early 1901 he went to Madrid and started an art magazine
together with a young writer, Francesc de Asis Soler. It was meant
as a platform for Spanish *art nouveau* and was tellingly titled "Arte
Joven" (Young Art). Benet Soler Vidal, whose family put up the
money for the project, was the editor, while Picasso was the art
director. It was not a particularly successful magazine and folded
after five issues; but it was eloquent of Picasso's views on art at that
period. Contributions were squarely in line with the "Modernista"
spirit, though they had a distinctly satirical and even nihilist flavour
to them. Picasso did the majority of the illustrations.[73] The maga-

zine was modelled on the Barcelona modernist organ "Pél y Ploma" (Brush and Pen), the presiding artist of which was Ramón Casas.[74] The aim was plainly to take contemporary art to Madrid, the conservative heart of Spain. When failure became inevitable, Picasso returned to Barcelona, and subsequently devoted his attention to Paris.

At that time his work took its bearings from what the Spanish avant-garde approved. He put his academic leanings aside and adopted the new creative approaches of the period in the way he had learnt: by copying. The works shown in his first exhibition at "Els Quatre Gats", for instance, consisted mainly of portraits (cf. p. 54) done after the example of Casas' famous pictures of prominent people.[75] The people Picasso portrayed were not as well known, but he used the same approach, drawing them from the knees up against a colourful background, using a mixture of charcoal and watercolour.

The Blue Dancer
Pierrot et danseuse
Paris, autumn 1900
Oil on canvas, 38 x 46 cm
Zervos XXI, 224; DB II, 23; Palau 507
Sutton Place (Surrey), Private collection

Gypsy Outside "La Musciera"
Bohémienne devant "La Musciera"
Barcelona, 1900
Pastel on paper, 44.5 x 59 cm
Zervos XXI, 167; DB II, 8; Palau 447
Private collection

The Embrace
L'étreinte
Paris, 1900
Oil on paper on cardboard, 51.2 x 55.3 cm
Zervos I, 26; DB II, 14; Palau 499
Moscow, Pushkin Museum

The Art of Youth 1898 – 1901 **60**

The Barcelona Bullring
L'entrée de la Plaza à Barcelone
Barcelona, 1900
Pastel on cardboard, 51 x 69 cm
Zervos XXI, 145; DB II, 9; Palau 454
Toyama (Japan), Toyama Prefectural Museum
of Modern Art

The Brutal Embrace
Frenzy
Paris, 1900
Pastel, 47.5 x 38.5 cm
Not in Zervos; Palau 500
Private collection; formerly Basel, Galerie Beyeler

Pages 62 and 63:
The Montmartre Fair
Baraque de foire, Montmartre
Paris, autumn 1900
Oil on canvas, 36.5 x 44.5 cm
Zervos XXI, 227; DB V, 63; Palau 504
Private collection

Montmartre Brasserie: The Flower Vendor
Brasserie à Montmartre
Paris, 1900
Oil on cardboard, 43 x 53.5 cm
Zervos XXI, 281; Palau 579
Paris, Private collection; formerly Galerie Rosengart

La Corrida
Course de taureaux (Corrida)
Barcelona, spring 1901
Oil on canvas, 47 x 56 cm
Zervos I, 88; DB IV, 5; Palau 557
Paris, Max Pellequer Collection

Bullfighting Scene (Corrida)
Course de taureaux (Corrida)
Barcelona, spring 1901
Oil on cardboard on canvas, 49.5 x 64.7 cm
Zervos VI, 378; DB IV, 6; Palau 559
Stavros S. Niarchos Collection

62   The Art of Youth   1898 – 1901

The Art of Youth 1898 – 1901 **63**

Portrait of Pedro Mañach. Paris, spring 1901
Oil on canvas, 100.5 x 67.5 cm
Zervos VI, 1459; DB V, 4; Palau 569
Washington (DC), National Gallery of Art

The Dwarf. Paris, 1901
Oil on cardboard, 104.5 x 61 cm
Zervos I, 66; DB IV, 2; Palau 602; MPB 4.274
Barcelona, Museu Picasso

Portrait of Gustave Coquiot
Portrait de Gustave Coquiot
Paris, spring 1901
Oil on cardboard, 46 x 38 cm
Zervos I, 85; DB VI, 16; Palau 571
Zurich, E.G. Bührle Collection

Above left:
Bedizened Old Woman
Femme aux bijoux
Barcelona, 1901
Oil on cardboard, 67.4 x 52 cm
Zervos VI, 389; DB IV, 4; Palau 600
Philadelphia (PA), Philadelphia Museum of Art,
The Arensberg Collection

Portrait of "Bibi la Purée"
Portrait de "Bibi la Purée"
Paris, 1901
Oil on canvas, 49 x 39 cm
Zervos VI, 360; DB V, 74; Palau 704
Paris, Musée National d'Art Moderne,
Centre Georges Pompidou

Portrait of Gustave Coquiot
Portrait de Gustave Coquiot
Paris, spring to summer 1901
Oil on canvas, 100 x 81 cm
Zervos I, 84; DB V, 64; Palau 605
Paris, Musée National d'Art Moderne,
Centre Georges Pompidou

Below left:
Overdressed woman
Femme dans la loge
Paris, 1901
Oil on canvas, 77 x 61 cm
Zervos XXI, 264; DB V, 71; Palau 648
Geneva, Charles Im Obersteg Collection

Woman with an Elaborate Coiffure (The Plumed Hat)
Femme au chapeau à plumes
Madrid, 1901
Oil on canvas, 46.5 x 38.5 cm
Zervos I, 39; DB III, 4; Palau 553
San Antonio (TX), Marion Koogler
McNay Art Institute

The Art of Youth 1898 – 1901 **67**

Woman with Blue Hat, Madrid, 1901
Pastel on cardboard, 60.8 x 49.8 cm
Not in Zervos
Private collection; formerly Galerie Rosengart

The Absinthe Drinker, Paris, 1901
Oil on cardboard, 65.5 x 50.8 cm
Zervos I, 62; DB V, 12; Palau 596
New York, Mrs. Melville Hall Collection

Stylistically, these works are strongly contoured with heavy outlines, and the facial features are highlighted with a few economical strokes. Picasso works in polarities. The overall shape is briskly established, but within it the face and body are differently treated. The long vertical lines or broad-area charcoal smudges are broken up with thick, obvious details. It is all done with great panache, but it is clearly simpler and even more schematic than pictures by Casas, where formal contrasts are far more subtly deployed. Picasso is out for rapid, foreground impact, and has reduced the structure of the models he is following to a principle, leaving the background a large bare space.

To reduce the given to a principle, and to define form in terms of linear contour and outline, were things that Picasso had learnt in his training; so the line-based art of *art nouveau* presented no problem to him. The menu he designed for "Els Quatre Gats" (p. 56) in 1899 is a good example. Every shape is rendered in clear line. Figures and background details work in plain zones of monochrome colour, or else are offset from each other by minor, stylized details. The illustration shows the speed and assurance with which Picasso had adopted a "Modernista" approach. There would be no real point in suggesting a specific influence on such a work.[76] Far too many of his works are much the same; Picasso was almost into serial production, and the tendency stayed with him later and repeatedly demonstrated the intensity with which he would pursue a subject or form. Themes such as an embrace or a kiss were to be repeated many times over, often varied only in some minor detail. He sketched poses and groupings over and over, deploying the results in various changing compositions.

But Picasso at that time did not confine himself to the repertoire of *art nouveau*. He was omnivorous in his taste for new aesthetic trends. Some of his drawings and paintings (cf. pp. 45 and 49) show him reworking the formal idiom of El Greco. The Greek-born painter had evolved his own distinctive style of elongated proportions and powerful colours in the late 16th and early 17th century in Spain. From El Greco Picasso borrowed the expressive elongation and the restless brushwork. He had seen original El Grecos in the Prado, of course; but his interest was also very much a product of the period. For centuries El Greco had been forgotten, and it was not till the 19th century that avant-garde artists rediscovered him. Charles Baudelaire was an admirer, Eugène Delacroix and Edgar Degas collected his work – though as late as 1881 a director of the Prado felt able to dismiss El Greco's paintings as "absurd caricatures". It was not till the "Modernistas" that this Spanish attitude really changed; Utrillo, above all, was instrumental in the revival of El Greco's fortunes.[77]

But it was Henri de Toulouse-Lautrec who made the most powerful impression on the youthful Picasso. His posters and paintings, draughtsmanlike in manner, economical, precise, often on the verge

Floral Still Life
Nature morte aux fleurs
Paris, 1901
Oil on canvas, 65 x 49 cm
Zervos I, 61; DB V, 22; Palau 642
London, Tate Gallery

Pierreuse
Pierreuse, la main sur l'épaule
Paris, spring 1901
Oil on cardboard, 69.5 x 57 cm
Zervos I, 63; DB V, 11; Palau 598; MPB 4.271
Barcelona, Museu Picasso

Portrait of a Woman
La Madrilène (Tête de jeune femme)
Paris, spring 1901
Oil on canvas, 52 x 33 cm
Zervos I, 64; DB V, 57; Palau 635
Otterlo, Rijksmuseum Kröller-Müller

Head of a Woman
Tête de femme
Paris, 1901
Oil on cardboard, 46.7 x 31.5 cm
Zervos I, 74; DB V, 59; Palau 631
Barcelona, Private collection

of being caricatures, held a particular appeal for Picasso. Toulouse-Lautrec was well known in Barcelona, but it was not till he visited Paris that Picasso saw originals and even bought posters to hang in his own studio.[78] As well as formal considerations , what interested him was the Frenchman's subject matter, the world of the cabaret and night club, the world of dancers and conviviality. Soon Picasso was producing his own pictures on these themes (cf. pp. 56 to 59).

In 1900, Picasso's interest in Toulouse-Lautrec peaked in his painting "Le Moulin de la Galette" (p. 58). Inside, there is a crowd; further on, beyond a diagonally cropped group of women seated at a table to the left, we see dancing couples as in a frieze. The subject and the treatment are reminiscent of a Toulouse-Lautrec done in 1889, which in turn was a reworking of Pierre-Auguste Renoir's 1876 painting of the merriment at the famous Moulin, transposing the colourful fun from the garden to the interior and to night.[79] Picasso follows Toulouse-Lautrec, and intensifies the effect by using the gas lighting to establish an atmosphere of half-light, a uniform duskiness in which the figures appear as patches of colour against a dark background. Correspondingly, the style of brush-work is more summary, working in large blocks and pinpointing only a few characteristics of the people shown. The people have in fact been stripped of their individuality and are merely props to illustrate social amusement.[80]

So Picasso was not merely imitating. He also tried to reconceive the originals he copied. Very soon he was trying to rework diverse influences in a single work. A good example painted on cardboard in 1901 is "Pierreuse" (p. 71).[81] A young woman wearing a red top and a decorative hat is seated at a blue table, leaning on both elbows, her right arm crooked to clasp her left shoulder. Her atti-tude is one of protective barring and signals that she is withdrawn within herself. Dreamily she gazes away into an undefined and indistinct distance.

A sense of transported absence is conveyed not only by the woman's pose but also by Picasso's compositional subtlety. The woman is leaning across to the left side of the picture, establishing a falling diagonal and thus introducing a quality of movement into the work. But it is movement that is meticulously counterbalanced and neutralized by the composition as a whole. The use of spatial areas is richly ambivalent. Inclining across the table, the woman seems to be coming nearer to us, and with her hat cropped more than once by the picture edge it is as if she were on the point of stepping out towards us. At the same time, though, her position on

The Kept Woman
(Courtesan with a Necklace of Gems)
L'hétaïre
Paris, 1901
Oil on canvas, 65.3 x 54.5 cm
Zervos I, 42; DB VI, 17; Palau 662
New York, The Metropolitan
Museum of Art

Woman Wearing a Necklace of Gems
Femme au collier de gemmes
Paris, 1901
Oil on cardboard, 43.7 x 36.1 cm
Zervos VI, 385; DB V, 48; Palau 660
Toronto, Art Gallery of Ontario

Lady in Blue
Femme en bleu
Madrid, early 1901
Oil on canvas, 133.5 x 101 cm
Zervos XXI, 211; DB III, 5; Palau 539
Madrid, Centro de Arte Reina Sofia

the other side of the table emphasizes inaccessibility. It is a painting of mood, and the contrastive use of colour, with the dichotomy of flat areas and broken-up form, serve to underline its mood. While the face and body are strongly outlined and colourfully painted in monochrome, the background is an iridescent tapestry of colour dabs. It is a restless patchwork of yellow, red, blue and green, and the pastose painting disturbs our eye and establishes productive unclarities. Picasso was using techniques borrowed from the pointillists, Vincent van Gogh, Paul Gauguin and the Nabis all in one, to make a style of his own.

The same applies to his portrait of Pedro Mañach (p. 64). It is an uncompromising frontal view. Mañach's right hand is on his hip, his left arm almost straight. The figure is a well-nigh pure study in

Right:
French Cancan
French Cancan
Paris, autumn 1901
Oil on canvas, 46 x 61 cm
Zervos XXI, 209; DB V, 55; Palau 508
Geneva, Raymond Barbey Collection

Women Chatting at the Races
Les courses
Paris, spring 1901
Oil on cardboard, 52 x 67 cm
Zervos XXI, 205; DB V, 31; Palau 587
France, Private collection

The Art of Youth 1898 – 1901 75

76 The Art of Youth   1898 – 1901

Mother and Child
Mère et enfant
Paris, spring 1901
Oil on canvas, 68 x 52 cm
Zervos XXI, 292; DB V, 10; Palau 576
Bern, Kunstmuseum Bern (on loan)

Woman Huddled on the Ground with a Child
Femme accroupie et enfant
Paris, 1901. Oil on canvas, 110.5 x 96.5 cm
Zervos I, 115; DB VI, 30; Palau 705
Cambridge (MA), Fogg Art Museum,
Harvard University

The Mother (Mother and Child)
La mère (Mère tenant deux enfants)
Paris, spring 1901
Oil on cardboard on panel, 74.4 x 51.4 cm
Zervos XXI, 291; DB V, 9; Palau 575
Saint Louis (MO), Saint Louis Art Museum

Mother and Child in Front of a Bowl of Flowers
Mère et enfant aux fleurs
Paris, spring to summer 1901
Oil on cardboard, 54 x 65 cm
Zervos I, 77; DB V, 7; Palau 629
Paris, Private collection

Still Life (The Dessert)
Nature morte (Le dessert)
Paris, 1901
Oil on canvas, 50 x 80.5 cm
Zervos I, 70; DB V, 72; Palau 659; MPB 4.273
Barcelona, Museu Picasso

outline, set against an ochre yellow and almost entirely undifferentiated background. Background and figure alike are done as large areas lacking finish, and the face too has been established with only a few lines and colours. It is a picture of contrasts, the yellow background offsetting the white and dark brown of the clothing; but the signal red of the tie, striking the sole aggressive note, has the effect of resolving polarities and bringing the whole work together. The influence of van Gogh's Provence work done late in life, and of the Pont-Aven school, is palpable.[82]

Of course contemporary critics were quick to notice Picasso's adoption of current avant-garde artistic styles. Reviewing the work shown in 1901 at the Galerie Vollard, Félicien Fagus wrote that Picasso had plainly been influenced by "Delacroix, Manet, Monet, van Gogh, Pissarro, Toulouse-Lautrec, Degas, Forain, perhaps even Rops".[83] The only thing wrong with this assessment is that it misses out an important name or two, such as that of Gauguin.

But the sheer number of influences on Picasso at that time need not only be seen in a negative light. It is normal for young artists to be influenced as they try to find their own style. And Picasso wasn't merely copying; he was quickly able to harmonize various influences into new wholes. If this had not been so, it would be hard to understand his early success on the art market. He had an excellent memory for formal qualities, one which stored them so deeply that they became part of his own way of thinking. He was imitating, yes – but he did so in order to find a style entirely his own.

77   The Art of Youth   1898 – 1901

The Two Saltimbanques (Harlequin and His Companion)
Les deux saltimbanques (Arlequin et sa compagne)
Paris, autumn 1901
Oil on canvas, 73 x 60 cm
Zervos I, 92; DB VI, 20; Palau 666
Moscow, Pushkin Museum

Harlequin Leaning on His Elbow
Arlequin accoudé
Paris, autumn 1901
Oil on canvas, 82.8 x 61.3 cm
Zervos I, 79; DB VI, 22; Palau 670
New York, The Metropolitan Museum of Art

4 The Blue Period
1901–1904

Picasso's works in the period from 1898 to 1901 were most diverse in character; it was plainly a time when he was getting his bearings, as is confirmed by the fact that he was forever examining the creative principles of contemporary progressive art. His examination was a deliberate and selective process; one of Picasso's great abilities was his discernment of the strengths and weaknesses of new artistic movements, his gift for borrowing what he could use. As a pupil he had early on perceived the shortcomings of academic art and realised that it was irreconcilable with his own convictions; now, similarly, he saw the dead ends of the avant-garde, the tendency of *art nouveau* to use superficial ornamentation and stiff linearity, the vapid esotericism of symbolism. In the year 1901 Picasso was already in a position to make a response and create something new of his own – the long series of works known as his Blue Period.

The term places in the foreground the monochrome tendency of the work. It is striking, certainly; but merely to identify the colouring is to say little. Nowadays the pictures are valued for their accessible formal repertoire, which has a unified, homogeneous quality to it; but the fact is that they are by no means simple, but rather products of complex, multi-layered artifice. They constitute no less than a résumé of European artistic progress since the mid–19th century[84] – though Picasso did forgo the newly-discovered potential of colour. In this respect he was diametrically at odds with Fauvism, which flourished at the same time.[85] So his contemporaries had initial difficulties making out the intention and value of Picasso's work. Picasso could of course have gone about things an easier way: a lesser talent would have been satisfied with what had been achieved so far and would have continued turning out art that spelled success with the public.

Though the fundamentals of the Blue Period were evolved in Paris, Barcelona remained the centre of Picasso's actual labours till he finally moved to the French capital in April 1904. In fact his work in Catalonia was interrupted only by a brief (and commercially dismal) stay in Paris from October 1902 to January 1903. His pictures, not merely melancholy but profoundly depressed and

Self-portrait "Yo"
Autoportrait "Yo"
Paris, summer 1901
Oil on cardboard on panel, 54 x 31.8 cm
Zervos I, 113; DB V, I; Palau 678
New York, Mrs. John Hay Whitney Collection

Self-portrait with Cloak
Autoportrait
Paris, late 1901
Oil on canvas, 81 x 60 cm
Zervos I, 91; DB VI, 35; Palau 715; MPP 4
Paris, Musée Picasso

82 The Blue Period 1901 – 1904

The Blue Roofs
Les toits bleus
Paris, 1901
Oil on cardboard, 40 x 60 cm
Zervos I, 82; DB V, 21; Palau 614
Oxford, Ashmolean Museum

The Blue Room
La chambre bleue (Le tub)
Paris, 1901
Oil on canvas, 51 x 62.5 cm
Zervos I, 103; DB VI, 15; Palau 694
Washington (DC), The Phillips Collection

Jeanne (Female Nude)
Jeanne (Nu couché)
Paris, 1901
Oil on canvas, 70.5 x 90.2 cm
Zervos I, 106; DB V, 52; Palau 606
Paris, Musée National d'Art Moderne,
Centre Georges Pompidou

cheerless, inspired no affection in the public or in buyers. Picasso had broken with Mañach, and his financial position was very bad indeed. The report that Picasso even burnt a large number of his drawings for heating that winter may be mere legend, but in terms of the art market he was certainly in the cold. And this isolation continued till 1905, when collectors began to take an interest in his work of the Blue and Rose Periods. It was not poverty that led him to paint the impoverished outsiders of society, but rather the fact that he painted them made him poor himself.[86] But he was neither lonely nor in critical straits. He was still an important figure in the Catalan scene. And he had his foothold in the Parisian Spanish community, and met new friends who consolidated his position, such as the writer Max Jacob.[87]

To understand Picasso's circumstances at that time helps us not only to grasp his life but also to grasp his subject matter. The beggars, street girls, alcoholics, old and sick people, despairing lovers, and mothers and children, all fit the despondent mood of the Blue Period so perfectly that it is as if Picasso had invented them. But of course all he invented was his treatment; otherwise he was squarely in the avant-garde line of development since the mid–19th century. The relinquishment of academic ideals and of the traditional valu-

Portrait of Jaime Sabartés (The Glass of
Beer)
Portrait de Jaime Sabartés (Le bock)
Paris, September to October 1901
Oil on canvas, 82 x 66 cm
Zervos I, 97; DB VI, 19; Palau 665
Moscow, Pushkin Museum

ations placed on supposedly higher or lower kinds of art, and the
new stress that was placed on autonomy of form, had by no means
implied indifference to content. It was just that content had
changed. The subjects now considered fit to paint were different
ones.

Gustave Courbet's realism located subjects in everyday village
life. Courbet liked to give plain physical work the full monumental
treatment, knowing the subject had hitherto not been taken seriously.[88] In Honoré Daumier's drawings, society's weaknesses were
lampooned, but Daumier also took the lives of smiths, butchers or
washerwomen seriously in paintings and graphic art that owed no
slavish debt to any classical norm.[89] And Impressionism, of course,
would be radically misunderstood if we saw it purely as formal

The Absinthe Drinker
La buveuse d'absinthe
Paris, 1901
Oil on canvas, 73 x 54 cm
Zervos I, 98; DB VI, 24; Palau 675
St. Petersburg, Hermitage

virtuosity, games played with colour, and atmospherics. Impressionism has all this to offer, but more too: the Impressionists did not
only paint sunny landscapes, or scenes recorded in the moods of
different seasons or times of day, they also discovered the modern
city as a source of subjects. If they recognised no hierarchy of formal values, they also knew no precedence of subjects. There were
no taboos in their approach to the new reality, no refusal to face
subjects that were beneath their dignity. Smoke-filled railway sta-
tions and cathedrals, boulevard life in Paris and night clubs and the
gloom of drinkers and whores, all appeared in their work. The
revolution in form was accompanied by a revolution in subject
matter. Their position as artistic outsiders prompted them to
examine social realities.[90]

85   The Blue Period   1901 – 1904

The Death of Casagemas
La mort de Casagemas
Paris, summer 1901
Oil on panel, 27 x 35 cm
Zervos XXI, 178; DB VI, 5; Palau 676; MPP 3
Paris, Musée Picasso

Picasso's Blue Period portrayals of beggars and prostitutes, workers and drinkers in bars, took up this line. His absinthe drinkers had antecedents in Degas and Toulouse-Lautrec.[91] And the Pierreuse staring dreamily into nowhere was of course a street girl. Many similar compositions followed from 1901 to 1904. Often they had thematic links to Degas and Toulouse-Lautrec, and links in terms of monumental treatment to Courbet, who – influenced by the revolutionary thinking of Pierre-Joseph Proudhon – had dared as early as 1856 to make two prostitutes by the Seine the subject of a large-scale painting.[92] Picasso's arresting "Woman Ironing" (p. 114) was also a product of a recent tradition, with affinities to works by Daumier and Degas.[93]

Of course it was not only the visual arts that were in flux. Political, philosophical and cultural thinking were expressed in literary form. Along with the work of Proudhon, there were the novels of the Naturalist Emile Zola. "Nana" in particular, the story of a prostitute, was well known, indeed notorious.[94] Just as Edouard Manet painted a "Nana" himself (Hamburg, Kunsthalle), so too Baudelaire and Zola responded to the new art in writing.[95]

We should also remember that the Paris milieu was not the sole influence on Picasso's Blue Period. Spanish culture played a considerable part too. After the 1868 revolution, which had led to a short-lived democratic republic[96], social injustice became a concern of Spanish art and writing too.[97] Of the various ideas that were imported into the country, anarchism was particularly influential; the Barcelona literary and artistic circles Picasso moved in were very interested in the tenets of anarchism, albeit in conjunction with other ideas too.[98] A self-portrait Picasso painted in the winter

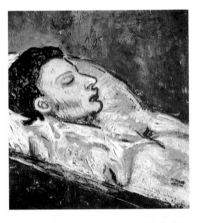

The Death of Casagemas (Casagemas in His Coffin)
La mort de Casagemas (Casagemas dans son cercueil)
Paris, summer 1901
Oil on cardboard, 72.5 x 57.8 cm
Zervos XXI, 179; DB VI, 6; Palau 677
Estate of the artist

Evocation (The Burial of Casagemas)
Evocation (L'enterrement de Casagemas)
Paris, summer 1901
Oil on canvas, 150.5 x 90.5 cm
Zervos I, 55; DB VI, 4; Palau 688
Paris, Musée d'Art Moderne
de la Ville de Paris

Portrait of Mateu Fernández de Soto
Portrait de Mateu Fernández de Soto
Paris, October 1901
Oil on canvas, 61 x 46.5 cm
Zervos I, 94; DB VI, 21; Palau 689
Winterthur, Oskar Reinhart Foundation

Portrait of Jaime Sabartés
Portrait de Jaime Sabartés
Paris, 1901
Oil on canvas, 44.5 x 36.8 cm
Zervos I, 87; DB VI, 34; Palau 706
Barcelona, Museu Picasso

of 1901/1902 (p. 80) captures the mood. It is as if Dostoyevsky's novels, Nietzsche's ideas and the theories of Mikhail Bakunin had stood godfather to the painting.

The "Modernista" painters and the post-modernists, foremost among them Nonell, used their work to explore social conditions following the collapse of the Spanish colonial empire and the consequent deterioration of the country's economic situation. Santiago Rusiñol used a subtle symbolism to describe Spain's ailing condition, painting dead and withered gardens time after time. Casas and Nonell, on the other hand, painted work that responded directly to political events and the miseries of the lower classes. Thus in 1894 Casas painted the public execution of anarchist bomber Santiago Salvador, while Nonell did numerous studies and paintings of slum life, men crippled in war, and social outcasts.[99] Together with Soler, Picasso had pursued radical ideas in "Arte Joven"; he attached especial importance to the writer Pio Baroja, whose tales lamented the lot of casual labourers and the unemployed.[100] The influence of anarchist literature and of Nonell's socio-critical art is apparent in many of Picasso's works of 1899 and 1900. But his new style of the Blue Period neither simply continued this line nor conformed with his sources. His formal approach was different for a start. Whereas Nonell (and Picasso himself in his "Arte Joven" days) had done compositions involving several figures and having a narrative character, the Blue Period works established just a handful of emphatic motifs. In Nonell's panoramic works, human misery was seen as a slice of real life in its real environment and implied comment on larger societal conditions. But in Picasso's case fate was an individual thing, endured in isolation.

"The Absinthe Drinker" (p. 85), an emotionally arresting painting, draws its power from this. Everything seems stony: the glass, the bottle, the woman herself. A sense of volume is conveyed by juxtaposing variant tones of the same colour within purely linear spaces. Spatial values are produced less by perspective than by the overlapping of forms. It is a meticulous, clear, balanced composition, with lighter and darker echoes of the skin tonalities unifying the effect. The tonal differences are so slight that the impression borders on the monochrome, serving solely to intensify the atmospheric charge. The draughtsman's forms make a more powerful impact than the painter's colouring. The long, talon-like hands gripping the angular face and upper arm, with the overall elongation of proportions, serve to emphasize the isolation and introspectiveness of the sitter.

The Blue House
La maison bleue
Barcelona, 1902
Oil on canvas, 51.7 x 41.5 cm
Zervos XXI, 280; DB VII, I; Palau 721
Zurich, Dobe Collection

Man in Blue
Homme en bleu (Portrait d'homme)
Paris and Barcelona, winter 1902/03
Oil on canvas, 90 x 78 cm
Zervos I, 142; DB VIII, I; Palau 782; MPP 5
Paris, Musée Picasso

Mother and Child from Behind
Mère et enfant
Barcelona, 1902
Oil on canvas, 40.5 x 33 cm
Zervos XXI, 367; DB VII, 18; Palau 749
Edinburgh, Scottish National Gallery of Modern Art

The Blue Period 1901 – 1904 **89**

Angel Fernández de Soto with a Woman
Angel Fernández de Soto avec une femme
Barcelona, about 1902/03
Watercolour and India ink on paper, 21 x 15.2 cm
Not in Zervos; MPB 50.494
Barcelona, Museu Picasso

"Crouching Beggar" (p. 93) shows Picasso developing his new stylistic resources. The crouching woman, cloaked in a blanket, her form contoured with flowing, forceful lines, is seen in some indeterminate location established by the mere indication of spatial levels. Blues of various kinds predominate. Even the ochre-brown blanket and the sallow face are shadowed with blue. The brushwork still juxtaposes thick and even, abrupt and smooth, as in the previous Paris paintings.

But the Blue Period Picasso did not merely pursue one-sided variations of an expressive approach. He produced very varied work, monumental, smoothly-constructed pieces alternating with detailed work the brushwork of which is nervy and dabbed. It is not only an art of considerable artifice, it is also an art which portrays

Reclining Nude with Picasso at Her Feet
Barcelona, about 1902/03
India ink and watercolour, 17.6 x 23.2 cm
Zervos XXI, 283; DB D IV, 5; MPB 50.489
Barcelona, Museu Picasso

The Mackerel (Allegorical Composition)
Le maquereau (Composition allégorique)
Barcelona, about 1902/03
Coloured India ink on cardboard, 13.9 x 9 cm
Not in Zervos; MPB 50.497
Barcelona, Museu Picasso

Two Figures and a Cat
Deux nus et un chat
Barcelona, about 1902/03
Watercolour and pencil on paper, 18 x 26.5 cm
Not in Zervos; MPB 50.497
Barcelona, Museu Picasso

an artificial world. For Picasso, confrontation with social reality was only a motivation; it was not an end in itself. For him it was more important to experiment, to try and test new visual approaches.

In "The Absinthe Drinker" the subject is not only the melancholy pub atmosphere and the dreariness of alcohol. The painting's meaning also lies in the autonomy of formal means. The erosion of defined spatiality, the abandoning of perspective construction, is only the most striking of several interesting features. It must be taken together with the accentuation of compositional fundamentals such as plenitude and emptiness, density and weight, emphasis and its lack. Picasso's composition uses three levels, the narrowest strip (contrary to usual practice) being the bottommost. It is also

91   The Blue Period   1901 – 1904

the brightest and thus, despite its weightless narrowness, none-theless possesses force and presence.

The other main motifs are similarly treated. The woman is seated to the right, but turned to the left in such a way that her head and cupped hand establish a vertical axis that is not quite the centre line of the composition but nevertheless roughly corresponds to the traditional golden section. This axis is also at odds with the vertical of the picture edge. The woman is not in the geometrical centre, but the figure does link the upper and lower zones with a certain weight, creating a stable tension between them. The bottle and glass echo this function.

If "The Absinthe Drinker" is thus a textbook work of eccentric composition, in "Crouching Beggar" Picasso emphasizes composi-tional centrality to express the woman's self-absorbed state. She is crouching right on the central vertical axis, the turns of her body turning about it. Solid motifs, with spatially flat planes in the back-ground, convey a sense of fullness and emptiness.

Ex-centricity and centralization were constants in this period. "The Blind Man's Meal" (p. 103) has a blind man up against the right of the composition, reaching across the table with unnaturally elongated arms, so that the rest of the picture seems somehow to be in his embrace or province. The radically monochromatic blue is married to a kind of formal crisscross procedure: the composi-

Study for "The Visit"
Etude pour "L'entrevue"
Paris and Barcelona, winter 1901/02
Pencil on paper, 45.9 x 32.8 cm
Zervos XXI, 369; Palau 737; MPP 447
Paris, Musée Picasso

Above:
The Visit (Two Sisters)
L'entrevue (Les deux sœurs)
Barcelona, 1902
Oil on canvas on panel, 152 x 100 cm
Zervos I, 163; DB VII, 22; Palau 739
St. Petersburg, Hermitage

Crouching Beggar
Miséreuse accroupie
Barcelona, 1902
Oil on canvas, 101.2 x 66 cm
Zervos I, 121; DB VII, 5; Palau 726
Toronto, Art Gallery of Ontario

Left:
Mother and Son on the Seashore
(The Fisherman's Farewell)
Les adieux du pêcheur
Barcelona, 1902
Oil on canvas, 46.3 x 38 cm
Zervos XXI, 365; DB VII, 19; Palau 741
Küsnacht, Agnes Adam-Doetsch Collection

Mother and Child on the Seashore
Mère et enfant au bord de la mer
Barcelona, 1902
Oil on canvas, 83 x 60 cm
Zervos VI, 478; DB VII, 20; Palau 746
USA, Private collection

tion uses striking echo techniques, the pallor in the blind man's neck answered by parts of the table, the paler blue patches on his clothing corresponding to the pale blues on the rear wall.

Though there is no clear line of evolution, certain Blue Period motifs and formal groupings do recur. In essence, Picasso was working within a limited range: men and women seated at tables, alone or in twos, meals being eaten, figures crouching or hugging themselves as they stand or sit, people with head in hand or arms crossed – this modest repertoire, in variations, accounts for the Blue Period work.

Of course, if there were no more to it, those with no prior interest would no longer have any particular reason to be interested in these pictures. In fact Picasso was a master of intensifying contrast and evocative effects. His mastery came from his assured grasp of certain formal and thematic antecedents, and of the various media (such as drawing, graphics or paint). One of his earliest etchings was "The Frugal Repast" (p. 108), done in 1904 and one of the masterpieces of 20th-century printed graphic art. In it, Picasso's approach to line etching resembles his handling of colour tones in

93 The Blue Period 1901 – 1904

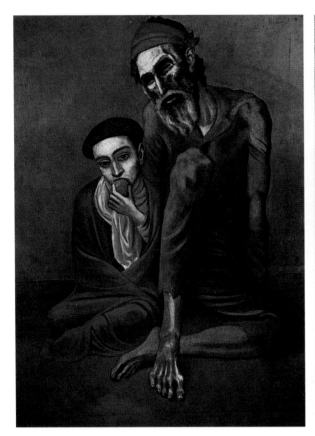

The Old Jew (Blind Old Man and Boy)
Le vieux juif (Le vieillard)
Barcelona, 1903
Oil on canvas, 125 x 92 cm
Zervos I, 175; DB IX, 30; Palau 936
Moscow, Pushkin Museum

The Old Guitar Player
Le vieux guitariste aveugle
Barcelona, autumn 1903
Oil on panel, 121.3 x 82.5 cm
Zervos I, 202; DB IX, 34; Palau 932
Chicago (IL), The Art Institute of Chicago

the paintings. Velvety black zones fade to grey and to bright clarity. As in "The Blind Man's Meal" Picasso plays with formal correspondences; but the cylindrical thinness of the arms, the elongated spread fingers, and the bony angularity of the figures with their dark and light areas, all recall El Greco. Not that the conspicuous influence of El Greco was the only presence in the Blue Period. It was not only the distortion of proportion that gave expressive force to these monochrome works, but also the grand, decorative linearity, a legacy of *art nouveau* and dialectically related to the subjects of the works. Monumentally conceived, solitary, emotionally intense figures, of course, were also standard fare in Symbolist art.

It is surely true that Picasso absorbed the influence of major artists such as Edvard Munch.[101] But another important influence was the minor French painter Eugène Carrière, who was well-known in Barcelona. A friend of Picasso's, Sebastián Junyent, was a pupil of Carrière, and Casas had earlier attended a Paris art school where Carrière taught.[102] His monochrome pictures using only a very few figures plainly influenced Picasso's numerous mother-and-child works. Other artists also influenced Picasso's monochrome

style. Indeed, it was a widely followed approach at the turn of the century, used by Symbolists, Impressionists and even Classicists. As well as Carrière's grey-brown paintings there were Pierre Puvis de Chavanne's allegorical works and James Abbott McNeill Whistler's tonal studies in blue and rose, seen in a large-scale Paris exhibition soon after the artist's death in 1903[103].

The colour blue was important in these experiments, and indeed, as we shall see, its meaning had a history. Its melancholy mood was often discussed in theoretical writings on art and in literature at the time. Painter-poet Rusiñol, one of the leading Catalan "Modernistas", published a short Symbolist tale, "El patio azul" (The Blue Courtyard), in the 10 March 1901 issue of Soler and Picasso's magazine "Arte Joven". The main character is a painter engaged in trying to capture the melancholy atmosphere of a courtyard surrounded by houses. In the process he meets a consumptive girl, who dies when he finishes his painting.[104] Shortly after, in his studio at Boulevard de Clichy 130 in Paris, Picasso painted "The Blue Room" (p. 82). He was joining the debate on the significance of the colour.

Blue not only denotes melancholy; it also carries erotic charges.[105]

Portrait of Señora Soler
Portrait de Madame Soler
Barcelona, 1903
Oil on canvas, 100 x 73 cm
Zervos I, 200; DB IX, 24; Palau 903
Munich, Staatsgalerie moderner Kunst

Portrait of Soler the Tailor
Portrait du tailleur Soler
Barcelona, summer 1903
Oil on canvas, 100 x 70 cm
Zervos I, 199; DB IX, 22; Palau 905
St. Petersburg, Hermitage

The Soler Family
La famille Soler
Barcelona, summer 1903
Oil on canvas, 150 x 200 cm
Zervos I, 203; DB IX, 23; Palau 904
Liège, Musée d'Art Moderne

Pages 98 and 99:
Nude with Crossed Legs
Femme nue aux jambes croisées
Barcelona, 1903
Pastel, 58 x 44 cm
Zervos I, 181; DB IX, 19
Private collection; formerly Basel, Galerie Beyeler

Celestina or Woman with a Cast
Celestina
Barcelona, March 1904
Oil on canvas, 81 x 60 cm
Zervos I, 183; DB IX, 26; Palau 958; MPP 1989–5
Paris, Musée Picasso

And it has a long tradition in Christian symbolic iconography, in which it stands for the divine.[106] German Romanticism gave blue the task of representing the transcendent ("The Blue Flower"), albeit in secular fashion.[107] Ever since the first third of the 19th century there had been a regular mania for blue, as it were, which peaked in 1826 in the tourist discovery of the Blue Grotto on Capri. As early as 1810, Goethe had advocated the use of dominant colours to set moods: blue light could be used for mourning, and one could look at one's surroundings through tinted glass in order to marshal divergent colours in a single tonality. In 1887 the French Symbolist painter Louis Anquetin actually adopted this method.[108]

Picasso's "The Visit" (p. 93) shows how consciously he was gathering these traditional values into a new synthesis. The attitudes and gestures of the figures are straight from Christian iconography. The visitation of Mary was portrayed in this way; and blue is the colour symbolically associated with the Virgin, the Queen of Heaven.[109] But Picasso was also at work on personal material in the painting. The women's heads are covered, as they are in many of his paintings of that period – and as they were at the women's prison of St. Lazare in Paris, to which Picasso had access in 1901 through a doctor he knew. It was an old building, in essence a converted 17th-century convent, and nuns of the Order of St. Joseph did the work of warders. Solitary confinement was a favourite punishment, though mothers were allowed to be with their children. It was a dismal place, full of women whose fates were desolate; and it made a profound impression on the young Spanish artist.[110] It was no coincidence that he chose the visitation, the meeting of Mary with the mother of John the Baptist, as a way of recording that impression. We have it from Picasso himself that "The Visit" shows an inmate and a nun, deliberately portrayed in equal fashion to emphasize their existential equality. Many of the mother-and-child pictures he painted at the time were affected by what he saw at St. Lazare too.[111]

The Blue Period peaked in "La Vie (Life)" (p. 105), a major composition which Picasso completed in May 1903. In many respects it is not only the major work of this phase but also the very sum of Picasso's art.[112] At first the structure seems straightforward, but in fact the history and message of the painting are complex. There are two groups of people, an almost naked couple and a mother with a sleeping babe, separated by half the picture's breadth. Between them we can see two pictures leaning against the wall, the lower showing a crouching person with head on knee, the upper – a kind of variant on the other – a man and woman crouching and holding each other. The top right corner of the upper picture has been cut off diagonally and slightly unevenly; it makes the impression of a study pinned up on the wall. The overall impression is of an artist's studio, so that we are tempted to see it as a representation of the life of the artist. But

Portrait of Sebastián Junyer-Vidal
Portrait de Sebastián Junyer-Vidal
Barcelona, June 1903
Oil on canvas, 125.5 x 91.5 cm
Zervos I, 174; DB IX, 21; Palau 898
Private collection

Couple in a Café
Ménage des pauvres
Barcelona, April 1903
Oil on canvas, 81.5 x 65.5 cm
Zervos I, 167; DB IX, 9; Palau 887
Oslo, Nasjonalgalleriet

Two Women at a Bar (Prostitutes in a Bar)
Pierreuses au bar
Barcelona, 1902
Oil on canvas, 80 x 91.4 cm
Zervos I, 132; DB VII, 13; Palau 754
Hiroshima, Hiroshima Museum of Art

The Blind Man's Meal
Le repas d'aveugle
Barcelona, autumn 1903
Oil on canvas, 95.3 x 94.6 cm
Zervos I, 168; DB IX, 32; Palau 920
New York, The Metropolitan Museum of Art

The Palace of Fine Arts, Barcelona
Le Palais des Beaux-Arts à Barcelone
Barcelona, 1903
Oil on canvas, 60 x 40 cm
Zervos I, 122; DB IX, I; Palau 942
Private collection

neither the subject nor the import of the work is easy to interpret. It is too fractured; nothing is what it seems, neither the place nor the people nor the action. Though the lovers at left seem intimate, their gestures are not. There is no trace of eye contact in the painting; all the characters are looking past one another into vacancy, with a melancholy air. They are not involved in a single action. And there are at least two different planes of reality.

And the location itself remains undefined, uncertain. The perspective angles are at odds with one another, the architectonic details ambiguous. It is an unreal and contradictory place, finally inaccessible to explanation, and the dominant blue even introduces a note of menace. Picasso has used Blue Period compositional techniques we can see in various pictures in one single, intense piece; and the same is true of his subjects. The embrace, seen here in a number of variations, was standard Picasso from 1900 to 1904, as was the mother and child, and the crouching posture. "La Vie" is a kind of pastiche of Picasso's Blue Period; yet it is no mere assemblage – rather, it is carefully planned, and its formal qualities and subject matter owed nothing to chance. Picasso did a number of instructive preliminary studies which show that a couple in a painter's studio were at the very heart of the composition from the start (cf. p. 104).[113]

103 The Blue Period 1901 – 1904

The other group, though, was only gradually fixed, and Picasso plainly first planned to position a bearded man at the right. Initially he gave the man standing with the woman his own features, as if the painting were of an autobiographical nature. Not till he was at work on the canvas did he make the decisive changes. But those changes themselves were directly related to matters in his own life. The man became his sometime friend Carlos Casagemas, who committed suicide in Paris in the year 1901 while Picasso was back in Spain. His unfulfilled passion for a young woman named Germaine, who was a model and lover for many in the Catalan artists' community, triggered his suicide. When Germaine spurned his affection, Carlos Casagemas tried first to kill her and then took his own life in the presence of a number of horrified friends.[114]

When Picasso heard the news in Spain, he was deeply affected. That same year he started to paint works that dealt with the dead man and his own relations with him. They were fictive, heavily symbolic paintings showing the dead Casagemas laid out, or even allegorically representing his funeral, attended by whores and the promiscuous sinners of Montmartre (p. 87). The fact that Picasso returned to Casagemas in the great 1903 composition means that the existential impact on him was profound. The biographical and non-personal strands in the work are in fact fully interwoven. During his first ever visits to Paris, Picasso led a bohemian life of drinking and sexual promiscuity with his Spanish friends.[115] His life style was partly a protest against conventionality in art and in life. The end of his friend Casagemas brought home to Picasso what was wrong with that life-style.

Study for "La Vie"
Etude pour "La vie"
Barcelona, May 1903
Pencil on paper, 14.5 x 9.5 cm
Not in Zervos; Palau 879; MPB 110.507
Barcelona, Museu Picasso

Study for "La Vie"
Etude pour "La vie"
Barcelona, May 1903
Ink and India ink on paper, 15.9 x 11 cm
Zervos VI, 534; DB D IX, 4; Palau 880; MPP 473
Paris, Musée Picasso

Study for "La Vie"
Etude pour "La vie"
Barcelona, 2 May 1903
India ink on paper, 26.7 x 19.7 cm
Zervos XXII, 44; DB D IX, 5; Palau 881
London, Penrose Collection

La Vie (Life)
La vie
Barcelona, spring to summer 1903
Oil on canvas, 196.5 x 128.5 cm
Zervos I, 179; DB IX, 13; Palau 882
Cleveland (OH), The Cleveland Museum of Art

106 The Blue Period 1901 – 1904

Portrait of Sebastián Junyer-Vidal
Portrait de Sebastián Junyer-Vidal
Barcelona, 1903
Oil on paper, 56 x 46 cm
Zervos I, 214; DB XI, 15; Palau 998; MPB 4.262
Barcelona, Museu Picasso

Portrait of Sebastián Junyent
Portrait de Sebastián Junyent
Barcelona, 1903
Oil on canvas, 73 x 60 cm
Not in Zervos; Palau 960; MPB 110.018
Barcelona, Museu Picasso

Left:
Mother and Child (The Sick Child)
Mère et enfant au fichu
Barcelona, 1903
Pastel on paper, 47.5 x 40.5 cm
Zervos I, 169; DB IX, 7; Palau 842; MPB 4.269
Barcelona, Museu Picasso

Woman with a Scarf
Femme au mouchoir
Barcelona, 1903
Oil on canvas on cardboard, 50 x 36 cm
Zervos I, 166; DB IX, 14
St. Petersburg, Hermitage

Portrait of Suzanne Bloch
Portrait de Suzanne Bloch
Paris, 1904
Oil on canvas, 65 x 54 cm
Zervos I, 217; DB XI, 18; Palau 981
São Paulo, Museu de Arte

Woman with Her Hair Up
(The Wife of the Acrobat)
Femme au casque de cheveux
(La femme de l'acrobate)
Paris, summer 1904
Gouache on cardboard, 42.8 x 31 cm
Zervos I, 233; DB XI, 7; Palau 977
Chicago (IL), The Art Institute of Chicago

Furthermore, Picasso's painting was in line with an artistic pre-occupation of the times. The subjects of early death, despair of one's vocation, and suicide were frequently dealt with, and much discussed in Barcelona's artistic circles.[116] Whether the allegorical dimension implied in the title by which we now know the painting was intended is doubtful, since the title was not given by Picasso.[117] The treatment of the figures goes beyond the typical attitudes of metaphoric figures; yet manifestly they are close kin to Symbolic art.[118] Casagemas stood for Picasso himself – who had originally portrayed himself in the picture and included the unambiguous motif of the easel. X-ray examination has revealed, furthermore, that Picasso used a canvas on which something had already been painted – and not just any canvas, but in fact his painting "Last Moments", seen at the Paris World Fair in 1900 and in other words a thematically and biographically extremely significant picture.[119]

It is idle to want to read an exact message into "La Vie". Yet Picasso's meaning is clear enough. All that mattered in biographical, artistic, creative and thematic terms in those years is present in this one picture. The melancholy and existential symbolism of that period in Picasso's life are richly expressed in this ambitious work.

The Frugal Repast
Le repas frugal
Paris, autumn 1904
Etching, 46.5 x 37.6 cm
Bloch I; Geiser 2 II a

Standing Nude
Jeune fille nue debout
Paris, about 1904 (or Barcelona, 1902?)
Oil on canvas, 110 x 70 cm
Zervos XXI, 366
Estate of Jacqueline Picasso

Picasso's technique of veiling the painting's meaning is in fact one of its signal qualities. He has managed to sidestep the vapidness of one-sided allegory; we are involved in this painting, drawn into it and – meditatively – into ourselves. The process opens up entirely new dimensions to historical painting.

Looking back, we can see the Blue Period works as a progression towards this goal, even though they were not specific preliminary studies, of course. For the first time we see in Picasso's art something that will strike us repeatedly in the sequel, a notable tension between the autonomy of the single work and the endeavour to gather the fruits of a line of development into one sum. "La Vie" is the first of a number of Picassos that stand out from the oeuvre by virtue of unusual formal and thematic complexity and an extraordinary genesis. The painting was both an end and a beginning: it was a prelude to paintings even more strictly monochromatic in their use of atmospheric blue and even more concerned with existential depths. The smooth, vast surfaces of the backgrounds, the

The Couple
Le couple
Paris, 1904
Oil on canvas, 100 x 81 cm
Zervos I, 224; DB XI, 5; Palau 985
Private collection

The Two Friends
Les deux amies
Paris, 1904
Gouache on paper, 55 x 38 cm
Zervos VI, 652; DB XI, 8; Palau 976
Paris, Private collection

clear structure pared down to the essentials, and the unifying contour, are all apt to the isolation of the figures – in other words, are cued by considerations of subject; yet still, Picasso is increasingly interested in other matters. Linear contour acquires an almost decorative flavour. Picasso tries out ways of concentrating formal options. He is plainly about to embark on something new.

109 The Blue Period 1901 – 1904

5 The Rose Period
1904–1906

The distance conferred by history places things in a new perspective and enables us to see a pattern in what strikes contemporaries as chaotic. Picasso is a good example of this.

For some years we have been in the habit of seeing his art of the years from 1901 to 1906 as a sequence of two periods, the Blue and the Rose. The terms are prompted by the dominant colours, and their use arouses certain expectations in us. But Picasso's contemporaries felt that what we see as two separate things in fact constituted a single unity. Though they clearly saw his overriding use of pinks, they did not consider that this justified the distinction of a new period, and spoke throughout of the Blue Period – as did the artist himself when looking back.[120] From our point of view the differences are most striking; but, at the time, nobody felt there to be any notable departure from the pre–1904 work to that of 1904 to 1906. In reality there are new departures but there is also common ground, and this is true both of Picasso's subjects and of formal considerations.[121]

After three years of portraying the poor and needy and lonely, though, Picasso struck out in new directions. "Woman with a Crow" (p. 113) shows him doing so. It is made entirely of polarities. The dynamic contour, the contrasting black and red and blue, the large and small, open and closed forms, the emphasis on the centre plus the lateral displacement, light juxtaposed with dark and the white paper gleaming through, the deep black of the crow's plumage against the woman's chalk-white face – all of these features are extraordinarily evocative. The figures seem almost engraved. The delicacy of the heads and the long, slender fingers of the woman emphasize the intimacy of gesture. It is a decorative picture, a work of arresting grace and beauty. Painted in 1904, it also records Picasso's new approach: in the period ahead, he chose subjects to match his newly aestheticized sense of form.

Connoisseurs and friends recognised as we do now that there was a unity to Picasso's new realm, and they gave his new phase the label "Harlequin Period"[122] after a prominent character in the new work. True, artistes were not new in Picasso in 1905; but now they were likelier to make solo appearances.[123] The seemingly bright and

Mother and Child and Four Studies of her Right Hand
Mère et enfant et études de mains
Paris, winter 1904
Black chalk on paper, 33.8 x 26.7 cm
Zervos I, 220; Palau 1019; DB D XI, 26
Cambridge (MA), Fogg Art Museum, Harvard University

Mother and Child
Mère et enfant (Baladins)
Paris, 1905
Gouache on canvas, 90 x 71 cm
Zervos I, 296; DB XII, 8; Palau 1021
Stuttgart, Staatsgalerie Stuttgart

merry world of the circus and cabaret and street artistes was as melancholy as that of the Blue Period's beggars and prostitutes and old people. Melancholy remained the core emotional note; but the form and message had changed.

It is true that the harlequins are outsiders too. But they have something to compensate for their low social rank – their artistry. Behind their gloom is great ability. They are downcast yet self-confident, presenting a dignified counter-image to the Blue Period's dejected figures passively awaiting their fates. And Picasso avails himself of their colourful costumes and graceful, decorative lines to create what can only be created by art: beauty.

It would doubtless be too simplistic to see Picasso's improved circumstances as the reason for his change from blue *tristesse* to rosy-tinted optimism.[124] But they must have played some part. He had made his final move to France in April 1904, taking a Montmartre studio on the Place Ravignan in May. It was one of a number in a barrack-like wooden building nicknamed the "bateau lavoir" from its similarity to the washboats on the Seine. Like Montmartre as a whole, it no longer had any central importance in the art scene: the focus had long shifted to Montparnasse. But in Impressionist days the likes of a Renoir had worked there.[125] Of course Picasso did not move solely among the artists of Montmartre and his old Spanish colony friends. He also knew the literary avantgarde in Paris.[126]

And he was increasingly establishing rewarding contacts with art dealers and collectors. In 1904 he exhibited at Berthe Weill's gallery, and in early 1905 he showed his first new pictures of travelling entertainers at Galerie Serrurière on the Boulevard Haussmann. He then agreed on terms with Clovis Sagot, a former circus clown who had set up a gallery in the Rue Laffitte. At this stage Picasso came to the attention of the wealthy American Leo Stein, and he and his sister, the Modernist writer Gertrude Stein, bought 800 francs' worth of Picassos. Shortly after, the dealer Ambroise Vollard even bought 2000 francs' worth. Other collectors such as the Russian Sergei Shchukin also invested.[127] Picasso's financial situation was improving noticeably. And his relationship with Fernande Olivier, which was to last for several years, introduced stability into his restless private life.[128]

Nonetheless, the Rose Period pictures are not merely records of a pleasant time in the artist's life. True, he often met other artists at Père Frédé's jokily named bar, the "Lapin agile", where the previous generation of artists had already been in the habit of gathering. And fashion required that one go to Medrano's circus on Montmartre.[129] But this is the small change of life, and Picasso's pictures speak plainly of his true concerns. "Woman with a Crow" was a portrait of Frédé's daughter Margot, who really did keep a pet crow.[130] In "At the 'Lapin Agile'" (p. 128) the scene is Picasso's favourite bar. Frédé himself appears as a musician in the back-

Meditation
Contemplation
Paris, autumn 1904
Watercolour and ink on paper, 34.6 x 25.7 cm
Zervos I, 235; DB XI, 12; Palau 1004
New York, Mrs. Bertram Smith Collection

Woman with a Crow
Femme à la corneille
Paris, 1904
Charcoal, pastel and watercolour on paper,
64.6 x 49.5 cm
Zervos I, 240; DB XI, 10; Palau 996
Toledo (OH), The Toledo Museum of Art

The Actor
L'acteur
Paris, late 1904
Oil on canvas, 194 x 112 cm
Zervos I, 291; DB XII, I; Palau 1017
New York, The Metropolitan Museum of Art

Woman Ironing
La repasseuse
Paris, spring 1904
Oil on canvas, 116.2 x 73 cm
Zervos I, 247; DB XI, 6; Palau 982
New York, The Solomon R. Guggenheim Museum

ground, and the harlequin is a self-portrait of Picasso.[131] Neither picture, however, is a straight representation of everyday reality. The woman with the crow is not so much a portrait as a type study, stylized beyond individuality. And in the bar scene Picasso is varying an approach he had used in his Blue Period for works such as "The Absinthe Drinker" (p. 85). In the new painting too, the people are gazing listlessly into vacancy, their bearing expressive of wearied lack of contact. The harlequin costume suggests that it is all a masquerade set up by an intellectual process: the creative artist poses as a performing artiste and in so doing takes artistry as his subject. The harlequins, street entertainers and other artistes of the Rose Period all enact the process of grasping the role of the artist. They were the product of complex reflection inspired not least by Picasso's relations with the literary world in Paris.

In later life, Picasso liked to present himself as essentially anti-

Portrait of Benedetta Canals
Portrait de Madame Benedetta Canals
Paris, autumn 1905
Oil on canvas, 88 x 68 cm
Zervos I, 263; DB XIII, 9; Palau 1152; MPB 4.266
Barcelona, Museu Picasso

Study for "Woman Combing Her Hair"
Etude pour "Femme se coiffant"
Paris, 1905
Pencil and charcoal on paper, 55.8 x 40.7 cm
Zervos I, 341
Norwich, Robert and Lisa Sainsbury Collection,
University of East Anglia

intellectual and purely interested in visual form. But at that early time in his career he was certainly interested in radical literary aesthetics, as his first encounter with writer André Salmon indicates. Picasso gave him a book of anarchic poetry by Fagus, the art critic. The poems were typical, in form and content, of what was then usual amongst the most progressive of the literati.[132] Picasso's acquaintance with Max Jacob had introduced him to this taste in 1901, and a few years later he was regularly at the "Closerie des Lilas", a Montparnasse café where the Parisian literary bohemia liked to meet. Under poet Paul Fort they met on Tuesdays for discussions, which were of particular interest to up – and – coming artists.[133]

Picasso's friend Guillaume Apollinaire was a prominent member of this group. The poet had recently published a play, "Les Mamelles de Tirésias" (The Breasts of Tiresias, 1903), which was subsequently to be of some significance for the Surrealists.[134] Apollinaire also wrote endless magazine articles dealing with the new political and cultural departures in Europe, preaching anarcho-syndicalism, anti-colonialism and anti-militarism. In 1905 he also took to writing art criticism, and this was to be of importance to Picasso. His features appeared in "Vers et prose" and mainly in "La Plume", a periodical which also held soirées at which everyone who was anyone in Parisian arts life liked to be seen. Apollinaire's consistent aesthetic radicalism strengthened Picasso's position. The poet repeatedly drew the public's attention to the Spaniard's work and so played an important part in Picasso's early recognition.[135]

One of Apollinaire's interests was directly related to Picasso's work. He liked to collect and edit erotica and pornographic literature, and established his own library of pornographic books, now in the Bibliothèque Nationale and still considered an authoritative collection. This breaching of a social taboo was partly inspired by contempt for bourgeois morality; Apollinaire created his

Head of a Woman in Profile
Tête de femme en profil. Paris, 1905
Etching, 29.2 x 25 cm
Bloch 6; Geiser 7 b

Boy with a Pipe
Garçon à la pipe
Paris, late 1905
Oil on canvas, 100 x 81.3 cm
Zervos I, 274; DB XIII, 13; Palau 1166
New York, Mrs. John Hay Whitney Collection

own programme of immorality, even starting a short-lived magazine titled "La Revue Immoraliste".[136]

Apollinaire and Picasso shared this taste to an extent. Picasso's early work often included erotic or downright pornographic scenes (pp. 90 and 91). In old age he returned to these themes, though not till then. It is not so much a reflection of Picasso's own life in a promiscuous milieu (though it is that too) as an extension of basically political convictions. Taboos set up by mindless social convention are breached by the freedom of art.[137]

Salmon was also important to Picasso through his critical and theoretical work on new movements in the visual arts, in which he emphasized the significant role played by Picasso. Salmon too was radical in political matters, interested in anarchism, and a friend of many revolutionaries. Artistically he was most attached to Symbolism. He played an important part in the arts world, and as secretary of "Vers et prose" he organized Paul Fort's soirées at the "Closerie des Lilas".[138] Like Salmon, Picasso's first literary acquaintance,

Young Girl with a Basket of Flowers
Fillette nue au panier de fleurs
Paris, autumn 1905
Oil on canvas, 155 x 66 cm
Zervos I, 256; DB XIII, 8; Palau 1155
New York, Private collection

Woman with a Fan
Femme à l'éventail
Paris, late 1905
Oil on canvas, 100.3 x 81.2 cm
Zervos I, 308; DB XIII, 14; Palau 1163
Washington (DC), National Gallery of Art,
Gift of W. Averill Harriman

Pages 118/119:
The Marriage of Pierrette
Les noces de Pierrette
Paris, 1905
Oil on canvas, 95 x 145 cm
Zervos I, 212; DB XI, 22; Palau 1093
Japan, Private collection

The Rose Period   1904 – 1906   **117**

The Acrobat's Family with a Monkey
Famille d'acrobates avec singe
Paris, spring 1905
Gouache, watercolour, pastel and India ink
on cardboard, 104 x 75 cm
Zervos I, 299; DB XII, 7; Palau 1058
Göteborg, Göteborgs Konstmuseum

Hurdy-gurdy Player and Young Harlequin
Joueur d'orgue de barbarie et petit arlequin
Paris, 1905
Gouache on cardboard, 100.5 x 70.5 cm
Zervos VI, 798; DB XII, 22; Palau 1073
Zurich, Kunsthaus Zürich

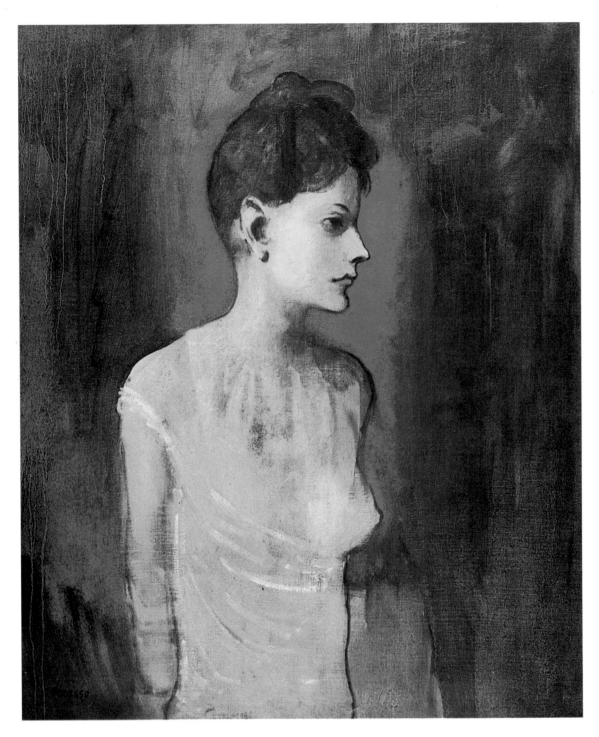

Woman Wearing a Chemise
Femme à la chemise
Paris, 1905
Oil on canvas, 73 x 59.5 cm
Zervos I, 307; DB XII, 5; Palau 1050
London, Tate Gallery

Seated Nude
Femme nue assise. Paris, early 1905
Oil on cardboard on panel, 106 x 76 cm
Zervos I, 257; DB XII, 3; Palau 1051
Paris, Musée National d'Art Moderne,
Centre Georges Pompidou

The Acrobats
Les saltimbanques
Paris, 1905
Etching, 28.8 x 32.2 cm
Bloch 7; Geiser 9 b

Circus Family (The Tumblers)
Famille de bateleurs
Paris, 1905
Watercolour and India ink on paper,
24.3 x 30.5 cm
Zervos XXII, 159; DB XII, 18; Palau 1031
Baltimore (MD), The Baltimore Museum of Art,
Cone Collection

Right:
The Death of Harlequin
La mort d'arlequin
Paris, 1906
Gouache on cardboard, 68.5 x 96 cm
Zervos I, 302; DB XII, 27; Palau 1182
Private collection

Clown and Young Acrobat
Bouffon et jeune acrobate
Paris, 1905
Charcoal, pastel and watercolour on paper,
60 x 47 cm
Zervos I, 283; DB XII, 29
Baltimore (MD), The Baltimore Museum of Art,
Cone Collection

Seated Harlequin
Arlequin assis
Paris, 1905
Watercolour and India ink; dimensions unknown
Zervos XXII, 237; DB XII, 10; Palau 1044
Paris, Private collection

Harlequin on Horseback
Arlequin à cheval
Paris, 1905
Oil on cardboard, 100 x 69.2 cm
Zervos I, 243; DB XII, 24; Palau 1065
Upperville (VA), Mr. and
Mrs. Paul Mellon Collection

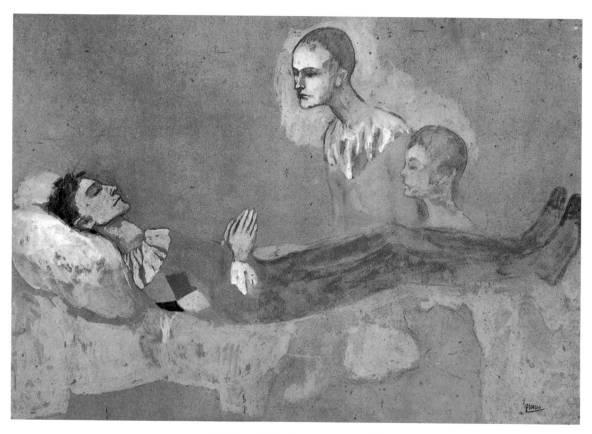

The Rose Period 1904 – 1906 **125**

Spanish Woman from Majorca
(Study for "The Acrobats")
Paris, 1905
Gouache and watercolour on cardboard,
67 x 51 cm
Zervos I, 288; DB XII, 34; Palau 1149
Moscow, Pushkin Museum

Max Jacob, was a regular visitor to the Montmartre studio, and even took a room there to work in for a spell. His major writings, founding works of Surrealist poetry, came a few years later, but in those early days at the "bateau lavoir" he was already set firmly against senseless norms.[139]

And another acquaintance was one of French literature's most dazzling personalities, Alfred Jarry. For him, as for many of his generation, the Dreyfus affair had shown up the weaknesses of French society and political life at the turn of the century. Public opinion had moved decidedly to the left. Jarry became a literary radical. In his own life he attempted to obey his maxims as an artist, and so became the very incarnation of the creative outsider. The three Ubu plays that began with the controversial satirical farce "Ubu Roi" in 1896 were his major achievement. Ubu is a personification of the philistine rampant who attains power and plunges the world into chaos through his reckless brutality. The safe, structured existential certainties of the middle classes are turned topsyturvy. The play later served as a model for the Dadaists and Surrealists and is seen as a precursor of absurd drama.[140]

In other words, Picasso was moving in left-wing literary and artistic circles. Anarchist ideas prompted the rejection of tradi-

Salomé
Paris, 1905
Etching, 40 x 34.8 cm
Bloch 14; Geiser 17 a

Mother's Toilette
La toilette de la mère
Paris, 1905
Etching, 23.5 x 17.6 cm
Bloch 13; Geiser 15 b

126   The Rose Period   1904 – 1906

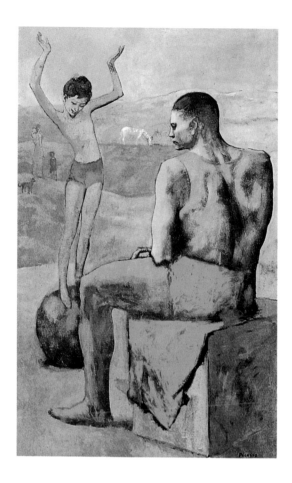

tional social structures and put unbridled individualism in their place. This individualism was expressed in a stylized role as outsider and artist. At this point we can return to Picasso's work. The Blue and Rose Period pictures of beggars, isolated people, harlequins, artistes and actors were a way of keeping "official" artistic values at arm's length, both thematically and formally. The paintings of Bonnat, Forain, Laurens, Béraud, Gervex, Boldini and others of their ilk presented society scenes and portraits of salon ladies.[141] The choice of an artistic milieu for the Rose Period works was a deliberate rejection of conventional subject matter. And that rejection went hand in hand with Picasso's quest for a new formal idiom. The subjects he painted came from a world he knew, and added up to a commentary of the role of the artist at that time; and the clowns and actors and artistes were widely viewed as symbols of the artistic life.

Traditionally, the fool or clown has a licence to utter unvarnished truth and so hold up a mirror to the mighty. During the Enlightenment the fool's fortunes were at their nadir; but, as the age of the middle class took a firm grip, the harlequin, pierrot or clown ac-

Acrobat and Young Equilibrist
Acrobate à la boule (Fillette à la boule)
Paris, 1905
Oil on canvas, 147 x 95 cm
Zervos I, 290; DB XII, 19; Palau 1055
Moscow, Pushkin Museum

Two Acrobats with a Dog
Deux saltimbanques avec un chien
Paris, spring 1905
Gouache on cardboard, 105.5 x 75 cm
Zervos I, 300; DB XII, 17; Palau 1035
New York, The Museum of Modern Art

Family of Saltimbanques (Study)
Famille de saltimbanques (Etude)
Paris, 1905
Gouache and charcoal on cardboard,
51.2 x 61.2 cm
Zervos I, 287; DB XII, 33; Palau 1126
Moscow, Pushkin Museum

At the "Lapin agile"
Au "Lapin agile" (Arlequin au verre)
Paris, 1905
Oil on canvas, 99 x 100.5 cm
Zervos I, 275; DB XII, 23; Palau 1012
Rancho Mirage (CA), Mr. and Mrs.
Walther H. Annenberg collection

The Rose Period 1904 –1906 **128**

quired a new, higher value. In France in particular he was seen as the epitome of the rootless proletarian, the People in person. After the 1848 revolutions, the new symbolic figure of the sad clown became familiar.

Baudelaire immortalized the figure in a prose poem. Edmond de Goncourt published a circus novel which dealt allegorically with the artistic life; his Brothers Zemganno are tightrope walkers and gymnasts, misunderstood by the public and often facing death, and acting throughout from an inner sense of vocation. Daumier portrayed entertainers as restless itinerants, at home nowhere. By the end of the century, the tragic joker had become a cult figure in Ruggero Leoncavallo's opera "Pagliacci". Street artistes and the

The Acrobats
La famille de saltimbanques (Les bateleurs)
Paris, 1905
Oil on canvas, 212.8 x 229.6 cm
Zervos I, 285; DB XII, 35; Palau 1151
Washington (DC), National Gallery of Art,
Chester Dale Collection

The Rose Period 1904 – 1906 **129**

circus were a favourite subject of progressive art, from Manet's 1860 "Street Musician" (New York, Metropolitan Museum) to the circus pictures of Toulouse-Lautrec and Georges Seurat.[142]

In adopting this line, Picasso was not only succumbing to the powerful influence of the French cultural scene. His interest in the subject had Spanish roots too. The Symbolist "Modernista" Rusiñol had written a play titled "L'Allegria que passa" which made a strong impression on Picasso when he did illustrations for it in "Arte Joven". His painting of an actor in harlequin costume, done at the close of 1904 (p. 114), draws upon Rusiñol's play.[143] Picasso subsequently did studies and paintings of a melancholy harlequin, a sad jester, not in the limelight but withdrawn into a life devoted to art, lived on the periphery of society and at odds with it. Formally speaking, these works betray the influence of Daumier. He too concentrated on a very few, striking figures.

Just as in the Blue Period a number of sketches, studies and paintings culminated in a major work, "La Vie" (p. 105), so too the harlequin phase produced the huge canvas "The Acrobats" (p. 129). It was Picasso's definitive statement on the artistic life. And, tellingly, it was another artist, the Austrian poet Rainer Maria Rilke (who in 1916 spent some months in the home of the then

The Harlequin's Family
Famille d'arlequin
Paris, spring 1905
Gouache and India ink on paper, 57.5 x 43 cm
Zervos I, 298; DB XII, 6; Palau 1039
Private collection

Acrobat and Young Harlequin
Acrobate et jeune arlequin
Paris, 1905
Gouache on cardboard, 105 x 76 cm
Zervos I,297; DB XII,9; Palau 1040
Brussels, Private collection

Boy with a Dog
Garçon au chien
Paris, 1905
Gouache and pastel on cardboard,
57.2 x 41.2 cm
Zervos I, 306; DB XII, 16; Palau 1033
St. Petersburg, Hermitage

Head of a Woman (Fernande)
Tête de femme (Fernande)
Paris, 1906
Bronze, 35 x 24 x 25 cm
Spies 6 II; Zervos I,323; Palau 1205; MPP 234
Paris, Musée Picasso

The Jester
Le fou
Paris, 1905
Bronze (after a wax original),
41.5 x 37 x 22.8 cm
Spies 4; Zervos I,322; Palau 1061; MPP 231
Paris, Musée Picasso

owner of the painting), who found the aptest words to convey an impression of the work, in the fifth of his "Duino Elegies": "But tell me, who are they, these wanderers, even more / transient than we ourselves . . ."[144]

X-ray examination has shown that the final picture was the fruit of long, painstaking labours, of frequent new starts and changes. It was begun at the start of the Rose Period in 1904. That composition, later painted over, was like a study now in Baltimore (cf. p. 124).[145] This shows a number of artistes' wives and children seen against a sketchily indicated landscape. With them, only slightly off the centre axis of the composition, stands a youth in harlequin costume, hands on hips, watching a girl balancing on a ball. Plainly the idea interested Picasso; he did an etching at the same time (p. 124) in which it appears in almost identical form. A copy of the etching served him when he came to transpose the scene to the canvas: he superimposed a grid in order to get everything just right.

That first version shows that Picasso wanted to draw all his approaches to the entertainer motif together into one composition.

All of the characters, even specific gestures and poses, appear in other Rose Period pictures, most famously "Acrobat and Young Equilibrist" (p. 127). But he was dissatisfied with the result, turned the canvas round, and painted over it. This changed the format into a vertical, and instead of a whole family there were now only two young acrobats. This picture too has survived in a gouache study now in the Museum of Modern Art, New York (p. 127).[146] Again the landscape is merely hinted at. The two youngsters facing us frontally almost fill the picture. The taller is in harlequin costume, while the other, still a child, has a dog with him.

Presumably Picasso felt that these figures were not sufficient to convey the various aspects of travelling entertainers' lives, for they too were painted over. Before resuming work on canvas he embarked on a set of preliminary studies. To an extent he fell back on his first idea. The centre was now occupied by a burly, seated man whom Picasso dubbed "El Tio Pepe Don José". A number of sketches tried out this compositional approach and the details involved.[147] At length the artist hit on a strategy that combined all three of the approaches he had been toying with, as we can see from a gouache now in the Pushkin Museum in Moscow (p. 128). Four male acrobats, standing, now provide the focus – among them Tio Pepe and two variants on the youngsters of the second version. What remained of the first version was a heavily adapted child motif, the young girl. In the background is a horse race. Picasso continued to sketch versions of the details till in summer 1905 he

Dutch Girl (La Belle Hollandaise)
Hollandaise à la coiffe (La belle Hollandaise)
Schoorl (Holland), summer 1905
Oil, gouache and blue chalk
on cardboard on panel, 77 x 66 cm
Zervos I, 260; DB XIII, 1; Palau 1134
Brisbane, Queensland Art Gallery

Three Dutch Girls
Les trois Hollandaises
Schoorl (Holland), summer 1905
Gouache and India ink on paper
on cardboard, 77 x 67 cm
Zervos I, 261; DB XIII, 2; Palau 1139
Paris, Musée National d'Art Moderne,
Centre Georges Pompidou

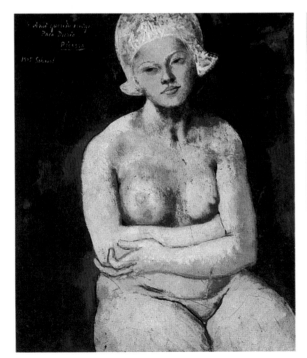

The Rose Period 1904 – 1906 **133**

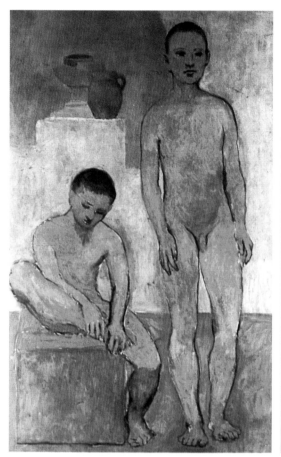

The Youths
Les adolescents
Gósol, spring to summer 1906
Oil on canvas, 151.5 x 93.5 cm
Zervos I, 305 and VI, 715; DB XV, 10; Palau 1241
Washington (DC), National Gallery of Art,
Chester Dale Collection

The Two Brothers
Les deux frères
Gósol, early summer 1906
Oil on canvas, 142 x 97 cm
Zervos I, 304; DB XV, 9; Palau 1233
Basel, Öffentliche Kunstsammlung Basel,
Kunstmuseum

finally painted over the canvas for the third time. At first he adopted the figural arrangement of the Moscow study; only with the fourth painting did Picasso at long last arrive at the version we now have. He put the man on the left in harlequin costume, replaced the boy's dog with a flower basket for the girl, and dressed the boy in a blue and red suit rather than a leotard. At bottom right he added a young seated woman. She too, rather than being a spontaneous inspiration, derived from a previously used motif (cf. p. 126). In other words, much as "The Acrobats" may make a unified impression, as if it had been achieved in one go, it in fact constitutes a synthesis of the motifs Picasso liked to paint during his Rose Period.

There are now six people; the background is not exactly defined. There are two blocks: the left-hand group, accounting for some two-thirds of the picture's breadth, consists of five people, while at right the young woman is sitting on her own. The contrast is heightened by subtle compositional means. The positioning of three of the figures at left very close together conveys a sense of

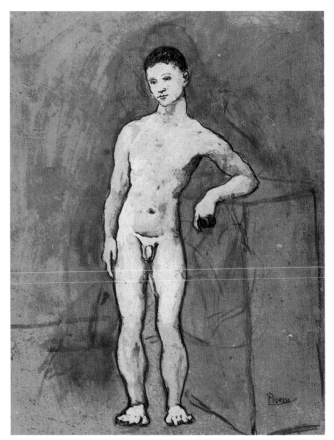
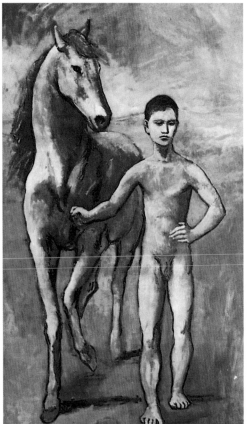

weight and unity, and the Mallorcan woman at right scarcely provides an effective counterbalance.

Picasso's palette consists basically of the three prime colours, plus
shadings in black and white to enrich the detail. The reds and blues
are graded in different degrees of brightness, but yellow only appears mixed with blues and browns, in unrestful presences that lack
much formal definition. Thus various degrees of sandy yellow account for the unreal, spatially undefinable landscape. The other
colours are caught up in similar spatial vagaries; depending on how
bright or aggressive or foregrounded they are, they are coupled
with darker, heavier shades that fade into the background. Only at
first glance does this make an evenly balanced impression. As soon
as we look more closely, things start to perplex us.

Take Tio Pepe, for instance, in whom Picasso's strategy of contrastive destabilization is most assertively seen. The massive red-
clad man is conspicuous – and conspicuously lacks the lower half
of his right leg! We can follow it only till just above the knee; and
the buff background only makes his lack the more obvious. This

Naked Youth
Garçon nu
Paris, 1906
Tempera on cardboard, 67.5 x 52 cm
Zervos I, 268; DB XIV, 8; Palau 1196
St. Petersburg, Hermitage

Boy Leading a Horse
Meneur de cheval nu
Paris, early 1906
Oil on canvas, 220.3 x 130.6 cm
Zervos I, 264; DB XIV, 7; Palau 1189
New York, The Museum of Modern Art

cannot be a mere mistake, nor quite without importance. A defect in a figure of such thematic and formal importance serves to destabilize the entire compositional logic, and, once alerted, we see that it is unreal through and through. The picture lacks a single point of view: the figures are spatially placed in a curiously all-round way, as if each zone of the picture were subject to its own perspective. Picasso is in fact once again telling us that artistic viewpoints are relative.

And he is doing it in a narrative mode that would well suit a historical picture. His de-clarified world is precisely the one these melancholy, uncommunicative characters would inhabit. And Picasso's departure from the laws of Nature is apt since it matches the manner in which acrobats earn their living by defying the law of gravity. The harlequin theme offered not only a visual means of approaching the life of the artist but also a pretext to review formal fundamentals. Almost all the paintings of this period suggest that this was the case, perhaps above all the Moscow picture of the equilibrist (p. 127), a balancing act in a compositional as well as thematic sense.

In that picture, the visual mainspring is not only the usual fundamentals of top and bottom, left and right, big and small, but also light and heavy, foreground and background. These conceptual qualities are the product of technical tricks; they can be manipulated to the very limits of possibility, and indeed toying with those limits can be visually most attractive. Picasso has positioned one extremely large figure at the right, the seated acrobat, and by way of contrast on the left a petite, delicate young artiste. If the man were to stand up he would be taller than the picture. His muscularity emphasizes the impression of power. But it is passive power, resting, and so far to the right that we might almost expect the picture to list to that side. The girl seems feather-light and dainty by comparison, higher up and further into the midfield. It is this placing that establishes a balance with the man. We should note in passing that Picasso is playing with his motifs, teasing our sense of the differing mass of sphere and cube. The tendency to experiment formally grew upon Picasso throughout the Rose Period.

In summer 1905, at the invitation of writer Tom Schilperoort, he made a journey. The writer had inherited some money, and asked Picasso to join him on the homeward trip to Holland. It happened that Picasso saw little of the Netherlands; they changed trains in Haarlem and Alkmaar, but otherwise the small town of Schoorl was all he saw. Still, it was an encounter with an entirely new landscape and way of life.[148] The few drawings and paintings he did on the trip were markedly different from the acrobat pictures. They drew on classical sources and ancient forms. From Picasso's spontaneous decision to accompany the Dutchman we can probably infer that his interest in the harlequins and artistes was at an end and that he was looking for new inspiration.

The Two Brothers
Les deux frères
Gósol, summer 1906
Gouache on cardboard, 80 x 59 cm
Zervos VI, 720; DB XV, 8; Palau 1229; MPP 7
Paris, Musée Picasso

Portrait of Fernande Olivier
with a Kerchief on her Head
Portrait de Fernande Olivier au foulard
Gósol, spring to summer 1906
Gouache and charcoal on paper, 66 x 49.5 cm
Zervos I, 319; DB XV, 45; Palau 1307
Richmond (VA), Virginia Museum of Fine Arts

Young Man from Gósol
Jeune espagnol
Gósol, early summer 1906
Gouache and watercolour on paper, 61.5 x 48 cm
Zervos I, 318; DB XV, 37; Palau 1322
Göteborg, Göteborgs Konstmuseum

"Three Dutch Girls" (p. 133) was the most important fruit of his journey. It readily betrays its model: even if the young women are wearing Dutch national costume, they are still grouped as the Three Graces traditionally were. Since the Renaissance, the classical group motif had been a much-imitated, much-adapted staple of European art.[149] Picasso was well acquainted with one version by the Flemish baroque artist Peter Paul Rubens, in the Prado in Madrid.[150] It was a picture that apparently enjoyed unusual popularity in Spanish artistic circles in Picasso's day.[151] The creative involvement with the motifs of antiquity plainly sprang from inner necessity. After his visit to Holland, Picasso's work was noticeably informed by the wish to create dense forms of statue-like balance and poise.

It was a wish that he articulated in numerous new studies and paintings in which the colourful palette of the acrobat pictures was replaced by a monochrome red. Most of the sketches, as their subjects suggest, must have been preliminaries for a large composition Picasso never painted, showing a horses' watering place.[152] "Boy Leading a Horse" (p. 135) was modelled on archaic figures of youths in the Louvre.[153] Not only this boy but also male nudes in other paintings and even portraits done at the time make a three-dimensional impression, abstracted and simplified, like sculptures transferred to canvas. At this time Pablo Picasso began to give greater attention to other media such as printed graphics or sculpture.

He had made an early attempt at sculpture in 1902, and "The Frugal Repast" (p. 108) in 1904 had shown him a master etcher at a date when he had only recently been taught the technique by the Spanish painter Canals.[154] Just as printed graphics had helped the pictures of acrobats on their way, so too three-dimensional work in wax or clay (cf. pp. 132 and 143) informed the formal vocabulary of the pictures that concluded the Rose Period. Picasso was developing in a new direction again.

Nude against a Red Background
Femme nue sur fond rouge
Paris, late 1906
Oil on canvas, 81 x 54 cm
Zervos I, 328; DB XVI, 8; Palau 1359
Paris, Musée de l'Orangerie

The Harem (Figures in Pink)
Le harem (Nus roses)
Gósol, early summer 1906
Oil on canvas, 154.3 x 109.5 cm
Zervos I, 321; DB XV, 40; Palau 1266
Cleveland (OH), The Cleveland Museum of Art

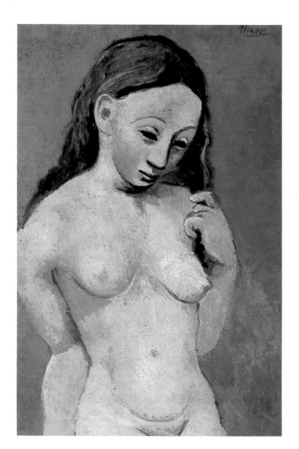

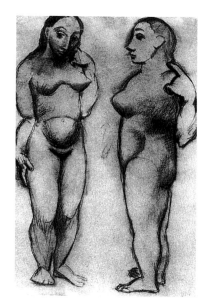

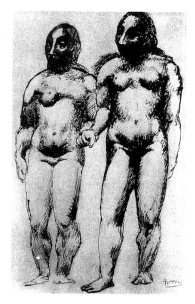

Two Nude Women
Deux femmes nues
Paris, autumn 1906
Pencil and charcoal, 63 x 47 cm
Zervos I, 365; Palau 1388

La Coiffure
La coiffure
Paris, spring to early autumn 1906
Oil on canvas, 175 x 99.7 cm
Zervos I, 313; DB XIV, 20; Palau 1213
New York, The Metropolitan Museum of Art

Two Nude Women
Deux femmes nues
Paris, autumn 1906
India ink and watercolour on paper,
48 x 31.5 cm
Zervos I, 359; DB D XVI, 21; Palau 1390
Geneva, Heinz Berggruen Collection

The Toilette
La toilette
Gósol, early summer 1906
Oil on canvas, 151 x 99 cm
Zervos I, 325; DB XV, 34; Palau 1248
Buffalo (NY), Albright-Knox Art Gallery

6 In the Laboratory of Art
1906/07

From the winter of 1905 on, Picasso did nothing but experiment –
till he made the breakthrough and created modern art's first truly
new idiom. Characteristically, though, he developed by moving
backwards, via a well-considered and multi-layered engagement
with tradition.

From 1905 on, Picasso strikingly gave central attention to nudes
– the basic academic test of an artist's skill. He also cut back his
deployment of colour once again. Now he was using it only to
reinforce forms that had been simplified to a concentrated essential.

1905 was the year when the Fauves provoked a scandal at the
autumn Salon. (In 1906, through Gertrude Stein, Picasso met the
most important of them, Henri Matisse and André Derain.[155]) He
also renewed his interest in Ingres, Gauguin and Cézanne. As well
as the Fauves with their revolutionary use of autonomous colour,
that autumn Salon had also had an Ingres retrospective and a small
show of ten Cézannes.[156] The latter's way of rendering form and
colour in accordance with the laws of painting rather than those of
Nature was very much in line with Picasso's new principles. The
academic classicism of Ingres, on the other hand, offered the perfection of draughtsmanlike form.

Furthermore, Picasso was significantly influenced by ancient
sculpture, particularly from ancient Iberia. In the Louvre there was
a section devoted to Iberian art, including artefacts that had been
discovered in 1903 in excavations at Osuna. Archaeological research at the time went hand in hand with a widespread interest in
primitive art, which was held to articulate the primal force of
human expression.[157] Picasso was more interested in what the
sculptures could tell him about form. Another kind of rudimentary
simplicity did enter his life in summer 1906, though, when he spent
a lengthy period in the Spanish province of Gósol amongst the
peasants.[158]

Increasingly Picasso was seeing the human form in terms of its
plastic volume. He simplified it, stripped it down to essentials, to
a very few blocks, stylizing it into something that was less and less
naturalistic. Any infringement of natural proportion he accepted

Woman Combing Her Hair
Femme se coiffant
Paris, 1906
Bronze (after a ceramic original),
42.2 x 26 x 31.8 cm
Spies 7 II; Zervos I, 329; Palau 1364; MPP 1981–3
Paris, Musée Picasso

Woman
Femme
Paris, early summer 1907
Oil on canvas, 119 x 93 cm
Zervos II**, 631; DR 75; Palau 1552
Basel, Beyeler Collection

Portrait of Gertrude Stein
Portrait de Gertrude Stein
Paris, winter 1905 to autumn 1906
Oil on canvas, 99.6 x 81.3 cm
Zervos I, 352; DB XVI, 10; Palau 1339
New York, The Metropolitan Museum of Art

Portrait of Allan Stein
Portrait d'Allan Stein
Paris, spring 1906
Gouache on cardboard, 74.3 x 59.1 cm
Zervos I, 353; DB XIV, 2; Palau 1198
Baltimore (MD), The Baltimore Museum of Art,
Cone Collection

with a shrug, even accentuating it in order to highlight the independence of art. This process peaked in a sense in two portraits: the autumn 1906 "Self-portrait with a Palette" (p. 147) and the "Portrait of Gertrude Stein" (p. 144), for which the writer sat repeatedly in 1905 and 1906 and which Picasso finally completed in the autumn of the latter year. Principles that later matured can be seen at work in the two works. In the picture of Stein, the solid mass of the subject affords an excuse to play with form: Picasso blithely ignores perspective, the relations of body parts to each other, and the logic of natural appearance. The head is an irregular block with eyes and a nose that look as if they have a life of their own. The style, though, is still suited to the sitter, and even expresses her all the better for being slightly distorted. The self-portrait goes further. Picasso deliberately abandons professional technique, and places his outlines and areas of colour rawly and inchoately before us, making no attempt to flesh out an appearance of a living person. There are no illusions in these lines and this

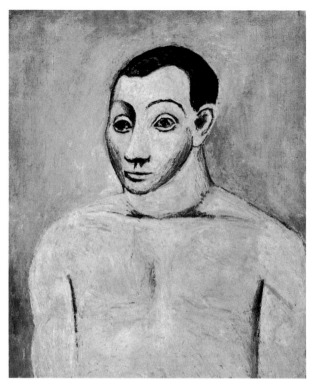 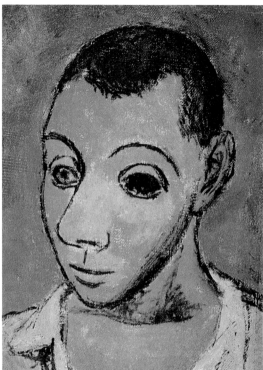

paint. They are simply there on the canvas to do the job of establishing a form.

Picasso pursued this path in a lengthy series of studies. In summer 1907 they culminated (at least for the time being) in the famous "Demoiselles d'Avignon" (p. 159). It has long been recognised as a key work in modern art. Yet for years, indeed decades, relatively little was known about how the work came to be painted – and so vague opinions, misconceived judgements and legends inevitably filled the gap. For instance, it is widely supposed that Picasso, under the influence of African art, was establishing a new vocabulary of de-formation which not only opened up new expressive opportunities for the visual arts but also represented a personal conquest of traumatic feelings. The artist's putative fear of venereal disease, the great mystery of sexual energy, and his private attitude to women, were all thought to have been exorcized by a ferocious effort of labour that left Picasso liberated. His possessed state was also adduced as the reason why the "Demoiselles" was never completed, merely abandoned at a critical point.[159]

Since it has been possible to view the preliminary studies in the Picasso estate, and to trace the path that led to "Les Demoiselles d'Avignon", this has all changed.[160] Speculation has yielded to fact. It is interesting to see how long it took Picasso to achieve the picture we now have.

Self-portrait
Autoportrait
Paris, autumn 1906
Oil on canvas, 65 x 54 cm
Zervos II*, 1; DB XVI, 26; Palau 1376; MPP 8
Paris, Musée Picasso

Self-portrait (Head of a Young Man)
Autoportrait (Tête de jeune homme)
Paris, autumn 1906
Oil on cardboard, 26.6 x 19.7 cm
Zervos I, 371; DB XVI, 27
Mexico City, Jacques and Natasha Gelman Collection

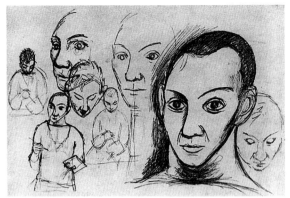

He began it in autumn 1906 after his return from Spain, doing sketches all that winter. In March 1907 he had a first composition ready, the study now in Basel (p. 155) which shows seven people in a brothel. Picasso subsequently altered the form and content significantly. The new compositional design (now in Philadelphia) cut the number of figures to five (cf. p. 155), and it was this version that the painter then transferred to canvas. He did not stop sketching further ideas, though; and it was not till July 1907 that he painted the final work we now have.[161]

It took him a full three-quarters of a year. And the intensity of labour can be proven by statistics: no fewer than 809 preliminary studies! Not only scrawls in sketchbooks but also large-scale drawings and even one or two paintings.[162] This is unparalleled in the history of art. His sheer application shows that Picasso cannot have been working in a possessed, spontaneous frame of mind. On the contrary, he worked in rational and impressively consistent fashion, unswervingly.

The sketches and studies are difficult to date or define, though, and a detailed account of the painting's evolution is therefore problematic.[163] "Normal" representative pictures appear alongside de-formed ones with no date to suggest a line for us to follow. For example, in a sketchbook he was using in March 1907 Picasso drew a sailor's torso and a masked face on the two sides of one and the same sheet. They were done one after the other, possibly even on the same day. The purest of position studies appear alongside sketches for the overall composition, again with no clear guidelines for dating. And there are even studies that have nothing at all to do with a brothel, and sketches that were not used for the painting in any way at all (pp. 153, 154 and 156).

This plural copiousness is instructive in itself. For one thing, it proves that Picasso was not influenced by "Negro" sculpture at all (as is still assumed in many quarters).[164] Picasso himself always denied it – and rightly so. The assumption rests on the fact that in summer 1907 he went to the Trocadéro Museum in Paris and was

Studies for "Self-portrait with a Palette"
Etudes pour "Autoportrait à la palette"
Paris, early autumn 1906
Pencil on paper, 31.5 x 47.5 cm
Zervos XXVI, 5; Palau 1377; MPP 524(r)
Paris, Musée Picasso

Studies for "Self-portrait with Palette"
Etudes pour "Autoportrait à la palette"
Paris, early autumn 1906
Pencil on paper, 31.5 x 47.5 cm
Zervos XXVI, 7; Palau 1378
Estate of the artist

Self-portrait with a Palette
Autoportrait à la palette
Paris, autumn 1906
Oil on canvas, 92 x 73 cm
Zervos I, 375; DB XVI, 28; Palau 1380
Philadelphia (PA), Philadelphia Museum of Art,
A. E. Gallatin Collection

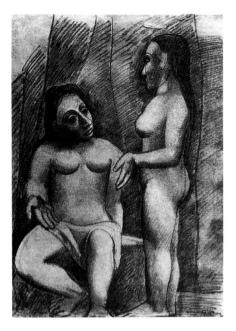

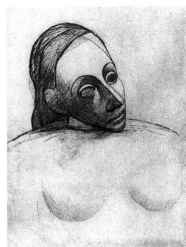

deeply impressed, indeed shocked, by a room of African sculpture, because the figures were made in much the same way as the deformed figures in his own work.[165] But those sculptures cannot have influenced him – because he had already arrived at the form he was after. Back in March 1907 he had done a head study that proves as much (p. 154), and he used it for the masked faces in the "Demoiselles". His shock in the museum was not caused by the sight of something new but by the recognition that what he thought he had invented already existed.[166]

We can follow Picasso's method clearly enough. There were two strands of evolution, one formal, one thematic. In Picasso's mind they were distinct, as we can see from the fact that most of the sketches only ever tackle one formal or one thematic problem. Picasso drew in any sketch-book as the ideas came to him, so that the most different of materials can be found together. But it was a useful working method in that it organically achieved the juxtapositions and synthesis Picasso was ultimately after. At irregular intervals he would therefore sketch combinations of distinct lines of development; some of these document the deconstruction of spatial and figural values and changes of content too. They are jottings; they record solutions to problems; and they establish a repertoire of images for the artist to use whenever he chooses. The yokings become ever more radical till at last the goal is in sight. The final stage involves work at the canvas itself.

As we can now see, in most of the individual sketches Picasso was striving for clear insight into the nature of artistic mimesis. Generally speaking, a line is drawn in such a way as to imitate the contour

Sitting Nude and Standing Nude
Femme nue assise et femme nue debout
Paris, autumn to winter 1906
Pencil and charcoal on paper, 63.6 x 47.6 cm
Zervos I, 368; DB XVI, 17; Palau 1406
Philadelphia (PA), Philadelphia Museum of Art,
The Arensberg Collection

Bust of Woman with Inclined Head
Buste de femme
Paris, winter 1906
Charcoal on paper, 62.5 x 47 cm
Zervos II**, 597 and VI, 877; Palau 1419
Estate of the artist

Standing Nude in Profile
Femme nue debout de profil
Paris, autumn to winter 1906
Pencil and charcoal; dimensions unknown
Zervos I, 369; Palau 1404

Seated Nude with Crossed Legs
Femme nue assise, les jambes croisées
Paris, autumn 1906
Oil on canvas, 151 x 100 cm
Zervos I, 373; DB XVI, 25; Palau 1397
Prague, Národni Gallery

Two Nudes
Femme nue de face et nue de profil
Paris, autumn 1906
Gouache on paper on canvas, 58.5 x 43.2 cm
Zervos I, 361; DB XVI, 14; Palau 1391
Locarno, Walter D. Floersheimer Collection

Woman Combing Her Hair
La coiffure
Gósol and Paris, late summer and autumn 1906
Oil on canvas, 126 x 90.7 cm
Zervos I, 336; DB XVI, 7; Palau 1363
New York, Schoenborn and Marx Collection

of an object; and when we look at that line we can identify it as a mimetic image because it resembles our own image of the object. Three things are involved in this process: the imagined image, the line, and the hand. If the hand does not obey the draughtsman's will, be it because he lacks the skill or the concentration, the lines will be distorted or meaningless. But lines can be used to convey meaning and character; concepts such as fat or thin, beautiful or ugly, become visually communicable. A line in itself lacks content or meaning. As Gertrude Stein might have put it: a line is a line is a line. But for that very reason lines can be made into figural complexes that are not mimetic and yet convey a conceptual image (cf. p. 154).

This was a truism to Picasso as to any draughtsman. The value of seeing it so clearly lay in recognising the twin poles of mimesis: on the one hand the ideal co-incidence of object and representation, and on the other hand the complete absence of any representational value. Every mimetic drawing contains elements of both extremes.

Picasso's conclusion, like all things of genius, was in essence very simple, but it has been of revolutionary importance for 20th-century art: the mimetic image is a compound of elements that do not intrinsically belong together. Their yoking is dictated by chance. So it must be possible to mix them quite differently and thus create forms that can still, it is true, be understood as representational in some sense, but which are pure art rather than a mimetic imitation of Nature.

The new formal language must contain as much of a representational nature as is necessary for it to be comprehensible, and at the same time must have as much non-referential visual material as possible without being entirely abstract. Picasso tried out his method on that most familiar of objects, the human body.

His studies of heads and faces are typical. The images we have of things already constitute an abstraction; so it takes little to draw a generalized representation of an object. In sketches done during winter 1906, the method Picasso used to draw a face was a simple, indeed conventional one. Two irregular lines indicated the breadth and shape of a nose, and parallel hatched lines on one side conveyed its size by means of shadow. The same procedure was then applied to other parts of the face (cf. p. 154). Now all that was

Two Nude Women Arm in Arm
Deux femmes nues se tenant
Paris, autumn 1906
Oil on canvas, 151 x 100 cm
Zervos I, 360; DB XVI, 13; Palau 1354
Switzerland, Private collection

Two Nudes
Deux femmes nues
Paris, late 1906
Oil on canvas, 151.3 x 93 cm
Zervos I, 366; DB XVI, 15; Palau 1411
New York, The Museum of Modern Art

required was to stylize all the principal and secondary lines, in a mechanistic fashion, and a far more artificial impression would be conveyed.

In May and June of 1907 he resumed this quest, to see how relatively minor alterations could change a faithful copy of Nature into something remote from it. He drew the bridge of the nose in strictly parallel lines, which devolved the hatched areas into a graphic autonomy. Then he angled the elliptical eyes and constructed a head out of unnatural straight lines and arcs. In March he had already tested distortions of this kind and had created a mask face. It still remained a head, conceptually speaking; but the random changes made it a new, unfamiliar image.

Picasso also used this same method of free combination of formal fundamentals in his use of colour in his oil studies. He changed the mimetic function and meaning of colours – such as skin colour and the way in which a three-dimensional effect was established – by juxtaposing lighter and darker areas (p. 158). In other studies he made his faces out of contrasts. Uniform prime colours remote from the reality of the subject were deployed in an anti-naturalist manner, the facial character heightened by a few complementary tonalities borrowed from colours in the background. In the process, Picasso travelled a great distance along the road of combining the colourist's and the draughtsman's evolutionary techniques (cf. pp. 156 and 157).

The final oil version of "Les Demoiselles d'Avignon" (p. 159) brought together the results of Picasso's experimentation in such a way that we can trace the entire spectrum of his options from the central figures out to the sides. It is the programmatic statement of a new formal vocabulary, created from the systematic scrutiny of conventional representational approaches and the development of a new synthesis out of them. It has not the slightest in common with specific historical styles of art such as Iberian or African sculpture.[167]

Everything in the picture is of fundamental importance, starting with the size of the canvas: the picture is often referred to as square, but is not, being in fact 243.9 x 233.7 cm in size. The marginal difference between the height and the breadth is significant because it leaves us irresolute: the picture is a rectangle but looks like a square. Everything in this picture teaches us of the inadequacy and randomness of customary concepts in visual representation.

The colour scheme is a synthesis of the monochromatic and the contrastive. The figures are painted in colours ranging from whitish yellow to brown, as are areas of the background; this contrasts with the blue that divides the right group from the left. The blue is agitated, disruptive, fractiously foregrounded; but on closer inspection we find that the contrast is less violent than it appears. Lighter or darker blues appear elsewhere, weakening the shock by establishing a sense of transition. And Picasso modifies the impact any-

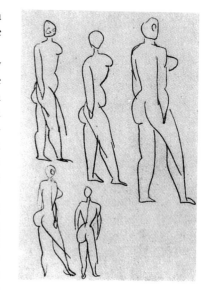

Female Nudes. Study for
"Les Demoiselles d'Avignon"
Femmes nues. Etude pour "Les Demoiselles d'Avignon"
Paris, autumn 1906
Pencil on paper, 26 x 20 cm
Zervos VI, 848; Palau 1425; MPP 1858
Paris, Musée Picasso

Group of Seven Figures. Study for
"Les Demoiselles d'Avignon"
Ensemble à sept personnages. Etude pour
"Les Demoiselles d'Avignon"
Paris, March 1907
Crayon on paper, 19.3 x 24.2 cm
Zervos XXVI, 97; Palau 1522; MPP 1861
Paris, Musée Picasso

Self-portrait
Autoportrait
Paris, spring 1907
Oil on canvas, 50 x 46 cm
Zervos II*, 8; DR 25
Prague, Národni Gallery

**Head of a Woman. Study for
"Les Demoiselles d'Avignon"**
Tête de femme. Etude pour
"Les Demoiselles d'Avignon"
Paris, winter 1906
Pencil on paper, 14.7 x 10.6 cm
Zervos II**, 603; Palau 1479; MPP 1859
Paris, Musée Picasso

**Head of a Woman. Study for
"Les Demoiselles d'Avignon"**
Tête de femme. Etude pour
"Les Demoiselles d'Avignon"
Paris, winter 1906
Pencil on paper, 32 x 24 cm
Zervos VI, 855; Palau 1481
Estate of the artist

**Head of a Woman. Study for
"Les Demoiselles d'Avignon"**
Tête de femme. Etude pour
"Les Demoiselles d'Avignon"
Paris, June to July 1906
Pencil on paper, 31 x 24 cm
Zervos VI, 968; Palau 1484
Private collection

The Sailor. Study for "Les Demoiselles d'Avignon"
Le marin. Etude pour "Les Demoiselles d'Avignon"
Paris, March 1907
Pencil on paper, 19.3 x 24.2 cm
Zervos XXVI, 100; Palau 1443; MPP 1861
Paris, Musée Picasso

Study for "Les Demoiselles d'Avignon"
Etude pour "Les Demoiselles d'Avignon"
Paris, March 1907
Charcoal on paper, 19.3 x 24.2 cm
Zervos XXVI, 101; Palau 1554; MPP 1861
Paris, Musée Picasso

Study for "Les Demoiselles d'Avignon"
Etude pour "Les Demoiselles d'Avignon"
Paris, June to July 1907
Pencil on paper, 31.2 x 24.7 cm
Zervos VI, 936; Palau 1466
Private collection

Page 155:
Study for "Les Demoiselles d'Avignon"
Etude pour "Les Demoiselles d'Avignon"
Paris, March to April 1907
Pencil and pastel on paper,
47.7 x 63.5 cm (sheet size)

Zervos II*, 19; DR 29; Palau 1511
Basel, Öffentliche Kunstsammlung Basel,
Kupferstichkabinett

Study for "Les Demoiselles d'Avignon"
Etude pour "Les Demoiselles d'Avignon"
Paris, spring 1907
Watercolour on paper, 17.5 x 22.5 cm
Zervos II*, 21; DR 31; Palau 1543
Philadelphia (PA), Philadelphia Museum of Art

In the Laboratory of Art   1906/07   **155**

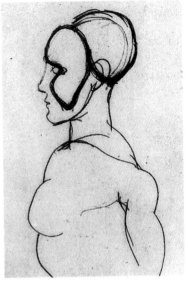

Female Nude. Study for
"Les Demoiselles d'Avignon"
Femme nue. Etude pour
"Les Demoiselles d'Avignon"
Paris, autumn 1906
Pencil on paper, 26 x 20 cm
Zervos VI, 903; MPP 1858
Paris, Musée Picasso

Female Nude. Study for
"Les Demoiselles d'Avignon"
Femme nue. Etude pour
"Les Demoiselles d'Avignon"
Paris, spring to summer 1907
Oil on canvas, 81 x 60 cm
Zervos II*, 24; DR 41; Palau 1550
Geneva, Heinz Berggruen Collection

way, by placing the contrastive blue zone almost in the position of
the classical golden section. In Renaissance art theory, to divide the
space in proportions such as these was to express ideal harmony –
which is the very opposite of what we first feel on seeing Picasso's
painting.

Compositionally, the placing of the subjects breaches conventional ideas of clarity and order. Critics tend to see two unequal parts
in this picture, the group of three women on the left and that of two
on the right defining these parts. But once we register the figures'
relations to the background we do better to identify three zones, increasing in size from left to right: first the woman at far left, then the

two frontally positioned women against the whitish-grey background, and then, seemingly split off by a harsh colour contrast, the two at the right. But this irregular tripartite scheme is at odds with a more orderly spatial division marked by the still life at the foot of the canvas: the table, seen as a triangular shape pointing upwards, coincides precisely with the centre axis. Logically, that axis is occupied by the middle one of the five women. The angle at which her arms are held behind her head restates the axis by inverting the triangle. Seen like this, the composition proves to be divided exactly in two. And to classical ways of thinking, symmetrical composition was a token of ideal order, of an austere kind.

Three grouping principles at least are at work in this painting. The use of all three together puts each into a new, relativized perspective. It is the same with the spatial values. The classical ideal of perspective as a means of establishing meaning has been conspicuously thrown overboard – thus the received wisdom claims, but it is too one-sided a way of seeing the picture. True, there is no perspective spatial depth in the work. But the overlapping of the figures most certainly does create some sense of space. And Picasso

Bust of a Woman or Sailor
Study for "Les Demoiselles d'Avignon"
Buste de femme ou de marin
Etude pour "Les Demoiselles d'Avignon"
Paris, spring 1907
Oil on cardboard, 53.5 x 36.2 cm
Not in Zervos; DR 28; MPP 15
Paris, Musée Picasso

Bust of a Woman
Buste de femme
Paris, spring to summer 1907
Oil on canvas, 64.5 x 50 cm
Zervos II*, 16; DR 33; Palau 1546
Prague, Národni Gallery

has also fixed a set point of view for us – albeit ironically, since the lower half of the painting looks up to the subjects, while in the upper it is impossible to be definite about the angle. The line separating these two ways of seeing is almost exactly the horizontal mid-composition line, where the classical code of central perspective required the viewer's horizon to be.

We also need to register the different ways of presentation within individual figures and objects. The bodies are seen at once from the front and the side, in a way not naturally possible. Lines, hatchings and blocks of colour are used to make random changes and de-formations in parts of the women's bodies, and Picasso's over-layering makes for entire areas of abstraction. In overall terms this is also true of the relation of the figures to the background, which the artist has treated as one of despatializing formal analogy.

Still, Picasso has not completely abandoned mimetic representation. The lines and colours still plainly show naked women in various positions. It is because this is still apparent that the deviations from a conventional aesthetic shock us. And the shock was only heightened, for Picasso's contemporaries, by the ostentatious and provocative nakedness of the women. The mask-like, barely human faces highlight the relativity of our ideas of beauty: the two

Les Demoiselles d'Avignon
Paris, June to July 1907
Oil on canvas, 243.9 x 233.7 cm
Zervos II*, 18; DR 47; Palau 1557
New York, The Museum of Modern Art

Study for "Three Women" (1908)
Etude pour les "Trois femmes" (1908)
Paris, 1907
Watercolour, gouache and pencil on paper,
61.5 x 47.3 cm
Zervos II**, 707
Mexico City, Jacques and Natasha
Gelman Collection

more recognisably human women in the centre begin to look lovely by comparison, though taken alone their cartoon faces and distorted bodies would be anything but beautiful. The face of the woman at left, also mask-like but less distorted than the two right-hand faces, is a halfway point between these extremes; just as the darker colouring he has used for her provides a compositional balance.

Picasso uses counterpoints and checks and balances of this kind throughout the painting, and this fact alone will suffice to demolish the widely-believed legend that the work is unfinished. A detailed analysis shows "Les Demoiselles d'Avignon" to be a meticulously considered, scrupulously calculated visual experience without equal. The formal idiom and utterly new style were by no means a mere relinquishing of prevailing norms in the visual arts but rather a subtly elaborated marriage of relinquishing and preservation. The same is true of the subject matter.

The first complete compositional plan, done in March 1907 and now in Basel (p. 155), shows an interior with seven people: five naked women and two clothed men. Studies of bearing, clothing and attributes tell us that the man on the left was envisaged as a student and the one in the middle as a sailor. This unambiguous scene, according to Picasso himself, showed a brothel in Barcelona's Carrer d'Avinyó: in other words, it had nothing in particular to do with the French town of Avignon. It was not till 1916 that Salmon put about the innocuous and simply wrong title by which the picture is now known; this title drew on in – jokes familiar among Picasso's circle of friends.[168] The fact that it is a brothel scene has prompted people to feel that Picasso had indeed been coming to terms with sexual troubles in painting the picture, a feeling they have felt confirmed in by the fact that Picasso studied venereal (particularly syphilitic) patients in St. Lazare.[169] Yet this view is not consistent. For one thing, Picasso painted prostitutes earlier, in pictures that alluded to works by Degas and Toulouse-Lautrec. And for another, after he did the Basel drawing he changed the composition so utterly that everything was dropped that could unambiguously suggest a brothel interior. This implies that the subject in itself no longer had any significance. The figure of a sailor with a death's-head shows that Picasso was initially planning a historical allegory.[170] But he departed from that as well, and in so doing put the conventional norms of the genre behind him.

Picasso's new idea for his subject was in fact a far more complex and inventive one. Just as he had examined traditional methods of representation and located a new solution, so too he examined the problem of iconography, of conveying content meaning through standard images, of re-using the idiom of existing visual ideas. There is a traditional model for the general theme of women showing off their bodily charms for a verdict. It shows three naked women standing in front of seated or standing males and goes by

Woman in Yellow
Femme au corsage jaune
Paris, spring 1907
Oil on canvas, 130 x 97 cm
Zervos II*, 43; DR 51
Private collection

the name of the judgement of Paris.[171] But Picasso had other antecedents in mind too.

Picasso's two frontal figures parody the conventional use of drapes and concealment to heighten the aesthetic impact of the naked female body. Here the drapes are used to emphasize the painter's departure from the norm. Since the Renaissance, the ancient sculptural ideal of the human form had provided a constant touchstone. In the 19th century and down to Picasso's time, one female figure of a deity had seemed the very epitome of ideal beauty: the Venus of Milo. Picasso's middle woman quite plainly is modelled on her, the one leg placed to the fore as in the sculpture. There is a Hellenistic version of the sculpture in the Louvre, the

Head of a Woman
Tête de femme
Paris, 1906/07
Wood, carved and partially painted,
39 x 25 x 12 cm
Spies II; Zervos II**, 611; Palau 1413;
MPP 1990-51
Paris, Musée Picasso

pose of which Picasso copied.[172] In any case it was a position that he was perfectly familiar with, since it was regularly used in academic life classes.[173]

The judgement of Paris, and Venus, were logical choices for Picasso: the first involved that ideal beauty which the second personified. And it was the problem of artistically presenting aesthetic norms that decided Picasso on a composition involving five different women. He had an ancient anecdote in mind. Zeuxis the painter, faced with the task of portraying the immortally beautiful Helen, took as his models the five loveliest virgins of the island of Kroton and combined their finest features in order to achieve a perfection of beauty that did not exist in Nature.[174]

The still life in the "Demoiselles" adds a theoretical statement. Critics have routinely commented that this detail seems unmotivated in what is supposedly a brothel scene, and have also pointed out that the fruit is done in a fairly true-to-life style unlike that of the figures. Picasso is alluding to another anecdote about Zeuxis, who was said to have painted fruit – grapes in particular – so skilfully that birds were fooled and pecked at them.[175] The Zeuxis tales are commonplaces of art history, but they also have an important place in that history, since Zeuxis is considered the forefather of illusionist art, the very kind of art and aesthetic rules that Picasso's non-normative painting "Les Demoiselles d'Avignon" swept aside.

Figure (Three views)
Figure
Paris, 1907
Wood, carved and painted; height: 25 cm
Spies 16; Palau 1441; Zervos II**, 608 to 610
Private collection

162 In the Laboratory of Art 1906/07

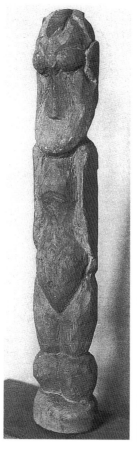

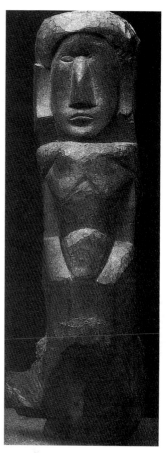

Impartial analysis shows the painting together with its preliminary studies to be radical in the true sense: Picasso re-conceived the entirety of the European art tradition from the roots up, and used its constituents to create a new visual language. It was not his intention to break with tradition. Rather, he was out to destroy convention – an altogether different undertaking. This painting, more than any other work of European Modernism, is a wholly achieved analysis of the art of painting and of the nature of beauty in art.

Standing Man (two views)
Homme debout
Paris, 1907
Wood, carved and painted, 37 x 6 x 6 cm
Spies 20; Zervos II**, 656 and 657
Private collection

Standing Nude
Femme nue debout
Paris, 1907
Wood, carved and painted, 31.8 x 8 x 3 cm
Spies 17; Zervos II**, 667; MPP 236
Paris, Musée Picasso

Standing Nude
Femme nue debout
Paris, 1907
Wood, carved and painted, 35.2 x 12.2 x 12 cm
Spies 15; Zervos II**, 668; MPP 237
Paris, Musée Picasso

7 Analytical Cubism
1907–1912

Looking back on the history of modern art from today's perspective, it is difficult to conceive of the bewilderment "Les Demoiselles d'Avignon" occasioned among Picasso's contemporaries. One German critic, Wilhelm Uhde, thought it "Assyrian" in some way or other; Georges Braque felt it was as if a fire-eater had been drinking petrol; and Derain ventured that some day Picasso would hang himself behind his picture.[176] Comments such as these seem all the more incomprehensible in view of the importance the painting was soon to have: Cubism derived its formal idiom from it. Most emphatically there were two sides to the work's reception.

The contemporary verdict is illuminating. After all, it was not the opinion of the general public – Picasso kept the picture under wraps, so it was not widely seen till the 1920s and thus not widely subject to the opinion of the public.[177] The bewilderment came from art dealers, fellow artists and friends, all of them insiders with progressive, avant-garde views, surely the ideal receivers of work so profoundly innovative. Why were they so helpless and shocked? Because the painting really was utterly new, something that had never before been seen. And yet, like all things revolutionary, the "Demoiselles d'Avignon" signalled not only a new start but also the end of a long process of development.

Picasso had evolved a new form by examining the idiom that had prevailed in European art since the Renaissance, dismantling its rules, and re-applying its mechanisms. In doing so he transcended that idiom and – logically – the principles underlying it. This was his declared aim, and he succeeded in achieving it.

Picasso marked the end of a historical process that had begun in the mid–18th century. At that time, writers on aesthetics, thinkers such as Denis Diderot or Gotthold Ephraim Lessing, had scrutinized and re-defined the meaning and function of painting. Since the Renaissance, art had been of a functional, content-oriented nature, serving to convey messages in visual form. The imitation of Nature and the illusionistic reproduction of the appearance of things was a way of making the world comprehensible. Paintings could tell stories by showing narrative actions, representing emotions, and expressing the movements of the soul. The dichotomy

Bust of Fernande
Buste de femme au bouquet (Fernande)
Horta de Ebro, summer 1909
Oil on canvas, 61.8 x 42.8 cm
Zervos XXVI, 419; DR 288
Düsseldorf, Kunstsammlung
Nordrhein-Westfalen

Woman with Pears (Fernande)
Femme aux poires (Fernande)
Horta de Ebro, summer 1909
Oil on canvas, 92 x 73 cm
Zervos II*, 170; DR 290
New York, Private collection

Three Women
Trois femmes
Paris, autumn 1907 to late 1908
Oil on canvas, 200 x 178 cm
Zervos II*, 108; DR 131
St. Petersburg, Hermitage

Landscape with Two Figures
Paysage aux deux figures
Paris, late 1908
Oil on canvas, 60 x 73 cm
Zervos II*, 79; DR 187; MPP 28
Paris, Musée Picasso

Analytical Cubism 1907 – 1912 **166**

between given reality and imitation produced numerous possible ways of communication.[178] In the 18th century this changed significantly. The frontiers of painting were defined anew and it was stripped of its narrative side; now it could only represent.[179] It was not long before the representational function of painting was questioned too, since it was essentially an illusionist process dependent on purely technical and unreliable processes. The philosophy of Kant, Hegel and Schopenhauer prompted a recognition of the absolute aesthetic impact of painting and the autonomous status of draughtsmanship and colour.[180]

This was a fundamental change. Where once content and form, message and image had needed to harmonize, now form became dominant, and indeed became the content. If ways of seeing, conceptualization, and cognition were to be considered inseparable, then the cognitive content of painting must logically enough be purely a matter of how the observer looked at it.[181] Inevitably, once this view gained ground, painting would tend to lose its mimetic character and become detached from the things which it claimed to represent. French 19th-century art and the art of post-Romantic

The Dance of the Veils (Nude with Drapes)
La danse aux voiles (Nu à la draperie)
Paris, summer 1907
Oil on canvas, 152 x 101 cm
Zervos II*, 47; DR 95
St. Petersburg, Hermitage

Nude with Raised Arms (The Dancer of Avignon)
Femme nue (La danseuse d'Avignon)
Paris, summer to autumn 1907
Oil on canvas, 150.3 x 100.3 cm
Zervos II*, 35; DR 53
Private collection

northern Europe underwent a parallel move towards greater abstraction.[182]

That evolution peaked in Picasso's "Demoiselles". It is the key work of Modernist art. Of course Picasso had his precursors – but the Impressionists' colourful attempts to capture the fleeting moment, and the Fauves' orgiastic use of colour, essentially remained faithful to the principle of mimesis. Random changes of natural form and colour, such as the Impressionists and Fauves used in their different ways, were psychologically prompted, and aimed at establishing moods. The natural original which the painting represented remained unaffected. Deviations were merely shifts in expressive emphasis.

Cézanne was of greater significance for High Modernism, though. However, his deconstruction of the given, and his treatment of form and colour, were stylistically determined. His reduction of natural shapes to geometrical solids upheld the traditional technical repertoire of the academies. Still, Cézanne did show what an individualist approach could accomplish. And his work served as a vital point of reference in the turning-point year of 1907: a

Woman with a Fan (After the Ball)
Femme avec éventail (Après le bal)
Paris, late spring 1908
Oil on canvas, 152 x 101 cm
Zervos II*, 67; DR 168
St. Petersburg, Hermitage

Seated Woman
Femme nue assise
Paris, spring 1908
Oil on canvas, 150 x 99 cm
Zervos II*, 68; DR 169
St. Petersburg, Hermitage

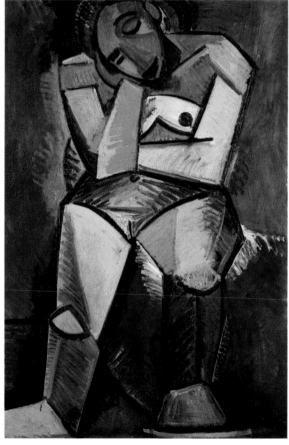

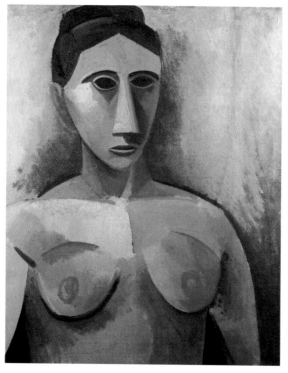

Bust of a Woman (Sleeping Woman)
Buste de femme accoudée (Femme dormante)
Paris, spring to summer 1908
Oil on canvas, 81.3 x 65.5 cm
Zervos XXVI, 303; DR 170
New York, The Museum of Modern Art

Bust of a Woman
Torse de femme
Paris, summer 1908
Oil on canvas, 73 x 60 cm
Zervos II*, 64; DR 134
Prague, Národni Gallery

Standing Nude
Femme nue debout
Paris, spring 1908
Gouache on paper, 62 x 46 cm
Zervos XXVI, 286; DR 154
Otterlo, Rijksmuseum Kröller-Müller

direct line of evolution runs from his "Bathers" to Matisse's "Blue Nude" (Baltimore, Museum of Art), Derain's "Bathers" (New York, Museum of Modern Art), and finally the "Demoiselles d'Avignon" (all three of which were painted in 1907).[183] It is a telling fact that it was a painter academic in the cast of his thinking – Picasso – who created the formal approach of the new art.

Picasso started not from colour but from form and form alone. This too reflected his place in history. In the 19th century, scientists made important discoveries relating to the human organs and the principles of sense perception. The physiological independence of cognitive processes was established, and this legitimized aesthetic views on the subject and indeed provided artists with a new impetus.[184] Experiments in colour vision conducted by the Frenchmen Joseph Plateau and Eugène Chevreul in 1834 and 1839 influenced painters from Delacroix to Georges Seurat. Hermann Helmholtz's "Physiology of Optics" (1867) and Wilhelm Wundt's "Physiological Psychology" (1886) were widely available in the French translations.

The Parisian literary avant-garde liked to discuss the ideas on the spatial sense which William James, taking Helmholtz further, had

Analytical Cubism 1907 – 1912 **169**

170 Analytical Cubism 1907 – 1912

Peasant Woman (Half-length)
La fermière (buste)
La Rue-des-Bois, August 1908
Oil on canvas, 81.2 x 65.3 cm
Zervos II*, 92; DR 194
St. Petersburg, Hermitage

Above left:
Head of a Man
Tête d'homme
Paris, autumn 1908
Gouache on panel, 27 x 21.3 cm
Zervos XXVI, 394; DR 152; MPP 25
Paris, Musée Picasso

Head of a Man
Tête d'homme
Paris, autumn 1908
Gouache on panel, 27 x 21.3 cm
Zervos XXVI, 392; DR 153; MPP 26
Paris, Musée Picasso

Peasant Woman (Full-length)
La fermière en pied
La Rue-des-Bois, August 1908
Oil on canvas, 81.2 x 65.3 cm
Zervos II*, 91; DR 193
St. Petersburg, Hermitage

Below left:
Head of a Woman
Tête de femme
Paris, spring 1909 (?)
Oil on canvas, 25 x 22 cm
Not in Zervos; DR 252
Berlin, Nationalgalerie, Staatliche Museen
zu Berlin-Preußischer Kulturbesitz

Head of a Man
Tête d'homme
Paris, spring 1909
Gouache on panel, 27.1 x 21.3 cm
Zervos XXVI, 412; DR 251; MPP 29
Paris, Musée Picasso

172 Analytical Cubism 1907 – 1912

Above left:
Friendship
L'amitié
Paris, winter 1907
Oil on canvas, 152 x 101 cm
Zervos II*, 60; DR 104
St. Petersburg, Hermitage

The Dryad (Nude in a Forest)
La dryade (Nu dans une forêt)
Paris, spring to autumn 1908
Oil on canvas, 185 x 108 cm
Zervos II*, 113; DR 133
St. Petersburg, Hermitage

Above right:
Seated Nude
Femme nue assise
Paris, winter 1908
Oil on canvas, 73 x 60 cm
Zervos II*, 118; DR 230
Houston (TX), Private collection

Below right:
Bathers
Baignade
Paris, spring 1908
Oil on canvas, 38 x 62.5 cm
Zervos II*, 93; DR 184
St. Petersburg, Hermitage

Below left:
Head of a Woman
Tête de femme
Paris, early 1908
Gouache on panel, 27 x 21 cm
Zervos XXVI, 393; DR 140
Estate of the artist

Standing Nude
Femme nue debout
Paris, spring 1908
Oil on panel, 27 x 21.2 cm
Zervos XXVI, 365; DR 157; MPP 23
Paris, Musée Picasso

Standing Nude
Femme nue debout tournée vers la droite
Paris, spring 1908
Gouache on panel, 27 x 21 cm
Zervos XXVI, 366; DR 158
Estate of the artist

173 Analytical Cubism 1907 – 1912

Green Bowl and Black Bottle
Bol vert et flacon noir
Paris, spring to summer 1908
Oil on canvas, 61 x 51 cm
Zervos II*, 89; DR 173
St. Petersburg, Hermitage

Below right:
Still Life with Fishes and Bottles
Nature morte avec poissons et bouteilles
Paris, early 1909
Oil on canvas, 73 x 60 cm
Zervos II*, 122; DR 213
Paris, Private collection

**Bowl of Fruit and Wine Glass
(Still Life with Bowl of Fruit)**
Compotier, fruits et verre
(Nature morte au compotier)
Paris, late 1908
Oil on canvas, 92 x 72.5 cm
Zervos II*, 124; DR 209
St. Petersburg, Hermitage

**Flowers in a Grey Jug and Wine Glass
with Spoon**
Bouquet de fleurs dans un pot gris
et verre avec cuillère
La Rue-des-Bois, August 1908
Oil on canvas, 81 x 65 cm
Zervos II*, 88; DR 196
St. Petersburg, Hermitage

Above left:
Pot, Wine Glass and Book
Pot, verre et livre
Paris, August to September 1908
Oil on canvas, 55 x 46 cm
Zervos II*, 87; DR 198
St. Petersburg, Hermitage

Pitcher and Three Bowls
Carafe et trois bols
Paris, summer 1908
Oil on cardboard, 66 x 50.5 cm
Zervos II*, 90; DR 176
St. Petersburg, Hermitage

Analytical Cubism 1907 – 1912 **175**

Green Bowl and Tomatoes
Bol vert et tomates
Paris, spring to summer 1908
Gouache on panel, 21 x 27 cm
Zervos XXVI, 362; DR 175
Estate of the artist

Above right:
Landscape
Paysage
La Rue-des-Bois, August 1908
(or Paris, July 1908)
Watercolour and gouache on paper,
64 x 49.5 cm
Zervos XXVI, 174; DR 183
Bern, Kunstmuseum Bern,
Hermann and Margrit Rupf Foundation

House in a Garden (House and Trees)
Maisonnette dans un jardin (Maisonnette et arbres)
La Rue-des-Bois, August 1908
(or Paris, winter 1908)
Oil on canvas, 92 x 73 cm
Zervos II*, 81; DR 190
Moscow, Pushkin Museum

expressed in his "Principles of Psychology" (1890). The book did not offer Picasso any direct inspiration to revise figurational procedures, and indeed he would have found little more in the physiological mechanics described than techniques of formal figuration which he had long been familiar with through drawing.[185] Still, these publications hallmarked the spirit of the age. It was a period when an artist might be in a position to rethink first principles. This was also true of the discovery of unfamiliar modes of expression – the contemporary enthusiasm for what was considered primitive or exotic art. We need only recall the influence Japanese woodcuts had on van Gogh and Toulouse-Lautrec, and the interest in archaic art which Picasso himself had recently demonstrated. This all resulted from the quest for new ways of creating visual images, traditional methods no longer seeming adequate to the needs of the age.[186] There is nothing more indicative of his contemporaries' helplessness, and their way of clinging to newly-established conventions, than the terms that were applied to Picasso's painting. To Uhde the "Demoiselles" seemed "Assyrian", and Henri ("Le Douanier") Rousseau, prized for his naive art, said Picasso's Cubism was "Egyptian". The inapt supposition that the new visual idiom drew on black, African art – though this did play some part for the Cubists later – was a product of this way of thinking too.[187] Of course Picasso saw it all, and was prompted to find a basic solution to the problem. He drew till he had devised a new formal language, which he then articulated in "Les Demoiselles d'Avignon" – showing how the old could be re-used to make something altogether new. If they were perplexed at first, his fellow artists soon understood what he was doing. Cubism became established, slowly but

Landscape
Paysage
La Rue-des-Bois, August 1908
(or Paris, September 1908)
Oil on canvas, 73 x 60 cm
Zervos II*, 82; DR 192
Private collection

House in the Garden
Maisonnette dans un jardin
La Rue-des-Bois, August 1908
Oil on canvas, 73 x 61 cm
Zervos II*, 80; DR 189
St. Petersburg, Hermitage

Analytical Cubism 1907 – 1912 **177**

surely: the first major peak that it reached is generally known as Analytical Cubism.

Picasso's famous portrait of art dealer Ambroise Vollard is an arresting example (p. 189). Amidst the complex criss-cross of lines and overlapping colour zones we are immediately struck by the head. It is done entirely in shades of yellow; and it also strikes us because, unlike the composition as a whole, it clearly represents the outline, structure and features of a human head. The oval broadens at the jowls. About the middle there are lines to denote eyebrows and the bridge of the nose. At right and left, narrow patches of white clearly indicate sideburns. We see the face of a man with a high, commanding forehead and a short beard already grey at the sides – a somewhat older man, presumably. The central lines delineate a strong, straight nose with a noticeable dent and broad nostrils. The thin upper lip also conveys the sitter's personality.

Picasso's painting fulfils the main requirements of a portrait: it represents the outer appearance of a certain individual in a recognisable way. But the artist is also displaying his skill at playing with the natural image. The lines are continued at random, no longer restricted to defining an available form. They have a life of their own. So do the colours: lighter and darker shades, with little regard for the subject, obey the curious rules of the composition instead. The subject is dissected, as it were, or analyzed. And hence this kind of Cubism has become known as "Analytical Cubism".[188]

Though the laws of the random afford common ground, the portrait of Vollard remains a distinctly different work from "Les Demoiselles d'Avignon". In the 1907 painting the aim was closed form; in the 1910 work it is open figuration. The dissolution of the subject establishes a kind of grid in which overlaps and correspondences can constantly be read anew. The essential characteristics of the subject are preserved purely because Picasso is out to demon-

Study for "Carnival at the Bistro"
Etude pour "Carnaval au bistrot"
Paris, winter 1908
Gouache on paper, 32 x 49.5 cm
Zervos VI, 1074; DR 219
Estate of the artist

Study for "Carnival at the Bistro"
Etude pour "Carnaval au bistrot"
Paris, winter 1908
Pencil on paper, 31.3 x 23.8 cm
Zervos VI, 1067; MPP 622
Paris, Musée Picasso

Study for "Carnival at the Bistro"
Etude pour "Carnaval au bistrot"
Paris, winter 1908
Watercolour and pencil on paper, 24.2 x 27.5 cm
Zervos VI, 1066; DR 217
Estate of the artist

Loaves and Bowl of Fruit on a Table
Pains et compotier aux fruits sur une table
Paris, winter 1908
Oil on canvas, 164 x 132.5 cm
Zervos II*, 134; DR 220
Basel, Öffentliche Kunstsammlung Basel, Kunstmuseum

Brick Factory in Tortosa
(Factory at Horta de Ebro)
Briqueterie à Tortosa (L'usine)
Horta de Ebro, summer 1909
Oil on canvas, 50.7 x 60.2 cm
Zervos II*, 158; DR 279
St. Petersburg, Hermitage

strate that the autonomy of line and colour is on a par with
straightforward representation, and just as convincing aestheti-
cally. His new approach put an end to the traditional scheme of
foreground, middleground and background, and the demarcation
of subject and setting, which were still present in the "Demoiselles". Between the two extremes lay a three-year transitional period. It began in 1908 and can be seen as the phase in which Cubism
was established.

The first works to follow the "Demoiselles" highlighted the
draughtsmanship and the correspondence of subject and background. Colour and line were juxtaposed or at times contraposed,
as in the famous "The Dance of the Veils (Nude with Drapes)"
(p. 167). Picasso's 1908 "Composition with a Skull" (p. 15) must
be seen as a continuation of this line. But in the two great nudes
that he worked on from spring to autumn 1908 the emphases were
clearly being placed differently. In both "Three Women" (p. 166)
and "The Dryad (Nude in a Forest)" (p. 172) the draughtsman's
lines are no longer so independent of the subject. Now, the lines
and colour zones are creating shapes of geometrical import. But the
perspective has been exploded, so that various points of view are
at work in the same composition. The light and shade are not
juxtaposed in a spatial relation; yet spaces and areas derived from
the construction of form evolve a spatial presence.

In midsummer 1908 Picasso made a breakthrough with his landscapes. "House in a Garden (House and Trees)" and the simply-
titled "Landscape" (both p. 177) take the principle of autonomous

Analytical Cubism 1907 – 1912 **180**

Houses on the Hill (Horta de Ebro)
Maisons sur la colline (Horta de Ebro)
Horta de Ebro, summer 1909
Oil on canvas, 65 x 81 cm
Zervos II*, 161; DR 278
New York, The Museum of Modern Art

The Reservoir (Horta de Ebro)
Le réservoir (Horta de Ebro)
Horta de Ebro, summer 1909
Oil on canvas, 60.3 x 50.1 cm
Zervos II*, 157; DR 280
New York, Mr. and Mrs. David Rockefeller
Collection

Two Nudes
Deux figures nues
Paris, 1909
Etching, 13 x 11 cm
Bloch 17; Geiser 21 III b

spatial values and evolve forms that make a stereometrically stylized impression. At the same time, the young French painter Braque had arrived at a similar position. He had met Picasso in spring 1907, and had seen "Les Demoiselles d'Avignon" at Picasso's studio that November. Though it startled him at first, the painting's impact stayed with him, and mingled with ideas derived from Cézanne. During two stays in southern France in summer 1908, painting the landscape near L'Estaque, Braque deconstructed representational and spatial values. The fundamental coincidence of his approach and that in Picasso's landscapes is arresting. But they were working independently of each other, with no direct contact.

At first glance, the motifs look like cubes – which is why the term "Cubism" was coined in the first place. In autumn 1908, Braque unsuccessfully submitted his new work for the Paris autumn Salon. Matisse, who was a member of the jury, observed to the critic Louis Vauxcelles that the pictures consisted of lots of little cubes. Vauxcelles adopted the phrase in a review he wrote in the magazine "Gil Blas" when Braque showed the paintings at the Kahnweiler gallery in November. And thus (as is so often the case) a misunderstanding produced a label; and by 1911 everyone was using the term "Cubism".[189]

In the winter of 1908, following Braque's exhibition, Picasso and Braque developed a give-and-take that often verged on collabora-

tion. The Spaniard's misgivings about the Frenchman vanished. (That spring he was still accusing Braque of pirating his inventions without making any acknowledgement.)[190] They did not share a studio, though; both artists worked resolutely on their own. But they did meet constantly to discuss their progress and learn from each other. They took trips – Picasso to Spain in 1909 and 1910, Braque twice to La Roche-Guyon in the Seine valley. Not till summer 1911 did they spend time together in Céret in the south of France, a popular artists' colony. They compared the fruits of their labours and debated new possibilities, often in a competitive spirit. Thus, for instance, Picasso's "Girl with a Mandolin (Fanny Tellier)" (p. 186) is plainly a response to a painting by Braque.[191] Both artists – and this is unique in the history of art – were developing a new style together. It was emphatically a give-and-take process: both artists have the same standing in the history of Cubism. The painstaking Braque, a slow worker, painted extraordinarily subtle works incomparable in their aesthetic effect. By contrast, Picasso was more restless and abrupt, jumping to and fro amongst various formal options. Both were experimenting in their own way, and both, independently, hit upon significant innovations. For Picasso, drawing and the investigation of form were always the focus of his interest.

One of the finest and most instructive of his games played with

Woman with a Mandolin
Femme à la mandoline
Paris, winter 1908
Oil on canvas, 91 x 72.5 cm
Zervos II*, 133; DR 236
St. Petersburg, Hermitage

Woman with a Mandolin
Femme à la mandoline
Paris, spring 1909
Oil on canvas, 100 x 81 cm
Zervos II*, 115; DR 271
Düsseldorf, Kunstsammlung
Nordrhein-Westfalen

Bather
Baigneuse
Paris, (early) 1909
Oil on canvas, 130 x 97 cm
Zervos II*, 111; DR 239
New York, Mrs. Bertram Smith Collection

Nude
Femme nue
Paris, early 1909
Oil on canvas, 100 x 81 cm
Zervos II*, 109; DR 240
St. Petersburg, Hermitage

Woman with Fan
La femme à l'éventail
Paris, early spring 1909
Oil on canvas, 101 x 81 cm
Zervos II*, 137; DR 263
Moscow, Pushkin Museum

Head of a Woman (Fernande)
Tête de femme (Fernande)
Paris, autumn 1909
Bronze, 40.5 x 23 x 26 cm
Spies 24 II; Zervos II**, 573; MPP 243
Paris, Musée Picasso

form is the still life "Loaves and Bowl of Fruit on a Table" (p. 179), painted in winter 1908/09, a drop-leaf table with loaves of bread, a cloth, a bowl of fruit and a lemon on it. The informing principle is not one of Cubist transformation, though, so much as a genuine metamorphosis – for the picture began by showing not objects in a still life but carnival merry-makers in a bistro! Picasso pursued his idea through a number of studies. The first showed a flat-perspective group of six at a drop-leaf table.[192] Subsequently he interwove the forms so as to blur the distinction between the subject and the background. His most conspicuous stylistic feature was the spatial extension of lines to include the figures in a veritable scaffolding of major diagonals and curves that dominated the entire picture. In other sketches (p. 178) he bunched lines together, and made visible progress in the deconstruction of form. The motifs and directional movements assembled into geometrical figures – trapeziums, rhombuses – which, taken individually, had already

become completely non-representational. Light and shadow likewise acquired a life of their own, appearing in contrastive shades of lighter and darker.

At this stage, Picasso had put mimesis aside and was free to define his forms anew. As he went on, formal similarities remained – though we would not perceive them if we did not have the preliminary studies. Thus the man's left arm propped on the table became a baguette, and his right arm became another, while the hand he was resting on the table became an upturned cup with no handle. The loaf in mid-table, cut into, was formerly the left forearm of a harlequin. The bust of the woman seated at left became the fruit bowl. These metamorphoses occurred in the smallest details; X-ray examination has shown that Picasso accomplished this fundamental transformation of what was once a figure composition in one bout of work on the canvas.

With such rethinking of visual possibilities in his mind, Picasso,

185 Analytical Cubism 1907 – 1912

186 Analytical Cubism 1907–1912

Bust of a Man (The Athlete)
Horta de Ebro, summer 1909
Oil on canvas, 92 x 73 cm
Zervos II*, 166; DR 297
São Paulo, Museu de Arte

Portrait of Manuel Pallarés
Barcelona, May 1909
Oil on canvas, 68 x 49.5 cm
Zervos XXVI, 425; DR 274
Detroit (MI), The Detroit Institute of Arts

Page 186 top:
Girl with a Mandolin (Fanny Tellier)
Jeune fille à la mandoline (Fanny Tellier)
Paris, late spring 1910
Oil on canvas, 100.3 x 73.6 cm
Zervos II*, 235; DR 346
New York, The Museum of Modern Art,
Nelson A. Rockefeller Bequest

Portrait of Georges Braque (?)
Paris, winter 1909. Oil on canvas,
61 x 50 cm. Zervos II*, 177; DR 330
Geneva, Heinz Berggruen Collection

Page 186 bottom:
Still Life with Aniseed Brandy Bottle
Nature morte à la bouteille d'anis del Mono
Horta de Ebro, August 1909
Oil on canvas, 81.6 x 65.4 cm
Zervos II*, 173; DR 299
New York, The Museum of Modern Art

Head of a Woman against Mountains
Tête de femme sur fond de montagnes
Horta de Ebro, summer 1909
Oil on canvas, 65 x 54.5 cm
Zervos II*, 169; DR 294. Frankfurt am Main,
Städelsches Kunstinstitut und Städtische Galerie

prompted by the southern light when he was in Spain during 1909, created pictures that approached perspective and optics as an interweaving of geometrical shapes and colour tonalities. Eloquent examples are "The Reservoir (Horta de Ebro)", "Houses on the Hill" and "Brick Factory in Tortosa" (pp. 180 and 181).

It is characteristic of Picasso (and a contrast to Braque) that he never saw Cubism purely in terms of painting. He tackled spatial values and planes in various media, using various motifs. Braque at that time restricted himself to relatively few kinds of picture, preferring those such as landscapes or still lifes that were conducive to abstracted formal games, and in his work he experimented with the manifold opportunities that monochrome painting afforded. Picasso, for his part, stuck to his usual repertoire of subjects. He tried to introduce them into his new experiments, and did not flinch from strong colour contrasts. Thus in 1909 he did a number of portraits that explored the analytic breakdown of form (cf. pp. 164 and 165). The areas of the human face defined by the placing of nose, mouth, cheeks, forehead and eyes, and resolved by light and shadow, were now a fabric of juxtaposed planes. And, as in 1906,

Picasso went into questions of volume in sculpture, to see if they too had autonomous values. In preparing the near-lifesize "Head of a Woman (Fernande)", a portrait of Fernande Olivier (p. 184), Picasso made his experiment using plaster; a small edition was later cast in bronze for Vollard.

In this sculpture, three-dimensional volume appears to be made of particles roughly equal in size. The ruling structural principle is an equilibrium of volume and emptiness. The most important points – the eye sockets, nose, lips – are done in accordance with their natural appearance. But in the forehead, cheeks and neck the natural lie of the features has been inverted – most noticeably in the neck and nape – so that a new rhythmic sense arises that introduces dynamics to the work.

Picasso used the same procedure in the three portraits of his dealers, the Germans Kahnweiler and Uhde and the Frenchman Vollard (above and right), painted in 1910. He did so in a way adapted to painting, by dissecting the space and fragmenting the image. This is the apogee of a line he had been following through a number of pictures in 1909, most doggedly in "Still Life with Aniseed Brandy Bottle" (p. 186). It says a lot for the non-representational autonomy of form in this work that for many years its

Portrait of Wilhelm Uhde
Portrait de Wilhelm Uhde
Paris, spring (to autumn) 1910
Oil on canvas, 81 x 60 cm
Zervos II*, 217; DR 338
Saint Louis (MO),
Joseph Pulitzer Jr. Collection

Portrait of Daniel-Henry Kahnweiler
Portrait de Daniel-Henry Kahnweiler
Paris, autumn to winter 1910
Oil on canvas, 100.6 x 72.8 cm
Zervos II*, 227; DR 368
Chicago (IL), The Art Institute of Chicago

Portrait of Ambroise Vollard
Portrait d'Ambroise Vollard
Paris, spring (to autumn) 1910
Oil on canvas, 93 x 66 cm
Zervos II*, 214; DR 337
Moscow, Pushkin Museum

Seated Nude
Femme nue assise
Paris, spring 1910
Oil on canvas, 92 x 73 cm
Zervos II*, 201; DR 343
London, Tate Gallery

Seated Nude in an Armchair
Femme nue assise dans un fauteuil
Paris, winter 1909
Oil on canvas, 91 x 71.5 cm
Zervos II*, 195; DR 332
St. Petersburg, Hermitage

Seated Woman in an Armchair
Femme assise dans un fauteuil
Paris, spring 1910
Oil on canvas, 94 x 75 cm
Zervos II*, 213; DR 344
Prague, Národni Gallery

Left:
The Guitar Player
Le joueur de guitare
Cadaqués, summer 1910
Oil on canvas, 100 x 73 cm
Zervos II*, 223; DR 362
Paris, Musée National d'Art Moderne,
Centre Georges Pompidou

Still Life with Bottle of Rum
La bouteille de rhum
Céret, summer 1911
Oil on canvas, 60.3 x 48.8 cm
Zervos II*, 267; DR 414
Mexico City, Jacques and Natasha
Gelman Collection

Man with a Moustache and a Clarinet
Homme moustachu à la clarinette
Céret and Paris, summer to autumn 1911
Ink, India ink and black chalk,
30.8 x 19.5 cm
Zervos XXVIII, 48; MPP 659
Paris, Musée Picasso

Standing Nude
Femme nue debout
Paris, autumn 1910
Charcoal on paper, 48.3 x 31.2 cm
Zervos II*, 208
New York, The Metropolitan Museum of Art

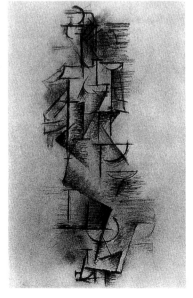

193 Analytical Cubism 1907 – 1912

subject was misinterpreted.[193] In the middle is a bottle of aniseed brandy. The translucent, reflective glass offered the artist a teasing visual surface, especially because of the fluting. In every painting, this analytic deconstruction of form inevitably led to the presence of non-representational elements; and this led Picasso and Braque to scrutinize the function of drawing and of signs.

The line outlines the object and establishes a visual sign. In a Cubist picture, though, this mimetic function is dissolved. Picasso and Braque now extended the scope of signs in pictures, and alongside representational images they included symbols and juxtaposed colourful structures without content. It was a new approach to a problem long familiar to painters, and the Cubists found new solutions. Titian and Velázquez had drawn strength from the combination of mimetic representation, in line and colour, and the sheer virtuosity of the artist's craft – a combination which accounts for much of their appeal to us today. In 1910, Picasso and Braque took the strategy to the borders of pure abstraction. Paintings such as "The Guitar Player" (p. 192) or "The Clarinet" (p. 196), compositions of great artistic charm, clearly demonstrate that beauty in art need not be pinned down to illusionist representation.

Cubism now entered a somewhat different phase, one that was heralded in 1911 and led the following year to new visual forms different in structure and principle. Braque, who had already used

Woman with a Guitar by a Piano
Femme à la guitare près d'un piano
Paris, (spring) 1911
Oil on canvas, 57 x 41 cm
Zervos II*, 237; DR 388
Prague, Národni Gallery

Woman with Guitar or Mandolin
Femme à la guitare ou mandoline
Paris, February 1911
Oil on canvas, 65 x 54 cm
Zervos II*, 257; DR 390
Prague, Národni Gallery

Man with a Guitar
Homme à la guitare
Paris, begun autumn 1911, finished 1913
Oil on canvas, 154 x 77.5 cm
Zervos XXVIII, 57; DR 427; MPP 34
Paris, Musée Picasso

The Mandolin Player
La mandoliniste
Paris, autumn 1911
Oil on canvas, 100 x 65 cm
Zervos II*, 270; DR 425
Basel, Beyeler Collection

single letters of the alphabet in Cubist paintings of 1909, now took to using entire words.[194] It was not a new idea; but in painting it had been restricted to producing the illusion of real lettering actually before the beholder.[195] Picasso borrowed this, and in "Still Life on a Piano ('CORT')" (pp. 198–199) transposed it to a new level of meaning. Whereas Braque retained the meanings of words and thus their value as communications, Picasso was pointing up the random quality of meaning in signs. The word "CORT" was a meaningless abbreviation for the name Alfred Cortot (a pianist). But it was also a witty riposte to Braque, who had included the words "Mozart" and "Kubelik" to suggest a concert. Picasso's still life also used musical instruments upon a piano, motifs which are directly related to concerts. It is an enigmatic picture, walking a thin line between meaning and nonsense and tantamount to a visual statement of epistemological tenets – and yet insisting on the truth of art.

195 Analytical Cubism 1907 – 1912

The Clarinet
La clarinette
Céret, (August) 1911
Oil on canvas, 61 x 50 cm
Zervos II*, 265; DR 415
Prague, Národni Gallery

Standing Nude
Femme nue debout
Paris, 1911
India ink on paper, 31 x 19 cm
Zervos XXVIII, 38

Cubist Nude
Femme nue debout
Cadaquès, summer 1910
Ink and India ink, 31.5 x 20.9 cm
Zervos XXVIII, 20
Stuttgart, Staatsgalerie Stuttgart

Violin Player with a Moustache
Violoniste moustachu
Céret and Sorgues, summer 1912
Ink, India ink, charcoal and pencil
on paper, 30.8 x 18.8 cm
Zervos XXVIII, 78; MPP 666
Paris, Musée Picasso

Analytical Cubism 1907 – 1912 **196**

Another innovation also originated with Braque. As a youngster he had been an apprentice house painter, and was familiar with a number of trade techniques, such as the "comb" – a template for mechanically establishing a whole area of parallel lines. Braque used it to imitate the graining of wood, and achieved a higher level of illusionism, conveying not only the appearance but also the material consistency of an object – a technical trick dazzlingly and absurdly used. Picasso borrowed the method for a number of still lifes (cf. pp. 208, 209 and 212), partly combined with letters. Cubism had changed considerably. A "simple" deconstruction of the mimetic, representational function of a picture had become an art which used the picture, itself a system of signs, to prove the random contingency of signs.

Violin "Jolie Eva"
Violon "Jolie Eva"
Céret or Sorgues, spring 1912
Oil on canvas, 60 x 81 cm
Zervos II*, 342; DR 480
Stuttgart, Staatsgalerie Stuttgart

Still Life on a Piano ("CORT")
Nature morte sur un piano ("CORT")
Céret, summer 1911 to spring 1912, Paris
Oil on canvas, 50 x 130 cm
Zervos II**, 728; DR 462
Geneva, Heinz Berggruen Collection

The Poet
Le poète
Sorgues-sur-Ouvère, summer to autumn 1912
Oil on canvas, 60 x 48 cm
Zervos II*, 313; DR 499
Basel, Öffentliche Kunstsammlung Basel,
Kunstmuseum, Gift of Maja Sacher-Stehlin

The Aficionado (The Torero)
L'aficionado (Le torero)
Sorgues-sur-Ouvère, summer 1912
Oil on canvas, 135 x 82 cm
Zervos II**, 362; DR 500
Basel, Öffentliche Kunstsammlung Basel,
Kunstmuseum

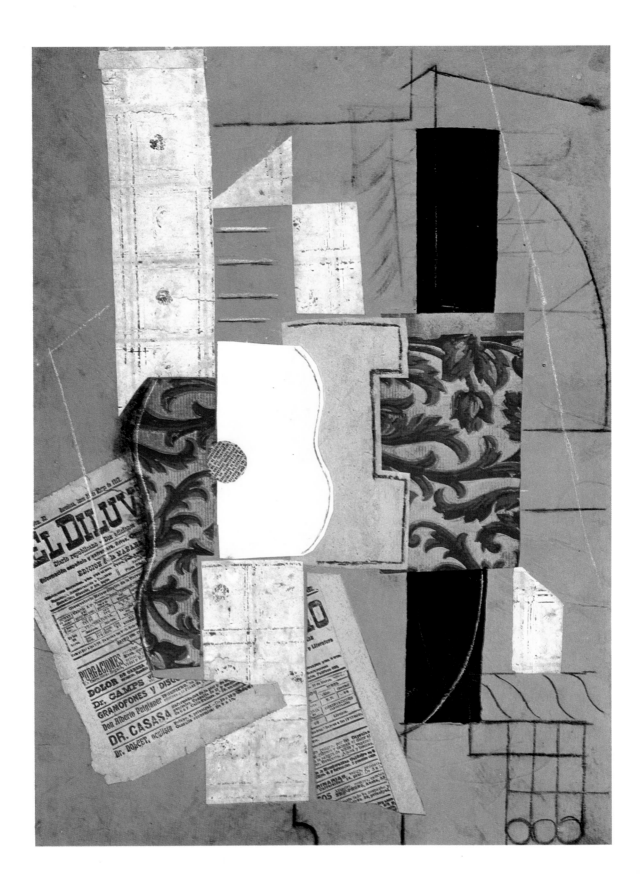

8 Synthetic Cubism
1912–1915

The work Picasso did in 1907 on "Les Demoiselles d'Avignon" placed him squarely in the contemporary vanguard. But in his radicalness he stood alone. From 1908 to 1911, together with Braque, he developed Cubism, and moved on to the frontiers of abstraction. Only a very few insiders were in a position to follow this progress, though. When the two artists created Synthetic Cubism from 1912 onwards, the situation had changed, and Cubism was no longer the property of the experts, a style hidden away in a handful of galleries, but rather the new sensational talking point among all who had an interest in contemporary art.

Late in 1911, a number of young artists calling themselves Cubists exhibited in the Salon des Indépendants and at the autumn Salon.[196] But Picasso and Braque were not the stars of these shows; they were not even to be seen. The most important artists of the Cubist group were Albert Gleizes, Jean Metzinger, Henri Le Fauconnier, Robert Delaunay, Roger de la Fresnaye and Fernard Léger. In 1912, the now expanded group again exhibited at both Salons. By now, public interest was even greater, and there was a scandal comparable only with that which had accompanied the arrival of the Fauves in 1905[197]. From our point of view, if we compare their work with what Picasso and Braque had just been doing, the fuss is difficult to understand. The Cubism that caught the public eye was by no means a genuinely revolutionary, innovative art. Almost all the pictures on show can be seen as pleasing variants on what the two true revolutionaries had been painting earlier, around 1908–1909. Only Delaunay and Léger had ideas of their own about abstraction from the representational.[198]

Nevertheless, the controversy raged in the press and even at political meetings. This rapid reception was doubtless assisted by the fact that the group offered the public a readily-grasped notion of Cubism. Their work was essentially geometrically abstract, taking its cue from the cube. Without taking Picasso's and Braque's latest work into account, the painters had gone back to Cézanne, and to the older work Braque had exhibited at Kahnweiler's in 1908[199].

The twin lines of development were plainly not running in synch. Artistic approaches, their significance for progress in art, and their

Various Studies: Guitars
Feuille d'études: guitares
(Etudes pour une sculpture)
1912/13
Ink, India ink and pencil on paper,
35.7 x 22.6 cm
Zervos XXVIII, 282; MPP 683
Paris, Musée Picasso

Guitar
La guitare
Céret, after 31 March 1913
Papiers collés, charcoal, India ink and chalk
on paper, 66.4 x 49.6 cm
Zervos II*, 348; DR 608
New York, The Museum of Modern Art,
Nelson A. Rockefeller Bequest

Guitar, Newspaper, Glass and Bottle
Guitare, journal, verre et bouteille
Céret, 1913
Papiers collés and ink on paper,
46.5 x 62.5 cm
Zervos II*, 335; DR 604
London, Tate Gallery

recognition in the public arena, were evolving in dislocated fashion. The reason must be sought in the new conditions of art and its reception in the early 20th century – which will also account for the shift in the evaluation of various Cubist artists that occurred during the debate of 1912.

In the 19th century it was the official Salons, and they (very nearly) alone, that decided the recognition of artists. Discussion divided according to whether artists were Salon or anti-Salon artists: we need only recall Courbet, or the Impressionists.[200] But since the turn of the century it had been commercial galleries and the press that steered the reception. Most important shows of avant-garde art were to be seen in the galleries. They acted as middlemen between the studios and the public, ensuring that the latest work was seen and providing journalists and critics with the material for reviews and essays. Of course the motives of the galleries were commercial, at least in part. Certain artists were promoted and marketed. This, after all, was the dawn of middle-class society's commercialization of art.[201]

Till the decisive Cubist breakthrough, Picasso's career too was one that depended on dealers' speculation. His early exhibition at Vollard's in 1901 represented an investment in his future productivity. Everyone who knew what was what realised, after all, that Salon art was being superseded by something new. Thus in early 1907 Vollard bought up everything of Picasso's, including all his sketches, for 2500 francs.[202] Both Picasso and Braque had contracts with the young German dealer Daniel Henry Kahnweiler, who paid a fixed price for their startling new work. An arrangement of this kind gave the artists a degree of security and also enabled them to

Bottle on a Table
Bouteille sur une table
Paris, after 8 December 1912
Papiers collés and charcoal on newspaper,
62 x 44 cm
Zervos II**, 782; DR 551; MPP 369
Paris, Musée Picasso

Synthetic Cubism 1912 – 1915 **204**

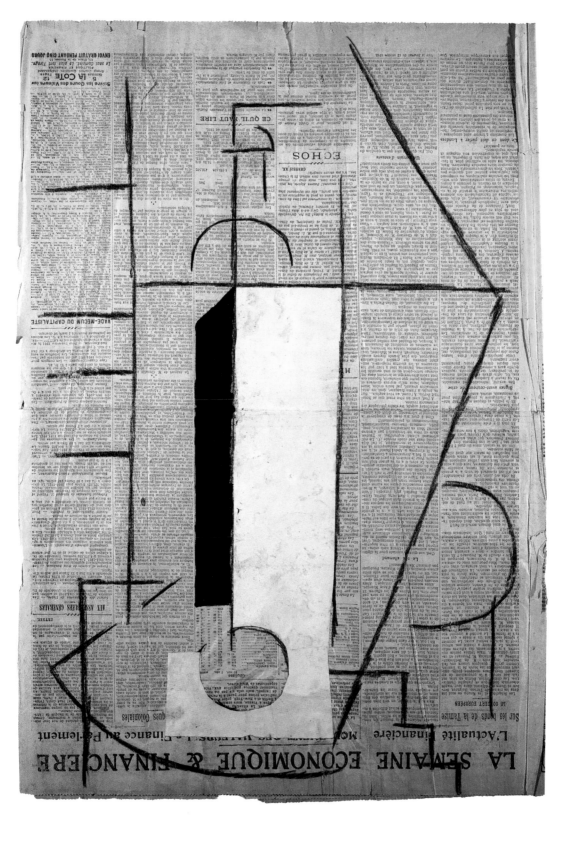

ignore the processes of official recognition. Picasso, in fact, never exhibited at a Paris Salon; instead, Kahnweiler sold his work to collectors, and introduced it to other galleries and dealers via his contacts. In 1911, both Picasso and Braque had exhibitions abroad – in the Galerie Thannhauser in Munich, for instance. These shows familiarized experts with their work but were largely ignored by the broader public.[203]

The official Cubist shows of 1911, at which Picasso and Braque were not represented, inevitably changed things. The public debate forced their work into the open and made it imperative to establish their significance in the evolution of Cubism. In 1912 Metzinger and Gleizes published "Du cubisme", a theoretical, popularizing view of Cubism that took Cézanne as the great exemplar.[204] But numerous writers in Picasso's circle published other views. That same year, Salmon published two books which are seen to this day as vital sources in the history of Modernist art: his "Histoire anecdotique du cubisme", and "La jeune peinture française". He was the first to stress Picasso's key position and the seminal importance of "Les Demoiselles d'Avignon" in the founding of Cubism. Then in 1913 Apollinaire's book "Les peintres cubistes" appeared, and made an attempt to distinguish and characterize groupings within the movement. Braque and Picasso were labelled "scientific" Cubists.[205]

All of this produced a fundamental revaluation of Cubism and the individual painters. Now Picasso stood centre-stage, vilified and acclaimed as the innovator *par excellence*. Though it does not fit the facts, Braque has been viewed ever since as Picasso's junior partner. This too can be accounted for if we look at the art scene

The Tavern (The Ham)
La guinguette (Le jambon)
Paris, winter 1912 (or spring 1914?)
Oil and wood shavings on cardboard,
29.5 x 38 cm (oval)
Zervos II**, 534; DR 704
St. Petersburg, Hermitage

of the time. Before Cubism, Picasso already had a name, while Braque was merely the young man among the Fauves. Though Picasso was the elder by a mere half year, he retained his advantage. From the start it was a financial advantage too: though both artists were under contract to Kahnweiler, the dealer paid Picasso four times what he paid Braque for his Cubist work.[206] This appears to have had no effect on the two artists' personal relations, though, and Picasso certainly seems to have considered Braque his equal. The letters they wrote each other – even if they were partly playing to the gallery, so to speak – record real friendship and mutual respect.[207]

Their exchange entered a new phase in 1912. Braque was continually trying to adapt craft techniques to Cubism, to put it on a new footing. The tactile sense could be appealed to in more ways than paint and a drawing pencil. He tested materials and methods familiar to the house decorator but new to art. Along with templates and other illusionist tricks, he mixed his paint with sand or plaster to create a rough, textured surface like that of a relief.[208] In

Still Life with Chair Caning
Nature morte à la chaise cannée
Paris, May 1912
Oil on oilcloth on canvas framed
with cord, 29 x 37 cm
Zervos II*, 294; DR 466; MPP 36
Paris, Musée Picasso

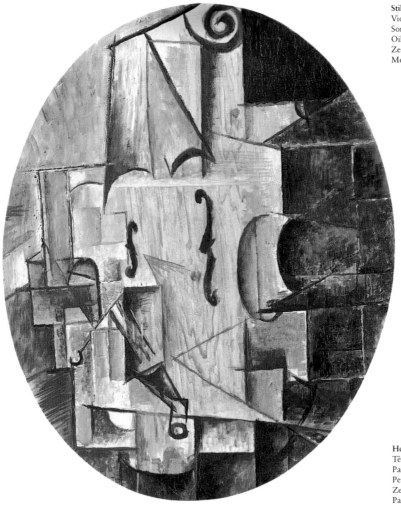

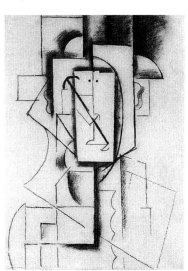

place of two-dimensional, surface mimesis on canvas or panel, Braque now used material textures of various kinds as an expressive value in itself. The next step, logically (as we can now see), was to redefine the visual function of technique and of the material(s) used.

In early 1912, following a stay at Sorgues, Braque showed Picasso his new work. It was three-dimensional. He had been cutting sculptural objects together, using paper or cardboard, and then painting or drawing over them. The spatial experiment was designed as a way of assessing illusionist techniques. He then applied the same ideas to two-dimensional work, retaining paper and cardboard as materials; and a new kind of work, the papiers collés, was born.[209] Subsequently he varied the textural effects and tried out further ways of developing them. In particular, he used pre-formed, printed, coloured and structured pieces of paper.

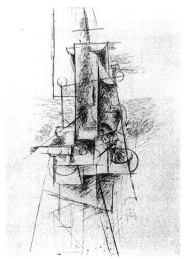

For Picasso, Braque's latest innovations provided the occasion to extend Cubism's visual system. Paintings such as the 1914 "Ma Jolie" (p. 241), personal in their allusive range, were the result. In these works, Picasso used letters and words as graphic, indeed iconic signs. The conventional meanings remain, since the letters can still be read, but the statement is puzzling. Picasso deploys messages that seem unambiguous but which become inaccessible once they appear in the context of his pictures. Thus in "Ma Jolie" the guitar, the make-believe music, the pipe, glass, playing card, dice, and the word "Bass", implying a drink, all provide ready associations with a café interior. The words "Ma Jolie" on the music would be perceived by contemporaries as a quotation from a popular chanson by Fragson; but the phrase also had a private meaning intended only for the artist's closest friends. It referred to Eva Gouel, a young woman who had entered the artistic milieu of

Montmartre as painter Louis Marcoussis's girlfriend and then became Picasso's partner.[110] Picasso similarly attached messages to his use of the house painter's "comb" template. In "The Poet" (p. 200) it not only provided texture, as it had for Braque. By using it for the poet's hair and moustache, Picasso introduced a mechanistic component into the representational process, well-nigh destroying all trace of illusionism and thereby redoubling the iconographic effect.

His approach to Braque's new papiers collés method was similar. The graphic structure of the printed paper produced a quality that was figuratively random in terms of a picture's import. In 1912 Picasso produced a number of masterly works of striking economy of means, one of the finest of them being the "Violin" (p. 217). Two scraps of newspaper, a few lines and charcoal hatchings – and the picture is finished. It is one of the loveliest and most intelligent Cubist pictures. First, Picasso clipped an irregular piece of newspaper and stuck it on cardboard. Then he drew a stylized violin's neck with the characteristic curled head. Following the precept of Analytical Cubism, he added formally deconstructed lines to suggest the parts of a violin. The newspaper text is still decipherable, but its original function and meaning have vanished. Though identifiably from a paper, it is seen purely as a graphic design, an image. The yellowing adds an extra interest, echoing the brownish colour of the violin. But Picasso did not merely defamiliarize his found material: the part of the newspaper from which he had clipped the first was reversed and placed at top right, where it acts as a background, this function being at odds with its identity as a newspaper fragment. We are offered an object and spatial dimensions – but, even as Picasso establishes them, he destroys them once again.

Violin Player
Violoniste
Sorgues-sur-Ouvère, summer 1912
Ink and India ink on paper, 30.7 x 19.5 cm
Zervos XXVIII, 102; MPP 673
Paris, Musée Picasso

Seated Man
Homme assis
1911/12
India ink and pencil on paper, 28.8 x 22.6 cm
Zervos XXVIII, 101; MPP 697
Paris, Musée Picasso

Man with Guitar (Study for a Sculpture)
Homme à la guitare (Etude pour une sculpture)
1912
India ink on paper, 30.5 x 19.5 cm
Zervos XXVIII, 126

Dove with Green Peas
Le pigeon aux petits pois
Paris, (spring) 1912
Oil on canvas, 65 x 54 cm
Zervos II*, 308; DR 453
Paris, Musée d'Art Moderne
de la Ville de Paris

Synthetic Cubism 1912–1915 **210**

The newspaper scraps are placed to mark an irregular vertical diagonal, a visual instability which the artist has echoed in the charcoal hatching. The tonal polarity creates a balance of the white card, the printed and yellowed paper, and the economical lines of the drawing. The form and content of the picture are at variance, but they are necessarily combined; and thus a subtle tension of great aesthetic and intellectual presence is created.

Picasso varied this stylistic approach in a number of *papiers collés* done in 1912. In one work (p. 205) he explored presence and vacancy by cutting an irregular rectangular shape out of a sheet of newspaper and then sticking the sheet upside-down on a sheet of cardboard. The art consists primarily in an intellectual rather than a technical process. Once again, Picasso deploys the first principles of representational art in absurd fashion. The table and bottle in the still life are presented with a few charcoal lines using the vacant space in the paper. Bottles are three-dimensional, and in terms of solid geometry cylinders. In transferring his bottle to the two dimensions of a picture, Picasso dispensed with any attempt at illusionist spatiality and rendered the bottle in two flat dimensions. Seen two-dimensionally, though, bottles are long rectangles; so that was the shape the artist cut out of the paper. The bottom of a bottle

Bowl of Fruit (The Fruit Dish)
Compotier et fruits
Céret, spring 1912
Oil on canvas, 55.3 x 38 cm
Zervos II*, 302; DR 475
New York, Private collection

Bottle of Pernod and Glass
Bouteille de Pernod et verre
Céret, spring 1912
Oil on canvas, 45.5 x 32.5 cm
Zervos II*, 307; DR 460
St. Petersburg, Hermitage

Violin, Glass, Pipe and Inkpot
Violon, verre, pipe et encrier
Paris, (May) 1912
Oil on canvas, 81 x 54 cm
Zervos II*, 306; DR 457
Prague, Národni Gallery

Page 214:
Violin
Violon accroché au mur
Paris, early 1913 (?)
Oil and sand on canvas, 65 x 46 cm
Zervos II**, 371; DR 573
Bern, Kunstmuseum Bern,
Hermann and Margrit Rupf Foundation

Violin and Sheet Music
Violon et feuille de musique
Paris, autumn 1912
Papiers collés on cardboard, 78 x 65 cm
Zervos II**, 771; DR 518; MPP 368
Paris, Musée Picasso

is circular, so Picasso's peculiar logic renders a circle in the two-dimensional projection. This circle is in fact a surviving area of newspaper in the cut-out section, displaced sideways. A few days later, in December 1912, Picasso made an exact counterpart of this picture, the bottle now represented – conversely – by the newspaper.[211]

During that period, Picasso also used other patterned materials such as wallpaper, advertisements, cloth and packaging, to good visual effect. Though unfamiliar materials were being introduced into the pictures, the iconic quality of presentation remained. The materials were integrated perfectly into the style and logic of Picasso's compositions, and were there primarily to add texture or patterning.[212] These *papiers collés* can thus be read as systems of signs producing a new level of effect. The best example is perhaps a painting done in Céret in 1913. According to its title, it shows a guitar (p. 220).

Pages 216 and 217:
Head of a Girl
Tête de jeune fille
Paris or Céret, early 1913
Pencil, charcoal and India ink
on paper, 63.5 x 48 cm
Zervos II**, 427; DR 589
Private collection

Violin
Violon
Paris, winter 1913
Papiers collés and charcoal on paper,
62 x 47 cm
Zervos XXVIII, 356; DR 524
Paris, Musée National d'Art Moderne,
Centre Georges Pompidou

Synthetic Cubism 1912 – 1915 **215**

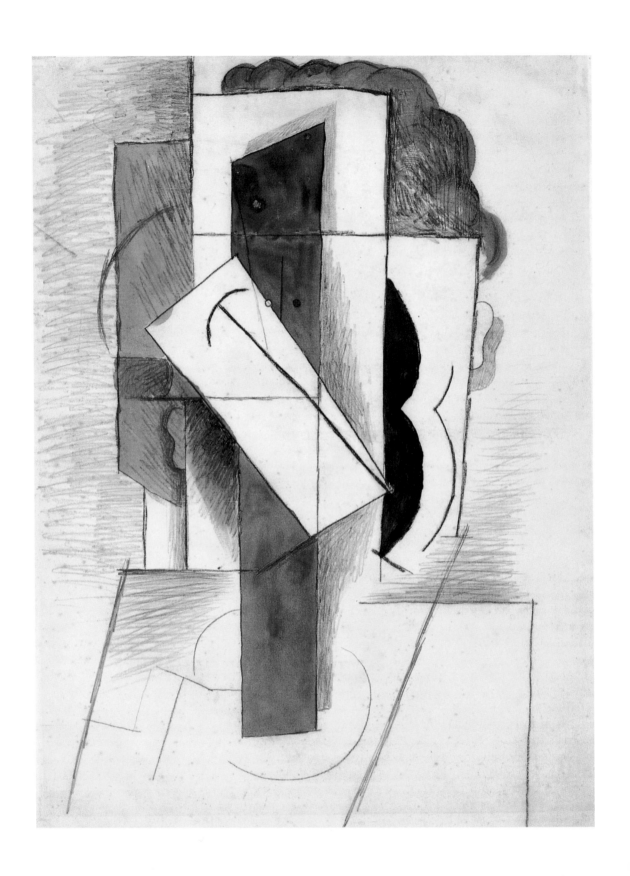

Guitar
Guitare
Paris, after 3 December 1912
Cardboard, paper, canvas, string and pencil,
22.8 x 14.5 x 7 cm
Spies 29; DR 556; Zervos II**, 779; MPP 245
Paris, Musée Picasso

Guitar
Guitare
Paris, after 3 December 1912
Cardboard, paper, canvas, string, oil
and pencil, 33 x 18 x 9.5 cm
Spies 30; DR 555; Zervos II**, 770; MPP 244
Paris, Musée Picasso

Geometrical Composition: The Guitar
Guitare
Céret, spring 1913
Oil on canvas on panel,
87 x 47.5 cm
Not in Zervos; DR 597; MPP 38
Paris, Musée Picasso

Mandolin and Clarinet
Mandoline et clarinette
Paris, early 1914
Painted pinewood and pencil,
58 x 36 x 23 cm
Spies 54; Zervos II**, 853; DR 632; MPP 247
Paris, Musée Picasso

Bottle of Vieux Marc, Glass and Newspaper
Bouteille de Vieux Marc, verre et journal
Céret, after 15 March 1913
Papiers collés, pins and charcoal on paper,
62.5 x 47 cm
Zervos II*, 334; DR 600
Paris, Musée National d'Art Moderne,
Centre Georges Pompidou

222

Bottle of Bass, Clarinet, Guitar,
Newspaper, Ace of Clubs
Bouteille de Bass, clarinette, guitare, violon,
journal, as de trèfle
Paris, winter 1913
Oil on canvas, 81 x 75 cm
Zervos II**, 487; DR 624
Paris, Musée d'Art Moderne,
Centre Georges Pompidou

223

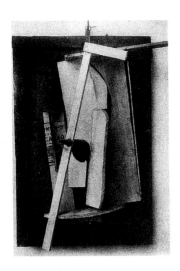  

The picture consists of a few irregular, angular areas of khaki, white and black. It is a copy of a *papier collé* that Picasso had recently done[213] – that is to say, it imitates an imitation. This defamiliarization is intensified by the use of angular shapes, since they are plainly at variance with the rounded shapes of what is supposedly the picture's subject, a guitar. And, further, the fundamentals of illusionism – light and shadow, perspective foreshortening – are not meaningfully deployed but are absurdly juxtaposed. The overlapping which at other times conveys spatial dimensions completes the defamiliarization in this picture so effectively that we would have no idea what it represented were it not for the title. The picture seems wholly abstract.

This defamiliarization still works entirely within the parameters of mimetic iconography. Picasso went about his work quite differently in the collage technique he devised at the time. In collage – unlike *papier collé* - an object is introduced into a context in such a way as to alter not only the medium but also the style and meaning of the motif.[214] "Still Life with Chair Caning" (p. 207), done in May 1912, is the cornerstone work of this new method. A composition in the manner of Analytical Cubism has been joined to a slant rectangular area showing the weave of a cane chair. This naturalistic component is at odds with the style of the rest. In fact it is not a representational piece of work by the artist, but a printed scrap of oilcloth. The semblance of reality is deployed as an illusion, identified as such, and exploited iconographically.

During this phase of Cubism, using new materials and techniques, Picasso was exploring the problem of spatial values in the illusion established by pictures. Many of his works therefore started from three-dimensional work. Alongside the *papiers collés* he began to make guitars out of cardboard (cf. pp. 218 and 219). The instrument is crudely but recognisably made: the brown colours of the cardboard, reminiscent of the wood of guitars,

Bottle and Guitar
Bouteille et guitare
Paris, autumn 1913
Wood, glued paper, plasticine cone;
dimensions unknown
Spies 56; DR 631; Zervos II**, 578
Probably destroyed (photo dated 1917)

Guitar and Bottle of Bass
Guitare et bouteille de Bass
Paris, spring to autumn 1913
Pieces of wood, glued paper, nails, charcoal,
89.5 x 80 x 14 cm
Spies 33 a; DR 630; Zervos II*, 575; MPP 246
Original state (photo dated 1917)
(Present state: see opposite page)

Guitar and Bottle
Guitare et bouteille
Paris, autumn 1913
String, cardboard and paper, 102 x 80 cm
Spies 48; DR 633; Zervos II**, 577

Guitar and Bottle of Bass
Guitare et bouteille de Bass
Paris, (spring to autumn) 1913
Pieces of wood, paper, charcoal and nails
on wooden board, 89.5 x 80 x 14 cm
Spies 33 b; Zervos II**, 575; DR 630; MPP 246
Paris, Musée Picasso

225

Study for "Woman in a Chemise Sitting in an Armchair"
Etude pour "Femme en chemise assise dans un fauteuil"
Paris, autumn 1913
Pencil, watercolour and gouache, 29 x 23 cm
Zervos II**, 785 and VI, 1263; DR 641
Private collection

Woman in a Chemise Sitting in an Armchair
Femme en chemise assise dans un fauteuil
Paris, autumn 1913 to spring 1914
Oil on canvas, 150 x 99.5 cm
Zervos II**, 522; DR 642
New York, Mrs. Victor W. Ganz Collection

Head of a Girl
Tête de jeune fille
Paris or Céret, winter to spring 1913
Oil on canvas, 55 x 38 cm
Zervos II**, 426; DR 590
Paris, Musée National d'Art Moderne, Centre Georges Pompidou

doubtless help us in the recognition. But inappropriate materials are used too, and spatial values subverted. The lid, bottom and side walls of the cardboard boxes are flattened to equal status. The basic Cubist rule of combining the representational and the random applies to these works too. But in contrast to Analytical Cubism, which dissected objects, here they are re-assembled. And for this reason a different term is used: Synthetic Cubism.[215]

Following this line, Picasso devised another new form, the assemblage. Basically it transposes the methods and effects of collage into three dimensions.[216] Two still-life works from 1913 are good examples: "Guitar and Bottle of Bass" (p. 225) and "Mandolin and Clarinet" (p. 221). The vehicle, structurally and visually, is wood. Picasso uses its tactile and visual properties, such as the graining and colour. By adding extra colour and drawing, he intensifies the effect, levels out spatial qualities, covers textures – but also contrasts his materials and techniques. It is a style that is nicely visible in the tondo "Glass, Pipe, Ace of Clubs and Dice" (p. 240). As well as wood, Picasso uses metal here; but it is painted over, and its original textural properties are no longer recognisable. The ace of clubs is sheet metal, the club symbol punched out. The dice is a

227 Synthetic Cubism 1912 – 1915

slant, cut-off section of a cylinder; only the painted motifs convey what it is meant to be.

Picasso also combined multi-level semantic defamiliarizations with tandem aesthetic and intellectual appeals in his only regular sculpture from this period, a famous serial work of which six copies were made: "The Glass of Absinthe" (p. 232). He made a wax and plasticine mould and variously painted the bronze casts. Absinthe (a vermouth brandy now banned because it is a health risk) was drunk from a glass goblet of the kind the sculpture shows. Picasso dissolved its transparent volume, with various highlights occasioned by the light, into isolated zones which he then juxtaposed, adding a genuine little spoon with a wax model of a sugar lump.

A great many things that are demonstrably wrong have been written about this yoking of different materials and methods of presentation. It is true that three formal levels meet in a mould: the reality of a genuine spoon, simple representation in the form of a wax copy of a sugar lump, and defamiliarization of the appearance of the glass.[217] But this is of no relevance in artistic terms, and is merely of practical significance. In the casting process of all six copies, the distinction between reality and simple representation inevitably vanished, because the spoon too now became only a

Violin and Clarinet
Violon et clarinette
Paris, early 1913
Oil on canvas, 55 x 33 cm
Zervos II**, 437; DR 575
St. Petersburg, Hermitage

Violin and Glass on a Table
Violon et verre sur une table
Paris, early 1913
Oil on canvas, 65 x 54 cm
Zervos II**, 370; DR 572
St. Petersburg, Hermitage

Violin at a Café (Violin, Glass, Bottle)
Violon au café (Violon, verre, bouteille)
Paris, early 1913
Oil on canvas, 81 x 54 cm
Zervos II**, 438 bis; DR 571
Galerie Rosengart

Ham, Glass, Bottle of Vieux Marc, Newspaper
Jambon, verre, bouteille de Vieux Marc, journal
Paris, (spring) 1914
Oil and sand on canvas, 38.5 x 55.5 cm
Zervos II**, 508; DR 705
Paris, Musée d'Art Moderne de la Ville de Paris

Bottle of Bass, Glass, Pack of Tobacco, Visiting Card
Bouteille de Bass, verre, paquet de tabac, carte de visite
Paris, early 1914
Papiers collés and pencil, 24 x 30.5 cm
Zervos II**, 456; DR 660
Paris, Musée National d'Art Moderne, Centre Georges Pompidou

Pipe, Bottle of Bass, Dice
Pipe, bouteille de Bass, dé
Paris, early 1914
Papiers collés and charcoal on paper, 24 x 32 cm
Zervos II**, 469; DR 664
Basel, Galerie Beyeler

representation of itself. The wax model of the genuine sugar lump was technically necessary because sugar, being porous, was unsuitable for bronze casting. All that really matters, in terms of the principles of Synthetic Cubism, is the contrast between conventionally faithful representation (the spoon and sugar) and Cubist methods. In all six copies this contrast is observed. The various painting merely served purposes of accentuation.

Thus the processes of deception underlying the art of illusion are excellently displayed in the assemblages and sculptures of Synthetic Cubism. Picasso arguably took this line of thinking to the logical extreme in his metal "Violin" (p. 242), done in 1915 and a full metre high. It is made of cut sheet metal, but the parts are wired in and colourfully overpainted so that the nature of the material is once again not immediately apparent. The volume of the metal components and the spatial values implied by the painting are at variance. The impact is further blurred because Picasso, partly harking back to the 1912 "Guitar", has interchanged spatial values. Parts that should occupy a foreground position in the object supposedly represented, and others that would be further from us in a conventional three-dimensional treatment, have exchanged places. The two holes in the soundboard are not depressions or

holes in the metal but added components. Reversing their state in the real world, they have here become small rectangular boxes lying on the board. Then there are the colours, white, black and blue areas alongside the brown ones suggesting the actual colour of a violin. Black areas seem suggestive of shadow, just as white ones imply bright light; yet this contrasts with the way things appear in reality. Graphic and spatial approaches, and the art of the painter, have all been combined in a sophisticated synthesis in this sculptural construction.

This playful approach to form can hardly be taken any further without exceeding the bounds of meaning – and evolving an altogether new artistic idiom. Constructions such as these thus took Cubism to the furthest limit of its options. The art scene had changed in the meantime. Cubism, still far from being publicly recognised as an apt response to the times, was now seen as the precursor of the artistic avant-garde throughout Europe. The dogmatic group centred on Metzinger and Gleizes no longer existed and the Cubist visual language had altered, acquiring international currency. In 1912, the Galerie La Boétie in Paris established a "Section d'Or" in which Marcel Duchamp and Juan Gris set the tone. Gris extended Analytical and Synthetic Cubism, while Duchamp's "Nude Descending a Staircase" found new ways of presenting motion. Braque and Picasso had invented a style which could now serve the formal needs of many different kinds of artists.[118]

The Futurist movement, for instance, sponteously proclaimed in Paris in 1909 by the Italian writer Filippo Tommaso Marinetti, was devoted to dynamism and movement, and played its own variations on the fragmentation technique of Analytical Cubism.[119] The

The Glass of Absinthe
Le verre d'absinthe
Paris, spring 1914
Painted bronze after a wax maquette with silver absinthe spoon, 21.5 x 16.5 x 8.5 cm
Spies 36 d; Zervos II**, 584; DR 756
New York, The Museum of Modern Art

The Glass of Absinthe
Paris, spring 1914
Painted bronze after a wax maquette with silver absinthe spoon, 21.5 x 16.5 x 8.5 cm
Spies 36 f; Zervos II**, 583; DR 758
Private collection

The Glass of Absinthe
Paris, spring 1914
Painted bronze after a wax maquette with silver absinthe spoon, 21.5 x 16.5 x 8.5 cm
Spies 36 e; Zervos II**, 582; DR 757
Philadelphia (PA), Philadelphia Museum of Art, A. E. Gallatin Collection

Below right:
Glass and Sliced Pear on a Table
Verre et poire coupée sur une table
Paris, April 1914
Gouache, pencil, wallpaper and paper on cardboard, 35 x 32 cm
Zervos II**, 481; DR 678
St. Petersburg, Hermitage

Bowl of Fruit with Bunch of Grapes and Sliced Pear
Compotier avec grappes de raisins et poire coupée
Paris, spring 1914
Gouache, tempera, pencil and wood shavings on cardboard, 67.6 x 52.2 cm
Zervos II**, 480; DR 680
St. Petersburg, Hermitage

Bottle of Bass, Glass and Newspaper
Bouteille de Bass, verre et journal
Paris, (spring) 1914
Tinplate, sand, wire and paper,
20.7 x 14 x 8.5 cm
Spies 53; Zervos II**, 849; DR 751; MPP 249
Paris, Musée Picasso

Violin and Bottle on a Table
Violon et bouteille sur une table
Paris, autumn 1915
Wood, string, nails, painted, and charcoal,
41 x 41 x 23 cm
Spies 57; Zervos II**, 926; DR 833; MPP 253
Paris, Musée Picasso

Bottle of Aniseed Brandy with Fruit Bowl and Grapes
Bouteille d'Anis del Mono et compotier
avec grappes de raisins
Paris, autumn 1915
Wood, tinplate, nails and charcoal,
35.5 x 27.5 x 26 cm
Spies 58; Zervos II**, 927; DR 834; MPP 254
Paris, Musée Picasso

Synthetic Cubism 1912 – 1915 **233**

Dutch painter Piet Mondrian exhibited at the 1911 Salon des Indépendants together with the other Cubists – but then accused Picasso, Braque and others of having failed to grasp the true aims of Cubism with the necessary precision. Mondrian advocated totally abstract art. With a number of others he started the "De Stijl" movement in Holland in 1917 – one of the core groups in European Constructivism.[220] The importance of Cubism was international. It inspired the avant-garde everywhere.

From 1908 on, thanks to the collector Sergei Shchukin, Picasso's latest Cubist work cold be seen in Moscow. Contemporary west European art was seen in a number of exhibitions not only in the main cities of Russia but also (for example) in Odessa, and was soon well known, spurring the abstract programmes of Suprematism (practised by Kasimir Malevich) and Rayonism (Michail Larionov).[221] The Swiss artist Paul Klee and the Germans August Macke and Franz Marc saw Cubism in Paris and subsequent developments such as Delaunay's Orphism; what they saw fed their own varieties of German Expressionism. In December 1911, Delaunay had exhibited in the first Blauer Reiter show in Munich's Thannhauser gallery. Klee and the American-born Lyonel Feininger subsequently took their impressions with them to the Bauhaus.[222] In Prague there was a veritable Cubist centre, with groups of artists organizing shows of French Cubism and doing their own Cubist paintings and sculptures.[223] As early as 1911, Alfred Stieglitz exhibited Picasso's work in his New York gallery, introducing the Spaniard to America.[224] The great Armory Show, held in New York in 1913, was the US breakthrough for many of the new European artists, among them the Nabis, the Fauves and the Cubists.[225]

So Cubism was a determining factor for many different kinds of Modernist art, as a model and a catalyst. Encouraged by Cubism, Wassily Kandinsky – precursor of total abstraction in art – was able to pursue his course. Yet Cubism did not directly initiate all of Modernism's artistic styles; abstract art in particular drew upon a complex variety of sources, including the decorative style of *art nouveau*. Taking that style as his point of departure, the German Adolf Hölzel painted almost abstract pictures as early as 1905. But it remains true that without the authority of Cubism, Modernism as we know it would quite simply not have existed.[226]

Moreover, Picasso and Braque had invented new media such as collage and assemblage, enriching the expressive repertoire. From Dada to the present, artists of every stylistic persuasion have used and developed these methods. Small wonder, then, that as Cubism gained ground it also founded international recognition of Picasso's special status in 20th-century art. In the second decade of the century he was already being seen as the artist who initiated the great Modernist breakthrough. Whenever new movements were started, it was Picasso and his work that served as a rallying cry. In a word: he became the hero of 20th-century art.[227]

Harlequin
Arlequin
Paris, autumn 1915
Oil on canvas, 183.5 x 105.1 cm
Zervos II**, 555; DR 844
New York, The Museum of Modern Art

Man with a Moustache
Homme à la moustache
Paris, spring 1914
Oil and glued printed fabric
on canvas, 65.5 x 46.6 cm
Zervos II**, 468; DR 759; MPP 40
Paris, Musée Picasso

Man with a Pipe (The Smoker)
Homme à la pipe (Le fumeur)
Paris, spring 1914
Oil and pasted paper on canvas,
138 x 66.5 cm
Zervos II**, 470; DR 760; MPP 39
Paris, Musée Picasso

Green Still Life
Nature morte verte
(Compotier, verre, bouteille, fruits)
Avignon, summer 1914
Oil on canvas, 59.7 x 79.4 cm
Zervos II**, 485; DR 778
New York, The Museum of Modern Art,
Lillie P. Bliss Collection

Still Life with Fruit, Glass and Newspaper
Nature morte avec fruits, verre et journal
Paris, summer 1914
Oil and sand on canvas, 34.5 x 42 cm
Zervos II**, 530; DR 781
Washington (DC), Mr. and Mrs. David
Lloyd Kreeger Collection

Portrait of a Young Girl
Portrait de jeune fille
(Femme assise devant une cheminée)
Avignon, summer 1914
Oil on canvas, 130 x 96.5 cm
Zervos II**, 528; DR 784
Paris, Musée National d'Art Moderne,
Centre Georges Pompidou

238 Synthetic Cubism 1912 – 1915

Glass, Pipe, Ace of Clubs and Dice
Verre, pipe, as de trèfle et dé
Avignon, summer 1914
Painted pieces of wood and metal on wooden board,
diameter 34 cm, depth 8.5 cm
Spies 45; Zervos II**, 830; DR 788; MPP 48
Paris, Musée Picasso

240

"Ma Jolie"
"Ma Jolie" (Pipe, verre, carte à jouer, guitare)
Paris, (spring) 1914
Oil on canvas, 45 x 41 cm
Zervos II**, 525; DR 742
Geneva, Heinz Berggruen Collection

241

Right:
Man with a Pipe
Homme au chapeau melon assis dans un fauteuil
(Homme à la pipe)
Paris, summer 1915
Oil on canvas, 130.2 x 89.5 cm
Zervos II**, 564; DR 842
Chicago (IL), The Art Institute of Chicago

Violin
Violon
Paris, 1915
Cut metal, painted, with iron wire,
100.1 x 63.7 x 18 cm
Spies 55; Zervos II**, 580; DR 835; MPP 255
Paris, Musée Picasso

242

9 The Camera and the Classicist 1916–1924

The work Picasso did from 1916 to 1924 was among the most baffling in his entire output. The public, his critics, and fellow artists were now familiar with him as the founder of Cubism and indeed of modern art, the painter who was most radical and consistent in casting aside the conventional laws of art and putting new rules in their stead. Mimetic copying of the given world could be seen as superseded. But now the great iconoclast bewildered the experts and general public alike by returning to a representational art of a monumental, statuesque kind.

Once again, Picasso's pictures were figural. Wholly in the classical tradition, and in accord with European forms of classicism, they were built on the line as the definition of form, offering generously – fashioned outlines large in conception and volume. But this alone could not have accounted for the confusion of Picasso's contemporaries. His return to tradition could have been dismissed as a relapse.[228] It was not so simple: one and the same artist was painting classicist nudes, portraits, scenes, and works in the spirit of Synthetic Cubism – at first sight quite incompatible – all in the same period. Thus the years from 1916 to 1924 are marked by the coexistence of polar opposites. And yet Picasso's work matched the mood of the age, and pursued his own intentions as an artist.

In August 1914 the First World War began. Braque and Derain, Picasso's closest artist friends, were called up. His dealer Kahnweiler, now an abominated German alien, remained in Switzerland for the duration of the war, and did not return to Paris from his exile until 1920. Apollinaire applied for and was granted French citizenship, so that he could volunteer; both he and Braque were wounded at the front. The poet was allowed back to Paris in 1916 because of his wound; he died in the 1918 'flu epidemic. Meanwhile, Picasso's companion Eva died in 1915[229]. Picasso himself, an established artist, moved in theatre and ballet circles, and thus, from 1916, had an entrée into high society. He knew the aristocracy and did frescoes for the Chilean millionaire Eugenia Errazuriz. He spent bathing holidays at society resorts such as Biarritz and Antibes. He travelled widely throughout Europe. His bohemian days in Montmartre were at an end, for good. And in summer

Olga Picasso in the Studio
(photograph, about 1917)

Portrait of Olga in an Armchair
(after the above photograph)
Portrait d'Olga dans un fauteuil
Montrouge, late 1917
Oil on canvas, 130 x 88.8 cm
Zervos III, 83; MPP 55
Paris, Musée Picasso

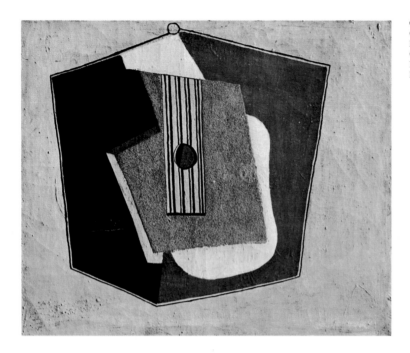

Guitar
Guitare
Paris, 1916
Oil on canvas, 54 x 65 cm
Not in Zervos
Private collection

Harlequin and Woman with Necklace
Arlequin et femme au collier
Rome, 1917
Oil on canvas, 200 x 200 cm
Zervos III, 23
Paris, Musée National d'Art Moderne,
Centre Georges Pompidou

Right:
Man Leaning on a Table
Homme accoudé sur une table
Paris, 1916
Oil on canvas, 200 x 132 cm
Zervos II**, 550; DR 889
New York, Private collection

The Camera and the Classicist 1916 – 1924 **246**

Woman in Spanish Costume (La Salchichona)
Femme en costume espagnol (La Salchichona)
Barcelona, 1917
Oil on canvas, 116 x 89 cm
Zervos III, 45; MPB 110.004
Barcelona, Museu Picasso

1918 he married. The previous year, working on a theatre project, he had met the Russian ballerina Olga Koklova.

Picasso followed her and the Ballets Russes to Rome, then to Madrid and Barcelona, and finally, in 1919, to London. These lengthy stays – eight weeks in Rome, three months in London – provided him with the chance to see more of Europe's heritage. He saw Naples and Pompeii; he saw the originals of the most important works of classical art; and in London he saw the Parthenon frieze, already familiar to him from plaster-cast copying exercises. He relished the masterpieces of the Renaissance in Rome, and took an interest in representations of Italian everyday life and lore which he bought in antique and junk shops.[230]

Changes in the art world accompanied those in his personal life, the current chauvinism influencing views of art too. Before the outbreak of war, in March 1914, Picasso's Rose Period masterpiece, "The Acrobats", had fetched a record price at a Paris auc-

The Peasants' Repast (after Le Nain)
Le retour du baptême (d'après Le Nain)
Paris, autumn 1917
Oil on canvas, 162 x 118 cm
Zervos III, 96; MPP 56
Paris, Musée Picasso

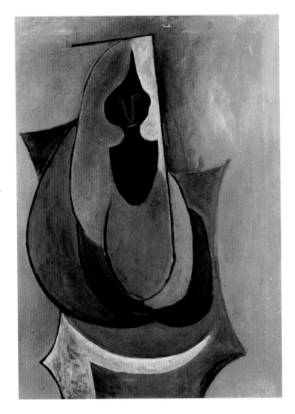

Study of a Cock
Etude d'un coq
Montrouge, 1917
Pencil on paper, 27.8 x 22.6 cm
Zervos III, 92

tion. The buyer was Munich's Thannhauser gallery, and the press spread the notion that the Germans were trying to use the absurd art of a few crazy foreigners to unsettle the art market.[231] Since then, sections of French public opinion had considered Cubism un-French, even an expression of things Teutonic and thus detested.

When the ballet "Parade" was first performed in Paris in 1917, with costumes and set design by Picasso, the audience called the performers "dirty boches".[232] During the war, political cartoons at times portrayed the German Kaiser and German militants as Cubists![233] This may well strike us as bizarre, since Kaiser Wilhelm II was hardly known for his avant-garde tastes, and none of the Cubist artists was German. But there was a tradition of detesting all things "boche", a tradition rooted in the Franco-Prussian War of 1870–71. It peaked in the First World War's victory over the German empire. It was connected with a French sense of classical tradition and an often crude rejection of the modern. France saw itself as the direct descendant of antiquity, the guardian of human values against the barbaric German enemy. Many factors and interests were interwoven with this image, among them campaigns for a restoration of the French monarchy. Not all of these factors were of real significance for the arts, but their effects were felt even among the cosmopolitan, internationalist Parisian avant-garde.[234]

A return to the classical tradition and a revival of classicism re-

sulted, not only in France: the return to the values of the ancient world was common in all the Mediterranean countries. French Cubists such as Braque and Léger, but also the Italian Futurist Gino Severini, and Giorgio de Chirico, the foremost artist of "pittura metafisica", returned to the repertoire of classical styles and subjects.[235] Barcelona had its classicism too, "Noucentisme", as Picasso found when he went to Spain in 1917: "The Barcelona Harlequin" (p. 256), in the Museu Picasso, suggests as much.[236] Interestingly, Apollinaire's 1917 defence of Cubism in the "Mercure de France" is also of a classical bent, stressing the "Latin" side of Cubist art.[237]

It is certain that these years of Modernism were by no means of a piece. Léger, for instance, was trying to combine the achievements of Cubism with classical forms, in order to place art at the service of political aims and take the side of the workers in the debates of the day. He was not alone in this. It was one of the main international currents in art in the 1920s: we need only recall George Grosz in Germany or Diego Rivera in Mexico, or even the utopias of radically abstract art.[238] And then there was a further, strong move towards rendering the formal features of avant-garde art purely decorative and thus combining it with a continuation of *art nouveau*. This particular line of evolution peaked in the great Paris arts and crafts exhibition of 1925, the abbreviated title of which gave this form its name – "Art deco".[239]

Seated Woman in an Armchair
Femme assise dans un fauteuil
Barcelona, 1917
Oil on canvas, 116 x 89.2 cm
Zervos III, 49; MPB 110.003
Barcelona, Museu Picasso

Bowl of Fruit
Compotier
Barcelona, 1917
Oil on canvas, 40 x 28.1 cm
Zervos III, 46; MPB 110.029
Barcelona, Museu Picasso

Figure with Bowl of Fruit
Personnage avec compotier
Barcelona, 1917
Oil on canvas, 100 x 70.2 cm
Zervos III, 48; MPB 110.006
Barcelona, Museu Picasso

View of the Columbus Memorial
Vue sur le monument de Colomb
Barcelona, 1917
Oil on canvas, 40.1 x 32 cm
Zervos III, 47; MPB 110.028
Barcelona, Museu Picasso

Remarkably enough, Picasso was very interested in the applied arts at that time, primarily in art design for the theatre. From 1916 to 1924 he was involved in no fewer than eight ballet or drama productions.[240] The first of these – designs for the curtain, set and costumes of the ballet "Parade" – was also the most important. In 1915 he had met the writer Jean Cocteau, who had an idea for a new ballet and had interested Sergei Diaghilev, the head of the Ballets Russes, in it. The avant-garde composer Erik Satie was engaged to write the music, and Picasso to design the ballet.

Though he had abandoned figural work in his Cubist phase, Picasso accepted the challenge. What decided him was Cocteau's concept, blending theatre, variety show and circus with technological features of modern city life. A travelling circus was to appear as a play within the play, accompanied by wailing sirens, clattering typewriters and public address voices. This idea derived from Futurist theatre but also from the tradition of circus images established since Toulouse-Lautrec, Seurat, and the Rose Period of Picasso.[241] He worked together with Cocteau, Satie and choreographer Léonide Massine, evolving an overall concept that adapted

"Parade": **Costume of the French Manager**
"Parade": Costume de manager français
Paris, 1917
Cardboard and cloth, painted,
approx. 200 x 100 x 80 cm
Spies 59; Zervos II**, 962
Original destroyed (photo dated 1917)

"Parade": **Costume of the American Manager**
"Parade": Costume de manager américain
Paris, 1917
Cardboard and cloth, painted,
approx. 200 x 100 x 80 cm
Spies 60; Zervos II**, 964
Original destroyed (photo dated 1917)

Cocteau's original idea somewhat. It was a chance for Picasso to marry Cubist style and figural representation in a novel way.

The curtain, an immense tableau, was such a marriage (cf. below and pp. 254–255). It shows a group of seven people in front of a theatre set; an eighth, a girl acrobat, is balancing on a white mare at left. The wings of the mythic Pegasus have been strapped onto the horse, who, licking her foal, seems unimpressed. The harlequin, torero, lovers, sailor and equilibrist are all familiar from Picasso's earlier work. They are presented two-dimensionally, with an emphasis on outline and in a manner plainly influenced by Picasso's collage work. Yet there is enough shadow and light in the scene to give an audience seated at some distance a distinctly evocative sense of spatial depth, combined with the Cubist effect of two-dimensionally flattened illusionist means of representation.

Plurality of styles remains a feature of Picasso's designs throughout. The costumes echo conventional clothing, as in the American girl's pleated skirt and sailor jacket. They use additive combinations of decorative items conceived in a two-dimensional spirit, but they also employ the means of Synthetic Cubism. This is particularly striking in the figures of the French and American managers (p. 252). Both figures are about three metres high, formed from various surfaces of painted papier maché, wood, cloth and even metal, slotted and notched into each other. The motifs – skyscrapers, Parisian boulevard trees – suggest the countries the managers come from, and underpin the Futurist principle of simultaneity. The managers are the formal idiom of Cubism in motion as they stomp their robotic way across the stage, personifying the mechanization and inhumanity of modern life.[242]

Self-portrait
Autoportrait
London, May to June 1919
Pencil and charcoal on paper, 64 x 49.5 cm
Zervos XXIX, 309; MPP 794
Paris, Musée Picasso

Design for the Curtain of "Parade"
Projet pour le rideau de "Parade"
Montrouge, 1917
Pencil on paper, 24.7 x 30 cm
Zervos II**, 949; MPP 1556
Paris, Musée Picasso

Pages 254/255:
Curtain for "Parade"
Le rideau de "Parade"
Paris, 1917
Tempera on cloth, 10.6 x 17.25 m
Zervos II**, 951
Paris, Musée National d'Art Moderne,
Centre Georges Pompidou

Harlequin with Violin ("Si tu veux")
Arlequin au violon ("Si tu veux")
Paris, 1918
Oil on canvas, 142 x 100.3 cm
Zervos III, 160
Cleveland (OH), The Cleveland Museum
of Art

Pierrot with a Mask
Pierrot
Paris, 1918
Oil on canvas, 92.7 x 73 cm
Zervos III, 137
New York, The Museum of Modern Art

Harlequin Playing a Guitar
Arlequin à la guitare
Paris, 1918
Oil on panel, 35 x 27 cm
Zervos III, 158
Geneva, Heinz Berggruen Collection

Harlequin Playing a Guitar
Arlequin jouant de la guitare
Paris, 1918
Oil on canvas, 97 x 76 cm
Zervos II**, 518; DR 762
Basel, Private collection

The Barcelona Harlequin
L'arlequin de Barcelone
Barcelona, 1917
Oil on canvas, 116 x 90 cm
Zervos III, 28; MPP 10.941
Barcelona, Museu Picasso

Pierrot with Mask
Pierrot au loup
Montrouge, 1918
Pencil on paper, 31 x 23 cm
Zervos III, 130

Three Dancers
Trois danseuses
London, 1919
Pencil on paper (three sheets glued together),
37 x 32.5 cm
Zervos XXIX, 432; MPP 840
Paris, Musée Picasso

Seven Dancers
(after a photograph; Olga in the foreground)
Sept danseuses
London, summer 1919
Ink on paper, 26.3 x 39.5 cm
Zervos III, 355
Estate of Jacqueline Picasso

Seven Dancers
(after a photograph; Olga in the foreground)
Sept danseuses
London, early 1919
Pencil on paper, 62.2 x 50 cm
Zervos III, 353; MPP 841
Paris, Musée Picasso

258 The Camera and the Classicist 1916 – 1924

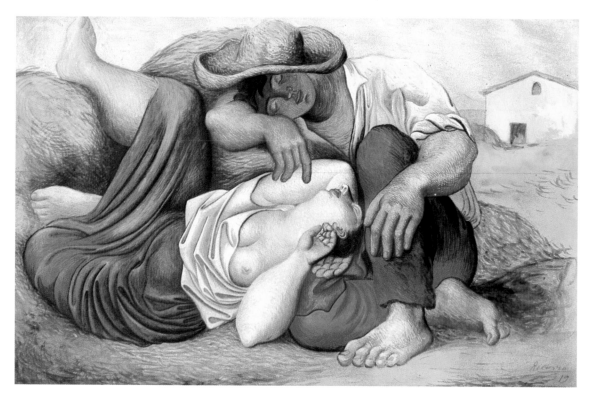

Sleeping Peasants
La sieste
Paris, 1919
Tempera, watercolour and pencil, 31.1 x 48.9 cm
Zervos III, 371
New York, The Museum of Modern Art,
Abby Aldrich Rockefeller Bequest

Study for "Sleeping Peasants"
Etude pour "La sieste"
Paris, 1919
Pencil on paper, 30 x 45.2 cm
Zervos III, 369

259 The Camera and the Classicist 1916 – 1924

Landscape with a Dead and a Living Tree
Paysage à l'arbre mort et vif
Paris, 1919
Oil on canvas, 49 x 64 cm
Zervos III, 364
Tokyo, Bridgestone Museum of Art

Picasso's designs for "Parade" were very complex. The classicist curtain can be read as a statement of the newly-awakened avant-garde interest in classical Latinate culture.[243] But the Cubist shapes, then widely detested, courted controversy. In the eyes of fellow artists, Picasso's "Parade" provided exemplary solutions to questions that were then interesting many artists throughout Europe, questions of how to create a new unity out of performance, choreography, music, set design and costumes. Robert and Sonia Delaunay, Marcel Duchamp, and Oskar Schlemmer did comparable work.[244]

This tenacious use of every possible stylistic option did not recur in Picasso's later stage designs. In 1919 he designed "Le Tricorne", a ballet set in 18th-century Spain. The curtain showed bullfight spectators, the stage set a stylized, two-dimensional landscape. The costumes (pp. 266–267) drew upon traditional Spanish costumes; though the combined frontal and upward angles of vision owe something to Cubism, the dominant note is superficial, decorative.[245] The same applies to "Pulcinella", a ballet with music by Stravinsky and choreography by Massine, produced in 1920. Picas-

so, in obedience to his commission, drew mainly on the Commedia dell'arte for his ideas. His stage set offered a view through the auditorium of a baroque theatre onto Naples by night.[246] In 1921 he used rejected "Pulcinella" designs for the ballet "Cuadro Flamenco".

During the work on "Pulcinella" disputes broke out between the artist and the theatre, and in 1922 they almost severed relations when Picasso came up with a near-abstract set design for "L'Après-midi d'une faune" . This replaced designs by Léon Bakst which had been lost; Diaghilev turned it down.[247] Not until 1924 did they work together again, when Picasso designed the curtain for another ballet, "Le Train bleu" (p. 292). This in a sense marked the nadir of Picasso's involvement with the theatre, in that the design was merely an enlargement of "Women Running on the Beach", a watercolour he had done in summer 1922[248]. The same year, however, he successfully married choreography and plot in his designs for a production of "Mercure". Like "Parade", this production again used the talents of Satie and Massine – though its success was doubtless due also to the ballet itself, which viewed antiquity

Still Life with a Guitar on a Table
in Front of an Open Window
La table devant la fenêtre
Saint-Raphaël, summer 1919
Gouache on paper, 31 x 22.2 cm
Zervos III, 401
Galerie Rosengart

Still Life in Front of a Window at Saint-Raphaël
Nature morte devant une fenêtre à Saint-Raphaël
Saint-Raphaël, summer 1919
Gouache and pencil on paper, 35.5 x 24.8 cm
Zervos III, 396
Geneva, Heinz Berggruen Collection

Pages 262 and 263:
The Bathers
Les baigneuses
Biarritz, summer 1918
Oil on canvas, 26.3 x 21.7 cm
Zervos III, 237; MPP 61
Paris, Musée Picasso

The Family of Napoleon III
(after a photograph)
La famille de Napoléon III
Paris, 1919. Pastel on paper, 62 x 48 cm
Not in Zervos. Private collection

Still Life with Pitcher and Apples
Nature morte au pichet et aux pommes
Paris, 1919
Oil on canvas, 65 x 43 cm
Not in Zervos; MPP 64
Paris, Musée Picasso

Basket of Fruit
Corbeille de fruits
Paris, 1918
Oil on plywood, 47.5 x 61.5 cm
Not in Zervos
Estate of Jacqueline Picasso

Still Life with Pitcher and Bread
Nature morte avec pichet et pain
Fontainebleau, 1921
Oil on canvas, 101 x 128 cm
Zervos IV, 285
Paris, Baron E. de Rothschild Collection

10

11

12

13

14

15

Costume Designs for the Ballet "Le Tricorne"
London, before 22 July 1919
Gouache, India ink and pencil on paper;
various formats
Paris, Musée Picasso

Ballet by Léonide Massine, after a novella
by Pedro de Alarcón. Music: Manuel de Falla.
Curtain, set and costumes: Pablo Picasso.
Performed by Sergei Diaghilev and his
"Ballets Russes".
Première: 22 July 1919,
Alhambra Theatre, London

1 "Le Tricorne": A Woman
Gouache and pencil on paper, 22.2 x 17.4 cm
Zervos XXIX, 401; MPP 1706

2 "Le Tricorne": A Woman
Pencil on paper, 25 x 16 cm
Zervos XXIX, 393; MPP 1700

3 "Le Tricorne": A Woman
Gouache, India ink and pencil, 22.5 x 17.5 cm
Zervos XXIX, 403; MPP 1705

4 "Le Tricorne": A Man
Gouache and pencil on paper, 22.5 x 17.5 cm
Zervos XXIX, 377; MPP 1695

5 "Le Tricorne": A Muleteer Carrying a
Sack of Flour
Gouache and pencil on paper, 26 x 19.7 cm
Zervos XXIX, 402; MPP 1688

6 "Le Tricorne": A Man from Aragon
Gouache and pencil on paper, 27 x 19.8 cm
Zervos III, 331; MPP 1685

7 "Le Tricorne": A Picador
Gouache and pencil on paper, 26.5 x 19.7 cm
Zervos III, 311; MPP 1691

8 "Le Tricorne": A Bailiff
Gouache, India ink and pencil on paper,
27 x 19.7 cm. Zervos III, 329; MPP 1682

9 "Le Tricorne": The Blue-Bearded Peasant
Gouache and pencil on paper, 27 x 19.5 cm
Zervos III, 332; MPP 1699

10 "Le Tricorne": An Old Man on Crutches
Gouache and pencil on paper, 26.5 x 19.7 cm
Zervos III, 335; MPP 1698

11 "Le Tricorne": A Lunatic
Gouache and pencil on paper, 26 x 19.8 cm
Zervos III, 317; MPP 1693

12 "Le Tricorne": The Miller
Gouache and pencil on paper, 26 x 19.5 cm
Zervos III, 320; MPP 1687

13 "Le Tricorne": The Partner of the Woman
from Seville
Gouache and pencil on paper, 27 x 20 cm
Zervos III, 313; MPP 1696

14 "Le Tricorne": The Mayor
Gouache, India ink and pencil on paper,
22,2 x 17.3 cm. Zervos XXIX, 380; MPP 1679

15 "Le Tricorne": The Chief Magistrate
Gouache and pencil on paper, 23.1 x 17.5 cm
Zervos XXIX, 379; MPP 1677

268 The Camera and the Classicist 1916 – 1924

Landscape near Juan-les-Pins
Paysage de Juan-les-Pins
Juan-les-Pins, summer 1920
Oil on canvas, 48 x 68 cm
Zervos IV, 107; MPP 68
Paris, Musée Picasso

Studies
Etudes
Paris, 1920
Oil on canvas, 100 x 81 cm
Zervos IV, 226; MPP 65
Paris, Musée Picasso

Left:
Portrait of Léonide Massine
Portrait de Léonide Massine
London, May to June 1919
Pencil on paper, 38 x 29 cm
Zervos III, 297
Chicago (IL), The Art Institute of Chicago

Portrait of Sergei Diaghilev and Alfred Seligsberg
(after a photograph)
Portrait de Serge Diaghilev et d'Alfred Seligsberg
London, early 1919
Charcoal and pencil on paper, 63.5 x 49.6 cm
Zervos III, 301; MPP 839
Paris, Musée Picasso

Portrait of Pierre-Auguste Renoir
(after a photograph)
Portrait de Pierre-Auguste Renoir
Paris, winter 1919
Pencil and charcoal on paper, 61 x 49.3 cm
Zervos III, 413; MPP 913
Paris, Musée Picasso

Portrait of Igor Stravinsky
(after a photograph)
Portrait d'Igor Stravinsky
Paris, 24 May 1920
Pencil on paper, 61.5 x 48.5 cm
Zervos IV, 60; MPP 911
Paris, Musée Picasso

269 The Camera and the Classicist 1916–1924

through the caricaturist style of Dadaist farce and afforded ample leeway for formal experimentation.

Picasso's curtain showed a harlequin playing a guitar and a pierrot with a violin. The lines and colour areas were sharply at variance; the colour zones did not coincide with the outlines of the figures. For the stage action, Picasso devised similar constructions which were called "practicables". They consisted of various panels cut to size, with figures of a geometrical/constructivist or simply playfully representational nature attached to them with wire. These "practicables" were moved by actors who remained unseen, so that three-dimensional poses could be struck outside the parameters of conventional choreography.[249]

Picasso had already created the visual form of these line-and-surface figures in 1918 or 1919. His work on "Mercure" was as closely related to independent painting and drawing as his designs for "Parade". Evidently Picasso's theatre designs were aimed at establishing new directions in the art. But the limits that were set by functional necessity and prescription were more than he would gladly put up with. Only twice were his ideas even remotely successfully adopted in practice, and in the early 1920s his interest in theatrical collaboration faded. His contribution to Cocteau's 1922 adaptation of "Antigone" consisted solely of a pared-back set design: three sketchy Doric columns on white wooden panelling. This was in line with Cocteau's call for classical simplicity, and indeed with the prevailing ideas of the time; but "Parade" and "Mercure" show just how much greater was the range covered by Picasso's own ideas.

It would be wrong to see his interest in the applied arts and the influence of a classicizing mood in the arts in France as the main cause of Picasso's own classicism. His concern for original classical artworks was in fact a return to models that had always been sig-

Sisley and His Wife
(after a painting by Renoir)
Le ménage Sisley
Paris, late 1919
Pencil on paper, 31 x 21.8 cm
Zervos III, 429
Geneva, Heinz Berggruen Collection

Sisley and His Wife
(after a painting by Renoir)
Le ménage Sisley
Paris, late 1919
Pencil on paper, 31 x 23.8 cm
Zervos III, 428; MPP 868
Paris, Musée Picasso

Italian Peasants
(after a photograph)
Paysans italiens
Paris, 1919
Pencil and charcoal on paper, 59 x 46.5 cm
Zervos III, 431
Santa Barbara (CA),
The Santa Barbara Museum of Art

The Lovers
Les amoureux
Paris, 1919
Oil on canvas, 185 x 140.5 cm
Zervos III, 438; MPP 62
Paris, Musée Picasso

The Schoolgirl
L'écolière
Paris, 1919
Oil on canvas, 93 x 75 cm
Not in Zervos
Douglas Cooper Collection

Girl with a Hoop
Fillette au cerceau
Paris, 1919
Oil and sand on canvas, 142 x 79 cm
Zervos III, 289
Paris, Musée National d'Art Moderne,
Centre Georges Pompidou

nificant for him. And during his Cubist years, for instance, he had repeatedly painted variations on works by Ingres, the great classicist.[250] There were many sides to Picasso's classicism.

The inadequacy of any one-sided view can be readily seen if we grasp the irreconcilability of his own works with the European classical ideal in art. Historically, classicism pledged explicit allegiance to the aesthetics of ancient Greece, implying a style of representation best described as idealized naturalism, a style that fundamentally took its bearings in mimetic fashion but aimed to beautify the image through symmetry and balanced proportions. The human form was always at the heart of classical art.[251] This remark applies to Picasso's work from 1916 to 1924 as well, of course. The human image is central to his work, the tendency to monumentalize it unmistakable. But symmetry and balanced proportions, those determining features of an idealizing treatment of natural form, are conspicuous not merely by their absence but by Picasso's constant refutation of them. He paints scenes; he paints heavy, three-dimensionally modelled nudes; but in contrast to classical tradition his treatment ignores principles of balance and

Pulcinella with a Guitar
Pulcinella à la guitare
Paris, 1920
Gouache and India ink on paper, 15.4 x 10.5 cm
Zervos IV, 66
France, Private collection

goes for monstrous and disproportioned physical mass. Classicist painters such as Ingres violated the natural physical proportions of the human body, it is true, but they were aiming at overall compositional harmony. That was quite manifestly not Picasso's goal.[252]

On the other hand, the dichotomies within his work are less gaping than might appear on a cursory first inspection. Back in 1914, his late Synthetic Cubism pictures were conventionally composed, plainly focussed on the centre. In pictures such as "Man with a Pipe (The Smoker)" (p. 237), a mixed-media work using oil and pasted paper, Picasso produced a figural image despite the use of various materials and an abstractive style. While the 1915 "Harlequin" (p. 235) transferred the appearance of collage and *papier collé* to work in oil, Picasso also reverted in that painting to the formal norms and techniques of representational art. The harlequin of the title is the main (if transfigured) subject, and thus central to the composition. The other zones of colour define the figure in a perfectly traditional manner, against a clear background.

Guitar, Bottle, Fruit Dish and Glass on a Table
Guitare, bouteille, compotier et verre sur une table
Paris, 1919
Oil on canvas, 100 x 81 cm
Zervos III, 165
Geneva, Heinz Berggruen Collection

273 The Camera and the Classicist 1916 – 1924

Mother and Child
Mère et enfant
Fontainebleau (?), 1921
Oil on canvas, 97 x 71 cm
Zervos IV, 289
Private collection

Mother and Child
Mère et enfant
Fontainebleau, 1921
Oil on canvas, 102.1 x 83.5 cm
Not in Zervos
Private collection

Picasso was exchanging the two poles of formal visual definition, the mimetic and the Cubist. This exchange was a return to first principles. A return seems logical since Cubism could go no further. To attempt to go on would have meant adopting total abstraction – a step that other artists did take at the time.

A new visual medium prompted Picasso's return: photography. Hitherto, this is a consideration that has been too little taken into account by Picasso's critics. Yet Picasso was an enthusiastic photographer as far back as Cubist days. He took a great many photographs of his studio, friends and fellow artists.[253] Though photography initially served merely to establish a documentary record, as pictures of paintings in different stages of completion suggest, Picasso will inevitably have noticed the distinctive features of the photographic image. The "Portrait of Olga in an Armchair" (p. 244) painted in 1917, the 1923 "Paul, the Artist's Son, on a Donkey" (p. 286), his studies of dancers (Olga among them: cf. p. 258) and of Diaghilev and Alfred Seligsberg or Renoir (p. 268), were all painted or drawn from photographs. Nor must we forget his many copies and variations of works of art seen in photographic reproduction, such as "Italian Peasants" or "Sisley and His Wife" (p. 270).[254] Line studies predominate among these works, reduced to essentials and almost completely disregarding shades of colours or indications of volume.

Woman and Child on the Seashore
Femme et enfant au bord de la mer
1921
Oil on canvas, 143 x 162 cm
Zervos IV, 311
Chicago (IL), The Art Institute of Chicago

Family on the Seashore
Famille au bord de la mer
Dinard, summer 1922
Oil on panel, 17.6 x 20.2 cm
Not in Zervos; MPP 80
Paris, Musée Picasso

275   The Camera and the Classicist   1916 – 1924

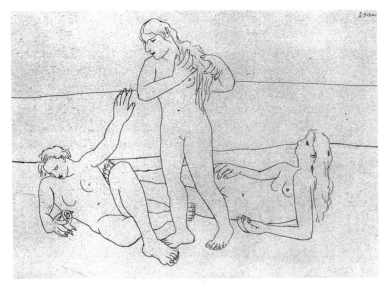

Three Bathers
Trois baigneuses
Juan-les-Pins, 3 September 1920
India ink on paper, 75 x 105 cm
Zervos IV, 182

Reclining Bather
Baigneuse allongée
Juan-les-Pins, 23 June 1920
Pencil on paper, 26.5 x 42 cm
Zervos IV, 162

Three Bathers
Trois baigneuses
Juan-les-Pins, summer 1920
Pencil on paper, 48 x 63 cm
Zervos IV, 105

Right:
Seated Nude Drying Her Foot
Femme nue assise s'essuyant le pied
1921
Pastel on paper, 66 x 50.8 cm
Zervos IV, 330
Geneva, Heinz Berggruen Collection

The Camera and the Classicist 1916 – 1924 **276**

Three Women at the Spring
Trois femmes à la fontaine (La source)
Fontainebleau, summer 1921
Oil on canvas, 203.9 x 174 cm
Zervos IV, 322
New York, The Museum of Modern Art

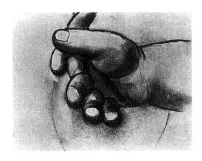

Study for "Three Women at the Spring"
Etude de main pour "Trois femmes à la fontaine"
Fontainebleau, summer 1921
Charcoal and red chalk on paper, 24.5 x 32.1 cm
Zervos IV, 326; MPP 967. Paris, Musée Picasso

Study for "Three Women at the Spring"
Etude pour "Trois femmes à la fontaine"
Fontainebleau, summer 1921
Pencil on panel, 21.5 x 27 cm
Not in Zervos; MPP 965
Paris, Musée Picasso

279 The Camera and the Classicist 1916 – 1924

Country Dance (Dancing Couple)
La danse villageoise
Paris, 1921 (1922?)
Fixed pastel and oil on canvas,
139.5 x 85.5 cm
Zervos XXX, 270; MPP 73
Paris, Musée Picasso

The Reading of the Letter
La lecture de la lettre
Paris, 1921
Oil on canvas, 184 x 105 cm
Not in Zervos; MPP 72
Paris, Musée Picasso

Three Musicians
Musiciens aux masques
Fontainebleau, summer 1921
Oil on canvas, 200.7 x 222.9 cm
Zervos IV, 331
New York, The Museum of Modern Art,
Mrs. Simon Guggenheim Fund

Three Musicians
Musiciens aux masques
Fontainebleau, summer 1921
Oil on canvas, 203 x 188 cm
Zervos IV, 332
Philadelphia (PA), Philadelphia Museum of Art

Still Life with Guitar
Nature morte à la guitare
Paris, 1922
Oil on canas, 83 x 102.5 cm
Zervos IV, 418
Galerie Rosengart

Packet of Tobacco and Glass
Paquet de tabac et verre
Paris, 1922
Oil on canvas, 33 x 41 cm
Zervos IV, 426
Switzerland, Private collection

The Bird Cage
La cage d'oiseaux
Paris, 1923
Oil and charcoal on canvas, 200.7 x 140.4 cm
Zervos V, 84
New York, Mrs. Victor W. Ganz Collection

Paul, the Artist's Son, on a Donkey
(after the photograph: see right)
Paul, fils de l'artiste, à deux ans
Paris, 14 April 1923
Oil on canvas, 100 x 81 cm. Zervos VI, 1429
Paris, Bernard Ruiz-Picasso Collection

Paul, the Artist's Son, on a Donkey
Photograph, 1923

Paul, the Artist's Son, in a Round Hat
Paul, fils de l'artiste
Paris, 14 April 1923
Oil on canvas, 27 x 22 cm
Zervos V, 180. France, Private collection

Linear austerity, a predilection for a purely linear style, was a feature of late 18th-century classicist art. People therefore assumed a link between that period and Picasso. But the similarity is only superficial. Rather, Picasso was trying to apply the stylistic resources of photography to painting and drawing. Black and white photography translates natural colours into a tonal scale from white through grey to black, and renders subjects in varying degrees of clarity or unclarity according to the depth of field. An impression of documentary precision is conveyed; in reality, the recorded scene is defamiliarized. Photography either radically polarizes available contrasts or blurs them if the focus or light are not right. The distance from the photographed subject can reinforce or distort the sense of perspective. At all events, the picture that results has a character all its own. It may be more precise than hand-drawn likenesses, but it is not faithful. And it was these peculiar features of photography that attracted Picasso to the medium.

The nature of his concerns can readily be deduced from the study after a photo of ballet impresarios Diaghilev and Seligsberg (p. 268), drawn in outline, with only occasional charcoal accentuation to suggest volume. Picasso has accentuated the very features a photograph highlights: eyes, nose, mouth, folds in clothing. The seated man seems rather too bulky below the waist compared with his build above it, an impression caused by the slightly distorted perspective of the angle from which the original picture was taken.

Picasso approached the unfinished portrait of his wife Olga (p. 244) in similar fashion. The figure is cropped at the knee and placed vertically in the right-hand two-thirds of the composition. In her left hand, resting lightly on her crossed left leg, she is holding

Paul Drawing
Paul dessinant
Paris, 1923
Oil on canvas, 130 x 97.5 cm
Zervos V, 177; MPP 81
Paris, Musée Picasso

Mother and Child
Mère et enfant
Dinard, summer 1922
Oil on canvas, 100 x 81 cm. Zervos IV, 371
Baltimore (MD), The Baltimore Museum of Art,
Cone Collection

Seated Woman in an Armchair
Femme assise dans un fauteuil
Paris, winter 1922
Oil on canvas, 81 x 65 cm
Zervos IV, 450
Los Angeles (CA), Private collection

Mother and Child. Mère et enfant
Dinard, summer 1922
Pencil on paper, 41 x 29 cm. Zervos IV, 369

a half-open fan. Her right arm, crooked at the elbow, is out-stretched across the back of the armchair. Her wide-open eyes are gazing dreamily into nowhere, or within her own inner depths. The lustreless dark brown dress contrasts with her light flesh, the colour of which is also the colour of the canvas ground. The armchair is covered in a striking fabric of red and yellow flowers, purple grapes and green leaves – a floral pattern which makes the loudest visual impact but is somewhat muted by the patterning of the dress and fan. These agitated areas of the picture do not distract from the true subject, the portrait, but in fact lend emphasis to it. This highlighting is further assisted by Picasso's indifference to the textural, material qualities of the fabrics: Olga's face, by contrast, is painted with great sensitivity. And that was what Picasso was out to do in this painting. The canvas, however, was not yet filled.

Picasso clearly intended to finish the picture. But doing so posed a problem: he would have had to complete the composition – and the photo afforded him no help in his quest for the right counter-balance in what remained to be painted. Everything in the photo was of roughly equal clarity, and thus of roughly equal status. A photograph is like a sampler of forms, all of equal value; it is only

Bust of a Woman
Buste de femme
Paris, 1923
Oil on canvas, 65 x 54 cm
Not in Zervos
Chicago (IL), Private collection

Head of a Woman
Tête de femme
Paris, 1923
Oil and sand on canvas, 46 x 38 cm
Zervos V, 45
Tokyo, Bridgestone Museum of Art

the response in the beholder's eye that introduces differentiation. A painting, however, unlike a photo, is built on a hierarchical sense of forms – otherwise it cannot easily be grasped. The camera is impartial towards its subjects and therefore able to open up surprising perspectives or even, in extreme cases, convey almost Cubist visual experiences using purely representational means. So Picasso abandoned work on the painting at this point. It is all the more attractive for being unfinished; the neutral canvas counteracts the tension between the woman's figure and the colourful, rather loud pattern of the armchair. Had he continued painting, Picasso would probably have become entangled in a formal jungle.

Picasso viewed the photograph as a thoroughly artificial original, the formal principle of which resided in a curiously dialectical relationship of polarities to levelled-out uniformities. Every recognisable detail was distinct from every other; yet the sheer number of details defied the eye. Polarity and uniformity were inseparable. Thus, the formal constituents of the image – line, surface, depth modelling – were themselves distinct. And what was true of photographs in general was also true of reproductions of artworks, images constituting a twofold defamiliarization, as it were. When

Acrobat
Saltimbanque
Paris, 1922
Gouache on paper, 16 x 11 cm
Not in Zervos. Private collection

Seated Woman in a Chemise
Femme assise dans une chemise
1923
Oil on canvas, 92.1 x 73 cm
Zervos V, 3
London, Tate Gallery

Seated Woman
Femme assise
Paris, 1 January 1923
Gouache on cardboard, 20.9 x 17.4 cm
Zervos VI, 1401
Oberlin (OH), Allen Memorial Art Museum

Picasso, working with photography, returned to the mimetic image, it was by no means a step back. His work from 1916 to 1924 was every bit as avant-garde as his Cubist work. He was altogether progressive in his approach. He was simply trying something different. At that time, a great deal of thought was going into the nature and potential of photography, and it had achieved recognition as an art from which other visual artists could in fact learn.

Painters and draughtsmen have always sought ways to make the purely technical problems of visual mimesis easier to solve. First aids such as the camera obscura were important forerunners of photography. When photography was invented in the late 1830s, artists such as Delacroix immediately used the new medium for their work. But it was merely an auxiliary aid.[255] Its value lay in its unique documentary reliability. Even to Baudelaire, progressive though his aesthetic thinking was, photography was not an art.[256] Ambitious photographers therefore set out to rival painting on its own territory, with the result that artistic photography till the beginning of the 20th century looked like a caricature of fine art.[257]

Of course, open-minded artists had long been availing themselves of photography's particular representational strengths. Degas borrowed the photographic sense of a cropped section of seen reality to create completely innovative compositions. The photographic movement studies by Eadweard Muybridge and Etienne Jules Marey in the last decades of the 19th century were an important

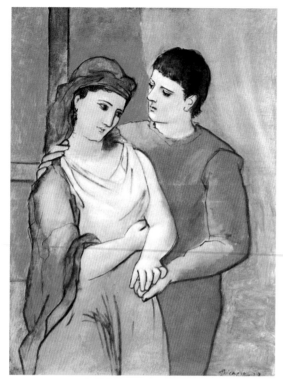

source of Futurism, and ultimately of abstract art too.[258] But not till the early 20th century did photographers strive for international recognition of their art on the basis of its distinctive features. Picasso was involved in these strivings almost from the outset. The American photographer Alfred Stieglitz was a major mover in the endeavour, founding the Photo Secession in New York in 1902, editing the journal "Camera Work" from 1903 on, and running the Little Galleries of the Photo Secession from 1905[259]. In 1907, the year Picasso painted "Les Demoiselles", Stieglitz took the photo he considered his best, "The Steerage", and was very pleased to find Picasso thought highly of it too. In 1911 Stieglitz organized the first American exhibition of Picasso's work at his gallery.[260]

In the USA, photography was soon an art form in its own right. The line of pure photography is linked with Edward Steichen, Walker Evans and Edward Weston. But painters such as Charles Sheeler also tried to use photographic forms in their art.[261] The nearest European equivalent was Germany's "Neue Sachlichkeit" (New Objectivity). From 1920 on, Dadaists, Surrealists, Soviet Constructivists and artists at the Bauhaus were all trying to bring new ideas to visual art with the help of experimental photography.[262]

And Picasso was trying to do the same. All of his figure drawings after 1916 were constructed according to the basic principles of photography – and for that reason they lack something we usually

The Lovers
Les amoureux
Paris, 1923
Oil on canvas, 130.2 x 97.2 cm
Zervos V, 14
Washington (DC), National Gallery of Art,
Chester Dale Collection

Woman with Blue Veil
La femme au voile bleu
Paris, 1923
Oil on canvas, 100.3 x 81.3 cm
Zervos V, 16
Los Angeles (CA), Los Angeles County Museum
of Art

Women Running on the Beach
(Curtain for the ballet "Le train bleu", 1924)
Deux femmes courant sur la plage (La course)
Dinard, summer 1922
Gouache on plywood, 32.5 x 42.1 cm
Zervos IV, 380; MPP 78
Paris, Musée Picasso

find in an art drawing: variability of line. Lines can be thick or thin, deep black or pale grey, and the gradations chosen can make the visual rhythm of a picture by emphasizing certain portions and not others. Not so in Picasso. From his portraits of composers Satie and Stravinsky (p. 268) to his copy of Renoir's portrait of "Sisley and His Wife" (p. 270), the lines are almost mechanically even. It is an astonishing effect, at once cold and utterly stylish.

Picasso was not only adopting the photographic contour. His paintings and drawings also borrowed the characteristic overemphasis of light-dark contrasts in defining volume, the juxtaposition of the linear and the spatial, even the distortions of perspective. He still used the visual artist's conventional methods, thus often mixing forms. In the Stravinsky portrait, for example, the composer's limbs are outsize, combining photographic distortion with the cartoonist's technique. In such works as "The Reading of the Letter" (p. 281) or the great nudes of 1921–22 (cf. p. 277), photographic harshness in the contrast of light and shadow is combined with a sculpturally modelled three-dimensionality, adding a slight distor-

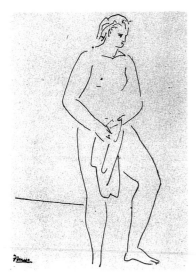

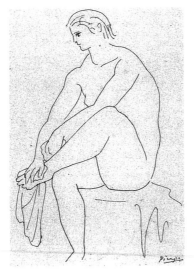

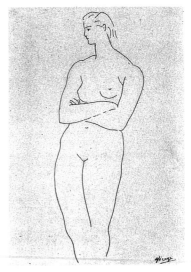

Standing Nude
Femme nue debout tenant une serviette
Cap d'Antibes, 1923
Pencil on paper, 35 x 26 cm
Zervos V, 50

Seated Bather Drying Her Feet
Baigneuse assise s'essuyant les pieds
Cap d'Antibes, 1923
India ink on paper, 35 x 26 cm
Zervos V, 55

Standing Nude with Crossed Arms
Femme nue debout les bras croisés
Cap d'Antibes, 1923
Pencil on paper, 35 x 26 cm
Zervos V, 51. Private collection

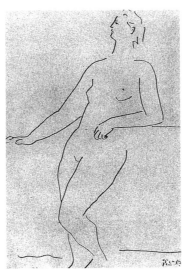

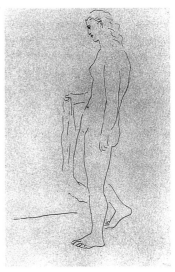

Seated Nude
Femme assise le bras gauche appuyé sur un rocher
Cap d'Antibes, 1923
Ink on paper, 35 x 26 cm. Zervos V, 56

Standing Nude Resting on One Arm
Femme nue debout appuyée
Cap d'Antibes, 1923
Ink on paper, 36 x 25 cm. Zervos V, 59

Standing Nude
Femme nue tenant une serviette
Cap d'Antibes, 1923
Ink on paper, 108 x 72 cm
Zervos V, 58

tion of perspective. These massive figures with dark eye sockets and seemingly machine-made bodies are the result.

Other pictures present linear figures seen against neutral, non-representational areas of colour. In these, Picasso blended the techniques of Synthetic Cubism with the kind of mimesis he was borrowing from photography. The combinations produced new formal modes such as we see in "The Lovers" (1923; p. 291). Paintings such as this represent an intermediate position which the artist tested for its functional values by using it in his theatre designs – for instance, in his work for the 1924 ballet "Mercure". But Picasso was a man to test his results over and over again. This he did by copying from photographs once more. In 1923 he painted "Paul, the Artist's Son, on a Donkey" (p. 286). The accentuation of different textures in the photo prompted a delightful composition. Picasso runs the gamut of visual methods, opposing lines to surface areas, smooth surfaces to textured ones, spatial depth to depthless zones. The shaggy fell of the donkey is a continuous fabric of dark

Greek Woman
La Grecque
Paris, 1924
Oil on canvas, 185 x 75 cm
Zervos V, 249
Private collection

Harlequin with a Mirror
Arlequin avec un miroir
1923
Oil on canvas, 100 x 81 cm
Zervos V, 142
Lugano-Castagnola, Thyssen-Bornemisza
Foundation

and light greys with white and black brush-strokes too. The boy's clothes are an irregular linear outline that defines a patch of colour and is economically detailed with a few more lines for folds.

In 1919 Picasso had already used a 1916 Ballets Russes publicity photo in order to combine dancers' poses and various techniques of creating three-dimensionality (pp. 258 and 692). In the first of these works he rendered the photo's shadow areas as hatching of the kind commonly used in engravings and etchings. In others he changed the photo's horizontal format into a vertical, tightened up the composition, even cut the number of figures and changed their poses. A dreamy gaze, fingers to chin, or upraised arms to keep a balance – to Picasso the attitudes were interchangeable.

In 1923 Picasso returned to the use of emphatic linear outline together with hatching for his portraits of the painter Jacinto Salvado in a harlequin costume Cocteau had handed on (pp. 296 and 297). In the unfinished version we can see how Picasso was aiming to unite the linear elements and the colouring of areas in a new synthesis. It was an experimental phase in his work, as the range of subjects indicates. He was using almost exclusively motifs drawn from his stock repertoire: harlequins, mothers with children, nudes, still lifes, studies of bullfights, portraits. New motifs were the beach scenes and bathers. These gave Picasso the chance to test his nudes in contexts of action.

Portrait of Olga (Olga in Pensive Mood)
Portrait d'Olga (Olga pensive)
Paris, 1923
Pastel and pencil on paper, 104 x 71 cm
Zervos V, 38; MPP 993
Paris, Musée Picasso

Portrait of Olga
Portrait d'Olga
Paris, 1923
Pastel and pencil on paper, 100 x 81 cm
Zervos V, 29
Washington (DC), National Gallery of Art,
Chester Dale Collection

He was also looking back to art history. Since his youth Picasso had copied from other originals. This predilection now peaked in multi-layered visual quotations and variations, copies, and borrowings. In 1917 he painted "The Peasants' Repast" (p. 249), conspicuously using a stylistic device he had been highly interested in during his earliest real period of artistic identity: the multitudinous dots and dabs of pointillism. But "The Peasants' Repast" is a product of combination, of synthesis, the composition not the artist's own but taken from a painting by the French artist Louis Le Nain, done in 1642 and now in the Louvre. As in the variations on the Ballets Russes publicity photos, Picasso altered his original, transforming the wide format into a concentrated vertical and adapting the proportional relations of the figures as he chose.

Right:
Seated Harlequin (The Painter Jacinto Salvado)
Arlequin assis (Le peintre Jacinto Salvado)
Paris, 1923
Oil on canvas, 130 x 97 cm. Zervos V, 17
Paris, Musée National d'Art Moderne,
Centre Georges Pompidou

Similarly in "Three Women at the Spring" (p. 279) he has adopted the technique suggested by photographic three-dimensionality, as the preliminary studies plainly show. On the other hand, though, his composition of figures clad in the garb of ancient statues is a variation on a portion of a work by the French baroque artist Nicolas Poussin.[263] Picasso's arresting motion study, "Women Running on the Beach" (p. 292), uses motif details from Raphael's Vatican frescoes and from an ancient Medean sarcophagus in the National Museum in Rome, both works Picasso saw in 1917[264]. In "Three Dutch Girls" (p. 133), painted in 1906, Picasso had already done a variation on the ancient sculptural group of the Three Graces, and he now did a number of etchings based on the same famous original.[265] He stepped up his work in printed graphics because the medium suited his new linear style. As well as doing illustrations for books by his friend Max Jacob – "Le Cornet à Dés" in 1917 and "Le Phanérogame" the following year – which

Seated Harlequin (The Painter Jacinto Salvado)
Arlequin assis (Le peintre Jacinto Salvado)
Paris, 1923. Oil on canvas, 125 x 97 cm
Zervos V, 37. Stavros S. Niarchos Collection

Seated Harlequin (The Painter Jacinto Salvado?)
Arlequin assis (Le peintre Jacinto Salvado?)
Paris, 1923. Oil on canvas, 130 x 97 cm
Zervos V, 135. Private collection

Seated Harlequin (The Painter Jacinto Salvado)
Arlequin assis (Le peintre Jacinto Salvado)
Paris, 1923. Tempera on canvas, 130.5 x 97 cm
Zervos V, 23
Basel, Öffentliche Kunstsammlung Basel,
Kunstmuseum

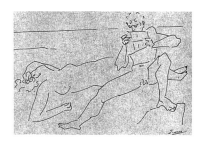

Female Nude and Pan-pipes Player
(Study for "The Pipes of Pan")
Etude pour "La flûte de Pan"
Antibes, summer 1923
India ink on paper, 23 x 31 cm. Zervos V, 109
USA, Private collection

Pan-pipes Player and Erotic Figures
(Study for "The Pipes of Pan")
Etude pour "La flûte de Pan"
Antibes, summer 1923
India ink on paper, 24.5 x 32 cm. Zervos V, 130

continued what he had begun in 1913 with three etchings for Jacob's "Le Siège de Jérusalem", he mainly did variations of motifs he had drawn or painted, such as "Three Women at the Spring".

The range of different techniques Picasso was using all shared a concern with identity of craftsmanship and form. As well as painting in oil on canvas, he painted on wooden panels as in centuries gone by. He even transferred pastel to canvas and combined it with oils: the "Country Dance (Dancing Couple)" (p. 280) and "The Reading of the Letter" (p. 281) are fine examples. The textural effect of pastel chalk on a rough canvas ground curiously reinforces tonal contrasts. As in earlier periods, the experiments were all subsumed into one major work recapitulating his experience throughout this period: "The Pipes of Pan" (1923; right).[266]

Over fifty studies in sketchbooks and on single sheets have survived, but the number of preliminary studies for the painting must have been far greater, for Picasso also used his 1920–1921 pencil and pastel drawings of bathers on the beach for his new purpose (cf. pp. 276 and 277). The variously posed women, most of them naked, were clearly originally meant to be part of an ambitious composition using a merely hinted-at landscape setting. But the artist broke off his work without managing to bring his ideas together satisfactorily. However, he had settled on the idea of tightly ordered groups of standing and seated figures. He returned to this idea in 1923, linking it to bacchanalian motifs from antiquity. The figure of a faun playing the Pan-pipes, in particular, was based on ancient sculpture.[267] Little by little his physical posture evolved – a kind of compromise between sitting, running and squatting (cf. right). The youth is half-kneeling on his left leg while his right is bent at the knee too. With both hands he is holding the pipes to his lips. At an intermediate stage in his work on this composition, Picasso added a woman to the scene, and a boyish Eros (cf. above), doubtless with a historical picture of amorous content in mind. But then he tautened the compositional concept, dropped the erotic content, and again accentuated the motif of bathing, admittedly not entirely jettisoning the erotic suggestiveness.

The result was the final big painting completed in summer 1923. The Pan-pipes player is posed as in the preliminary studies. Beside

The Pipes of Pan
La flûte de Pan
Antibes, summer 1923
Oil on canvas, 205 x 174.5 cm
Zervos V, 141; MPP 79
Paris, Musée Picasso

Still Life with Mandolin
Nature morte à la mandoline
Juan-les-Pins (?), 1924
Oil on canvas, 97.5 x 130 cm
Zervos V, 224
Amsterdam, Stedelijk Museum

him, in a frontal pose turned slightly to the right, also in bathing trunks, stands another youth. His right leg is casually bent at the knee. Between them we see the vast blues of sea and sky. The different shades emphasize the spatial depth. Rough brown, beige and sandy areas provide a backdrop to the youths, foregrounding them through the contrast, accentuating the spatiality, and rounding out the centripetal composition. The two figures illustrate Picasso's methods of three-dimensional modelling: darker and lighter shades, variously contrasting, to indicate a range of volume qualities from flat to round, together with the natural proportions of the bodies, heighten the picture's evocativeness.

Mandolin and Guitar
Mandoline et guitare
Juan-les-Pins, summer 1924
Oil and sand on canvas, 140.6 x 200.2 cm
Zervos V, 220
New York, The Solomon R. Guggenheim Museum

Book, Bowl of Fruit and Mandolin
Livre, compotier et mandoline
1924
Oil on canvas, 100 x 80.4 cm
Zervos V, 379
Munich, Staatsgalerie moderner Kunst

If Picasso seems to have eased off the violation of natural proportion seen in other nudes from this time, this is due to a more subtle approach to the problem. Like classically-minded 19th-century artists such as Ingres or Anselm Feuerbach, he combines an arbitrary elongation of bodily proportion with questions of posture and bearing, so that his figures balance each other out and establish a strong sense of harmony. The noticeable departures from ideals of beauty underline this; for in reality the violations are considerable – the pipes player, if he were to stand upright, would be taller than the other youth and would occupy the entire height of the canvas.

Like Picasso's entire output from 1916 to 1924, this picture was a variation on others, uniting in one place subject-matter with shades of antiquity, classical models, a classicist mode of composition, and a style derived from photography and blended with Synthetic Cubism.

301 The Camera and the Classicist 1916 – 1924

Paul as Pierrot (The Artist's Son)
Paul en Pierrot (Le fils d'artiste)
Paris, 28 February 1925
Oil on canvas, 130 x 97 cm
Zervos V, 374; MPP 84
Paris, Musée Picasso

Paul as Harlequin
Paul en arlequin
Paris, 1924
Oil on canvas, 130 x 97.5 cm
Zervos V, 178; MPP 83
Paris, Musée Picasso

10 A Juggler with Form
1925–1936

In 1928, in the Paris studio of the Spanish sculptor Julio Gonzáles, Picasso made four constructions using iron wire and sheet metal, three of which have survived (pp. 324 and 325). Gonzáles had been familiarizing his countryman with soldering technique since that March, so that by October Picasso was able to play with some ideas he had for a sculpture. These pieces are models towards a large-scale work he was planning. They are thus fairly small, from 38 to 60 centimetres high, and economical in their use of iron wire of various thicknesses. The straight wires were arranged in long parallels or at acute or obtuse or right angles, and wires bent into arcs or ellipses were added, the whole soldered complex creating an intricate visual image. The impact draws as much upon the combination of linear and spatial elements as on the interplay of straight and curved forms and the varying thickness of the wire.[268]

At first glance these constructions look complicated and confusing. But on closer inspection we see two fundamental features. On the one hand, they present a juxtaposition of geometrical shapes, rectangles, triangles and ellipses grouped spatially into irregular stereometric configurations – extended pyramids, squashed cubes. These figures overlap and interpenetrate each other, so that we see new ones depending on where we stand. On the other hand, at points there are details – small spheres, discs, irregular tricorn ends – recalling, however remotely, the human figure. This encourages us to read the works entirely differently: what looked totally abstract at first now seems to be a stylized representational figure.

The works are like picture puzzles. Picasso's remarkable and noteworthy handling of the fundamentals of sculpture is striking. The use of wire translates form into an issue of linear definition. This is a principle of the draughtsman, not the sculptor. The work created in this way is on a sheet of metal, like a plinth, yet the shapes are in the open, challenging our sense of the tactile impressions that should be conveyed by sculpture. Our literally tactile "grasp" of the work is now transferred to the understanding eye. It is wholly a matter for the intellect, and depends on association. Picasso's approach has serious implications for three-dimensionality, which is fundamental to all sculpture. From any angle, these

Head of a Woman
Tête de femme
Boisgeloup, 1931
Bronze, 128.5 x 54.5 x 62.5 cm
Spies 133 II; MPP 302
Paris, Musée Picasso

The Sculptor
Le sculpteur
Paris, 7 December 1931
Oil on plywood, 128.5 x 96 cm
Zervos VII, 346; MPP 135
Paris, Musée Picasso

Woman with Mandolin
Femme à la mandoline
1925
Oil on canvas, 130 x 97 cm
Zervos V, 442
Los Angeles (CA), Walter Annenberg Collection

Woman with Sculpture (The Sculptress)
La statuaire (La femme sculpteur)
Juan-les-Pins, summer 1925
Oil on canvas, 131 x 97 cm
Zervos V, 451
New York, Mr. and Mrs. Daniel Saidenberg
Collection

The Dance
La danse
Monte Carlo, June 1925
Oil on canvas, 215 x 142 cm
Zervos V, 426
London, Tate Gallery

works become non-spatial patterns of lines. True, we can change our point of view by standing elsewhere, as with any genuinely volumed sculpture; but what we see is not a new spatial shape but a new pattern of lines. Unlike traditional sculpture, these works require an act of the intellect to complete the spatial transfer. The plinth helps us get our bearings. Strictly speaking, these works are three-dimensional transfers of two-dimensional graphics. They were given the label "spatial drawings" by Kahnweiler.[269]

It is an apt label, as Picasso's preliminary studies show (p. 325). These possess practically the same degree of three-dimensionality. The sculptures evolved from pure draughtsmanship. In 1924, Picasso did well over fifty linear ink drawings in a sketchbook, using curved and straight lines and adding solid circles at the bridge points (p. 324).[270] As we know from statements the artist made in 1926, maps of the night sky inspired these drawings. Picasso was fascinated by astronomical charts, which represented stars as thick dots and joined them up with thin lines to show constellations.[271] The representational and the abstract interacted. It was only an act of assertive recognition that gave significance to the meaningless figure. Picasso took the same approach. He used a technical method to craft concrete forms empty of content, and then imposed meaning on them in an arbitrary act of the maker's will.

307   A Juggler with Form   1925 – 1936

The ambiguity of formal meaning, the open expressive significance of an art object, the fundamental doubts concerning images conveyed by draughtsmanship – all these basic issues entered into Picasso's picture puzzles, on page and plinth alike. It was a new approach to something that had repeatedly concerned Picasso since his Rose Period: thinking about the nature of art became itself the occasion for an artwork and its meaning. But now, unlike in earlier periods, the principle was foregrounded and stood alone. The genre of artwork, its material form, was now primarily of a pragmatic nature. The nature of Picasso's work underwent a clear change, compared with the period immediately preceding this phase.

From 1916 to 1924, because he was testing the visual media, painting and drawing predominated. Autonomous art and applied art were as polarized as cause and effect. From 1925 to 1936, Picasso tackled sculpture, with an intense copiousness of production that can only be called explosive. He juxtaposed all the two- and three-dimensional forms of expression, or used them sequentially. The unceasing alternation of media was matched by an interplay of forms. In 1928, for instance, he did two small plaster figurines, later cast in bronze (p. 326). The restless shapes, shifting sharply from thick to thin, from open form to closed, have been made into figures largely abstract in character yet still reminiscent

Seated Woman
Femme assise
Paris, 1927
Oil on canvas, 130 x 97 cm
Zervos VII, 77
New York, The Museum of Modern Art

Seated Woman
Femme assise
Paris, 1926/27
Oil on canvas, 130 x 97 cm
Zervos VII, 81
Toronto, Art Gallery of Ontario

The Kiss (The Embrace)
Le baiser
Juan-les-Pins, summer 1925
Oil on canvas, 130.5 x 97.7 cm
Zervos V, 460; MPP 85
Paris, Musée Picasso

310 A Juggler with Form 1925 – 1936

The Bottle of Wine
La bouteille de vin
1925/26
Oil on canvas, 98.5 x 131 cm
Zervos VI, 1444
Basel, Beyeler Collection

Musical Instruments on a Table
Instruments de musique sur une table
1925
Oil on canvas, 162 x 204.5 cm
Zervos V, 416
Madrid, Centro de Arte Reina Sofía

Musical Instruments on a Table
Instruments de musique sur une table
Juan-les-Pins, summer 1926
Oil on canvas, 168 x 205 cm
Zervos VII, 3
Basel, Beyeler Collection

of human shapes. Everything is rounded; the flux of form seems fluid, as if a dynamic process were arrested and frozen. Legs, breasts, heads, eyes, noses protrude in a transitional smoothness from what seems an almost amorphous mass. These figures also took their origins from drawings, this time of an illusionist, three-dimensional nature rather than a purely linear character.

Sketchbooks dating from 1927 show endless variations of a basic figure (pp. 318 to 321). This is Picasso looking back; but he is doing so in pursuit of a decided transformation of form. The subject of bathers, of which he had already done numerous studies in 1920–1921, is now dealt with purely in terms of formal impact. The parts of the body are elongated or compressed or thinned out almost to lines in a process that seems mechanical, but are also conveyed in organic softness – the mechanical and organic loosely or tightly combined into a whole. At last, in 1928, Picasso rigorously dissected the structures, and on his drawing paper he worked on configurations geometrical in leaning. They are angular and straight, flat and solid, spheres and elliptical shapes that look

The Artist and his Model
Le peintre et son modèle
Paris, 1926
Oil on canvas, 172 x 256 cm
Zervos VII, 30; MPP 96
Paris, Musée Picasso

as if they were made of stone (p. 326). The sculptures that resulted were organic in form – and that was how the "Metamorphoses" (p. 326) came about. In paintings, though, Picasso revised the thematic function of his abstraction, placing it in bathing scenes where the compositions feature a veritable ballet of amorphous shapes on the beach (pp. 320, 321, 330, 331).

Some years later, in 1932, this chain of variations culminated in the oil "Bather with Beach Ball" (p. 356). The visual opulence of this work at once proves it a peak achievement, a final point along a development, the sum of a long series of studies, experiments and insights. The composition, seemingly simple and yet subtle, is typical Picasso in its use of correspondences and contrasts. Angular forms are juxtaposed with rounded ones; naturalistic features appear alongside abstract. Spheres and shapes like clubs, thick, sweeping, dense, form a figure that has a distantly human appearance. Legs apart, arms crossed as she leaps, the bather has just caught a ball that makes a distinctly tiny impression beside her bulky body. The figure almost completely fills the canvas, this, with Picasso's use of a vertical diagonal, making the sense of movement all the more dynamic. Taken with the clumsiness of this body, the crass pattern of the bathing suit, the beach cabin and the blue sea, Picasso's view of life at the seaside is distinctly humorous.

But for Picasso form in itself was devoid of content; so he considered himself at liberty to interchange forms and substitute other contents. A 1931/1932 set of variations on a female portrait is almost programmatic in this respect. His starting point for a large number of drawings, graphic works, sculptures and paintings was the head of a woman with what is known as a Greek profile, an arc that might have been drawn with compasses tracing the line from brow to skull to a falling curtain of hair. The chin seems an exact reversal of the forehead. Picasso treats these two areas as equivalent in formal terms; he takes them apart and reassembles them into new, capricious forms. In one sculptured bust (p. 338, below right), for instance, he fashions the hair and brow into a solid, fleshy roll. He leaves this in the position where we would expect to see this kind of shape in a face, and simply scratches in a few parallel lines to indicate a hair-do and nose. The eyes and mouth, by contrast, are in an almost conventional albeit coarsely mimetic style. The head is a synthesis of the mimetic and the arbitrary.

In a work done on 2 January 1932 Picasso drew on the fruits of his sculptural work and transferred those insights, with slight variations of detail, to paint (p.345). This picture, "Reading", shows a seated woman, her body disassembled and reconstructed. Picasso proceeded to work variations on this process. One shows a woman

The Milliner's Workshop
Les modistes (L'atelier de la modiste)
Paris, January 1926
Oil on canvas, 172 x 256 cm
Zervos VII, 2
Paris, Musée National d'Art Moderne,
Centre Georges Pompidou

Still Life with Bust and Palette
Nature morte au buste et à la palette
1925
Oil on canvas, 97 x 130 cm
Zervos V, 380
Basel, Private collection

Still Life with a Cake
Nature morte à la galette
Paris, 16 May 1924
Oil on canvas, 98 x 130.7 cm
Zervos V, 185
Mexico City, Jacques and Natasha
Gelman Collection

Still Life with Ancient Bust
Nature morte à la tête antique
1925
Oil on canvas, 97 x 130 cm
Zervos V, 377
Paris, Musée National d'Art Moderne,
Centre Georges Pompidou

Studio with Plaster Head
Tête et bras de plâtre
Juan-les-Pins, summer 1925
Oil on canvas, 98.1 x 131.2 cm
Zervos V, 445
New York, The Museum of Modern Art

A Juggler with Form   1925 – 1936   315

The Studio
L'atelier
Paris, winter 1927
Oil on canvas, 149.9 x 231.2 cm
Zervos VII, 142
New York, The Museum of Modern Art

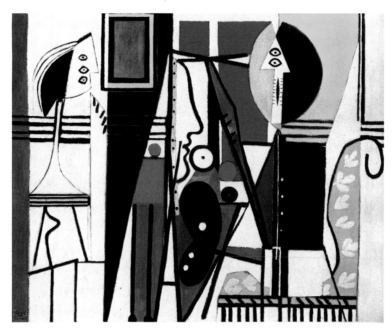

The Artist and His Model
Le peintre et son modèle
Paris, 1928
Oil on canvas, 129.8 x 163 cm
Zervos VII, 143
New York, The Museum of Modern Art

Left:
Figure
Figure
Cannes, 1927
Oil on canvas, 128 x 98 cm
Zervos VII, 67
Estate of Jacqueline Picasso

Pages 318 and 319:
Sketchbook No. 95
Cannes, September 1927
Pencil on paper, 30.3 x 23 cm
Zervos VII, 90–107; Glimscher 95;
MPP 1990–107
Paris, Musée Picasso

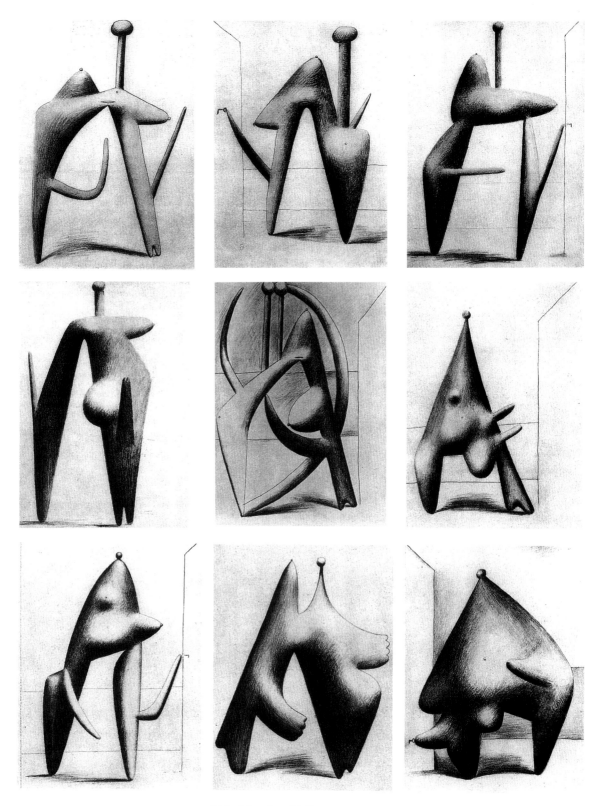

318 A Juggler with Form 1925 – 1936

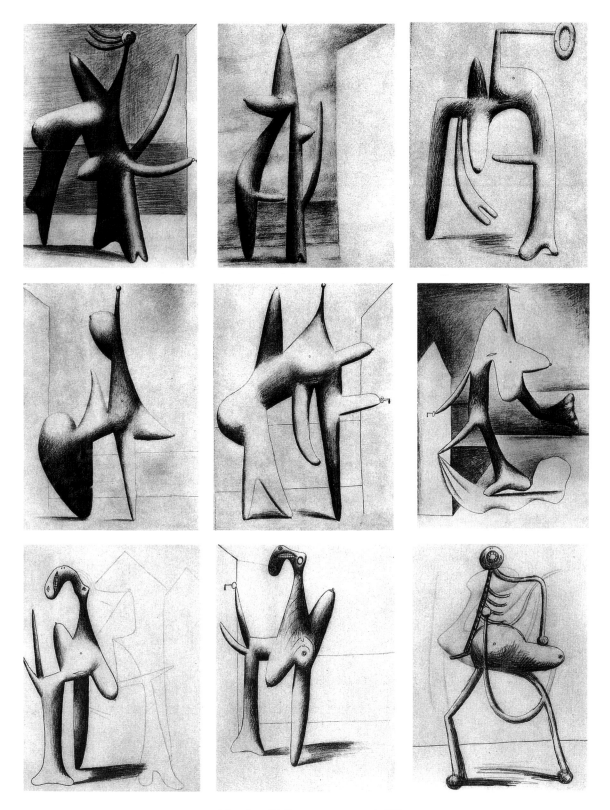

A Juggler with Form   1925 – 1936   **319**

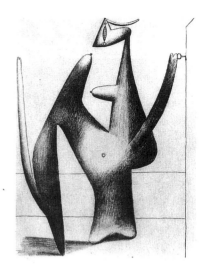

Sketchbook No. 95
Cannes, September 1927
Pencil on paper, 30.3 x 23 cm
Zervos VII, 108; Glimscher 95;
MPP 1990–107. Paris, Musée Picasso

Left:
Bather
Baigneuse
Dinard, 6 August 1928
Oil on canvas, 22 x 14 cm
Not in Zervos; MPP 106
Paris, Musée Picasso

Below:
Bathers on the Beach
Baigneuses sur la plage
Dinard, 12 August 1928
Oil on canvas, 21.5 x 40.4 cm
Zervos VII, 216; MPP 108
Paris, Musée Picasso

Ballplayers on the Beach
Joueurs de ballon sur la plage
Dinard, 15 August 1928
Oil on canvas, 24 x 34.9 cm
Zervos VII, 223; MPP 109
Paris, Musée Picasso

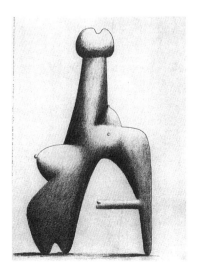

Right:
Bather Opening a Beach Cabin
Baigneuse ouvrant une cabine
Dinard, 9 August 1928
Oil on canvas, 32.8 x 22 cm
Zervos VII, 210; MPP 107
Paris, Musée Picasso

Left:
Sketchbook No. 95
Cannes, September 1927
Pencil on paper, 30.3 x 23 cm
Zervos VII, 109; Glimscher 95;
MPP 1990–107. Paris, Musée Picasso

A Juggler with Form   1925–1936   **321**

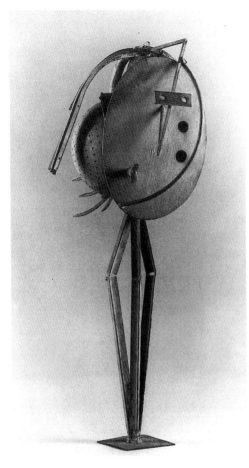

Right:
Guitar
Guitare
Paris, spring 1926
String, newspaper, sackcloth and nails
on painted canvas, 96 x 130 cm
Zervos VII, 9; MPP 87
Paris, Musée Picasso

Guitar
Guitare
Paris, May 1926
Cardboard with India ink, string, tulle
and pencil on cardboard, 13.8 x 12.6 cm
Spies 65 E; MPP 92
Paris, Musée Picasso

Guitar
Guitare
Paris, 29 April 1926
Cardboard, tulle, string and pencil
on cardboard, 12.5 x 10.4 cm
Spies 65 A; MPP 88
Paris, Musée Picasso

Head of a Woman
Tête de femme
Paris, 1929/30
Iron, sheet metal, colander and springs,
painted, 100 x 37 x 59 cm
Spies 81; MPP 270
Paris, Musée Picasso

Woman in a Garden
La femme au jardin
Paris, spring 1929
Iron, soldered and painted white,
206 x 117 x 85 cm
Spies 72 I; MPP 267
Paris, Musée Picasso

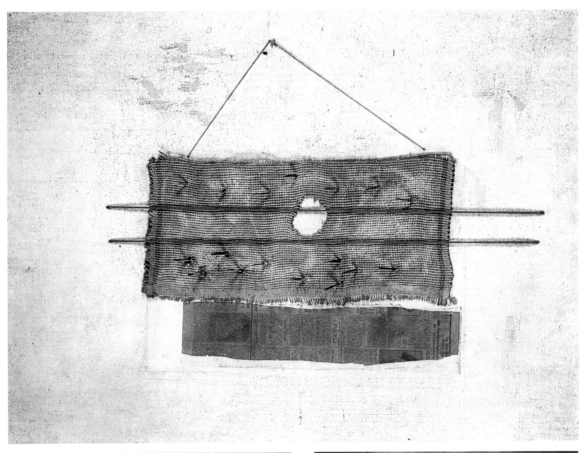

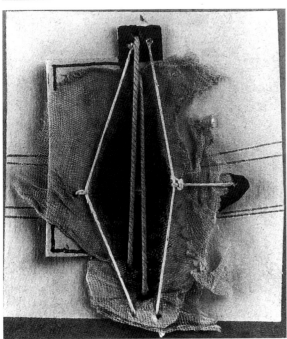

A Juggler with Form 1925 – 1936 **323**

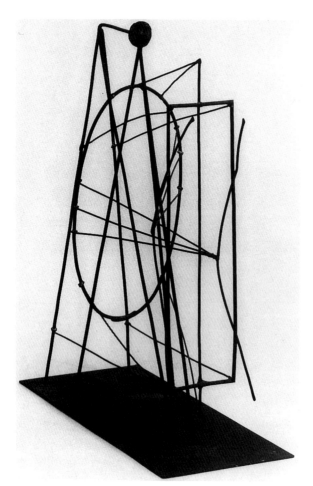

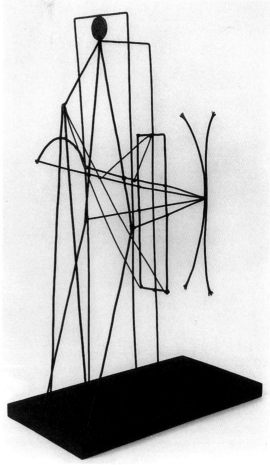

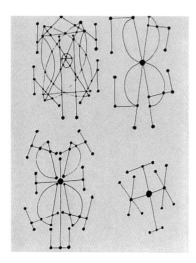

Studies for Balzac's "Le Chef-d'œuvre inconnu"
Juan-les-Pins, 1924
Ink on paper, 10 x 11.5 cm
Zervos V, 281. Private collection

seated in a red armchair (p. 359), her arms, hands, torso, breasts and head spherical or club-like shapes, as if hewn from stone. Picasso was transferring the tactile qualities of sculpture into his painting. In the combination of semi-abstract, stylized forms with clear reminiscences of the human body, such paintings continue the 1927–1928 variations on the subject of bathers which Picasso had repeatedly drawn (pp. 318–321, 326).

This series peaked in April 1932 in the painting "Woman with a Flower" (p. 351). Two-dimensional areas of colour, boldly and sweepingly outlined, are juxtaposed with similar areas that bear witness to a modelling, three-dimensionalizing instinct. The head is like a kidney, with lines for mouth, nose and eyes. The picture is related to a sculpture done the previous year (p. 338) in which the long, irregular cylinder of the stand looks like an Alice in Wonderland neck and supports a head made of a number of smoothly interlocking heart-shaped solids. The eyes are scratched in as flat, pointed ovals. The mouth is a declivity walled about by a roll of flesh. And the nose has been displaced.

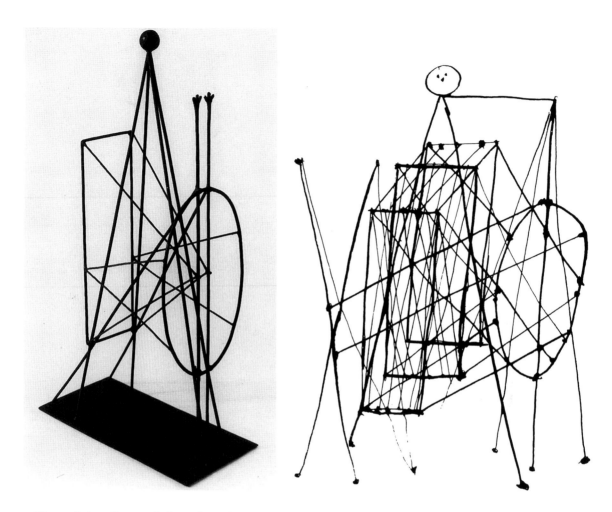

Picasso's juggling with form found support at that period in another new movement that had emerged from Dada: Surrealism. In summer 1923 Picasso met the leader of the movement, the writer André Breton, and did an etching of him. In 1924 Breton published the first Surrealist Manifesto. In it he proposed that the subconscious was a more valid mode of perceiving reality than rational thought and sense. He advocated dreams and the visions of madness as an alternative to reason. He was inspired by Sigmund Freud's psychoanalytic writings, and by the poetry of Rimbaud, Mallarmé, Lautréamont and Apollinaire, from whose work the label of the new movement was indirectly derived. Surrealism's aim was to reveal the subconscious realm of dreams by exploring avenues opened up by psychoanalysis. It disregarded the causal order of the perceptible world and set out to counter it with an unlimited use of the irrational. In this way, individual life would undergo a revolutionary transformation: feeling and expressive potential would be infinitely enhanced and extended.

The Surrealists were opposed to all artistic procedures based on

Figure (Maquette for a Memorial to Apollinaire)
Figure (Maquette pour un monument
d'Apollinaire)
Paris, autumn 1928
Iron wire and sheet metal, 50.5 x 18.5 x 40.8 cm
Spies 68; MPP 264. Paris, Musée Picasso

Figure (Maquette for a Memorial to Apollinaire)
Figure (Maquette pour un monument
d'Apollinaire)
Paris, autumn 1928
Iron wire and sheet metal, 60.5 x 15 x 34 cm
Spies 69; MPP 265. Paris, Musée Picasso

Figure
Figure
Paris, autumn 1928
Iron wire and sheet metal, 37.7 x 10 x 19.6 cm
Spies 71; MPP 266. Paris, Musée Picasso

Figure (Maquette for a Memorial to Apollinaire)
(Sketchbook No. 96, sheet 21)
Figure. Etude pour un monument d'Apollinaire
Dinard, 3 August 1928
India ink on paper, 30 x 22 cm
Zervos VII, 206
Geneva, Marina Picasso Foundation

326 A Juggler with Form 1925 – 1936

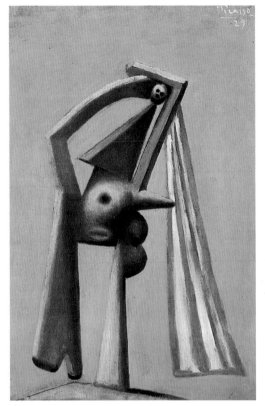

Woman with Veil
Femme au voile
1929
Oil on canvas, 40.9 x 26.5 cm
Zervos VII, 254. Private collection

Head
Tête
1929
Oil on canvas, 73 x 60 cm
Zervos VII, 273. Baltimore (MD), The Baltimore Museum of Art

Left:
Bather with Beach Ball
(Sketchbook No. 96, sheet 2)
Dinard, 27 July 1928
Pencil and India ink on paper, 38 x 31 cm
Zervos VII, 200
Geneva, Marina Picasso Foundation

Bather with Beach Ball
(Sketchbook No. 96, sheet 3)
Dinard, 27 July 1928
Pencil and India ink on paper, 38 x 31 cm
Zervos VII, 201
Geneva, Marina Picasso Foundation

Bather (Metamorphosis I)
Baigneuse (Métamorphose I)
Paris, 1928
Bronze, 22.8 x 18.3 x 11 cm
Spies 67 II; MPP 261
Paris, Musée Picasso

Bather (Metamorphosis II)
Baigneuse (Métamorphose II)
Paris, 1928
Plaster original, 23 x 18 x 11 cm
Spies 67 A II; MPP 262
Paris, Musée Picasso

conscious reason. In its place they put chance, trivia, and a revaluation of plain everyday sensation. Originally a literary movement, it quickly embraced the visual arts too, and a number of new techniques were developed. The most important of them were frottage, which (like brass rubbing) calls for the production of visual, textural effects by rubbing, and grattage, a kind of reverse frottage, in which paint is thickly applied and then scraped off revealing the layer underneath. Nor should we forget *Ecriture automatique*, the Surrealists' rediscovery of automatic writing and equivalent procedures in painting and drawing whereby what mattered was to suspend rational control and allow the subconscious to express itself directly via the text or image produced.[272]

One of their points of reference was also Picasso, as a pioneer of art and inventor of new methods. His playful approach to the meaning of form, his loose disdain for convention, made him appear a fellow spirit. A sculptural construction of Picasso's was reproduced in the first number of their periodical, "La Révolution surréaliste", in December 1924. In the second, in January 1925, two pages of the sketchbook of "Constellations" (cf. p. 324) which he had done in summer 1924 at Juan-les-Pins were reproduced. The fourth issue used Picasso's painting "The Dance" (p. 306) and – reproduced for the first time in France – "Les Demoiselles d'Avignon". In 1925 Picasso exhibited at the first joint Surrealist show in the Galerie Pierre in Paris. He did portraits of Surrealist writers for their books, and in 1933 one of his collages was taken for the title page of the new magazine, "Minotaure" (p. 377).[273]

This contact, though continuing for several years, was not without conflict. When the ballet "Mercure" was first performed in 1924, with Picasso's set design and costume, several Surrealists protested at his involvement, claiming the event was merely a benefit show for the international aristocracy. It is true that Etienne Comte de Beaumont was involved in producing the ballet. But Breton, Louis Aragon and other Surrealists, impressed by the fertility of Picasso's imagination, published an apology in the "Paris Journal" headed "Hommage à Picasso".[274] Picasso, for his part, accused the Surrealists of not having understood him, in a lengthy statement on the aims and intentions of his art published in 1926. To prove his point, he referred to the interpretations the Surrealists had written to accompany the sketchbook drawings printed in their

Large Nude in a Red Armchair
Grand nu au fauteuil rouge
Paris, 5 May 1929
Oil on canvas, 195 x 129 cm
Zervos VII, 263; MPP 113
Paris, Musée Picasso

Reclining Woman
Femme couchée
Paris, April 1929
Oil on canvas, 46.3 x 61 cm
Zervos VII, 260
Paris, Musée National d'Art Moderne,
Centre Georges Pompidou

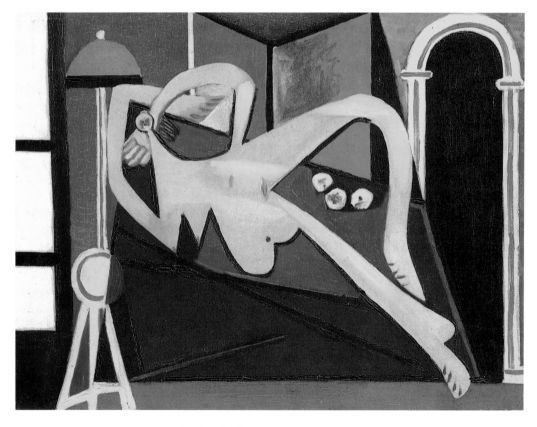

Bather
Baigneuse
Dinard, 15 August 1928
Oil on canvas, 24.5 x 35 cm
Zervos VII, 224; MPP 1900–14
Paris, Musée Picasso

magazine in 1924[275]. In the 1950s, he observed that his work before 1933 had been free of Surrealist influences.[276]

We might reply by pointing to the publication of his work in Surrealist periodicals, and to his close personal relations with certain members of the group, such as Paul Eluard, a lifelong friend. The fact is that Surrealist influences in his art are many and various. From de Chirico to Joan Miró, he registered Surrealist painting precisely, taking it as a model, and was particulary inspired by Surrealist sculpture, especially works by Alberto Giacometti.[277]

Not that the borrowings were ever isolated occurrences. Picasso adapted what he took to his own purposes, and combined it with borrowings from altogether different kinds of art. Thus his 1931/32 sculptures of women's heads are related to Matisse's bust "Jeannette V", made between 1910 and 1913, and also to the mask-like "Portrait of Professor Gosset" done by Raymond Duchamp-Villon in 1918, in which Cubist and Futurist elements are combined.[278] Picasso was also inspired by designs for female busts

and full-length figures the sculptor Jacques Lipchitz was doing after 1930. The latter's broken-form sculptures, called "transparents", alongside Picasso's own sketches of "constellations", were the most important source for the wire constructions of 1928[279].

Like the Surrealists, Picasso too explored the visual potential of tactile qualities. There are a number of affinities in technical methods, the use of montage, and the further development of collage and assemblage. Yet still the tensions that existed between Picasso and the Surrealists were the product of deep-seated differences. It is no exaggeration to say that their respective aims and intentions were in fact diametrically opposed. For that very reason there were superficial overlaps in the approach to artistic experiment and the transformation of conventional techniques and modes of expression. The assemblages Picasso did in spring 1926, which were published that summer in "La Révolution surréaliste", point up the differences of creative method nicely. The assemblages consist of just a few, simple, everyday things. Scraps of linen and tulle, nails,

The Swimmer
La nageuse
Paris, November 1929
Oil on canvas, 130 x 162 cm
Zervos VII, 419; MPP 119
Paris, Musée Picasso

Pages 332 and 333:
The Blue Acrobat
L'acrobate bleu
Paris, November 1929
Charcoal and oil on canvas, 162 x 130 cm
Not in Zervos; MPP 1990-15
Paris, Musée Picasso

The Acrobat
L'acrobate
Paris, 18 January 1930
Oil on canvas, 162 x 130 cm
Zervos VII, 310; MPP 120
Paris, Musée Picasso

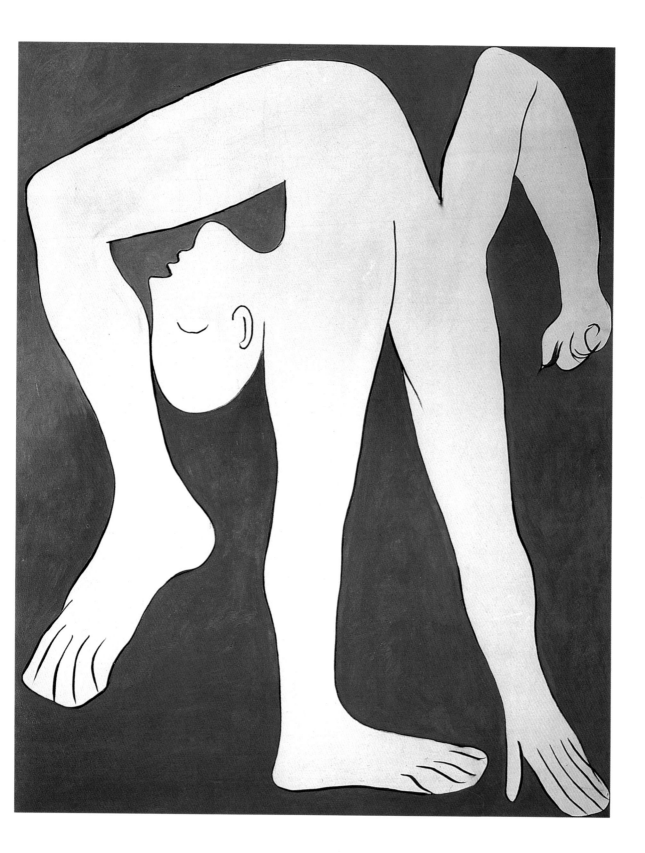

Seated Woman (Figure)
Femme assise (Figure)
Paris, 1930
Oil on panel, 66 x 49 cm
Zervos VII, 314
Basel, Beyeler Collection

Bust of a Woman with Self-portrait
Buste de femme et autoportrait
Paris, February 1929
Oil on canvas, 71 x 60.5 cm
Zervos VII, 248
Private collection

Woman with Doves
La femme aux pigeons
Paris, 1930
Oil on canvas, 200 x 185 cm
Not in Zervos
Paris, Musée National d'Art Moderne,
Centre Georges Pompidou

336

The Crucifixion (after Grünewald)
La crucifixion (d'après Grünewald)
Boisgeloup, 19 September 1932
Ink and India ink on paper,
34.5 x 51.5 cm
Zervos VII, 55; MPP 1075
Paris, Musée Picasso

The Crucifixion
La crucifixion
Paris, 7 February 1930
Oil on plywood, 51.5 x 66.5 cm
Zervos VII, 287; MPP 122
Paris, Musée Picasso

A Juggler with Form 1925 – 1936 **337**

Head of a Woman
Tête de femme
Boisgeloup, 1931
Bronze, 71.5 x 41 x 33 cm
Spies 110 II; MPP 292
Paris, Musée Picasso

Bather
Baigneuse
Boisgeloup, 1931
Bronze, 70 x 40.2 x 31.5 cm
Spies 108 II; MPP 289
Paris, Musée Picasso

**Head of a Woman
(Marie-Thérèse Walther)**
Tête de femme (Marie-Thérèse Walther)
Boisgeloup, 1931
Bronze, 128.5 x 54.5 x 62.5 cm
Spies 133 II; MPP 302
Paris, Musée Picasso

Bust of a Woman
Buste de femme
Boisgeloup, 1931
Bronze, 78 x 44.5 x 54 cm
Spies 131 II; MPP 298
Paris, Musée Picasso

string, buttons and newspaper are put together to make almost abstract images.[280]

In "Guitar" (p. 323, top), for instance, Picasso has arranged a piece of sackcloth, a scrap of newspaper, two long nails and some string in such a way that what looks like a random collection of objects takes on the appearance of a "picture". By referring to the title we can read this picture as representational. The cut-out circle in the middle of the cloth echoes the hole in a guitar's soundboard, and the two nails loosely suggest the strings. The yellowed newspaper denotes the side and bottom of the instrument, and the string must presumably represent the (oddly angled) neck. The image is wholly non-naturalistic, and the form contrasts with that of an actual guitar. But in its details there are enough similarities to establish the concept of a guitar. Picasso is continuing the line of Synthetic Cubism here, seeing the picture as a system of signs, the arbitrary nature of which leaves the imagination leeway for untrammelled invention. The possibility of recognition is anchored in concepts and definitions, and happens entirely in the intellect.

Surrealism does exactly the opposite. It too primarily operates with a conceptual system, but its techniques and aims alike depend on the irrational. Scarcely controlled creative acts may produce random results, or logical and meticulous labour may produce im-

Nude in Front of a Statue
Femme nue devant une statue
4 July 1931
Etching, 31.2 x 22.1 cm
Bloch 139; Geiser 205

Nude with Raised Knee
Femme nue à la jambe pliée
9 July 1931
Etching, 31.2 x 22.1 cm
Bloch 141; Geiser 208

ages beyond rational interpretation; that is not the point. In the former case, form expresses the artist's subconscious and appeals to the beholder's emotions. In the latter, the beholder's subconscious is activated via feeling even though he has no rational access to the work. In terms of form and the meaning of form, however, emotion plays no part at all in Picasso's work.

This is not to say that no feeling is involved in the impact of his work. But it is different. For the Surrealists, form is the trigger of a chain of associations which are suggestive of emotional states and linked to the spiritual condition of instinctual mankind. In Picasso, form is free, autonomous. He appeals to the emotions to prompt conflict or even shock, starting an intellectual process in the course of which we reflect not on ourselves but on art. That was the aim of the picture-puzzle line-and-point sketches of summer 1924 which led to the wire sculptures of autumn 1928 (cf. pp. 324 and

Table of Etchings
Table des eaux-fortes
Paris, 4 July 1931
Etching, 37.5 x 29.8 cm
Bloch 94; Geiser 135 I b

325). These works avowedly play off the abstract against the representational, the spatial against the graphic. But Picasso had a particular reason, drawn from the theory of art, for using linear studies to make constructions. Their form reveals his purpose.

Linearity and space are dialectically juxtaposed. The iron rods stand for tactile, material volume. But they also look like lines, and seem two-dimensional. Since we interpret them as denoting outlines, they establish figures. But the material they outline is air — neither visible nor palpable. Paradoxically, these sculptures use a substance the spatial content of which is literally *immaterial*. What Picasso has sculpted is *nothing-ness*. This was what he was after.

Pitcher and Bowl of Fruit
Pichet et coupe de fruits
Paris, 22 February 1931
Oil on canvas, 130 x 162 cm
Zervos VII, 322
New York, The Museum of Modern Art

Large Still Life on a Pedestal Table
Grande nature morte au guéridon
Paris, 11 March 1931
Oil on canvas, 195 x 130.5 cm
Zervos VII, 317; MPP 134
Paris, Musée Picasso

A Juggler with Form 1925 – 1936 **340**

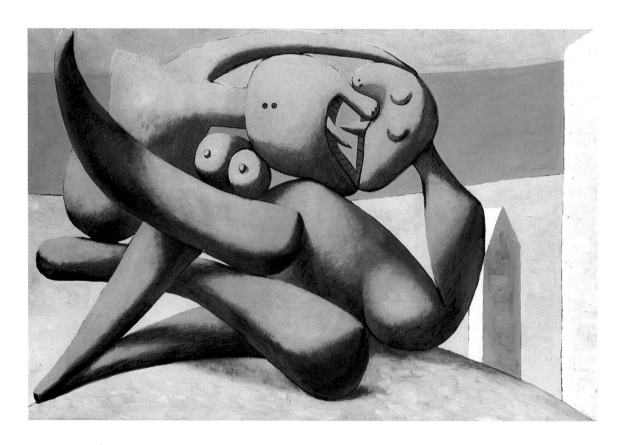

Figures at the Seashore
Figures au bord de la mer
Paris, 12 January 1931
Oil on canvas, 130 x 195 cm
Zervos VII, 328; MPP 131
Paris, Musée Picasso

The maquettes were done in response to a commission. The Association of Friends of Apollinaire planned to erect a memorial to the poet on the tenth anniversary of his death, and approached Picasso, who aptly tackled the project in the spirit of a phrase Apollinaire had written: "the statue made of nothing, of vacancy". Apollinaire was thinking of a monument to a poet; so it seemed doubly appropriate to Picasso to borrow this thought from his friend. The evident relation to the human figure derives its meaning from this consideration too: Picasso evolved his idea in order to put the 19th century's outmoded notions of memorials aside, for good. The representational, figural echo alludes to the tradition of monuments, but in a radical form that departs conspicuously from the tradition. Unfortunately Picasso's idea was too daring and progressive for his contemporaries. The committee turned it down.[281]

Not till much later did the artist have the chance to realize his ideas, at least in part. In 1962 he himself had two large-scale versions of the four maquettes made, one 115 centimetres high, the other 200, intended as intermediate stages towards a finished version on a monumental scale. In 1973, shortly before his death, one version over four metres high was put up in the Museum of Modern Art, New York. No longer able to see it for himself, Picasso followed the progress of the work through reports and photo-

graphs. Finally, in 1985, when the Picasso Museum was opened in Paris, another version almost five metres high was put up there.[282]

The basic idea remained alive in Picasso's œuvre. In 1931 he used 16 of the 1924 sketches to illustrate a bibliophile edition of Honoré de Balzac's tale "Le Chef-d'œuvre inconnu". Again the line-and-point constructs, neutral in themselves, were placed in a theoretical context. Balzac's story of the unknown masterpiece is about translating the absolute into art. It tells of a 17th-century painter whose ambition is to express an ideal, perfect illusion of life, beyond all specifics of form, colour and perspective. When he has been at work on his masterpiece for ten years, friends – among them the French painter Poussin – persuade him to let them see it. What the shocked group see, instead of the portrait of a lady they have been led to expect, is a chaotic jumble of colours and lines.[283]

At that time, Picasso was particularly interested in the applied art of book illustration. The subjects he searched out were closely connected with his own work towards self-reflexive art. He employed a variety of etching processes (cold needle, line etching and aquatint) for this work, which included thirteen classicist etchings also for Balzac's novella, thirty etchings done in 1930 for publisher Albert Skira for an edition of Ovid's "Metamorphoses" which appeared the following year, and one hundred plates done between

Woman Throwing a Stone
Femme lançant une pierre
Paris, 8 March 1931
Oil on canvas, 130.5 x 195.5 cm
Zervos VII, 329; MPP 133
Paris, Musée Picasso

1930 and 1937 which became the "Suite Vollard" in 1939. The same familiar repertoire of subjects recurred: painter and model, bullfight, bathers, nudes, acrobats. The works have titles such as "Sculptor Resting with Model in his Arms" or "Sculptor with Model at a Window". Sculptors or painters with models account for the greatest part of these works. Painters and sculptors, themselves drawn naturalistically, can make abstract figures from real originals, Picasso is saying – or naturalistic images from abstract models. These sequences of graphics, deconstructed twofold, bring home the work of the artist. This applies to the return to antiquity too, a constant in Picasso's work since his youth. It was not only the classical style that provided a point of reference for formal matters, but also the subject matter of myths illustrated.

Ovid's "Metamorphoses", the most illustrated of all books after the Bible, deals with the entirety of the ancient world's mythology. Its presence in European art has been a long and signal one. On a political level, it moves from the beginning of the world to the new Golden Age under Emperor Augustus (Ovid's contemporary). In a

Reading
La lecture
Boisgeloup, 2 January 1932
Oil on canvas, 130 x 97.5 cm
Zervos VII, 358; MPP 137
Paris, Musée Picasso

Reclining Nude
Femme nue couchée
Boisgeloup, 4 April 1932
Oil on canvas, 130 x 161.7 cm
Zervos VII, 332; MPP 142
Paris, Musée Picasso

sense the "Metamorphoses" are sublime propaganda. The book, true to its title, tells of heroes and heroines transformed into animals, plants, streams, stars and so forth.[284] Metamorphoses of this order are the proper province of the creative artist. If he wishes he can use the aesthetic norms and subjects of antiquity; but he can also make a faun into an artist, transform a stone into organic substance, and then metamorphose it back to a stone.

As always, Picasso did not observe the bounds of one artistic genre. He combined elements from various sources, and transferred his figurations and motifs from drawings to printed graphics, from etchings to paintings. Thus in the 1933 "Silenus Dancing in Company" (p. 365) we have a gouache and India ink variation on a baroque theme.[285] In late 1931, in "The Sculptor" (p. 304), Picasso transferred to an oil painting the 1931/32 female busts from the painter-and-model theme, and transposed the formal puzzle component to both figures, the artist and the statue created by him. The motifs are repeated in a distinctly different 1933 treatment in ink, India ink, watercolour and gouache which again shows the sculptor and his work (p. 364).

Beach Game and Rescue
Jeu de plage et sauvetage
Paris, November 1932
Oil on canvas, 97 x 130 cm
Zervos VIII, 64
Switzerland, Private collection

The Rescue
Le sauvetage
Paris, December 1932
Oil on canvas, 130 x 97 cm
Zervos VIII, 66
Basel, Beyeler Collection

The Red Armchair
Femme assise dans un fauteuil rouge
Paris, 16 December 1931
Oil and enamel paint on plywood,
130.8 x 99 cm
Zervos VII, 334
Chicago (IL), The Art Institute of Chicago

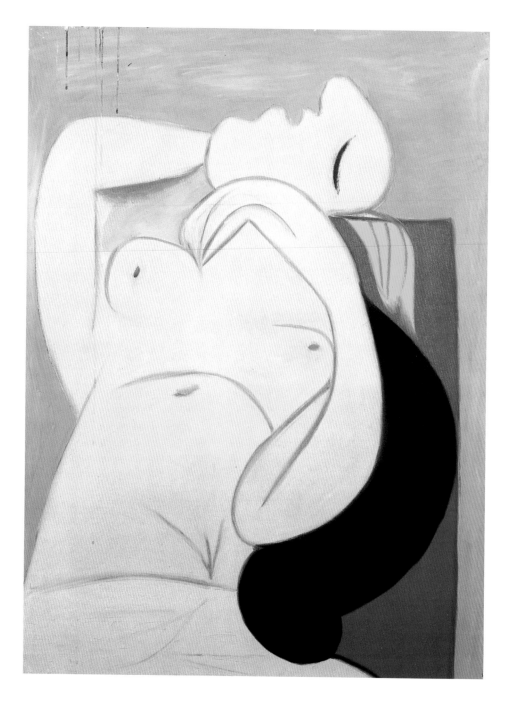

Sleep
Le sommeil
Paris, 23 January 1932
Oil on canvas, 130 x 97 cm
Zervos VII, 362
Estate of Jacqueline Picasso

Reclining Nude
Femme nue couchée
Boisgeloup, 6 August 1932
Oil on canvas, 24 x 35 cm
Not in Zervos
Rome, Private collection

Reclining Nude
Femme nue couchée
Boisgeloup, 19 June 1932
Oil on canvas, 38 x 46 cm
Not in Zervos
Paris, Musée National d'Art Modern,
Centre Georges Pompidou

Woman with a Flower
Femme à la fleur
Boisgeloup, 10 April 1932
Oil on canvas, 162 x 130 cm
Zervos VII, 381
New York, Mr. and Mrs. Nathan
Cummings Collection

350

Reclining Nude with Flowers
Femme nue couchée aux fleurs
Boisgeloup, July 1932
Oil on canvas, 101.6 x 92.7 cm
Zervos VII, 407
New York, Peter A. Rübel Collection

The Mirror
Le miroir
Boisgeloup, 12 March 1932
Oil on canvas, 130.7 x 97 cm
Zervos VII, 378
Private collection

Girl Before a Mirror
Jeune fille devant un miroir
Boisgeloup, 14 March 1932
Oil on canvas, 162.3 x 130.2 cm
Zervos VII, 379
New York, The Museum of Modern Art,
Gift of Mrs. Simon Guggenheim

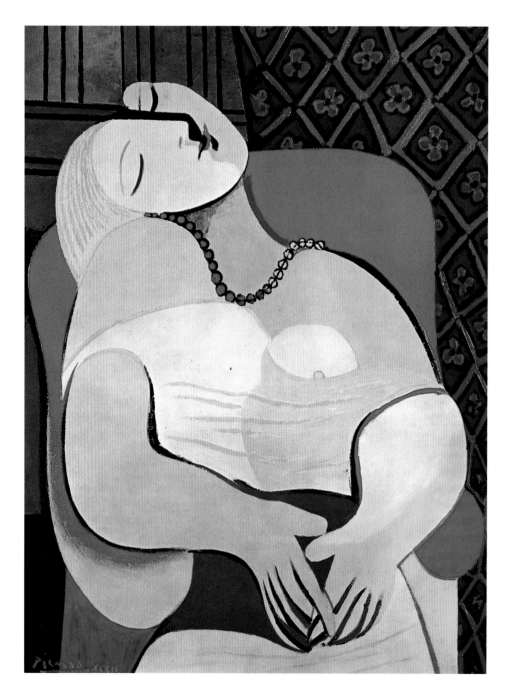

The Dream
Le rêve
Boisgeloup, 24 January 1932
Oil on canvas, 130 x 98 cm
Zervos VII, 364
New York, Mrs. Victor W. Ganz Collection

Nude in a Red Armchair
Femme nue dans un fauteuil rouge
1932
Oil on canvas, 130 x 97 cm
Zervos VII, 395
London, Tate Gallery

Bather with Beach Ball
Baigneuse au bord de la mer
Boisgeloup, 30 August 1932
Oil on canvas, 146.2 x 114.6 cm
Zervos VIII, 147
New York, The Museum of Modern Art

356

Seated Bather
Baigneuse assise au bord de la mer
Paris, early 1930
Oil on canvas, 163.2 x 129.5 cm
Zervos VII, 306
New York, The Museum of Modern Art,
Mrs. Simon Guggenheim Fund

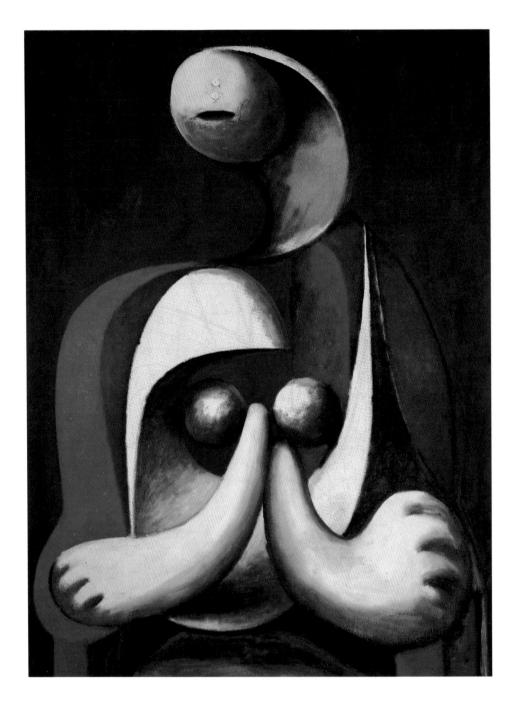

Seated Woman in a Red Armchair
Femme assise dans un fauteuil rouge
Boisgeloup, 1932
Oil on canvas, 130 x 97.5 cm
Not in Zervos; MPP 139
Paris, Musée Picasso

Woman in a Red Armchair
Femme au fauteuil rouge
Boisgeloup, 27 January 1932
Oil on canvas, 130.2 x 97 cm
Zervos VII, 330; MPP 138
Paris, Musée Picasso

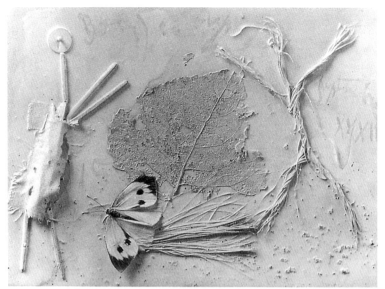

Composition with Butterfly
Composition au papillon
Boisgeloup, 15 September 1932
Cloth, wood, plants, string, nails,
butterfly and oil on canvas, 16 x 22 x 2.5 cm
Spies 116; MPP 1982–169
Paris, Musée Picasso

Woman with Leaves
Femme au feuillage
Boisgeloup, 1934
Bronze, 37.9 x 20 x 25.9 cm
Spies 157 II; MPP 314
Paris, Musée Picasso

Figure
Figure
Tremblay-sur-Mauldre (?), 1935
Ladle, hoes, wood, string and nails,
112.1 x 61.5 x 29.8 cm
Spies 165; MPP 316
Paris, Musée Picasso

Bust of a Bearded Man
Buste d'homme barbu
Boisgeloup, 1933
Plaster original, 85.5 x 47 x 31 cm
Spies 152 I; MPP 312
Paris, Musée Picasso

A Juggler with Form 1925 – 1936 **361**

Dying Bull
Taureau mourant
Boisgeloup, 16 July 1934
Oil on canvas, 33.3 x 55.2 cm
Zervos VIII, 228
Mexico City, Jacques and Natasha
Gelman Collection

Bullfight (Corrida)
Course de taureaux (Corrida)
Boisgeloup, 27 July 1934
Oil on canvas, 50 x 61 cm
Not in Zervos
Private collection

A Juggler with Form   1925 – 1936   **362**

Bullfight (Corrida)
Course de taureaux (Corrida)
Boisgeloup, 22 July 1934
Oil on canvas, 54.3 x 73 cm
Zervos VIII, 219
Private collection

Bullfight (Corrida)
Course de taureaux (Corrida)
Boisgeloup, 22 July 1934
Oil on canvas, 97 x 130 cm
Zervos VIII, 229
Private collection

363   A Juggler with Form   1925 – 1936

Silenus Dancing in Company
Silène en compagnie dansante
Cannes, 6 July 1933
Gouache and India ink on paper,
34 x 45 cm
Not in Zervos
Geneva, Heinz Berggruen Collection

A large number of Picasso's etchings are responses to Rembrandt. In three, the Dutch baroque painter appears with his model, but many other plates in the "Suite Vollard" document Picasso's approach to Rembrandt. One unfinished Rembrandt etching shows the artist and his model. Picasso not only played numerous variations on the theme of a female nude seen from the rear together with an artist seen frontally. He was also interested in formal aspects of the Rembrandt work. He adopted the contrast of richly cross-hatched areas with plain outline drawing, using it elsewhere with different subjects.[286] Both types of quotation – of form and of motif – acted as an analysis of the artist himself. Picasso was placing himself on a par with Rembrandt – a high ambition indeed, for Rembrandt is widely seen as *the* master of etching, and in Picasso's time was considered the greatest artist of all time. Picasso was asserting that he himself was Rembrandt's legitimate successor, that he himself was the most important 20th-century artist.

There is a contrast to Surrealist intentions and techniques. Picasso transfers a clearly definable content to his pictures, his system of signs directly related to the message to be conveyed. In Surrealism, the visual sign is an enigma, an instrument of encodement; deep and inward meditation is required to decode the image. For Picasso, form and content are mutually determinant, in a way that is ultimately perfectly traditional. They serve either the exploration of visual problems or the analysis of a subject. Picasso's titles define the content; Surrealist titles add a layer of obfuscation.

In summer 1925, in his painting "The Dance" (p. 306), Picasso reworked studies drawn that spring when visiting the Ballets Russes in Monte Carlo, purely representational ones playing off

365 A Juggler with Form 1925 – 1936

Woman Facing to the Right
Femme de 3/4 gauche
Boisgeloup, 12 July 1934
Oil on canvas, 55 × 33 cm
Zervos VIII, 243
Basel, Galerie Beyeler

Woman with Cap
Femme au béret
Boisgeloup, 12 July 1934
Oil on canvas, 55 × 38 cm
Not in Zervos
Paris, Maya Ruiz-Picasso Collection

linear effects against economical three-dimensionality. He now combined this interplay with what he had learnt from the papiers collés, finding a way of heightening the ecstatic dynamism of the action in the most evocative of styles. But there is far more to the picture. In a gap towards the top right, silhouetted against the blue sky, we see the profile of Ramón Pichot, a friend of Picasso's who had recently died. The painting is dedicated to him. What looks like a pure celebration of *joie de vivre* turns out to portray the old Spanish custom of dancing around the dead when they are laid out.[287] This redefinition of the subject is perfectly matched to the redefinition of form; as in the later maquettes for the Apollinaire memorial, the picture-puzzle component has a distinct function.

That year, Picasso created another masterpiece of formal metamorphosis, "The Kiss" (p. 309), a truly awful picture – but wonderful too! A manifesto of new ways of expression, it presents the aggressive, violent and primitive aspects of the act of love with a brutality scarcely ever attempted before. It makes demands on us. We have to disentangle what we see, gradually discovering at the

Confidences
Confidences
1934
Oil, papiers collés and gouache
on canvas, 194 x 170 cm
Zervos VIII, 268
Paris, Musée National d'Art Moderne,
Centre Georges Pompidou

top, amidst the seeming chaos of loud colours and contrasts, mouths locked in a devouring kiss; a figure at left, holding another in an embrace; an exploded backbone atop straddled legs. But what looks like a mouth or eye, soulfully intimate, is in fact a vagina about to be "eaten", and at the bottom of the picture we are provocatively confronted with an anus – balancing the composition in ribald parody of classical laws of composition. Not until late work done in the 1960s did Picasso again treat sexuality thus.

A picture as aggressive as "The Kiss" was of course not merely the articulation of an artistic programme. It came out of personal experience. Picasso's marriage to Olga was not a happy one. They shared few interests, neither communicating nor enriching each other's lives. Art here mirrors reality, expresses it vividly.

A similar process is at work in the female bust that recurs frequently in the sculptures, drawings, graphics and paintings from 1931 on. The features are those of Marie-Thérèse Walter, Picasso's young lover. In January 1927, aged 45, he had met the girl, then aged just 17, outside Lafayette's, a Paris department store. The

Nude in a Garden
Femme nue dans un jardin
Boisgeloup, 4 August 1934
Oil on canvas, 162 x 130 cm
Not in Zervos; MPP 148
Paris, Musée Picasso

story goes that he used the corniest approach in the book: "You have an interesting face, Mademoiselle. I should like to paint you. My name is Picasso." The name meant nothing to her, but she agreed. Within months she was his lover. But he was still married, and had to keep the relationship secret. In the years that followed there was many an undignified scene and incident. It was not till 1935 that Picasso finally left his wife, when Marie-Thérèse gave birth to their daughter Maja.[288] The artist called it the worst time of his life. But it was also the climax of a fraught situation that had been affecting the subjects and formal approaches of his art for years. We need only look at the 1932 painting "Girl Before a Mirror" (p. 353). The girl is Marie-Thérèse. Picasso preferred this picture of his lover to all the others. In the paradoxical tension between the motif of tranquil contemplation and the agitated style in which it is painted, Picasso has conveyed far more than an everyday moment. Marie Thérèse is studying her reflected image closely; but

Woman at the Sideboard
Femme au buffet
Juan-les-Pins, 9 April 1936
Oil on canvas, 55 x 46 cm
Not in Zervos; MPP 151
Paris, Musée Picasso

this simple attitude is transformed by the wild colours and assertive lines. It is as if we were seeing her at once clothed, naked, and revealed in X-ray image. The picture is full of sexual symbolism.[289]

In other works of the period, distress and violent feeling are apparent in the visible tension. From 1930 on, we frequently find the Christian motif of the crucifixion, partly using historical originals such as Matthias Grünewald's Isenheim altarpiece, of which Picasso did a small painting (p. 337) and a 1932 series of India-ink variations. Above all, he dealt with relations between the sexes, in numerous variations on his artist-and-model subject but also in a new version of his bullfight pictures: the motif of the Minotaur. Picasso approached the mythical subject in characteristic fashion. In Greek myth, the Minotaur was the son of Pasiphaë – wife of Minos, King of Crete – by a white bull. The king had the half-human, half-animal creature confined to a labyrinth, and every ninth year (at the close of every Great Year) seven Athenian youths

369   A Juggler with Form   1925 – 1936

Lady in a Straw Hat
Le chapeau de paille au feuillage bleu
Juan-les-Pins, 1 May 1936
Oil on canvas, 61 x 50 cm
Not in Zervos; MPP 155
Paris, Musée Picasso

and seven Athenian maidens were offered up to the Minotaur – till finally Theseus, with Ariadne's help, slew the beast. In the 19th century the Minotaur was increasingly divorced from its mythic context, and the Surrealists took it as a symbolic figure. André Masson portrayed it, and a Surrealist magazine started in 1933, to which Picasso contributed, had its name for a title.[290] Picasso used the subject as a vehicle for personal and historical material.

The various states of the "Minotauromachy" etching, and the India-ink and gouache studies of 1936 (pp. 376 to 379), allude both to the ancient tradition and to the modern. The Minotaur invades the sculptor's studio. He is also seen dragging the dead mare, a symbol of female sexuality, from his lair. He is plagued by demons, and is vanquished by Theseus. But the creature can always be identified with the dual nature of the artist. This owes something to Nietzsche's "The Birth of Tragedy", in which Nietzsche saw art as essentially a duality, possessing Apollonian and Dionysian features. His view was an un-historical one, projected upon Greek

Head of a Woman (Olga Picasso)
Tête de femme (Olga Picasso)
Paris, 10 March 1935
Oil on canvas, 61 x 50.5 cm
Not in Zervos
Buffalo (NY), Albright-Knox Art Gallery

antiquity; but the interpretative structure it provided has proved widely useful. Picasso equated his sculptor with the Apollonian spirit, but all things intoxicated and impassioned were Dionysian. Both aspects of the creative duality appeared in his work.[291]

Of course we must remember that the violence in many of these works also reflected contemporary politics. France and indeed all of Europe was radically unstable at the time, and Fascism was on the rise. Spain had been in the hands of a military dictatorship since 1923, and it was not till 1931 that an elected government replaced it. Since 1930, the Surrealists had been increasingly committed to the Communist Party, but Picasso refused to be directly involved in politics. This does not mean that he took no interest in political events or was ignorant of social conditions, though it is true that his purchase in 1932 of Boisgeloup, a château 60 kilometres north of Paris, and his employment of a private secretary and a chauffeur, can be taken as indications of his middle-class established status.[292]

The key picture in political terms is the composition showing the

371   A Juggler with Form   1925 – 1936

372 A Juggler with Form 1925 – 1936

Minotaur in the clutches of a gryphon figure (p. 378, bottom), Picasso's variation on a famous ancient model, the Hellenistic Pasquino group, showing the dead Patroclus in the arms of Menelaus.[293] It was done as a study for the curtain for Romain Rolland's play "14 juillet", performed in Paris in summer 1936 in honour of the election victory of the French People's Front. Like the bullfight, the use of the Minotaur motif shows the subject's symbolic value in Picasso's eyes, as an expression of social concern. The parallels with the increasingly critical political situation, and Picasso's preoccupation with the Minotaur and bullfight complex, eloquently suggest the multitude of meanings these themes can convey.[294] From 1925 to 1936, Picasso used a stock of formal and thematic approaches that could be used for a great variety of purposes. It was an art of transfer. Unlike the previous period, this one did not end in a single work gathering all the strands together in one great synthesis, but in the end the times compelled him to create such a work. In 1937 he painted his great masterpiece "Guernica".

373 A Juggler with Form 1925 – 1936

Interior with a Girl Drawing
Deux femmes
Paris, 12 February 1935
Oil on canvas, 130 x 195 cm
Zervos VIII, 263
New York, The Museum of Modern Art,
Nelson A. Rockefeller Bequest

Young Woman Drawing (The Muse)
La muse
1935
Oil on canvas, 130 x 162 cm
Zervos VIII, 256
Paris, Musée National d'Art Moderne,
Centre Georges Pompidou

Right:
Woman Reading
Femme lisant
Paris, 9 January 1935
Oil on canvas, 161.5 x 129.5 cm
Zervos VIII, 260; MPP 149
Paris, Musée Picasso

**Woman with a Candle, Fight Between
Bull and Horse**
Femme à la bougie, combat entre taureau et cheval
Boisgeloup, 24 July 1934
Ink, India ink and pencil on canvas
on panel, 31.5 x 40.5 cm
Zervos VIII, 215; MPP 1136
Paris, Musée Picasso

Minotauromachy
La minotauromachie
Paris, begun 23 March 1935
Etching and grattoir, 49.8 x 69.3 cm
Bloch 288, V; Baer 373, VII
Paris, Musée Picasso

Minotaur and Horse
Minotaure et cheval
Boisgeloup, 15 April 1935
Pencil on paper, 17.5 x 25.5 cm
Zervos VIII, 244; MPP 1144
Paris, Musée Picasso

Design for the Cover of "Minotaure"
Maquette pour la couverture de "Minotaure"
Paris, May 1933
Collage: Pencil on paper, corrugated cardboard,
silver foil, silk ribbon, wallpaper overpainted
with gold and gouache, doilies, browned canvas
leaves, drawing pins and charcoal on wooden
board, 48.5 x 41 cm. Not in Zervos
New York, The Museum of Modern Art

Pages 378 and 379:
Wounded Minotaur, Horse and Figures
Minotaure blessé, cheval et personnages
Paris, 10 May 1936
Gouache, ink and India ink on paper,
50 x 65 cm. Zervos VIII, 288; MPP 1165
Paris, Musée Picasso

Study for the Curtain for "14 juillet"
by Romain Rolland
Etude pour le rideau de scène du "14 juillet"
de Romain Rolland
Paris, 28 May 1936
Gouache and India ink, 44.5 x 54.5 cm
Zervos VIII, 287; MPP 1166
Paris, Musée Picasso

Minotaur and Dead Mare Outside a Cave,
with Young Veiled Girl
Minotaure et jument morte devant une grotte
face à une jeune fille au voile
Juan-les-Pins, 6 May 1936
Gouache and India ink on paper, 50 x 65.5 cm
Not in Zervos; MPP 1163
Paris, Musée Picasso

Faun, Horse and Bird
Faune, cheval et oiseau
Paris, 5 August 1936
Gouache and India ink on pape 44.2 x 54.4 cm
Not in Zervos; MPP 1170
Paris, Musée Picasso

378   A Juggler with Form   1925 – 1936

A Juggler with Form   1925 – 1936   379

Face
Visage
1928
Lithograph, 20.4 x 14.2 cm
Bloch 95; Geiser 243;
Mourlot XXIII; Rau 23
Alling, Walther Collection

Pablo Picasso

Carsten-Peter Warncke

Pablo Picasso
1881–1973

**Edited by
Ingo F. Walther**

PART II
The Works 1937–1973

I I War, Art and "Guernica" 1937

"Guernica", filling an entire wall, is surely the best-known 20th-century work of art (pp. 400/401). It relates to a specific historical event, and expresses Picasso's political commitment. For this reason, art and politics, the creative hallmarks of the work and its historical circumstances, must be treated as inseparable.

By 1936 at the latest, Picasso's lack of interest in current political events was at an end. In April that year, the alliance of Socialists and Communists known as the Popular Front came to power in France, a development matching what had already been a reality for some months in Spain. Since the end of the military dictatorship and the proclamation of the republic on 14 April 1931, Spain had been undergoing violent social and political upheaval. In 1934 the moderate Republican and Socialist government was replaced by a coalition of Monarchists and right-wing republicans, which rescinded reforms. This prompted a miners' revolt and a general strike – bloodily put down by the army, under the supreme command of General Franco and with the assistance of Fascist Italy. In November 1934 the Falange, the Spanish wing of the international Fascist movement, was constituted. Not till 19 February 1936 did the political tide turn, when the Popular Front won the election and was able to form a government – legally and with full democratic legitimacy. The first months of that government were marked by conflict on all sides, the Falange in particular trying to crush the workers' movement via terrorist methods.

The assassination of the leader of the Monarchists on 13 July 1936 signalled the start of open revolt. On 17 July civil war began with the rebellion of the army (under Franco) in Spanish Morocco, a rebellion which spread to Spain itself on 18 July. The Republican government found itself facing an alliance of Nationalists, Falangists and anti-Republicans, led by the forces of Franco, who, helped by Italy and Nazi Germany, transferred his troops from the North African colony to Spain. The war was to last till 28 March 1939 and cost one and a half million lives. The Falangist side was aided by Italian and German troops, particularly the notorious Condor Legion, a German air force unit. The Republican government was supported by the Soviet Union and by numerous volunteers from

Page 382:
Pablo Picasso with Bread Fingers
Photograph by Robert Doisneau
Vallauris, Villa La Galloise, 1952

Pages 384 and 385:
Provoking the Bull on Horseback
("La Tauromaquia", 25)
(cf. p. 541)

Mother with Dead Child on a Ladder
Study for "Guernica" (21)
Paris, 10 May 1937 (V)
Pencil and crayon on paper,
45.7 x 24.4 cm. Zervos IX, 15
Madrid, Museo Nacional del Prado,
Cason del Buen Retiro

many countries; the official government policies of France and Great Britain, however, dictated non-intervention.[295]

From the outbreak of civil war, Picasso was on the side of the legitimate Republican government, which appointed him director of the Prado in Madrid, Spain's most important art gallery, in July 1936. In January 1937 the government commissioned him to paint a mural for the Spanish pavilion at the Paris World Fair, due to open in July. At the same time, he moved to a new studio in the Rue des Grands-Augustins in Paris (the street where Balzac's tale "Le Chef-d'œuvre inconnu" was set). At first Picasso intended to meet the commission with a representation of the freedom of art, using a studio scene with painter and model.[296] But when the news of the bombing of the holy Basque town of Guernica reached him, he changed his mind. On 26 April 1937 the town was totally destroyed in just three and a half hours by Falangist forces, Spanish, Italian and German troops, under German command. The town was of no military importance; its destruction was an act of pure terrorism. But it rapidly acquired political significance as reports of the atrocity appeared in the world press. Guernica was transformed by those reports into a symbol of modern total warfare.

And Guernica also became synonymous with the horrors of the civil war. For it was not the first time something of the sort had happened. In November 1936, for example, large numbers of the civilian population were systematically killed in the several weeks of bombardment that accompanied the attempt to take Madrid. And on 31 March 1937 the small Basque town of Durango was almost totally destroyed by German aircraft.[297] With these new impressions of war vivid in his mind, Picasso abandoned his original idea for the mural and began sketch work on a new idea on 1 May 1937. By mid-June the finished work was being mounted on the wall of the Spanish pavilion at the World Fair, and the building was officially opened on 12 July. The pavilion showcased Republican Spain in mortal jeopardy; and Picasso's painting fitted perfectly, though he made his statements exclusively in symbolic form. There was no specific depiction of warfare in the work, nor was there any emphasis on political events. In fact Guernica, the great symbol of the terror of war, had prompted an allegorical composition.[298]

The painting is monumental in effect but not oppressive. The horizontal-format composition uses seven figures, or figure groups; it is clearly yet subtly divided up. Two presentations occupy the left and right sides, with a flat triangle between. In the middle, unnaturally posed, stands a wounded horse, its neck wrenched to the left, its mouth wide open in pain. To the right, from a square space, are a stylized human head in profile and an arm holding a lighted oil lamp over the scene. Above the horse's head is an ambivalent motif: a large eye of God, surrounded by a circlet of irregular jags, with a lightbulb for a pupil – standing for sunlight as well as electric light. To the right of the horse a woman is hurrying, her pose

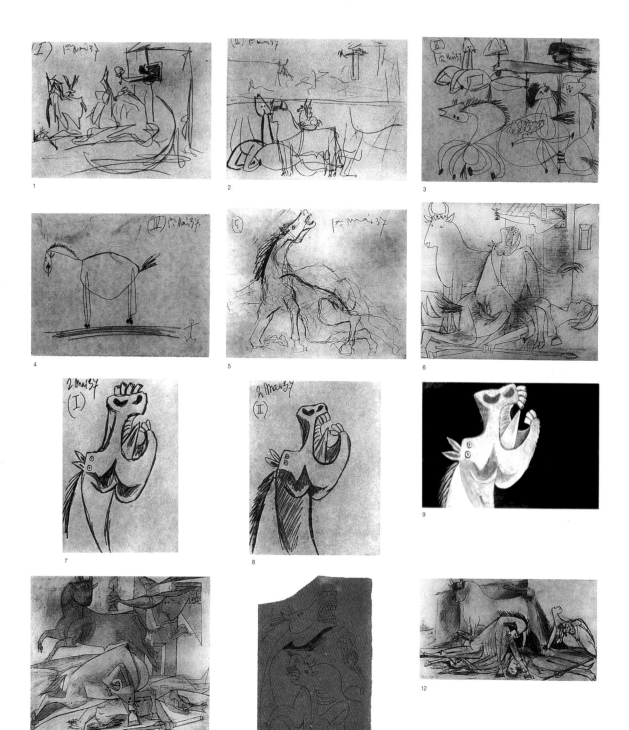

1

2

3

4

5

6

7

8

9

10

11

12

plainly conceived to fit the falling diagonal: this is where the central group is completed, in compositional terms. A counterpart to this figure is a warrior statue on the ground to the left below the horse, its arms outstretched, a broken sword in one hand. The statue has been smashed into hollow pieces.

Picasso avoids the involuntary rigidity of precision composition. The sun and lamp are to the left, the equally striking white house wall to the right of the painting's central vertical axis. Above the smashed statue stands a unified group. A mother is kneeling before a bull, screaming, holding her dead child in her arms. A corresponding figure at the right edge of the canvas has its head flung back, mouth open to cry out, and arms stretched heavenwards in a gesture of profound emotion. The use of dark and light areas and irregular jags suggests that we see this as a falling, burning figure against a house in flames. The spatial situation of the composition has been systematically unsettled by various lines leading into the depths and by irregular perspective foreshortening. The dark-light use heightens this unsettling effect of destabilization, since no definite source of light can be made out. The scene is happening neither inside nor out: it is, so to speak, everywhere.[299]

Picasso reconciled primal forms of expression, his own formal idiom, and motifs and images that were readily understandable, familiar through a long tradition. In painting "Guernica" as an allegorical history, he was using a traditional picture genre. And quite clearly the tripartite structure of the composition was an echo of the exalted triptych, the classical form of Christian altar paintings. Picasso's use of the form was utterly contemporaneous: the triptych had long since become a secular mode, and had been used in both abstract and representational art for a variety of purposes.

The great triptychs of the German painters Max Beckmann and Otto Dix were important for Picasso. Beckmann and Dix had conveyed the turmoil of the age and the horror of war in allusive yet highly realistic works.[300] Picasso, for his part, proved a virtuoso in code-shifting in traditional modes and methods. Though it is readily taken in as a whole, "Guernica" is nonetheless a work of multilayered complexity. Therein lies its attraction and greatness. It is far more than agitprop art. The preliminary studies, by a Picasso who was already fully aware of his significance in the history of art, enable us to follow the evolution of the work exactly. Forty-five dated studies and a number of photographs showing the different states of the work in progress (pp. 389 to 399) provide unparalleled documentation.[301] The labours they bear witness to were carried out with the utmost concentration. From the start on 1 May to the completion on 4 June, Picasso took just five weeks. For a work on so monumental a scale, and of such formal and thematic complexity, it is staggeringly fast. But the explanation lies in Picasso's characteristic way of working, manoeuvring motifs from his own repertoire and from the stock of European art through the ages.

13 Study for "Guernica"
Paris, 8 May 1937 (II)
Pencil on paper,
24 x 45.5 cm. Zervos IX, 12

14 Study for "Guernica"
Paris, 9 May 1937 (I)
Pencil and ink on paper,
24 x 45.3 cm. Zervos IX, 14

15 Study for "Guernica"
Paris, 9 May 1937 (II)
Pencil on paper,
24 x 45.3 cm. Zervos IX, 18

16 Study for "Guernica"
Paris, 9 May 1937 (II)
Pencil on paper,
45.3 x 24 cm. Zervos IX, 16

17 Horse. Study for "Guernica"
Paris, 10 May 1937 (I)
Pencil on paper,
24.1 x 45.6 cm. Zervos IX, 17

18 Study for "Guernica"
Paris, 10 May 1937 (II)
Pencil on paper,
45.3 x 24.3 cm. Zervos IX, 21

19 Study for "Guernica"
Paris, 10 May 1937 (III)
Pencil on paper,
45.4 x 23.9 cm. Zervos IX, 20

20 Study for "Guernica"
Paris, 10 May 1937 (IV)
Pencil and crayon on paper,
24.2 x 45.6 cm. Zervos IX, 19

21 Study for "Guernica"
Paris, 10 May 1937 (V)
Pencil and crayon on paper,
45.7 x 24.4 cm. Zervos IX, 15

22 Study for "Guernica"
Paris, 11 May 1937
Pencil on paper,
23.9 x 45.5 cm. Zervos IX, 23

23 Study for "Guernica"
Paris, 13 May 1937 (I)
Pencil and crayon on paper,
45.4 x 24 cm. Zervos IX, 22

13

14

15

16

17

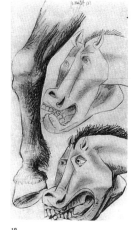

18

19

20

21

22

23

The first state (11 May) merely placed the outlines of the key figures on the canvas, not necessarily in their final positions. The bull stands over and to the right of the mother with the dead child. Beside the bull, one arm of the reclining warrior rises like the outstretched arm of a man crucified. This is plainly the central motif; the horse is turning to the warrior, too. To the right, Picasso has already drawn in the figure with the lamp, the hurrying figure, and the burning figure, but the details are different; for instance, the hurrying woman is carrying a dead body. Familiar sources in the European art tradition have influenced this composition. Peter Paul Rubens' great allegorical painting "The Horrors of War" (in Florence) provided forms and subjects for Picasso's treatment of the topic. The lying man with outstretched arms, the mother with child, the frieze effect, the overall impact of extended arms and dynamically interlinked forms, all derived from Rubens.[302]

But the figure at right with uplifted arms is no mere variant on Europa in Rubens' painting. It combines two figures against a burning house wall in Raphael's Vatican fresco of the Borgo fire.[303] And yet another traditional image influenced the woman with the dead child in her lap: the pietà of the Virgin holding the dead Christ.[304] The woman's head and the lamp are also variations on a historical motif: light as a symbol of Enlightenment, represented by an allegorical female form bearing a torch. The most famous figure of this kind is the Statue of Liberty in New York, by the French sculptor Frédéric-Auguste Bartholdi.[305] The mother with the dead child alludes to the ancient Pasquino group which Picasso had already drawn upon for his Minotaur works (p. 378). The bull and horse themselves, of course, relate to the Minotaur and bullfight complex which Picasso had been using since the mid-1930s, not least to convey political statements.

The work Picasso did on the studies and on the final canvas of "Guernica" shows how he altered what were at first unambiguously political symbols in order to endow them with universal validity. When he began work on 1 May 1937, his idea of the total picture was still fairly vague. However, sketchy as some of the preliminary work was, it did include everything of moment: the standing bull at the left, the horse in the middle, the house wall at right with the figure bearing a lamp. By 9 May, after much work on detail, the composition was ready to be transferred to the huge canvas. The last of the studies shows, however, that the first canvas state had taken the development of the idea further and was not merely a one-to-one transfer. In the sketch (p. 391 no. 15), the bull's head is turned to the right, and a large wheel has been introduced to the centre of the composition; houses are grouped around an area strewn with prostrate soldiers and the dead, not very readily distinguishable, and at right by the house wall a single arm is stretched out. The picture makes a cluttered and unclear overall impression. The first canvas state is calmer,

24 Study for "Guernica"
Paris, 13 May 1937 (II)
Pencil on paper,
23.9 x 45.4 cm. Zervos IX, 24

25 Study for "Guernica"
Paris, 13 May 1937 (III)
Pencil and crayon on paper,
23.9 x 45.5 cm. Zervos IX, 25

26 Study for "Guernica"
Paris, 20 May 1937
Pencil and gouache on paper,
23.1 x 29.2 cm. Zervos IX, 28

27 Study for "Guernica"
Paris, 20 May 1937
Pencil and gouache on paper,
23.2 x 29.2 cm. Zervos IX, 29

28 Study for "Guernica"
Paris, 20 May 1937
Pencil and gouache on paper,
29 x 23.1 cm. Zervos IX, 27

29 Study for "Guernica"
Paris, 20 May 1937
Pencil and gouache on paper,
23.1 x 29 cm. Zervos IX, 26

30 Study for "Guernica"
Paris, 20 May 1937
Pencil and gouache on paper,
29 x 23.2 cm. Zervos IX, 32

31 Study for "Guernica"
Paris, 24 May 1937
Pencil and gouache on paper,
29.2 x 23.1 cm. Zervos IX, 31

32 Study for "Guernica"
Paris, 24 May 1937
Pencil and gouache on paper,
29.2 x 23.2 cm. Zervos IX, 33

33 Study for "Guernica"
Paris, 24 May 1937
Pencil and gouache on paper,
23.1 x 29.3 cm. Zervos IX, 30

24

25

26

27

28

29

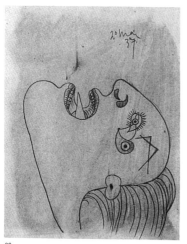

30

31

32

and the figural groupings, few in number but clearly articulated, enrich the impact of the subject.

But Picasso's reasons for altering his compositional concept once it was on canvas were not merely formal. The first state marks a caesura in terms of content too. In the sketch, crudely stylized though the presentation is, we can still make out a real market square, and so make the connection with the Basque town of Guernica. On canvas, we can no longer identify any place. Only the burning house suggests a particular inhabited place; but it stands more generally for human shelter, and its violent destruction.

Another photograph shows that in the second canvas state the lying warrior's outstretched hand was circled with a halo of fire, and many of the individual figures were painted in, in large areas of black or grey. Next Picasso got rid of the outstretched arm and transformed the aureole into the eye of God. Given the shift in the compositional weight, he turned the warrior so that his head was now at the left. The removal of the arm and clenched fist, with the aureole that emphasized them, was done for reasons of content. The gesture was an international symbol for the struggle of the Left, used by Communists and, in Spain, particularly by the Popular Front. A motif that came with so unambiguous a connotation would have reduced the entire painting to agitprop.[306]

In the next state, Picasso deliberately used the contrasts of large black, grey and white areas to define his motifs further. The photo shows how he tried out his effects before fixing them on canvas, taping wallpaper remnants over critical zones, removing them after testing the impressions, then painting in relevant details. The absence of the warrior's arm had left an empty space in the centre. To fill it, Picasso changed the position of the horse. Now it stood erect, mouth open, head tossed back to the left. This had the effect of placing sheer animal suffering, the primal scream of pain, at the heart of the composition: primaeval, emotional, a formulation directly communicating the main concern of the work.

The motif was a quotation from Picasso himself. In a gouache of 10 May 1936 on the minotaur theme (p. 378) the horse appears in the very same position as now in "Guernica"; Picasso simply transferred the lance and wound from the minotaur to the horse. This variant on a figural grouping he had been using since 1924 shows the continuity in Picasso's repertoire of motifs.[307] Picasso also changed other parts, reducing the falling figure at right by the burning wall and redefining the lamp and sun in the middle. The final version of the painting had essentially now been arrived at.

In the fifth state, its body realigned, the bull is emphatically on the left, transformed in attitude and bearing into a protector of the mother and child. Blacks, whites and greys are now deployed across the canvas with more consistent deliberation than ever. The dead body in the arms of the hurrying woman has been definitively abandoned. Yet the overall impact still does not seem quite to add

34 **Study for "Guernica"**
Paris, 27 May 1937
Pencil and gouache on paper,
23.2 x 29.3 cm. Zervos IX, 36

35 **Study for "Guernica"**
Paris, 27 May 1937
Pencil and gouache on paper,
23.2 x 29.3 cm. Zervos IX, 34

36 **Study for "Guernica"**
Paris, 28 May 1937
Pencil, crayon and gouache
on paper, 23.2 x 29.3 cm. Zervos IX, 38

37 **Study for "Guernica"**
Paris, 28 May 1937
Pencil, crayon, gouache and collage
on paper, 23.1 x 29.2 cm. Zervos IX, 37

38 **Study for "Guernica"**
Paris, 28 May 1937
Pencil, crayon and gouache
on paper, 23.2 x 29.3 cm. Zervos IX, 35

39 **Study for "Guernica"**
Paris, 31 May 1937
Pencil, crayon and gouache
on paper, 23.2 x 29.3 cm. Zervos IX, 39

40 **Study for "Guernica"**
Paris, 3 June 1937
Pencil, crayon and gouache
on paper, 23.2 x 29.3 cm. Zervos IX, 40

41 **Study for "Guernica"**
Paris, 3 June 1937
Pencil, crayon and gouache
on paper, 23.2 x 29.3 cm. Zervos IX, 44

42 **Study for "Guernica"**
Paris, 3 June 1937
Pencil, crayon and gouache
on paper, 23.2 x 29.3 cm. Zervos IX, 41

43 **Study for "Guernica"**
Paris, 3 June 1937
Pencil and gouache on paper,
23.2 x 29.2 cm. Zervos IX, 45

44 **Study for "Guernica"**
Paris, 4 June 1937
Pencil and gouache on paper,
23.2 x 29.2 cm. Zervos IX, 42

45 **Study for "Guernica"**
Paris, 4 June 1937
Pencil and gouache on paper,
23.2 x 29.2 cm. Zervos IX, 43

34

35

36

37

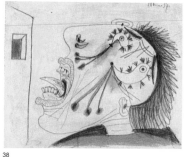

38

39

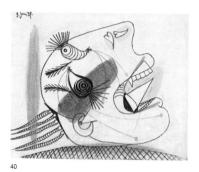

40

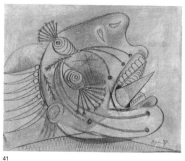

41

42

43

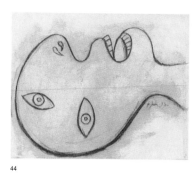

44

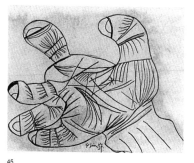

45

up: centre and sides are played off against each other, true, but at left the figure of the lying warrior makes for a diffused effect.

In states six and seven we see Picasso establishing a more cogent solution, formally and in terms of content. He left the warrior's head where it was, but turned it to look up, and, echoing a still life of 1925 (p. 315), changed the figure into a smashed statue. He used short parallel strokes to indicate the horse's coat, which introduced a dynamic restlessness to the texture of the centre. Finally Picasso reworked some of the details in the seventh state, eliminating (for example) at the very last moment the anecdotal detail of the tear rolling down the hurrying woman's cheek. The work as completed on 4 June was a composition uniquely unified in modern art, and of unparalleled conviction. Its impact derives not only from the subtle complexity of the composition and content but also from the stylized, schematic manner in which the figures are presented, at once timelessly ancient and universally accessible.

Prior to, during and after his work on "Guernica", Picasso did a series of political pictures that dealt quite differently with Franco's war on the legitimate government of Spain. These etchings bore the title "Dreams and Lies of Franco" (p. 410). In two sheets of nine scenes each, Picasso (for the only time in his entire oeuvre) used a series of pictures to indicate a time sequence. They were intended to be sold separately as single postcards in support of the aid campaign for the Spanish Republicans. On 8 and 9 January 1937 Picasso etched fourteen of the eighteen scenes, then after a break reworked them in aquatint on 25 May and completed the work on 7 June, when he added the remaining four scenes. By then he had abandoned the idea of selling individual pictures in postcard format and had decided to sell the series as a whole.[308]

This also involved a stylistic change, linked to his work on the newly completed "Guernica". Unlike the latter, "Dreams and Lies of Franco" was intended as satirical, partisan agitprop ridiculing Franco, branding his campaign as anti-human, cruel and senseless. Picasso subordinated his style to his political aims. Positive characters retained their natural form; Franco appeared deformed and surreal. Picasso illustrated stages in Franco's vanquishing at the hands of the Spanish people. For printing reasons, the scenes appear in reverse order and should be followed right to left.

In the first scene, the Caudillo appears as a perverse Christian knight, a parody of the legendary El Cid or Miguel de Cervantes' Don Quixote. Derided by the sun, he gashes his own horse. In the second, the general is tightrope walking, his monstrously erect phallus a burlesque of his machismo, his boastful stance as a glorious warrior. The third panel shows Franco using a pick in the attempt to smash a female bust (for Picasso a symbol of art and perfection): the general is a threat to culture. In the fourth scene, Franco, dressed as a woman, represents cowardice. In the fifth he is attacked by a bull, symbolic of the defeat of Fascism. The sixth

Guernica (1st state)
Paris, 11 May 1937
Oil on canvas, 349.3 x 776.6 cm
Zervos IX, 58
Madrid, Museo Nacional del Prado,
Cason del Buen Retiro

Guernica (2nd state)
Paris, May 1937
Oil on canvas, 349.3 x 776.6 cm
Zervos IX, 59
Madrid, Museo Nacional del Prado,
Cason del Buen Retiro

Guernica (3rd state)
Paris, May 1937
Oil on canvas, 349.3 x 776.6 cm
Zervos IX, 60
Madrid, Museo Nacional del Prado,
Cason del Buen Retiro

Guernica (4th state)
Paris, May 1937
Oil on canvas, 349.3 x 776.6 cm
Zervos IX, 61
Madrid, Museo Nacional del Prado,
Cason del Buen Retiro

397 War, Art and "Guernica" 1937

shows the Caudillo praying to the monstrance of high finance, in a barbed-wire compound. In the seventh, a parody of the biblical creation of the world, the general, exhausted by his labours, is resting amongst vermin. In the eighth, mounted on Pegasus, he is setting off to the sun: but he has transfixed the winged horse, symbol of poesy, with the shaft of his banner. So in scene nine we see him mounted on a pig, again setting off to the sun: the change symbolic of Franco's fall and the salvation of Spain. The tenth scene shows Pegasus dead, slain by Franco. The eleventh and twelfth show a dead woman and a dead horse, victims of Franco, the horse cradling its fallen rider with its neck. In the thirteenth, the bull is presented as Franco's enemy, killing him in the fourteenth. The last four scenes, added later, deploy figures from the "Guernica" repertoire and illustrate the sufferings of Franco's victims in the civil war.

Picasso was using motifs of his own but also others from Spanish art: figures and scenes from paintings by Velázquez and Francisco de Goya, particularly his bullfight sequence "Tauromachia". Picasso's form and content suited a direct attack on a political enemy; his style employed elements of caricature.

In "Guernica" it is entirely different. Any direct evocation of an identifiable contemporary reality or even a political grouping has been carefully avoided. The symbolic idiom is deliberately generalized. The bull and horse, through their association with bullfighting, stand for Spain: the horse is the people suffering, the bull the people triumphant, but both are victims of aggression and destructive violence. All the figures in "Guernica" are victims. The meaning of the painting, deliberately stated in general terms borrowed from Rubens' great painting, lies in its representation of the destruction of human civilization by war.

The form of the work matches its fundamental simplicity of statement perfectly. There is neither caricature nor propaganda in it. Picasso's allegory is rigorously done. The blacks, greys and whites echo the old use of grisaille in altarpieces. Nothing in the work is specific to the medium of paint: it is a draughtsman's creation. The simultaneity of perspective and figures, the juxtaposition of linear and volumed representation, and varying frontal and profiled angles of vision, are all stylistic devices Picasso had already developed in earlier work. Nevertheless, the simple primaeval power of the picture, so seemingly archaic in tone yet so sophisticated in composition, did mark a new departure. Once again, Picasso's stylistic quest had been catalysed by examination of source material.

In this case, the key is the fourth sketch of 1 May, the first detail study for "Guernica" (preceded by three compositional drafts). The study shows a horse (p. 389 no. 4). It is drawn as a child would draw a horse, its physical proportions purely symbolic, all four legs and both eyes equally visible. In the third sheet (p. 389 no. 3) there are seemingly infantile uses of line as well. These, however, are a response to surrealist figural work. Both strands – children's draw-

Guernica (5th state)
Paris, May 1937
Oil on canvas, 349.3 x 776.6 cm
Zervos IX, 62
Madrid, Museo Nacional del Prado,
Cason del Buen Retiro

Guernica (6th state)
Paris, May 1937
Oil on canvas, 349.3 x 776.6 cm
Zervos IX, 63
Madrid, Museo Nacional del Prado,
Cason del Buen Retiro

Guernica (7th state)
Paris, May 1937
Oil on canvas, 349.3 x 776.6 cm
Zervos IX, 64
Madrid, Museo Nacional del Prado,
Cason del Buen Retiro

Guernica (final state)
Paris, 4 June 1937
Oil on canvas, 349.3 x 776.6 cm
Zervos IX, 65
Madrid, Museo Nacional del Prado,
Cason del Buen Retiro

399 War, Art and "Guernica" 1937

ings and Surrealism – were interwoven and important influences. In "Guernica" Picasso combined his linear style, widely termed classical, with surreal recordings of the subconscious; and the foundation on which the combination was established was the basic idiom of children's drawings. Children's principles determined his contouring, the use of detail motifs, and the perspective.

For Picasso, the idiom of children's drawings was evidently a completely new discovery. His early professional training had given him no opportunity to draw in a childlike way himself, nor had his own children prompted in him an awareness of the child's way of seeing the world. This is all the more remarkable since Picasso had

portrayed his little son Paul drawing and painting (p. 287). It was not till the Thirties that Picasso, under the influence of Surrealism, occasionally admitted the child's manner to his work, as in "The Crucifixion" (1930; p. 337).[309] Taking a detour through another style in art, Picasso came to value the expressive power of children's art. The Surrealists, looking for modes of expression that were untainted by existing mental and cultural pressures, had discovered children's creative powers for themselves.[310] And that discovery in turn helped Picasso. Thus "Guernica", for Picasso, became a great synthesis of the very various artistic approaches he had been taking since his period of so-called classicism.

Guernica
Paris, 1 May to 4 June 1937
Oil on canvas, 349.3 x 776.6 cm
Zervos IX, 65
Madrid, Museo Nacional del Prado,
Cason del Buen Retiro

War, Art and "Guernica" 1937 **401**

12 The Picasso Style
1937–1943

In "Guernica" Picasso had arrived at the formal idiom with which we automatically associate his name. It was to inform a diverse range of works without ever again breaching his system from within. Thus his work from 1937 till his death can be seen as expressing that one style – though of course shifts in emphasis indicate changes in the artist's major interests.

The first phase saw the years in which Picasso tested the possibilities of his new style. Initially individual in character, this process of evolution ran its course at a time that could hardly have been more turbulent, dangerous or uncertain, a time of great political crisis in Europe followed by the Second World War. Picasso's art did reflect the existential menace of the age, but only indirectly. Considered dispassionately, his work seems to reverse its profile. "Guernica" had been a commissioned work, with a brief to articulate history. Under the powerful pressure of events, form had become a counter-world, art a counter-attack. This in itself was an eminently political stance. And the full dimensions of that stance become apparent if we assess the hallmarks of the Picasso style.

Since the great experiment of "Les Demoiselles d'Avignon", the subsequent further development of Cubism, and the years of so-called classicism, two mutually contradictory principles of depiction had coexisted in Picasso's art. They may be labelled dissociation and figuration.[311] Figuration is mimetic, representational art, handed down by tradition; dissociation is autonomous art, non-representationally departing from its subjects in the given world. In Picasso's work they alternate and exert a mutual influence. Figuration informed his work from the outset, even in work influenced by Surrealism. He used techniques of dissociation even in the years from 1916 to 1924 to offset his classical approaches; they were decisive in his engagement with Surrealism. The path to a synthesis was always implicit in his dual system.

Within the overall system of depiction, figuration and dissociation represent polar opposites. The former reproduces the subjective viewpoint, shows the subject as the beholder sees it. The laws of perspective apply: a subject viewed from the front cannot reveal its rear. That aspect of its appearance is left to the imagination,

Woman with Cap and Checked Dress
Femme au béret et à la robe quadrillée
Paris, 4 December 1937
Oil on canvas, 55 x 46 cm
Not in Zervos
Private collection; formerly Galerie Beyeler, Basel

figuration relying upon the associative cooperation of the beholder. Dissociation, by contrast, includes the whole subject, shows the rear as well as the frontal view if it so wishes. In this respect it is more objective. But the gain in terms of dissociative images is countered by a loss: the various elements can no longer be accommodated within a defined area, and the principle of a containing outline has to be abandoned. That principle belongs to figurative art: it includes everything in unified outlines, ensures that every subject is distinct from every other. The basic task for any depictive art seeking a synthesis of the two approaches is obvious. It has to introduce the gains of dissociative art into the realm of figuration, and vice versa. Picasso's new style did just that, using contoured, linear, figurative outlines without feeling compelled to represent the exact specifics of the given subject.

He had been working on this since the mid-Thirties. Children's art influenced him importantly; it did not depict objects in the conventional manner of the single subjective viewpoint, but it did use clearly defined outlines. Children try to depict features of an object that seem important. Their representations bear little resemblance to the originals as we in fact see them in everyday experience. Form in children's art is a kind of sign language, a system of figurative symbols. Children are not out to produce art; they are engaging with the reality before them. This, of course, is the fundamental difference between children's art and Picasso's style.

Two portraits of seated women done in 1937 before his work on

Portrait of Dora Maar
Portrait de Dora Maar
Paris, 1 October 1937
Oil and pastel on canvas,
55 x 45.5 cm
Not in Zervos; MPP 194
Paris, Musée Picasso

Portrait of Dora Maar
Portrait de Dora Maar
Paris, 23 November 1937
Oil on canvas, 55.3 x 46.3 cm
Zervos IX, 136; MPP 166
Paris, Musée Picasso

Portrait of Dora Maar Seated
Portrait de Dora Maar
Paris or Mougins, 1937
Oil on canvas, 92 x 65 cm
Zervos VIII, 331; MPP 158
Paris, Musée Picasso

"Guernica" afford clear illustrations of this. Both of them show lovers: Marie-Thérèse Walter (p. 407) and Dora Maar (p. 404). The former is dated 6 January 1937, and that of photographer Dora Maar was doubtless painted not long after. The most striking visual trick at first inspection, in both paintings, is the treatment of the faces. The outlines are profiles, but the features are seen frontally too, which is impossible in real circumstances. This dual angle of vision had been familiar in Picasso's art since the 1920s. It occurred in figure portrayals that combined the dissociative and the figurative principles. Parts of the body were dismembered, so to speak; and in the portraits of these two women Picasso transformed their clothing into autonomous visual imagery. In this he was following principles unknown to children's art: perspective and balanced proportion. Both principles are fundamental to figurative art. Picasso had already developed ways of deploying both principles freely, as he chose, in the dissociative formal idiom of Cubism. Now, with the input of ideas gleaned from children's drawings, his options had been extended to include the figurative symbolism characteristic of children's art.

The portrait of his daughter Maya, done on 16 January 1938 (p. 425), clearly reveals how capriciously Picasso handled this new system. The little girl is sitting on the floor, a doll in her arm. Her legs and skirt are rendered as geometrical blocks, unnaturally crossed; the legacy of Cubist dissociation is unmistakable. Her face

Portrait of Marie-Thérèse Walter
Portrait de Marie-Thérèse Walter
Paris, 4 December 1937
Oil and pencil on canvas,
46 x 38 cm. Not in Zervos; MPP 167
Paris, Musée Picasso

Portrait of Marie-Thérèse Walter with a Garland
Portrait de Marie-Thérèse Walter à la guirlande
Paris, 6 February 1937
Oil on canvas, 61 x 46 cm
Not in Zervos
Paris, Maya Ruiz-Picasso Collection

Portrait of Marie-Thérèse Walter
Portrait de Marie-Thérèse Walter
Paris, 6 January 1937
Oil on canvas, 100 x 81 cm
Zervos VIII, 324; MPP 159
Paris, Musée Picasso

shows the familiar combination of profile and frontal angles, the two angles not additively juxtaposed in Cubist manner but simultaneously present, as in a superimposed photograph.

By contrast, in Dora Maar's face we see the two angles in juxtaposition; the nose is both in its normal position and in profile. In the portrait of Marie-Thérèse Walter the profile view was the point of departure. It was merely extended by adding a second eye and a heightened, whiter area to suggest a cheek. In the picture of his daughter, as in the women's portraits, Picasso more or less retained the natural proportions. There is just one striking exception: the girl's right arm was painted as a child might have painted it, a short stump ending in sketchy shapes that stand for five spread fingers.

For Picasso, what was interesting in children's drawings was only the principle of formal construction. For this reason, comparison of his own work with children's drawings, though it may seem an obvious one to draw, does not make a great deal of sense. The resemblance is only superficial and only ever relates to individual features. Denunciation of Picasso's work as infantile is a cliché of contemporary art opinion. In 1937, indeed, the official German guide to the Paris World Fair declared that "Guernica" "looks as if it had been drawn by a four-year-old".[312] The Fascists used this defamatory response as freely as comparisons with the work of the mentally retarded if they wanted to disparage art.

Cubist dissociation, figuration and childlike symbolism are the three foundations on which the formal idiom of the "Picasso style" was built. They made possible a vast potential of variation. Every one of these formal systems consists of a number of characteristic features which only define a system once they appear together. But these features can be used separately, or combined with others. This fact is illustrated by the three portraits we have been examining too. In each one the artist has established an imaginary space. In none of them is it genuinely illusionist; rather, Picasso is playing with the notion of three-dimensionality, and its imitation. In the "Portrait of Marie-Thérèse Walter" zones of different colour are juxtaposed in such a way as to suggest depth. Lighter and darker shades indicate the floor, ceiling and walls. The way that they interact is suggestive of central perspective, so that there is an element of caprice in the spatial sense of the picture. In the portrait of Dora Maar, Picasso juxtaposes areas of parallel lines which, taken together, convey spatiality, since the lines run in such a way as to suggest depth. Though nothing here is indicative of exact perspective either, the illusion strikes us as more persuasive, since the basic grid of perspective foreshortenings is there. In the portrait of little Maya, two horizontal bands of white and brown suggest space. They are colours only, without any perspective construction; but the child's pose prompts us to interpret the colours as part of a room. In part, the composition depends on our powers of association, which is a traditional method in establishing backgrounds.

Great Bather with Book
Grande baigneuse au livre
Paris, 18 February 1937
Oil, pastel and charcoal on canvas,
130 x 97.5 cm
Zervos VIII, 351; MPP 160
Paris, Musée Picasso

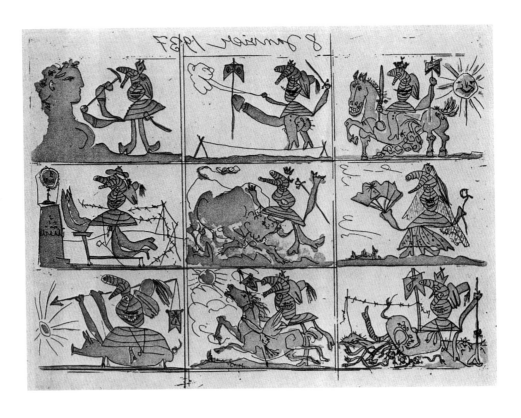

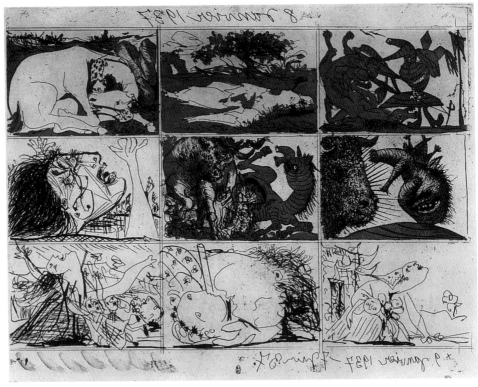

Head of a Faun
Tête de faune
1937/38
Oil on canvas, 55 x 46 cm
Not in Zervos
Estate of the artist

Head of a Faun
Tête de faune
1937/38
Oil on canvas, 76 x 56.5 cm
Not in Zervos
Private collection

Dreams and Lies of Franco I
Sueño y mentira de Franco I
Paris, 8 January 1937
Etching and aquatint, 31.4 x 42 cm
Bloch 297; Baer 615

Dreams and Lies of Franco II
Sueño y mentira de Franco II
Paris, 8 and 9 January to 7 June 1937
Etching and aquatint, 31.4 x 42 cm
Bloch 298; Baer 616

What is true of the construction of spatial values is also true of the presentation of figures – for instance, in another picture of Maya also painted in January 1938 (p. 424). The child herself and the toy boat in her hands are established with blocks of bright juxtaposed colour, but details such as the hair style and clothes are reproduced figuratively. The face is a schematic design of purely linear, crudely drawn eyes, nose and mouth, using triangular areas of white, green, red, blue and yellow colour. These areas have no intrinsic figural meaning whatsoever; indeed, they are at odds with figural representation. But once they are there, as parts of the face, we respond to them as we would to the modelled three-dimensionality of differently-lit parts of a face.

A diametrically opposed method is at work in a study of a seated woman done on 27 April 1938 in India ink, gouache and crayon (p. 417). It is a study in both the autonomy and the functionality of the line. The woman's head is done in the familiar combination of frontal and profile; and, in the process, the line as an instrument for conveying form has taken on an independent life of its own. Admittedly an identifiable image of a body has been produced, and thus a certain representational value; but the picture is a fabric of webs and meshes. This use of lines totally alters the character of the image. The line is no longer subordinated to representation of the sitter; rather, the seated figure is an excuse to play with lines. Naturally enough, most of the forms are angular. In the December

Weeping Woman
La femme qui pleure
Paris, 18 October 1937
Oil on canvas, 55.3 x 46.3 cm
Not in Zervos; MPP 165
Paris, Musée Picasso

Woman Crying
La suppliante
Paris, 18 December 1937
Gouache and India ink on panel, 24 x 18.5 cm
Not in Zervos; MPP 168
Paris, Musée Picasso

413

Weeping Woman
Femme en pleurs
Paris, 26 October 1937
Oil on canvas, 60 x 49 cm
Zervos IX, 73
London, Tate Gallery

Woman with Cockerel
Femme au coq
Paris, 15 February 1938
Oil on canvas, 145.5 x 121 cm
Zervos IX, 109
Baltimore (MD), The Baltimore Museum of Art

1938 "Seated Woman in a Garden" (p. 423) Picasso went on to combine autonomy of block with autonomy of line. Since "Guernica", Picasso had essentially been ringing the same changes on the fundamentals of visual presentation as he had been doing in the Cubist phase.

What did make a considerable difference was the fact that his free variation was now always contained within a defined outline, a figural shape. This is particularly apparent if we look at "Women at Their Toilette" (pp. 426/427), done in spring 1938. This cartoon for a tapestry combined the papiers collés technique with conventional oil on canvas, thus, true to Picasso's new synthesis, combining dissociative Cubism's technical achievements with the painting method of traditional figurative art. He found he could use this variation of formal principles to communicate statements. In the "Portrait of Maya with Her Doll" Cubist, figurative and childlike approaches to form complement each other in a way that seems wholly apt to the subject – a child. The interchange of defining characteristics is apt in a similar way. The doll, for instance, has a more human face than the child: its big eyes, tiny nose and full, slightly pouting lips add up to a schematic, stylized baby-face. Using sophisticated juxtapositions of this kind, Picasso contrived to load simple compositions with details of defining quality.

We see this vividly if we compare the portraits of Marie-Thérèse Walter and Dora Maar. Marie-Thérèse's hat and dress consist of

Man with Ice Cream Cone
Homme au cornet de glace
Mougins, 14 August 1938
Oil on canvas, 61 x 50 cm
Zervos IX, 206
Geneva, Fondation Marina Picasso

Man in a Straw Hat Holding an Ice Cream Cone
Homme au chapeau de paille et au cornet de glace
Paris or Mougins, 30 August 1938
Oil on canvas, 61 x 46 cm
Zervos IX, 205; MPP 174
Paris, Musée Picasso

Seated Woman
Femme assise
Paris, 27 April 1938
Gouache, crayon and ink on paper,
76.5 x 55 cm. Zervos IX, 133
Basel, Beyeler Collection

Still Life with Red Bull's Head
Nature morte: Bougie, palette,
tête de taureau rouge
Paris, 26 November 1938
Oil on canvas, 97 x 130 cm
Zervos IX, 239
New York, Mr. and Mrs. William
A. M. Burden Collection

lined patterns that give a mood of yielding softness. The rounded contours of her body give the same impression. The sitter is manifestly being portrayed as a calm, gentle, unaggressive personality. Dora Maar strikes us quite differently, though. Using the pattern of her dress as a pretext, Picasso emphasizes angularity, and the note of aggressiveness this strikes is reinforced by the signal red and dark violet shades. Maar's long fingers are like daggers; and her face, done in loud, bright yellows, greens and reds in a crescendo of intensity, only underlines the shrill impact.

The colours and poses in both portraits are similar, yet the overall image is entirely different. One is all calm and *joie de vivre*; the other is nervousness and tension. In both portraits the artist has succeeded in conveying that most intangible of things, a human personality. And he has done it without stressing facial expressions or poses, which customarily establish the character of a sitter.

Another important work that used the new method of depiction grew out of the work on "Guernica". After he had completed that enormous canvas, Picasso did a number of studies on the time-honoured subject of grief, showing a woman weeping into a handkerchief. Using his combined dissociative and figurative method, he dissected the faces into lines and experimented with various colour bases applied in different ways.[313] When he had tried out combinations to his satisfaction, he produced an oil of moderate size which he completed on 26 October 1937 (p. 414). Again the composition combines a frontal and profile view of the face. Furthermore, the face has also been splintered into shards contoured with thick lines, and these shards, painted in shades of varying degrees of aggressiveness, serve to heighten an overall impression of shattered nervousness (as in the portrait of Dora Maar). The handkerchief, hand

The Cock
Le coq
Paris, 29 March 1938
Pastel, 77.5 x 54 cm
Zervos IX, 113
New York, Mr. and Mrs. Ralph
F. Colin Collection

Still Life with Candle, Palette and Black Bull's Head
Nature morte avec bougie, palette et tête de taureau noire
Paris, 1938
Oil on canvas, 97 x 130 cm
Zervos IX, 240
Estate of the artist

Still Life with Candle, Palette and Red Head of Minotaur
Nature morte avec bougie, palette et tête de Minotaure rouge
Paris, 27 November 1938
Oil on canvas, 73 x 92 cm
Not in Zervos
Estate of the artist

and face interconnect (and in this respect extend the method used in "Les Demoiselles d'Avignon"); the treatment defies the natural definition of the individual motifs. This is the most fractured portion of the picture, and the rest of the head, and the background, are juxtaposed in relative tranquillity and clarity of definition. The composition perfectly conveys the act of crying; it catches the expression of profound emotional crisis exactly. Picasso can well afford to dispense with conventional attention to detail. Only the one or two rounded shapes suggest tears; the anecdotal flavour of big

419 The Picasso Style 1937–1943

The Sailor
Le marin
Mougins, 31 July 1938
Oil on canvas, 58.5 x 48 cm
Zervos IX, 191
Geneva, Heinz Berggruen Collection

Man with Ice Cream Cone
Homme au cornet de glace
23 July 1938
India ink on paper, 30.5 x 23 cm
Zervos IX, 188

round sobbed tears has been carefully avoided. Here, it is the shattered form that conveys the shattered feelings.

Given the associative relation of Picasso's forms to the emotional content, he succeeds in presenting things which are fundamentally open to analogy – the aim of figurative painting. But the Picasso style is actually far richer in technical scope, and in a position to reformulate the traditional aims of visual presentation – without by any means dropping historical work, genre scenes or other conventional types of painting.

A signal example of this is "Night Fishing at Antibes" (p. 430), a large composition painted in 1939. Real experience lay behind it; Picasso spent the last summer of peace with Dora Maar at Antibes on the Côte d'Azur, and in the evenings he would watch the fishermen going out to fish by acetylene lamp. The painting that resulted is anecdotal at heart. Dora Maar is to be seen to the right of the harbour, with her bike, eating an ice cream. Beside her is Breton's wife Jacqueline Lamba, and at the very back we can make out the Palais Grimaldi. The centre of the picture is occupied by the

Woman in a Straw Hat
Femme au chapeau de paille sur fond fleuri
Paris, 25 June 1938
Oil on canvas, 73 x 60 cm
Not in Zervos
Galerie Rosengart

fishermen, spearing childishly-scrawled fish from the deep green waters. The contrast of darkness and colour establishes a night-time scene both cheerful and yet enigmatic.

Picasso was thus able to deploy his formal means to achieve very different results. His work from 1937 to 1943 saw him continually testing those differences. One of the most important pictures of the period was the "Nude Dressing Her Hair" (p. 439), painted in May and June 1940 in his studio at Royan. In the bottom quarter of the canvas Picasso has placed a violet trapezoid, with two dark green vertical trapezoids at the sides, a thin, almost black triangle at the top, and a large, not quite regular rectangular area of olive green between the two dark green sides. This suggests a space or room: the illusion is almost of a view through a peephole, framing the subject, a seated woman with her arms behind her head. She occupies almost the entire canvas, so that she not only has a monumental quality but also makes the space seem cramped. The use of this tight compositional grid introduced a note of disquiet: the figure's attitude calls for elbow room, but space is precisely

Pages 422 and 423:
Seated Woman in an Armchair
Femme assise dans un fauteuil
31 May 1938
Oil on canvas, 188 x 129.5 cm
Not in Zervos. Estate of Jacqueline Picasso

Seated Woman in a Garden
Femme assise dans un jardin
Paris, 10 December 1938
Oil on canvas, 131 x 97 cm
Zervos IX, 232. New York,
Mr. and Mrs. Daniel Saidenberg Collection

Pages 424 and 425:
Maya with a Boat
Maya au bateau
Paris, 30 January 1938
Oil on canvas, 61 x 46 cm
Not in Zervos
Galerie Rosengart

Portrait of Maya with Her Doll
Portrait de Maya avec sa poupée
Paris, 16 January 1938
Oil on canvas, 73.5 x 60 cm
Zervos IX, 99; MPP 170. Paris, Musée Picasso

The Picasso Style 1937–1943 **421**

Women at Their Toilette
(Cartoon for a tapestry)
Femmes à leur toilette
Paris, spring 1938
Pasted wallpaper and gouache
on paper, 299 x 448 cm
Zervos IX, 103; MPP 176
Paris, Musée Picasso

Above:
Woman with Mauve Hat
Femme au chapeau mauve
Royan, 27 October 1939
Oil on canvas, 55 x 46 cm
Zervos IX, 363. Private collection;
formerly Galerie Beyeler, Basel

Right:
The Yellow Sweater (Dora Maar)
Le chandail jaune (Dora Maar)
Royan, 31 October 1939
Oil on canvas, 81 x 65 cm
Not in Zervos
Geneva, Heinz Berggruen Collection

Self-Portrait
Royan, 11 August 1940
Pencil on paper, 16 x 11 cm
Zervos XI, 82

what this painting, in a direct appeal to our emotions, denies her. Picasso has emphasized this disquiet. The figure's bodily proportions are unnatural. The feet still follow nature, albeit in crudely simplified form; but thighs, knees and calves are harshly juxtaposed, angular areas of light beige and dark brown. The figure is rendered with extreme foreshortening, a capricious use of perspective, and a playful rethinking of the elements of visual presentation. Whole parts of the body (such as the left thigh) are simply left out. The face is no longer an overlapping yoking of frontal and profile views as in the portraits of Dora Maar or Marie-Thérèse; rather, the silhouette and full-face are crudely juxtaposed at different heights. There is a curious duality in the way the figure has been done. It might be described as mechanization of the organic, and stylizing of the mechanical, both principles so interwoven that it is difficult to make out what is happening in the picture.

Though Picasso was plainly performing a variation on stylistic approaches he had already tested, "Nude Dressing Her Hair" was not spontaneously done. In fact a large number of sketches and studies preceded it. In various sketch-books there are a total of well over 200.[314] One of these books, started at Royan on 10 January 1940 and finished there on 26 May the same year, sheds particularly instructive light on Picasso's work methods. It not only contains studies for "Nude Dressing Her Hair". The first drawings are

hasty sketches after Delacroix's famous painting "The Women of Algiers" (1834), which Picasso knew well from visits to the Louvre. In these sketches, Picasso was internalizing the compositional options made available by Delacroix's painting; in the process he redistributed the components in geometrically rounded or conical form (p. 438 no. 2). If Picasso had not expressly noted the original he was following, we should scarcely be able to identify any connection. In other sketches, Picasso schematically rendered details of the original. Then at length a study of Delacroix's two seated women prompted him to a figural idea of his own (p. 438 no. 3). What is most striking in this sketch is the use of profile and frontal views of the face at split levels – the very device he was to use in the finished "Nude Dressing Her Hair" and which he had already employed in "Seated Woman in a Garden" (p. 423). In the next sketch Picasso further dissected the forms. There is a twofold rationale to such a method: it connotes both distance (and thus independence of the given subject) and the presence of a specific original. Because the forms being conjoined are discrete and distinctly abstract, the leeway for further metamorphosis is considerable. This left Picasso the option of projecting physical forms into the largely neutral shapes of his first sketches, and then rendering his further studies specific in the same way, by establishing legs, arms, and a chest and abdomen.

Still Life with Bull's Head
Nature morte avec tête de taureau
29 January 1939
Oil on canvas. Zervos IX, 238
Cleveland (OH), The Cleveland Museum of Art

Left:
Night Fishing at Antibes
Pêche de nuit à Antibes
Antibes, August 1939
Oil on canvas, 205.7 x 345.4 cm
Zervos IX, 316
New York, The Museum of Modern Art,
Mrs. Simon Guggenheim Fund

Plainly – and this is what makes the process so utterly fascinating – the associations were not altogether free. It is even possible to follow them and recreate a thought process. As he reshaped the figure, Picasso was toying with a motif he had long been using, that of the female nude with arms raised and crooked behind her head, a classic nude pose which he had already used in a key position in "Les Demoiselles d'Avignon". Picasso worked on "Nude Dressing Her Hair" for a full six months. It was typical of his work methods that in the process he was continually taking his bearings from a particular point of departure, in this case Delacroix's painting.

At heart, all Picasso's paintings to the end of the Second World War were interrelated. When the "Nude Dressing Her Hair" was finished, he adapted the pose and compositional grid to "Boy with Lobster" (p. 443). It was not an isolated case of adaptation. Indeed, the range of subjects he covered was palpably limited if we compare with earlier periods, and he introduced few new motifs. This is an indication of Picasso's interest in experiment at the time, of course: he used and re-used the same motifs, but placed his emphases differently. Thus he did a large number of portraits of seated women, and an immense number of busts and portraits. The sheer quantity ought not to blind us to the fact that even among the limited range of motifs there were interrelations. The sitting position in the portraits of Dora Maar, Marie-Thérèse, and his daughter Maya, and the preliminaries for the "Nude Dressing Her Hair", was a single position, somewhat varied. The location of a style was merely one aspect (a formal one) of this output; Picasso's serial work also had an unmistakable, strongly self-referential component. His fruitful interest in the work of contemporaries had waned. This, however, was less the fault of the artist than of the

Above:
Reclining Woman with a Book (Marie-Thérèse Walter)
Femme couchée lisant (Marie-Thérèse Walter)
Le Tremblay-sur-Mauldre, 21 January 1939
Oil on canvas, 96.5 x 130.5 cm
Zervos IX, 253; MPP 177. Paris, Musée Picasso

Head of a Woman
Tête de femme
7 January 1939
Oil and Ripolin on paper, 43 x 29 cm
Zervos IX, 250. Private collection

Right:
Marie-Thérèse Leaning on One Elbow
Marie-Thérèse accoudée
Paris, 7 January 1939
Oil on canvas, 65 x 46 cm
Not in Zervos
Paris, Maya Ruiz-Picasso Collection

Portrait of Marguerite Walter (Mémé)
Portrait de Marguerite Walter (Mémé)
Royan, 21 October 1939
Oil and pencil on canvas, 41 x 33 cm
Zervos IX, 367
Paris, Maya Ruiz-Picasso Collection

Portrait of Jaime Sabartés as Spanish Grandee
Portrait de Jaime Sabartés en grand d'Espagne
Royan, 22 October 1939
Oil on canvas, 45.7 x 38 cm
Zervos IX, 366; MPB 70.241
Barcelona, Museu Picasso

Head of a Woman
Tête de femme
Royan, 30 November 1939
Oil on canvas, 65 x 54.5 cm
Zervos IX, 375; MPP 183. Paris, Musée Picasso

age: it was, after all, a time of pre-war crises, the Second World War, and the occupation of France by the Germans.

The political situation forced Picasso into isolation. First, he was cut off from his homeland by the Spanish Civil War and the victory of Franco's Falangists. And then, after the German invasion of France, the Paris art scene changed in a way that peculiarly affected Picasso, the great practitioner of Modernism. As in the First World War, when everything was in a state of flux and upheaval, but even more so now because of the alien occupational rule, the arts in France were dominated by the summons to traditional French values. Independence in the arts was now viewed with deep suspicion. What the journalists and arts officers wanted instead was applied art. Maurice de Vlaminck, once a leading member of the Fauves, was foremost in this new line, branding Picasso (in a malicious article written for "Comoedia" magazine in 1942) as the pre-eminent modern artist who must bear the responsibility for the decline of the arts. The old, defamatory clichés revealingly made their appearance in the piece, particularly the claim that Picasso was a pernicious foreigner whose un-French spirit was having a destructive influence on the culture of the great French nation.

A group that had previously been marginalized, a group whose anti-modern position had rendered it unimportant for the evolution of the arts, was now dominant in the official scene in France. As in Fascist countries, so too in France, political change had

Seated Woman with Bird
Femme assise avec oiseau
17 June 1939
Oil on canvas, 92 x 73 cm
Not in Zervos. Private collection

Seated Woman with Red and Blue Hat
Femme assise au chapeau bleu et rouge
17 June 1939
Oil on canvas, 92 x 73 cm
Not in Zervos. Estate of the artist

Bust of a Woman Wearing a Striped Hat
Buste de femme au chapeau rayé
Paris, 3 June 1939
Oil on canvas, 81 x 54 cm
Not in Zervos; MPP 180
Paris, Musée Picasso

Cat Catching a Bird
Chat saisissant un oiseau
Paris, 22 April 1939
Oil on canvas, 81 x 100 cm
Zervos IX, 296; MPP 178
Paris, Musée Picasso

brought with it the triumph of reactionaries in the arts. Not that the Modernists did not defend their position vigorously. André Lhote and Jean Bazaine immediately protested in print against Vlaminck's article. The major Modernist artists remained visible in gallery exhibitions (if they were French). Two fronts were defined. On the one side were the reactionary, nationalist advocates of traditional art, and those artists who collaborated with the Nazis. They all agreed to go on a study tour of Germany in 1941, and in 1942

Cat Eating a Bird
Chat dévorant un oiseau (Chat à l'oiseau)
Le Tremblay-sur-Mauldre, April 1939
Oil on canvas, 96.5 x 128.9 cm
Zervos IX, 297
New York, Mr. and Mrs. Victor W. Ganz
Collection

Café at Royan
Le café à Royan
Royan, 15 August 1940
India ink on paper, 21.5 x 27 cm
Zervos XI, 87

Café at Royan
Café à Royan (Le café)
Royan, 15 August 1940
Oil on canvas, 97 x 130 cm
Zervos XI, 88; MPP 187
Paris, Musée Picasso

437 The Picasso Style 1937–1943

1 **Study for "Women of Algiers"** (after Delacroix)
Royan, January 1940
Pencil on paper, 10.5 x 15.5 cm
Zervos X, 206

2 **Study for "Women of Algiers"** (after Delacroix)
Royan, January 1940
Pencil on paper, 10.5 x 15.5 cm
Zervos X, 204

3 **Study for "Nude Dressing Her Hair"**
(Carnet 106). Royan, January 1940
Pencil on paper, 15.5 x 10.5 cm
Zervos X, 209

4 **Study for "Nude Dressing Her Hair"**
(Carnet 106). Royan, January 1940
Pencil on paper, 15.5 x 10.5 cm
Zervos X, 214

5 **Study for "Nude Dressing Her Hair"**
(Carnet 106). Royan, January 1940
Pencil on paper, 15.5 x 10.5 cm
Zervos X, 216

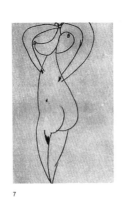

6 **Study for "Nude Dressing Her Hair"**
(Carnet 106). Royan, January 1940
Pencil on paper, 15.5 x 10.5 cm
Zervos X, 220

7 **Study for "Nude Dressing Her Hair"**
(Carnet 106). Royan, January 1940
Pencil on paper, 15.5 x 10.5 cm
Zervos X, 225

8 **Study for "Nude Dressing Her Hair"**
(Carnet 106). Royan, January 1940
Pencil on paper, 15.5 x 10.5 cm
Zervos X, 241

9 **Study for "Nude Dressing Her Hair"**
(Carnet 106). Royan, January 1940
Pencil on paper, 15.5 x 10.5 cm
Zervos X, 249

10 **Study for "Nude Dressing Her Hair"**
(Carnet 106). Royan, January 1940
Pencil on paper, 15.5 x 10.5 cm
Zervos X, 510

11 **Study for "Nude Dressing Her Hair"**
(Carnet 106). Royan, January 1940
Pencil on paper, 19 x 11.8 cm
Zervos X, 511

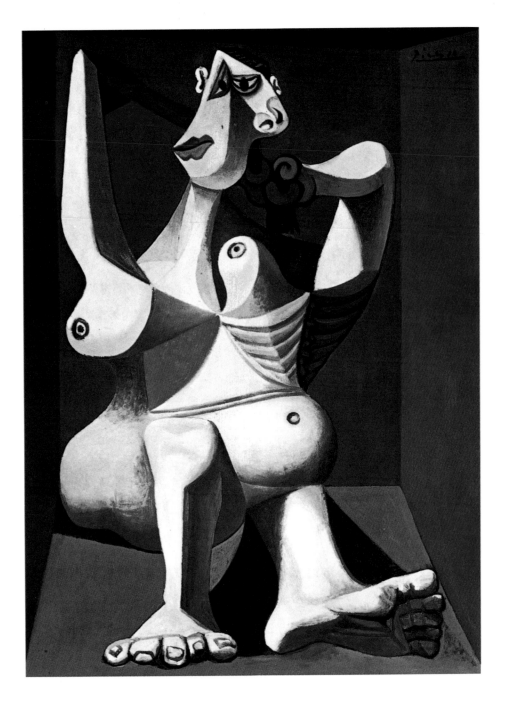

Nude Dressing Her Hair
Femme se coiffant
Royan, 6 March to June 1940
Oil on canvas, 130 x 97 cm
Zervos X, 302
New York, Mrs. Bertram Smith Collection

439

440 The Picasso Style 1937–1943

Woman with Hat Seated in an Armchair
Femme au chapeau assise dans un fauteuil
Paris, summer 1941. Oil on canvas,
130.5 x 97.5 cm. Zervos XI, 374
Basel, Öffentliche Kunstsammlung Basel,
Kunstmuseum

Seated Woman (Dora Maar)
Femme assise (Dora Maar)
Paris, June 1941. Oil on canvas,
99.8 x 80.5 cm. Not in Zervos
Munich, Staatsgalerie moderner Kunst

Left:
Seated Woman in an Armchair
Femme assise dans un fauteuil
September 1941. Oil on canvas,
130 x 97 cm. Zervos XI, 283

Seated Woman in an Armchair
Paris, 12 October 1941
Oil on canvas, 80.7 x 65 cm
Zervos XI, 340. Düsseldorf,
Kunstsammlung Nordrhein-Westfalen

Seated Woman in an Armchair
October 1941
Oil on canvas, 130 x 97 cm
Zervos XI, 94. Private collection

Seated Woman in an Armchair
23 October 1941. Oil on canvas,
92 x 73 cm. Zervos XI, 343

constituted an honorary committee for a large-scale show of work by Nazi sculptor Arno Breker at the Orangerie des Tuileries. As well as Vlaminck, this group included Derain, Dunoyer de Segonzac and Othon Friesz, to name only the more familiar artists. On the other side were young French artists, such as Charles Lapicque and Bazaine, who exhibited in a 1941 show of Modernist painting. Like other radical Modernists, such as Alfred Manessier, Nicolas de Staël and Jean Dubuffet, their endeavours all tended to the continuation of pure abstraction.[315]

For Picasso there was no room – as a contemporary artist, that is, rather than a mere cult figure of the Modernist movement. Thus he was doubly isolated during the war. Furthermore, he personally felt very deeply affected by the consequences of the occupation. In autumn 1940 he moved entirely to the Rue des Grands-Augustins studio, which was to be his sole space through the dark years till 1944. After his years of travels to the Côte d'Azur, or lengthy sojourns at Royan on the Atlantic coast, he was now compelled to lead an unsatisfying life in occupied Paris, cut off from an arts scene with any life to it, and confronted every day with the troubles of wartime, such as the impossibility of heating in winter. Throughout that difficult time, Picasso adhered to a policy of non-intervention. He took no sides: he refrained from direct involvement in the Résistance (in contrast to his friend Paul Eluard), but also kept a polite

Bull's Head on a Table
Tête de taureau sur une table
Paris, 6 April 1942
Oil on canvas, 116 x 89 cm
Zervos XII, 35
Milan, Emilio Jesi Collection

distance from the Germans. True, his studio was open to German visitors; but when they came he would give them postcard reproductions of "Guernica", and on one famous occasion, when a German officer asked Picasso, "Did you do that?" the artist replied, "No, you did." Moreover, when he ran out of fuel, he declined to accept special favours as a non-French national, and observed: "A Spaniard is never cold."[316]

His work recorded the wartime situation indirectly. The version of "Still Life with Steer's Skull" (1942; p. 445) now in Düsseldorf records the German commandant's order to black out Paris at night. The gloomy, claustrophobic "L'Aubade" (p. 446) conveys the oppressive mood of the war years too. The subtly allusive mode of these paintings reflects a practice common among contemporaries. The younger French abstract artists, for instance, preferred

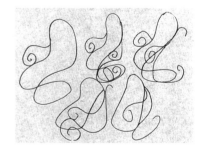

Study for a Rocking Chair
Etude pour un fauteuil à bascule
Paris, 1943
Pencil on paper, 22 x 14 cm
Zervos XIII, 71

Boy with Lobster
Jeune garçon à la langouste
Paris, 21 June 1941
Oil on canvas, 130 x 97.3 cm
Zervos XI, 200; MPP 189
Paris, Musée Picasso

the French national colours of red and blue for their non-representational paintings, for expressly political reasons.[317]

Though his personal situation was a melancholy one, Picasso's fame abroad was then growing apace. "Guernica" was of key significance in the process. In 1938 the painting embarked on its travels, being exhibited first in London and then in the USA. In America in particular, Picasso came to be recognised as the foremost modern artist in those years. In 1937, the newly-founded Museum of Modern Art in New York bought "Les Demoiselles d'Avignon", and in 1940, together with the Art Institute of Chicago, mounted the major retrospective "Picasso. 40 Years of his Art", which was seen in no fewer than ten major American cities. In the eyes of the Americans, the tour established Picasso as the most important living artist of the century.[318]

443 The Picasso Style 1937–1943

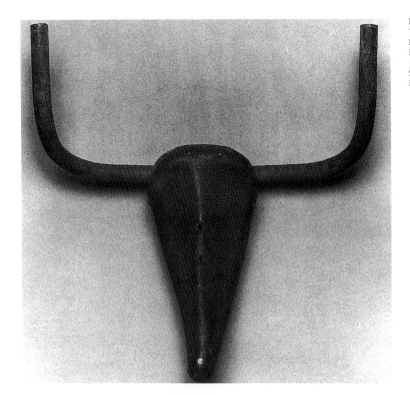

Head of a Bull
Tête de taureau
Paris, spring 1942
Bicycle saddle and handlebars,
33.5 x 43.5 x 19 cm
Spies 240 I; MPP 330
Paris, Musée Picasso

Death's Head
Tête de mort
Paris, 1943
Bronze, 25 x 21 x 31 cm
Spies 219 II; MPP 326
Paris, Musée Picasso

Right:
Still Life with Steer's Skull
Nature morte avec crâne de bœuf
Paris, 5 April 1942
Oil on canvas, 130 x 97 cm
Not in Zervos
Düsseldorf, Kunstsammlung
Nordrhein-Westfalen

L'Aubade
L'Aubade (Nu allongé avec musicienne)
Paris, 4 May 1942
Oil on canvas, 195 x 265.4 cm
Zervos XII, 69
Paris, Musée National d'Art Moderne,
Centre Georges Pompidou

Still Life with Guitar
Nature morte à la guitare
Paris, 1942
Oil on canvas, 100 x 81 cm
Not in Zervos
Private collection

Right:
Female nude
Femme nue
1941
Oil on canvas, 92 x 65 cm
Zervos XI, 198
Paris, Courtesy Galerie Louise Leiris

448 The Picasso Style 1937–1943

449 The Picasso Style 1937–1943

Bust of a Woman
Buste de femme
7 October 1943
Oil on canvas, 73 x 60 cm
Zervos XIII, 139
Private collection. Paris, Courtesy Galerie Louise Leiris

450

Seated Nude Woman Gazing at a Sleeping Man
Femme nue assise contemplant un homme endormi
Paris, 20 January 1943
India ink on paper, 49 x 65 cm
Zervos XII, 219; MPP 1327
Paris, Musée Picasso

Sleeping Man and Seated Woman
Homme couché et femme assise
Paris, 19 January 1943
India ink on paper, 51 x 65.5 cm
Zervos XII, 218
Geneva, Fondation Marina Picasso

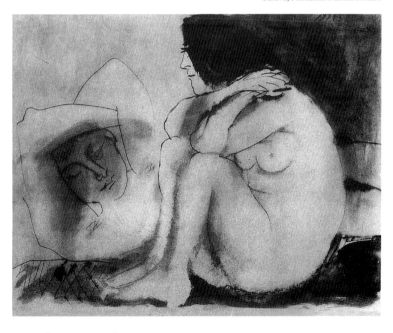

451 The Picasso Style 1937–1943

War
La guerre
Vallauris, 1952
Oil on hardboard, 4.5 x 10.5 m
Zervos XV, 196
Vallauris, Temple de la Paix

Peace
La paix
Vallauris, 1952
Oil on hardboard, 4.5 x 10.5 cm
Zervos XV, 197
Vallauris, Temple de la Paix

13 Politics and Art
1943–1953

His whole life long, Picasso was a man who throve on exchange with other people, and his isolation during the occupation was not easily to be borne. His work of the period alluded cautiously to the universal doom, and articulated with increasing directness that inner sense of involvement which cried out for expression. "L'Aubade" (p. 446) was Picasso's way of presenting an ambiguous statement in idyllic garb. It shows a seated figure playing a mandolin and a reclining nude. The unbroken blocks of colour and the draughtsman's precise outlines are by no means in harmony; rather, they create an atmosphere of conflict. The figures seem contorted and fractured, the inside of anatomy turned out; fully physical though they are, they reveal the skeletal figure of Death.

The Temple of Peace at Vallauris
Photograph, 1952

Picasso's style neatly met the time's requirements of subtlety and allusiveness. Open political commitment, or indeed direct accusation, would have put him in personal jeopardy. To the more sensitive observers of the age, such as the German writer Ernst Jünger, the existential depth of such paintings was perfectly apparent: "Never had it been so powerfully and oppressively clear to me that the homunculus is more than an idle product of the imagination. The image of Man is foreseen as by a magus, and few sense the terrible profundity of the decision taken by the painter. Though I repeatedly tried to turn our talk to this subject, he evaded it, doubtless on purpose."[319]

Of course Picasso evaded it. Open discussion of the problem would have forced him to take an unambiguous stand. The writer, after all, was wearing the uniform of the army of occupation, and their talk turned upon the real political background of aesthetic approaches. For Picasso, it was important to retain the ambiguity of form as a mask disguising his critique of the times. He refashioned for his own ends Surrealist techniques using camouflage, satirical incongruity and imagery that made its appeal to the unconscious. He was not only painting; he was also writing prose, and experimenting with his own brand of calligraphy, a meaningless kind of hieroglyphic automatic writing with which he filled pages.

In January 1941 Picasso wrote "Desire Caught by the Tail" – a

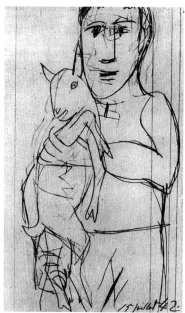

play (first published in 1944)[320] about the privations of the Parisians during the occupation. The hero of the piece is Big Foot, who endeavours to win the favour of the Tart. The Onion is his rival. The Tart has a Cousin and two friends, Fat Anxiety and Thin Anxiety. In addition we meet Round Piece, the Two Bow Wows, Silence and the Curtain. The farce, in six acts, is about basic passions and instincts. The characters try in vain to stave off cold and starvation and assuage their need for love.[321]

The play was performed (if not publicly) on 14 May 1944, before the end of the German occupation. Friends and acquaintances on the arts scene gave a rehearsed reading in Michel Leiris's flat. Albert Camus directed the reading; Jean-Paul Sartre played Round Piece, Leiris read Big Foot, the writer Raymond Queneau the Onion, and the female parts were taken by Simone de Beauvoir, Dora Maar, Louise Leiris and actress Zanie Aubier. A number of people came to hear the reading, among them Braque and Jacques Lacan. Tellingly, the writers and philosophers were in the majority. Pressured by circumstances, Picasso was returning to the literary scene, which had meant so much to him before, especially in his Blue and Rose Periods. After the reading he invited the actors and audience round to his studio, where he showed them the original manuscript of Alfred Jarry's farce "Ubu Cocu", one of the cycle of Ubu plays including the famous "Ubu Roi". Jarry's work was the very epitome of artistic anarchy in the opening years of the 20th century, and the source of Picasso's farce.[332]

But the days of salon revolutions were long over. Picasso's friends Robert Desnos and Max Jacob had died in concentration camps; others had actively fought for the liberation of France. Picasso

Study for "Man with Sheep"
Etude pour "L'homme au mouton"
Paris, 19 August 1942
India ink on paper, 18.2 x 9.5 cm
Zervos XII, 125. Private collection

Man with Sheep
L'homme au mouton
Paris, February or March 1943
Bronze, 222.5 x 78 x 78 cm
Spies 280 II; MPP 331
Paris, Musée Picasso

Politics and Art 1943–1953 **455**

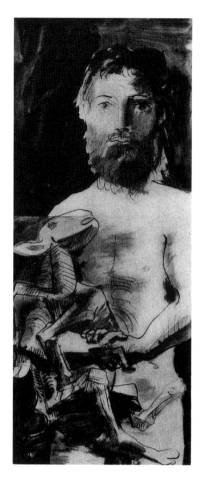

renewed his contacts with intellectual circles, mainly in order to share in their espousal of Résistance aims. The Allied landings and the reconquest of France, followed by the end of the Second World War, marked a turning point in Picasso's life. Suddenly he became what he had not been (to the same extent) before: a public figure. Ever since he had been recognised as the founder of modern art, his fame had spread, albeit within the cultural sector only. He was internationally known, though purely as an artist. With the entry of the Allies into Paris, two factors enhanced his status: the growth of his overseas reputation, and the post-war reinstatement of Modernism at the heart of the arts and political life. Picasso, rather than any other, was the artist whose studio soldiers, gallery owners and reporters wanted to visit. Photographers such as Lee Miller and Robert Capa documented his life and work in entire series of pictures; and these photos, widely seen in the mass media, earned Picasso enormous popularity. As the leading practitioner of an art condemned by the Fascists, and as a man who had not yielded an inch to them, Picasso became a cult figure. Anything he said was eagerly noted, printed and parroted.

He was of great importance for the new political and arts scene in liberated France. Just six weeks after the Allies entered Paris, the autumn salon – the "Salon de la Libération" – opened its doors, on 6 October 1944. It was the first programmatic expression of Picasso's central importance: he had no fewer than 74 paintings and five sculptures in the exhibition. It was in fact the first Salon he had ever shown at; his participation constituted the first official recognition by his French fellows. His political stance and his standing as an artist went hand in hand – and provoked immediate reactions, too.

Study after "Man with Sheep"
Etude d'après "L'homme au mouton"
Paris, 30 March 1943
India ink wash drawing on paper,
130.5 x 50.7 cm
Zervos XII, 241; MPP 1319
Paris, Musée Picasso

The Charnel House (1st state)
Le charnier
Paris, (1944)-1945
Charcoal on canvas, 199.8 x 250.1 cm
Zervos XIV, 72

The Charnel House
Le charnier
Paris, (1944)-1945
Oil and charcoal on canvas, 199.8 x 250.1 cm
Zervos XIV, 76
New York, The Museum of Modern Art

The Charnel House (3rd state)
Le charnier
Paris, (1944)-1945
Charcoal on canvas, 199.8 x 250.1 cm
Zervos XIV, 75

457 Politics and Art 1943–1953

Woman in Green
Femme en vert
Paris, 1943
Oil on canvas, 129.5 x 96.5 cm
Zervos XIII, 49
USA, Private collection

Woman Washing Her Foot
Femme se lavant le pied
Paris, 6 May 1944
Pencil on paper, 50.5 x 38.3 cm
Zervos XIII, 291
Chicago (IL), The Art Institute of Chicago

Artistic and political reactionaries, the stragglers of Pétain's regime, attempted to tear down his pictures from the walls, and prompted a scandal. The French society of authors took Picasso's side. The day before the Salon opened, there was news that only served to exacerbate tempers: Picasso had joined the Communist Party of France.[323]

He had abandoned his lifelong reluctance to commit himself to political sides. It was a logical consequence of recent history, the expression of his ideals. Since Franco's Spain had become a no-man's-land for an unforeseeable time, Picasso found a new home (as he himself put it) in the French Communist Party, amongst leading lights of the new France such as Sartre or Louis Aragon.[324] Publicly, Picasso repeatedly stated his view that an artist was not a one-dimensional creature involved exclusively in making art, but also a political being with an active interest in the problems of the

Woman with Brooch
Femme à la broche
17 March 1944
Oil on canvas, 80 x 59.7 cm
Zervos XIII, 237
Private collection

Head of a Boy
Tête de jeune garçon
Paris, 13 August 1944
India ink on paper, 60 x 55 cm
Zervos XIV, 33
Geneva, Fondation Marina Picasso

age. Picasso claimed that in his art he had always aimed to fight like a revolutionary; art, he said, was not so much something to prettify the home as a weapon in a political struggle.[325] And indeed, many of the works that followed in rapid succession attest to Picasso's involvement in the concerns of the times.

Not that those works were an art of direct statement. For instance, in 1945 Picasso painted a number of still lifes that glance at the privations and fears of life during the occupation. Surely the most important of these is "Pitcher, Candle and Enamel Saucepan" (p. 469). Tellingly, with the 1942 "L'Aubade" it was one of ten paintings which the artist, at the suggestion of his friend, museum curator Jean Cassou, gifted to the Musée National d'Art Moderne in May 1946.[326] The picture shows three objects only. It draws upon crucial formal insights that Picasso had developed in his great "Guernica". Here too, tried and tested stylistic modes serve to

459 Politics and Art 1943–1953

The Bull
Le taureau
Paris, 18 December 1945
Lithograph, 28.9 x 41 cm
Mourlot 17 IV; Baer 87; Rau 92

The Bull
Le taureau
Paris, 17 January 1946
Lithograph, 28.9 x 41 cm
Bloch 389; Mourlot 17 XI; Baer 95; Rau 100

question and undermine what appears unambiguous, but at the same time to render it universally valid. A number of perspective viewpoints – front, side and rear – jointly establish unified, clear outlines that do not correspond with the picture's spatial values. On a brown tabletop we see a pitcher, a burning candle and an enamel saucepan, lined up at only slightly different degrees of visual depth. The bright yellow of the brass candlestick is the strongest colour, strikingly contrasted by the acid blue of the saucepan. Shades of grey, green and brown, and large patches of white, lend stability to this restless colourfulness, so that the overall impression of the canvas is one of subdued colour. The power of the pure

Bullfight Scenes
Scènes de corrida
Paris, 15 December 1945
Lithograph, 40 x 60 cm
Bloch 1343; Mourlot 11; Rau 105

Sketch Sheet: Bulls
Feuille d'études de taureaux
18 January 1946
India ink on paper, 21 x 35 cm
Zervos XIV, 135

colours seems muted, despite the decidedly aggressive use of the yellow and blue. Thus the expressive values of the colours waver between the bright and the subdued. They are unstable. Similarly with the light: the candle's big flame and black shadow convey an appearance of brightness, yet the lit sides of the three objects are on the sides away from the light. It is not light with any real illuminative power; it is symbolic light. The painting's symbolism is simple, using everyday household objects to suggest the difficulty of life under the occupation.[327]

Even the large-scale 1948 composition "The Kitchen" (pp. 478/479) reflects that everyday, basic privation. It shows the

461 Politics and Art 1943–1953

The Sideboard at the "Catalan"
Le buffet du "Catalan"
Paris, 30 May 1943
Oil on canvas, 81 x 100 cm
Zervos XIII, 26
Stuttgart, Staatsgalerie Stuttgart

kitchen at Picasso's studio flat in the Rue des Grands-Augustins. Against a sad, grey, non-spatial background we see a variety of utensils and furniture. Spanish tiles and birdcages, plates and stove hotplates are the principal subjects. But the overall impression is one of fragility, indeed of utter emptiness. Personal experience of going without, in the home and workplace, has become a generalized warning. The ochre yellow New York version (p. 477) is no less melancholy, for the greater warmth of the colour is counter-

Glass and Pitcher
Verre et pichet
Paris, 23 July 1944
Oil on canvas, 33 x 41 cm
Zervos XIV, 5
New York, Private collection

acted by the greater austerity in the positioning of the objects. Other still lifes of the period use their motifs with even blunter directness of moralizing intent. They tend to be dominated by a skull, a painted version of a sculpture Picasso did in 1943 in his studio in the Rue des Grands-Augustins (p. 444).[328] There are also objects that recall war and menace – very evocatively, for instance, in "Skull, Sea Urchins and Lamp on a Table" (1946; p. 469). Black, white and grey areas, awkwardly constrictive and jostling, predominate, and the three spiky sea urchins on the plain plate seem reminiscent of some mediaeval weapon, such as a mace.

Symbolic form, a compacted artistic treatment of given reality, and translation of the everyday wretchedness of war into an urgent though not superficial visual idiom, are all to be found in a major Picasso done at the very end of the war: his great composition "The Charnel House" (p. 457). It was inspired by a Spanish film about a family killed in their kitchen. When Picasso went to work on the

Tomato Plant
Plant de tomates
Paris, 10 August 1944
Oil on canvas, 92 x 73 cm
Zervos XIV, 26
Switzerland, Private collection;
formerly Galerie Rosengart

463 Politics and Art 1943–1953

painting from February to May 1945, it was with the first photographs of liberated German concentration camps in mind[329] – though this dimension only entered the work at a late stage, as the composition was already fixed in formal terms before any of the photographs were published. This only lends additional weight to the painting's statement, though, taking as it does political terror as its subject.

The picture shows a heap of corpses after an execution. One figure, still tied to a post, is collapsing onto the others. It was only during the course of Picasso's work on the painting that the location became more precisely defined. Greyish blue, white and black areas denote walls, floor and posts, a set of architectonic props that suggest both exterior and interior, as in "Guernica". The still life of kitchen utensils at top left is not only a glance at the film original; it also underlines the everyday banality and ubiquity of terror. It

Satyr, Faun and Centaur (Triptych)
Study for "La joie de vivre"
Antibes, autumn 1946
Oil and Ripolin on cement,
250 x 360 cm
Zervos XIV, 242–244
Antibes, Musée Picasso

Still Life
Nature morte
10 April 1947
Oil on canvas, 81 x 100 cm
Zervos XV, 46
Estate of Jacqueline Picasso
Paris, Courtesy Galerie Louise Leiris

can hit anyone, anywhere, any time. Even more than in "Guernica" the monochrome scheme, the linearity and the use of areas of unbroken colour serve to make a universal of the statement. First Picasso sketched in the simple outlines of his stylized figures, heaping them so that the lines are interwoven, creating a tangled network that defies distinction of separate forms. Later he filled in some of the segments, so establishing an equilibrium of figural and spatial motifs. (Only the line-drawing still life remains different.) The heap of bodies can be seen as replicating the destruction of individual identity in the world of totalitarian terror. Human beings cannot even preserve their individual physical identities; even their bodies are taken from them.

The painting was done with an etching from Goya's series "Desastres de la Guerra" in mind.[330] In other words, it was using preformulated artistic modes of response to war. It cannot really be seen as a direct expression of political commitment; though Picasso often expressed political positions at this time, as an artist he retained his independence. But six years later things looked somewhat different when he painted "Massacre in Korea" (pp. 500/501). The Korean War had begun six months earlier. The painting was Picasso's protest at the American invasion. Shown at the May Salon in Paris, it took sides in a war of ideologies. And its formal idiom was an unambiguous, partisan one, using handed-down simple symbols and only sparingly heightening the figural naturalism with cautious touches of the dissociative. We see the good and evil sides in straightforward confrontation on an extremely broad format. Four naked women, rigid with fear, and their four similarly naked children (the nakedness symbolizing defencelessness), are being aimed at by six soldiers armed to the teeth

La joie de vivre (Pastorale)
Antibes, autumn 1946
Oil on hardboard, 120 x 250 cm
Zervos XIV, 289
Antibes, Musée Picasso

Page 468:
Still Life with Skull, Book and Oil Lamp
Nature morte au crâne, livre et lampe à pétrole
Paris, 1 March 1946
Oil on plywood, 54 x 65 cm
Not in Zervos; MPP 1990–22
Paris, Musée Picasso,
Dation Jacqueline Picasso

Still Life with Leeks, Fish Head, Skull and Pitcher
Nature morte aux poireaux, tête de poisson,
crâne et pichet
13 March 1945 and 3 December 1946
Oil on canvas, 81 x 116 cm
Zervos XIV, 94. Estate of Jacqueline Picasso
Paris, Courtesy Galerie Louise Leiris

468 Politics and Art 1943–1953

Pitcher, Candle and Enamel Saucepan
Pichet, bougeoir et casserole émaillée
Paris, 16 February 1945
Oil on canvas, 82 x 106 cm
Zervos XIV, 71
Paris, Musée National d'Art Moderne,
Centre Georges Pompidou

Skull, Sea Urchins and Lamp on a Table
Crâne, oursins et lampe sur une table
Antibes or Paris, 27 November 1946
Oil on plywood, 81 x 100 cm
Zervos XIV, 290; MPP 198
Paris, Musée Picasso

469 Politics and Art 1943–1953

Plate: "Head of a Faun", 15 October 1947
White clay, decoration with engobe, glazed,
32 x 38 cm. Basel, Galerie Beyeler

Plate: "Brown and Blue Face", 29 October 1947 (VIII)
White clay, decoration with engobe, glazed,
31 x 38 cm. Basel, Galerie Beyeler

Plate: "Bullfight Scene", 1947
White clay, decoration with engobe, glazed,
32 x 38 cm. Basel, Galerie Beyeler

Plate: "Bullfight Scene", 1947
White clay, decoration with engobe, glazed,
32 x 38 cm. Basel, Galerie Beyeler

Politics and Art 1943–1953 **471**

Head of a Woman
Tête de femme
8 January 1947
Oil on canvas, 73 x 60 cm
Not in Zervos
Paris, Courtesy Galerie Louise Leiris

Still Life on a Table
Nature morte sur une table
Paris, 4 April 1947
Oil on canvas, 100 x 80 cm
Not in Zervos
Private collection; formerly Galerie Rosengart

(symbolizing far superior power). The soldiers' postures seem at once mechanical and archaic; they are ancient warriors transmuted into death-bringing robots.[331] A green, sweeping, simplified landscape featuring only a single ruined house is the backdrop to the composition.

For his work on it, Picasso drew upon a number of cognate works, in particular Edouard Manet's famous painting "The Execution of Emperor Maximilian in Mexico" (Mannheim, Kunsthalle). From it Picasso took the figure grouping and particularly the figure of the death squad commander. He also borrowed from the work that inspired Manet, Goya's familiar "3rd May 1808" (Madrid, Museo Nacional del Prado). The twofold grouping and the threatening anonymity of the soldiers have been taken directly from Goya, as has the figure of a fallen victim, transformed in Picasso's painting into a child crouching on the ground.

Goya too was inspired by antecedent works, Jacques-Louis David's "Rape of the Sabine Women" and "The Oath of the Horatii" (both in the Louvre in Paris). Picasso drew on David's paintings for particular features such as the striding stance of one soldier and details of mediaeval or ancient weaponry.[332] This blatant use of other paintings is in line with the one-dimensionality of the painting's form and content. It is very different from other pictures of similar subject. This is the result of aiming simultaneously at two objectives. Only the title places the painting in the Korean War; as in his other anti-war pictures, Picasso has carefully avoided using specific details that would tie down his statement to a particular place and time. The form has become programmatic.

Plainly a naturalistic, representational image is in the foreground. What counts for Picasso is the message. Consistently, he has presented the action as a picture within a picture: all round, there is a margin of unpainted canvas, which gives the work a fictive, mask-like quality. It is worth examining this defamiliarization. Mimetic representation was far more in line with public expectation than the formal idiom of Modernism, and could therefore count on a more approving response. In this we see the predicament of political, ideological art. Since the early days of Stalin, international Communism had been advocating realism as the only acceptable mode of artistic work. The French Communist Party toed this line too. It was an urgent dilemma for Picasso, as became clear at the 1945 Party congress, which gave him an accolade as man and artist but nonetheless called for realism in art.

Communist ideology saw art as a weapon in a political struggle that embraced every area of human activity. It is true that Picasso saw matters in exactly the same light, and considered himself a Communist artist painting Communist art; but his idea of what this meant was a different one from the Party's. To his way of thinking, politics served moral ends. For this reason his commitment was always expressed in humanitarian causes, and never in the dis-

Seated Woman in an Armchair
Femme assise dans un fauteuil
1948
Oil on canvas, 100.5 x 81 cm
Zervos XV, 103
Private collection; formerly Galerie Beyeler, Basel

David and Bathsheba (after Lucas Cranach the Elder)
David et Bethsabée (d'après Lucas Cranach)
Paris, 29 May 1949
Lithograph, 76 x 56 cm
Bloch 442; Mourlot 109; Rau 194

David and Bathsheba (after Lucas Cranach the Elder)
David et Bethsabée (d'après Lucas Cranach)
Paris, 30 March 1947
Lithograph, 64 x 49 cm
Bloch 441; Mourlot 109 IV; Rau 187

The Dove
La colombe
Paris, 9 January 1949
Lithograph, 54.5 x 70 cm
Bloch 583; Mourlot 141; Rau 414

Politics and Art 1943–1953 **476**

charging of official Party duties. He attended Communist peace
conferences in Breslau (1948), Paris (1949), Sheffield (1950) and
Rome (1951); but he preserved a distance from art whose form was
dictated by the Party, and always insisted on his own independence
as an artist.[333] "Massacre in Korea" was a special case, an attempt
to reconcile opposite points of view. Certainly he did work that
served propagandist purposes in those years, but it was applied art
– such as the dove in flight which he designed for the Sheffield
congress, a conventional enough image for the concept of universal
peace.[334]

477 Politics and Art 1943–1953

The Kitchen
La cuisine
Paris, November 1948
Oil on canvas, 175 x 252 cm
Zervos XV, 107; MPP 200
Paris, Musée Picasso

The latent conflict between Picasso's ideas on art and those of the French Communist Party became open after the death of Stalin, when (at Louis Aragon's request) he did a portrait of the dead leader for the arts magazine "Les Lettres françaises". The portrait, though relatively true to life, was stylized in Picasso's manner; it was used on the magazine cover, but was out of line with the precepts of socialist realism, and furthermore ignored the features which Stalin iconography had established as characteristic.[335] To Picasso's bewilderment, the portrait was consequently seen by Communist Party members as a mockery of Stalin. The divergence of opinion between the artist and the Party was too great to permit long-term collaboration. Picasso did remain a member of the Party, and on 1 May 1962 received the Order of Lenin for the second time. But the differences and alienation between his own and Party cadre thinking became so profound that in November 1956, with a number of others, he published an open letter in "Le Monde" protesting against Soviet intervention in Hungary.[336]

Essentially, the Communist Party was using Picasso for propagandist reasons. In this respect he shared the fate of many intellectuals and artists who were so repelled by the Second World War and the atrocities perpetrated by the Fascists that they felt it necessary to espouse political causes openly. Everyday politics passed over their idealism blithely enough. And in the Cold War, with the two power blocs set hard and fast, individuals were only tolerated as extras on the political stage. Attempts to unite the arts and politics and thus to transform the state into something better proved to be illusory. Progressive Communist artists in particular found that things went much as they had with the utopian Modernists, Constructivists and satirical realists of the Twenties. Their ideas

Claude with a Ball
Claude à la balle
Paris, 15 December 1948 (II)
Oil on canvas, 100 x 81 cm
Zervos XV, 109
Paris, Maya Ruiz-Picasso Collection

Claude in Polish Costume
Claude en costume polonais
Paris, 23 October 1948
Oil on canvas, 120 x 50 cm
Zervos XV, 101

Claude in the Arms of His Mother
Claude dans les bras de sa mère
Paris, 30 October 1948
Oil on canvas, 92 x 73 cm
Zervos XV, 110

only had any impact in brief periods of transition. Since the final years of the Tsarist age, important Picassos had been in Russia, but it was not till the 1970s that Soviet arts policy honoured him not only as a prominent Party member but also as an artist.[337] Picasso's commitment to the Communist cause was necessarily no more than an episode in the immediate post-war years.

Still, Picasso persisted in expressing his general humanitarian and political concerns in his work. During the period when he was questioning Party sovereignty in the arts, he was painting a deconsecrated 14th-century chapel at Vallauris. Outraged by the Korean War, he had decided to make the chapel a temple of peace. From April to September 1952, in over 250 sketches, he designed two huge murals for the chapel, on the subject of war and peace. The murals (p. 452) were completed that December, though they were not installed till 1954. Tellingly, Picasso again took his bearings for the twin allegorical works from the art of the past.[338] War is symbolized by a kind of frieze in which a horse-drawn chariot is taking the field against a monumental figure armed in ancient fashion and bearing the scales and shield of justice and peace. Behind the chariot, attacking warriors seen in black silhouette are engaged in carnage. The death's-heads carried by the charioteer point to the only outcome of battle. By contrast, the other mural affords a prospect of unsullied happiness. It shows mothers and playing children, around the central figure of Pegasus, pulling a plough at the bid-

Paloma
Vallauris, January 1951
Oil on canvas; dimensions unknown
Not in Zervos
Private collection

Claude Writing
Claude écrivant
Vallauris, 1951
Oil on canvas, 46 x 38 cm
Not in Zervos
Paris, Maya Ruiz-Picasso Collection

El Greco:
Portrait of Jorge Manuel Theotokopulus,
about 1600–1605
Oil on canvas, 81 x 56 cm
Seville, Museo de Bellas Artes

ding of one child and so personifying the fertile world of peace. Both pictures, in their own ways, continue the childlike elements in "Guernica" and link them to forms Matisse had used in his Arcadian paintings.[339]

Matisse was then the other great exponent of Modernism and the only artist among his fellows whom Picasso considered his equal. In 1943 he had moved to Vence, where he decorated the chapel of a convent, designing the stained-glass windows, the candlesticks and crucifix, the chasubles and murals. The Chapel of the Rosary was consecrated on 25 June 1951. Picasso was not personally present at the ceremony, but he did visit his sick fellow artist shortly beforehand.[340] To make his murals Matisse had transferred drawings onto glazed tiles, so establishing a sort of equivalent to the spatial work Picasso had done in Antibes in 1946, when he had spent two months of hard concentration painting twenty-two murals onto plywood and hardboard for the Palais Grimaldi. These economically drawn works, sometimes using extensive blocks of colour, describe an Arcadian realm of peaceful Mediterranean contentment, using motifs drawn from ancient mythology (cf. p. 467). There is a sense of serene joy in these deliberately simple pictures. The subject of *joie de vivre* was borrowed from Matisse. The Antibes series was completed in 1947 with "Odysseus and the Sirens", whereupon the Paris administrative centre for the nation's museums redubbed the building "Musée Picasso".[341] Though the Antibes and Vallauris works are doubtless not among the artist's most important, they clearly show his interest in art seen in public spaces.

Political commitment was only one aspect of Picasso's creative efforts at that time. The distinctive dichotomy in his activities was not least a result of particular artistic interests. This is clearest in the sculptures he did between 1943 and 1953. One of his most famous and characteristic, done in 1943 during the darkest period of the occupation, when Picasso felt utterly isolated, was the "Head of a Bull" (p. 444). The skeletal head and horns of a bull are conveyed by two found objects which in themselves are meaningless, a bicycle saddle and handlebars. Picasso subsequently had this assemblage cast in bronze, thus reassessing the original materials, eliminating the contrasts and opening out the ambivalence of form. It was a continuation of what he had done in "The Glass of Absinthe" (p. 232), that famous product of synthetic Cubism. The absolute economy of the "Head of a Bull" was breathtaking, and remains stunning to this day. And from then on Picasso retained the basic principle of metamorphosis of formal meaning and interpretation in all his sculptural work.

"Baboon and Young" (p. 488), done in October 1951, achieved a comparable popularity. It was immediately cast in bronze in a limited edition of six. Picasso was inspired by two toy cars which the art dealer Kahnweiler gave to his son Claude, and used them

Portrait of a Painter (after El Greco)
Portrait d'un peintre (d'après El Greco)
Vallauris, 22 February 1950
Oil on plywood, 100.5 x 81 cm
Zervos XV, 165
Lucerne, Angela Rosengart Collection

for the head of the ape, bottom to bottom so that the gap between the two becomes the slit of the baboon's mouth, the radiator the whiskers, the roof the receding forehead, and the two front windows the eyes – to which Picasso added two plaster balls as pupils. Picasso then used coffee cup handles as ears and an immense jug for the body. The arms and the remainder of the baboon's body, and her young, were modelled in plaster. Finally, the outstretched tail was another found item: a car suspension spring curled at one end.[342]

Picasso proceeded similarly with his 1950 "Nanny Goat" (pp. 484 and 485), the "Woman with Baby Carriage" and "Girl Skipping" (moulded the same year but not finished till 1954; pp. 486 and 489) and the still life "Goat Skull, Bottle and Candle" (p. 484), done between 1951 and 1953. For the "Nanny Goat" he used a large round basket for the belly, metal strips for the lean flanks, carved vinewood for the horns, and cardboard for the ears. The fibrous wooden part of a palm leaf served for the smooth brow and the hairless backbone. The legs and feet were made of wood too; a lighting appliance was the behind; folded cardboard and metal tubing became the genitals and anus, twisted wire the tail; and two ceramic vessels functioned as an udder. For the "Girl Skipping" a Vallauris ironmonger bent a length of iron rod to the shape required for the skipping rope (and the figure's support). The girl's body is made of two wicker baskets, ceramics, baking tins and plaster; and the feet are clad in ordinary shoes. For the "Woman with Baby Carriage" Picasso used a real push-chair but constructed the figures of metal parts, roof tiles, baking tins and bits of pottery.

Right:
Nanny Goat
Chèvre
Vallauris, 1950
Plaster (Wicker basket, ceramic ware, palm leaf, metal, wood, cardboard and plaster),
120.5 x 72 x 144 cm
Spies 409 I; MPP 339
Paris, Musée Picasso

Goat Skull, Bottle and Candle
Crâne de chèvre, bouteille et bougie
Vallauris, 1951–1953
Bronze, 79 x 93 x 54 cm
Spies 410 II a; MPP 341
Paris, Musée Picasso

Nanny Goat
Vallauris, 1950
Bronze (original opposite), 120.5 x 72 x 144 cm
Spies 409 II; MPP 340. Paris, Musée Picasso

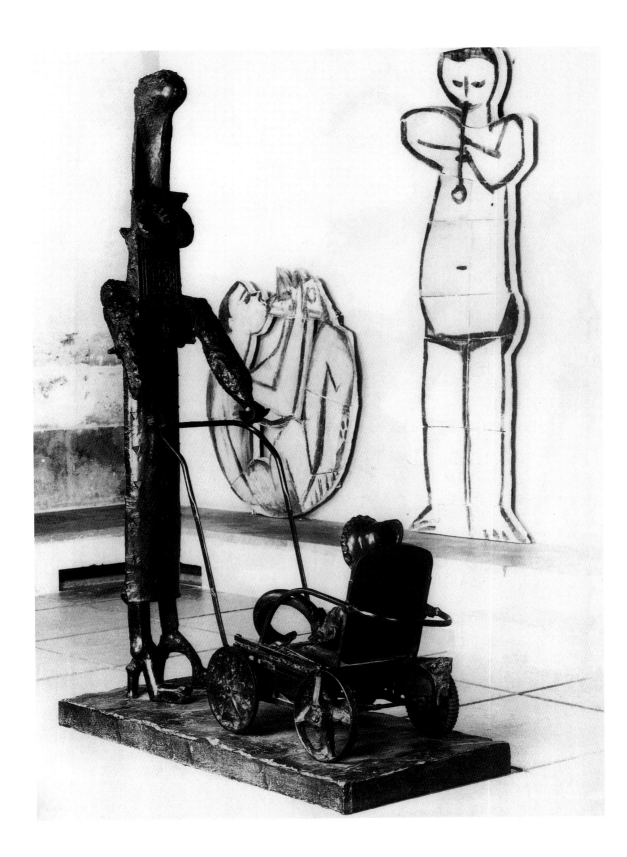

His older idea of using bicycle handlebars as an animal's horns reappeared in "Goat Skull, Bottle and Candle", on a goat skull made of baked clay, plaster and screws. For the beams of light shed by a burning candle he used nails.[343]

Using the technique of the *objet trouvé*, a method much beloved by the Surrealists, Picasso succeeded in ringing fascinating changes. His formal analogies render the external qualities of figures ambiguous, and indeed challenge them.[344] There are few better places than his sculptural work to see the intellectual vigour of Picasso's art. Every detail is sophisticated in conception. In the "Girl Skipping", for instance, we see a small child still unsure of how to use the rope: her awkwardness is expressed in the instability of the sculpture, but especially by the outsize shoes – and by the fact that she is wearing them on the wrong feet.

Picasso's use of objects in his sculpture was radically different from that of other modern artists. The "ready-made" of a Marcel Duchamp, for example, is provocative in conception. The placement of objects is less a matter of form than of what the objects signify. A bicycle wheel on a stool, or a bottle-dryer declared as art – these things do not revalue the objects; rather, they aim criticism at the very concept of art.[345] Picasso, by contrast, is fundamentally returning to a pre-modern artistic idiom. In the mid-16th century the Mannerist painter Giuseppe Arcimboldo had assembled various kinds of object into allegorical portraits and figures. It was an art of analogy and similitude. In a portrait made of vegetables, for instance, a cucumber could stand for a nose. This mode of characterization was later to become the province of satirical drawings in particular. It was a marginal, little-noted kind of art, but in it an underground tradition lived on, only to be rediscovered by the Surrealists when they hit upon the bizarre inventions of Arcimboldo.[346] Picasso for his part was not copying objects mimetically but using the real things for sculptural purposes, expanding the principle considerably.

In this context it is necessary to consider the genesis of form. Basically there are two possibilities: either the seen object prompts a spontaneous idea of metamorphosis, or, conversely, a planned concept comes first and the objects are sought out to fit it. It was in this latter way that the "Nanny Goat" was made; Picasso went in search of objects to fit his idea. On the other hand, the look of the toy cars spontaneously prompted the idea of the baboon.[347] In all his sculptures, though, the idea is central – an intellectual exercise, which the artwork provides material substance for, as it were. We can see this particularly in Picasso's approach to the tactile qualities of surfaces. In distinguishing between *objets trouvés* and bronze casts of them, in choosing either to gather a variety of materials or to use his own, he was establishing specific effects. In the use of original objects, the meaning of form is in the foreground; in bronze casts, that meaning is subordinate to qualities of appear-

Woman with Baby Carriage
Femme à la voiture d'enfant
(La femme à la poussette)
Vallauris, 1950
Bronze (from an assemblage of plaster, fired clay, metal, baking tins and child's pushchair),
203 x 145 x 61 cm
Spies 407 II; MPP 337
Paris, Musée Picasso

487 Politics and Art 1943–1953

Baboon and Young
Le guenon et son petit
Vallauris, October 1951
Ceramic ware, two toy cars,
metal and plaster, 56 x 34 x 71 cm
Spies 463 I; MPP 342
Paris, Musée Picasso

Girl Skipping
Petite fille à la corde
Vallauris, 1950
Plaster, ceramic ware, wicker basket,
baking tins, shoes, wood and iron,
152 x 65 x 66 cm
Spies 408 I; MPP 336
Paris, Musée Picasso

489 Politics and Art 1943–1953

Gustave Courbet:
Girls by the Seine, 1857
Oil on canvas, 173.5 x 206 cm
Paris, Musée du Petit Palais

Girls on the Banks of the Seine (after Courbet)
Les demoiselles au bord de la Seine
(d'après Courbet)
Vallauris, February 1950
Oil on plywood, 100.5 x 201 cm
Zervos XV, 164
Basel, Öffentliche Kunstsammlung Basel,
Kunstmuseum

Left:
Round Vase: "Four Fish"
Vallauris, 1 July 1950
Red clay, decoration with carving and engobe
Height: 28 cm. Basel, Galerie Beyeler

Above:
Plate: "Goat's Head in Profile", 1950
White clay, relief painted with oxidized paraffin,
glazed. Diameter: 25.5 cm. Basel, Galerie Beyeler

Left:
Plate: "Goat's Head in Profile", 1950
White clay, relief painted with oxidized paraffin,
white enamèl glaze. Diameter: 25.5 cm
Private collection

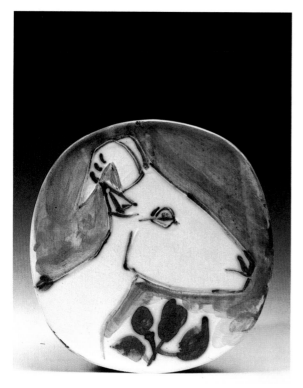

Pages 494 and 495:
Vase: "Flute Players and Dancers" (two views)
Vallauris, May 1950. Red clay, moulded on the wheel,
decoration with carving and engobe. Height: 70 cm
Private collection

493 Politics and Art 1943–1953

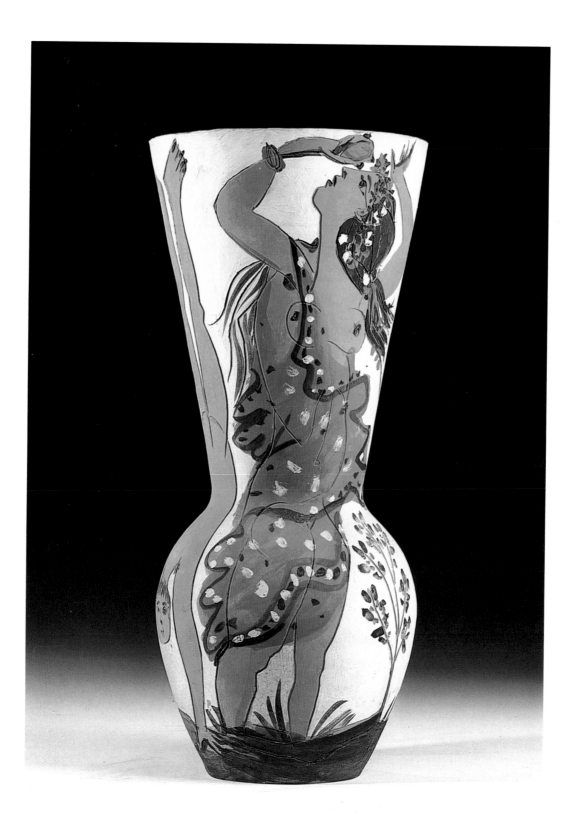

Right:
Nude Wringing Her Hair
Femme nue se tordant les cheveux
Vallauris, 7 October 1952
Oil on plywood, 154 x 120 cm
Not in Zervos
Chicago, Private collection

Seated Woman with a Bun
Femme au chignon assise
30 January 1951
Oil and Ripolin on plywood, 108.5 x 89.5 cm
Zervos XV, 177
Paris, Courtesy Galerie Louise Leiris

ance – say, the juxtaposition of rougher and smoother textures. It is practically the creation of a new object. If Picasso, as he continued to work on a sculpture such as "Goat Skull, Bottle and Candle", painted various casts, thus disguising and redefining the true qualities of the metal, it was basically an approach of synthetic Cubism.[348]

As they came into existence, these works defined new areas of meaning, playing with visual form, three-dimensionality and surface structure. Qualities of plasticity, though not unimportant, were distinctly of secondary significance. Whether Picasso carried out an idea in paint or sculpture was essentially a pragmatic question. Thus he was able to alternate between the forms. "Goat Skull, Bottle and Candle", for instance, itself inspired by a 1939 still life (p. 431), prompted two further paintings in 1952 (pp. 502 and 503). The prime importance of the idea, consistently enough, can be seen in the genesis of his works, traceable through the invariable

497 Politics and Art 1943–1953

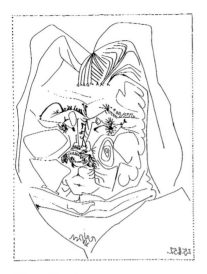

Balzac. 25 November 1952
Lithograph, 70 x 53 cm
Bloch 724; Mourlot 226; Rau 559

Mediterranean Landscape
Paysage méditerranéen
Vallauris, 10 September 1952
Ripolin on shipboard, 81 x 125 cm
Zervos XV, 229. Formerly Galerie Beyeler, Basel

preliminary sketches. The best illustration of this is the large-scale sculpture "Man with Sheep" (p. 455), done in early 1943. Unlike the *objets trouvés* and the assemblages, the figure was wholly modelled in clay on an iron frame, in conventional style, and then moulded in plaster for subsequent bronze casting. This work was preceded by a large number of studies, beginning as early as 15 July 1942. At first the figure was not full-length: Picasso sketched a man holding a sheep's forelegs in his left hand and the hind with his right (p. 454). The final form evolved through a large number of detail and compositional studies, in the course of which Picasso drew upon an ancient statue of a man carrying a calf, as well as on the motif – familiar since childhood – of Christ as the good shepherd. The figure became a personification of peace, in response to the war.[349] Of greater interest is Picasso's protracted irresolution (as sketches of September 1942 confirm) whether to use the idea as a painting or a sculpture. At first he thought both were possible. The sketches envisaged a historical painting, while purely linear sketches done in August 1942 (p. 455) suggest Picasso was thinking of a graphic solution. We have his own word for it that it was only at a late stage that he thought of sculpture.[350] The finished group still reveals this indeterminacy. The figure is still marked by the strong contrast between the rough surface of face and torso and

the smoothness of the long legs. As Picasso himself noted, he had miscalculated the statics, and the model threatened to collapse under the excessive weight of the clay – so that he had to take his plaster cast from an unfinished state, despite his wish to work more on the legs and feet.[351]

This may seem to imply an astounding indifference to his own work on Picasso's part. Taking a cast in these circumstances was an admission of defeat. Judged by the artist's aims, "Man with Sheep" is strictly speaking a failure. But we must bear Picasso's attitude to sculpture in mind. Compared with the intellectual act of evolving the concept, the work of producing the final object was a negligible business. What counted was the artist's mind and will. Speaking of "Head of a Bull" (p. 444), Picasso commented that he would be perfectly happy if one day someone retrieved his artwork from the garbage and used it for bicycle parts.[352]

A further indicator of the view Picasso took of his own work is

Smoke Clouds at Vallauris
Fumée à Vallauris
Vallauris, 12 January 1951
Oil on canvas, 59.5 x 73.5 cm
Zervos XV, 174; MPP 202
Paris, Musée Picasso

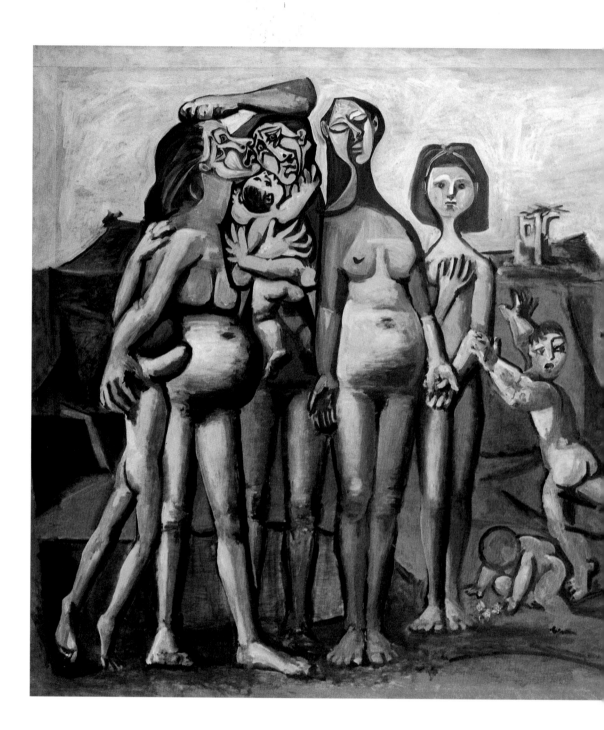

Massacre in Korea
Massacre en Corée
Vallauris, 18 January 1951
Oil on plywood, 109.5 x 209.5 cm
Zervos XV, 173; MPP 203
Paris, Musée Picasso

Goat Skull, Bottle and Candle
Crâne de chèvre, bouteille et bougie
Paris, 25 March 1952
Oil on canvas, 89 x 116 cm
Zervos XV, 201; MPP 206
Paris, Musée Picasso

his sense of himself as demiurge creating new worlds of his own through his new techniques and genres. His command of the various aspects of technique his art involved was absolute. Staying on the Côte d'Azur at the small town of Vallauris, an old pottery centre, Picasso acquired skills in ceramic art. In 1946, at an exhibition of work by potters who lived there, Suzanne and Georges Ramie challenged Picasso to produce ceramic ware of his own. His subconscious went to work on the new form, and by the following summer he was full of ideas of his own.

Initially he worked at "Madoura", the Ramies' workshop; then in 1948, with Françoise Gilot, he moved into the newly-purchased Villa La Galloise in Vallauris, and set up a ceramic workshop of his own in an old perfumery in the town. Within a year he had produced over 2,000 ceramic pieces, eloquent proof of the extraordinary energy with which he tackled his new technique. The Vallauris years from 1947/48 to 1954 marked Picasso's most intensive work with ceramics.[353] Painters and sculptors had tended to ignore the ancient art, and in Europe it had never recovered the high status it

had had in ancient Greece, which produced vase paintings in black
and red which are among the great achievements of Occidental
art.[354] Matisse and other Fauves had worked with clay on occasion,
but restricted their efforts to painting ware made by potters.[355]

Picasso's approach was a different one from the outset. He acquired both the potter's and the ceramic painter's skills. His ceramic work includes painted plates and vases, but also sculptures
made by joining preformed pieces, as well as moulded objects.[356] At
first he devoted himself to painting finished pieces – making bullfight scenes, still lifes or animal portrayals out of mere plates. The
given form of the objects was always his point of departure in
evolving ideas, but it became so involved in the decorative trans-
mutation that a new thing resulted. The numerous bullfight scenes
show this well. Picasso would paint a corrida in the base of the
plate and either use the rim for a distinct colour frame or else dab
specks of paint to suggest a grandstand full of spectators.

Clay as a material met Picasso's aims, which centred upon types
of formal metamorphosis, very well. It was capable of being

Goat Skull, Bottle and Candle
Crâne de chèvre, bouteille et bougie
Paris, 16 April 1952
Oil on canvas, 89 x 116 cm
Zervos XV, 198
London, Tate Gallery

Politics and Art 1943–1953 **503**

Portrait of Madame H.P. (Hélène Parmelin)
Portrait de Madame H.P.
Vallauris, 1952
Oil on plywood, 147 x 115 cm
Zervos XV, 214
London, Marlborough Gallery

Seated Woman
Femme nue accroupie
Vallauris, 9 July 1953
Oil on canvas, 130.2 x 95.9 cm
Zervos XV, 292
Saint Louis (MO), The Saint Louis Art Museum

Right:
Portrait of Madame H.P. (Hélène Parmelin)
Portrait de Madame H.P. sur fond vert
Vallauris, 1952
Oil on plywood, 145.5 x 96.5 cm
Zervos XV, 215
Paris, Edouard Pignon Collection

moulded into infinitely various forms, remained pliable throughout the process, and was thus at the constant disposal of the artist's ideas. Thus, for example, a compact vase became a kneeling woman, and the body, stem and spout of one vessel became a bird. The decorative images were complemented with careful use of relief – added strips of clay and indentations. Picasso used paint to reinforce and decoratively highlight the form and function of the ware, but also deployed its illusionist effects to redefine forms: jugs became stagey scenarios suggestive of spatial depth, or were transformed into human or animal shapes.

Picasso's playful mastery of new techniques can also be seen in his revived commitment to printed graphics, and in particular lithography, which had hitherto played only a marginal part in his interests.[357] Now, working together with members of Fernand Mourlot's Paris workshop, Picasso produced over 200 lithographs between November 1945 and 1950, exploring an entire range of new technical possibilities. Planographic printing inspired Picasso. It was possible to duplicate line drawings, crayon studies or India-ink work, and to print from different surfaces, from limestone to sheet zinc, which created particular effects and expressive potential. The work process happened in stages, which permitted interruptions to scrutinize the state of the work in hand. Originally lithography had been purely a reproductive art because, unlike woodcuts, copper engravings or etchings, it can produce an absolutely faithful copy of an original drawing. The specific technique does not necessarily affect or change colours and lines. It was this that appealed to Picasso. He used the plates and paper, crayons and oils unconventionally, and regularly turned lithographic orthodoxy topsy-turvy, making seemingly difficult or senseless demands on Tuttin the printer. Broad though their thematic range is, Picasso's lithographs ultimately have but one true subject: the artist's own virtuosity.

We see that virtuosity in the famous series of bullfight scenes, variations on a single theme printed from a single type of plate, increasingly radical in the simple sense of form, detailed and realistic or else purely linear as if to satisfy oriental ideals (p. 460). We see it in Picasso's portraits of his young lover Françoise Gilot. From silhouette sketches of bullfight scenes (p. 461) to portrait sketches, Picasso is forever demonstrating his mastery of complex methods. That demonstrative will is present throughout the lithographic work. He used the draughtsman's entire repertoire, from classical outlines to painterly gradations of grey values, deploying his craft deliberately and affording us a full documentation of his creative process.[358] This may account for the thematic disunity and qualitative unevenness of Picasso's lithographs.

It was a period of considerable revival for the graphic arts. Many artists were working in the medium, in an attempt to meet the expansionist demands of a market keyed to the mass media.[359] Pi-

Woman Playing with a Dog
Femme et chien jouant
Vallauris, 8 March 1953
Ripolin on plywood, 81 x 100 cm
Zervos XV, 246
Lucerne, Picasso Collection,
Donation Rosengart

casso took up a position all his own, satisfying commercial demands but at the same time using the medium to profile himself.
One work dating from 1949 nicely illustrates his practice and its
impact. Picasso had been asked to design a poster for the world
peace conference in Paris. Aragon, visiting the studio in the Rue des
Grands-Augustins, chose a lithograph of a dove (p. 476) which
Picasso had done on 9 January 1949. Reproduced millions of times
on posters, it was to become probably Picasso's most popular
graphic work. Ironically, though, it had never been meant as pro-

Nude in the Studio
Femme nue dans l'atelier
Vallauris, 30 December 1953
Oil on canvas, 89 x 116.2 cm
Zervos XVI, 96
Geneva, Heinz Berggruen Collection

Right:
Seated Woman with Dog
Femme assise avec chien
Vallauris, 3 February 1953
Oil on plywood, 130 x 97 cm
Zervos XV, 236. Private collection;
formerly Galerie Rosengart

The Shadow
L'ombre
Vallauris, 29 December 1953
Oil and charcoal on canvas, 129.5 x 96.5 cm
Zervos XVI, 100; MPP 208
Paris, Musée Picasso

The Shadow on the Woman
L'ombre sur la femme
Vallauris, 29 December 1953
Oil on canvas, 130.8 x 97.8 cm
Zervos XVI, 99
Toronto, Art Gallery of Ontario

paganda. It was simply one of a number of pictures of doves with no ideological implications at all. The dove was of course a conventional symbol of peace; Picasso had liked the motif ever since early youth. In 1943, during the war, he had painted "Child with Doves" (p. 449), expressing the longing for peace. The lithograph of 9 January 1949 was an experiment in nuance, an attempt at using thinned India ink on a zinc plate to achieve subtle effects. The white plumage of the dove, with gentle touches of brown, was the perfect subject. Aragon, for his part, chose the picture because it had an Impressionist flavour and was thus in line with a kind of art then seen as folk-like and thus acceptable. The Communist appropriation and popularization of his work had nothing to do with Picasso's own intentions and was in fact at odds with them.[360]

In the immediate post-war years, the reception of his work continued to be governed by misunderstanding. The dissatisfaction of the Party, which tolerated Picasso's art for opportunist reasons, was matched by vituperative right-wing defamation. Both the 1944 autumn Salon in Paris and the great London exhibition of Matisse and Picasso in 1945 prompted imprecations that were widely parroted.[361] At the same time a number of cultural commentaries influenced by José Ortega y Gasset's "The Dehumanization of the Arts" (1925) were appearing in many places. At heart, the attacks

were all targeted at a supposed destruction of the image of mankind by the societal non-answerability of art[362] – a lightly veiled demand that art and artists be subordinated to ideologies, to the binding value systems of specific political creeds. It was not only because of his fame, his avowed political commitment, and his distinctive formal idiom that Picasso attracted many of the attacks aimed at modern art. More than any other, he epitomized the autonomy of the modern artist who refuses to be squeezed into the moulds of others.

Thus his art at that time, like his life, was Janus-faced. Freedom and commitment, expansionism and withdrawal, went hand in hand. Picasso tended increasingly to retreat from Paris, where he had lived and worked for half a century, and spend his personal and creative time on the Côte d'Azur. His new-found political and artistic freedom was accompanied by a new partnership, with a young painter, Françoise Gilot; in 1947 and 1949 their children Claude and Paloma were born.[363] His exploration of new artistic media and techniques was a counterbalance to his political involvement. If he was to be avowedly committed, adopting political positions with all the limited vision that that could often imply, then Picasso would also be absolute in his art, a creative human being who recognised no constraints.

Child Playing with a Toy Truck
Enfant jouant avec un camion
Vallauris, 27 December 1953
Oil on canvas, 130 x 96.5 cm
Zervos XVI, 98; MPP 1900–25
Paris, Musée Picasso,
Dation Jacqueline Picasso

In Front of the Garden
Devant le jardin
Vallauris, 1953
Oil on canvas, 150.5 x 98.5 cm
Zervos XVI, 97
Private collection

Pages 510 and 511:
Jug: "Figurehead", 1952
White clay, decoration with carving and engobe
Height: 21 cm. Breadth: 24 cm
Basel, Galerie Beyeler

Jug: "Woman's Face", 10 July 1953
White clay, decoration with knife carvings and engobe, partially glazed. Height: 35 cm
Basel, Galerie Beyeler

14 The Presence of the Past
1954–1963

On 2 and 3 June 1954 at Vallauris, Picasso painted two portraits of a mystery woman called "Madame Z" (pp. 514 and 515). One shows her in three-quarter profile, in a crouch, arms crossed around her knees; the other is a bust profile pure and simple. Both are profiles in the sense that they convey the characteristics of the sitter; but they are also experiments in the complementary effects of draughtsmanly methods in painting. The canvas in each case has been divided up into large, irregular blocks of colour; the figures themselves are mere outlines, defined with a few economical lines. Black and white contrast baldly, with each other and with the strong colours. Hatched areas pick up the line emphasis of the portraits. The use of correspondences extends into details: crudely painted dark grey patches of shadow match other zones of restless brushwork, and both are at variance with the clear lines and even areas of colour. Some months later, in October 1954, Picasso returned to his subject in two further versions of the crouching woman (pp. 514 and 515) in which he pursued his play with form. The June composition was the point of departure for both works, in which Cubist dissociation and elements of the synthetic "Picasso style" interact. Picasso was now highlighting different colour effects. Blue, violet and grey alongside white and matt orange, in one, produce a gradation of tonalities; in the other painting, green and blue bluntly juxtaposed with red and yellow explode in contrastive brightness. One more time, in January 1959, Picasso returned to the subject in a series of fairly small canvases. The changes we see him making in the compositional nature of the subject serve to explore the tensions between colourful zones and white. It is the colour areas that vary, red in one painting, green in the next. The figure and the interior setting are placed with just a few lines and simple blocks; Picasso was plainly little interested in conveying the specific nature of his subject, as had still been the case in the 1954 portraits. Now the pictures are things of haste, done for effect. They reduce the art of painting to first principles. The craftsman's mastery is of secondary importance. And the series principle triumphs too.

All of this is characteristic of Picasso's work from the later 1950s on, a period customarily seen as one in which he expressed personal

Portrait of Jacqueline
Portrait de Jacqueline
21 October 1955
India ink and pencil on paper,
65 x 50 cm. Zervos XVI, 485

Jacqueline in Turkish Costume
Jacqueline en costume turc
Cannes, 20 November 1955
Oil on canvas, 100 x 81 cm
Not in Zervos
Paris, Catherine Hutin-Blay Collection;
Courtesy Galerie Louise Leiris

Jacqueline in a Crouch
Jacqueline accroupie
Vallauris, 8 October 1954
Oil on canvas, 146 x 114 cm
Not in Zervos. Private collection

Portrait of Jacqueline Roque with Arms Crossed
Portrait de Jacqueline Roque
aux mains croisées
Vallauris, 3 June 1954
Oil on canvas, 116 x 88.5 cm
Zervos XVI, 324; MPP 1990–26
Paris, Musée Picasso,
Dation Jacqueline Picasso

experience in his creative work.[364] There is some justice in this view of course. In the "Madame Z" cycle that justice is self-evident: the woman is Jacqueline Roque, whom Picasso met in summer 1953 when his relationship with Françoise Gilot was coming to a gradual end, and whom he would marry in 1961. Picasso's private life also entered his work in pictures of Claude and Paloma, his two children by Françoise (pp. 516 and 517). But, as in the Jacqueline portraits, the meaning of these paintings is not solely a personal one. Both works, dating from 1954, show the children drawing, once on their own, once under the eye of a female figure. In painting his own children drawing, Picasso was reflecting upon his own art: the paintings were not so much original works as new versions of older ones. The motif went back to 1923 when he portrayed his son Paul (p. 287). The scene including a watchful mother, dated 17 May 1954, was a variation on a 1943 painting showing a mother helping her child in its first attempts to walk,[365] in turn a variation on the 1937 "Great Bather with Book" (p. 409).

Personal material and constant repetition were twin faces of the same phenomenon. Picasso was now scarcely concerned to mirror the outside world. Instead, he took his own work as the centre of the creative universe. As in the Twenties and Thirties, this self-reflexive vein led him to the studio itself, and archetypal scenes of the artist at work with his model, as subjects.

In 1955 Picasso bought La Californie, a sumptuous 19th-century

villa splendidly situated on the hills above Cannes, with a view right across to Golfe-Juan and Antibes. He established a studio on the upper floor, and in the numerous 1955–1956 studio scenes motifs from that studio blend with the villa's architectural features. La Californie's opulent *art nouveau* decor, the garden with its palms and eucalyptus trees, the furniture, the painting paraphernalia, all prompted detailed, assured, harmonious paintings, among the finest of Picasso's old age, combining simple representation with the techniques of his Cubist period in sophisticated ways (cf. p. 531). An overall formal unity was supplied by the prevailing linearity of La Californie's interior. The cupboards, windows, walls, easels and paintings constituted a loose ensemble, the elements of which lent weight to each other. In the picture done on 30 March 1956, Picasso used a simple but witty device to underline his own creative inventiveness, placing at the centre of the studio scene a fresh, virgin canvas awaiting the artist. The pure, white, empty space contrasts with the rest of the picture and is also its prime subject. The picture within a picture was one of Picasso's traditional motifs; through it, he grants us access to the very essence of the creative process. Picasso is showing us his power. He can make a world out of nothing.

The marginally later "Jacqueline in the Studio" (p. 530) makes the same point in a slightly different way: Picasso's partner, seen in a villa interior, is positioned against an empty canvas in such a way

Jacqueline in a Crouch
Jacqueline accroupie
Vallauris, 8 October 1954
Oil on canvas, 146 x 114 cm
Zervos XVI, 329. Private collection

Portrait of Jacqueline Roque with Flowers
Portrait de Jacqueline aux fleurs
Vallauris, 2 June 1954
Oil on canvas, 100 x 81 cm
Zervos XVI, 325. Estate of Jacqueline Picasso

that we cannot be certain whether her image is Jacqueline herself or a portrait of her within the portrait.

As Picasso well knew, creative power such as his had its less happy side: freedom accompanied by a sense of compulsion, the virgin canvas crying out to be painted on, for the artist to supply constant proof of his power. But still his studio picture is optimistic, showing that Art can vanquish the void: beside the blank canvas, two others in varying degrees of completion are on the floor. Not that work already done can serve as a substitute for present work; it is no more than proof of past productiveness. This insight may explain the frenetic output of Picasso's late years. At times he painted three, four, even five pictures in a single day, driven by the compelling urge to prove himself anew over and over again.

In his old age, Picasso transferred to his art the task of expressing the vitality which was ebbing from his life. And his tireless activity was also a way of confirming his own accomplishment, perhaps even going further: more, it had to be more. Hence, for instance,

Claude and Paloma Drawing
Claude et Paloma dessinant
Vallauris, April 1954
Oil on canvas, 92 x 73 cm
Zervos XVI, 272
Newark (NJ), Private collection

Left:
Claude Drawing, Françoise and Paloma
Claude dessinant, Françoise et Paloma
Vallauris, 17 May 1954
Oil on canvas, 116 x 89 cm
Zervos XVI, 323; MPP 209
Paris, Musée Picasso

517 The Presence of the Past 1954–1963

Portrait of Sylvette David
Portrait de Sylvette David
1954
Oil on canvas, 100 x 81 cm
Zervos XVI, 274
Basel, Galerie Beyeler

Portrait of Sylvette David
Portrait de Sylvette David
Vallauris, 22 May and 4 October 1954
Oil on panel, 130 x 97 cm
Zervos XVI, 315
Chicago (IL), The Art Institute of Chicago

the new graphic works which, when successful, articulated lifelong fascinations in a succinct and impeccably judged manner – for instance, the 1957 etching series "La Tauromaquia".[366] All of the etchings are precise records of carefully-observed scenes, using just a few dabs and strokes, quickly but perfectly done (pp. 540 and 541). All but the title leaf were aquatint etchings, which enabled Picasso to use solid-printed blocks. The complexity of the process is essentially at odds with spontaneity or the snapshot recording of bullfight scenes, and it is this incongruity that lends Picasso's series its particular genius. Using the most economical of means he achieves a maximum of effect. A handful of lines mark the extent of the arena and grandstand; dabs represent the spectators; and grey and black patches add up to the precision-placed image of a torero, say, driving his banderillas into the neck of an attacking bull. Picasso's style succeeds particularly well in conveying the physical bulk of the bull, its dynamic presence, and its nimble movements. The renderings may appear hasty, but in fact Picasso's images are the product of many years of interest in the subject. It was an interest that united personal experience and art history. Picasso was taking his bearings from Goya, transposing the older painter's classic treatment of the bullfight theme into modern terms and, in the process, proving himself Goya's equal.[367]

Similar proof was provided by over a hundred sheet-metal, col-

Portrait of Sylvette David
Portrait de Sylvette David
21 April 1954 (II)
Pencil on paper, 31 x 24 cm
Zervos XVI, 277; MPP 1429
Paris, Musée Picasso

Portrait of Sylvette David
Portrait de Sylvette David
21 April 1954 (I)
Pencil on paper, 31 x 24 cm
Zervos XVI, 278; MPP 1428
Paris, Musée Picasso

Portrait of Sylvette David
Portrait de Sylvette David
21 April 1954 (III)
Pencil on paper, 32 x 24 cm
Zervos XVI, 284. Private collection

Portrait of Sylvette David in a Green Armchair
Portrait de Sylvette David au fauteuil vert
Vallauris, 18 May 1954
Oil on canvas, 81 x 65 cm
Zervos XVI, 308. New York, Private collection

519 The Presence of the Past 1954–1963

Left:
The Toilette
La coiffure
Vallauris, 7 March 1954
Oil on canvas, 130.5 x 97 cm
Zervos XVI, 262. Lucerne, Picasso Collection,
Donation Rosengart

In the Studio
Dans l'atelier
17 January 1954 (I)
India ink on paper, 24 x 32 cm
Zervos XVI, 183. Private collection

Reclining Woman
Femme couchée
Paris, 26 November 1954
Oil on canvas, 130.5 x 162 cm
Not in Zervos
Estate of Jacqueline Picasso
Paris, Courtesy Galerie Louise Leiris

521   The Presence of the Past   1954–1963

Bullfight Scene
Scène de tauromachie (Le torero soulevé)
Nice, summer 1955
Oil on canvas, 79.5 x 190.4 cm
Not in Zervos. Estate of Jacqueline Picasso

Bullfight Scene
Scène de tauromachie (Le picador soulevé)
Nice, summer 1955
Oil on canvas, 79.5 x 190.4 cm
Not in Zervos. Estate of Jacqueline Picasso

Women of Algiers (after Delacroix)
Femmes d'Alger (d'après Delacroix)
Paris, 1 January 1955
Oil on canvas, 45.8 x 55.2 cm
Zervos XVI, 346. Private collection

Women of Algiers (after Delacroix)
Les femmes d'Alger (d'après Delacroix)
Paris, 14 February 1955
Oil on canvas, 114 x 146 cm
Zervos XVI, 360
New York, Mrs. Victor W. Ganz Collection

Page 524:
Beach at La Garoupe (first version)
La plage à La Garoupe (première version)
Nice, summer 1955
Oil on canvas, 80 x 190 cm
Not in Zervos. Private collection

Beach at La Garoupe (second version)
La plage à La Garoupe (deuxième version)
Nice, summer 1955
Oil on canvas, 80 x 190 cm
Not in Zervos. Private collection

Still Life on a Chest of Drawers
Nature morte sur une commode
Nice, summer 1955
Collage and oil on canvas, 80 x 190 cm
Not in Zervos. Private collection

Page 525:
Great Reclining Nude with Crossed Arms
Femme nue allongée
Nice, summer 1955
Oil, charcoal and papiers collés on canvas,
80 x 190 cm. Not in Zervos; MPP 1990–27
Paris, Musée Picasso

Great Reclining Nude with Crossed Arms
Femme nue allongée
Nice, summer 1955
Oil on canvas, 80 x 190 cm
Not in Zervos. Estate of Jacqueline Picasso

Great Reclining Nude (The Voyeurs)
Femme nue allongée (Les voyeurs)
Nice, 24 August 1955
Oil on canvas, 80 x 192 cm
Not in Zervos. Estate of Jacqueline Picasso

Jacqueline in Turkish Costume
Jacqueline en costume turc
Cannes, 29 November 1955
Oil on canvas, 81 x 65 cm
Not in Zervos
Estate of Jacqueline Picasso
Paris, Courtesy Galerie Louise Leiris

Female Nude in a Turkish Cap
Femme nue au bonnet turc
Cannes, 1 December 1955
Oil on canvas, 116 x 89 cm
Zervos XVI, 529
Paris, Musée National d'Art Moderne,
Centre Georges Pompidou,
Gift of Kahnweiler-Leiris

lapsable sculptures done between 1959 and 1963, continuing what had begun in a smith's workshop at Vallauris in 1954. As early as "Goat Skull, Bottle and Candle" (p. 484), for instance, the bottle was not the usual full-volumed object, but rather sheet metal sol-- dered together. Picasso was out to challenge spatial perception with contrastively juxtaposed kinds of visual experience. Now, he continued this line with three-dimensional works, taking the transfer from the two-dimensional plane to spatial p,resence as their first principle. He cut out paper shapes, folded them as he required, then, blowing up the size with meticulous precision, had a smithy make sheet-metal versions. The last stage was to paint them in such a way as to establish spatial effects that he had sketched in on his paper maquettes. These metal creations were a variation on what he had been doing in his sculptural collage work in the synthetic Cubism phase, but also harked back to the wire constructions thought out for the Apollinaire memorial in 1928 (cf. pp. 324 and 325):[368] the graphic and the sculptural constructs coincided in such a way as to question principles of transfer.

The extent to which Picasso was drawing on his own work in these sheet-metal sculptures can be demonstrated down to details of motif. The 1961 "Football Player" (p. 566) is a perfect example of this. The figure, seen in mid-game, has his left arm raised, his right swung down in an arc. There is a classical contrapposto in the position of the legs, the left providing the vertical axis of the composition, the right wide and high. The figure has been foreshortened as in a picture, the limbs appearing in different sizes – a fact which we have been trained by convention to interpret as registering different distances from the point of view. The impression is one of power and energy, heightened by the S-shape of the figure. The footballer is plainly about to put his full force into a kick. However, no player would strike quite this attitude. Not that the movement in itself is impossible; but it is untypical, because in kicking a long shot no player would raise the arm on the same side of his body as the leg he is standing on, or lower the arm on the same side as the leg he is taking the kick with – the energy that went into the opposed movements would cancel out, and little power would be left to go into the kick itself. A real football player would automatically behave in exactly the opposite way. Picasso's figure only makes sense if we imagine him moving forwards as he jumps. His unstable position recalls a dancer; and in fact the figure originated in a dance environment. The artist was drawing on studies he had drawn of the Ballets Russes in 1919 and which he had worked on further in the Twenties.[369] Calling the figure a football player is sleight of hand. The trick is made plausible purely by the painted shirt, shorts and boots. Sculpture such as this is not intended as a mimetic representation of reality; rather, it sets out to play with the basics of visual experience. And deception is the fundamental principle of this art.

Seated Nude
Femme nue accroupie
Cannes, 2 January 1956
Oil on canvas, 130 x 97 cm
Zervos XVII, 1
Paris, Galerie Louise Leiris

Jacqueline in the Studio
Jacqueline dans l'atelier
Cannes, 2 to 8 April 1956
Oil on canvas, 114 x 146 cm
Zervos XVII, 67. Lucerne, Picasso Collection,
Donation Rosengart

Woman in the Studio
Femme dans l'atelier
Cannes, 11 May to 10 June 1956
Oil on canvas, 65 x 81 cm
Zervos XVII, 107. Private collection;
formerly Galerie Beyeler, Basel

530 The Presence of the Past 1954–1963

This was nothing new in the Fifties; Picasso was reworking principles he had already established. We might analyse the great figural group of "Bathers" (pp. 537 and 538/539), which Picasso made in 1956, in much the same terms. In it, the emphatically simple principle of construction becomes the true subject. The stereometric quality of the group links it to the block-and-line works of the Twenties; the importance of the material recalls the assemblages of the Forties and early Fifties; and, like the collapsible sheet-metal sculptures, the roots of the work lie in the material collages of synthetic Cubism. The sculpture looks back to Picasso's own innovations in technique; and the subject is retrospective in character too, recalling the series of pictures of bathers which Picasso did in the Twenties. In several of those compositions (cf. pp. 320, 321, 330 and 331) he was playing with relief-like volume and geometrically-inspired forms. The plasticity of the 1956 "Bathers" results from the transfer to another material.[370] At times, Picasso's habitually self-referential mode can seem hermetic.

His self-referential habit distinguished the Picasso of old age fundamentally from earlier Picassos. His great fame and his withdraw-

The Studio at "La Californie", Cannes
L'atelier de "La Californie" à Cannes
Cannes, 30 March 1956
Oil on canvas, 114 x 146 cm
Zervos XVII, 56; MPP 211
Paris, Musée Picasso

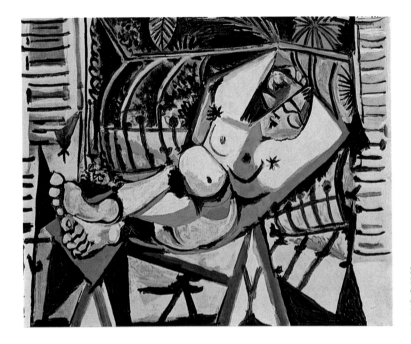

Nude in Front of the Garden
Femme nue devant le jardin
Cannes, 29 to 31 August 1956
Oil on canvas, 130 x 162 cm
Zervos XVII, 158
Amsterdam, Stedelijk Museum

al from public life were the twin poles of his existence: inevitably, they accompanied an artistic isolation that was far-reaching. This is only paradoxical at first glance. As a popular figure – comparable to film stars or politicians who are constantly in the limelight – Picasso had been mythologized into a living legend, stripped of everyday normality in the public mind. He left Paris in order to work undisturbed in the pleasant climate of the south; and his isolation inevitably grew. The situation was complicated by the fact that the post-occupation now beginning in political and cultural life, which had claimed Picasso as the figurehead of rehabilitated and revitalized Modernism, had obscured a fact which was already becoming apparent in the 1940s: Picasso was no longer in the contemporary mainstream of developments in art.

Since Surrealism, innovation in modern art had been taking quite different courses. Be it in the USA or in France, the prevailing mode was abstract art, of one kind or another. The various abstract camps had already been dominant in the French arts opposition during the occupation years, and after the Second World War abstract art bore all before it. 1947 was the turning-point in public terms. In that year, independently of each other, young artists exhibiting at galleries in New York and Paris made apparent the special expressive potential of the new formal idiom.[371] They all dispensed with the figure – which for Picasso, whether he retained or deconstructed it, nonetheless always remained central; and this departure was associated with automatic processes linked to the subconscious, to which Picasso, whose work proceeded along intellectual lines, had a fundamental antipathy. Building on Surrealist

Two Women on the Beach
Deux femmes sur la plage
Cannes, 16 February 1956
Oil on canvas, 92 x 73 cm
Zervos XVII, 36
Paris, Musée National d'Art Moderne,
Centre Georges Pompidou

Man and Woman at the Beach
Homme et femme sur la plage
Cannes, 18 April 1956
Oil on canvas, 89 x 116 cm
Zervos XVII, 78. Private collection

Nude in a Rocking Chair
Femme nue à la chaise à bascule
Cannes, 26 March 1956
Oil on canvas, 195 x 130 cm
Zervos XVII, 55
Sydney, Art Gallery of New South Wales

ideals and the improvisations of Paul Klee, the young international abstract artists evolved new techniques allowing subconscious processes ungoverned by the will into their work. Tachism, lyrical abstraction, Abstract Expressionism: these were the major labels attached to a new style of painting that deliberately bypassed prevailing norms and advocated radical individualism. From the dripping method of the American Jackson Pollock, who covered entire canvases with paint dripped from holed buckets, to the action painting of French artist Georges Mathieu, often covering huge surfaces in a rapid frenzy with crowds looking on, elevating speed itself to a cardinal principle, abstract art was busy foregrounding anti-intellectual processes.[372] Emotion, moods, the pure impact of colours and shapes, regardless of rational criteria in art, also informed the paintings of a Hans Hartung or Serge Poliakoff. The psychologization of creative principles peaked in the work of Jean Dubuffet, who took the work of the mentally handicapped as his model. Even in art that retained the figure, expressive tendencies were dominant: for example, in the work of the COBRA group.[373]

The tragedy of late Picasso was that these currents in art dominated, indeed smothered the scene till 1960. To the general public, he became a figure to be identified with, almost a guardian of

Spring
Le printemps
20 March 1956
Oil on canvas, 130 x 195 cm
Zervos XVII, 45
Paris, Musée National d'Art Moderne, Centre Georges Pompidou

Bacchanal
Bacchanale
22 September 1955 (II)
India ink and gouache on paper,
50.7 x 65.8 cm
Zervos XVI, 430; MPP 1990–92
Paris, Musée Picasso

tradition – quite the opposite of what he intended. Compared with the brusque unfamiliarity of a new art that made no concessions, Picasso's work came to seem comprehensible and accessible, and to afford a familiar point of orientation amidst the chaos. Tellingly, his "Sylvette" pictures (pp. 518 and 519) were immensely popular. In 1954 he had met a young woman, Sylvette David, who sat for him. He did over forty drawings and oils of her; they were very quickly published and seen in reproductions all over the world.[374] Two factors influenced the fame and impact of the series. One was the look of the girl herself, her hair in the pony tail then fashion-

Women of Algiers (after Delacroix)
Les femmes d'Alger (d'après Delacroix)
Paris, 17 March 1955
Lithograph, 23.5 x 34 cm
Mourlot 266; Rau 610

Bathers on the Beach at La Garoupe
Baigneurs sur la plage à La Garoupe
Cannes, 1957
Oil on canvas, 194.2 x 258.7 cm
Not in Zervos
Geneva, Musée d'Art et d'Histoire

The Bathers
Les baigneurs
Cannes, 1956
Six figures, bronze, from
wooden originals
Spies 503–508; MPP 352–357
Paris, Musée Picasso

Pages 538/539:
The Bathers
Les baigneurs
Cannes, 1956
Six figures: wooden original
Spies 503–508 I
Stuttgart, Staatsgalerie Stuttgart

From left:
The diver (La plongeuse),
264 x 83.5 x 83.5 cm
Man with clasped hands
(L'homme aux mains jointes),
213.5 x 73 x 36 cm
The fountain man (L'homme fontaine),
227 x 88 x 77.5 cm
The child (L'enfant),
136 x 67 x 46 cm
Woman with outstretched arms
(La femme aux bras écartés),
198 x 74 x 46 cm
The young man (Le jeune homme),
176 x 65 x 46 cm

The Presence of the Past 1954–1963 **537**

The Bullfighters Enter the Arena ("La Tauromaquia", 3)
Paseo de cuadrillas. Cannes, spring 1957
Etching, 20 x 30 cm. Bloch 953

The Picador Attacks ("La Tauromaquia", 12)
El picador obligando al toro con su pica
Cannes, spring 1957. Etching, 20 x 30 cm. Bloch 962

The Banderillas Go In ("La Tauromaquia", 14)
Clavando un par de banderillas. Cannes, spring 1957
Etching, 20 x 30 cm. Bloch 964

The Matador Decrees the Bull's Death ("La Tauromaquia", 16)
El matador brinda la muerte del toro. Cannes, spring 1957
Etching, 20 x 30 cm. Bloch 966

Capework ("La Tauromaquia", 17)
Suerte de muleta. Cannes, spring 1957
Etching, 20 x 30 cm. Bloch 967

The Injury ("La Tauromaquia", 18)
La cogida. Cannes, spring 1957
Etching, 20 x 30 cm. Bloch 968

Aiming the Deathblow ("La Tauromaquia", 19)
Citando a matar. Cannes, spring 1957
Etching, 20 x 30 cm. Bloch 969

The Deathblow ("La Tauromaquia", 20)
La estocada. Cannes, spring 1957
Etching, 20 x 30 cm. Bloch 970

The Torero Proclaims the Death of the Bull ("La Tauromaquiá", 21)
Después de la estocada el torero señala la muerte del toro
Cannes, spring 1957. Etching, 20 x 30 cm. Bloch 971

Dragging Out the Dead Bull ("La Tauromaquia", 23)
El arrastre. Cannes, spring 1957
Etching, 20 x 30 cm. Bloch 973

Provoking the Bull on Horseback ("La Tauromaquia", 25)
Citando al toro con el rejón. Cannes, spring 1957
Etching, 20 x 30 cm. Bloch 975

Bullfighting on Horseback ("La Tauromaquia", 26)
Alanceando a un toro. Cannes, spring 1957
Etching, 20 x 30 cm. Bloch 976

Lucien Clergue:
Pablo Picasso (photograph), Cannes 1956

Jaime Sabartés with a Pin-up
Jaime Sabartés avec une pin-up
Cannes, 4 December 1957
Colour heliogravure with India ink,
35.6 x 26 cm. Not in Zervos; MPB 70.674
Barcelona, Museu Picasso

The Bay of Cannes
La baie de Cannes
Cannes, 19 April to 9 June 1958
Oil on canvas, 130 x 195 cm
Zervos XVIII, 83; MPP 212
Paris, Musée Picasso

Bust of a Woman (after Lucas Cranach the Younger)
Buste de femme (d'après Lucas Cranach le Jeune)
1958. Colour linocut, 65 x 53.5 cm. Bloch 859

Woman with Raised Arm
Femme accroupie au bras levé
Cannes, 12 January 1956
Lithograph, 43 x 60 cm
Mourlot 275; Rau 618

Still Life with Bull's Head
Nature morte à la tête de taureau
Cannes, 25 May to 9 June 1958
Oil on canvas, 162.5 x 130 cm
Zervos XVIII, 237; MPP 213
Paris, Musée Picasso

The Dining Room at Vauvenargues
La salle à manger à Vauvenargues
Vauvenargues and Cannes,
23 March 1959 and 23 January 1960
Oil on canvas, 195 x 280 cm
Zervos XVIII, 395
Paris, Galerie Louise Leiris

547   The Presence of the Past   1954–1963

Portrait of Jacqueline
Portrait de Jacqueline
13 February 1957
Collage and charcoal on paper,
64 x 51 cm
Not in Zervos
Estate of Jacqueline Picasso

Portrait of Jacqueline in Profile
Portrait de Jacqueline de profil
17 April 1959
Oil on canvas, 61 x 49.5 cm
Zervos XVIII, 445. Private collection

Portrait of Jacqueline in Profile
Portrait de Jacqueline de profil
17 April 1959 (II)
Oil on canvas, 55 x 46 cm
Zervos XVIII, 446. Private collection

Portrait of Jacqueline in Profile
Portrait de Jacqueline de profil
17 April 1959 (III)
Oil on canvas, 46 x 38 cm
Zervos XVIII, 447. Private collection

Portrait of Jacqueline in Profile
Portrait de Jacqueline de profil
17 April 1959 (IV)
Oil on canvas, 55 x 46 cm
Zervos XVIII, 448. Private collection

The Presence of the Past 1954–1963 **549**

The Studio
L'atelier (Les pigeons perchés)
Vauvenargues, 2 April 1960
Oil on canvas, 50 x 61 cm
Zervos XIX, 199. Estate of the artist

Faun and Goat
Faune et chèvre
1959. Colour linocut, 53 x 64 cm. Bloch 934

550

The Fall of Icarus
La chute d'Icare. Cannes, 1958
Mural, 8 x 10 m. Not in Zervos
Paris, Palais de l'UNESCO, Delegates' Lobby

Left:
Seated Nude
Femme nue accroupie
Vauvenargues or Cannes,
21 (III) and 24 June 1959
Oil on canvas, 146 x 114 cm
Zervos XVIII, 488. Private collection;
formerly Galerie Beyeler, Basel

Seated Nude
Femme nue assise
Cannes, 8 February 1959
Oil on canvas, 100 x 81 cm
Zervos XVIII, 322
Private collection

Reclining Nude Under a Pine Tree
Femme nue couchée sous un pin
Cannes, 20 January 1959
Oil on canvas, 195 x 280 cm
Zervos XVIII, 323
Chicago (IL), The Art Institute of Chicago

553 The Presence of the Past 1954–1963

El Bobo (after Velázquez and Murillo)
El bobo (d'après Velázquez et Murillo)
Vauvenargues, 14 and 15 April 1959
Oil and enamel paint on canvas, 92 x 73 cm
Zervos XVIII, 484. Private collection

Bathsheba
Bethsabée
30 January 1960
Oil on canvas, 140 x 194 cm
Zervos XIX, 157. Private collection

The Presence of the Past 1954–1963 **554**

Nude on a Sofa
Femme nue sur un divan
Vauvenargues, 3 February 1960
Oil on canvas, 195 x 130 cm
Zervos XIX, 162
New York, Private collection

Reclining Nude on a Blue Divan
Femme nue couchée sur un divan bleu
Vauvenargues, 20 April 1960
Oil on canvas, 89 x 115.5 cm
Zervos XIX, 279
Paris, Musée National d'Art Moderne,
Centre Georges Pompidou,
Gift of Louise and Michel Leiris

Bather with Sand Shovel
Nu sur la plage et pelle
Vauvenargues, 12 April 1960
Oil on canvas, 114 x 146 cm
Zervos XIX, 236. Paris,
Bernard Ruiz-Picasso Collection

Right:
Seated Nude Against Green Background
Femme nue accroupie sur fond vert
Vauvenargues, 11 May 1960
Oil on canvas, 130 x 97 cm
Zervos XIX, 293. Private collection;
formerly Galerie Beyeler, Basel

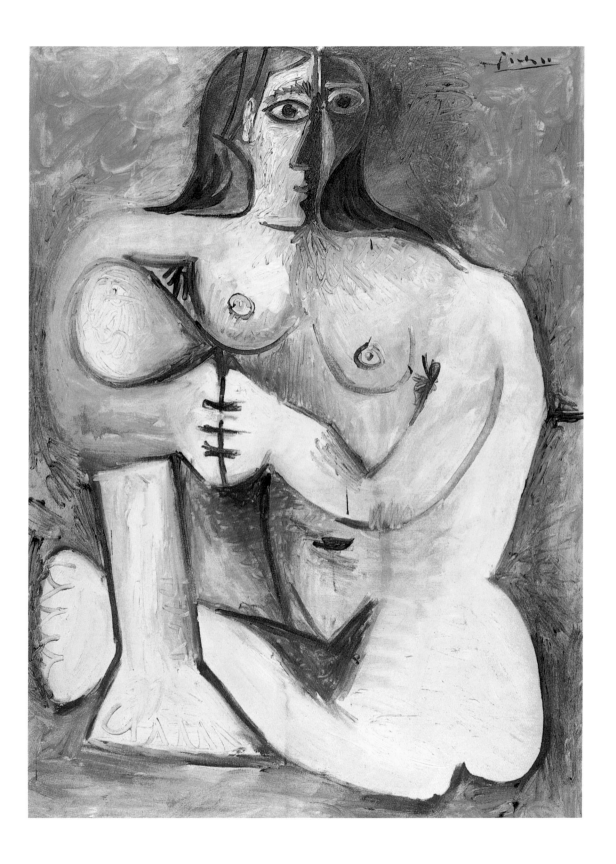

Study for "Le Déjeuner sur l'herbe" (after Manet)
Le Déjeuner sur l'herbe (d'après Manet)
Vauvenargues, 3 March to 20 August 1960
Oil on canvas, 129 x 195 cm
Zervos XIX, 204; MPP 215
Paris, Musée Picasso

Edouard Manet:
Le Déjeuner sur l'herbe, 1863
Oil on canvas, 208 x 264.5 cm
Paris, Musée d'Orsay

able, the hallmark of an entire generation of young women. The other was that the "Picasso style" rendered the defamiliarization tactics of modern painting accessible. Picasso did both naturalist representations of his sitter and abstractive, schematic, anti-figural renderings of the real image. The latter subversively took the details of head and body apart into lines and blocks, reassembling them in new forms subject to the artist's caprice. It was a textbook illustration of the principles of dissociation; and, since it referred constantly to the real figure of the sitter, it was an act of artistic creation that could readily be understood. Even those who disliked deformed figures had to acknowledge and respect Picasso's artistry. He had become the great go-between, easing relations between the shockingly new and established tradition.

To see Picasso thus was of course to misunderstand him. He would doubtless have been unaffected by the process if his work and person had not been assigned an absolute status. Everything he did was hailed with rapture. Apart from attacks of the familiar sort, he was now exempt from even the smallest criticism, public comments on Picasso, paeans and panegyrics, tending to make a demi-god of him.[375] It was good for business, of course, sending his prices soaring, even for minor work. But it had a devastating effect on the artist's creative spirit. He had always been one to assimilate and process new stimuli: his engagement with Surrealism, for in-

Study for "Le Déjeuner sur l'herbe" (after Manet)
Etude pour "Le Déjeuner sur l'herbe" (d'après Manet)
Vallauris, 29 June 1954
Pencil on paper, 21 x 27 cm
Zervos XVI, 319; MPP 1887
Paris, Musée Picasso

stance, a movement so very different in nature from his own art, was extraordinarily productive, because it prompted him to constant re-examination of his own approach. Such fertile interchange was now a thing of the past. He was out of sympathy with contemporary art; in the eyes of young artists he was a grand old man of yesteryear, admired for his onetime achievements but of no present use except perhaps as an ideological guide. Though his work still

Le Déjeuner sur l'herbe (after Manet)
Le Déjeuner sur l'herbe (d'après Manet)
Vauvenargues, 4 March and 30 July 1960
Oil on canvas, 60 x 73 cm. Zervos XIX, 205
Private collection; formerly Galerie Beyeler, Basel

559   The Presence of the Past   1954–1963

Le Déjeuner sur l'herbe (after Manet)
Le Déjeuner sur l'herbe (d'après Manet)
Vauvenargues, 29 February 1960
Oil on canvas, 130 x 195 cm
Zervos XIX, 203. Private collection;
formerly Galerie Beyeler, Basel

Le Déjeuner sur l'herbe (after Manet)
Le Déjeuner sur l'herbe (d'après Manet)
Mougins, 16 July 1961
Oil on canvas, 89 x 116 cm
Zervos XX, 91. Lucerne, Picasso Collection,
Donation Rosengart

The Presence of the Past 1954–1963 **560**

served as a point of reference, it was his early work the younger artists went to, not the later. Henry Moore, for instance, took his bearings from the sculptural metamorphoses Picasso had done in the late Twenties;[376] Francis Bacon evolved new figure images from Picasso's achievements of the Thirties.[377]

Picasso's isolation from the art scene, and the cult that attached to his own person, only served to confirm traits that were already his. His work took on an avowedly universal character. He turned, for instance, to new modes of graphic art. He made engravings on celluloid,[378] and in particular from the late 1950s on he turned to linocuts.[379] At the time the technique was enjoying unusual popularity. Picasso used it primarily for work in colour, playing off large blocks against small, and used the printing plate webs as a linear grid, employing an approach that had been developed for woodcuts by other 20th-century artists (cf. pp. 546, 573, 580 and 581).[380]

Picasso's interest in public art was revived in autumn 1957 when he agreed to paint a work for the delegates' foyer at UNESCO

Le Déjeuner sur l'herbe (after Manet)
Le Déjeuner sur l'herbe (d'après Manet)
Mougins, 26 July 1961 (VI)
Crayon on cardboard, 27 x 37 cm
Zervos XX, 107. Private collection

Le Déjeuner sur l'herbe (after Manet)
Le Déjeuner sur l'herbe (d'après Manet)
Mougins, 17 June 1961
Oil on canvas, 60 x 73 cm
Zervos XX, 34. Private collection;
formerly Galerie Rosengart

headquarters in Paris. It was his first commission to do a mural since "Guernica".[381] As with the Spanish Civil War painting, Picasso's first thought was of a subject concerning the artist's role. But what he in fact painted, in 1958, was a seaside scene with standing and reclining figures and one dark figure plunging with outstretched limbs into the great blue waters. Georges Salles gave the work the title "The Fall of Icarus" (p. 551) in order to add a profounder intellectual dimension.[382] The central figure evolved from a child's plaything, a swallow made of folded paper. Picasso was evidently deeply indebted to the simple technique of folding paper; it also governed his work in sheet-metal sculpture.[383] Picasso returned to this motif in a stage set design he did in 1962 for a Paris Opera House production of a ballet, "The Fall of Icarus".[384]

Work of this nature placed Picasso alongside the other masters of classical Modernism. Fernand Léger, for instance, had painted the great hall of the United Nations building in New York in 1952.[385] Léger's art in turn inspired Picasso to paint frieze-like compositions featuring crudely stylized figures seen against vast areas of bright colour. These works (cf. pp. 524 and 525) were marked by a simple allegorical tone and a quality of populist humanism. Léger's large-scale paintings rendered everyday life in a pronounced, accessible style by combining elements of classic Modernism with aspects of folk or propagandist art.[386] Picasso, tending towards compositions in strong colours, was also toying with Fauvism. He was after an

Bust of a Seated Woman
Buste de femme assise
Vauvenargues, 2 April 1960
Oil on canvas, 116 x 88 cm
Zervos XIX, 225. Private collection

Bust of a Seated Woman
Buste de femme assise
Vauvenargues, 2 April 1960
Oil on canvas, 100 x 81 cm
Zervos XIX, 255
Colmar, Musée d'Unterlinden

Reclining Nude
Femme nue couchée
5 December 1960
Oil on canvas, 114 x 146 cm
Zervos XIX, 406. Private collection

Reclining Nude
Femme nue allongée
Mougins, 11 December 1961 (III)
Oil on canvas, 92 x 73 cm
Zervos XX, 149. Private collection

The Presence of the Past 1954–1963 **563**

Woman and Dog Under a Tree
Femme et chien sous un arbre
Mougins, 13 December 1961
and 10 January 1962
Oil on canvas, 162 x 130 cm
Zervos XX, 160. Private collection

entrée into the practices of contemporary art, even though it was at variance with his own aims; and so expressive traits of style, pure colour effects, and actionist aspects, all began to be increasingly noticeable in his work. But unfortunately real dynamics and expressive force were frequently sacrificed to mere bustle, as he continued to produce work for the sake of it. The 1959 variations on a portrait of Jacqueline (p. 549) prove the point. The artist was trying to meet the Picasso mystique halfway by boosting production; but the quality suffered all too often. He had always tried and tested his ideas in long series of studies; now, at the expense of artistic discipline, he extended the principle tremendously. His habit of returning to his own work, of reworking earlier innovations, was now merely ticking over, no more than an end in itself.

The sterility that was now in Picasso's work can be measured by the paraphrases of old masters done at this time (and only at this time). Starting from a single original, he would produce entire series of variations. In a sense, this process began in 1947 with the

various states of his lithograph after Lucas Cranach's "David and Bathsheba" (p. 476). In the winter of 1954, in his Paris studio in the Rue des Grands-Augustins, he established paraphrase as his new working principle. From 13 December 1954 to 14 February 1955 he did fifteen oil variations on Delacroix's "The Women of Algiers" (cf. p. 523), accompanied by a number of drawings, etchings and lithographs (p. 536).[387] Picasso did not retain the composition, colours or style of the original, but drew freely upon its formal repertoire to suit himself. Delacroix's painting shows three harem women and a servant woman seen from behind. It is a striking picture, deriving its impact from the contrast of dark interior and highlighted figures bright against the dusk.

From the outset, Picasso made changes in this basic pattern, transposing one seated figure from the original right to the left side, placing the servant in the foreground, or introducing new figures. In January 1955 his concept was in place. He could go on. Now, the composition was dominated by the polarity between a clothed

Three Standing Women
Trois femmes debout
Cannes, 1961
Cut and folded paper,
each 44 x 26.5 cm
Spies 600, 580 1a, 601. Private collection

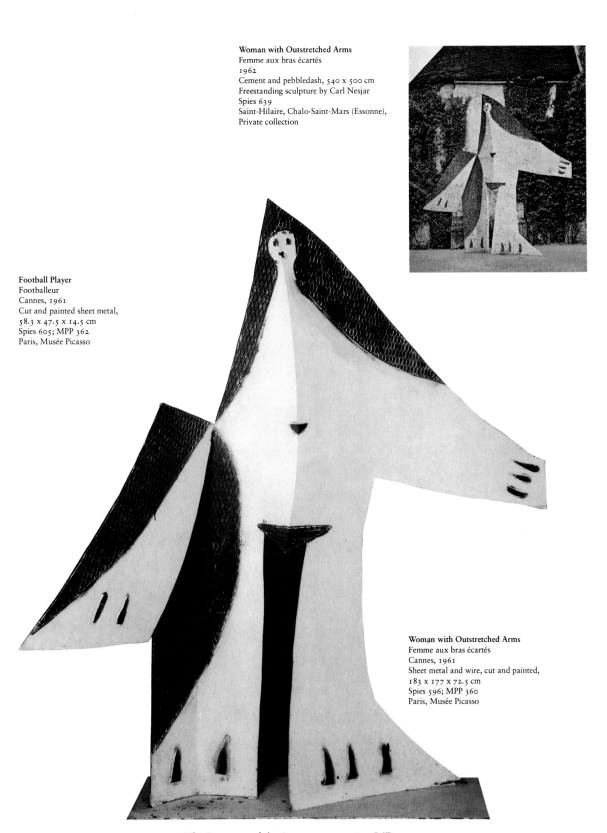

Woman with Outstretched Arms
Femme aux bras écartés
1962
Cement and pebbledash, 540 x 500 cm
Freestanding sculpture by Carl Nesjar
Spies 639
Saint-Hilaire, Chalo-Saint-Mars (Essonne),
Private collection

Football Player
Footballeur
Cannes, 1961
Cut and painted sheet metal,
58.3 x 47.5 x 14.5 cm
Spies 605; MPP 362
Paris, Musée Picasso

Woman with Outstretched Arms
Femme aux bras écartés
Cannes, 1961
Sheet metal and wire, cut and painted,
183 x 177 x 72.5 cm
Spies 596; MPP 360
Paris, Musée Picasso

Seated Woman with Hat
Femme assise au chapeau
27 January 1961
Oil on panel, 115.5 x 89 cm
Zervos XIX, 422
Galerie Rosengart

568

Woman with Hat
Femme au chapeau
Cannes, 1961 and 1963
Cut and folded sheet metal,
painted (1963) in several colours,
126 x 73 x 41 cm. Spies 626 2a
Basel, Beyeler Collection

569

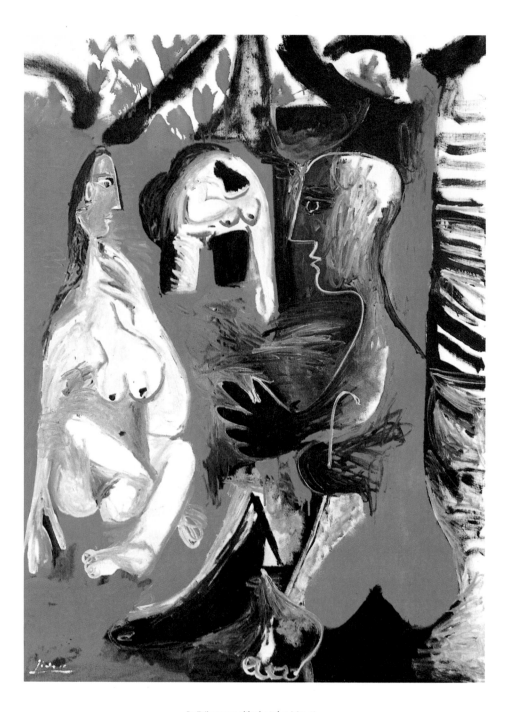

Le Déjeuner sur l'herbe (after Manet)
Le Déjeuner sur l'herbe (d'après Manet)
Mougins, 30 July 1961
Oil on canvas, 130 x 97 cm
Zervos XX, 113
Humlebæk (Denmark), Louisiana Museum

570

Flute Player
Joueur de flûte
Mougins, 31 December 1962
Oil on canvas, 162 x 130 cm
Zervos XXIII, 96
Geneva, Heinz Berggruen Collection

Woman with Big Hat
Femme au grand chapeau
Mougins, 3 January to 27 July 1962
Oil on canvas, 130 x 97 cm
Zervos XX, 185. Private collection;
formerly Galerie Rosengart

Bust of a Woman with Hat
Buste de femme au chapeau
Mougins, 1962
Coloured linocut, 63.5 x 52.5 cm
Bloch 1072

Family Portrait
Portrait de famille
Mougins, 19 June to 19 October 1962
Lithograph with crayon, 56 x 76 cm
Zervos XXIII, 4; Rau 748; MPP 1532
Paris, Musée Picasso

Family Portrait
Portrait de famille
Mougins, 6 July and 16 October 1962
Lithograph with crayon, 50 x 66 cm
Zervos XXIII, 3; Mourlot 387; Bloch 1032;
Rau 753. Private collection

The Presence of the Past   1954–1963   **574**

Family Portrait
Portrait de famille
Mougins, 21 June and 11 October 1962 (III)
Lithograph with crayon, 56 x 76 cm
Zervos XXIII, 5; Mourlot 384; Bloch 1030;
Rau 750. Private collection

Family Portrait
Portrait de famille
Mougins, 21 June and 9 October 1962 (III)
Lithograph with crayon, 56 x 76 cm
Zervos XXIII, 2; Mourlot 383; Bloch 1029;
Rau 749. Private collection

575   The Presence of the Past   1954–1963

The Rape of the Sabine Women (after David)
L'enlèvement des Sabines (d'après David)
Mougins, 4 to 8 November 1962
Oil on canvas, 97 x 130 cm
Zervos XXIII, 69
Paris, Musée National d'Art Moderne,
Centre Georges Pompidou

The Rape of the Sabine Women
L'enlèvement des Sabines
Mougins, 24 October 1962
Oil on canvas, 46 x 55 cm
Zervos XXIII, 6
Prague, Národni Gallery

The Rape of the Sabine Women (after David)
L'enlèvement des Sabines (d'après David)
Mougins, 9 January and 7 February 1963
Oil on canvas, 195.5 x 130 cm
Zervos XXIII, 121
Boston (MA), Museum of Fine Arts

The Presence of the Past 1954–1963 **576**

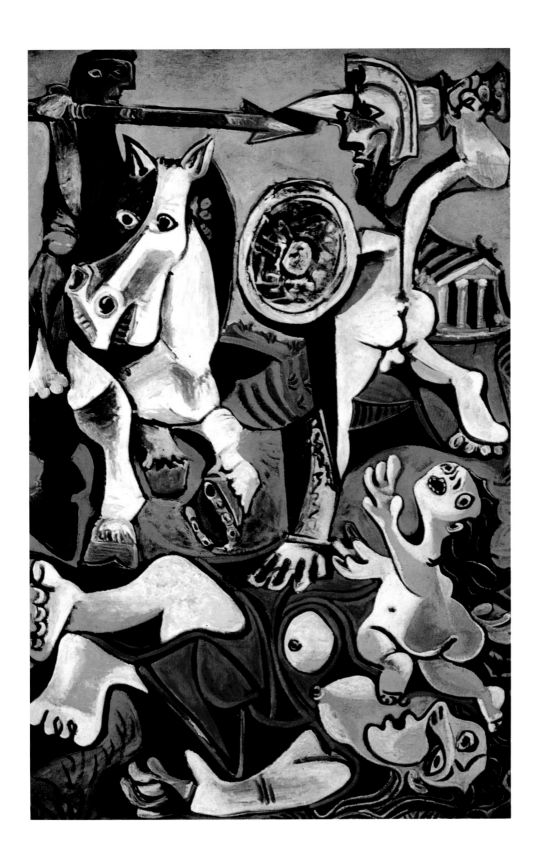

Head of a Woman
Tête de femme
Cannes, 1961
Cut, folded and painted sheet metal,
39 x 24 x 11.2 cm
Spies 620.2. Private collection

woman seated at left and a nude reclining at right. The servant, turning away, and a further nude at the rear completed the group. The changes were not entirely the product of caprice; Picasso had taken the foreground grouping from a picture of odalisques by Jean-Auguste Dominique Ingres.[388]

The seated figure at the rear was also taken from an Ingres, the "Turkish Bath", which Picasso had already been importantly inspired by in his work on "Les Demoiselles d'Avignon".[389] He was deliberately juxtaposing Ingres and Delacroix in a new context, the combination attesting his considerable insight into art history. In their day, the two painters stood for the opposing aesthetic positions of Romanticism and Classicism, but met in their presentation of oriental subject matter.[390] This common ground was introduced by Picasso, both formally and in terms of the motifs, into his series of paraphrases – to great and unifying effect. The series peaked in the picture painted on 14 February 1955. The exotic brightness of the Orient is handled contrastively and colourfully, the seductive

Head
(Maquette for Sculpture in Chicago Civic Center)
Mougins, 1962 to 1964
Iron and sheet metal, 104.7 x 69.9 x 48.3 cm
Spies 643 2b
Chicago (IL), The Art Institute of Chicago

eroticism of the two main figures nakedly presented. Picasso has combined subtle illusionist approaches with abstractive methods. His new articulation of a traditional theme also alludes to the odalisque paintings of Matisse.[391]

Over the next few years he extended his paraphrase series considerably, but the quantity of output was not always matched by the quality. In 1957 he did over fifty variations on Velázquez's "Las Meninas". They were followed by over 150 sketches and drawings, and 27 paintings, done after Manet's "Le Déjeuner sur l'herbe" from 1959 to 1962. Finally, he did a number of larger works adapting Jacques-Louis David's "Rape of the Sabine Women".[392]

Manet's famous painting, which shocked its 19th-century audience and prompted a scandal when first exhibited, shows two naked or near-naked women with two clothed men in a country setting (cf. p. 558). Manet had painted his work as something of a pastiche, drawing on Giorgione's "Concert in the Country" (in the Louvre) and a detail from a copper engraving by Raimondi after a

Still Life by Lamplight
Nature morte sous la lampe
Mougins, 1962
Coloured linocut, 53 x 63.8 cm
Bloch 1101

design by Raphael.[393] The figure group of the "Déjeuner" had begun to interest Picasso in June 1954 because his own treatments of painters and models used a similar grouping. At that time he did a number of sketches after Manet, returning at the end of the Fifties to more concentrated work on the material.[394] He did variations on the composition of the "Déjeuner" in oils, graphics and drawings, emphasizing the contrast between the female nudes and the male figures, which he subjected to greater or lesser degrees of decon-struction (pp. 558 to 561). In most of the pictures, he used only one man with the women – transparently a version of his own painter and model theme. He tried to harmonize form and subject by trans-lating the motif's undisguised eroticism into an intensified expres-sionism of style, rendering the figures and the landscape as inter-penetrating, dynamic equivalents. The range in his variations, the formal concentration, are slighter than in "Women of Algiers", without a comparable intellectual depth or unity. Most of the "Dé-jeuner" paraphrases repeat the same superficial version of the same

Woman with Hat
Femme au chapeau
1963
Coloured linocut, 53 x 40 cm
Bloch 1145

Le Déjeuner sur l'herbe (after Manet)
Le Déjeuner sur l'herbe (d'après Manet)
Mougins, 13 March 1962
Coloured linocut, 53.3 x 64.5 cm
Bloch 1027

581   The Presence of the Past   1954–1963

The Artist and His Model
Le peintre et son modèle
Mougins, 3 (I) and 4 March 1963
Oil on canvas, 50 x 108 cm
Zervos XXIII, 158

The Artist and His Model
Le peintre et son modèle
Mougins, 3 (II) and 4 March 1963
Oil on canvas, 50 x 108 cm
Zervos XXIII, 160

scene. There was manifestly no rigorously thought-out concept underpinning Picasso's work on the series.

And the variations on "The Rape of the Sabine Women" are similarly one-dimensional. There was a pre-David treatment of the subject by Nicolas Poussin on which Picasso drew for his own work, borrowing the emotionalism of the figures and stressing the fight, the brutality, and the suffering of the women, as his principal factors in form and content.[395] After trying out the poses in monochrome versions (cf. p. 576) he tested colour contrasts in order to establish which intensified the emotional impact best (p. 576) before finally painting a simplified, cropped version in vertical format that uses only four figures: two warriors, a dead mother, and her

The Artist in His Studio (initial stage)
Le peintre dans son atelier
Mougins, 14 and 15 March 1963
Oil on canvas, 60 x 93 cm
Zervos XXIII, 172

The Artist in His Studio
Le peintre dans son atelier
Mougins, 4 April 1963
Oil on canvas, 60 x 93 cm
Zervos XXIII, 172

screaming child (p. 577). The allusions to Picasso's own war paintings, from "Guernica" through "Massacre in Korea" to "War" and "Peace" (pp. 400/401, 500/501 and 452), are unmistakable.

The difference to earlier periods in Picasso's work is striking, to say the least. Taking his bearings from the art of the past, for Picasso, always implied locating incentives and ideas – be it the odalisques of Ingres for early Cubism or ancient sculpture and baroque paintings for the late Rose Period and his so-called Classicism. This ongoing and extremely fruitful process peaked in Picasso's late years in his ceramic art of the Forties and Fifties. His ware, and the artwork with which it was decorated, was no imitation of a classical original (cf. pp. 492 to 495). It was not a copy of ancient stor-

584   The Presence of the Past   1954–1963

Rembrandt and Saskia
Rembrandt et Saskia
Mougins, 13 March 1963
Oil on canvas, 130 x 162 cm
Zervos XXIII, 171

The Artist and His Model (initial stage)
Le peintre et son modèle
Mougins, 8 March 1963 (II)
Oil on canvas, 96 x 132 cm
Zervos XXIII, 169

The Artist and His Model (final state)
Le peintre et son modèle
Mougins, 16 May 1963
Oil on canvas, 96 x 132 cm
Zervos XXIII, 169

age, cultic or drinking vessels, nor did the decorative style have anything in common with the technique or form of black and red vase paintings.[396] Picasso varied the first principles and translated into a modern idiom whatever was capable of analogy. His thick-bellied vases with sheer conical necks were decorated with figures organically adapted to the shapes of the vessels. Maenads, nymphs and fauns, generously and tellingly outlined and economical in detail, people the surfaces of the ware. In its modernity, Picasso's ceramic art was one of classical harmony, in compositions of great beauty.

Picasso did other variations of old masters in the Forties. Even as the fighting was raging around Paris in 1944, he was at work on an adaptation of Poussin's "Bacchanal.[397] In 1947, among other things, he modelled a lithographic series on Cranach's painting "David and Bathsheba". In 1950 he painted versions of Gustave Courbet's "Women on the Banks of the Seine" and El Greco's "Portrait of a Painter".[398] These were followed between 1955 and

Seated Woman in a Black Armchair
Femme assise dans un fauteuil noir
Mougins, 19 November and 18 December 1962
Oil on canvas, 130 x 97 cm. Zervos XXIII, 85
Private collection; formerly Galerie Beyeler, Basel

Seated Woman in an Armchair
Femme assise dans un fauteuil
Mougins, 20 November and 13 December 1962
Oil on canvas, 130 x 97 cm
Zervos XXIII, 84. Stanford (CA), Private collection

1957 by portraits of Jacqueline as "Lola of Valence" (after Manet's painting), an etching copy of Rembrandt's "Man in the Golden Helmet", an India-ink drawing after Cranach's "Venus and Cupid", and a painting after portraits of El Bobo, the court dwarf, by Velázquez and Murillo.[399] Essentially these works remained within the parameters laid down in 1917 with "The Peasants' Repast" (p. 249), after Le Nain's original, adapting compositions and subjects by concentrating attention on particular aspects of them. The variations are modern in that they bring the past works up to date, and in this Picasso was entering a tradition stretching from Delacroix's copies of Rubens to van Gogh's paintings after Gustave Doré: one early 20th-century masterpiece of this kind was Matisse's 1915 "Variation on a Still Life by Jan Davidsz. de Heem".[400]

The paraphrases do, however, have the effect of highlighting the increasingly tautological and almost autistic tendency of Picasso's collage-guided art to repeat itself in the late Fifties. Simply to metamorphose a picture was not in itself invariably adequate as the informing concept behind hundreds of works. The high standard Picasso had set in matching form and content could not always be maintained. In many of the paintings and studies of the period, he was plainly satisfied with having filled the canvas. It was a trivial reversal of the priorities of the artist: what ought to have been the *sine qua non* had become the *raison d'être*.

Great Profile
Grand profil
Mougins, 7 January 1963
Oil on canvas, 130 x 97 cm
Zervos XXIII, 117
Düsseldorf, Kunstsammlung Nordrhein-Westfalen

The Artist and His Model
Le peintre et son modèle
Mougins, 6 December 1963
Aquatint and gouge, 41.8 x 47.6 cm
Bloch 1143

The Artist and His Model
Le peintre et son modèle
Mougins, 7 December 1963
Etching and aquatint,
34.5 x 42.2 cm. Bloch 1144

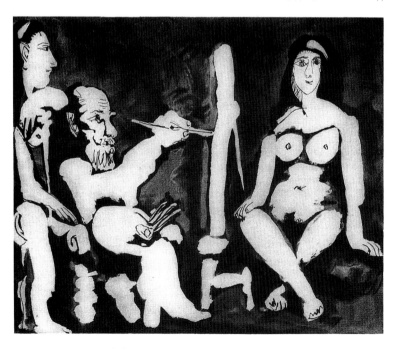

The Artist and His Model
Le peintre et son modèle
Mougins, 10 and 12 June 1963
Oil on canvas, 195 x 130.3 cm
Zervos XXIII, 286
Munich, Staatsgalerie moderner Kunst

589 The Presence of the Past 1954–1963

The Artist and His Model
Le peintre et son modèle
Mougins, 2 March 1963 (I)
Oil on canvas, 38 x 46 cm
Zervos XXIII, 154

The Artist and His Model
Le peintre et son modèle
Mougins, 2 March 1963 (II)
Oil on canvas, 73 x 92 cm
Zervos XXIII, 155

The Artist and His Model
Le peintre et son modèle
Mougins, 2 March 1963 (III)
Oil on canvas, 72.5 x 91.5 cm
Zervos XXIII, 156

The Artist and His Model
Le peintre et son modèle
Mougins, 2 March 1963 (IV)
Oil on canvas, 72.5 x 91.5 cm
Zervos XXIII, 157

The Artist and His Model (initial stage)
Le peintre et son modèle
Mougins, 9 March 1963 (I)
Oil on canvas, 65 x 80.5 cm
Zervos XXIII, 170

The Artist and His Model (final state)
Le peintre et son modèle
Mougins, 9 and 31 March 1963
Oil on canvas, 65 x 80.5 cm
Zervos XXIII, 170

The Artist and His Model (initial stage)
Le peintre et son modèle
Mougins, 5 March 1963 (III)
Oil on canvas, 89 x 116 cm
Zervos XXIII, 163

The Artist and His Model (final state)
Le peintre et son modèle
Mougins, 11 September 1963
Oil on canvas, 89 x 116 cm
Zervos XXIII, 163

The Artist and His Model (first stage)
Le peintre et son modèle
Mougins, 17 March 1963
Oil on canvas, 65 x 92 cm
Zervos XXIII, 205
Paris, Musée National d'Art Moderne,
Centre Georges Pompidou

The Artist and His Model (second stage)
Le peintre et son modèle
Mougins, 20 March 1963
Oil on canvas, 65 x 92 cm
Zervos XXIII, 205
Paris, Musée National d'Art Moderne,
Centre Georges Pompidou

The Artist and His Model (final state)
Le peintre et son modèle
Mougins, 9 April 1963
Oil on canvas, 65 x 92 cm
Zervos XXIII, 205
Paris, Musée National d'Art Moderne,
Centre Georges Pompidou

Right:
The Artist and His Model
Le peintre et son modèle
Mougins, 29 March and 1 April 1963
Oil on canvas, 130 x 162 cm
Zervos XXIII, 196
New York, Private collection

The Artist and His Model
Le peintre et son modèle
Mougins, 3 and 8 April 1963
Oil on canvas, 130 x 195 cm
Zervos XXIII, 202

The Presence of the Past   1954–1963   **592**

The Presence of the Past   1954–1963   **593**

The Artist
Le peintre
Mougins, 10 March 1963 (II)
Oil on canvas, 61 x 50 cm
Zervos XXIII, 176. Private collection

The Artist
Le peintre
Mougins, 10 March 1963 (I)
Oil on canvas, 61 x 50 cm
Zervos XXIII, 175. Private collection

The Artist
Le peintre
Mougins, 10 (III) and 12 March 1963
Oil on canvas, 100 x 73 cm
Zervos XXIII, 177. Private collection

Right:
The Artist and His Model
Le peintre et son modèle
Mougins, 28 March and 7 May 1963
Oil on canvas, 130 x 162 cm
Zervos XXIII, 195
Basel, Courtesy Galerie Beyeler

The Artist and His Model
Le peintre et son modèle
Mougins, 30 March and 3 September 1963
Oil on canvas, 130 x 162 cm
Zervos XXIII, 197. Madrid,
Museo Español de Arte Contemporáneo

The Presence of the Past 1954–1963 595

Left:
Portrait of Jacqueline
Portrait de Jacqueline
Mougins, 22 April to 30 May 1963
Oil on canvas, 92 x 60 cm
Zervos XXIII, 219
Galerie Rosengart

Above:
Seated Woman with Yellow and Green Hat
Femme assise au chapeau jaune et vert
Mougins, 6 January 1962
Oil on canvas, 162 x 130 cm
Zervos XX, 179
Paris, Catherine Hutin-Blay Collection

Woman with Mirror
Femme au miroir
Mougins, 7 January 1963
Oil on canvas, 116 x 89 cm
Zervos XXIII, 116. Private collection

The Artist and His Model
Le peintre et son modèle
Mougins, 16 June 1963 (II)
Oil on canvas, 54 x 81 cm
Zervos XXIII, 288. Private collection

The Artist and His Model in a Landscape
Le peintre et son modèle dans un paysage
Mougins, 28 April (II) and 4 May 1963
Oil on canvas, 89 x 130 cm
Zervos XXIII, 223
Castellón, H. Graffman Collection

1

2

3

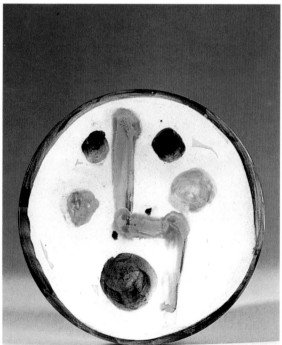

4

600   The Presence of the Past   1954–1963

5

6

7

8

The Presence of the Past 1954–1963 **601**

Las Meninas (after Velázquez)
Les Ménines (d'après Velázquez)
Cannes, 17 August 1957
Oil on canvas, 194 x 260 cm
Zervos XVII, 351; MPB 70.433
Barcelona, Museu Picasso

15 The Case of "Las Meninas" 1957

From 17 August to 30 December 1957, Picasso did a series of 58 very different large-scale oils related to "Las Meninas" (illus. right), painted by the Spanish artist Diego Velázquez in 1656 and so titled after the two maids at court included in it.[401] Picasso took an interest in this famous work for various reasons. Velázquez was and still is considered one of the major figures in European art. Picasso had considered himself one of this company too ever since (at the very latest) the directors of the Louvre invited him, shortly after the Second World War, to hang works of his own alongside major works in the collection, for a single day, in order to establish the stature of his art through the comparison.[402]

Being Spanish, Velázquez might in that respect be seen as a precursor of Picasso. The modern artist had seen "Las Meninas" in the original when he was in Madrid, studying at the Royal Academy of Art. At that time, the works of Velázquez were his preferred objects of study (cf. Chapter 2). In the 1950s, furthermore, the work of Velázquez underwent a revival thanks to Francis Bacon's variations on the portrait of Pope Innocent X. The English painter's series is one of the outstanding accomplishments of figural art since the Second World War.[403] But Picasso was especially attracted to "Las Meninas" because it dealt with his central theme of painter and model. Velázquez's painting is incomparable in its meditation upon the historical and societal preconditions of artistic activity.

The vertical-format rectangular picture shows a gloomy room lit only from windows at the side: the artist's studio. Ten figures are in this space, making a somewhat lost impression, all in the lower half of the composition, with dark vacancy above them. They are positioned at three points of depth: in the foreground, as if in a frieze, are a Spanish princess and her retinue, consisting of two maids-of-honour, two court dwarfs, and a peaceful dog. At left, somewhat behind this group, stands the painter himself at his easel, at work on a huge canvas, his brush at his palette. In the middle-ground there are two servants. And at the very rear, through an open door, we can see the chamberlain of the court, in glaring light.

Different though the postures and attitudes of these people are, they are almost all giving their attention to the same place, to some

Diego Rodriguez de Silva y Velázquez:
Las Meninas, 1656
Oil on canvas, 318 x 276 cm
Madrid, Museo Nacional del Prado

vis-à-vis. The mirror at the rear reveals that this is the king and queen. Thus the painting unambiguously, albeit subtly, expresses the facts of everyday life for Velázquez, painter at court. Life at court was strictly hierarchical. The composition preserves that hierarchy, and marginalizes the painter. While at work he is giving his attention to those people who are at the heart of court life and determine his activity as artist.[404] The other figures are also subordinate to the king and queen, most strikingly the Infanta, second to them in rank, whose gaze is fixed on them. If the boy at right departs from the norm, absorbed in a world of his own and kicking the dog, it is because, as a court dwarf, he has a certain licence: he is one of those fools whose presence at court was traditionally tolerated. In other words, Velázquez's painting is a portrait of social relations. The subtle darks and lights and graded colour values serve to strengthen the message. Velázquez showed himself in this work to be the "true painter of reality", as Picasso put it.[405] That was what constituted his attraction for the modern artist.

Picasso now set about restructuring that reality. In contrast to his previous procedure when paraphrasing Delacroix's "Women of Algiers" (p. 523), the largest full-scale composition came first this time (p. 602), and not last. It was conceived programmatically, as an exposé of the new subject. The nature of the transformation is clear from two changes: the format has been revised, and the status of the painter has been upgraded. Now the format is a broad horizontal, the picture itself more narrative in flavour. Though the painter is still at left, off-centre, he and his easel now occupy a good third of the canvas breadth and almost its entire height. The painter and easel are done in the "Picasso style", as if Picasso were deliberately contrasting his own style with that of the 17th-century painter. On the other hand, the dwarf and dog are in the infant style Picasso had evolved for "Guernica". The chamberlain at rear, the maids-of-honour and servants, and the king and queen in the mirror, are all crudely and hastily established in a manner also reminiscent of children's drawings. The colour and light, crucial factors in the original, have undergone a total change: the new work is a grisaille based on contrasts of white and grey, and the greys, unlike the colours in Velázquez's painting, do not reflect the light.

Everything in this new version has become unambiguous. The figures are frontally positioned or in clear profile. One will has borne all before it: Picasso's. He is lord of his world, empowered to do whatsoever he chooses. The rival royal power has ceased to matter. Picasso is free to treat his subject as he wishes. In this, he has not only established the parameters for his treatment of "Las Meninas"; the subject seems in fact well-nigh exhausted. The paintings that followed the large-scale opening version of 17 August either deal with parts and details or produce variations on the horizontal format.

First, from 20 August to 4 September, there were eleven pictures

15 **Infanta Margarita María**
Cannes, 5 September 1957
Oil on canvas, 35 x 27 cm
Zervos XVII, 366; MPB 70.447

1 **Las Meninas** (after Velázquez)
Cannes, 17 August 1957
Oil on canvas, 194 x 260 cm
Zervos XVII, 351; MPB 70.433

All 58 variations on "Las Meninas":
Barcelona, Museu Picasso

2 **Infanta Margarita María**
Cannes, 20 August 1957
Oil on canvas, 100 x 81 cm
Zervos XVII, 353; MPB 70.434

3 **María Augustina Sarmiento**
Cannes, 20 August 1957
Oil on canvas, 46 x 37.5 cm
Zervos XVII, 352; MPB 70.435

4 **Infanta Margarita María**
Cannes, 21 August 1957
Oil on canvas, 100 x 81 cm
Zervos XVII, 356; MPB 70.436

5 **Infanta Margarita María**
Cannes, 22 August 1957
Oil on canvas, 33 x 24 cm
Zervos XVII, 354; MPB 70.437

6 **Infanta Margarita María**
Cannes, 26 August 1957
Oil on canvas, 41 x 32.5 cm
Zervos XVII, 357; MPB 70.438

7 **Infanta Margarita María**
Cannes, 27 August 1957
Oil on canvas, 40.5 x 33 cm
Zervos XVII, 355; MPB 70.439

8 **Infanta Margarita María**
Cannes, 27 August 1957
Oil on canvas, 33 x 24 cm
Zervos XVII, 361; MPB 70.440

9 **Infanta Margarita María**
Cannes, 27 August 1957
Oil on canvas, 33 x 24 cm
Zervos XVII, 359; MPB 70.441

10 **Infanta Margarita María**
Cannes, 28 August 1957
Oil on canvas, 33 x 24 cm
Zervos XVII, 358; MPB 70.442

11 **Infanta Margarita María**
Cannes, 28 August 1957
Oil on canvas, 18 x 14 cm
Zervos XVII, 360; MPB 70. 443

12 **Infanta Margarita María**
Cannes, 4 September 1957
Oil on canvas, 35 x 27 cm
Zervos XVII, 365; MPB 70.444

13 **Central Group**
Cannes, 4 September 1957
Oil on canvas, 35 x 27 cm
Zervos XVII, 363; MPB 70.445

14 **The Whole Group**
Cannes, 4 September 1957
Oil on canvas, 46 x 37.5 cm
Zervos XVII, 364; MPB 70.447

605 The Case of "Las Meninas" 1957

The Pigeons
Cannes, 12 September 1957
Oil on canvas, 100 x 80 cm
Zervos XVII, 400; MPB 70.457
(cf. no. 25 opposite)

16 **Infanta Margarita María**
Cannes, 6 September 1957
Oil on canvas, 41 x 32.5 cm
Zervos XVII, 367; MPB 70.448

17 **Infanta Margarita María**
Cannes, 6 September 1957
Oil on canvas, 46 x 37.5 cm
Zervos XVII, 362; MPB 70.449

18 **The Pigeons**
Cannes, 6 September 1957
Oil on canvas, 100 x 80 cm
Zervos XVII, 394; MPB 70.450

19 **The Pigeons**
Cannes, 6 September 1957
Oil on canvas, 100 x 80 cm
Zervos XVII, 395; MPB 70.451

20 **The Pigeons**
Cannes, 7 September 1957
Oil on canvas, 33 x 24 cm
Zervos XVII, 398; MPB 70.452

21 **The Pigeons**
Cannes, 7 September 1957
Oil on canvas, 100 x 80 cm
Zervos XVII, 396; MPB 70.453

22 **The Pigeons**
Cannes, 7 September 1957
Oil on canvas, 80 x 100 cm
Not in Zervos; MPB 70.454

23 **The Pigeons**
Cannes, 11 September 1957
Oil on canvas, 130 x 97 cm
Zervos XVII, 397; MPB 70.455

24 **The Pigeons**
Cannes, 12 and 14 September 1957
Oil on canvas, 100 x 80 cm
Zervos XVII, 399; MPB 70.456

25 **The Pigeons**
(see opposite page)

26 **The Pigeons**
Cannes, 12 September 1957
Oil on canvas, 145 x 113 cm
Zervos XVII, 401; MPB 70.458

27 **Infanta Margarita María**
Cannes, 14 September 1957
Oil on canvas, 100 x 81 cm
Zervos XVII, 368; MPB 70.459

28 **The Whole Group**
Cannes, 15 September 1957
Oil on canvas, 129 x 161 cm
Zervos XVII, 369; MPB 70.460

29 **María Augustina Sarmiento and
Infanta Margarita María**
Cannes, 17 September 1957
Oil on canvas, 32.5 x 41 cm
Zervos XVII, 371; MPB 70.461

30 **The Whole Group**
Cannes, 17 September 1957
Oil on canvas, 129 x 161 cm
Zervos XVII, 370; MPB 70.462

16   17   18
19   20   21
22
23   24
25   26   27
28   29   30

which, with a single exception, focussed on the Infanta, the central figure in Velázquez's composition. What attracted Picasso most was the girl's bright dress. In Velázquez it was the brightest element of light in the picture, countering the glare from the open door at the rear. In his own paraphrases, Picasso tended to use a mono-chrome composition that revised the light and shadow and the figure. In the full-figure picture of the Infanta done on 21 August (p. 605, no. 4) the brightness from the open door affords a kind of touchstone for the princess's dress, while the colour studies that followed (nos. 5 to 12) concentrated on the face. Picasso's aim was plainly to transmute Velázquez's subtly tonal work not only in terms of style, composition and motifs but also in terms of colour.

There followed an intermezzo of nine brightly colourful pictures done from 6 to 12 September. At first sight they seem to have nothing at all to do with the picture by Velázquez. Picasso had been giving all his concentration to the paraphrases and had quit the studio at La Californie for the purpose, moving up to the loft.[406] There, undisturbed by the everyday life of the household, he was alone with a view of the Mediterranean and with his sole compan-ions, the pigeons. Taking the loft window as frame and backdrop, he now painted the pigeons a number of times, in fluent, alla prima work that recalled both the Fauves and the relaxed manner of Raoul Dufy. These paintings (pp. 606 and 607) record both the artist's independence and his engagement with colour. Picasso de-liberately turned aside from his main route in order to study the expressive power of pure, bright colour. What this study produced may be seen in a further portrait of the Infanta done on 14 Septem-ber (p. 607, no. 27). This picture set the tone for everything else that followed.

Picasso now tried to render the chiaroscuro factor in the original Velázquez through contrasts of darker and lighter shades of colour, in dissected, complex patterns; and from 18 September on he at-tempted to transfer this principle to the whole composition (p. 609, no. 31). But the result was not convincing, and on 9 October he embarked on a small set of detail studies (nos. 35 to 39) – essen-tially, he was back at square one. He tested colour combinations on the Infanta, her maid, and the figures at right. The major depar-ture in this new series came when he transformed the dwarf into a piano player (no. 40), a motif from the Picasso repertoire.[407]

A further series of studies of the maid to the right of the Infanta in the Velázquez tested the potential of expressionist modes. Once again Picasso detoured into a different subject, this time three land-scapes and a portrait of Jacqueline. Not till 30 December did he return to the motifs Velázquez offered, with a study of the right-hand maid (p. 610, no. 58). This not only marked a return to the tonal values of the original but also tried to render those values in relaxed brushwork such as is sometimes characteristic of Veláz-quez's own style. But here the entire series suddenly breaks off.

45 **Isabel de Velasco and María Bárbola**
Cannes, 8 November 1957
Oil on canvas, 130 x 96 cm
Zervos XVII, 385; MPB 70.477

31 **The Whole Group**
Cannes, 18 September 1957
Oil on canvas, 129 x 161 cm
Zervos XVII, 372; MPB 70.463

32 **The Whole Group**
Cannes, 19 September 1957
Oil on canvas, 162 x 130 cm
Zervos XVII, 373; MPB 70.464

33 **The Whole Group**
Cannes, 2 October 1957
Oil on canvas, 162 x 130 cm
Zervos XVII, 374; MPB 70.465

34 **The Whole Group**
Cannes, 3 October 1957
Oil on canvas, 129 x 161 cm
Zervos XVII, 375; MPB 70.466

35 **Isabel de Velasco**
Cannes, 9 October 1957
Oil on canvas, 65 x 54 cm
Zervos XVII, 377; MPB 70.467

36 **María Augustina Sarmiento**
Cannes, 9 October 1957
Oil on canvas, 65 x 54 cm
Zervos XVII, 376; MPB 70.468

37 **María Augustina Sarmiento and
Infanta Margarita María**
Cannes, 10 October 1957
Oil on canvas, 92 x 73 cm
Zervos XVII, 379; MPB 70.469

38 **María Augustina Sarmiento**
Cannes, 10 October 1957
Oil on canvas, 73 x 55 cm
Zervos XVII, 378; MPB 70.470

39 **María Augustina Sarmiento**
Cannes, 10 October 1957
Oil on canvas, 115 x 89 cm
Zervos XVII, 380; MPB 70.471

40 **The Piano**
Cannes, 17 October 1957
Oil on canvas, 130 x 97 cm
Zervos XVII, 404; MPB 70.472

41 **Nicolasico Pertusato**
Cannes, 24 October 1957
Oil on canvas, 61 x 50 cm
Zervos XVII, 382; MPB 70.473

42 **Isabel de Velasco, María Bárbola,
Nicolasico Pertusato and the Dog**
Cannes, 24 October 1957
Oil on canvas, 130 x 96 cm
Zervos XVII, 383; MPB 70.474

43 **Isabel de Velasco, María Bárbola,
Nicolasico Pertusato and the Dog**
Cannes, 24 October 1957
Oil on canvas, 130 x 96 cm
Zervos XVII, 384; MPB 70.475

44 **Isabel de Velasco, María Bárbola,
Nicolasico Pertusato and the Dog**
Cannes, 24 October 1957
Oil on canvas, 130 x 96 cm
Zervos XVII, 381; MPB 70.476

31

32
33

34

35
36

37

38
39

40

41
42

43

44
45

609   The Case of "Las Meninas"   1957

46

47

48

49

50

51

52

54

55

56

57

58

The Case of "Las Meninas" 1957 **610**

46 Infanta Margarita María
   and Isabel de Velasco
   Cannes, 15 November 1957
   Oil on canvas, 130 x 96 cm
   Zervos XVII, 386; MPB 70.478

47 The Whole Group
   Cannes, 15 November 1957
   Oil on canvas, 130 x 96 cm
   Zervos XVII, 387; MPB 70.479

48 The Whole Group
   Cannes, 17 November 1957
   Oil on canvas, 35 x 27 cm
   Zervos XVII, 388; MPB 70.480

49 María Augustina Sarmiento
   Cannes, 17 November 1957
   Oil on canvas, 24 x 19 cm
   Zervos XVII, 389; MPB 70.481

50 Isabel de Velasco
   Cannes, 17 November 1957
   Oil on canvas, 24 x 19 cm
   Zervos XVII, 392; MPB 70.482

51 Isabel de Velasco
   Cannes, 17 November 1957
   Oil on canvas, 27 x 22 cm
   Zervos XVII, 393; MPB 70.483

52 Isabel de Velasco
   Cannes, 17 November 1957
   Oil on canvas, 24 x 19 cm
   Zervos XVII, 390; MPB 70.484

53 Isabel de Velasco and Nicolasico Pertusato
   Cannes, 17 November 1957
   Oil on canvas, 24 x 19 cm
   Zervos XVII, 391; MPB 70.485

54 Landscape
   Cannes, 2 December 1957
   Oil on canvas, 14 x 17.5 cm
   Zervos XVII, 407; MPB 70.486

55 Landscape
   Cannes, 2 December 1957
   Oil on canvas, 14 x 18 cm
   Zervos XVII, 406; MPB 70.487

56 Landscape
   Cannes, 2 December 1957
   Oil on canvas, 16 x 22 cm
   Zervos XVII, 405; MPB 70.488

57 Portrait of Jacqueline
   Cannes, 3 December 1957
   Oil on canvas, 116 x 89 cm
   Zervos XVII, 408; MPB 70.489

58 Isabel de Velasco
   Cannes, 30 December 1957
   Oil on canvas, 33 x 24 cm
   Zervos XVII, 444; MPB 70.490

Towards the end, Picasso's work on the series was slow, and it finally stagnated. And in December 1957, after all, he was already busy with preliminary work for the Paris UNESCO building mural.[408]

So Picasso's variations on "Las Meninas" finally came to nothing. It is true that he succeeded in articulating the core idea of his new version: that the artist occupies a new, changed position in modern, liberal society. The large composition that opened the series expressed this idea powerfully. The Picasso style is in a sense the very definition of modern art, providing the contemporary artist with an entire range of available approaches. And Picasso, revising the original in colour terms too, was aiming to outdo his illustrious forerunner. He tackled the task with furious energy, and even interposed sequences of works devoted to particular problems (the pigeons) into the "Meninas" series. And with these experiments behind him he painted a lovely figure portrait of the Infanta (no. 27) which can be considered a success in its own right.

But to transfer his colourist concepts to the overall composition was a more complex undertaking. And in the end Picasso conceded defeat. Limits constrained the autonomy of colour; and the compositions of 18 September and 2 and 3 October (nos. 31, 33 and 34) all illustrate the same dilemma – colour was still of secondary importance, subordinated to form. Interestingly, Picasso scarcely went further than simple colour contrasts or the deployment of one or two glowing colours in a monochrome structure. He was the prisoner of his own lifelong principles. For Picasso, who saw visual form from a draughtsman's point of view, colour was always secondary. The series of pigeon paintings interposed in the "Meninas" paraphrases highlight the shortcoming this imposed on him: though he was painting the pictures with the aim of composing in pure colour, he nowhere attained that aim with any fullness. Only the picture of 11 September (no. 23) articulates the effects of a specific colour scale, systematically placing violet against blue and green. But the structure is a simple one, confined to a clearly defined area within the composition. There is no fundamental orchestration of colour such as might use a scale of gradations to highlight certain tonalities and climactic colour values at vital points in the composition – nor does Picasso achieve this in his "Meninas" variations. Thus the last series too, which begins in crude colour polarities and then moves through mixed shades in quest of subtler nuances, produces no satisfying result in the end. Ultimately, Picasso's variations on Velázquez's "Las Meninas", viewed in terms of a working method, and judged with Picasso's own vast ambitions in mind, must be considered a record of failure.

16 The Old Savage
1963–1973

In September 1958 Picasso bought the château at Vauvenargues. Increasingly it became a refuge from an inquisitive public that veritably besieged La Californie. The 14th-century château was near Aix-en-Provence at the foot of Mont Sainte-Victoire, featured in many of Cézanne's paintings. Then in June 1961 Picasso moved into Notre-Dame-de-Vie, a villa near the village of Mougins, in the hills above Cannes. It was to be his last residence and place of work.[409] He had long been a classic of modern art, but still attempted to influence the public reception of his work. For instance, when the Museu Picasso in Barcelona was opened in 1970, prominent members of the Franco regime tried to use the occasion as a means of legitimation. However, their plans for a state ceremony were brought to nothing by Picasso, who vetoed all such ideas, wary of affording political enemies any purchase.[410]

Picasso had long taken a special interest in the work of the Norwegian artist Carl Nesjar. In the Fifties, Nesjar had engraved Picasso studies in concrete with the help of a sand-blaster. Now, in the 1960s, he developed a method of making immense concrete casts of Picasso's sculptures. For Picasso it was the fulfilment of a lifelong dream – ever since the Twenties he had been fired by ideas for large-scale sculptural work. From 1962 to 1964, commissioned by Skidmore, Owings and Merrill, an American architectural firm, he designed the maquette for a 20-metre sculpture. As in the 1928 memorial for Apollinaire (pp. 324 and 325), Picasso established an interplay of volume and surface in this "civic" work, and created linear effects by using wires. The final work was done in Corten steel and installed at the Chicago Civic Centre in 1967 (p. 579).[411]

The art scene had undergone a complete change. The Sixties were a period of great upheaval and transition in the Western world, not least in the visual arts. The total international hegemony of abstract art waned, as its shortcomings became increasingly, painfully apparent. Everywhere, voices were raised in opposition to a non-representational art felt to be sterile, uncommitted, escapist. The new departure of the Sixties was dominated by Pop Art and the New Realism.[412] Both schools made uninhibited use of every conceivable visual idiom, particularly advertising and comic strips. The con-

Man with a Hat
Buste d'homme au chapeau
Mougins, 23 November 1970
Oil on canvas, 81 x 64.5 cm
Zervos XXXII, 310
Geneva, Fondation Marina Picasso

Seated Old Man
Vieil homme assis
Mougins, 26 September 1970 (I)
and 14 November 1971
Oil on canvas, 144.5 x 114 cm
Zervos XXXII, 265; MPP 221
Paris, Musée Picasso

tinued evolution of classical Modernism played a decisive part in this. Assemblages, collages and ready-mades were now being used to expose social taboos and brand societal mistakes. Thus everyday objects such as soup cans or washpowder boxes became icons of mass society's consume-and-dispose mentality. They were made in series format, or presented in monumental autonomy. The best-known works are those of the American Pop artists Andy Warhol, Claes Oldenburg, Roy Lichtenstein and Robert Rauschenberg, whose assemblages and other artefacts matched what French artists such as Arman and César had been doing.[413] The new departure also constituted an end to creative one-sidedness – even the actionist legacy of Surrealism was continued in new socially critical forms such as the happening.[414] And in the train of such developments came conceptual art.

Picasso's attitude to contemporary art was divided. Most of its formal repertoire had been familiar to him for years – indeed, he had invented some of the techniques himself. Time seemed to be coming full circle in the oddest of ways. Picasso, who had at one time set out to revolutionize art and articulate the contradictions inherent in the creative act, found himself viewed as the Establishment and bracketed with Salon artists such as Bernard Buffet, who appropriated the achievements of Modernism to manufacture snappy arts and crafts.[415] Thus Picasso, at the end of his life, was squeezed right out to the periphery. On the one hand media acclaim, on the other withdrawal from public life; old age and its physical frailty, an art scene that made uninhibited demands on him and his art – he was facing formidable challenges. And to capitulate would have been tantamount to throwing in the towel for good.

Instead, he riposted with an art of revolt. The art of Picasso's old age articulates the will to survive. From 1963 on, conflicts within and without became ever more visible in his work. He did several hundred studies and paintings on his old subject of "The Artist and His Model" (pp. 582 ff.). An intense, indeed obsessive preoccupation with the subject of the artist's identity followed; this was not new in Picasso, but the single-mindedness and energy with which he pursued his subject was unusual even for him. Contemporaries were staggered by the sheer bulk of his production, and the statistics are indeed astounding. For example, from 16 March to 5 October 1968 he did 347 etchings, from January 1969 to the end of January 1970 no fewer than 167 paintings, and from 15 December 1969 to 12 January 1971 194 drawings. 156 etchings followed from January 1970 to March 1972, 172 drawings from 21 November 1971 to 18 August 1972, and a further 201 paintings from 25 September 1970 to 1 June 1972. These figures represent only the works published to date. And all this by a man aged 87 to 91![416]

This formidable productiveness is obviously eloquent of fantastic vitality. The public was amazed at the world's most famous artist's undiminished activity.[417] But behind that amazement lay a damning

The Sculptor
Le sculpteur
Mougins, 26 and 27 February 1964 (II)
Aquatint and gouge, 38 x 27.5 cm
Bloch 1196

1 **The Artist**
Le peintre
Mougins, 10 October 1964
Gouache and India ink
overpainted on a print,
98 x 75 cm. Zervos XXIV, 215
Private collection

In 1964 the French publisher Spitz put a reproduction of the painting "The Artist" (right) on the market. 30 complimentary copies of this print were sent to Picasso. He kept one for his archive and overpainted the remaining 29 with gouache and India ink, producing a set of variations all done between 10 and 24 October 1964 (see below and pp. 616/617). Picasso commented:

"I could do thousands of them. Working like that is wonderful, over a painter who's already there. Essentially there is nothing more terrible for a painter than a blank canvas."

The Artist
Le peintre
Mougins, 30 March 1963 (II)
Oil on canvas, 92 x 73 cm
Zervos XXIII, 198
Private collection

2 **The Artist**
Le peintre
Mougins, 10 October 1964 (II)
Gouache and India ink,
overpainted on a print,
98 x 75 cm. Zervos XXIV, 216
Private collection

3 **The Artist**
Le peintre
Mougins, 10 October 1964 (III)
Gouache and India ink,
overpainted on a print,
98 x 75 cm. Zervos XXIV, 217
Private collection

4 **The Artist**
Le peintre
Mougins, 11 October 1964
Gouache and India ink
overpainted on a print,
98 x 75 cm. Zervos XXIV, 218
Private collection

5 **The Artist**
Le peintre
Mougins, 11 October 1964 (II)
Gouache and India ink,
overpainted on a print,
98 x 75 cm. Zervos XXIV, 219
Private collection

6   **The Artist**
Mougins, 13 October 1964 (I)
Gouache and India ink, overpainted
on a print, 98 x 75 cm
Zervos XXIV, 220

7   **The Artist**
Mougins, 13 October 1964 (II)
Gouache and India ink, overpainted
on a print, 98 x 75 cm
Zervos XXIV, 221

8   **The Artist**
Mougins, 13 October 1964 (III)
Gouache and India ink, overpainted
on a print, 98 x 75 cm
Zervos XXIV, 222

9   **The Artist**
Mougins, 16 October 1964
Gouache and India ink, overpainted
on a print, 98 x 75 cm
Zervos XXIV, 223

10   **The Artist**
Mougins, 16 October 1964 (II)
Gouache and India ink, overpainted
on a print, 98 x 75 cm
Zervos XXIV, 224

11   **The Artist**
Mougins, 16 October 1964 (III)
Gouache and India ink, overpainted
on a print, 98 x 75 cm
Zervos XXIV, 225

12   **The Artist**
Mougins, 17 October 1964 (I)
Gouache and India ink, overpainted
on a print, 98 x 75 cm
Zervos XXIV, 226

13   **The Artist**
Mougins, 17 October 1964 (II)
Gouache and India ink, overpainted
on a print, 98 x 75 cm
Zervos XXIV, 227

14   **The Artist**
Mougins, 17 October 1964 (III)
Gouache and India ink, overpainted
on a print, 98 x 75 cm
Zervos XXIV, 228

15   **The Artist**
Mougins, 18 October 1964 (I)
Gouache and India ink, overpainted
on a print, 98 x 75 cm
Zervos XXIV, 229

16   **The Artist**
Mougins, 18 October 1964 (II)
Gouache and India ink, overpainted
on a print, 98 x 75 cm
Zervos XXIV, 230

17   **The Artist**
Mougins, 18 October 1964 (III)
Gouache and India ink, overpainted
on a print, 98 x 75 cm
Zervos XXIV, 231

18 **The Artist**
Mougins, 19 October 1964
Gouache and India ink, overpainted
on a print, 98 x 75 cm
Zervos XXIV, 232

19 **The Artist**
Mougins, 19 October 1964 (III)
Gouache and India ink, overpainted
on a print, 98 x 75 cm
Zervos XXIV, 233

20 **The Artist**
Mougins, 19 October 1964 (IV)
Gouache and India ink, overpainted
on a print, 98 x 75 cm
Zervos XXIV, 234

18   19   20

21 **The Artist**
Mougins, 19 October 1964 (V)
Gouache and India ink, overpainted
on a print, 98 x 75 cm
Zervos XXIV, 235

22 **The Artist**
Mougins, 21 October 1964 (I)
Gouache and India ink, overpainted
on a print, 98 x 75 cm
Zervos XXIV, 236

23 **The Artist**
Mougins, 21 October 1964 (II)
Gouache and India ink, overpainted
on a print, 98 x 75 cm
Zervos XXIV, 237

21   22   23

24 **The Artist**
Mougins, 21 October 1964 (III)
Gouache and India ink, overpainted
on a print, 98 x 75 cm
Zervos XXIV, 238

25 **The Artist**
Mougins, 23 October 1964 (I)
Gouache and India ink, overpainted
on a print, 98 x 75 cm
Zervos XXIV, 239

26 **The Artist**
Mougins, 23 October 1964 (II)
Gouache and India ink, overpainted
on a print, 98 x 75 cm
Zervos XXIV, 240

24   25   26

27 **The Artist**
Mougins, 24 October 1964 (I)
Gouache and India ink, overpainted
on a print, 98 x 75 cm
Zervos XXIV, 241

28 **The Artist**
Mougins, 24 October 1964 (II)
Gouache and India ink, overpainted
on a print, 98 x 75 cm
Zervos XXIV, 242

29 **The Artist**
Mougins, 24 October 1964 (III)
Gouache and India ink, overpainted
on a print, 98 x 75 cm
Zervos XXIV, 243

27   28   29

Landscape at Mougins
Paysage à Mougins
Mougins, 26 December 1963
Oil on canvas, 130 x 162 cm
Zervos XXIII, 95. Private collection

verdict: logically, it implied that productivity itself was being ranked above quality, as if the aged Picasso's heroic performance required the astonished applause that might greet a circus act. The reason for this lay in the work itself. If we consider the endless portrayals of the painter and model scene, of nudes, of sex, or the portraits and so forth, we are confronted with an art plainly at odds with aesthetic ideals of creating beauty. Overhasty painting, blotches and dribbles, mock-primitive figures dismembered beyond recognition, colours that can be genuinely painful to look at, all guarantee that these pictures come as a shock. The praise they earned for the physical endurance they attested was no more than an expression of helplessness before their formal character.

And yet it is impossible to ignore the evocativeness of that character. Picasso forces us to enter into a dialogue with his art; and, true to himself, he does so with consistent, unremitting logic. If his work now dispenses with subtlety, casts nuanced colours to the winds, and is brutally unambiguous in form and content, it does most certainly prompt unmistakable reactions. There is nothing

618 The Old Savage 1963–1973

monolithic about this last phase in Picasso's work, though. True, the 1963 series of artist and model paintings makes a homogeneous impression on first inspection, consisting of slight variations on a repeated constant in terms of the group composition and motifs. All the paintings look spontaneous, as if the artist had deliberately avoided pausing for thought and the whole meaning resided in a spur-of-the-moment quality. But paintings such as these, several of which might often be done in a single day (cf. p. 590), were accompanied by others that might be worked on in several stages, sometimes with month-long interruptions (p. 583).[418]

In 1964, working with great concentration over a number of days, Picasso painted a portrait of his wife Jacqueline (p. 622, top left). In preliminary works he had tried out effects of colour blocks, paint and line. Now, in the portrait, he combined the principles he had gleaned from those experiments. Then in May he took the painting as a point of departure for a variation in which he played off painting and draughtsmanlike elements more contrastively against each other (p. 622, top right). Both procedures – rapidly

The Artist and His Model
Le peintre et son modèle
Mougins, 26 October (II) and
3 November 1964
Oil on canvas, 146 x 89 cm
Zervos XXIV, 246
New York, Mr. and Mrs. Morton
L. Janklow Collection

The Artist and His Model
Le peintre et son modèle
Mougins, 25 October 1964
Oil on canvas, 195 x 130 cm
Zervos XXIV, 245
Switzerland, Gilbert de Botton Collection

1

2

3

4

5

6

7

8

9

620 The Old Savage 1963–1973

1 Head of a Man
  Tête d'homme
  Mougins, 4 December 1964 (II)
  Oil on canvas, 55 x 46 cm
  Zervos XXIV, 295. Private collection

2 Head of a Man
  Tête d'homme
  Mougins, 4 December 1964 (III)
  Oil on canvas, 55 x 46 cm
  Zervos XXIV, 297. Private collection

3 Head of a Man
  Tête d'homme
  Mougins, 4 December 1964 (IV)
  Oil on canvas, 55 x 46 cm
  Zervos XXIV, 298. Private collection

4 Head of a Man
  Tête d'homme
  Mougins, 5 December 1964 (III)
  Oil on canvas, 46 x 38 cm
  Zervos XXIV, 301. Private collection

5 Head of a Man
  Tête d'homme
  Mougins, 5 December 1964 (V)
  Oil on canvas, 46 x 38 cm
  Zervos XXIV, 303. Private collection

6 Head of a Man
  Tête d'homme
  Mougins, 10 December 1964 (I)
  Oil on canvas, 35 x 27 cm
  Zervos XXIV, 309. Private collection

7 Head of a Man
  Tête d'homme
  Mougins, 10 December 1964 (III)
  Oil on canvas, 35 x 27 cm
  Zervos XXIV, 311. Private collection

8 Head of a Man
  Tête d'homme
  Mougins, 10 December 1964 (V)
  Oil on canvas, 61 x 50 cm
  Zervos XXIV, 314. Private collection

9 Head of a Man with Hat
  Tête d'homme au chapeau
  Mougins, 10 December 1964 (VII)
  Oil on canvas, 61 x 50 cm
  Zervos XXIV, 308. Private collection

10 Head of a Man
  Tête d'homme
  Mougins, 10 December 1964 (VI)
  Oil on canvas, 55 x 46 cm
  Zervos XXIV, 315. Private collection

11 Head of a Man
  Tête d'homme
  Mougins, 11 December 1964 (II)
  Oil on canvas, 92 x 65 cm
  Zervos XXIV, 316. Private collection

10

11

painting a spontaneous artist and model scene, or patiently evolving and adapting a composition – were typical of Picasso's lifelong method of working. But now he intensified his labours in a way that went far beyond his norm.

On 30 March 1963, for example, he painted an artist at work (p. 615). From 10 to 24 October 1964 he then did 29 variations on the theme, changing the artist's headgear or facial features, making him bearded or wrinkled, old or young, in a broad range of transformations. In these revisions of a single subject, the point of departure always remained clearly in sight. It is, in fact, always the same picture: he was using 29 original-size reproductions of his own oil of 30 March 1963 (cf. pp. 614 to 617) which a French publisher had sent him. In overpainting in this way, he was emphasizing the contingent, temporary status of an individual work.

This repeated work on a reproduction highlights the heart of Picasso's concerns in his late work: he was out to destroy the concept of the finished work. Series were no longer intended as attesting evolution towards a work, as his extremely sketchy oils of male faces indicate. Here, he was performing an equivalent to the overpainting of reproductions: it was only the context of a sequence that produced meaning in an individual work. The constituents underwent little variation but their juxtaposition changed, underlining the infinite possible ways of combining formal fundamentals (left and above). These pictures are not finished products; they merely document the basic options available to creative work. Alluding directly to the textbook character of the series principle, Picasso uses rudimentary, indeed childlike forms of expression. The pictures seem the kind of scrawl that anyone could do. Technique has been pared to a minimum; caprice reigns triumphant. We are witnessing a creative spirit free of technical constraint and asserting that the traditional concept of art is null and void.

Consistently enough, Picasso does not communicate content in

622   The Old Savage   1963–1973

Left:
Jacqueline, Seated with Her Cat
Jacqueline assise avec son chat
Mougins, 26 to 28 February and
1 to 3 March 1964
Oil on canvas, 195 x 130 cm
Zervos XXIV, 101. Estate of Jacqueline Picasso

Jacqueline, Seated with Her Cat
Jacqueline au chat assise dans un fauteuil
Mougins, 4 May 1964
Oil on canvas, 130 x 81 cm
Zervos XXIV, 141. Estate of Jacqueline Picasso

Standing Nude
Femme nue debout
Mougins, 23 April 1963 (I)
Oil on canvas, 81 x 54 cm
Zervos XXIII, 215. Private collection

Seated Nude in an Armchair
Femme nue assise dans un fauteuil
Mougins, 23 April 1963 (II)
Oil on canvas, 92 x 73 cm
Zervos XXIII, 216. Private collection

Seated Nude in an Armchair
Femme nue assise dans un fauteuil
Mougins, 23 April 1963 (III)
Oil on canvas, 100 x 65 cm
Zervos XXIII, 217. Private collection

Nude in an Armchair
Femme nue dans un fauteuil
Mougins, 2 May and 7 June 1964
Oil on canvas, 116 x 80.5 cm
Zervos XXIV, 138. Estate of Jacqueline Picasso

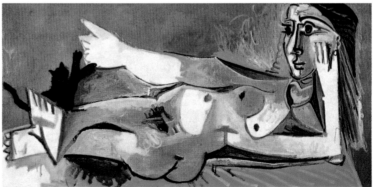

Reclining Nude Playing with a Cat
Femme nue couchée jouant avec un chat
Mougins, 7 and 23 March 1964
Oil on canvas, 97.5 x 195 cm
Zervos XXIV, 133
Wuppertal, Von der Heydt-Museum

623 The Old Savage 1963–1973

Reclining Nude
Femme nue couchée
Mougins, 9 and 18 January 1964
Oil on canvas, 65 x 100 cm
Zervos XXIV, 25
Galerie Rosengart

Reclining Nude Playing with a Cat
Femme nue couchée jouant avec un chat
Mougins, 17 February 1964
Oil on canvas, 128 x 194 cm
Zervos XXIV, 94. Private collection

Reclining Nude
Femme nue couchée
Mougins, 28 January and 13 March 1964
Oil on canvas, 130 x 194 cm
Zervos XXIV, 69. Private collection

Reclining Nude Playing with a Cat
Femme nue couchée jouant avec un chat
Mougins, 8 March 1964
Oil on canvas, 128 x 194 cm
Zervos XXIV, 132. Private collection

Reclining Nude Playing with a Cat
Femme nue couchée jouant avec un chat
Mougins, 8 and 22 March 1964
Oil on canvas, 119 x 194 cm
Zervos XXIV, 134. Private collection

Reclining Nude with Flower and Cat
Nu couché à la fleur et chat
Mougins, 18 March 1964
Oil on canvas, 113 x 193 cm
Zervos XXIV, 131. Private collection

625 The Old Savage 1963–1973

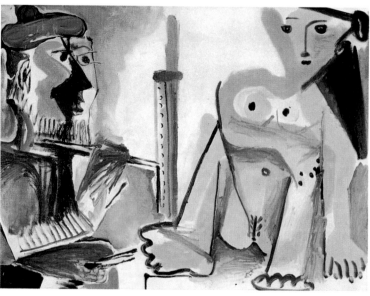

Seated Nude
Femme nue assise
Mougins, 7 January 1965 (II)
Oil on canvas, 116 x 89 cm
Zervos XXV, 7
USA, The Beverly and Raymond
Sackler Collection

The Artist and His Model
Le peintre et son modèle
Mougins, 14 (II) and 15 November 1964
Oil on canvas, 89 x 130 cm
Zervos XXIV, 269. Private collection

Right:
Seated Nude in an Armchair
Femme nue assise dans un fauteuil
Mougins, 3 and 5 August 1965 (I)
Oil on canvas, 116 x 89 cm
Zervos XXV, 6
Paris, Courtesy Galerie Louise Leiris

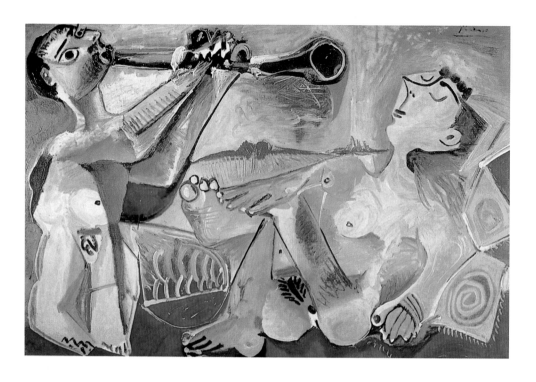

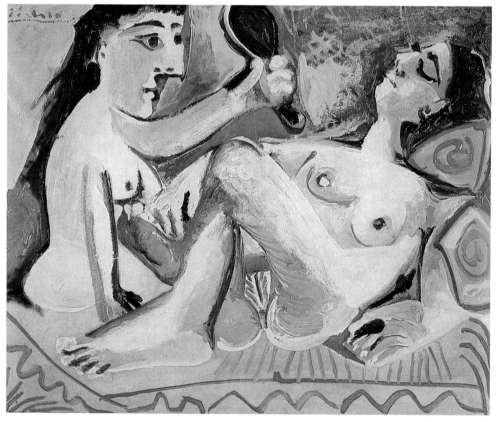

628 The Old Savage 1963–1973

Left:
L'aubade
Mougins, 19 and 20 January 1965
Oil on canvas, 130 x 195 cm
Zervos XXV, 19
Geneva, Musée du Petit Palais

The Two Friends
Les deux amies
Mougins, 20 and 26 January 1965
Oil on canvas, 81 x 100 cm
Zervos XXV, 18. Berne, Kunstmuseum Bern,
Gift of Walter and Gertrud Hadorn

Right:
Seated Nude Leaning on Pillows
Femme nue assise appuyée sur des coussins
Mougins, 19 (IV) and 20 December 1964
Oil on canvas, 54 x 65 cm
Zervos XXIV, 338. Private collection

Large Nude
Grand nu
Mougins, 20 to 22 February
and 5 March 1964
Oil on canvas, 140 x 195 cm
Zervos XXIV, 95
Zurich, Kunsthaus Zürich

629 The Old Savage 1963–1973

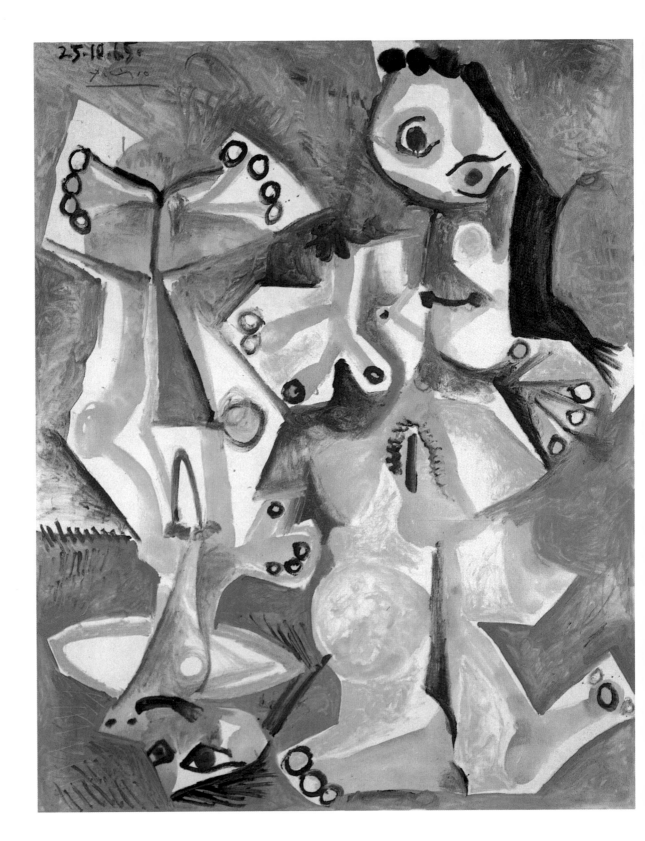

Left:
Nude Man and Woman
Homme et femme nus
Mougins, 25 October 1965
Oil on canvas, 162 x 130 cm
Zervos XXV, 183. St. Moritz, Private collection
Paris, Courtesy Galerie Louise Leiris

Woman Pissing
La pisseuse
Mougins, 16 April 1965 (I)
Oil on canvas, 195 x 97 cm
Zervos XXV, 108
Paris, Musée National d'Art Moderne,
Centre Georges Pompidou,
Gift of Louise and Michel Leiris

Pages 632 and 633:
Seated Man (Self-portrait)
Homme assis (Autoportrait)
Mougins, 3 and 4 April 1965
Oil on canvas, 99.5 x 80.5 cm
Zervos XXV, 95. Estate of Jacqueline Picasso
Paris, Courtesy Galerie Louise Leiris

Portrait of Jacqueline
Portrait de Jacqueline
Mougins, 4 and 5 April 1965
Oil on canvas, 99.5 x 80.5 cm
Zervos XXV, 97. Estate of Jacqueline Picasso
Paris, Courtesy Galerie Louise Leiris

Landscape
Paysage
Mougins, 7 May 1965
Oil on cardboard, 50 x 80 cm
Zervos XXV, 126
Private collection

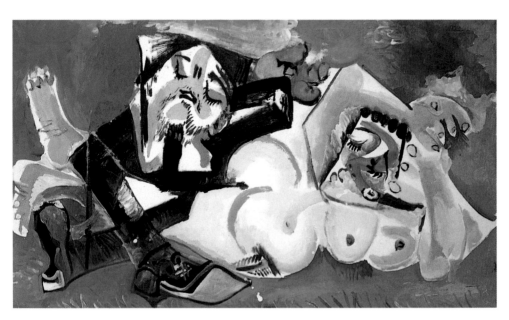

The Sleepers
Les dormeurs
Mougins, 13 April 1965
Oil on canvas, 114 x 195 cm
Zervos XXV, 106
Paris, Galerie Louise Leiris

Flute Player and Watermelon Eater
Joueur de flûte et mangeur de pastèque
Mougins, 6 June 1965 (I)
Oil on canvas, 162 x 130 cm
Zervos XXV, 158
Paris, Courtesy Galerie Louise Leiris

Head of a Woman and Head of a Man
Tête d'homme et de femme
Mougins, 22 May 1967
Oil on canvas, 65 x 54 cm
Zervos XXV, 368
Paris, Courtesy Galerie Louise Leiris

**Musketeer (Domenico Theotocopulos
van Riyn da Silva)**
Mousquetaire
Mougins, 28 March 1967
Oil on plywood, 101 x 81.5 cm
Zervos XXV, 323. Budapest, Ludwig Collection;
formerly Galerie Rosengart

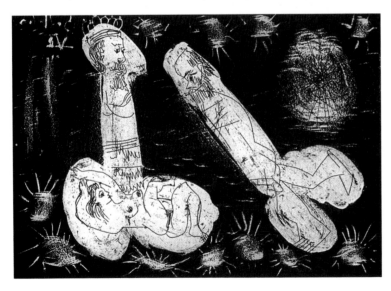

Untitled
Sans titre
Mougins, 15 November 1966 (VI)
Aquatint and etching, 22.5 x 32.5 cm
Bloch 1418; Baer VI, 1446

The Old Savage   1963–1973   **636**

Above:
Nude Man and Woman
Homme et femme nue
Mougins, 22, 28 February and 1 March 1967
Oil on canvas, 100 x 81 cm
Zervos XXV, 292
New York, Gelman Collection

Right:
L'aubade
Mougins, 18 June 1967
Oil on plywood, 161.7 x 122 cm
Zervos XXVII, 28
Galerie Rosengart

Flowers and Man with Umbrella
Fleurs et buste d'homme au parapluie
Mougins, 14 November 1968
Oil on canvas, 97 x 146 cm
Zervos XXVII, 373. Paris, Galerie Louise Leiris

his pictures now. There is no narrative or representational statement; his art has become a kind of performance. The questionable
status of form is in the foreground (as it had been for years). Thus
an irregular line may zigzag down the bridge and ridge of the nose,
the upper lip, the mouth and the chin. The line may be an unnatural
green, but it is in the right place. Then it is joined by a similar,
yellow line which implies a relation with the physical human face
but does not coincide with its natural lines. The overpaintings of
reproductions proceed similarly. On 30 March 1963 (p. 615) Picasso painted a male face, economically established with a few
generous brush-strokes in blue and white, seen simultaneously
from the front and in profile. With so Spartan a starting point, there
was ample scope for variation. What counted was the act of painting itself. The surface area, after all, could be obliterated and re-

Reclining Nude with Necklace
Femme nue couchée au collier
Mougins, 8 October 1968 (I)
Oil on canvas, 113.5 x 161.7 cm
Zervos XXVII, 331. London, Tate Gallery

Right:
Nude and Smoker
Femme nue debout et homme à la pipe
Mougins, 10 November 1968
Oil on canvas, 162 x 130 cm
Zervos XXVII, 369
Galerie Rosengart

The Old Savage 1963–1973 **640**

peopled with altogether different figures. Thus the oils done in the late Sixties and early Seventies, too, were merely variations on a few elementary motifs, stripped of technical sophistication.

However, the principle of metamorphosis and costume transformation is illustrated, especially in paintings from 1963 and 1969. In "Rembrandt and Saskia" (13/14 March 1963; p. 585). Picasso has done the lower part of the male figure two-dimensionally, providing a strong block of black in the centre of the painting. On 18 and 19 February 1969 he varied the same pose in two paintings showing men smoking, with a small Cupid (pp. 654 and 655). The brushwork has undergone radical change. In the 18 February picture, linearity of form is foregrounded, and the colour blocks are therefore filled with broad brushstrokes. In that of 19 February, the blocks of colour are themselves stressed once again – though with the crucial difference that now the act of painting, the imprecise movement of the hand, is being emphasized. The two paintings are complementary. While the motifs in that of 18 February are linear and the colours of secondary importance, Picasso proceeds in that of 19 February in exactly the contrary fashion. He fills the canvas with undefined bright colours, then, the good draughtsman, indicates forms that translate the colour composition into a figural painting. The vigorous brush-work and the seemingly expressive style are masks, to deceive us: they are there to confuse, to subvert

Musketeer with Pipe
Mousquetaire à la pipe
Mougins, 13 October 1968 (I)
Oil on canvas, 146 x 97 cm
Zervos XXVII, 341
Paris, Galerie Louise Leiris

Seated Man with Pipe
Homme assis à la pipe
Mougins, 15 September 1968 (II)
Oil on plywood, 100 x 81 cm
Zervos XXVII, 312
Paris, Courtesy Galerie Louise Leiris

Left:
Musketeer with Pipe
Mousquetaire à la pipe
Mougins, 16 October 1968 (I)
Oil on canvas, 162 x 130 cm
Zervos XXVII, 340
Paris, Galerie Louise Leiris

The Old Savage 1963–1973 **643**

Suite 347, Plate 298
Mougins, 31 August 1968
Etching, 17 x 20.5 cm
Bloch 1778

perception. There is next to no systematic orchestration of colour aimed at heightening of impact. Instead, paint squeezed straight from the tube onto the canvas has triumphed. Indeed, Picasso's use of paint is distinctly sloppy, leaving blotches and inchoate breaches wherever we look.

Things make a similar impression in the graphic work. Never before had Picasso done as many etchings as he did in the last years of his life. The command of Picasso the craftsman was plainly un-diminished. Using various etching and aquatint techniques, linear and otherwise, he was still drawing figures with a single line and a

Suite 347, Plate 1
Mougins, 16 to 22 March 1968
Etching, 39.5 x 56.5 cm
Bloch 1481

The Old Savage 1963–1973 **644**

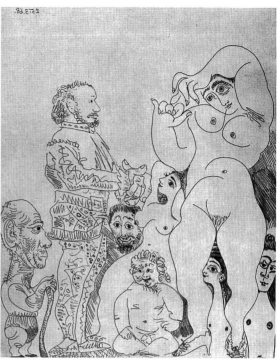

Suite 347, Plate 6
Mougins, 24 March 1968 (II)
Etching, 42.5 x 34.5 cm
Bloch 1486

Suite 347, Plate 8
Mougins, 25 March 1968
Etching, 42.5 x 34.5 cm
Bloch 1488

Suite 347, Plate 290
Mougins, 20 and 22 August 1968
Etching, 28 x 39 cm
Bloch 1770

Pages 646 and 647:
The Smoker
Homme à la pipe
Mougins, 22 November 1968
Oil on canvas, 146 x 88.8 cm
Zervos XXVII, 377
Galerie Rosengart

Musketeer with Pipe and Flowers
Mousquetaire à la pipe et fleurs
Mougins, 5 November 1968
Oil on canvas, 145.5 x 97 cm
Zervos XXVII, 364
Galerie Rosengart

steady hand as late as summer 1971[419]. This may be the best place to identify Picasso's subtle intentions. Many of the etchings betray formal inconsistencies, with carefully worked areas appearing alongside negligently scrawled details, and there are visible gaps in Picasso's handling of compositional questions. But the sheer number of his supposed slips is enough to preclude all possibility of spontaneity in his work.

The main subject is sexuality. It is so obsessive that the public has continued to find this area of Picasso's work problematic to this day. Picasso was probing at a great social taboo. The public recep-

Bust of a Man
Buste d'homme
Mougins, 7 July 1969
Oil on canvas, 65 x 54 cm
Zervos XXXI, 301. Private collection

Head of a Man
Tête d'homme
Mougins, 6 July 1969
Oil on paper, 65.7 x 50.8 cm
Zervos XXXI, 297
Galerie Rosengart

tion of his late work (this only proves how disturbing this work seems) has been masterly in its repression of this part of his œuvre. In 1980, for instance, the great retrospective at the Museum of Modern Art in New York almost entirely excluded his sexual material. It still strikes many as so provocative that on the occasion of the first retrospective of his late work, in 1988, debate centred on whether Picasso was a pornographer.[420] Whenever it has not been possible to avoid the sexual pictures, the orthodox Picasso reception has dictated that biographical reasons be adduced for Picasso's obsessive treatment of sex, implying that Picasso had to get a dirty old man's fantasies out of his system.[421]

None of this is convincing, and in fact the truth of the matter is far more intractable. Picasso's explicit pictures were part of the Sixties revolution.[422] The rebellion against taboos at that time must almost inevitably have reminded him of similar currents earlier in his life. Tellingly, he started from works in which, agreeing with his friend Apollinaire's radical views, he had used pornography to combat encrusted bourgeois morality (cf. Chapter 5). It was not that Picasso's 1968 etchings were a direct contribution to the struggles of the young generation: the work was not political in nature. But he did nonetheless, in his seclusion, follow events on television, and the general mood of rebellion confirmed him in his own refractory individualism.

Picasso's sexual etchings and paintings followed a line of thought that involved transformational effects, among them those of costume. Behind this lay not only the anarchist mood of early studies done in 1902 (cf. pp. 90 and 91) but also the major artist and model series done in the late Twenties and early Thirties. Again, in his work of the Sixties and Seventies, Picasso combined allusions to the art of the past with themes and motifs that were constants in his own repertoire: the theatre, the circus, ancient mythology. Though this late work initially strikes us as rudimentary and chaotic, the form and content are in fact subtly judged. Thus in 1966 we find him commenting on sexuality in his etchings by peopling sexual organs with figures (p. 636). Gustav Klimt had already availed himself of this method at the beginning of the century.[423] Still, in almost all Picasso's pictures the voyeurist element is dominant. The artist and his female nude model are almost invariably being observed by ugly old men in various kinds of costume (pp. 644 and 645). This has led people to infer that it is the old Picasso we are seeing, humorously burlesquing his own physical impotence by casting himself in the role of voyeur.

No doubt the artist was expressing personal problems; but too simple a one-to-one identification would be wrong. It would be apt, in fact, to drawings of a like nature done in the Fifties (cf. p. 521). In the late work, the observers are of too various a sort, and

Bust of a Man
Buste d'homme
Mougins, 22 September and 2 November 1969
Oil on canvas, 130 x 97 cm
Zervos XXXI, 487
Paris, Courtesy Galerie Louise Leiris

Couple
Couple
Mougins, 14 December 1969 (II)
Oil on canvas, 130 x 97 cm
Zervos XXXI, 545
Paris, Courtesy Galerie Louise Leiris

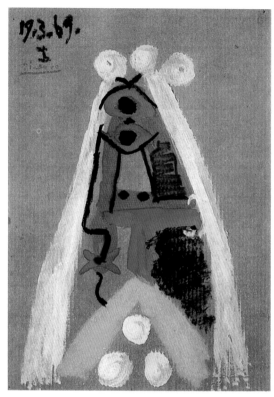

Bust of a Man
Buste d'homme
Mougins, 20 March 1969 (I)
Oil on corrugated cardboard, 131 x 50.8 cm
Zervos XXXI, 106. Private collection

The Bride
La mariée
Mougins, 19 March 1969 (I)
Oil on corrugated cardboard, 88 x 64 cm
Zervos XXXI, 104. Private collection

Bust of a Man
Buste d'homme
Mougins, 20 March 1969 (II)
Oil on corrugated cardboard,
129.5 x 50.8 cm
Zervos XXXI, 107. Private collection

at times the figures exchange roles, too. A baroque nobleman will become an artist and paint the beautiful model himself. The painter always remains the creator. This fact expresses Picasso's view of art as an act of (pro)creation presented to a public itself incapable of creative endeavour. In view of the intimacy of the act of (pro)creation, it is tantamount to shamelessness if the urge to expose is constantly being satisfied, the private secrets revealed. Picasso rarely expressed the role of the modern artist, under constant observation by the omnipresent mass media, with such illuminating force. The painter under public scrutiny (i.e. Picasso himself) is obliged constantly to play new roles. He is the knight and the sailor, the circus artiste and the nobleman, but above all he is the "new Rembrandt". In the work of his old age, Picasso took the 17th-century Dutch painter as the artist *par excellence* with whom it was possible to identify. "Rembrandt and Saskia" (p. 585) heralded a lengthy series of paintings which to a greater or lesser extent constituted masked self-portraits of Picasso. He was returning to the outmoded idea of the productive, creative person as genius.

The Old Savage 1963–1973 **653**

Pages 654 and 655:
Musketeer and Cupid
Mousquetaire et Amour
Mougins, 18 February 1969
Oil on canvas, 194.5 x 130 cm
Zervos XXXI, 67
Cologne, Museum Ludwig;
formerly Galerie Rosengart

Rembrandtesque Figure and Cupid
Personnage rembranesque et Amour
Mougins, 19 February 1969
Oil on canvas, 162 x 130 cm
Zervos XXXI, 73
Lucerne, Picasso Collection,
Donation Rosengart

Left:
Large Heads
Grandes têtes
Mougins, 16 March 1969
Oil on canvas, 194.5 x 129 cm
Zervos XXXI, 102
Aachen, Ludwig Collection;
formerly Galerie Rosengart

656 The Old Savage 1963–1973

L'aubade
Mougins, 14 June 1970 (IV)
Chalk on cardboard, 25 x 33.5 cm
Zervos XXXII, 127
Paris, Courtesy Galerie Louise Leiris

Man in an Armchair
Homme dans un fauteuil
Mougins, 27 June 1969
Oil on plywood, 130 x 81 cm
Zervos XXXI, 288
Paris, Courtesy Galerie Louise Leiris

Left:
Pierrot and Harlequin
Pierrot et arlequin
Mougins, 16 December 1969 (II)
Crayon on paper, 32.5 x 41 cm
Zervos XXXI, 551
Paris, Galerie Louise Leiris

Smoker and Nude
Fumeur et femme nue
Mougins, 21 June 1969
India ink and crayon on paper,
24 x 32 cm. Zervos XXXI, 268
Paris, Galerie Louise Leiris

Pages 658 and 659:
Man in an Armchair
Homme au fauteuil
Mougins, 16 October 1969
Oil on canvas, 116 x 89 cm
Zervos XXXI, 465
Paris, Courtesy Galerie Louise Leiris

Seated Man with Sword and Flower
Homme assis à l'épée et à la fleur
Mougins, 2 August (II) and 27 September 1969
Oil on canvas, 146 x 114 cm
Zervos XXXI, 449
Private collection; formerly Galerie Beyeler, Basel

Musketeer with Dove
Mousquetaire à la colombe
Mougins, 1969
Oil on canvas, 195 x 130 cm
Zervos XXXI, 155
Ito (Japan), Ikeda Museum of 20th Century Art

The Man with the Golden Helmet
(after Rembrandt)
L'homme au casque d'or (d'après Rembrandt)
Mougins, 8 April 1969
Oil on canvas, 145.5 x 114 cm
Zervos XXXI, 143. Private collection;
formerly Galerie Rosengart

661

662 The Old Savage 1963–1973

Left:
Reclining Nude with a Man Playing the Guitar
Femme nue couchée et homme
jouant de la guitare
Mougins, 27 October 1970
Oil on canvas, 130 x 195 cm
Zervos XXXII, 293; MPP 224
Paris, Musée Picasso

Flute Player and Female Nude
Joueur de flûte et femme nue
Mougins, 21 October 1970 (II)
Oil on canvas, 114 x 146 cm
Zervos XXXII, 285
Paris, Courtesy Galerie Louise Leiris

Woman in an Armchair
Femme au fauteuil
Mougins, 7 January 1970 (IV)
Oil on canvas, 130 x 97 cm
Zervos XXXII, 11
Paris, Courtesy Galerie Louise Leiris

Man and Woman
Homme et femme
Mougins, 27 November 1970
Oil on canvas, 100 x 81 cm
Zervos XXXII, 311
Paris, Courtesy Galerie Louise Leiris

Pages 664 and 665:
Cavalier with Pipe (The Matador)
Matador
Mougins, 14 October 1970
Oil on canvas, 145.5 x 114 cm
Zervos XXXII, 273; MPP 223
Paris, Musée Picasso

Seated Girl
Jeune fille assise
Mougins, 21 November 1970
Oil on plywood, 130.3 x 80.3 cm
Zervos XXXII, 307; MPP 225
Paris, Musée Picasso

Mother and Child
Maternité
Mougins, 30 August 1971
Oil on canvas, 162 x 130 cm
Zervos XXXIII, 168; MPP 226
Paris, Musée Picasso

Fatherhood
Paternité
Mougins, 29 September 1971
Oil on canvas, 146 x 114 cm
Zervos XXXIII, 167
Estate of Jacqueline Picasso

Left:
The Family
La famille
Mougins, 30 September 1970
Oil on canvas, 162 x 130 cm
Zervos XXXII, 271; MPP 222
Paris, Musée Picasso

Man and Woman
Homme et femme
Mougins, 12 July 1971 (II)
Oil on canvas, 116 x 88.5 cm
Zervos XXXIII, 100; MPP 1990-43
Paris, Musée Picasso,
Dation Jacqueline Picasso

The Old Savage   1963–1973   **667**

Picador
Buste de picador
Mougins, 11 April 1971 (II)
Oil on canvas, 92 x 73 cm
Zervos XXXIII, 59
Paris, Courtesy Galerie Louise Leiris

Card Player
Le joueur de cartes
Mougins, 30 December 1971 (II)
Oil on canvas, 114 x 146 cm
Zervos XXXIII, 265
Humlebæk (Denmark), Louisiana Museum

Right:
Couple
Mougins, 23 December 1970 (IV)
to 25 June 1971
Oil on plywood, 163.5 x 131.5 cm
Zervos XXXIII, 73; MPP 1990–41
Paris, Musée Picasso,
Dation Jacqueline Picasso

The Old Savage 1963–1973 **668**

Seated Man with Cane
Homme assis à la canne
Mougins, 13 September 1971 (II)
Oil on canvas, 130 x 97 cm
Zervos XXXIII, 180; MPP 1990–46
Paris, Musée Picasso,
Dation Jacqueline Picasso

Head of a Man with Straw Hat
Tête d'homme au chapeau de paille
Mougins, 26 July 1971
Oil on canvas, 91.5 x 73 cm
Zervos XXXIII, 117; MPP 1990–44
Paris, Musée Picasso,
Dation Jacqueline Picasso

Seated Man
Homme assis
Mougins, 27 June 1971
Oil on canvas, 100 x 81 cm
Zervos XXXIII, 179
Paris, Courtesy Galerie Louise Leiris

The Old Savage   1963–1973   **671**

17 The Legend of the Artist

The mythologization of Picasso into a titanic Hero of Modern Art has tended to obscure his work. But it is a process with a lengthy tradition. From time immemorial, the extraordinary creative powers of artists have been assimilated into heroic ideas. Since the Renaissance, when artists were released from their deprecating definition as mere craftsmen, imagination and obsessive inventiveness have been considered their characteristic traits. In this view, the creative artist is inspired, and produces his work in an uncontrollable frenzy that verges on madness. The legend has it that the artist comes into this world a prodigy. His genius can be seen in the fact that essentially he needs no teacher, and develops by virtue of innate powers. Tales relating to Raphael are matched by the claim, *de rigueur* in every Picasso biography, that his father gave the young Pablo his brush and paints, never to paint himself again.[424]

For this reason, his academic training was long ignored or dismissed as unimportant. This is complemented in the Picasso myth by an emphasis on the virtuosity of his craftsmanship, a technical command well above the norm. An artist of genius, after all, can establish the most astounding shapes and likenesses in seconds. Through this ability, he also has absolute mastery of every conceivable means of expression, style, and creative insight. Being a genius, the artist is daemonically close to insanity, his creative power thus deriving from a spirit either divine or deranged. In physical terms that power is seen in sexual prowess at once fearsome and magnificent. The artist possesses unusual energy, best seen in his attitude to his work. Obsessed by his ideas, he enters into the world of his work entirely, labours for hours and days without pause, no longer registers the petty concerns of the real world.[425]

Much of this is quite plainly a description of the real Picasso. Because this is so, it is difficult to distinguish fiction from reality, role-playing from authentic personality. Time after time, in consequence, the old heroic image of Picasso continues to be perpetuated. Modernist innovation is attributed to him far beyond what is historically verifiable. He is stylized into the major figure in a cult of genius that remains with us to this day. It is of course true that in his long life Picasso produced a formidable quantity of work,

The Young Painter
Le jeune peintre
Mougins, 14 April 1972 (III)
Oil on canvas, 91 x 72.5 cm
Zervos XXXIII, 350; MPP 228
Paris, Musée Picasso

Head
Tête
Mougins, 3 July 1972
Chalk and crayon on paper,
66 x 50.5 cm
Zervos XXXIII, 438
Galerie Rosengart

Seated Man
Homme assis
Mougins, 28 June 1971
Oil on canvas, 129.5 x 96.5 cm
Zervos XXXIII, 77
Paris, Courtesy Galerie Louise Leiris

more than perhaps any other artist, and that his creative curiosity was boundless. He was active in painting, sculpture, graphic art and craft, in fact in every branch of the visual arts bar architecture. And he remained tirelessly active till the very end of his life. So it was that his work came to be seen as infinite in extent.

Astoundingly, Picasso's thematic range was slight. Again and again we encounter the artist and his model, bullfights, bathers, figures from classical mythology, or portraits. In the course of his career he established a repertoire which he deployed and redeployed constantly. His amazing ability to ring the changes obscured perception for many years of his true creative character. But there was a limit to variation in his work. What invariably prevailed was form: his work always evolved from the line, from the principles of the draughtsman. For Picasso, sculpture, painting and graphics were not primary categories in their own right. His versatility resided primarily in the range of means he brought to bear on what he wanted to express. At heart, his interests were single-minded in the extreme: he was out to test the representational values of form. There is no autonomy of colour in Picasso; nor do spatial values have any real independence in his work. He always considered colour a means of reinforcing the expressive power of form, either by emphasizing or by diluting the impact. In his extensive sculptural output there are practically no works of a conventional kind, apart from stray figures carved in wood in 1907 (pp. 162 and 163). His sculptural work developed from drawings, establishing spatial

presence through illusionist effects. Pure abstraction never meant anything to him, even though some of his pictures – such as the 125 lithographic illustrations to Pierre Reverdy's book "Le chant des morts" (1946–48) – show that he was well aware of the possibilities open to abstract art.[426]

Picasso's works were links in a chain of experiments. Hence the artist's many statements denying the finished character of individual works, seeing them rather as parts of an evolutionary process. Every picture, artefact and sketch he did records a visual experience, and thus possesses a value of its own, as a fragment of the whole. Views of Picasso depend largely on the criteria involved in the viewing. If we were to judge him by conventional standards, the vastly ambitious scale of his productivity and versatility would be cut down by the fact that the many thousands of studies led to relatively few final works of any substantial complexity.

The concept of what constitutes a work of art has itself undergone change. We no longer check to see whether prior intentions have been enacted according to plan. Anything can be a work of art. Yet even by these new criteria, Picasso's unusual œuvre is unique in extent, if not in diversity. His rivals include Edgar Degas, who produced not only paintings and drawings but also graphics and sculptures of genuine innovative importance,[427] and Max Ernst, the Surrealist whose work included drawings, paintings, sculptures and montages that introduced new departures into modern art.[428]

The view of Picasso as the pre-eminent genius of the century is

Page 674:
Seated Man
Homme assis
Mougins, 13 September 1971 (I)
Oil on canvas, 130 x 97 cm
Zervos XXXIII, 75
Paris, Courtesy Galerie Louise Leiris

Two Heads
Deux têtes
Mougins, 14 July 1971
Oil on canvas, 100 x 81 cm
Zervos XXXIII, 102
Paris, Courtesy Galerie Louise Leiris

Above:
Man Writing
Buste d'homme écrivant
Mougins, 7 July 1971 (II)
Oil on canvas, 100 x 81 cm
Zervos XXXIII, 92; MPP 1990–42
Paris, Musée Picasso

Man and Flute Player
Homme et flûtiste
Mougins, 10 April 1972
Oil on canvas, 81 x 65 cm
Zervos XXXIII, 343
Paris, Courtesy Galerie Louise Leiris

Mardi gras
Mougins, 15 February 1972 (III)
Oil on canvas, 146 x 114 cm
Zervos XXXIII, 318
Paris, Courtesy Galerie Louise Leiris

due not least to his willingness to fulfil public expectations of artists. In Henri Georges Clouzot's revealingly titled film "The Mystery of Picasso" (1956), for instance, the artist demonstrates his working methods to the camera, and thus to millions: it is an eloquent proof of his approach to the myth. He is not only constantly at work on the canvas, in order to convey his conviction that a work is continually involved in a process of creation and destruction, but he also shows the artist's caprice at work, making changes as he chooses, and in this respect conforms to the legend. It seems there is neither rhyme nor reason in his choice of a particular point to begin painting; but then, with astounding speed, he has painted

Musician with Guitar
Musicien à la guitare
Mougins, 26 May 1972
Oil on canvas, 194.5 x 129.5 cm
Zervos XXXIII, 397; MPP 229
Paris, Musée Picasso

an entire composition. The rapidity of the act of creation, and the emergence of a rational result from a seemingly irrational process, are both essential factors in the myth of the virtuoso genius. The artist as magus was a role Picasso quite deliberately played.[429]

He was not the only artist to do this. Rubens, for example, liked to play the part of lord and master in the realm of art when visitors were present. A Danish doctor named Sperling, who sought him out in his Antwerp studio, reported that while they talked Rubens continued painting, dictated a letter, and listened to readings of classical literature. Much the same was reported of Julius Caesar and later of Napoleon.[430] For Picasso, this role-playing afforded a

677   The Legend of the Artist

way of concealing creative conflict behind a multitude of masks, and of confirming his own preeminence. As early as the Thirties he was seeing himself as the new Rembrandt, and from the Fifties on the charades of historical role-playing became an important creative strategy for him, a process centred on the subject of the artist and his model, including the concept of the artwork as the artist's child, the idea that creativity is a kind of sexual act, and the banal notion that the model was the artist's lover.[431]

Picasso's own life seemed to afford the public concept of the artist as social outsider ideal proof. The artist is permitted to live out liberties denied to others trammelled by societal constraints.[432] In the work of his old age in particular, Picasso presented himself to a shamelessly voyeuristic public as a man of unfailing potency: a compulsively, feverishly productive artist wholly immersed in his work. This was both a mask and a vital means of self-preservation. His work, forever expanding into new genres, substantiated his image as a universal genius. Like a new Michelangelo, Picasso ap-

Landscape
Paysage
Mougins, 31 March 1972
Oil on canvas, 130 x 162 cm
Zervos XXXIII, 331; MPP 227
Paris, Musée Picasso

Bust of a Man
Buste d'homme
Mougins, 12 February 1972 (II)
Oil on canvas, 100 x 80.8 cm
Zervos XXXIII, 315
Estate of Jacqueline Picasso
Paris, Courtesy Galerie Louise Leiris

Reclining Nude and Head
Femme nue couchée et tête
Mougins, 25 May 1972 (I) and 7 April 1973
Oil on canvas, 130 x 195 cm
Zervos XXXIII, 398
Private collection

The painting above, "Reclining Nude and Head",
is the last Picasso worked on. He applied the
creamy white, to brighten the impression, on the
evening of 7 April 1973. The following day, 8
April, he died shortly before midday. For this information, given to me in May 1973, I am indebted to one of the curators of the exhibition
"Picasso 1970–1972" at the Palais des Papes,
Avignon, where the last oils Picasso painted were
shown. He received the picture, not yet dry, immediately before Picasso's death, to prepare it for
hanging in the exhibition, which was opened on
23 May 1973. Picasso's widow Jacqueline later
confirmed the information. To date, no oils from
1973 have been exhibited or published. Probably
Picasso only drew, and perhaps did a little work in
watercolour, in the final months of his life.   I.F.W.

peared before the public as painter, sculptor, writer. His work inevitably varied in quality – but then, Michelangelo's sonnets were
by no means comparable, in literary value, with his majestic accomplishments in sculpture, painting and architecture.

Of greater interest in relation to Picasso's status in art history is
the clearly apparent factor of conscious strategy. This is at odds
with prevalent notions of the artist working barely consciously on
the products of his own imagination. But in Picasso's œuvre we
plainly see a rational, logical, consistent method. At core he was an
intellectual artist. For a long time, his ways of articulating his ideas
obscured this crucial fact. In a real sense, Picasso transferred ideas
into art, and created unified harmonies of idea and artwork, form
and content, which are fundamentally traditional in nature and
highlight his classical character.[433]

In this respect he was essentially different from modern concept
art and the father of the movement, Marcel Duchamp. In concept
art, the concept precedes and accompanies the work, which in turn
refers to the concept. A verbal key or explanation is required if the
whole is to be grasped. Picasso's work, by contrast, shows. The statement is made visible. His work is inherently comprehensible. There
is no gap between abstract content and concrete form. Uniquely in
the 20th century he was capable of radical innovation on the one
hand but on the other of continuing traditional lines. Thus in "Les
Demoiselles d'Avignon" he vanquished the representational picture,
while in "Guernica" he revived the genre of historical painting in a
new form.

Picasso's true greatness and significance lie in his dual role as
revolutionary and traditionalist at once. He gave a new vitality to
art even as he preserved the creative presence (outside the museums) of its history. For this reason he became the pre-eminent
figure in 20th-century art.

APPENDICES
by Ingo F. Walther

Pablo Picasso 1881–1973
A Chronology

Doña María Picasso y Lopez, mother of Picasso. "If you become a soldier," she told her son, "you will be a general. If you become a monk, you will be Pope." About 1906

36, Plaza de la Merceded, Málaga, the house where Picasso was born

Don José Ruiz Blasco, Picasso's father, was a painter and taught drawing at the College of Arts and Crafts at Málaga. It was he who gave his son his first tuition and "brought him up" to be a genius

1880 On 8 December Don José Ruiz Blasco (1838–1913) marries Doña María Picasso y Lopez (1855–1939) in Málaga. Don José is a painter, curator of the municipal museum, and an art teacher at San Telmo School of Arts and Crafts. He comes of an old, respected family from the northwest province of Léon. Doña María is an Andalusian of part Arab blood.

1881 The first of the couple's three children is born on 25 October at 36 (now 15), Plaza de la Merceded, Málaga: Pablo Diego José Francisco de Paula Juan Nepomucéno Maria de los Remedios Crispín Crispriano Santísima Trinidad. In his artist life the son will at first sign himself with his father's name as Pablo Ruiz but from about the turn of the century will change to the matronymic Pablo Picasso.

Left: Picasso with pipe. About 1908–1910

1884 In December Pablo's elder sister, Dolorès (1884–1958), known as Lola, is born at Málaga.

1887 In October Pablo's second sister, Concepción (1887–1891), known as Conchita, is born at Málaga.

1888/89 Father and son go to the bullfights. The boy begins painting with his father's guidance. At eight he paints his first picture, "The Little Picador".

1891 The family move to Corunna in northwest Spain, on the Atlantic coast, where Ruiz is taking up a new position as professor at Da Guarda Art School. Pablo goes to grammar school. He paints and draws and helps his father with the latter's paintings. Sister Conchita dies.

1892 Enters drawing class at Corunna Art School, where his father teaches. Draws his father, his mother and landscapes.

1893 Qualifies for figure drawing class at the Art School.

1894 Writes and illustrates diaries (pp. 30 ff.) signed "P. Ruiz". Goes on to classes for drawing after classical plaster casts (pp. 36 ff.) and after nature, and for painting. Ruiz, recognising his son's great gift, gives him his own brush and palette, resolving never to paint again himself.

1895 In spring Ruiz is called to La Lonja Academy of Art in Barcelona as professor of figure drawing. The family join him in the autumn. At the Prado in Madrid, Pablo discovers the Spanish masters. Sum-

Pablo Picasso aged four in 1885

Pablo in 1888, aged seven, with Lola (Dolorès), the elder of his sisters

Pablo Picasso in 1896, aged 15, shortly after arrival in Barcelona

José Ruiz Blasco: "Dovecote", 1878. Oil on canvas, 102 x 147 cm. Málaga, Ayuntamiento. Painted by Picasso's father, who gave up painting himself when he recognised Pablo's ability

"The Little Picador", 1889. Oil on panel, 24 x 19 cm. Zervos VI, 3; Palau 4. Paris, Claude Picasso Collection. The first oil by Picasso, painted at the age of eight

View of Horta de Ebro, 1898

mer holiday with family at Málaga. In the autumn they move to 3, Calle Cristina, Barcelona. Enters Academy of Art. Goes straight in to upper classes, passing the entrance exams with flying colours. Paints "The Barefoot Girl" (p. 35) and his first major picture, "First Communion" (p. 38). Given permission to copy in the province's Academy of Art museum.

1896 "First Communion" is exhibited in Barcelona. Summer holidays in Málaga. Paints landscapes (p. 46), bullfights and family portraits, including "Portrait of Aunt Pepa" (p. 45). Moves into his first studio at 4, Calle de la Plata, Barcelona, with his friend Manuel Pallarés from Horta de Ebro (now Horta de San Juan) in Tarragona province.

1897 "Science and Charity" (pp. 50/51), his second major oil, is praised at the national art exhibition in Madrid and wins a gold medal in Málaga. Spends the summer there again. In a new Barcelona artists' café, "Els Quatre Gats" (The Four Cats), he paints portraits of local artists on the walls. These are reviewed in "La Vanguardia". His father's brothers send money for him to study in Madrid. Passes entrance exam for upper grade at San Fernando

Royal Academy in Madrid, but in the winter, disappointed by the tuition, he leaves it again, to his father's annoyance.

1898 Scarlet fever in spring. Returns to Barcelona. Convalesces at Horta in the Ebro valley with his friend Manuel Pallarés. Paints landscapes there. His painting "Costumbres de Aragón" wins medals in Madrid and Málaga.

1899 Returns to Barcelona in February. With Santiago Cardona i Turró he takes a studio at 2, Calle d'Escudillers Blancs. Works as a painter and illustrator for magazines. In the intellectual and artistic circles at "Els Quatre Gats" he meets painters Carles Junyer-Vidal, Isidre Nonell, Joaquim Sunyer Miró and Carlos Casagemas, sculptor "Manolo" Hugué (1872–1945), the brothers Fernández de Soto, and writer Jaime Sabartés (1881–1968), who becomes a close friend and

Picasso's first studio in Paris in 1900, at 49, Rue Gabrielle

Picasso with Pedro Mañach (p. 64) and Torres Fuentes in his studio in Boulevard de Clichy, in front of a portrait of Picasso by Francisco Iturrino. Paris, 1901

The home and studio of Pedro Mañach at 130, Boulevard de Clichy, Paris, where Picasso lived temporarily after his return from Spain

later his secretary. Painter Ramón Casas (1866–1932) introduces him to the work of Swiss draughtsman and graphic artist Théophile Steinlen (1859–1923) and French painter and graphic artist Henri de Toulouse-Lautrec (1864–1901). Does a charcoal self-portrait (p. 54) and his first etching, "El Picador", which is known as "El Zurdo" (The Lefthander) because it is back-to-front. Casas and Miguel Utrillo start the magazine "Pél y Ploma" (Brush and Pen).

1900 With Carlos Casagemas he moves into a studio at 17, Calle Riera de San Juan, Barcelona. Enters poster competitions. Exhibition of 150 drawings at "Els Quatre Gats" is widely reviewed. Exhibits "Derniers moments" at Paris World Fair. Drawings published in "Joventut" and "Catalunya artistica" magazines. In October he goes to Paris with Casagemas and uses Nonell's Montmartre studio at 49, Rue Gabrielle. Looks at work by Cézanne, Toulouse-Lautrec, Degas, Bonnard and others at the commercial galleries. Dealer Berthe Weill buys three pastel bullfight scenes. Dealer Pedro Mañach (p. 64) offers him a contract sum of 150 francs a month for his pictures, and becomes Picasso's first regular dealer. Paints "Le Moulin de la Galette" (p. 58), probably his first Paris picture. Spends Christmas with his family in Barcelona and the New Year with Casagemas in Málaga.

1901 In February the lovesick Casagemas commits suicide. Picasso, distraught, paints "The Death of Casagemas", "The Burial of Casagemas" (pp. 86–87) and

other related works. Goes to Madrid to co-edit "Arte Joven" magazine, which folds after a few issues. In May returns to Paris with Jaume Andreu Bonsoms and moves into Casagemas's old studio at 130, Boulevard Clichy. Through Mañach he meets the French writer Max Jacob (1876–1944). From now on he only signs his work with the matronymic "Picasso". Following Paris night life scenes such as "The Absinthe Drinker" (p. 85) he increasingly turns to subjects of poverty, old age and

The main hall of "Els Quatre Gats" in Barcelona, about 1899/1900

Picasso (centre), Mateu F. de Soto and Carlos Casagemas on the roof of 3, Carrer de la Mercè in Barcelona. About 1900

loneliness, and then the world of the circus (pp. 78 f.). His almost monochrome blue-green palette heralds the Blue Period: "The Blue Room" (p. 82), portraits of Jaime Sabartés and Mateu Fernández de Soto (p. 88), "Woman with Blue Hat" (p. 68), "Self-Portrait with Cloak" (p. 80) and various mother and child paintings (p. 77). In April he shows "Woman in Blue" at the Exposición General de Bellas Artes in Madrid. Exhibits pastel work in a "Pél y Ploma" show in Barcelona with work by Ramón Casas. First Paris show in June, together with Francisco Iturrino (1864–1924), at the Galerie Ambroise Vollard. The self-portrait "Yo Picasso" (p. 6), included there, is very well reviewed in the "Revue Blanche". 15 pictures are sold before the exhibition opens.

1902 In January his contract with Mañach expires. Returns to Barcelona, to a studio at 6, Calle Nueva (now 10, Calle Conde del Asalto). Paints more "blue" pictures such as "The Visit" (p. 93) and "Two Women at a Bar" (p. 102). First sculpture: "Femme assise". In October he goes to Paris for the third time, this time with Sebastiàn Junyer-Vidal. Shortage of money compels him to change his lodgings frequently. For a while he lives with Max Jacob in the latter's rooms at 87, Boulevard Voltaire. Does almost exclusively drawings because he cannot afford canvas. In April exhibits 30 paintings and pastels at Berthe Weill's in Paris; in November he exhibits "blue" pictures in a group show, and receives an enthusiastic "Mercure de France" review.

Picasso aged 22. Photo by Ricardo Canals, with Picasso's inscription: "To my friends Suzanne and Henri [Bloch] 1904"

Picasso in Montmartre, Place Ravignan, 1904

1903 At the start of the year he returns to Barcelona and continues working in the studio at 17, Calle de la Riera de San Juan, this time together with the painter Angel Fernández de Soto. He is particularly productive, and in 14 months he does over 50 paintings and a number of small sculptures. After extensive preliminary work he paints a key work of the period, "La Vie" (p. 105), and then "Celestina" (p. 99), a one-eyed procuress who figures in a dramatized novel by Spanish writer Fernando de Rojas (1465–1541). The elongated figures in some pictures recall the work of El Greco (1541–1614): "Poor People on the Seashore" (p. 101), "The Blind Man's Meal" (p. 103), "The Old Guitar Player" (p. 94). The intense blues express the decay and fragility of old age.

1904 In April he moves finally to Paris with Junyer-Vidal, with whom he rents a studio at 13, Rue Ravignan (now Place Emile Goudeau). Max Jacob, with the washboats on the Seine in mind, dubs the dilapidated house the "Bateau-lavoir". Picasso remains in it till 1909. There he meets the writers Guillaume Apollinaire (1880–1918), Alfred Jarry (1873–1907) and André Salmon (1881–1969), Dutch painter Kees van Dongen (1877–1968) and a number of French artists. Brief relationship with "Madeleine", perhaps the "Woman with Her Hair up" (p. 106). Meets the beautiful Fernande Olivier, who is first his model and then, for the next seven years, his lover. With friends he often goes to Médrano's circus in Montmartre (which prompts acrobat and artiste subjects in his work) and a bar called "Au Lapin Agile". Margot, the

Three views of the famous "Bateau-Lavoir" at 13, Rue Ravignan – a tumbledown building housing a number of artists' studios where Picasso lived for five years. In the bottom photo, Picasso has marked his studio window with an arrow. 1904

The "Lapin Agile" in Montmartre. Postcard, about 1872. Below: interior view, with Frédé the landlord in the foreground with a guitar. On the wall is Picasso's painting "Au Lapin Agile" (p. 128). About 1905

daughter of the bar owner Frédé, is Picasso's model for "Woman with a Crow" (p. 113). With help from Ricardo Canals (1876–1931) he etches "The Frugal Repast" (p. 108). October: last exhibition at Berthe Weill's. The Blue Period ends and is superseded by the Rose Period: "The Actor" (p. 114), "Woman Wearing a Chemise" (p. 122).

1905 February: group show at Galerie Serrurier, at which he exhibits the first Rose Period works, which Apollinaire reports on in two magazines. Circus subjects continue to interest Picasso in paintings such as "The Acrobats" (p. 129) and "Mother and Child" (p. 110) but also in his series of acrobat etchings which Vollard later prints (pp. 124, 126). A sculpture, "The Jester" (p. 132), is cast in bronze at Vollard's prompting. The Russian dealer Sergei Shchukin begins wholesale buying of Picassos, among them "Woman with a Fan" (p. 117). The American writer Gertrude Stein (1874–1946), whose salon Picasso visits, also buys his pictures. Summer in Schoorl near Alkmaar, Holland, as the guest of a young writer, Tom Schilperoort, and there he paints pictures of young Dutch women (p. 133). In Paris that autumn he paints "Young Girl with a Basket of Flowers" (p. 117) and "Boy with a Pipe" (p. 116). In October the Fauves cause a scandal at the Salon d'Automne. Late that year Picasso paints "The Death of Harlequin" (p. 125).

1906 At the start of the year he paints "Boy Leading a Horse" (p. 135). In the Louvre he sees an exhibition of Iberian sculpture excavated near Osuna in the province of Seville. It makes a deep impression on him, influencing his style of

Fernande Olivier, 1905

Fernande Olivier, Picasso and Ramón Reventos in "El Guayaba" in Barcelona, which served Juan Vidal y Ventosa, who took the photo, as a studio. Taken the day before Picasso and Fernande left for Gósol, May 1906

painting in a more relief-like, three-dimensional direction, as in "Portrait of Gertrude Stein" (p. 144) painted that autumn. Through Stein he meets Henri Matisse (1869–1954) and soon after André Derain (1880–1954), both members of the Fauves group. Vollard buys most of the "rose" pictures for 2,000 francs, affording Picasso a life free of financial worry for the first time. May: with Fernande Olivier he visits his parents in Barcelona and then goes on to Gósol, a village in the Pyrenees in Lérida province. There he paints "The Two Brothers" (p. 137), studies of landscapes and peasants ("Young Man from Gósol", p. 138), and toilette motifs (pp. 140 ff.). August: hasty return to Paris because of the risk of typhoid fever. Further pictures of women at their toilette (pp. 139, 150) and a sculpture (p. 143) are influenced by Iberian sculpture, as is the "Self-portrait with Palette" (p. 147) and "Two Nudes" (p. 151).

1907 Paints a "Self-portrait" (p. 152) expressing a fundamental change of style. March: Matisse and Derain exhibit at the first Salon des Indépendants. Over several months, Picasso does studies (809 have survived) and heavily divergent preliminary versions using various techniques (pp. 153–158) in preparation for "Les Demoiselles d'Avignon" (p. 159), the large-scale painting which he completes in July: the first Cubist painting, anticipating the "invention" of Cubism by Georges Braque (1882–1963), who took his bearings from statements by Paul Cézanne (1839–1906) that visible reality could be reduced to cubes, cones and spheres. Even Picasso's friends are surprised by his picture (not publicly exhibited till 1916). In the Ethnological Museum he is impressed by African sculpture, the influence of which shows in "The Dance of the Veils" and "Nude with Raised Arms" (p. 167) and in primitivist wooden sculptures (pp. 162 ff.). Art dealer

Daniel-Henry Kahnweiler (1884–1979), German by origin and proprietor of a new Paris gallery since the beginning of the year, visits Picasso at the Bateau-Lavoir. He is dumbfounded by "Les Demoiselles d'Avignon" and becomes Picasso's dealer and subsequently a good friend. October: Picasso visits the Cézanne memorial exhibition, Salon d'Automne. Through Apollinaire he meets Braque.

1908 After a large number of studies, he paints "African" nudes, under the influence of black sculpture (p. 169). Paints various versions of the large-format "Three Women" (p. 166). In late summer, with Fernande, he goes to La Rue-des-Bois, north of Paris, and there paints figures such as "Peasant Woman" (p. 171) and landscapes, which he continues in Paris in the autumn ("The Dryad", p. 172). The first Cubist landscapes

Fernande Olivier and Benedetta Canals (p. 115) in Canals' studio, 1904

Gósol in the Pyrenees, where Picasso spent the summer of 1906

Gertrude Stein (p. 144) in her Paris flat in the Rue des Fleurs. About 1905

A Chronology **687**

Picasso in the "Bateau-Lavoir". Behind him, sculptures from New Caledonia, 1908

Studies for "Les Demoiselles d'Avignon". Paris, March 1907. Pencil on paper, 19.3 x 24.2 cm each. Zervos II**, 634, 635; Palau 1528, 1532; MPP 1861. Paris, Musée Picasso

The studio at Horta de Ebro, with portraits of Fernande at the rear (p. 164). Summer 1909

painted by Braque at L'Estaque near Marseilles are turned down by the Salon d'Automne but exhibited by Kahnweiler in November, when they excite great interest. Matisse's comment about "little cubes" gives rise to the term "Cubism". Picasso buys "Portrait of Yadwigha" (cf. photo p. 501) by Henri "Le Douanier" Rousseau (1844–1910) and in November gives a banquet in his honour at the Bateau-Lavoir. The collaboration of Picasso and Braque becomes a friendship. In the winter he paints "Seated Nude" and "Bathers" (p. 173). December: group show in Paris, including three works by Picasso.

1909 The picture "Carnival at the Bistro" evolves into the still life "Loaves and Bowl of Fruit on a Table" (p. 179). May: visits family and friends in Barcelona. Spends summer with Fernande at Horta de Ebro, where he sees his old friend Manuel Pallarés (portrait p. 187) and spends the most productive period in his career as an artist. The landscapes there, such as "The Reservoir" (p. 181), portraits of Fernande such as "Woman with Pears" (p. 164), and still lifes, lead to analytical Cubism, which dispenses with central perspective and splits up form into shards. September:

return to Paris, move from Bateau-Lavoir to a flat at 11, Boulevard de Clichy near the Place Pigalle. There he entertains friends and has Braque as a neighbour. "Head of a Woman (Fernande)" cast in bronze (p. 184). The New Artists' Association in Munich organizes a show at the Galerie Thannhauser, the first in Germany that Picasso exhibits at.

1910 Finishes the famous Cubist portraits of Vollard the art dealer, of German collector and critic Wilhelm Uhde (1874–1947) and, in the autumn, of Kahnweiler (pp. 188 ff.). June: travels to Barcelona with Fernande, then on to spend summer at Cadaqués, on the Mediterranean in the province of Gerona, where Derain and his

André Salmon in Picasso's studio at the "Bateau-Lavoir", in front of the first version of "Three Women" (p. 166). Late spring 1908

"Still Life with Fruit Bowl", Paris, 1909. Etching, 13 x 11 cm. Bloch 18; Geiser 22 IIIb

Picasso wearing Braque's French army uniform, photographed by Braque, 1909

688 A Chronology

Horta de Ebro, where Picasso spent summer 1909, the most productive period in his career (pp. 164–165 and 180–181)

Cadaqués, where Picasso and Fernande spent July 1910 and met André Derain

The "Cubists' House" at Céret, where Picasso spent part of summer 1911 (with Fernande), 1912 (with Eva) and 1913

wife are also holidaying. There he paints "The Guitar Player" (p. 192). Etches illustrations to Max Jacob's novel "Saint Matorel", published by Kahnweiler in 1911. Throughout his life, graphic book decorations in etching, copper engraving, lithograph, linocut and other techniques remain a major artistic interest. Does his first Cubist sculpture: "Head of a Woman". His pictures are exhibited in April in Budapest, in May in Paris, in the autumn (together with work by Braque) in Düsseldorf, Munich and, from November, in London.

1911 July: to Céret, in the French eastern Pyrenees, where he stays in his friend Manolo Hugué's house, working. In August Braque, Fernande and Max Jacob join him. In Cubist compositions like "Still Life with Bottle of Rum" (p. 193) he adopts Braque's use of typographical lettering. Braque compares their working relationship with climbers roped up. Picasso has to restore to the Louvre two Iberian sculptures which he has bought in good faith from a thief. Apollinaire, who acts as intermediary, falls under suspicion. Picasso's relations with Fernande cool. Through Gertrude Stein and her brother Leo he meets Eva Gouel (Marcelle Humbert) and falls in love, calling her "Ma Jolie". He exhibits at group shows in January at Galerie Paul Cassirer in Berlin, in May at the Berlin Secession and in Düsseldorf, and in October at the Stedelijk Museum in Amsterdam. In March 83 watercolours and drawings dating from 1905 to 1910 are exhibited in New York, his first US show.

Picasso in his studio at 11, Boulevard de Clichy. On the wall above his head the drawing "Female Nude" (p. 193). Winter 1910/1911

A Chronology **689**

Picasso in the studio at Sorgues. Behind him "The Aficionado" (p. 201). Summer or autumn 1912

The studio at 242, Boulevard Raspail. On the wall a guitar being played by a newspaper guitarist. Spies 28 (but now lost). Paris, early 1913

Picasso in Montparnasse. About 1912

1912 At the beginning of the year he paints a large number of still lifes. Explores the use of new materials to make his first spatial construction, a "Guitar" (pp. 218 ff.). In his first collage, "Still Life with Chair Caning" (p. 207), he uses printed oilcloth to represent the cane. Uses other trompe-l'œil effects in paintings too. "Du Cubisme", a book by the painters Albert Gleizes (1881–1953) and Jean Metzinger (1883–1956), is published. Eva Gouel becomes Picasso's lover. With her he travels to Céret in May and in June on to Avignon, and rents "Les Clochettes", a villa in nearby Sorgues, where they are joined by Braque and his wife. There he paints "The Poet" (p. 200) and "The Aficionado" (p. 201). Braque does the first "papier collé", a technique which Picasso adopts in the autumn. He does montages of newspaper, labels, advertising texts, stuck on paper and overdrawn in charcoal, such as "Bottle on a Table" (p. 205). Returns to Paris with Eva. Moves from Montmartre to 242, Boulevard Raspail in Montparnasse. In December he signs a three-year exclusive contract with Kahnweiler. Major solo and group exhibitions in Moscow, with the "Blauer Reiter" in Munich, at the Berlin Secession, in Leipzig, London, the Cologne "Sonderbund", Amsterdam, and at the third unjuried show in Berlin.

1913 Paints a Cubist portrait of Apollinaire at the start of the year, for his poetry collection "Alcools". Apollinaire's book "Les peintres cubistes" appears in Paris. Picasso spends spring and summer at Céret with Eva, at times joined by Braque, Max Jacob or Spanish painter Juan Gris (1887–1927). Paints "Geometric Composition: The Guitar" (p. 220). May:

Marcelle Humbert, whom Picasso called Eva, in a kimono. Eva died in December 1915. Paris, about 1911/1912

Les Clochettes, the house in Sorgues where Picasso lived with Eva in 1912

travels to Barcelona for his father's funeral. His mother moves in with his sister Lola Gómez. The papiers collés lead on to synthetic Cubism and works such as "Guitar" (p. 220). August: return to Paris. Moves to 5, Rue Schoelcher. After preliminary sketches he paints "Woman in a Chemise Sitting in an Armchair" (p. 227). Painter Fernand Léger (1881–1955) publishes an important article on Cubism in the Berlin magazine "Der Sturm". An autumn exhibition organized by "Der Sturm" gives considerable space to French painters. Apollinaire reproduces Picasso's work in the magazine "Les Soirées de Paris". Russian artist Vladimir Tatlin (1885–1953) visits Paris for several months to study Picasso's constructions in his studio, and is inspired to Cubist "engineering art" of his own. February: large retrospective at Galerie Thannhauser in Munich. Exhibits in the International Exhibition of Modern Art in New York, Boston and Chicago and in group shows in Moscow in March/April, in Budapest in April/May, in London in October, and in Cologne, Prague and Berlin in December.

1914 In January Kahnweiler publishes "Le siège de Jérusalem", a book of poems by Max Jacob with graphic illustrations by Picasso. The 1905 "The Acrobats" (p. 129) fetches 11,500 francs at auction. Further papiers collés such as "Pipe, Bottle of Bass, Die" (p. 230). Six variously painted bronze casts are taken from Picasso's sculpture "The Glass of Absinthe" (p. 232). June: travels to Avignon with Eva. The Braques and Derains spend the summer nearby. Paints still lifes and portraits ("Portrait of a Young Girl", p. 239) in bright colours and pointillist technique.

Picasso in the studio of Franck Haviland, one of the first collectors of black art, about 1914/15

Picasso posing as a boxer in the studio at 5, Rue Schoelcher. About 1914/15

2 August: First World War begins. Braque and Derain are called up. Apollinaire volunteers. Kahnweiler's gallery is impounded because he is a German and he moves first to Italy and subsequently to Switzerland. When Picasso returns to Paris in late October he is now a foreigner caught between his French chosen homeland and his German supporters. In the first six months of the year he exhibits at group shows in London, Moscow, Prague, Bremen, Berlin and Munich. Galerie Miethke in Vienna shows 57 Picassos. December: new paintings and drawings by Braque and Picasso are exhibited in New York.

1915 Does realistic pencil portraits of Jacob and Vollard. In February Jacob converts to Catholicism and Picasso acts as sponsor. Eva, whose health had been poor the previous year, falls ill in spring and is taken to hospital in the suburb of Auteuil in November, where Picasso visits her every day despite the distance. He paints "Harlequin" (p. 235) nonetheless, geometrical in form and in bright colours on a black background, and considers it his best treatment of the theme. Makes a wire and sheet metal "Violin" (p. 242). Writer Jean Cocteau (1889–1963) visits, with composer Edgar Varèse (1885–1965), and a long-standing friendship results. Eva dies

on 14 December. Picasso confides his sorrows to Gertrude Stein. Exhibits in group shows from February to June in Rome, in May/June in Philadelphia. In October/November the Lluis Plandiura Collection is shown in Barcelona, including early Picassos.

1916 In Zurich the writers Hugo Ball (1886–1927), Hans Arp (1887–1966) and

Picasso's studio at 5, Rue Schoelcher. On the chair is "The Barefoot Girl" (1895; p. 35). 1914

"Self-portrait", 1915. Ink on paper, 15 x 11 cm. Zervos XXIX, 163

A Chronology **691**

In the Rue Schoelcher studio. Behind him "Man Leaning on a Table" (p. 247). About 1915/16

Picasso in 1915

"Portrait of Ambroise Vollard" – Picasso's dealer. Paris, August 1915. Pencil on paper, 46.7 x 32.1 cm. Zervos II**, 922. New York, The Metropolitan Museum of Art

Advertising photograph for the Ballets Russes. In the centre Olga Koklova, later Picasso's first wife (cf. p. 258). About 1916/17

692 A Chronology

Portrait sculpture of Picasso by his friend Pablo Gargallo, 1917. Terracotta, 21 x 23 cm. Musée de Céret

Picasso in 1917

Picasso in 1916

Tristan Tzara (1896–1963) start the Dada movement at the Cabaret Voltaire. Picasso does five illustrations for a foreword by Ball. May: Cocteau brings Russian impresario Sergei Diaghilev (1872–1929) with him to Picasso's home. Diaghilev had brought his Ballets Russes with him to Paris in 1909. He is planning a ballet titled "Parade", using a libretto by Cocteau, choreography by Léonide Massine (1896–1979) and music by Erik Satie (1866–1925). Picasso's agreement to design the production initiates a long, fruitful collaboration. Does "Man Leaning on a Table" (p. 247), a mixture of collage and painting. In July the 1907 "Les Demoiselles d'Avignon" (p. 159) is publicly exhibited in Paris for the first time. Moves to Montrouge, a southern suburb of Paris, to 22, Rue Victor Hugo. Helps arrange a banquet on 31 December in honour of Apollinaire, who has published the novel "Le poète assassiné". Picasso does a number of drawings of him, and paints a portrait of Cocteau, who has work by Picasso, Matisse and Amedeo Modigliani (1884–1920) exhibited in the Salle Huyghens in Paris.

1917 February: to Rome with Cocteau to join Diaghilev's troupe, with which he continues to work until 1924. Designs costumes and set for the ballet "Parade" (pp. 252–255). Meets the Russian composer Igor Stravinsky (1882–1971). Visits Pompeii, Naples and Florence. Falls in love with prima ballerina Olga Koklova. 18 May: "Parade" is premièred at the Théâtre du Châtelet in Paris. In the programme, Apollinaire uses the term "surrealism" for the first time. On account of Olga he accompanies the troupe to performances in Madrid and Barcelona, where painter friends welcome his temporary return

home. Olga becomes Picasso's lover, leaves the Ballets Russes, and returns to Montrouge with him. He paints realistic portraits of her from photographs: "Portrait of Olga in an Armchair" (p. 244). Does further pointillist work: "Woman in Spanish Costume" (p. 248) and "The Peasants' Repast" (p. 249) after Louis Le Nain. In Paris, Jacob's poetry collection "Le cornet à dés" is published, 14 copies including an engraving by Picasso.

1918 Picasso's association with the Ballets Russes gains him an entrée into high society, and his own life style undergoes a permanent change. In the spring he and Olga move into the Hotel Lutétia. Friendship with Eugenia Errazuriz, a wealthy Chilean. Paints harlequins in classical and synthetic Cubist style (pp. 256 f.). In May he and Vollard are the witnesses when Apollinaire marries Jacqueline Kolb. After a performance of Bronislava Nijinska's (1891–1972) ballet "Le Renard", with music by Stravinsky, he meets the writers Marcel Proust (1871–1922) and James Joyce (1882–1941). On 12 July he marries Olga in the Russian church in Paris, with Cocteau, Jacob and Apollinaire as his witnesses. Spends the honeymoon and summer at Eugenia Errazuriz's villa at Biarritz. Paints and draws beach scenes ("The Bathers", p. 262). In Kahnweiler's absence, Paul Rosenberg becomes his dealer. November: Apollinaire dies of 'flu following a wound. The Picassos move into a flat occupying two comfortable floors in the Rue La Boétie. Joint exhibition with Matisse in January at the Galerie Paul Guillaume in Paris. Jacob's novel "Le phanérogame" is published with an etching by Picasso.

Picasso with Max Jacob outside the Café de la Rotonde. About 1915

Olga Koklova, Picasso and Jean Cocteau during a tour of "Parade" in Rome, 1917

Picasso with stage painters, sitting on the curtain for "Parade" (cf. pp. 254–255). Rome, 1917

A Chronology **693**

Picasso's 1917 studio at 22, Rue Victor Hugo, Montrouge

Picasso in Pompeii, 1917

The Picasso room in the Moscow home of the Russian collector Sergei Shchukin. The paintings are almost all illustrated in Chapters 4 and 5. Pre-1917

1919 At the start of the year he paints "Girl with a Hoop" (p. 272) and "Guitar, Bottle, Fruit Dish and Glass on a Table" (p. 273). In spring the Spanish painter and graphic artist Joan Miró (1893–1983) visits, and Picasso helps by buying a painting. May to July: with the Ballets Russes in London. Designs the costumes, set and curtain (which he paints himself) for "Le Tricorne", with music by the Spanish composer Manuel de Falla (1876–1946) and choreography by Massine. 22 July: première at the Alhambra Theatre (pp. 266 ff.). Draws dancers (p. 258), among them his wife Olga. From August he and Olga are at Saint-Raphaël on the Côte d'Azur. Paints "Sleeping Peasants" (p. 259) and Cubist still lifes in watercolour. Rosenberg exhibits the latter with drawings at his Paris gallery in October. May/June: exhibits in a group show in Barcelona. November: does the cover for "Feu de joie", a book of poems by the French writer Louis Aragon (1897–1982). December: Diaghilev invites him to design the ballet "Pulcinella". First lithographs using Saint-Raphaël subjects. In Paris, Jacob's "Le Défense de Tartuffe", a book of verse and prose, is published. 25 copies again include an engraving by Picasso.

1920 Designs the costumes (inspired by Commedia dell'arte) and set for the ballet "Pulcinella", with a libretto and choreography by Massine (portrait p. 268) and music by Stravinsky after Giovanni Battista Pergolesi (1710–1736). 15 May: première at the Paris opera house. Draws portraits of composers Stravinsky (p. 268), Satie and de Falla (p. 696). In June he and Olga travel to Saint-Raphaël and on to Juan-les-Pins on the Côte d'Azur. There he

Renoir. Photograph dating from 1912 which served Picasso for his 1919 drawing (p. 268)

Picasso and Olga in the studio of the stage painter who did the curtain for "Le Tricorne" (pp. 267). London, 1919

paints colourful gouaches using Commedia dell'arte motifs, landscapes, and neoclassical works. Returns to Paris in late September. Kahnweiler, having returned to Paris early in the year, has opened a new gallery under the name of his partner, André Simon. His study of Cubism has meanwhile been published in Munich. Picasso does new lithographs of French writers Raymond Radiguet (1903–1923) and Paul Valéry (1871–1945). One of the latter is used for the title page of Valéry's book "La jeune Parque". In October/November he exhibits in shows in Barcelona and Rome and at Rosenberg's in Paris.

1921 Birth of his son Paolo (Paul) on 4 February. Picasso is prompted to two self-portraits and a return to the subject of "Mother and Child" (pp. 274 f.). April: the first monograph on Picasso's work, by Maurice Raynal, is published in Munich, and in Paris a year later. Designs the ballet "Cuadro flamenco", with music arranged by Manuel de Falla, which is performed only once in Paris in May. In May, June and November the collections of Uhde and Kahnweiler, containing numerous Picassos

"The Window in St. Raphaël". Invitation to an exhibition at Galerie Rosenberg. Paris, 1919. Lithograph, 13.2 x 8.4 cm. Bloch 35; Geiser 221; Mourlot I; Rau I

In July 1917 Picasso celebrated his return to Barcelona with painter friends in Layetana's Gallery. At his feet: Angel F. de Soto. Seated: Maeztu and F. Iturrino. Standing, from left: Padilla, Feliu Elies, Román Jori, Xavier Nogués, Soglio, M. Humbert, L. Plandiura, A. Riera, G. Anyés, J. Colomer, Ricardo Canals. Top: Miguel Utrillo, S. Segura and Aragay

Left:
Léonide Massine as the miller in "Le Tricorne",
with Vera Nemchinova, 1919

Léonide Massine as the Chinese
conjuror in "Parade", 1917

"Picasso's living room in the Rue La Boétie" (from left: Jean Cocteau, Olga, Erik Satie and Clive Bell). Paris, 21 November 1919. Pencil on paper, 49 x 61 cm. Zervos III, 427; MPP 869. Paris, Musée Picasso

A Chronology 695

"Portrait of Manuel de Falla", Paris, 9 June 1920. Pencil and charcoal on paper, 63 x 48 cm. Zervos IV, 62; MPP 915. Paris, Musée Picasso

"Olga", Juan-les-Pins, 26 July 1926. Charcoal on canvas, 130 x 97 cm. Zervos V, 99

"Portrait of Erik Satie", Paris, 19 May 1920. Pencil and charcoal on paper, 62.3 x 47.7 cm. Zervos IV, 59; MPP 910. Paris, Musée Picasso

Picasso, about 1920–1922

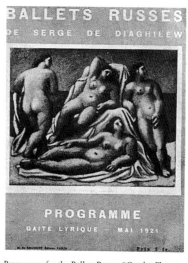

Programme for the Ballets Russes "Cuadro Flamenco" with a reproduction of a painting by Picasso. London, May 1921

Olga Picasso with Paul, 1923. Photo by Man Ray

and confiscated by the French government during the war, are auctioned off. Spends the summer with Olga and Paul at a villa in Fontainebleau, working hard on large-scale compositions in various styles such as "Three Musicians" (pp. 282–283) and "Three Women at the Spring" (p. 279). September: returns to Paris. Solo exhibitions in January at the Leicester Gallery in London and in the autumn at Rosenberg's in Paris.

1922 A collector named Doucet buys "Les Demoiselles d'Avignon" (p. 159) for

25,000 francs. Picasso spends the summer with Olga and Paul at Dinard on the coast of Brittany. Paints them as mother and child. "Women Running on the Beach" (p. 292) is later used as a design for the curtain of the ballet "Le Train Bleu" in 1924. In September they return to Paris because Olga is ill. Designs set and masks for Cocteau's adaptation of Sophocles' "Antigone" in the Théâtre de l'Atelier in Paris in December. Paints "Still Life with Guitar" (p. 284) in the style of the papiers collés. Three etchings, including a portrait of the author, for the poetry collection "Cravates de chanvre" by Pierre Reverdy

(1889–1960). Solo exhibition at Galerie Thannhauser in Munich in the autumn. In November exhibits in "Les inconnus", a show mounted by Kahnweiler at his new Galerie Simon in Paris.

1923 Paints alternately in Cubist and neoclassical style as in the portraits of painter Jacinto Salvado as a harlequin (pp. 296–297). In May the New York magazine "The Arts" publishes an English translation of the first major interview with Picasso, conducted in Spanish by Marius de Zayas. A French version follows only in

"View of Dinard", Dinard, 1922. Ink on paper, 41 x 29 cm. Zervos IV, 375. Picasso, Olga and Paul spent summer 1922 there

Picasso with his son Paul in Dinard, 1922

A beach party at La Garoupe. At left, Olga holding the hand of Comte Etienne de Beaumont. Picasso is seated in the centre, wearing a hat and looking rather bored. Antibes, 1923

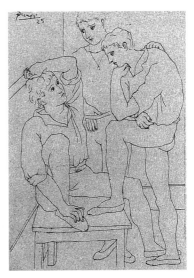

"Three Ballet Dancers", Monte Carlo, 1925. Ink on paper, 35 x 25 cm. Zervos V, 429

1925. In July, at a Dada event in Paris, Picasso as Cubist is declared dead; Breton defends him. Spends the summer with Olga and Paul at Cap d'Antibes near Nice. His mother visits, and he paints her portrait. Paints "The Pipes of Pan" (p. 299) and draws studies of bathers (p. 293). Meets American artist Gerald Murphy (1888–1964) and his wife. Etches a portrait of surrealist writer André Breton (1896–1966) for the title page of his new book "Clair de terre". Returns to Paris in September. Paints his son Paul on a donkey and drawing (pp. 286–287) and his wife Olga (p. 295). Solo shows at Thannhauser's in Munich and Rosenberg's in New York. Exhibits in group shows at Simon's in Paris and the Arts Club in Chicago.

1924 Makes a "Guitar" construction using painted tin and wire. Begins a series of large, ornate still lifes such as "Still Life with Mandolin" and "Mandolin and Guitar" (p. 300). Solo exhibition at Rosenberg's in Paris. Designs for the set and costumes of the ballet "Mercure" by Count Etienne de Beaumont, with music by Erik Satie, which is given a charity performance at the Théâtre de la Cigale, Paris, on 18 June, by Léonide Massine's ballet troupe. The audience and critics are not convinced, but Picasso is defended by a large number of surrealists on 20 June in a "Hommage à Picasso" in "Les Soirées de Paris". Uses the 1922 "Women Running on the Beach" (p. 292) for a curtain design for another ballet, "Le Train Bleu", by Cocteau, with music by Darius Milhaud (1892–1974), set by sculptor Henri Lau-

rens (1885–1954), costumes by fashion designer Coco Chanel (1883–1971) and choreography by Bronislava Nijinska. It is premièred by the Ballets Russes at the Paris Théâtre des Champs-Elysées on 20 June. Summering with Olga and Paul at Juan-les-Pins he does a number of ink drawings, and the portrait "Paul as Harlequin" (p. 303). October: the "Manifeste du surréalisme" by André Breton appears. In December in Paris writers Pierre Naville and Benjamin Péret (1899–1959) publish the first number of a new magazine, "La Révolution surréaliste", with a reproduction of the "Guitar" construction. Pierre Reverdy publishes a monograph on Picasso.

1925 Spring in Monte Carlo with Olga and Paul during the Ballets Russes season. He does realistic sketches of the dancers. In June he completes his painting "The Dance" (p. 306). In it the first signs of tension between him and Olga are apparent. With Olga and Paul he spends the summer at Juan-les-Pins again. Paints "Studio with Plaster Head" (p. 315) using props from Paul's puppet theatre, "Woman with Sculpture" (p. 307), and "The Kiss" (p. 309). November: exhibits at the first surrealist group show at Galerie Pierre in Paris, with Hans Arp, the Italian Giorgio de Chirico (1888–1978), the German Max Ernst (1891–1976), the Swiss Paul Klee (1879–1940), the Frenchman André Masson (1896–1987), the Spaniard Joan Miró, the American Man Ray (1890–1976) and the Frenchman Pierre Roy (1880–1950). During the year, "La Révolution surréaliste" publishes ink drawings done in Juan-les-Pins the previous summer, the 1907 "Les Demoiselles d'Avignon" and the recently completed "The Dance", as well as an article by Breton on Surrealism and painting which discusses Picasso. Picasso contributes a lithograph portrait of the author to Raymond Radiguet's "Les joues en feu".

1926 In Paris, Christian Zervos starts the magazine "Cahiers d'Art". Working with Picasso over many years, Zervos creates his life's work, a 34-volume catalogue of Picasso's work. Picasso paints "The Milliner's Workshop" (p. 313) in curvilinear grisaille, and "The Artist and His Model" (p. 312). In the spring he constructs a number of guitars as assemblages or montages

Marie-Thérèse Walter as she was when Picasso met her aged 17. About 1927

Picasso and Olga in Cannes. Summer 1927

With Olga and Paul at Saint-Raphaël. Summer 1927

using objets trouvés such as shirtcloth, floorcloth, nails and string, in a style that leads on from Cubism to Surrealism. One such "Guitar" (p. 323) is reproduced in "La Révolution surréaliste". June/July: Galerie Rosenberg exhibits twenty years of Picassos. Waldemar George's "Picasso dessins", reproducing 64 drawings, appears in a special edition including a 1925 lithograph "Tête de femme". Summer at Juan-les-Pins and Cap d'Antibes. Paints a large still life, "Musical Instruments on a Table" (p. 310). In a volume of collected writings entitled "Rappel à l'ordre", Cocteau publishes an article on Picasso. In October Picasso travels to Barcelona, where "La Publicidad" runs an interview with him. One ill-considered comment leads to a quarrel with Cocteau. In Paris, Zervos publishes "Picasso. Œuvres 1920–1926" with an additional engraving by the artist.

1927 Picasso tells 17-year-old Marie-Thérèse Walter, a total stranger: "My name is Picasso – I should like to paint you." Soon she is his lover, at first secretly. On 11 May Picasso's fellow-countryman, Bateau-Lavoir neighbour and friend, the painter Juan Gris, born in Madrid in 1887, dies in Paris. Spends the summer in Cannes with Olga and Paul. Produces a portfolio of India ink drawings of large bathing women, and other work of an emphatically sexual nature, the "Metamorphoses" (p. 326). Returns to Paris in the autumn and paints the two-headed "Seated Woman" (p. 308). In the winter he returns to studio subjects with "The Studio" (p. 317) and etchings. These latter, ink drawings done in 1924, and woodcuts

done in 1926, serve as illustrations for a new edition of Honoré de Balzac's (1799–1850) "Le chef-d'œuvre inconnu", commissioned by Vollard (p. 324). Solo exhibitions at Rosenberg's in Paris, Alfred Flechtheim's in Berlin and the Galerie Pierre in Paris. Exhibits in group shows in Barcelona and New York.

1928 The large collage "Minotaurus" takes up a theme that will continue to occupy him over the next few years, as does "The Artist and His Model" (p. 317). For the first time since 1914 he returns to sculpture, with "Bather. Metamorphosis I" (p. 326). Two versions of it are reproduced in the "Cahiers d'Art" together with other sculptures and constructions. Picasso resumes contact with Spanish sculptor Julio Gonzalez (1876–1942) and visits him at his Paris studio to learn his techniques of metal construction, even working occasionally in his studio. He does metal work, such as the maquette for an Apollinaire memorial (pp. 324 f.), which is rejected by the memorial committee. Spends the summer holidays with Olga and Paul at Dinard in Brittany, and secretly meets Marie-Thérèse Walter. Produces a series of small-format, colourful works (commonly referred to as his Dinard Period) showing bodily parts, limbs or organs combined in various ways, as in the bathers series (pp. 320–321, 330). Uhde writes on "Picasso et la tradition française" and Tériade describes a visit to Picasso in "L'Intransigeant". André Level's book on Picasso uses the lithograph "Face" (p. 380), probably a portrait of Marie-Thérèse Walter.

1929 Works with Gonzalez in the latter's studio on sculptures and wire constructions, among them the large "Woman in a Garden" (p. 322). Paints a series of aggressive pictures such as "Bust of a Woman with Self-portrait" (p. 335) and "Great Nude in a Red Armchair" (p. 329) which express the crisis phase his marriage to Olga has now entered. In spring the Spanish painter Salvador Dalí (1904–1989) visits him for the first time. Last family summer at Dinard. Zervos publishes an article on Picasso's designs for an Apollinaire memorial in the "Cahiers

d'Art" and reproduces the designs. Apollinaire's "Contemporains pittoresques" includes an etching by Picasso. November: the Museum of Modern Art is opened in New York.

1930 Continues working on metal sculptures in Gonzalez's studio. Paints a "Seated Bather" (p. 357) in Surrealist manner. In February he completes "The Crucifixion" (p. 337), which Pierre Daix describes as "a translation of fantastic Expressionism into the realm of historical painting". April: a Picasso special issue of the magazine "Documents" is published, with numerous essays and illustrations. June: buys Château Boisgeloup in Departement Eure, some fifty miles northwest of Paris. During the summer in Juan-les-Pins he does a number of reliefs using sand. Commissioned by the young Swiss publisher Albert Skira he does the illustrations for a new edition of Ovid's "Metamorphoses". Several of the 30 etchings show a face resembling Marie-Thérèse Walter's. After the return to Paris in the autumn he rents a flat for her at 44, Rue La Boétie, while he continues to live at number 23 with his family. The Spanish critic Eugenio d'Ors publishes a monograph on Picasso with a lithograph. Picasso's Blue Period gouache "The Blind Man" is bought by the Toledo museum for 110,000 francs. In the USA there are a number of important exhibitions. In January the New York Museum of Modern Art's first special exhibition, "Painting in Paris", includes 14 Picassos, and the Reinhardt Gallery in New York puts on a Derain and Picasso joint show. In March the Arts Club of Chicago includes 15 paintings in a show. In Oc-

Picasso in his studio, with the 1928 "Bather" (p. 321) on the floor. About 1928

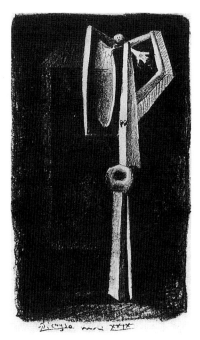

"Figure", May 1929. Lithograph, 23.7 x 13.8 cm. Bloch 96; Geiser 246; Mourlot XXVI; Rau 29

Sculptures by Picasso in his Boisgeloup studio, 1933. Photo: Gallatin

The 17th-century Château Boisgeloup near Gisors (Eure), which Picasso bought in 1930

Gertrude Stein, Picasso, Paul, a couple (the Kahnweilers?) and Alice B. Toklas. About 1933

tober the John Becker Gallery in New York exhibits gouaches and drawings. In November Picasso's work is again seen at the Reinhardt Gallery in New York. For a March group show of collages at the Galerie Goëmans in Paris, which includes work by Picasso, Aragon writes a catalogue preface under the title "La peinture au défi". In October Picasso is awarded the prize of the Carnegie Foundation in Pittsburgh for the 1918 "Portrait of Olga in Profile".

1931 Paints still lifes such as "Large Still Life on a Pedestal Table" (p. 341), which alludes to the body of Marie-Thérèse, and "Pitcher and Bowl of Fruit" (p. 340). In May he starts establishing a large sculpture studio at Boisgeloup, and increasingly devotes his time to solid sculpture. He does heads and busts (p. 338) and at the same time drawings and graphics (p. 339) on the same themes. His relationship with Marie-Thérèse prompts this work and also a series of etchings done at Juan-les-Pins in the summer. In December he paints "The Sculptor" (p. 304) contemplating a bust of Marie-Thérèse, and in "The Red Armchair" (p. 348) she appears with two

faces. His exhibitions include "Picasso's Abstractions" in New York in January, "Thirty Years of Pablo Picasso" in London in April, and a show at Rosenberg's in Paris in June. The new edition of Ovid's "Metamorphoses" with 30 etchings is published by Skira in Lausanne. In Paris, Vollard publishes the new edition of Balzac's "Le Chef-d'œuvre inconnu", using 13 Picasso etchings and 67 woodcuts, exactly 100 years after the first edition was published in 1831.

1932 At the start of the year he paints a series of seated or reclining blonde women, generally asleep, using Marie-Thérèse as model (pp. 344, 345, 349–355). While Olga and Paul are at Juan-les-Pins, he spends the summer working at Boisgeloup on new sculptures, busts and female figures with the ample proportions of his new model, Marie-Thérèse. He is visited there by Braque, Gonzalez, Kahnweiler, Zervos, and writers Michel Leiris (1901–1990) and Paul Raynal (1885–1971). Returns to the subject of the crucifixion and adapts Mathias Grünewald's Isenheim altar crucifixion (p. 337). January: the Harvard Society for Contemporary Art in Cambridge (MA) exhibits his etchings for Ovid's "Metamorphoses". Picasso himself selects 236 works dating from 1901 on for the large-scale June/July retrospective at the Galerie Georges Petit in Paris, which is marked by a special issue

of "Cahiers d'Art" and an interview with Tériade in "L'Intransigeant". The show is met with misgivings and even rejection amongst the critics, as is an expanded exhibition seen in September/October at the Kunsthaus in Zurich. In October, Zervos publishes the first volume of his catalogue, which lists Picasso's work from 1895 to 1906. The Catalonian provincial government buys part of the Lluis Plandiura collection, including some twenty early Picasso paintings, for the Museu Picasso in Barcelona.

1933 In the first half of the year, in Paris, he does a great many graphic works, mainly etchings, mostly on the subject of the sculptor's studio and frequently including Marie-Thérèse. He also deals with the Minotaur subject (a monstrous creature with a human body and bull's head). This work constitutes a significant part of the 100-plate "Suite Vollard" (1930–1937), named for the publisher. On 1 June the first issue of the magazine "Minotaure", edited by Tériade and published by Skira, appears, with a cover collage by Picasso (p. 377). The issue includes an article on Picasso by Breton, with illustrations including the 1932 drawings after Grünewald's

A Chronology **699**

"Reclining Sculptor with Model in His Arms and Sculpted Head", Paris, 2 April 1933. Etching, 19.3 x 26.7 cm. Bloch 171; Geiser 324

Illustration for the "Lysistrata" of Aristophanes, 17 January 1934. Etching, 21.1 x 13.9 cm. Bloch 272; Geiser 392 II B

"Sculptor and Model with Fighting Bull", 31 March 1933. Etching, 19.4 x 26.7 cm. Bloch 166; Geiser 319

1934 Further etchings on the subject of the sculptor's studio, featuring Rembrandt in some (p. 22). At Boisgeloup he does sculptures like "Woman with Leaves" (p. 360). In August/September he pays a long visit to Spain with Olga and Paul, taking in Irún, San Sebastián, Burgos, Madrid, El Escorial (with its important collection of Spanish masters), Toledo, Saragossa and Barcelona. In the museum of Catalan art in Barcelona he looks at Romanesque ecclesiastical art. In mid-September he returns to Paris and produces a wealth of paintings, drawings and etchings of bullfight scenes (pp. 362 ff.). Does four etchings of "Blind Minotaur Led Through the Night by a Girl" (p. 702). January: group exhibition with Braque, Gris and Léger at the Arts Club of Chicago. February: solo show of 79 works at the Wadsworth Atheneum (Hartford, CN). He also exhibits at the Museo de Arte Moderno in Buenos Aires. A new translation of the "Lysistrata" of Aristophanes, published in New York, is illustrated with six etchings and 34 lithographs by Picasso (see above). He contributes an etching, "Murder", to Benjamin Péret's poetry collection "De Derrière les fagots", published in Paris (see right), and another etching to Georges Hugnet's "Petite Anthologie poétique du Surréalisme".

Right:
Picasso in his studio at 23, Rue de La Boétie. Behind him "Portrait of Yadwigha" (1885) by Henri "Le Douanier" Rousseau, which Picasso bought in Montmartre in 1908 for 5 francs and remained very attached to throughout his life.
Photo by Brassaï, 1932

crucifixion. Summer in Cannes with Olga and Paul. Buys a car and drives to Barcelona with his family to visit relations and old friends. In the museum he sees his own pictures from the dissolved Plandiura collection. September: returns to Paris amd paints bullfight scenes such as "Death of the Toreador" (p. 364). That autumn his former lover Fernande Olivier's memoirs of the years 1904 to 1913 appear as "Pi-

casso et ses amis". Wary of Olga's jealousy, Picasso tries unsuccessfully to ban the sale of the book. Tristan Tzara's collection of essays "L'Antitête" is published, with Picasso's etching "Three Graces on the Beach". The first volume of Bernhard Geiser's catalogue "Picasso. Peintre-Graveur", listing engravings and lithographs done from 1899 to 1931, is published in Berne. The second volume follows in 1968.

"Head of a Woman", about 1933/34. Monotype, 26.8 x 19.3 cm

"Blind Minotaur Led Through the Night by a Girl", Paris, November 1934. Aquatint and etching, 24.7 x 34.7 cm. Bloch 225; Geiser 437 IV c

1935 In February paints "Interior with a Girl Drawing" (p. 374) and then for almost a year no further painting. In the spring he does his most important cycle of etchings, the "Minotauromachy" (p. 376), combining Minotaur and bullfight motifs. Begins to write and illustrate Surrealist poetry; some are printed with an introduction by Breton in a special issue of the "Cahiers d'Art". When Marie-Thérèse becomes pregnant, Olga leaves Picasso in June and moves with Paul to the Hôtel Californie in Rue Berri, while Marie-Thérèse lives with her mother, Mémé. Divorce proceedings are started but deferred for financial reasons. Picasso calls this period "the worst in my life" and in July he requests Jaime Sabartés, his friend since 1899, to join him from South America. On 5 October Picasso's second child is born, to Marie-Thérèse Walter. This daughter is named María de la Concepción (after Picasso's second sister, who only lived to be four years old) and known as Maya. In November Sabartés and his wife return from South America to Paris. They move into the Rue La Boétie and Sabartés becomes Picasso's secretary, devoting the rest of his life to him. In February/March Picasso papiers collés are exhibited at the Galerie Pierre in Paris. In March/April he exhibits in a group show, "Les Créateurs du Cubisme", at the Galerie des Beaux-Arts in Paris.

1936 As the year begins he becomes friends with the Surrealist poet Paul Eluard (1895–1952), with whom he has been acquainted for some time. Through him he meets a young Yugoslavian photographer, Dora Maar. With Marie-Thérèse

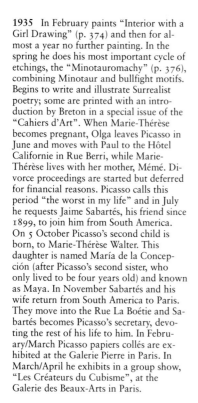

"Murder" (inspired by David's "Death of Marat"), Boisgeloup, 7 July 1934. Pencil on paper, 39.4 x 50.4 cm. Zervos VII, 216; MPP 1135. Paris, Musée Picasso

and Maya he goes to Juan-les-Pins, where he paints Marie-Thérèse repeatedly that April (p. 372). He does further drawings, watercolours and gouaches on the Minotaur theme (pp. 378 f.), continuing with these after their return to Paris in May. Commissioned by Vollard, he does a large number of etchings together with Lacou-

rière, in the latter's studio, for Buffon's (1707–1788) "Histoire naturelle". Designs the curtain (pp. 26 and 378) for a production of Romain Rolland's (1866–1944) play "14 Juillet" (1902) on Bastille Day in the Alhambra theatre. After the outbreak of the Spanish Civil War on 18 July he sides against Franco, supporting the Re-

"Man with a Mask, Woman Holding a Child", Juan-les-Pins, 23 April 1936. Ink and India ink wash drawing on paper, 65 x 50 cm. Zervos VIII, 278; MPP 1158. Paris, Musée Picasso

Illustration for "Grand Air" by Paul Eluard, 4 June 1936. Etching, 41.5 x 31.5 cm. Bloch 289

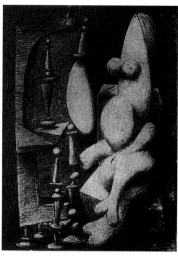

"Female Nude at the Dressing Table", Juan-les-Pins, 12 April 1936. Pencil on paper, 64 x 48 cm. Zervos VIII, 275; MPP 1153. Paris, Musée Picasso

Picasso in 1935

Marie-Thérèse Walter with their daughter Maya. Juan-les-Pins, April 1936

Picasso at Boisgeloup with his St. Bernard, 1935

publicans, who subsequently appoint him director of the Prado in gratitude, in which capacity he uses his authority to help preserve the Spanish heritage of art treasures. In early August he goes to Mougins near Cannes, where he meets the Eluards, Zervos, Man Ray, and the Surrealist poet René Char (1907–1988). He also meets Dora Maar (née Markovic) again, who speaks fluent Spanish, and they become lovers. Near Mougins he discovers the village of Vallauris, which was a potters' colony even in antiquity. He relinquishes Château Boisgeloup, where he had his own sculpture studio, to Olga, and

moves to Tremblay-sur-Mauldre, some 25 miles west of Paris near Montfort-l'Amaury, where Vollard places a studio at his disposal. Marie-Thérèse and Maya live there till 1940. January: major retrospective in Barcelona, subsequently seen in Bilbao and Madrid, at Rosenberg's in Paris in March, at Zwemmer's in London in May/June, and at Valentine's in New York in October/November. Exhibits in "Cubism and Abstract Art" in New York in March and in the International Surrealist Exhibition in London in June. Eluard's collections of poetry "La Barre d'appui" and "Les Yeux fertiles" feature Picasso etch-

ings, the latter also having a portrait of the author drawn by Picasso.

1937 Expresses his opposition to Franco in his two "Dreams and Lies of Franco" etchings (p. 410) and an aggressive poem. In Barrault's storehouse, an old building at 7, Rue des Grands-Augustins, he establishes a new studio. Early in the year he paints a series of portraits of Marie-Thérèse (pp. 406 f.) and "Great Bather with Book" (p. 409). Commissioned by the Republican government of Spain, he paints the immense mural "Guernica" (pp.

Picasso's dealer Ambroise Vollard

"Portrait of Ambroise Vollard" ("Suite Vollard", plate 99), Paris, early March 1937. Aquatint, 34.7 x 24.7 cm. Bloch 232; Baer 618 Bd

In 1937 Picasso rented the top two floors of 7, Rue des Grands-Augustins as a studio and apartment. It was there that he painted "Guernica". He kept the studio on till spring 1967

Above and right:
Picasso at work on "Guernica". Photo: Dora Maar, 1937

Left:
In the Rue des Grands-Augustins studio, 1937

400–401) for the Spanish pavilion at the Paris World Fair. The painting is inspired by a German air raid on the Spanish town on 26 April. In May, after 45 preliminary studies (pp. 389–395), he begins work on the painting in his new studio. Dora Maar records the painting's progress in photographs (pp. 704–705). At the World Fair, opened on 12 July, his sculptures "Head of a Woman" (1932) and "Woman with Vase" (1933) are also exhibited. Zervos devotes a special issue of "Cahiers d'Art" to "Guernica", using Dora Maar's photographs and printing a number of essays and poems. Spends summer at Mougins with Dora and the Eluards, painting Dora (pp. 404–405) and Eluard's wife Nusch. Returns to Paris in September. In October he travels to Switzerland and visits the sick Paul Klee in Bern. Paints "Weeping Woman" (p. 412) and "Woman Crying" (p. 414), echoes of the Guernica material.

"Guernica" in the Spanish pavilion at the Paris World Fair, 1937

April: exhibition of drawings, gouaches and pastels at Valentine's in New York. June: joint show with de Chirico at Zwemmer's in London. November: "20 Years in the Evolution of Picasso 1903–1923" at Seligmann's Gallery in New York. The Museum of Modern Art buys "Les Demoiselles d'Avignon" for $24,000. A further 23 works are seen in New York in "Picasso from 1901 to 1937" at Valentine's. In June he has 32 pictures in "Les Maîtres de l'Art Indépendant" at the Petit Palais in Paris.

1938 In January he paints two portraits of his daughter, "Maya with a Boat" (p. 424) and "Portrait of Maya with Her Doll" (p. 425), and in February "Woman with Cock" (p. 415). The same motif appears in drawings and pastels (p. 418). In spring he does a large collage, "Women at Their Toilette" (pp. 426–427), then draw-

Picasso in his studio with "Guernica". Photo: Dora Maar, 1937

"Woman with Tambourine", Paris, 1938. Etching and aquatint, 66.5 x 51.4 cm. Bloch 310

Picasso mixing paint for work on "Guernica". Photo: Dora Maar, 1937

ings using webs of radiating and concentric lines sometimes reminiscent of wickerwork and presently giving way to a series of pictures of seated women (pp. 417 and 423). Spends summer at Mougins with Dora Maar and the Eluards. Paints portraits of Dora and of Nusch Eluard, and "Man with Ice Cream Cone" and "Man with a Straw Hat Holding an Ice Cream Cone" (p. 416). Returns to Paris in September. Buys the studio at 7, Rue des Grands-Augustins. Spends October with Zervos and his wife in Vézelay, a village in the Departement of Yonne with an old Benedictine monastery and church. In November paints "Still Life with Red Bull's Head" (p. 418). In winter he has a severe bout of sciatica and is confined to bed for weeks. In October, the exhibition of "Guernica" and numerous accompanying studies in London excites considerable interest. The show continues to Leeds and Liverpool. In October/November work by Picasso and Matisse is exhibited at the Museum of Modern Art in Boston. In November an exhibition of 21 paintings of the period 1908–1934 is seen at Valentine's in New York. "L'indicatif présent ou l'infirme tel qu'il est" by Luc Decaunes and "Solidarité" by Paul Eluard are published in Paris, each with a Picasso etching. Gertrude Stein publishes a study of Picasso.

1939 On 13 January Picasso's mother María Picasso y Lopez dies in Barcelona at the age of 84. Two weeks later the city is taken by Franco's forces. On 26 January he paints portraits of Marie-Thérèse Walter (p. 432) and Dora Maar in the same pose. In April he paints "Cat Catching a Bird" and "Cat Eating a Bird" (p. 436). In

July/August he is at Antibes with Dora Maar and subsequently also Sabartés in a flat belonging to Man Ray. On 22 July he is in Paris briefly for the funeral of Ambroise Vollard, killed in an accident. In August he paints "Night Fishing at Antibes"

Picasso with Dora Maar, painter and photographer, at Golfe-Juan, 1937

Picasso with Paul Eluard by the sea, 1938

(p. 430). At the end of August all three return to Paris, and in September, after the outbreak of the Second World War, go on to Royan, where the Gironde meets the Atlantic, and move into the Hôtel du Tigre. Marie-Thérèse and Maya are already living nearby. With some interruptions, Picasso remains there till August 1940. In October he is in Paris for a fortnight, and the French photographer Brassaï (1899–1984) photographs him for an article in "Life" magazine. At Royan he paints Sabartés in the garb of a Spanish grandee with a ruff (p. 433). January: exhibition of still lifes at Rosenberg's in Paris and of drawings at the Arts Club of Chicago. May/June: "Picasso in English Collections" in London. He exhibits in a group show at the Kunsthalle in Bern. The exhibition of "Guernica" with studies, seen the previous year in England, is now shown (from May on) in New York, Los Angeles, Chicago and San Francisco. On 15 November a 344-work retrospective, "Picasso: Forty Years of His Art", opens at the Museum of Modern Art in New York. The exhibition, its contents varying, subsequently travels to a number of American cities. "Pour la Tchécoslovaquie" by Czech writer František Langer (1888–1965), Paul Claudel (1868–1955), Paul Valéry and others is published in Paris with a linocut by Picasso. In the early days of the war, French soldiers billetted at Boisgeloup destroy or damage sculptures by Picasso.

1940 At Royan he sets up a studio with a view of the Atlantic in his villa, "Les Voiliers". In the next few months he moves to and fro between Royan and Paris. He fills entire sketchbooks with studies of a nude

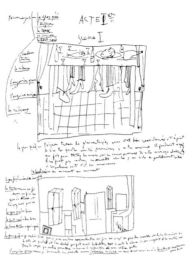

Picasso at the Café de Flore, Paris, 1940

The first page of Picasso's farce "Le Désir attrapé par la queue". January 1941. André Breton commented that "it is like theatre in an ear-ring."

Picasso and Sabartés in the Royan studio in front of "Woman Dressing Her Hair" (p. 439). 1940

dressing her hair (p. 438) and finishes the painting (p. 439) at Royan in June. He also paints still lifes of the fish market and "Café at Royan" (p. 437). In May German troops advance into Belgium and France, occupying Paris and Royan too in June. At the end of August, Picasso returns to Paris with Dora. Marie-Thérèse and Maya follow in the autumn and move to the Boulevard Henri IV. Picasso leaves the flat in Rue La Boétie and moves into his studio at 7, Rue des Grands-Augustins. A member of the Résistance, he declines preferential treatment by the occupying Germans. The story goes that when a German officer was shown a photograph of "Guernica" and asked, "Did you do that?" Picasso replied, "No, you did". In the artist's presence, the Germans draw up an inventory of numerous works he has deposited in the vaults of a Paris bank. Dealers Rosenberg and Kahnweiler leave, for the USA or unoccupied France. In April Yvonne Zervos exhibits Picasso watercolours and gouaches at her Paris Galerie M.A.I. Writer and art critic Jean Cassou (1897–1986) publishes an essay on Picasso. André Breton's "Anthologie de l'humour noir", Iliazd's (i.e. Ilya Zdanevich) "Afat" and Pierre Naville's "Le Miroir de merveilleux" are published in Paris with illustrations by Picasso.

1941 In January he writes a six-act Surrealist play, "Le Désir attrapé par la Queue", a facsimile of which is published two years later before a subsequent edition with three drawings and a title page self-portrait. He turns back to the subject of seated women, painting several works on the subject in the summer (pp. 440 f.) as

well as "Boy with Lobster" (p. 443). At weekends he visits Marie-Thérèse and Maya in the Boulevard Henri IV. He is not allowed to leave Paris to use his sculpture studio at Boisgeloup, so he sets one up in his bathroom in the Rue des Grands-Augustins. There he does a number of small sculptures and a big "Head of a Woman" with Dora Maar as model. A bronze cast is placed in a Paris cemetery in 1959 in honour of Apollinaire. March: solo exhibition at the Bignou Gallery in New York. Georges Hugnet's monograph on Picasso is published in Paris with six engravings.

1942 On 27 March sculptor Julio Gonzalez, his friend of many years and fellow artist, dies. Picasso attends the funeral at Arcueil and is deeply distressed. He paints seven pictures of bulls' skulls, as brightly coloured as church stained glass, and makes a "Head of a Bull" (p. 444) with a bicycle saddle and handlebars. In April he paints "Still Life with Steer's Skull" (p. 445) and on 4 May completes "L'Aubade" (p. 446). In June, in an article in "Comoedia" magazine, painter Maurice de Vlaminck (1876–1958) accuses him of having led French painting astray. Art critic André Lhote (1885–1962) takes Picasso's part, as do many young painters and intellectuals. In July he begins numerous studies for "Man with a Sheep" (p. 454). In August he paints two portraits of Nusch Eluard. Her husband rejoins the Communist party and goes underground. Buffon's "Histoire naturelle" is published in Paris, with Picasso's 31 animal aquatint drawings done in 1936. Georges Hugnet's "Non vouloir" also appears, with five illustrations by Picasso.

1943 In January he gives Dora Maar a copy of the "Histoire naturelle" with many pages additionally overpainted. Does a "Death's Head" in plaster and casts it in bronze (p. 444). Does further drawings of a man with a sheep. Meets the young painter Françoise Gilot, who visits him regularly in his studio, where he is now painting more once again: child paintings such as "First Steps" and "Child with Doves" (p. 449). With Cocteau he attends the funeral of painter Chaim Soutine (1893–1943). Frequents "Le Catalan" restaurant and meets old friends there (cf. p. 462). Towards the end of the year, Françoise Gilot appears in his pictures. Exhibitions at Rosenberg's in New York and at the Fogg Art Museum in Cambridge (MA). Georges Hugnet's "Le Chèvre-feuille" is published in Paris, with an etching and six engravings by Picasso.

1944 Picasso's friends, the Surrealist poet Robert Desnos (1900–1945) and Max Jacob, are transported to concentration camps, where Jacob dies within days and Desnos in 1945. On 19 March at the home of Louise and Michel Leiris a private reading of Picasso's "Le Désir attrapé par la queue" is given under the direction of Albert Camus (1913–1960). Among those taking part are Jean-Paul Sartre (1905–1980) and his partner, the writer Simone de Beauvoir (1908–1986). Picasso overcomes great technical difficulties and completes "Man with Sheep" (p. 455), a sculpture over two metres high modelled in wet clay on an iron frame, immediately moulded in plaster and then later cast in bronze. June: solo exhibition at the Sociedad de Arte Moderno in Mexico. In Au-

Picasso wearing a trench coat in the Rue des Grands-Augustins studio in the hard wartime winter of 1943

"Self-portrait", Royan, 11 August 1940. Pencil on paper, 16 x 11 cm. Zervos XI, 81. Aachen, Ludwig Collection

Françoise Gilot (aged 21) in spring 1943 when Picasso (aged 61) met her

gust, during the Paris rising, he joins Marie-Thérèse in Boulevard Henri IV. After the liberation of Paris on 25 August he returns to the Rue des Grands-Augustins, where he is visited by his friends and many British and Americans. In October he joins the French Communist party, stating that he is not only an artist but also a revolutionary. That October he exhi-

bits at the Salon d'Automne for the first time, this time titled the Salon de la Libération. His show of 74 paintings and five sculptures in a separate room prompts demonstrations and protests against his art and politics. In November he attends a memorial service for dead Résistance fighters at Père Lachaise cemetery in Paris. Two books of poetry, Desnos's "Contrée" and

Eluard's "Au Rendez-vous allemand", are published in Paris, each with a graphic work by Picasso.

1945 Completes "The Charnel House" (pp. 456 f.), which Pierre Daix sees as a continuation of the theme of "Guernica". Zervos makes a photographic record of

"Paper sculptures", Paris, December 1943. Torn paper, varying in height from 12 to 30 cm. Zervos XIII, 197; Spies 256, 257, 259–261

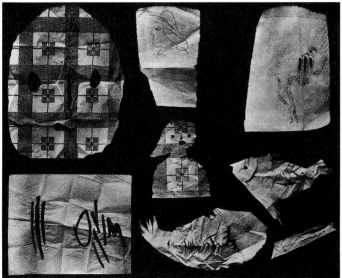

Picasso soon after the liberation in his Paris studio, 1944

Picasso wearing a Catalan cap, about 1944

Picasso in Toulouse, 1945. Inscribed to his friend Jaime Sabartés

the painting's evolution till completion in May. In February and March Picasso paints still lifes such as "Pitcher, Candle and Enamel Saucepan" (p. 469) and "Still Life with Leeks, Fish Head, Skull and Pitcher" (p. 468). In May, writer and politician André Malraux (1901–1976) visits

him and he describes his wartime experiences. Does three realistic portrait drawings of Maurice Thorez (1900–1964), secretary general of the Communist party. At the party congress in June, Roger Garaudy (born 1913) criticizes Picasso's kind of art. Designs the curtain for "Le Rendez-vous",

a ballet by Jacques Prévert (1900–1977) with music by Joseph Kosma (1905–1969) and choreography by Roland Petit (born 1924). 15 June: première at the Théâtre Sarah Bernhardt in Paris. In July he goes to Cap d'Antibes with Dora Maar, which angers Françoise Gilot, who turns down a room he has rented for her at Golfe-Juan and goes to Brittany. Buys a house at Ménerbes, a village in the Vaucluse region of Provence, paying for it with a still life and giving it to Dora Maar as a present. November: Braque introduces him to Fernand Mourlot. At the Mourlot brothers' printing establishment in Paris he acquires fundamental skills in lithographic technique, and is particularly impressed by the possibility of preserving different states in the evolution of a print, as in his lithograph of a bull (p. 460). By 1949 he has done some 200 lithographs, including colour ones, the first being a portrait of Françoise, who has returned to him. February/March: exhibition of drawings and paintings at the Buchholz Gallery in New York. June/July: show at Louis Carré's in Paris. December: joint exhibition of works with Henri Matisse at the Victoria and Albert Museum in London. Three volumes of poetry published in Paris – Eluard's "A Pablo Picasso", Char's "Le Marteau sans maître", and "Jours de Gloire" by Paul Valéry and others – carry graphics by Picasso.

This photograph was taken on 16 June 1944 in Picasso's studio in the Rue des Grands-Augustins. He had invited those who took part in the first reading of "Le Désir attrapé par la queue" (Desire Caught by the Tail) to thank them and to have a group photograph taken by Brassaï. The reading itself had taken place on 19 March at the home of Louise and Michel Leiris, attended by the leading artists and intellectuals of Paris. Some are no longer in this photo, however. With their parts in brackets, they are, standing (from left): Jacques Lacan, Cecile Eluard, Pierre Reverdy, Louise Leiris (The Two Bow Wows), Zanie Aubier (The Tart), Picasso, Valentine Hugo, Simone de Beauvoir (Her Cousin). Seated: Jean-Paul Sartre (Round Piece), Albert Camus, Michel Leiris (Big Foot), Jean Aubier (The Curtain) and Picasso's Afghan hound Kazbek. Not on the photo were: Dora Maar (Thin Anxiety), Germaine Hugnet (Fat Anxiety), Raymond Queneau (The Onion) and Jacques Bost (Silence).

1946 In March he visits Françoise Gilot at printer Louis Fort's in Golfe-Juan, and together they visit Matisse in Nice. In late April he returns to Paris with Françoise, now his lover. In May he paints a number of portraits of her, and in June, with Mourlot, does ten lithographs of her head. In July he goes to Ménerbes with her, to the

Picasso with Eluard (right) walking through Paris after liberation in 1944

Marie-Thérèse Walter with daughter Maya

Picasso with an owl brought from Antibes in his Paris studio, 1947

house he had given Dora Maar, and then on to Cap d'Antibes and Golfe-Juan. Françoise is pregnant. The curator of the Antibes museum offers him the use of rooms in the Palais Grimaldi as a studio. He works there for several months on murals, still lifes with sea creatures, local figures, and "La Joie de vivre" (p. 467). He gives these pictures to the museum, which is renamed Musée Picasso. Revisits the potters' village of Vallauris and meets the Ramiés. During the year he is distressed by the death of Gertrude Stein in Paris on 27 July and of Nusch Eluard in Switzerland on 28 November. At the end

of November Picasso and Françoise return to Paris. In February/March he exhibits "The Charnel House" and "Memorial for the Spanish" in "Art et Résistance" at the Musée National d'Art Moderne in Paris. In June/July the Galerie Louis Carré in Paris shows "Dix-neuf Peintures" of his. Alfred H. Barr's "Picasso: Fifty Years of His Art" (an expanded version of the 1939 exhibition catalogue) is published in New York. In Paris, Sabartés publishes his memoirs as "Picasso: Portraits et souvenirs". The Spanish original version, "Picasso, retratos y recuerdos", is not published in Madrid till 1953.

1947 In the first six months he does over 50 lithographs in Mourlot's workshop, some using new techniques, with owls, fauns, centaurs, bacchantes or doves as subjects. He also returns to the theme of the seated woman, and does variations on "David and Bathsheba" (p. 476) by Lucas Cranach the Elder (1472–1553). In May, at Jean Cassou's prompting, he gives the Musée d'Art Moderne in Paris ten important paintings, the first to be included in a French museum collection apart from one picture in Paris and two in Grenoble. On 15 May his son Claude is born, his first child by Françoise. In June they go to

Picasso's hands, 1947

Picasso with Paul Eluard in the Antibes Picasso Museum with the painting "La joie de vivre" (p. 467), 1947

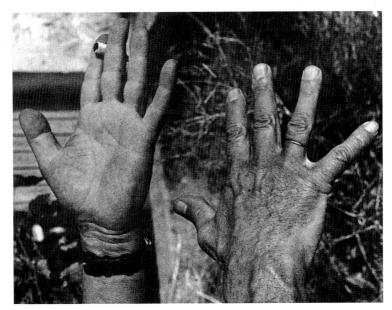

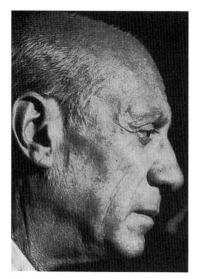

Picasso in 1948

Picasso at the world peace congress in Breslau, August 1948

Picasso in his studio with "The Charnel House" (p. 457) at the rear. Winter 1948

"Seated Woman in an Armchair", Paris, 3 January 1949. Lithograph. Bloch 588; Mourlot 137; Rau 395

Picasso's poster for the Paris peace congress in 1949, with the dove motif (p. 476) that quickly became famous

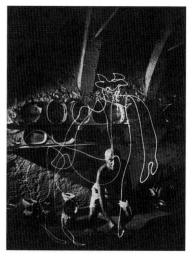

Picasso "drawing" with a torch. Vallauris, 1949. Photo by Gjon Mili

Golfe-Juan near Cannes. In August, in Georges Ramié's "Madoura" workshop at Vallauris, Picasso studies ceramic techniques and is soon having startling new ideas about technique and the form and colour of pots, pitchers, plates, about animal and figural motifs: it is a revival of the ancient pottery tradition of Vallauris. By the following year he has done some 2,000 items of ware. Designs the set for a production of Sophocles' "Oedipus", directed by Pierre Blanchar (1896–1963) at the Théâtre des Champs-Elysées in Paris in De-

cember. First exhibition of Picasso lithographs at Curt Valentin's gallery in New York, which also publishes Juan Larrea's "Guernica: Pablo Picasso" with photographs by Dora Maar. For "Dos contes" by Ramón Reventos he does four copper engravings and subsequently four etchings for the French translation. Does graphic illustrations for a new edition of Gleizes/Metzinger's 1912 study "Du Cubisme", and an etching for a French book of "Cinq Sonnets" by Francesco Petrarch (1304–1374).

1948 In summer he moves to Vallauris and produces a great deal of ceramic ware. He is living with Françoise and Claude at a villa called "La Galloise". In August he attends an international peace congress in Breslau, and visits Warsaw, Cracow and Auschwitz. Draws Russian writer Ilya Ehrenburg (1891–1967), an old friend and the initiator of the congress. The French government awards him a medal and the President of Poland confers a decoration upon him. In October he returns to Paris with Françoise, who is again pregnant. At

The ceramics studio at Vallauris, 1950   Above and right: in the Paris studio, 1950

home he paints two versions of "The Kitchen" (pp. 477–479). February/March: group show with Gris and Braque at the Kunsthalle in Basel and then in Berne. September/October: group show with Gris and Miró at Museum of Modern Art in San Francisco, then Portland (Oregon). Solo shows: "Œuvres de Provence 1945–1948" at Louise Leiris' in Paris in November, lithographs at the Galerias Layetanas in Barcelona in December. In November he has his first major exhibition of 149 ceramics in the Maison de la Pensée Française in Paris. For this show he designs a poster for the first time. Does 125 lithographs for Reverdy's calligraphic poems, "Le Chant des morts", and 41 etchings and aquatints for a manuscript edition of twenty poems by the Spanish poet Luis de Góngora y Argote (1561–1627). Does graphics for "Escrito" by Iliazd and "La fosse commune" by Ivan Goran Kovachich. Belgian producer Paul Haesaerts makes a documentary film, "Visite à Picasso", at Vallauris and the Musée Picasso in Antibes. Skira publishes a portfolio with colour illustrations of Picasso's ceramics, with an introduction by Georges and Suzanne Ramié.

1949 On 8 January he does the lithograph "The Dove" (p. 476), which Aragon chooses in February for the poster of the world peace congress in Paris in April. The image becomes world famous. Picasso names his daughter Paloma, born on 19 April, after the peace dove. His interest in the mother and child motif revives. Returns to Vallauris and buys a former perfumery in Rue du Fornas which he converts into separate painting and sculpture studios plus storage space for ceramics. Collects material for montages and assemblages. Uses a long iron bar and other metal waste for a "Pregnant Woman". From autumn on and in the following year he works harder on sculpture. Solo shows: March/April new work at Buchholz in New York, April at the Gallery of Arts in

Picasso with Françoise Gilot and nephew Javier Vilató on the beach at Golfe-Juan, 1948. Photo by Robert Capa

Toronto, and in July 64 new works at the Maison de la Pensée Française in Paris. A new edition of Prosper Mérimée's (1803–1870) "Carmen" is published with 38 copper engravings and four aquatints by Picasso. Further graphics for two poetry books, "Elégie d'Ihpétonga" by Ivan Goll (1891–1950) and "Poésie de mots inconnus" by Ronke Akinsemoyin and others. Kahnweiler publishes "Les Sculptures de Picasso", with photographs by Brassaï and Dora Maar. Fernand Mourlot publishes the first volume of his catalogue of the lithographic works, "Picasso Lithographe", covering the years 1919 to 1947; three further volumes follow, up to 1964. Christian Zervos publishes "Dessins de Picasso 1892–1948" in Paris.

1950 Picasso is given the freedom of Vallauris. In gratitude he gifts the community a bronze cast of his 1944 "Man with Sheep", which is installed in August. In January he paints his children Claude and Paloma (pp. 480–481) and in February variations on "Women on the Banks of the Seine" (pp. 490–491) after Gustave Courbet (1819–1877) and "Portrait of a Painter" (p. 483) after El Greco. Does assemblages of found objects of various kinds: a goat, a woman with baby carriage, and a girl skipping (pp. 484–486 and 489). Owls are his favourite ceramic motif, and already have been for some years. In October he attends the world peace congress in Sheffield. The poster is a dove in flight, after a Picasso lithograph of

9 July. In November he is awarded the Lenin Peace Prize. Solo exhibitions in July/August at Knokke-Le-Zoute (Belgium) and in November/December (sculptures and drawings) at the Maison de la Pensée Française in Paris. Exhibits at group shows: "Quattro Maestri del Cubismo" at the Venice Biennale and "From Fantin to Picasso" in Rotterdam. He contributes 32 illustrations to "Corps perdu" by the Afro-Caribbean writer Aimé Césaire (born 1913), nine lithographs to Tristan Tzara's "De Mémoire d'homme", and one graphic each to Robert Godet's "L'âge de soleil" and "Une Visite à Vallauris" by René Batigne and Georges Salles. The second volume of Mourlot's "Picasso Lithographe" appears, covering the years 1947 to 1949 and including two lithographs by the artist.

1951 Winter in Vallauris, where he paints "Massacre in Korea" (pp. 500–501) in protest against the American invasion. It is exhibited in Paris at the Salon de Mai but meets with a lukewarm reception. In June Paul Eluard marries his second wife, Dominique Lemor, at Saint-Tropez, and Picasso and Françoise are the witnesses. The chapel at Vence near Nice which Matisse has decorated is opened with considerable publicity and consecrated by the bishop. Picasso is not present, but visits Matisse on his sickbed. He is in Paris for periods, has to move from the flat in the Rue La Boétie and moves to 9, Rue Gay-Lussac, though he retains the studio in the Rue des

Jacqueline Roque, about 1950

Picasso with his unfinished sculpture of a "Goat" (p. 485) in 1952

"Youth", Vallauris, 9 June 1950. Lithograph, 50.2 x 64.8 cm. Bloch 657; Mourlot 188 II; Rau 503. The picture was used for the world youth peace conference poster in Nice in 1950

Portrait of Stalin by Picasso in "Les Lettres Françaises", 12–19 March 1953

Grands-Augustins. In Vallauris he uses chance finds in sculptures such as "Baboon and Young" (p. 488). "Goat Skull, Bottle and Candle" (p. 484) is an experiment in intersecting planes. Attends world peace congress in Rome. In late autumn he returns to Paris with Françoise. His 70th birthday is marked by a large retrospective in Tokyo, exhibitions of sculptures and drawings in Paris, and a show of drawings and watercolours at the Institute of Contemporary Arts in London. Eluard's poetry collection "Le Visage de la paix" carries a lithograph by Picasso, the last occasion they work together. "Dons des féminines" by Valentine Penrose uses an etching.

1952 In April in Vallauris he starts sketching and design work for two immense mural paintings, "War" and "Peace" (p. 452), which he completes late in the year at Vallauris. In 1954 they are installed in the Peace Temple there as planned. In Vallauris he paints the "Portrait of Madame H. P." (p. 505), the wife of his painter friend Edouard Pignon. A young woman, Jacqueline Roque, starts as assistant to Suzanne Ramié. Relations with Françoise cool. In late October he goes to Paris alone. Paul Eluard, one of his closest friends, dies on 18 November, and Picasso attends the funeral. Several lithograph portraits of Balzac. One is included in a new edition of "Le Père Goriot" (p. 498). In early December he returns to Vallauris. Finishes his play "Quatre Petites

Filles" (begun in 1947), which is published in 1968. February/March: solo exhibition at Curt Valentin's gallery in New York.

1953 During the year he is to and fro between Paris and Vallauris, as are Françoise and the children. On 5 March Stalin (born 1879) dies. Requested by Aragon to supply a portrait for "Les Lettres françaises", Picasso innocently uses a photo dating from 1903 and showing the young Stalin, which angers the Communist party and ultimately leads to a breach. Summer in Vallauris with Françoise and the children inspires pictures of children playing (p. 509) and a "Seated Woman" (p. 504) showing Françoise. He carves and paints small wooden dolls for Paloma. In August, at the invitation of the Lazermes, whom he has met through his friend Manolo, he travels with Maya and later Paul to Perpignan at the foot of the eastern Pyrenees. There he again meets Jacqueline Roque, a divorcée. Goes to bull fights at Collioure. At nearby Céret the Communists throw celebrations in his honour. When he returns to Vallauris in September, Françoise leaves us, taking the children to Paris and moving into a new flat in Rue Gay-Lussac, where Picasso sometimes visits. In October he terminates an intermittent relationship with Geneviève Laporte. In November in Vallauris he is occupied with a large number of drawings on the subject of the artist and his model. Sabartés gives his personal library to the Museo de Málaga and his collection of works by Picasso

to the city of Barcelona. January: exhibits in "Le Cubisme, 1907–1914" in Paris. Major retrospective in May/July at the Galleria Nazionale d'Arte Moderne in Rome, an enlarged version of which goes to Milan in the autumn. June: 170 works on show in Lyon. December: exhibits at the Museo de Arte Moderno in São Paulo. Contributes six copper engravings to Maurice Toesca's "Six Contes fantastiques". Producer Luciano Emmer films him at work on the Peace Temple at Vallauris.

1954 Continues the artist and model series (p. 521), incorporating motifs from the world of the circus and from mythology. Meets an English 19-year-old, Sylvette David, who models for 39 drawings and paintings within one month (pp. 518–519). In June and October he paints portraits of Jacqueline Roque (pp. 514–515). Does collapsible sculptures made of wood and cut and folded sheet metal, overpainted and spatially intersecting, as well as heads and busts of Sylvette David and Jacqueline Roque. These are preliminaries to later large-scale work in concrete. Spends much of the summer in Perpignan again, where he is joined for periods by his son Paul and Paul's wife-to-be Christine and Maya, by Françoise Gilot with Claude and Paloma, and by Jacqueline Roque with her daughter Catherine. Living in the Rue de l'Ange, he is host to many friends. In September he and Françoise separate for good, and she

Sylvette David aged 19 when Picasso met her in Vallauris and did 39 portraits of her. The portraits confirmed the English girl's pony-tail as teenage girls' preferred hair style worldwide (pp. 518–519).

"Pages at Play", Vallauris, 19 February 1951. Lithograph, 31.8 x 42.5 cm. Bloch 685; Mourlot 199; Rau 523

A Chronology 713

Picasso drawing in Clouzot's film "Le Mystère Picasso", Nice, 1955. Photo: André Villers

Picasso during the shooting of George Clouzot's film "Le Mystère Picasso" in Nice, 1955

returns to Paris with the children. Goes to Vallauris with Jacqueline and then to Paris, where she moves in with him in the Rue des Grands-Augustin. Picasso is deeply affected by the death on 3 November of his highly-esteemed friend Matisse ("Really there is only Matisse"). In the same year he has lost other old friends: Henri Laurens on 5 May, André Derain in

an accident on 8 September, and Maurice Raynal. In December, with Matisse's odalisques in mind and inspired by the beauty of Jacqueline (pp. 512 and 526–527), he begins a series of variations (pp. 523 and 536) on "Women of Algiers" by Eugène Delacroix (1798–1863), producing a total of 15 paintings and two lithographs. Numerous solo and group exhibitions in

New York, Basel, Barcelona, Céret, San Antonio (Texas), Cannes and Stockholm. For a short period, the important Maison de la Pensée Française retrospective "Deux périodes, 1900–1914 et 1950–1954" includes 37 paintings from the former collection of Sergei Shchukin.

1955 On 11 February Picasso's wife Olga dies at Cannes and is buried there. In May Picasso goes with Jacqueline, Paul and Maya to Perpignan, where they meet the Leirises and Cocteau and go to bullfights at Céret. In June he buys La Californie, a 19th-century villa in Belle Epoque style in large grounds of its own on a hill above Cannes, with views of Golfe-Juan as far as Cap d'Antibes. He later places sculptures in the partly tropical gardens. The high-ceilinged, light studio prompts a series of "interior landscapes". Numerous friends visit him there. He goes to bullfights at Arles and Nîmes. In the summer, Henri-Georges Clouzot (1907–1977) makes the film "Le Mystère Picasso" in the studios at Nice, showing him drawing or painting various works (pp. 522 and 524–525). Solo exhibitions in January/February at the Contemporary Arts Association in Houston (Texas), in May/June (drawings and bronzes) at Marlborough Fine Art in London, from June to October (graphic work) at the Bibliothèque Nationale in Paris, and in December (ceramics) at Syra's in Barcelona. From June to October a large retrospective of some 150 paintings from 1900 to 1955 is at the Musée des Arts Décoratifs in Paris, and then, in similar format, travels to Munich, Cologne

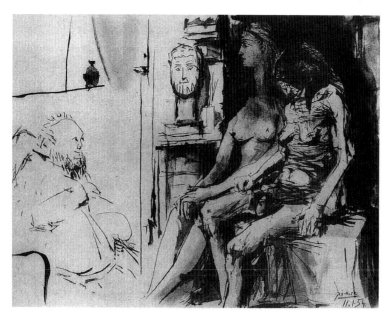

"The Artist and His Model", 11 January 1954. India ink on paper, 24 x 32 cm. Zervos XVI, 178

With Paloma and Claude, Vallauris 1951. Photo: Edward Quinn

Bathing with Claude and Paloma, 1955. Photo: Roger Hauert

and Hamburg. Exhibits in February in a group show in Paris in honour of the Spanish poet Antonio Machado (1875–1939). In December he has 57 works in the 3rd Hispano-American Art Biennale in Barcelona, and graphic work, with Braque and Marc Chagall (1887–1985), at the Sala Gaspar in Barcelona. Tristan Tzara's book of poems "A Haute Flamme", published in Paris, carries six copper engravings by Picasso. In Stuttgart, Hans Bolliger and Bernhard Geiser publish a study of Picasso's graphic work from 1899 to 1954.

1956 At the beginning of the year he paints "Seated Nude" (p. 529) and then returns to the subject of bathers in "Two Women on the Beach" (p. 533). In the summer he continues this with a number of wooden assemblages, "The Bathers", which are then cast in bronze (pp. 537–539). Following the interior landscapes he paints the studio at La Californie (p. 531) and "Jacqueline in the Studio" (p. 530). To mark his 75th birthday on 25 October, the potters of Madoura workshop in Vallauris throw a party, and Ilya Ehrenburg organizes an exhibition of paintings in

"Bathers on the Beach at La Garoupe", Cannes, 16 September 1956. Oil on canvas, 54 x 65 cm. Zervos XVII, 160

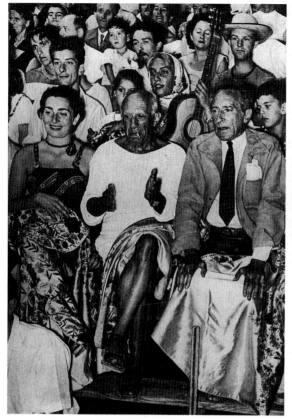

Picasso with Jacqueline and Jean Cocteau at a bullfight in Vallauris, 1955. Daughter Maya with the guitar, with Paloma beside her, and to the right, behind Cocteau, Claude. Photo: Brian Brake

Picasso, by Roger Hauert. Vallauris, 1955

Moscow. In November, together with Edouard Pignon, Hélène Parmelin and other members, he signs a protest to the French Communist party (published in "Le Monde") against the Soviet presence in Hungary. "Le Mystère Picasso" is screened at the Cannes film festival. Solo exhibitions in July (paintings, drawings and graphics) in Cannes, in October (lithograph originals) in Barcelona, Malmö and London, in November in Castres and Oslo, in December (book illustrations) in Nice. Fernand Mourlot publishes the third volume of "Picasso Lithographe" in Paris, including two lithographs by the artist, and Maurice Jardot publishes "Picasso. Dessins d'un demi-siècle" with an additional lithograph.

1957 At the start of the year he does a number of painted ceramics, some sculptures, a large number of portraits of Jacqueline, and several landscapes. In the spring he etches the 26-plate "Tauromaquia" series (pp. 540–541). From mid-August he is occupied with variations on "Las Meninas", painted in 1656 by Diego

Velázquez (1599–1660), which he first saw in 1895 in the Prado in Madrid. As early as 1952 he told Sabartés of his idea of copying the painting. It shows the Spanish Infanta with her court ladies in attendance and contains a self-portrait of the artist (p. 603). Picasso works hard for several months, on the top floor of La Californie, on 58 variations on the picture, finishing in late December (pp. 602–610). In the autumn he is commissioned by UNESCO to paint a mural for the new Paris headquarters. He does his first studies in December, filling two sketchbooks, initially with bathers and nudes. The Norwegian painter and sculptor Carl Nesjar (born 1920) introduces him to a technique of his own devising called "bétongrave", sculpting concrete with a sand-blaster. Nesjar, working from drawings by Picasso, does the first concrete reliefs for three interior walls in an Oslo government building: a beach scene, fisherman and faun and satyr, and heads done in wood or carved, painted sheet iron intended for later scale enlarging. Solo show of new paintings at the Galerie Louise Leiris in Paris in March/April, paintings and sculptures

from 1898 to 1956 at the New York Museum of Modern Art in May to mark his 75th birthday (the exhibition later travels to the Art Institute of Chicago and the Museum of Art in Philadelphia), gouaches and watercolours from 1898 to 1957 in Arles from July to September, and paintings, sculptures, drawings and ceramics in Barcelona in October/November. "Dans l'atelier de Picasso" by Jaime Sabartés contains six lithographs. He also illustrates books by Antonin Artaud (1896–1948), Pierre André Benoît and Michel Leiris.

1958 Picasso's sister Lola (Gómez) dies in Barcelona. In January he finishes the huge mural for UNESCO. It consists of a large number of tiles and covers an area of 100 square metres. It now shows a diver being watched by bathers. It is exhibited in March in the school yard at Vallauris and installed in Paris in the UNESCO building in September (p. 551). Georges Salles dubs it "The Fall of Icarus". Paints various versions of "The Bay of Cannes" (pp. 544–545) seen from La Californie, further studio interiors, and many pictures of Jacque-

Picasso with (from left) Vidal Ventosa, Jacqueline, Juan Gaspar and Antoni Clavé at Vallauris, 1955

Picasso with Jacqueline on the platform in Cannes, 1956. Photo: Jacqueline Picasso

"Daniel-Henry Kahnweiler", Cannes, 3 June 1957. Lithograph, 65 x 49.5 cm. Bloch 835; Mourlot 296; Rau 643

line that reflect the happiness of their private life. In September, with new buildings encroaching on the villa and inquisitive tourists thronging the perimeter, Picasso buys the roomy old château of Vauvenargues near Aix-en-Provence, a 14th-century building which was the home of the French writer of that name (1715–1747) in the 18th century. It is just below Mont Sainte-Victoire, which Cézanne made famous through his paintings. Picasso works there intermittently from 1959 to 1961. He experiments with linocuts. Solo shows: January/February in Philadelphia, ceramics in Paris from March to June and from July to October in Céret, in July/September in Liège, in November/December in New York, where the Blue Period "Mother and Child" is sold for $150,000, and in the royal palace in Copenhagen. Sabartés publishes "Les Ménines et la vie"; it and other books by Char, Benoît and Tzara include graphic work by Picasso.

1959 In January he writes a long poem in Spanish, "Trozo de piel", which Camilo José Cela (born 1916) publishes in 1961. His "Bust of a Woman" (p. 546), done as six linocut variations on a work by Lucas Cranach the Younger (1515–1586) in various colours, is a virtuoso performance. In February he works at Vauvenargues for the first time, then alternates between Vauvenargues and La Californie. Paints "The Dining Room at Vauvenargues" (p. 547), a parody of "El Bobo" (p. 554) by Bartolomé Estéban Murillo (1618–1682), and several portraits of Jacqueline (p. 549). In June a bronze cast of the 1941 "Head of a Woman" modelled on Dora Maar is placed beside the Church of Saint-Germain-des-Prés in Paris as a memorial

Picasso in a kilt, about 1958

Top: Picasso with his pigeons at the time of "Las Meninas" in the loft of La Californie.
Below: With Paloma and Claude on the terrace of La Californie, Cannes, 1957

Picasso with canvases, a pitcher and a plywood flute player at La Californie. Cannes, 1956. Photo: Jacqueline Picasso

Pages 718/719:
The studio at La Californie, Cannes, 1957.
Photo: André Villers. Arles, Musée Rèattu

Picasso's shaving stand in the Rue des Grands-Augustins. On the wall a lithograph portrait of Kahnweiler. About 1957/58

"Woman with Flowered Blouse" (Jacqueline), Cannes, 27 December 1958. Lithograph, 63 x 48 cm. Bloch 847; Mourlot 307 III; Rau 665

Jacqueline and Picasso leaving La Californie to move to Vauvenargues, 1958.
Photo: David Douglas Duncan

Picasso and Jacqueline celebrating his 80th birthday in Vallauris, October 1961

Picasso's studio at "Notre-Dame-de-Vie", Cannes, about 1966

Picasso looking out of the window of Vauvenargues. Photo: Jacqueline Picasso

to Apollinaire. In August he begins on a set of variations on Manet's "Le Déjeuner sur l'herbe". These paintings and drawings are to occupy him for two full years. He does further linocuts on Mediterranean subjects such as bacchanals, centaurs and fauns. In October, with Jacqueline and other friends, he is involved in the making of Cocteau's film "Le Testament d'Orphée". In May/June his variations on Velázquez's "Las Meninas" are exhibited at the Galerie Louise Leiris in Paris and the originals of the "Tauromaquia" graphic series at the Sala Gaspar in Barcelona. Other solo shows in March/April in Boston, May/June at the Musée

Cantini in Marseilles, September/October in the Swedish-French Gallery in Stockholm, November/December at Saidenberg's in New York ("Faces and Figures, 1900 to 1959"), and December (22 lithographic originals) at the Prisma in Madrid.

1960 At the start of the year he returns to women bathing and washing their feet, to drawings and paintings on the subject of the artist and his model, which is to dominate his work in the Sixties. In April in Vauvenargues he paints "Bather with Sand Shovel" (p. 556). The separate pre-

sentation of discrete parts of the visual image anticipates the structure of large metal sculptures he is planning. In August he completes a further version after Manet's "Déjeuner sur l'herbe", begun in March and following upon many others (pp. 558–561 and 570). In October, influenced by Catalan folk art, he starts on design work and drawings for mural decorations at the Colegio Oficial de los Arquitectos de Barcelona, which Carl Nesjar

Right:
Picasso with a pistol and cowboy hat given him by Gary Cooper, La Californie, Cannes, 1958. Photo: André Villiers. Arles, Musée Rèattu

720 A Chronology

The Museu Picasso in Barcelona, in the 15th-century Berenguer d'Aguilar Palace. It was opened on 9 March 1963

In the Mougins studio, 1963

later installs on interior and exterior walls of the building in concrete relief. Late in the year he experiments with folding cardboard cut-outs as maquettes for large-format cut sheet metal sculptures. In London, Roland Penrose organizes an Arts Council major retrospective of 270 works (1895 to 1959) at the Tate Gallery (from July to September), for which Picasso himself chooses 100 pictures from his own collection. Solo exhibitions of graphic work: January to March in Nice, June to August at Mülhausen in Alsace; 45 linocuts at Galerie Louise Leiris in Paris in June/July and then in Barcelona; in November/December 30 hitherto unseen works at the Sala Gaspar in Barcelona, and new drawings and watercolours of bullfights at Louise Leiris in Paris. From August to October there is a large-scale group exhibition of ceramics by Picasso, Matisse, Chagall, Georges Rouault (1871–1958), Léger and Cocteau at the International Ceramics Museum in Faenza (Italy), the cradle of faience ware. Picasso does four etchings for Jacqueline's book "Température" and illustrations for books by Benoît, Char, and the Chilean poet Pablo Neruda (1904–1973).

1961 In January he starts preparatory sketchwork on his new subject, the rape of the Sabine women. On 2 March he mar-

ries Jacqueline Roque at Vallauris. It is a simple wedding. After first creating cardboard maquettes (p. 565) he makes large-surface metal sculptures in cut and painted sheet metal such as "Woman with Outstretched Arms" (p. 567) and "Footballer" (p. 566). Disappointed by the changing character of Cannes, he quits first Vauvenargues and then La Californie, moving in June to Notre-Dame-de-Vie, a large country house at Mougins, in the hills a few miles north of Cannes. There he works on a new series after Manet's 1863 painting "Le Déjeuner sur l'herbe". Picasso's 80th birthday on 25 October is celebrated throughout the art world, and by himself and friends some days later at Vallauris. The University of California Art Gallery in Los Angeles mounts a major exhibition of 170 works, titled "Bonne Fête, Monsieur Picasso!" Jaime Sabartés writes the introduction to "A los toros avec Picasso", which reproduces 103 India ink drawings and four lithographs of bullfight scenes. Luis Miguel Dominguin, a bullfighter friend of Picasso's, dedicates his book "Toros y toreros", which carries a lithograph by Picasso, to the artist. René Char and other writers publish a Festschrift, "25 octobre 1961", illustrated with an etching. David Douglas Duncan (born 1916) publishes a book presenting several hundred "unknown" Picassos from the artist's own collection. Solo shows of linocuts in Cincinnati (January), graphic work in Paris and Madrid (January/February), drawings in Barcelona (April), ceramics in Madrid (May) and in Málaga (December), and from June to August in Bremen.

1962 In January he paints Jacqueline as a "Seated Woman with Yellow and Green Hat" (p. 597), initiating a series of over seventy portraits (paintings, drawings, ceramics and graphic works). In April the Colegio Oficial de los Arquitectos de Barcelona unveils Picasso's concrete murals. On 1 May he is awarded the Lenin Peace Prize for a second time. Makes further sheet metal heads of women. In August, for the dancer and Paris opera house ballet director Serge Lifar (1905–1986), he paints a gouache design for the set of the ballet "Icare", as well as several variations on the "Rape of the Sabine Women" (pp. 576–577) after Jacques Louis David (1748–1825). Nesjar does a larger, six-metre-high concrete version of the metal "Woman with Outstretched Arms" for the garden of Daniel-Henry Kahnweiler at Saint-Hilaire (p. 567). His energy and enthusiasm undiminished, he produces over a hundred graphics during the year, most of them linocuts (pp. 573 and 580–581): female portraits, still lifes, and variations on the themes of "Déjeuner sur l'herbe" and the artist and his model. For his linocuts he develops a new cutting and printing technique that permits brilliant results

hitherto impossible. In New York two further exhibitions mark Picasso's 80th birthday after the event: "Picasso: An American Tribute" in April/May, featuring over 300 works in nine galleries, and from May to September the "Picasso 80th Birthday Exhibition" at the Museum of Modern Art. There are various further solo shows at Worcester (MA), Paris, Lyon, Vallauris and Barcelona. Jean Cocteau's monograph "Picasso de 1916 à 1961" is published, with 25 lithographs.

1963 At the start of the year he does 13 portraits of Jacqueline, including the "Great Profile" (p. 587). In February he starts on an artist and model series, and paints 45 pictures between March and June alone (pp. 582–585). On 9 March the Museu Picasso is opened in Barcelona in the 15th-century Aguilar Palace in Calle Montcada. From May to September he works on crayon drawings after "Bathsheba at her Toilet" by Rembrandt (1606–1669). Again he loses two long-standing friends, Braque on 31 August and Cocteau on 11 October. Embarks on a new collaboration with Aldo Crommelynck, whom he met twenty years earlier at Lacourière's workshop, and his brother Piero. They set up a copper engraving printing workshop in Mougins. There Picasso produces the graphics in his "Embraces" and "Artist and Model" series, again surprising his collaborators by his innovative technical approach and use of mixed media. For his friend Douglas Cooper, collector and art historian, he designs mural decorations for Château Castille at Remoulins, in the Rhone valley near Avignon. Nesjar does them in concrete relief. Solo shows: July to September at the Musée de l'Athénée in Geneva; in the summer "Picasso. Les Potiers" in Vallauris and "Picasso: Deux époques" at Galerie Rosengart in Lucerne; and in December 15 recent linocuts at the Sala Gaspar in Barcelona.

1964 The entire 24th volume of Christian Zervos's catalogue of Picasso's works is devoted to the year 1964 (pp. 614 ff.). From January to May he paints a series of some twenty pictures of a nude woman with a cat, most of them featuring Jacqueline as model (pp. 623–625). In the spring Picasso's ex-lover Françoise Gilot, co-authoring with the American art critic Carlton Lake, publishes her intimate memoirs of life with Picasso. Picasso's attempts to prevent publication of the French translation only increase the book's sales. The photographer Brassaï, who has followed Picasso at work for many years, publishes "Conversations avec Picasso", illustrated with his own photographs. Picasso makes a metal sculpture of a "Head" (p. 579) in response to an American commission. The finished version, 20 metres high, is completed in 1965 and placed at the Chicago Civic Centre in 1967. In the closing months of the year, Picasso paints about a hundred pictures on the artist and model theme (pp. 619 and 626). During the year there are major retrospectives in Japan and Canada. "Picasso and Man", at the Art Gallery of Ontario in Toronto in January/February, shows 273 works covering the years 1898 to 1961 and is seen subsequently at the Musée des Beaux-Arts in Montreal. In Tokyo, the National Museum of Modern Art's exhibition of works from 1899 to 1963 runs from May to July and then travels to Kyoto and Nagoya. Galerie Louise Leiris in Paris exhibits recent paintings dating from 1962/63 in January/February, and coloured linocuts in May/June. Other exhibitions are held in Barcelona, Ottawa, Vallauris and Lausanne. Fernand Mourlot publishes the fourth colume of "Picasso Lithographe" in Paris, containing two lithographs by the artist.

1965 In February Picasso paints a number of turbulent landscapes. Continues the artist and model series, producing some thirty paintings in March alone (pp. 626–628). He then turns to the new subject of a man holding a child or eating a watermelon, a family scene which he does in paint and in graphic modes. In May he paints further landscapes. "Vivre avec Picasso", the French version of Françoise Gilot's memoirs, is published, causing bad feeling and cutting Picasso off from his children Claude and Paloma, who are no longer allowed to visit him. The distress doubtless contributes to giving Picasso a stomach ulcer, for which he undergoes an operation at the American hospital in Neuilly-sur-Seine outside Paris in November. This is the artist's last stay in Paris. Nesjar does further concrete sculptures to designs by Picasso. On the shores of Lake Vänern near Kristinehamm in Sweden a "Head of a Woman" is mounted on a concrete pillar 15 metres high and almost two metres in diameter. A "Cut-open Figure" is installed in Vondel Park in Amsterdam. A group of four figures based on Manet's "Déjeuner sur l'herbe" is put up in the Moderna Museet in Stockholm, and further works in Oslo and Marseilles. In April/May an exhibition of "Apollinaire et le cubisme" is on in Lille. He exhibits at the Kunstverein in Frankfurt (May to July), and the Musée des Augustins in Toulouse mounts "Picasso et le théâtre" (June to September). In June there are new productions of three ballets Picasso originally designed: "Parade" (1917), "Le Tricorne" (1919) and "L'après-midi d'un faune" (1922). In July/August the Sala Gaspar in Barcelona exhibits paintings, drawings and graphics. In September he exhibits at Kiruna (Sweden), and in December has lithographs in a group show, "L'atelier Mourlot", in London. Jean Adhémar's "L'atelier Mourlot",

Louis Aragon's "Shakespeare", Hélène Parmelin's "Le Peintre et son modèle" and a Festschrift for Kahnweiler by Werner Spies and others all carry graphic works by Picasso.

1966 After convalescing, he begins to draw once more in the spring, and to paint. Figures of flute players, watermelon eaters and Spanish musketeers convey a cheerful mood. In August he resumes graphic work. By the following spring he has done 60 first-rate engravings, though they are not printed up for several years. On 28 September his friend André Breton dies in Paris. On 25 October almost the entire art world joins Picasso in celebrating his 85th birthday. The occasion is marked with exhibitions in many countries, some of which commemorate 60 years of his graphic work or 20 of his ceramics. The most important retrospective to date, "Hommage à Picasso" in Paris, including over 700 works, is opened in November by his personal friend André Malraux, Minister of the Arts in France since 1959. The paintings are exhibited at the Grand Palais, the drawings, sculptures and ceramics at the Petit Palais, and 171 graphic works in the Bibliothèque Nationale. The retrospective is a great success, attracting over a million people, who take a particular interest in the sculptural works. Many of these, from Picasso's own collection, are on public display for the first time. True to habit, Picasso does not attend the exhibition himself. In the same year, Pierre Daix and Georges Boudaille publish their catalogue of the paintings from 1900 to 1906, and Hans Bolliger and Kurt Leonhard publish their second volume on the graphic works, 1955–1965. Hélène Parmelin's "Notre-Dame-de-Vie" is published, with a linocut by Picasso.

1967 On 20 January some two hundred Catalonian academics and students pay homage to Picasso in Barcelona. He draws the watermelon eater, the flute player, the man with the sheep, and mythological scenes. In spring he declines membership of the French Legion of Honour. He is obliged to give up the studio in the Rue des Grands-Augustins because he has not used the apartment which comes with it for twelve years. He goes on with the series of "musketeers". For the first time he paints a female nude leaning forward and frontally foreshortened, and he does a series on this theme up till October. In the second half of the year he does a large number of pencil and India ink drawings: nudes, and the "embrace" and "kiss" themes. The immense "Head of a Woman" is put up at the Chicago Civic Center. A major exhibition of over 200 sculptures and 32 ceramics is shown from June to August at the Tate Gallery in London and from October at the Museum of

Picasso's children Claude, Paloma and Paul with Paul's son Bernard at a tribute to Picasso, 1966

Picasso's dealer Daniel-Henry Kahnweiler, 1966

Modern Art in New York. Further solo exhibitions: February/March at the Art Center in Fort Worth (Texas) and the Museum of Fine Arts in Dallas (Texas), March/April at the Stedelijk Museum in Amsterdam, March/April "Master Graphics" at the Wallraf-Richartz Museum in Cologne, July to September new work at Museum Unterlinden in Colmar, and in November 70 graphic works from 1905 to 1965 at the Musée des Beaux-Arts, Le Havre. René Char's "Les Transparents" and Douglas Cooper's "Picasso théâtre" are published, each illustrated with graphics by Picasso.

1968 In January he does paintings on the subject of "Nude with a Bird" and drawings on "The Turkish Baths", inspired by the 1862 painting by Jean Auguste Dominique Ingres (1780–1867). On 13 February Picasso's friend and secretary Jaime Sabartés, who was born in the same year of 1881, dies. In his memory, Picasso gifts the 58 pictures after Velázquez's "Las Meninas" and a Blue Period portrait of Sabartés to the Museu Picasso in Barcelona, the cornerstone of whose holdings had been laid in 1953 by Sabartés's own gift of Picassos. From 16 March to 5 October Picasso is working inconceivably hard at Mougins on a series of 347 graphic works, mainly etchings, using a variety of motifs

Picasso in Arles. Photo: Jacqueline Picasso

Picasso at "Notre-Dame-de-Vie" in Mougins.
Photo: Jacqueline Picasso

from the world of the circus, bullfighting, the theatre and commedia dell'arte, and finally a number of erotic scenes inspired by Ingres which strike a humorous note (pp. 644–645). The graphics are printed by the brothers Crommelynck in Mougins and exhibited at Galerie Louise Leiris in Paris in December under the title "Suite 347".
Late in the year he again paints musketeers smoking (pp. 641–643 and 646–647). A huge concrete bust of Sylvette is installed at the University of New York. In Bern, Georges Bloch publishes the first volume of his catalogue of the graphic work, to be followed by three further volumes, and Bernhard Geiser publishes volume two of "Picasso. Peintre-graveur". The variations on "Las Meninas" which Picasso gave the Museu Picasso in Barcelona are exhibited there in May. Further solo shows in Chicago, Baden-Baden, Málaga and Vienna.

1969 Returns to painting with a renewed expressive power. His large output includes faces with staring expressions such as "Large Heads" (p. 652), couples kissing (p. 648), men with swords or pipes (pp. 654–655) and still lifes (p. 649). His fantastic "El entierro del conde de Orgaz", written between 1957 and 1959, is now published in Barcelona, with a foreword by the poet Rafael Alberti (born 1902) and with twelve etchings, three aquatints and a copper engraving of recent date as illustrations. In October Yvonne and Christian Zervos visit Picasso in Mougins and are so taken with the beauty and copiousness of his new creative output that they decide the work must be exhibited and persuade Picasso to agree. The "Suite 347" graphics travel from Paris to Zurich, thence to Hamburg, Cologne, Stockholm, Nagoya (Japan) and Toronto.

Further solo exhibitions: April to June "Picasso d'aujourd'hui" in Arles, June/July "Figures peintes 1969" at the Galerie "Cahiers d'Art" in Paris, from July to October "The Artist and His Model" at the Staatliche Kunsthalle in Baden-Baden, in summer at Lucerne. In November the 1906/07 gouache "Head of a Red Woman" fetches 280,000 francs in Paris, and a version of "Les Demoiselles d'Avignon" is sold for 350,000. In December he exhibits 194 drawings at the Galerie Louise Leiris, most of them in colour, and every one of them is sold the day the show opens, for prices from 30,000 to 60,000 francs.

1970 He gifts all the paintings and sculptures that remained with his family in Barcelona and were in the keeping first of his mother and then of his sister Lola to the Museu Picasso in Barcelona, requesting however that there be no ceremony to mark the gift. The works mainly date from his youth in Corunna and Barcelona, and from the period when he was working with Diaghilev and the Ballets Russes in 1917. On 20 January Yvonne Zervos dies. The exhibition of 167 paintings and 45 drawings done in 1969, which she curated, runs from May to October in the Papal Palace at Avignon. The public are greatly impressed by the 88-year-old's creative vitality. On 12 September Zervos, who drew up the catalogue, dies of a heart attack. Picasso has thus lost two of his most loyal friends and advocates in a short space of time. In May the Bateau-Lavoir in Paris, where he lived and worked from 1904 to 1909, is destroyed by fire. During the year he does some 200 drawings, and in the autumn numerous paintings such as "The Family" (p. 666) and versions of "The Matador" (pp. 664–665). Major ex-

hibitions: October/November "Picasso: Master Printmaker" at the Museum of Modern Art in New York; from December to February 1971 "The Cubist Epoch" (including work by Picasso) at the County Museum of Art in Los Angeles and subsequently (April to June 1971) at the Metropolitan Museum of Art in New York; from December to March 1971 "Four Americans in Paris: The Collections of Gertrude Stein and Her Family", featuring 47 works from her collection, 38 by Picasso, at the Museum of Modern Art, New York. The "Suite 347" graphics travel on to Barcelona, Toulouse, Caen, London, Regensburg, Stuttgart, Ferrara, Chicago and Helsinki.

1971 In the winter he gives the Museum of Modern Art in New York his first sheet metal and wire construction, the 1912 "Guitar". In May he gives 57 of his latest drawings to the Musée Rèattu at Arles, where he was always fond of going to bullfights. In August he paints "Mother and Child", in September "Fatherhood" (p. 667). He is honoured in many ways on the occasion of his 90th birthday on 25 October. At the Louvre in Paris, President Georges Pompidou (1911–1974) opens an exhibition of eight Picasso paintings from different French public collections, an honour never ever paid to a living artist. He is given the freedom of the city of Paris. The Musée National d'Art Moderne exhibits major work done before the First World War from the St. Petersburg Hermitage and the Pushkin Museum in Moscow. The Communist party holds a rally at the Palais des Sports. The Vallauris potters celebrate lavishly. In New York, the Marlborough and Saidenberg galleries exhibit loaned works to review 70 years of Picasso's work. There are special exhibitions throughout the world: in Spain, Japan,

Canada, Great Britain, Switzerland and Germany as well as France and the US. In London, schoolchildren holding reproductions of the 1901 "Child Holding a Dove" (p. 12) gather on the steps of the Tate Gallery and celebrate the day by releasing ninety doves. Lucien Clergue's film about Picasso is on French television. One of the great works of world literature, Fernando de Rojas' dramatized novel about a procuress "La Celestina", first published in 1499 in Burgos, is issued by the brothers Crommelynck with 66 etchings and aquatints from the "Suite 347". In Stuttgart, Werner Spies publishes "Picasso. Das plastische Werk". Georges Bloch publishes the third volume of his catalogue of the graphic works, covering the years 1966 to 1969.

1972   During the year he does mainly drawings and graphics at Mougins, but also paintings (pp. 672 – 680) and in June/July a number of self-portraits in chalk and crayon (pp. 8 and 672), some of them rendering the head as a death mask. Gives the Museum of Modern Art in New York an enlarged two-metre model of the wire construction he did in 1928 as a maquette for a memorial to his friend Apollinaire (pp. 324–325). A four-metre-high finished version is put up in the museum's

grounds. From January to April the museum exhibits Picasso drawings and graphics from its own holdings. In December the Galerie Louise Leiris in Paris exhibits 172 new drawings. Further exhibitions include books with original graphic work at the Museu Picasso in Barcelona (October/November) and "Picasso. Œuvre gravée 1904–1968" at the Galerie Municipal in Montreuil near Paris (December). In Barcelona Juan Eduardo Cirlot's study of the work of the young Picasso is published.

1973   Galerie Louise Leiris has now been exhibiting Picasso's most recent work consistently since 1953, making a significant contribution to the consolidation of his reputation. From December 1972 to January 1973 the gallery exhibits 172 drawings done between November 1971 and August 1972, and in January/February 1973 156 graphic works done between late 1970 and March 1972. On 8 April Pablo Picasso dies, aged 91, at his villa, Notre-Dame-de-Vie, in Mougins, of oedema of the lung resulting from a bout of 'flu in December 1972. The evening before, he was still working on a painting (p. 680). On 10 April he is buried in the grounds of Château Vauvenargues near Aix-en-Provence. The 1933 bronze

"Woman with a Vase", which was exhibited at the 1937 World Fair in Paris, is placed on his grave. On 12 April his grandson Pablito attempts suicide and dies three days later. At Picasso's wish, his widow Jacqueline and son Paul donate his valuable personal collection of paintings to the French state. It includes works by Le Nain, Chardin, Corot, Courbet, Degas, Cézanne, Renoir, Rousseau, Matisse, Derain, Braque, Gris and Miró. The first major memorial exhibition is held from May to September at the Papal Palace in Avignon, with 201 paintings of the period 1970 to 1972, selected by the artist himself. There are numerous other exhibitions in Cleveland, Bern, Paris, Céret, Montpellier, Hanover, Geneva, Barcelona and Metz. After Picasso's death, the prices for his works climb to dizzying heights. The Mellon Foundation pays $1 million for the 1910 "Female Nude" for the National Gallery of Art in Washington, DC. In New York, $720,000 are paid for the 1906 "Jeune Homme au bouquet".

1974   The French state accepts the Picasso bequest. The authenticity of a number of paintings is disputed. Maya Widmayer, daughter of Marie-Thérèse Walter and Picasso, and Claude and Paloma Picasso, his

Picasso in the garden of La Californie with "Head of a Woman" (1936; Spies 128). Photo: Jacqueline Picasso

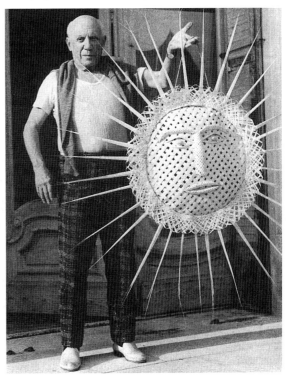

Picasso holding the sun in his hand. Photo: Jacqueline Picasso

children by Françoise Gilot, are his (illegitimate) heirs. In July lawyers are called in to sort out the estate, and a valuator to draw up an inventory of the works left by the artist at his death. In October the Spanish government appoints a panel of lawyers to examine legal means of having "Guernica" returned to Spain. From October to December 67 watercolours, drawings and gouaches dating from 1897 to 1972 are exhibited at the Sala Gaspar in Barcelona.

1975 The Museu Picasso in Barcelona is expanded by acquisition of a third, adjoining building in Calle de Montcada, where the works of Picasso's youth and any future donations are to be housed and a Picasso research centre established. Michel Guy, Secretary of State at the French Ministry of the Arts, calls on Jacqueline Picasso at Mougins in January and afterwards, with her consent, announces the establishment of a Musée Picasso in the Hôtel Salé in Paris. The children object on the grounds that the inventory has not yet been completed or the claims on the estate officially agreed. Nevertheless, the Paris municipal council agrees on the foundation of the museum in March. On 5 June Paul Picasso, born in 1921 of Picasso and his wife the Russian dancer Olga Koklova, dies in Paris.

1976 In July, Dominique Bozo is appointed curator of the Musée Picasso, and

President Georges Pompidou opening a Picasso exhibition at the Louvre in Paris on 21 October 1971, an honour never before paid any living artist

architect Roland Simounet is commissioned to design the interior. On 23 November Picasso's friend André Malraux, French Minister of the Arts from 1959 to 1969, dies at Creteil near Paris.

1977 In June a contract is agreed between Picasso's six heirs: his three natural children Maya, Claude and Paloma, his two grandchildren from Paul's two marriages, and Jacqueline. In July Jacqueline contests the contract, which is not finally signed till September. The value of the works left by Picasso is assessed at 1,251,673,000 francs. Of this, 20% goes to the state. On 20 October Marie-Thérèse

Walter, Picasso's partner from 1927 to 1936 and mother of their daughter Maya, commits suicide at Cap d'Antibes. Late in the year a large Picasso exhibition is held at the Juan-March Foundation in Madrid. A sculpture made in honour of Picasso by sculptor Miguel Berrocal (born 1933) is put up in a public park in Málaga which now bears Picasso's name. Negotiations for the return of "Guernica" to Madrid remain unsuccessful as yet.

1978 In July 48 works from the Picasso bequest of 1973, including ten monochrome works by Degas, are exhibited in the Louvre.

1979 On 11 January art dealer Daniel-Henry Kahnweiler, born in Mannheim in 1884 and a lifelong supporter of Picasso, dies in Paris. A large number of important Picassos are given to the French state in place of death duties. They are exhibited in Paris at the Grand Palais and form the core of the future Musée Picasso's collection.

1980 The largest Picasso retrospective to date is held at the Museum of Modern Art in New York to mark the museum's 50th anniversary.

1981 "Guernica", first exhibited in 1937 at the Paris World Fair and subsequently in the Museum of Modern Art, New York, on permanent loan, is assigned to the Museo Nacional del Prado in Madrid under the terms of Picasso's will. It is now returned there, to the Casón del Buen Retiro, a 17th-century royal summer residence now part of the Prado.

1985 The Musée Picasso at the Hôtel Salé in Paris is opened. At this time the holdings include 203 paintings, 191 sculptures, 85 ceramics and over 3,000 drawings and graphic works.

1986 The Royal Academy of Arts in London exhibits Picasso's sketchbooks for the first time in Europe. On 15 October Picasso's widow Jacqueline (born 1926) commits suicide. Ingo F. Walther's monograph "Pablo Picasso" is published and translated into eleven languages; it becomes the best-selling book on Picasso world wide.

1990 The Musée Picasso in Paris receives 162 further works from the estate of Jacqueline Picasso in place of death duties, including 47 paintings which are exhibited in Paris, Marseilles, Bordeaux, Strasbourg, Calais and Amiens from 12 September 1990 to 20 January 1992. Of the 20 most expensive paintings in the world at this date, priced at a total of some 4,000 million, six are by van Gogh and seven by Picasso.

One wall in the "Picasso 1970–1972" exhibition at the Palais des Papes, Avignon, with his last oils. Opened shortly after his death, the show lasted from 23 May to 23 September 1973. In the photo are "Couple" (p. 669), "Seated Man with Cane" (p. 671), "Seated Man" (p. 674) and in the middle on the easel the painting Picasso worked on the evening before his death, "Reclining Nude and Head" (p. 680). Photo: Mario Atzinger

Notes

1 For example: Wilfried Wiegand: Pablo Picasso. Reinbek 1973; Hélène Parmelin: Picasso says . . . , London 1969, South Brunswick (NY) 1969; Brassaï: Picasso and Company. Garden City (NY) 1966, London 1967; Edward Quinn: Photographs from 1972. New York 1980; David D. Duncan: Picasso and Jacqueline. London 1980; Françoise Gilot and Carlton Blake: Life with Picasso. New York 1964, London 1965

2 Juan Antonio Gaya Nuño: Bibliografía crítica y antológica de Picasso. San Juan 1966; Ray A. Kibbey: Picasso. A Comprehensive Bibliography. New York and London 1977

3 Peter Saul, "Saul's Guernica", 1973; Equipo Crónica: "El Intruso", 1969. In: Udo Kultermann: The New Painting. Boulder 1977, ill. XI and 105

4 Walt Disney: Picasso-Raub in Barcelona. Stuttgart 1985 (= Abenteuer aus Onkel Dagoberts Schatztruhe, vol. 4)

5 The wedding picture of Jules and Cathérine is a detail of "Circus Family", and a reproduction of "Seated Harlequin" hangs in their house in the Black Forest

6 Lexikon des Internationalen Films. Reinbek 1987, vol. 1, p. 24

7 Werner Spies (ed.): Pablo Picasso. Werke aus der Sammlung Marina Picasso. Munich 1981, p.10

8 Spies (note 7), ibid.; Eunice Lipton: Picasso Criticism 1901-1939. The Making of an Artist Hero. Diss. New York 1975, New York 1976, pp. 45, 50

9 Brassaï (note 1), p. 24 and opposite p. 100

10 From: André Verdet: Picasso. Geneva 1956, p. 3

11 Werner Spies: Das Auge am Tatort. Munich 1979, pp. 66 f.

12 Christian Zervos: Pablo Picasso. 34 vols., Paris 1932-1978; Werner Spies: The Sculpture by Picasso. London 1971; Georges Bloch: Pablo Picasso. Catalogue of the Printed Graphic Work. 4 vols., Bern 1968-1979; Georges Ramié: Céramique de Picasso. Paris 1974

13 Alfred H. Barr: Picasso. Fifty Years of His Art. New York 1946; William Rubin (ed.): Pablo Picasso. A Retrospective. The Museum of Modern Art. New York 1980; Picasso. Œuvres recues en paiement des droits de succession. Paris 1980; Late Picasso (exibition catalogue). Tate Gallery, London 1988

14 Cf. Franz Roh: Streit um die moderne

Kunst. Auseinandersetzung mit Gegnern der neuen Malerei. Munich 1962, pp. 122–126

15 Danièle Giraudy: Pablo Picasso. La mémoire du regard. Paris 1986

16 Parmelin (note 1), p. 86

17 Juan Eduardo Cirlot: Pablo Picasso. Birth of a Genius. New York 1972, London 1972, pp. 13–27; Josep Palau i Fabre: Picasso. The Early Years, 1881-1907. New York 1980, Oxford 1981, pp. 38–104

18 Wiegand (note 1), p. 10. See also: Jürgen Glaesemer (ed.): Der junge Picasso. Frühwerk und blaue Periode (exibition catalogue). Berne 1985, p. 30

19 Cirlot (note 17), p. 9

20 Parmelin (note 1), p. 86

21 Wolfgang Kemp: " . . . to introduce everywhere a truly constructive type of drawing instruction". In: Zeichnen und Zeichenunterricht der Laien, 1500-1870. Ein Handbuch. Frankfurt am Main 1979; Reiner Hespe: Der Begriff der Freien Kinderzeichnung in der Geschichte des Zeichen- und Kunstunterrichtes von ca. 1890-1920. Frankfurt am Main 1985

22 Kemp (note 21), pp. 15–36

23 Kemp (note 21), ill. 3

24 Kemp (note 21), pp. 37–146

25 Kemp (note 21), pp. 149–323; Hespe (note 21), pp. 60 ff.

26 Roland Penrose: L'Œil de Picasso. Paris 1967, pp. 18 ff. Palau (note 17), p. 32

27 Kemp (note 21), pp. 283 ff.; Hespe (note 21), pp. 67 ff.

28 Cf. Augusti Duran i Sanpere: Populäre Druckgraphik Europas. Spanien vom 15. bis zum 20. Jahrhundert. Munich 1971

29 As Cirlot (note 17), p. 13 – For illustrations of paintings by Picassos father cf. Rubin (as note 18), p. 35

30 Kemp (note 25), loc cit.; Hespe (note 25), loc cit.; Theodor Fontane reports for example in his "Wanderungen durch die Mark Brandenburg", Part One, Berlin ³1987, p. 111, how when Schinkel was a youth his father would draw birds for him to copy

31 Ernst Hans Gombrich: Art und Illusion. New York 1961, fig. 106

32 Palau (note 17), fig. 172. For the method of Crane cf. Hespe (note 21), fig. 37

33 Cirlot (note 17), pp. 14 ff.; Palau (note 17), pp. 38 ff.

34 Hespe (note 21), p. 15

35 Kemp (note 21), pp. 121 ff.; Albert Boime:

The Academy and French Painting in the Nineteenth Century. London 1971; Gombrich (note 31), pp. 156–178

36 Boime (note 35), especially pp. 24 f.

37 As Palau (note 37), fig. 42 f.

38 Cf. Boime (note 35), fig. 7 and 8

39 Cirlot (note 17), fig. 31, 50, 467–473; Palau (note 17), fig. 78, 121

40 Cirlot (note 17), pp. 25 f.

41 Thieme-Becker: Allgemeines Lexikon der bildenden Künstler von der Antike bis zur Gegenwart. Vols. 1–37, Leipzig 1907-1950, vol. 16, 1923, pp. 397 f., and Boime (note 35), fig. 9,10

42 Palau (note 17), p. 84; Juan Antonio Gaya Nuño: Ars Hispaniae. Historia universal del arte del Siglo XIX. Madrid 1966, pp. 88–93

43 Wiegand (note 1), pp. 14 f.

44 Boime (note 35), pp. 36 f.

45 Palau (note 17, pp. 86–131; see also Cirlot (note 17), p. 25

46 Palau (note 17), p. 89

47 Boime (note 35), fig. 20, 26, 28

48 Wiegand (note 1), p. 10

49 Kemp (note 21), fig. 145; Gombrich (note 31), pp. 146–178, fig. 125

50 Parmelin (note 1), p. 86; Cirlot (note 17), pp. 6 f.; Palau (note 17), p. 32

51 Boime (note 35), pp. 34 f.

52 Palau (note 17), p. 48

53 Arnold and Marc Glimcher: Je suis le cahier. The Sketchbooks of Picasso. New York 1986

54 For Picasso's father cf. Glaesemer (note 18), pp. 30–43

55 Palau (note 17), pp. 96 ff. and 122 ff.

56 Nuño (note 41), pp. 333 ff. ; Rudolf Zeitler: Propyläen Kunstgeschichte. Die Kunst des 19. Jahrhunderts. Berlin 1990, passim

57 Wiegand (note 1), p. 16. See also Cirlot (note 17), pp. 133 ff.

58 Palau (note 17), pp. 134–141

59 Palau (note 17), pp. 134 f.

60 Palau (note 17), pp. 154–370; Glaesemer (note 18)

61 Palau (note 17), pp.132–152; Wiegand (note 1), p. 19; Theodor Schieder (ed.): Handbuch der Europäischen Geschichte, vol. 6. Stuttgart 1968, pp. 505–535

62 Palau (note 17), p. 112

63 Palau (note 17), pp. 96–104; Glaesemer (note 18), p. 93

64 Palau (note 17), pp. 96–104; Glaesemer (note 18), pp. 46 f., 96 f.

65 Palau (note 17), p. 126
66 Palau (note 17), pp. 131 f.
67 Palau (note 17), pp. 126 ff., 156 ff.; Glaesemer (note 18), pp. 47–49; Juan Antonio Gaya Nuño: Art Hispaniae. Arte del Siglo XX. Madrid 1977, pp. 31 ff., 104 ff.
68 Palau (note 17), p. 121
69 Palau (note 17), pp. 126 f.; Glaesemer (note 18), p. 132
70 Palau (note 17), p. 101
71 Pierre Daix, in: Glaesemer (note 18), pp. 43 ff.; Palau (note 17), pp. 200 ff.
72 Palau (note 17), pp. 204 ff., Glaesemer (note 18), p. 194
73 Ron Johnson, in Glaesemer : (note 18), pp. 156 ff., Palau (note 17), pp. 216 ff.
74 Palau (note 17), pp. 216 ff.
75 Palau (note 17), pp. 182 ff.; Francesc Fontbona, in: Glaesemer (note 18), pp. 48 f.
76 Anthony Blunt and Phoebe Pool: Picasso. The Formative Years. London 1962, fig. 8–14
77 Wiegand, (note 1), p. 22 with note 23
78 Daix (note 71), pp. 55 f.; Blunt/Pool (note 76), fig. 32–38
79 Palau (note 17), p. 208; Daix (note 71), p. 55: Elda Fezzi: L'opera completa di Renoir, Milan 1972, no. 248, 249; Douglas Cooper: Toulouse-Lautrec. Stuttgart 1955, pp. 88 f.
80 Daix (note 71), p. 55
81 Cf. Palau (note 17), pp. 236, 248
82 Daix, in: Glaesemer (note 18), p. 58
83 Wiegand (note 1), p. 34; Lipton (note 8), pp. 21 ff.; Glaesemer (note 18), pp. 232 f.
84 Wiegand (note 1), p. 41
85 Cf. Marcel Giry: Le Fauvisme. Fribourg 1981, pp. 55 ff.
86 In general for this period: Pierre Cabanne: Le siècle de Picasso. Vol. 1, Paris 1975, pp. 103 ff.; Palau (note 17), pp. 228–370; Pierre Daix and Georges Boudaille: Picasso. The Blue and Rose Periods. Greenwich (CT) and London 1967, pp. 191–235; Glaesemer (note 18)
87 Palau (note 17), pp. 258 f.
88 In general Jack Lindsay: Gustave Courbet. His Life and Art, Somerset 1973. Especially: James Henry Rubin: Realism and Social Vision in Courbet & Proudhon. Princeton 1980, pp. 3 ff. and 58 ff.; Sarah Faunce and Linda Nochlin (ed.): Courbet Reconsidered. New Haven (CT) and London 1988, pp. 17 ff., 77 ff.; Klaus Gallwitz and Klaus Herding (ed.): Malerei und Theorie. Das Courbet Colloquium 1979. Frankfurt am Main 1980, pp. 233 ff., 49 ff.
89 Wiegand (note 1), p. 48; in general: Karl Eric Maison: Honoré Daumier, Catalogue raisonné of paintings, water-colours and drawings. 2 vols., Paris 1968; André Rossel: H. Daumier prend parti. Œuvres politiques et sociales. Paris 1971; Matthias Arnold: Honoré Daumier. Leben und Werk. Stuttgart 1987; Jean Adhémar: Honoré Daumier. Paris 1954
90 Cf.: Norma Broude (ed.): World Impressionism. New York 1990, especially pp. 9–35; Alice Bellony-Rewald: The Lost World of the Impressionists. London 1976, p. 165 ff.
91 Franco Russoli and Fiorella Minervino: L'opera completa di Degas. Milano 1970, no. 399, fig. XXXVI; Cooper (note 79), pp. 90 f. – on the photos which Toulouse-Lau-

trec has made for copying, cf.: Van Deren Coke: The Painter and the Photograph from Delacroix to Warhol. Albuquerque 1964, p. 91
92 Faunce/Nochlin (note 88), pp. 133 f., no. 32
93 Luigi Barzini and Gabriele Mandel: L'opera pittorica completa di Daumier. Milan 1971, passim; Russoli/Minervino (note 91), no. 364–368, 408, 595, 596, 625
94 Werner Hofmann: Nana. Mythos und Wirklichkeit. Cologne 1973, especially pp. 21 ff.
95 Wolfgang Drost: Baudelaire und die Bildende Kunst. Diss. Tübingen 1957; F.W. Heemings and Robert J. Niess (ed.): Emile Zola. Salons. Geneva and Paris 1959; Emile Zola: Schriften zur Kunst. Die Salons von 1866 bis 1896. Frankfurt am Main 1988; Johan Rewald: Cézanne et Zola. Paris 1936
96 Schieder (note 61), Vol. 5, Stuttgart 1981, pp. 912–925
97 Patricia Leighten: Re-Ordering the Universe. Picasso and Anarchism, 1897–1914. Princeton 1989, pp. 15 ff.
98 Leighten (note 97), pp. 17 ff.
99 Leighten (note 97), pp. 19 ff.; Blunt/Pool (note 76), pp. 11 ff.
100 Leighten (note 97), pp. 26 ff.
101 Blunt/Pool (note 76), pp. 18 ff.; Hans H. Hofstätter: Symbolismus und die Kunst der Jahrhundertwende, Cologne 1965, pp. 150 ff.; Symbolismus in Europa (exhibition catalogue). Baden-Baden 1976; Bildwelten des Symbolismus. Neuss 1985; on the predecessors of the most important poses of Symbolist art, see also Hans Jürgen Hansen: Das pompöse Zeitalter. Oldenburg and Hamburg 1970, pp. 113 ff.
102 Blunt/Pool (note 76), ill. 91, 92 and text
103 Wiegand (note 1), p. 45; Hofstätter (note 101), pp. 128 ff. Andres McLaren Young, Margaret MacDonald, Robin Spencer and Hamish Miles: The Paintings of James McNeill Whistler. 2 vols., New Haven (CT) and London 1980
104 Glaesemer (note 18), pp. 208 ff., 215 ff.
105 For example "Blaue Stunde" by Max Klinger, which was correctly pointed out in this connection by Wiegand (note I), pp. 46 f.: Max Klinger 1857–1920. Wege zum Gesamtkunstwerk. Mainz 1984, no. 23, p. 269
106 Lexikon der christlichen Ikonographie, Vol. 2, Freiburg im Breisgau 1970, pp. 7 ff.; Dorothea Forstner: Die Welt der Symbole, Innsbruck ²1967, p. 125
107 Latest complete description: Hans Gercke (ed.): Blau: Farbe der Ferne. Heidelberg 1990
108 Wiegand (note 1), p. 45
109 Lexikon (note 106); Forstner (note 106), ibid.
110 Anatoly Podosik, in Glaesemer (note 18), pp. 177–191
111 Podosik (note 110), pp. 186 ff.
112 Wiegand (note 1), pp. 186 ff.; Daix/Boudaille (note 86), pp. 58 ff.; Palau (note 17), pp. 339 ff.; Blunt/Pool (note 76), pp. 20 f.
113 Palau (note 17), pp. 340 f.; Glaesemer (note 18), pp. 186–194
114 Marilyn McCully, in Glaesemer (note 18), pp. 166–176
115 Daix, in Glaesemer (note 18), pp. 58 ff.

116 McCully (note 114), p. 170
117 McCully (note 114), p. 176
118 Wiegand (note 1), p. 50, note 75
119 McCully (note 114), pp. 168 ff.
120 Gilot/Lake (note 1), p. 77
121 Cabanne (note 86), pp. 153 ff.; Palau (note 17), pp. 380–437; Daix/Boudaille (note 86), p. 65
122 Wiegand (note 1) pp. 54 f.; Daix/Boudaille (note 86), p. 65
123 Cf. Daix/Boudaille (note 86), pp. 193, 197 f.; Blunt/Pool (note 76), p. 21
124 Wiegand (note 1), p. 54; Daix/Boudaille (note 86), p. 65
125 Palau (note 17), pp. 371 ff.; Jeanine Warnod: Bateau-Lavoir. Wiege des Kubismus. 1892–1914. Geneve 1976
126 Palau (note 17), p. 374; Warnod (note 125), pp. 50 ff. ; Wiegand (note 1), p. 42; Rubin (note 13), p. 56
127 Daix/Boudaille (note 86), p. 78; Wiegand (note 1), pp. 50 ff.; Palau (note 17), pp. 434 ff.
128 Wiegand (note 1), p. 42; Daix/Boudaille (note 86), p. 54; Palau (note 17), p. 376; Warnod (note 125), pp. 73 ff. and passim. Also, a personal account, which is however of no value for art history: Fernande Olivier: Picasso and His Friends. New York 1965
129 Warnod (note 125), pp. 14 ff., 55 ff., 64
130 Daix/Boudaille (note 86), no. XI 10
131 Daix/Boudaille (note 86), no. XII 23
132 Leighten (note 97), pp. 52 f.
133 Palau (note 17), p. 394
134 Œuvres complètes de Guillaume Apollinaire. 4 vols., Paris 1965–1966, here: Vol. 3
135 Leighten (note 97), pp. 53–63; in general: Hajo Düchting: Apollinaire zur Kunst. Texte und Kritik 1905–1918. Cologne 1989; Leroy C. Breunig and Susan Suleiman (ed.): Apollinaire on Art. Essays and Reviews. 1902–1918, London 1972
136 Leighten (note 97), p. 60
137 For this reason one must rule out superficial and derivative works such as Mary Mathews Gedo: Art as Autobiography. Chicago (IL) and London 1980
138 Leighten (note 97), pp. 69–73
139 G. Kamber: Max Jacob and the Poetics of Cubism. Baltimore and London 1971; P. Andreu: Vie et mort de Jacob. Paris 1982
140 Leighten (note 97), pp. 63–69; Keith Beaumont: Alfred Jarry. A Critical and Biographical Study. Leicester 1984
141 Daix/Boudaille (note 86), p. 66
142 Wiegand (note 1), pp. 55 f.; Denis Rouart and Daniel Wildenstein: Edouard Manet. Catalogue raisonné. 2 vols., Lausanne and Paris , Vol. 1, no. 52: Cooper (note 79), pp. 33 ff.; Richard Thomson: Seurat. Oxford 1985, pp. 147 ff., 214 ff. In general: Roland Berger and Dietmar Winkler: Der Zirkus in der bildenden Kunst. Stuttgart 1983; Francis Haskell: The Sad Clown. Some Notes on a 19th Century Myth, in: Ulrich Finke (ed.): French 19th-Century Painting and Literature. Manchester 1972, pp. 2–16
143 Palau (note 17), p. 399
144 Wiegand (note 1), p. 56; Palau (note 17), p. 416; Daix/Boudaille (note 86), p. 76
145 The following text refers to:: E. A. Carmen jr.: Picasso. The Saltimbanques (exhibition catalogue). Washington (DC) 1980, and

ibid.: The Saltimbanques, Sketchbook no. 35, 1905. In: Glimcher (note 53), pp. 9–50

146 Daix/Boudaille (note 86), no. XII.17

147 Palau (note 17), p. 143. fig. 1106; Zervos (note 12), vol. 22, no. 217

148 Palau (note 17), pp. 417 ff.; Daix/Boudaille (note 86), p. 272

149 Edgar Wind: Pagan Mysteries in the Renaissance. London 1958, pp. 31 ff.; Andor Pigler: Barockthemen. Budapest ²1974, vol. 2, pp. 102 ff.

150 P.P. Rubens. Des Meisters Gemälde, ed. by Rudolf Oldenbourg, Berlin and Leipzig n.d. (1921), p. 434

151 When Picasso visits "El Guayaba" in Barcelona together with Fernande in 1906, he is confronted by a whole series of reproductions, including the "Mona Lisa" and Rubens "Three Graces". In a photo taken at this time, Picasso is sitting directly under this picture postcard – Palau (note 17), p. 438; Blunt/Pool (note 76), frontispiece; see also the ill. in the appendix, p. 687

152 Palau (note 17), pp. 432–435; Daix/Boudaille (note 86), pp. 282–286

153 Blunt/Pool (note 76), fig. 162, 163

154 Daix/Boudaille (note 86), p. 80

155 Wiegand (note 1), pp. 60, 63; Palau (note 17), pp. 466–485; Daix/Boudaille (note 86), pp. 92 ff.; Rubin (note 13), pp. 58 f. – Giry (note 85), pp. 91 f.

156 Rubin (note 13), p. 58

157 Standard work: James Johnson Sweeney: Picasso and Iberian Sculpture. In: "Art Bulletin" 23 (1941), pp. 191–198

158 Wiegand (note 1), pp. 58 f.; Palau (note 17), pp. 438–465; Daix/Boudaille (note 86), pp. 85–92

159 Wiegand (note 1), pp. 60–64; Palau (note 17), pp. 486–508: Rubin (note 13), pp. 86 f.; Barr (note 13); Günter Bandmann: Pablo Picasso. Les Demoiselles d'Avignon. Stuttgart 1965; Michael Hoog: Les Demoiselles d'Avignon et la peinture à Paris en 1907–1908. In: "Gazette des Beaux-Arts" 82 (1973), pp. 209–226; Leo Steinberg: The Philosophical Brothel. In: "The Art News" 71 (1972), pp. 20–29, 38–47; Gedo (note 137), pp. 75 ff.

160 Les Demoiselles d'Avignon (exhibition catalogue). Musée Picasso, Paris. 2 vols., Paris 1988

161 Catalogue of the "Demoiselles" (note 160), vol. 2, pp. 367 ff., 489 ff., 547 ff.

162 Completely reproduced in: Catalogue of the "Demoiselles" (note 160), vol. 1

163 Cf. the still inadequate descriptions in the catalogue (note 161)

164 Cf. Catalogue of the "Demoiselles" (note 161)

165 William Rubin: From Narrative to "Iconic" in Picasso. In: "Art Bulletin" 65, (1983), pp. 615–649, bases his argument concerning this influence on his pre-dating of the Trocadero visit, which according to Picasso himself took place in the fall of 1907, to the summer, i. e. before the painting was finished. This is now the prevailing opinion – cf. catalogue of the "Demoiselles" (note 161)

166 It has been established that Picasso saw so-called "Negro" sculptures as early as 1906 in Martisse's studio, without being influenced to take over their forms directly. – Wiegand (note 1), p. 60. This entire unoriginal thesis has been solidly fixed in Picasso research since Barr (note 13, under the influence of a thencurrent publication: Robert Goldwater: Primitivism in Modern Art. New York and London 1938. A more recent, expanded treatment of it is: William Rubin: "Primitivism" in 20th Century Art (exhibition catalogue). New York 1984

167 This was already viewed correctly by Pierre Daix in his pioneering investigation, in which he also proves that African sculptures with forms similar to Picasso's did not reach France until 1920 – Pierre Daix: "Il n'y a pas d'art nègre dans Les Demoiselles d'Avignon". In: "Gazette des Beaux-Arts" 86 (1970), pp. 247–270

168 Catalogue of the "Demoiselles" (note 160), vol. 2, p. 642

169 Michel Leja: "Le Vieux Marcheur" and "Les Deux risques". Picasso, Prostitution, Venereal Disease and Maternity 1899–1907. In: "Art History" 8 (1985), pp. 66–81; all of this is again treated extensively by Rubin. In: Catalogue of the "Demoiselles" (note 160), vol. 2, pp. 419 ff.

170 Catalogue of the "Demoiselles" (note 160), vol. 1, and the explications in vol.2

171 The direct model was a painting by Rubens in London, a variant of which hangs in the Prado in Madrid and well-known to Picasso – Rubens (note 150), pp. 344, 432

172 Mario Denti: Due "demoiselles" di tradizione ellenistica. Sul ruolo dell'arte antica nella formazione del Cubismo. In: Prospettiva 47 (1986), pp. 75–87

173 Boime (note 35), fig. 13

174 Cicero: De inventione II, 1 – Werner Spies has pointed out the connection (note 7), pp. 23 f.

175 Pliny the Younger: Naturalis historia, vol.35, §§ 65 and 66

176 Bandmann (note 159), pp. 26 ff.; Catalogue of the "Demoiselles" (note 160), vol. 2, pp. 647–688 (a complication of all the relevant remarcs by contemporaries, from Apollinaire to Vollard)

177 Not until 1924 did the patron of the arts Jacques Doucet buy the picture at the instigation of the Surrealists Breton and Aragon, who reproducced it in 1925 in their journal "La Révolution surréaliste" for the first time in France. Cf. note 224

178 The standard exposition is in Rensselaer W. Lee: Ut pictura poesis. The humanistic theory of painting. In: "Art Bulletin" 22 (1940), pp. 197–269

179 Norman Bryson: Word and Image. French Painting of the Ancien Régime. Cambridge (MA) 1981, especially pp. 154–178; M.H. Abrams: Spiegel und Lampe. Romantische Theorie und die Tradition der Kritik. Munich 1978, especially pp. 261 ff.

180 Clearly and concisely reviewed by Werner Busch, in: "Kritische Berichte" 9 (1981), pp. 35–50

181 Cf. Gottfried Boehm: Einleitung. In: Konrad Fiedler: Schriften zur Kunst I. Munich 1971, pp. XXI-LXI

182 Werner Hofmann: Grundlagen der modernen Kunst. 1966, especially pp. 166 ff.; Robert Rosenblum: Modern Painting and the Northern Romantic Tradition. London 1975

183 Hajo Düchting: Paul Cézanne. 1839–1906. Nature into Art, Cologne 1989, especially pp. 227 ff.; Catalogue of "Demoiselles" (note 160), vol. 1, pp. 6–10

184 Boehm (note 181), pp. XXVII ff.; Marianne L. Teuber: Formvorstellung und Kubismus oder Pablo Picasso und William James. In: Kubismus. Künstler-Themen-Werke- 1907–1920 (exibition cat.) Cologne 1982, pp. 9–57, especially. pp. 12 ff.

185 Here Teuber overestimates the direct formal influence of the drawings of objects that are included in James' book to illustrate his theses (note 184), p. 38

186 Cf. Rubin: "Primitivism" (note 166)

187 On Rousseau's static characterization of Cubism, cf. Warnod (note 125), p. 125, and in general Rubin: "Primitivism" (note 166)

188 The concept was minted by Daniel-Henry Kahnweiler: The Rise of Cubism. New York 1949

189 William Rubin: Picasso and Braque. Pioneering Cubism. New York 1989, p. 345. On the general history of the collaboration between Picasso and Braque, ibid. pp. 9–56, 336–414; Pierre Daix: Le journal du Cubism. Geneva 1982, pp. 43–67, 98–109; John Golding: Cubism. A History and an Analysis. 1907–1914. London ²1968, pp. 47–137

190 Rubin, Picasso and Braque (note 189), p. 342

191 In spring 1910 Braque painted a "Woman with Mandolin" as the first vertical oval in Cubism (a horizontal oval had preceded it shortly before) – Nicole Worms de Romilly and Jean Laude: Braque, le cubisme, fin 1907–1914. Paris 1982, no. 71 and no. 65. He painted a variant of it in the traditional vertical-rectangle format – Romilly no. 72. Picasso immediately responded with a woman playing the mandolin in a vertical oval – Pierre Daix and Joan Rosselet: Le Cubisme de Picasso. Neuchâtel 1979, no. 341. Then he also painted a variant on Braque's vertical-rectangle painting using this motif – see also Rubin: Picasso and Braque (note 189), no. 107–112

192 Christian Gelhaar: Pablo Picassos Stilleben "Pains et compotier aux fruits sur une table". Metamorphosen einer Bildidee. In: "Pantheon" 28 (1970), pp. 127–140

193 Rubin, Picasso and Braque (note 189), p. 18

194 The first painting is a still life with the letters "Gil B" (for "Gil Blas") – Romilly (note 191), no. 53. On the friendly competition in 1912 using this element of style, cf. Rubin: Picasso and Braque (note 189), p. 21. Picasso was referring directly to Braque's painting "Violin, Mozart, Kubelick" – Romilly (note 191), no. 121

195 On the abovementioned still life, cf. the exhibition catalogue "Stilleben in Europa" Münster and Baden-Baden 1979, passim (with numerous examples); Norbert Schneider: The Art of the Still Life. Still Life Painting in the Early Modern Period. Cologne 1990, especially pp. 186 ff.

196 Daix: Cubism (note 189), pp. 82 ff.; Golding (note 189), pp. 28 ff.

197 Daix: Cubism (note 189), pp. 69 ff.; Golding (note 189), pp. 24 ff.

198 Daix: Cubism (note 189), pp. 138–160

199 Daix: Cubism (note 189), pp. 70 ff.

200 Daix: Cubism (note 189), p. II. On the significance and history of the "Salons" Georg

Friedrich Koch: Die Kunstausstellung. Ihre Geschichte von den Anfängen bis zum Ausgang des 18. Jahrhunderts. Berlin 1967, especially pp. 251–274 (19th century)

201 Daix: Cubism (note 189), p. II.
202 Rubin: Picasso and Braque (note 189), p. 336
203 Rubin: Picasso and Braque (note 189), pp. 346 ff. On Kahnweiler's person and his business policy, cf. Pierre Assouline: Der Mann, der Picasso verkaufte. Daniel-Henry Kahnweiler und seine Künstler. Bergisch-Gladbach 1990; Patrick-Gilles Persin: Daniel-Henry Kahnweiler. L'aventure d'un grand marchand. Paris 1990
204 Daix: Cubism (note 189), p. 96
205 Daix: Cubism (note 189), p. 96
206 Rubin: Picasso and Braque (note 189), p. 389
207 Rubin: Picasso and Braque (note 189), pp. 41–45
208 Rubin: Picasso and Braque (note 189), p. 14
209 Rubin: Picasso and Braque (note 189), pp. 24–35
210 Daix: Cubism (note 189), p. 67. The first painting in which Picasso used the words "Ma Jolie" to refer to his love for Eva Gouel was produced in winter 1911/12 – Rubin: Picasso and Braque (note 189), no. 201; Daix/Rosselet (note 191), no. 430
211 Daix/Rosselet (note 191), comments on no. 551 and 552. They prove that a different newspaper was used for no. 552 than for no. 551
212 Rubin: Picasso and Braque (note 189), p. 30
213 Cf. Daix/Rosselet (note 191), no. 596 and 597
214 Rubin: Picasso and Braque (note 189), pp. 30 f. On collage and its history in 20th-century art: Herta Wescher: Die Collage. Cologne 1968; Prinzip Collage, Neuwied and Berlin 1968; Helen Hutton: The Technique of Collage. New York 1968
215 This concept, like that of "analytical Cu-. bism" was minted by Kahnweiler (note 188), p. 34
216 William C. Seitz (ed.): The Art of Assemblage. New York 1961. This is the epochal catalogue of an exhibition in The Museum of Modern Art in New York. After the exhibition this term came into general use
217 cf. Spies (note 12), p. 72
218 Daix: Cubism (note 189), pp. 86–93; Golding (note 189), pp. 159 ff.
219 Daix: Cubism (note 189), pp. 78–81. On this movement: Maurizio Calvesi: Der Futurismus. Cologne 1987; Futurismo & Futurismi. Catalogue of the exibition in the Palazzo Grassi in Venice. Milano 1986
220 Daix: Cubism (note 189), pp. 94 f. For "De Stijl" in general: Carsten-Peter Warncke: The Ideal as Art. De Stijl 1917–1931. Cologne 1990; Mildred Friedman (ed.): De Stijl: 1917–1931. Visions of Utopia. Oxford ²1986
221 Daix: Cubism (note 189), pp. 115–117. In general on this: Camilla Gray: Das große Experiment. Die russische Kunst 1863–192. Cologne 1974
222 Daix: Cubism (note 189), pp. 118 f.
223 Daix: Cubism (note 189), pp. 120 f.
224 Rubin: Picasso and Braque (note 189), p. 359. Stieglitz visited Picasso in the same year to his Paris studio – ibid., p. 366. As

early as 1910 an article by Gelett Burgess – who had visited in Paris avant-garde in their studios, including Picasso – appeared in the American journal "Architectural Record". The "Demoiselles d'Avignon" was reproduced for the first time in this publication (note 160), vol. 2

225 Daix: Cubism (note 189), pp. 122–124
226 Wolfgang Venzmer: Adolf Hölzel. Leben und Werk. Stuttgart 1982, pp. 74 f. In general for the history of abstract art: Maurice Tuchman and Judi Freeman (ed.): Das Geistige in der Kunst. Abstrakte Malerei 1890–1985. Stuttgart 1988
227 Cf. Lipton (note 8), pp. 121 ff.
228 Wiegand (note 1), pp. 85–92; Cabanne (note 86), pp. 283–398
229 Rubin (note 13), pp. 178 f., 196–199
230 Rubin (note 13), pp. 196–199; Giovanni Carandente. In: Ulrich Weisner (ed.): Picassos Klassizismus. Werke 1914–1934, Bielefeld 1988, pp. 51 ff.
231 Rubin (note 13), pp. 398; Kenneth E. Silver. In: Weisner (note 230), p. 78
232 Rubin (note 13), p. 197
233 Silver (note 231), p. 78
234 Silver (note 231), pp. 77 f.; Kenneth E. Silver: Esprit de Corps. The Art of the Parisian Avant-Garde and the First World War. Princeton 1989
235 Elizabeth Cowling and Jennifer Mundy (ed.): On Classic Ground. Picasso, Léger, de Chirico and the New Classicism 1910–1930. London 1990
236 Marilyn McCully. In: Weisner (note 230), pp. 43–50
237 Silver (note 231), p. 83
238 Wiegand (note 1), p. 88 f.; Giulio Carlo Argan: Die Kunst des 20. Jahrhunderts, 1880–1940. Berlin 1990 (Propyläen Kunstgeschichte), pp. 192–231
239 Martin Battersby: The Decorative Twenties. London 1969; Nancy J. Troy: Modernism and the Decorative Arts in France. New Haven (CT) 1991
240 Douglas Cooper: Picasso Theatre. New York ²1987; William S. Liebermann: Picasso and the Ballet. New York 1946
241 Angelika Herbert-Muthesius: Bühne und Bildende Kunst im Futurismus. Diss. Heidelberg 1985; Cooper (note 240), p. 22
242 Sabine Vogel: Pablo Picasso als Bühnenbild- und Kostümentwerfer für die Ballets Russes. Diss. Cologne 1983, pp. 75–101; Liebermann (note 240), p. 272
243 Silver (note 231), p. 82
244 Wolfgang Storch: Bühne und Bildende Kunst im 20. Jahrhundert. Hannover 1968, pp. 46–82
245 Cooper (note 240) pp. 37–43
246 Cooper (note 240) pp. 43–49
247 Cooper (note 240) pp. 52 f.
248 Cooper (note 240) pp. 61 f.
249 Cooper (note 240) pp. 55–61
250 Odalisque, after Ingres, 1907 – Rubin (note 13), p. 219. On the significance of Ingres as a model for the development of the "Demoiselles d'Avignon", cf. the Catalogue of the "Demoiselles" (note 160)
251 Kurt Bauch: Klassik-Klassizität-Klassizismus. In: "Das Werk des Künstlers" I. (1939/40). pp. 429–440
252 On the significance for Cubisme of Ingres' arbitrary treatment of human proportions,

cf. Daix: Cubism (note 189), p. 20
253 Numerous proofs in Rubin: (note 13), pp. 122 ff.
254 Rubin (note 13), ill. 415, 414, 438, 443, 445, 450, 451, 491. The photograph used by Picasso for painting his Olga in an armchair is now in the Musée Picasso in Paris (ill. p. 245). So far Daix, in Weisner (note 230), pp. 14 ff., has been the only one to explore this connection
255 On the history of photography from the "camera obscura" to Niépce – Helmut Gernsheim: Geschichte der Photographie. Die ersten hundert Jahre. Frankfurt am Main 1983, pp. 11 ff., 42 ff.; Beaumont Newhall: Geschichte der Photographie. Munich 1989, pp. 8–26. On the history of photography as a source of models for painters, cf., besides Coke (note 91), in particular: Erika Billeter (ed.): Malerei und Photographie im Dialog von 1840 bis heute. Zurich 1977
256 Gernsheim (note 255), pp. 293 f.; Michel F. Braive: Das Zeitalter der Photographie. Von Niépce bis heute. Munich 1965, pp. 139–147
257 Gernsheim (note 255), pp. 723 ff.; Newhall (note 255), pp. 75 ff., 145 ff.
258 Gernsheim (note 255), pp. 568 ff.
259 Gernsheim (note 255), pp. 730 ff.; Newhall (note 255), pp. 155 ff., 173 ff.
260 Rubin: Picasso and Braque (note 189). pp. 359, 366
261 Gernsheim (note 255), pp. 733 ff., Newhall (note 255), pp. 173–198; François Mathey: Le réalisme américain. Geneva 1978, pp. 119–148
262 Newhall (note 255), pp. 205–222; Emilio Bertonati: Das experimentelle Photo in Deutschland 1918–1940. Munich 1978; Deren van Coke: Avantgarde-Fotografie 1919–1939. Munich 1982; Jeanine Fiedler (ed.): Fotografie am Bauhaus. Berlin 1990; Hans Gotthard Vierhuff: Die Neue Sachlichkeit. Malerei und Fotografie. Cologne 1980; Les Réalismes. 1919–1939 (exhibition catalogue). Centre Georges Pompidou and Berlin, Munich 1980
263 Silver, in: Weisner (note 230), pp. 85 f., Rubin (note 13), no. 421
264 Carandente, in: Weisner (note 230), p. 59; Guntram Koch and Hellmut Sichtermann: Römische Sarkophage. Munich 1982, no. 180 (pointed out by U. Heinen, Cologne)
265 Bloch (note 12), vol. 1, no. 51, 57–61
266 Brigitte Leal, in: Weisner (note 230), pp. III ff.; Zervos (note 12), vol. 5, no. 107–130
267 Jürgen Thimme: Picasso und die Antike. Karlsruhe 1974, pp. 16 f.
268 Spies (note 12), pp. 89 f.; Christa Lichtenstern: Pablo Picasso. Denkmal für Apollinaire. Frankfurt am Main 1988
269 Daniel-Henry Kahnweiler: Les Sculptures de Picasso. Paris 1949
270 Zervos (note 12), vol. 5, no. 269 ff.; Spies (note 12), p. 92; Lichtenstern (note 268), pp. 48 ff.
271 Wiegand (note 1), p. 94; Lichtenstern (note 268), p. 50
272 Robert Short: Dada und Surrealismus. Zurich 1984; Robert Lebel, Michel Sanouillet and Patrick Waldberg: Der Surrealismus. Cologne 1987
273 Rubin (note 13), pp. 224 f., 252–255, 276

f., 306 ff.; Wiegand (note 1), pp. 94 ff.; László Glózer: Picasso und der Surrealismus. Cologne 1974; John Golding: Picasso and Surrealism. In: Roland Penrose and John Golding (ed.): Picasso in Retrospect 1881–1973. London 1973

274 Rubin (note 13), p. 225
275 Wiegand (note 1), pp. 95 f.
276 Wiegand (note 1), p. 96
277 Glózer (note 273), pp. 51 ff.
278 Christa Lichtenstern: Picasso "Tête de Femme". Zwischen Klassik und Surrealismus. Frankfurt am Main 1980, pp. 31 ff.
279 Lichtenstern (note 278), p. 57
280 Wiegand (note 1), p. 96
281 Spies (note 12), pp. 93 f.; Lichtenstern (note 268), pp. 20–23
282 Lichtenstern (note 268), pp. 35–45. Only three of the four original models have survived
283 Bloch (note 12), no. 82 ff.; Dore Ashton: A Fable of Modern Art. Berkeley 1991
284 Jean Seznec: The Survival of the Pagan Gods. New York 1953; M.D. Henkel; Nederlandsche Ovidius-Illustraties van de 15e tot de 18e eeuw. In: "Oud Holland" 39 (1921), pp. 149–187; Pigler (note 149), vol. 2, passim
285 Cf. Pigler (note 14), vol. 2
286 Bloch (note 12), vol. 1, no. 207, 208, 214. Bloch (loc cit.), no. 188 variates Rembrandt's etching "Der Zeichner nach dem Modell" from 1639 – K.G. Boon: Rembrandt. Das graphische Werk. Vienna and Munich 1963, plate 151 (B. 192). In general for this: Janie Cohen: Picasso-Rembrandt-Picasso (exibition catalogue). Amsterdam 1990
287 Lichtenstern (note 268), pp. 82 f.
288 Wiegand (note 1), pp. 100 f. ; Rubin (note 13), pp. 253, 276 f., 307; Lichtenstern (note 278), pp. II ff.; Gilot (note 1), passim
289 Lichtenstern (note 278), pp. 34 f.
290 Glózer (note 273), pp. 46 ff.; Jan Runnquist: Minotaurus. Stockholm 1963
291 Alexandra Parigoris, in: Weisner (note 230), p. 28; Martin Vogel: Apollinisch und Dionysisch. Geschichte eines genialen Irrtums. Regensburg 1966
292 Wiegand (note 1), pp. 100 f.; Gilot (note 1), pp. 165 ff., 310 ff.
293 Helmut Knirim: Tradition und individuelle Schaffensweise. Studien zum Werk Picassos. Frankfurt am Main 1980, pp. 39 f.
294 Wiegand (note 1), pp. 102 ff.
295 Schieder (note 61), vol. 7, Stuttgart 1979, pp. 663–685
296 Max Imdahl: Picassos Guernica. Frankfurt am Main 1985, p. 47
297 Guernica. Kunst und Politik am Beispiel Guernica. Picasso und der Spanische Bürgerkrieg (exibition catalogue). Berlin 1975, pp. 22 f.
298 Imdahl (note 296); Guernica (note 297); Anthony Blunt: Picasso's "Guernica". London 1969; Ellen C. Oppler (ed.): Picasso's Guernica. New York and London; Herschel B. Chipp: Picasso's Guernica. Berkeley 1988
299 Imdahl (note 296) writes on p. 54 that the location is a "cellar viewed from inside and outside". This is surely an oversimplification. Chipp's interpretation is preferable (note 298), pp. 134 f.
300 Cf. Klaus Lankheit: Das Triptychon als Pa-

thosformel. Heidelberg 1959
301 Chipp (note 298), pp. 70 ff.; Rudolf Arnheim: Picassos Guernica. The Genesis of a Painting. Berkeley 1962; Zervos (note 12), vol. 9, no. 1–65
302 Alice Doumain Tankard: Picasso's Guernica after Rubens' Horrors of War. Philadelphia (PA) 1984
303 Knirim (note 293), p. 127
304 Guernica (note 297), p. 60
305 Guernica (note 297), p. 59; Knirim (note 293), p. 123
306 Guernica (note 297), pp. 52 f.
307 Cf. Jean-Clarence Lambert: Picasso. Dessins de tauromachie 1917–1960. Paris 1960; in detail also the literature mentioned in notes 296–298
308 Werner Spies: Pablo Picasso. Traum und Lüge Francos. Frankfurt am Main 1968, pp. 28 ff.
309 Zervos (note 12), vols. 7 and 8, passim; Rubin (note 13), passim
310 Cf. René Passeron: Encyclopédie du Surréalisme. Paris 1975; José Pierre: Le surréalisme. Paris 1973
311 Imdahl (note 296), pp. 22–40. The terms already in: Max Raphael: Raumgestaltungen. Der Beginn der modernen Kunst im Kubismus und im Werk von Georges Braque. Frankfurt am Main/New York 1986, pp. 128 ff. (written in 1943)
312 Guernica (note 297), p. 66
313 Zervos (note 12), vol. 9, no. 46–57, 70–77; Arnheim (note 301), no. 46–61
314 Zervos (note 12), vol. 10, no. 202–249, 331–358, 387–428, 458–485, 510, 511, 512; Christian Zervos: Carnet de dessins de Picasso. Paris 1948; Glimcher (note 53), no. 106, 109, 110, 112
315 Laurence Bertrand Dorléac: Die französische Kunstszene zwischen 1940 und 1944. In: Picasso im Zweiten Weltkrieg, 1939 bis 1945 (exibition catalogue), Museum Ludwig, Cologne 1988, pp. 129–143
316 Cabanne (note 86), vol. 2, p. 51–92; Rubin (note 13), pp. 350–352; Wiegand (note 1), pp. 115–121
317 Dorléac (note 315) pp. 141 f.
318 In 1946 Alfred H. Barr published a revised edition of this catalogue (note 13). It subsequently became a standard work on Picasso and had considerable influence on the public image of the artist. On the history of Picasso's art in the USA, cf. Rubin (note 13), pp. 348 f.; Picasso im Zweiten Weltkrieg (note 315), pp. 261–263
319 Picasso im Zweiten Weltkrieg (note 315), p. 280
320 Rubin (note 13), p. 351; Wiegand (note 1), p. 121; Picasso im Zweiten Weltkrieg (note 315), pp. 286–289
321 Completely reproduced in: Marie-Laure Bernadac: Picasso écrits. Paris 1989, pp. 258 ff.
322 Rubin (note 13), p. 353
323 Cabanne (note 86), vol. 2, pp. 106–143; Wiegand (note 1), pp. 122–129
324 Rubin (note 13), p. 353; Wiegand (note 1), pp. 122 f.
325 Wiegand (note 1), p. 122
326 Rubin (note 13), p. 381
327 Cf. Picasso's own comment on this in: Pierre Daix: Picasso und der Krieg. In: Picasso im Zweiten Weltkrieg (note 315), p. 88
328 Zervos (note 12), vol. 14, no. 87, 88, 93–100

329 Zervos (note 12), vol. 14, no. 72–76; Rubin (note 13), p. 380
330 Picasso im Zweiten Weltkrieg (note 315), p. 60
331 See for this Kahnweiler's opinion, in: Wiegand (note 1), p. 126
332 See the models in: Kindlers Malerei Lexikon. Munich 1976, vol. 3, pp. 168, 172, vol. 5, p. 146, vol. 8, p. 315
333 Wiegand (note 1), pp. 122 f.
334 Ernst-Gerhard Güse and Bernd Rau: Pablo Picasso. Die Lithographien. Stuttgart 1988, pp. 20–22, catalogue no. 144, 145, 146, 159–161, 504–507, 536, 537, 543–549
335 Rubin (note 13), p. 384; Wiegand (note 1), p. 129
336 Rubin (note 13), p. 417
337 Felix Philipp Ingold: Picasso in Russland. Materialien zur Wirkungsgeschichte. Zurich 1973
338 Claude Roy: Pablo Picasso. La guerre et la paix. Paris 1954. For the tradition of these themes in art, cf. Pigler (note 149), p. 491
339 Pierre Schneider: Matisse. Paris 1984, pp. 241–275
340 Schneider (note 339), pp. 670–674
341 Dor de la Souchère: Picasso in Antibes. New York and London 1960
342 Spies (note 12), pp. 179 and 251
343 Spies (note 12), pp. 250, 240–246, 260
344 Spies (note 12), pp. 250 f.
345 Arturo Schwarz: Marcel Duchamp. New York 1975, text to the notes 60–63; Anne d'Harnoncourt and Kynaston McShine: Marcel Duchamp. Munich 1989, passim
346 The Arcimboldo Effect (exhibition catalogue), Palazzo Grassi, Venice. Milano 1987
347 Cf. Spies (note 12), pp. 250 f.
348 Spies (note 12), p. 260
349 Spies (note 12), pp. 204–208; Lichtenstern (note 278), pp. 45 f.
350 Cf. Zervos (note 12), vol. 12, no. 87–96, 115–141, 152, 220, 221, 238–241, 291, 297–306; Spies (note 12), p. 206
351 Spies (note 12), pp. 206–208
352 Wiegand (note 1), p. 118
353 Picasso in Vallauris. Paris 1951; Georges Ramié: Céramique de Picasso. Paris 1984
354 Cf. Erika Simon: Die griechischen Vasen. Munich 1976
355 Cf. Tamara Préaud and Serge Gauthier: Die Kunst der Keramik im 20. Jahrhundert. Fribourg and Würzburg 1982
356 André Fremigier: La gloire de Picasso. In: "Revue de l'art" 1968/69, pp. 115–122; Daniel-Henry Kahnweiler: Picasso. Keramik. Hannover 1970; Pablo Picasso Céramiques. Collection Jacqueline Picasso. Vallauris 1986; Picasso Céramiques (exhibition catalogue), Galerie Beyeler, Basel. Basel 1990
357 Fernand Mourlot: Picasso. Litographs. Boston (MA) 1970; Güse/Rau (note 334)
358 Wiegand (note 1), pp. 129–133
359 Wiegand (note 1), pp. 131 f.
360 Güse, in: Güse/Rau (note 334), pp. 20–22
361 Wiegand (note 1), p. 121 f.
362 Wiegand (note 1), p. 122 and note 192
363 Cabanne (note 186), vol. 2, pp. 93–231; Rubin (note 13), pp. 380–385
364 Especially characteristic of this is: Pierre Dufour: Picasso 1950–1968. Biographical and Critical Study. Geneva 1969
365 Zervos (note 12), vol. 13, no. 36; Rubin (note 13), p. 374

366 Jaime Sabartés: A los toros avec Picasso. Monte Carlo and Cologne 1961; Jean-Clarence Lambert: Picasso. Dessins de tauromachie 1917–1960. Paris 1960. Picasso created this series to illustrate the book, published in 250 copies: José Delgado alias Pepe Illo: La Tauromaquia, o Arte de torear, Barcelona 1959 – Bloch (note 12), vol. 1, no. 950–976 and p. 308 no. 95

367 Tomás Harris: Goya. Engravings and Lithographs. 2 vols., Oxford 1964; Pierre Gassier and Juliet Wilson: The Life and Complete Work of Francisco Goya. New York 1981, no. 1149–1243; Pierre Gassier: The Drawings of Goya. The Sketches, Studies and Individual Drawings. London 1975, pp. 327–429. The connection with Goya is also visible in the book illustrated by Picasso, because its first edition from 1804 was already used by Goya as a source

368 Spies (note 12), p. 270

369 Cf. Zervos (note 12), vol. 3, no. 346, vol. 5, no. 200 ff. On 3 June 1961 Picasso also created a lithograph entitled "Football", which is a variation on this figurine – Güse/Rau (note 334), no. 721

370 Spies (note 12), p. 296

371 Seit 45. Die Kunst unserer Zeit, vol. 1, Brussels 1970, p. 15

372 Seit 45. (note 371), pp. 13–158

373 Seit 45 (note 371), pp. 161–298; Seit 45, vol. 2, pp. 8–96

374 Klaus Gallwitz: Picasso at 90: The Late Work. New York and London 1971

375 The only serious and thorough – though narrowed by its Marxist approach – critique of Picasso's late work was published by: John Berger: The Success and Failure of Picasso. Harmondsworth and Baltimore (MD) 1965, New York 1989

376 Cf. Robert Melville: Henry Moore. Sculptures and Drawings. 1921–1969. London 1971

377 Francis Bacon (exhibition catalogue). London 1985. For Moore and Bacon in context: Susan Compton: Englische Kunst im 20. Jahrhundert. Malerei und Plastik. Munich 1987, pp. 296–309, 328–341

378 Bloch (note 12), vol. 1, no. 864 ff.

379 Bloch (note 12), vol. 1, no. 906 ff.

380 Hans Platte: Farbige Grafik unserer Zeit. Stuttgart 1960; M. Rothenstein: Linocuts and Woodcuts. London 1962; Theodor Musper: Der Holzschnitt in fünf Jahrhunderten. Stuttgart 1964; W. Schürmeyer: Holzschnitt und Linolschnitt. Ravensburg 1964

381 Gaetan Picon: La chute d'Icare de Pablo Picasso. Geneve 1971

382 Spies (note 12), p. 300

383 Cf. Picon (note 381), pp. 99–103. Spies (note 12), p. 270, believes that Matisse's cut-out coloured papers were the decisive influence, but these works have a totally different formal structure. See on this: Jean Guichard-Meili: Matisse, gouaches découpées. Paris 1983

384 Cooper (note 240), fig. 416 f.

385 Nicholas Serota (ed.): Fernand Léger (exhibition catalogue). Munich 1988, p. 70

386 Werner Schmalenbach: Léger, Cologne 1977, especially no. 43–48

387 John Richardson: Picasso's Atelier and Other Recent Works. In: "Burlington Maga-

zine" 99 (1957), pp. 183–193; Gallwitz (note 374), pp. 136–142

388 Georges Wildenstein: The Paintings of J.A.D. Ingres. London 1954, no. 228

389 Daix: Cubism (note 189), pp. 20 f.

390 James Harding: Artistes Pompiers. French Academic Art in the 19th Century. London 1979, pp. 69–90

391 Picasso himself: "Matisse is dead, and he has willed me his Odalisques", Gallwitz (note 374), p. 116

392 Gallwitz (note 374), pp. 113–150

393 Rouart/Wildenstein (note 142), vol. 1, no. 67

394 Zervos (note 12), vol. 16, no. 316–319; Douglas Cooper: Les déjeuners. Paris 1962; Gallwitz (note 374), pp. 145–148

395 Gallwitz (note 374), pp. 148–350

396 Cf. Simon (note 354)

397 Gallwitz (note 374), pp. 125 f.

398 Rubin (note 13), pp. 395–403

399 Rubin (note 13), pp. 432–433

400 Daix: Cubism (note 189), p. 133

401 Jaime Sabartés: Picasso. Les ménines et la vie. Paris 1958; Gallwitz (note 374), pp. 142–144

402 Gallwitz (note 374), p. 117

403 Bacon (note 377), no. 9, 12, 13, 16, 25, 26

404 Cf. Jonathan Brown: Velázquez. Painter and Courtier. New Haven (CT) and London 1986, pp. 253–264

405 Quoted from Gallwitz (note 374), p. 143

406 Sabartés (note 401), pp. 10 f., 17 f.

407 Cf. for example Zervos (note 12), vol. 4, no. 298

408 Picon (note 381), pp. 23–45

409 Cabanne (note 86), pp. 295–458; Wiegand (note 1), pp. 125–144; Rubin (note 13), pp. 418–421

410 Wiegand (note 1), p. 123

411 Spies (note 12), pp. 311–315; Lichtenstern (note 268), pp. 84–88

412 Seit 45 (note 371), vol. 2, pp. 156–301; Tilman Osterwold: Pop Art. Cologne 1991

413 Seit 45 (note 371), pp. 201–242, 243–276; Osterwold (note 412), pp. 145–201

414 Jürgen Schilling: Aktionskunst. Lucerne 1978; W. Nöth: Strukturen des Happenings. Hildesheim and New York 1972

415 "The surprising artistic success of Buffet can probably be compared only with that of Pablo Picasso" – H. Read, in: Kindlers Malerei Lexikon (note 332), p. 193

416 Gert Schiff: Picasso. The Last Years, 1963–1973. New York 1983, p. 12

417 Gallwitz (note 374), p. 183; Schiff (note 416), p. 11

418 Cf. Zervos (note 12), vol. 23 ff.

419 Cf. Bloch (note 12), vol. 4, no. 2002–2009

420 Late Picasso. Paintings, Sculpture, Drawings, Prints 1953–1972 (exhibition catalogue). London 1988; Guy Scarpetta: Picasso Porno, in: "Art Press" 122 (1988), pp. 26 f.

421 Cf. Late Picasso (note 420); Gallwitz (note 374), pp. 151–181

422 Cf. Osterwold (note 412) and Seit 45 (note 371), vol. 2

423 Gottfried Fliedl: Gustav Klimt, 1862–1918. The World in Female Form. Cologne 1989, p. 120

424 Wiegand (note 1), p. 147; Ernst Kries and Otto Kurz: Die Legende vom Künstler. Vienna 1934, pp. 26. f.; Ingo F. Walther: Pablo Picasso 1881–1973. Genius of the Century.

Cologne 1986, p. 8

425 Cf. Kris/Kurz (note 425), pp. 95–100, 103–118

426 Mourlot (note 357), vol. 2, no. 117; Wiegand (note 1), pp. 130 f.; Güse/Rau (note 334), no. 220–344

427 John Rewald: Degas' Complete Sculpture. Catalogue Raisonné. San Francisco 1990; Jean Adhémar and Françoise Cachin: Degas. Radierungen. Litographien. Monotypien. Munich 1973

428 Finally: Werner Spies (ed.): Max Ernst (exhibition catalogue). London, Stuttgart and Düsseldorf 1991

429 Kris/Kurz (note 424), pp. 69–87; Margot and Rudolf Wittkower: Künstler – Außenseiter der Gesellschaft. Stuttgart ²1989, pp. 307–309

430 Hans Gerhard Evers: Peter Paul Rubens. Munich 1942, p. 31. Cf. also the biography in Plutarch, to whose description of Caesar is the basis of the theme treated by Rubens

431 Kris/Kurz (note 424), pp. 114–126; Wittkower (note 429), pp. 169–171

432 Wittkower (note 429), pp. 172–216

433 Cf. Erwin Panofsky: Idea. Berlin ³1975

C.-P. W

Bibliography

FULL TITLES OF CATALOGUES QUOTED IN THE CAPTIONS:
BAER: B. Baer: Catalogue raisonné de l'œuvre gravé et des monotypes 1935–1945. Suite aux catalogues de B. Geiser. Bern 1986. – BLOCH: G. Bloch: Pablo Picasso. Catalogue of the Printed Graphic Work 1904–1972. 4 vols. Bern 1968–1979. – DB: P. Daix and G. Boudaille: Picasso. The Blue and Rose Periods. A Catalogue Raisonné of the Paintings. Greenwich (CT) 1967 and London 1967. – DR: P. Daix and J. Rosselet: Picasso: The Cubist Years, 1907–1916. A Catalogue Raisonné of the Paintings and Related Works. Boston (MA) and London 1979. – GEISER: B. Geiser: Picasso. Peintre-Graveur. Catalogue illustré de l'œuvre gravé et lithographié 1899–1934. 2 vols. Bern 1933–1968. – MOURLOT: F. Mourlot: Picasso Lithographs. Boston (MA) 1970. – MPB: Museu Picasso: Catàleg de pintura i dibuix. Barcelona 1984. – MPP: M.L. Besnard-Bernadac, M. Richet and H. Seckel (eds.): The Musée Picasso. Catalogue of the Collection. 2 vols. Vol. I: Paintings, Papiers collés, Picture Reliefs, Sculptures, Ceramics. Vol. II: Drawings, Watercolours, Gouaches, Pastels. London 1986–1988. – PALAU: J. Palau i Fabre: Picasso. The Early Years, 1881–1907. New York 1980, Oxford 1981. – RAU: B. Rau: Pablo Picasso. Die Lithographien. Stuttgart 1988. – SPIES: W. Spies: The Sculpture by Picasso. With a Catalogue of the Works. London 1971. – ZERVOS: C. Zervos: Pablo Picasso. Vol. I-XXXIII. Paris 1932–1978 (Catalogue of the Works 1895–1972). The abbreviation Cat. indicates exhibition catalogue.

1. Bibliographies:
GAYA NUÑO, J.A.: Bibliografía critica y antológica de Picasso. San Juan (Puerto Rico) 1966. – KIBBEY, R.A.: Picasso. A Comprehensive Bibliography. New York and London 1977.

2. Catalogues raisonnés:
BAER, B.: Catalogue raisonné de l'œuvre gravé et des monotypes 1935–1945. Suite aux catalogues de B. Geiser. Bern 1986 (= Baer). – BESNARD-BERNADAC, M.L., M. RICHET and H. SECKEL (eds.): The Musée Picasso. Catalogue of the Collection. Vol. I: Paintings, Papiers Collés, Picture Reliefs, Sculptures, Ceramics. Vol. II: Drawings, Watercolours, Gouaches, Pastels. London 1986–1988 (= MPP). – BLOCH, G.: Pablo Picasso. Catalogue of the Printed Graphic Work, 1904–1972. 4 vols. Bern 1968–1979 (= Bloch). – CZWIKLITZER, C.: Picasso's Posters. New York 1971 (= Bloch). – DAIX, P. and G. BOUDAILLE: Picasso: The Blue and Rose Periods. A Catalogue Raisonné of the Paintings. Greenwich (CT) and London 1967 (= DB). – DAIX, P. and ROSSELET, J.: Picasso: The Cubist Years, 1907–1916. A Catalogue Raisonné of the Paintings and Related Works. Boston (MA) and London 1979 (= DR). – GEISER, B.: Picasso. Peintre-Graveur. Catalogue illustré de l'œuvre gravé et lithographié, 1899–1934. 2 vols. Bern 1933–1968 (= Geiser). – GIRAUDY, D. (ed.): Antibes: Catalogue raisonné des peintures, dessins, sculptures, céramiques, tapisseries au Musée d'Antibes. Antibes 1981. – GLIMCHER, A. and M. (ed.): Je suis le cahier. The Sketchbooks of Picasso. New York 1986. – GOEPPERT, S., H.C. GOEPPERT-FRANK and P. CRAMER: Pablo Picasso. Catalogue raisonné des livres illustrés. Geneva 1983. – LASARTE, J.A. DE (ed.): Museo Picasso. Catálogo I. Barcelona 1975. – LECALDANO, P. (ed.): The Complete Paintings of Picasso. Blue and Rose Periods. London and New York 1971, Harmondsworth 1987. – MINERVINO, F.: L'opera completa di Picasso cubista. Milan 1972. – MOURLOT, F.: Picasso Lithographs. Boston (MA) 1970 (= Mourlot). – Museu Picasso: Catàleg de pintura i dibuix. Museu Picasso. Textos de M. A. Capmany, M.T. Ocaña, J. Ainaud. Barcelona 1984 (= MPB). – PALAU I FABRE, J.: Picasso. The Early Years 1881–1907. New York 1980, Oxford 1981 (= Palau). – PALAU I FABRE, J.: Picasso Cubism 1907–1917. New York and London 1990. – RAMIÉ, A.: Picasso. Catalogue of the Edited Ceramic Works 1947–1971. Vallauris 1988. – RAMIÉ, A.: Picasso, Keramik. Bern 1980. – RAU, B.: Pablo Picasso. Die Lithographien. Stuttgart 1988. – RUBIN, W. (ed.): Picasso in the Collection of the Museum of Modern Art. New York 1972, 1980. – SPIES, W.: Sculpture by Picasso. With a Catalogue of the Works. New York 1971, London 1972 (= Spies). – ZERVOS, C.: Pablo Picasso. Vol. I-XXXIII (Vol. II in two parts; catalogue of works from 1895–1972;

catalogue of paintings; the sculptures, drawings, graphic works and ceramics are incomplete). Paris 1932–1978 (= Zervos).

3. Artist's writings, collections of quotations:
ARMITAGE, M. (ed.): Picasso. Two Statements. New York 1936. – ASHTON, D. (ed.): Picasso on Art: A Selection of Views. New York and London 1972, Harmondsworth 1980. – BERNADAC, M.L. and C. PIOT (eds.): Picasso écrits. Paris 1989. – HAASE, J. (ed.): Worte des Malers P. Picasso. Zurich 1970. – PARMELIN, H.: Picasso Says . . . London and South Brunswick (NY) 1969. – PICASSO, P.: Poemas y declaraciones. Mexico City 1944. – PICASSO, P.: Poems. San Francisco (CA) 1956. – PICASSO, P.: Wort und Bekenntnis. Die gesammelten Dichtungen und Zeugnisse. Zurich 1954, Berlin 1957, Zurich 1960. – PICASSO, P.: Hunk of Skin. San Francisco (CA) 1968. – PICASSO, P.: The Four Little Girls. London 1970, Millwood (NY) 1973. – PICASSO, P.: Worte und Gedanken von Pablo Picasso. Basel 1967. – PICASSO, P.: Desire Caught by the Tail. New York 1962, London 1970. – PICASSO, P.: Über Kunst. Zurich 1988.

4. Memoirs, written and photographic documentation:
APOLLINAIRE, G.: The Cubist Painters. New York 1944. – BERNADAC, M.-L.(ed.): Picasso vu par Brassaï. Paris 1987 (Cat.). – BERNADAC, M.-L.(ed.): Faces of Picasso. Paris 1991 (Cat.). – BRASSAÏ: Picasso and Company. Garden City (NY) 1966, London 1967. – BUCHHEIM, L.-G.: Picasso. A Pictorial Biography. New York and London 1959. – BURNS, E.: Gertrude Stein on Picasso. New York 1970. – COCTEAU, J.: Picasso. Paris 1923. – COCTEAU, J.: Le rappel à l'ordre. Paris 1926. – CRESPELLE, J.P.: Picasso and His Women. New York 1969. – CRESPELLE, J.P.: La vie quotidienne à Montmartre au temps de Picasso 1900–1910. Paris 1978. – DUNCAN, D.D.: The Private World of Pablo Picasso. New York and London 1958. – DUNCAN, D.D.: Goodbye Picasso. New York 1974. – DUNCAN, D.D.: The Silent Studio. New York 1976. – DUNCAN, D.D.: Viva Picasso, a Centennial Celebration 1881–1981. New York 1980. – DUNCAN, D.D.: Picasso and Jacqueline. London 1988. – ELUARD, P.: A Pablo Picasso. New York 1947. – GEORGES-MICHEL, M.: De Renoir à Picasso: Les Peintres que j'ai connus. Paris 1954. – GILOT, F. and C. LAKE: Life with Picasso. New York 1964, London 1965. – GILOT, G.: Henri Matisse – Pablo Picasso. New York and London 1990. – HUELIN Y RUIZ-BLASCO, R.: Pablo Ruiz Picasso. Su infancia, su adolescencia, y primeros anos de juventud, todo ello precedido de datos historicos, anecdotas, curiosedades y recuerdos de la familia Ruiz-Blasco. Madrid 1975. – JEDLICKA, G.: Begegnungen mit Künstlern der Gegenwart. Erlenbach and Zurich 1945. – KAHNWEILER, D.-H.: Confessions esthétiques. Paris 1963. – KAHNWEILER, D.-H.: Entretiens avec Picasso. Paris 1964. – KAHNWEILER, D.-H.: My Galleries and Painters. The Documents of 20th Century Art. New York and London 1971. – LAPORTE, G.: Sunshine at Midnight: Memories of Picasso and Cocteau. New York and London 1975. – LAPORTE, G.: Un amour secret de Picasso. Monaco 1989. – MALRAUX, A.: Picasso's Mask. New York 1976. – McCULLY, M. (ed.): A Picasso Anthology. Documents, Criticism, Reminiscences. London 1981. – MILI, G.: Picasso's Third Dimension. Photographs. New York 1970. – MOURLOT, F.: Gravés dans ma mémoire. Paris 1979. – OLIVIER, F.: Picasso and His Friends. New York 1965. – OLIVIER, F.: Souvenirs intimes. Paris 1988. – OTERO, R.: Forever Picasso: An Intimate Look at His Last Years. New York 1974. – PARMELIN, H.: Picasso Plain: An Intimate Portrait. New York 1963. – PENROSE, R.: Portrait of Picasso. London 1956, New York 1957, New York and London 1971. – Picasso à Antibes. Text by J. Sabartés, Photographs by M. Sima. Paris 1948. – PONGE, F. and P. DESCARGUES: Picasso. Photographs by E. Quinn. New York 1974. – PRÉVERT, J.: Portraits de Picasso. Photographs by André Villers. Milan 1959, Paris 1981. – QUINN, E.: Picasso at Work: An Intimate Photographic Study. Introduction and Text by R. Penrose. New York 1964, London 1965. – QUINN, E.: Picasso. Photographs from 1951–1972. New York 1980. – QUINN, E.: Picasso avec Picasso. Paris 1987. – ROSENGART, A. and S.: Besuche bei Picasso. Lucerne 1973, Stuttgart 1990. – SABARTÉS, J.: Picasso. An Intimate Portrait. New York 1948, London 1949. – SABARTÉS, J.: Picasso. Do-

cuments iconographiques. Geneva 1954. – SALMON, A.: Souvenirs sans fin. 2 vols. Paris 1955f. – STEIN, G.: Picasso. New York and London 1939, New York 1946, Boston (MA) 1960. – STEIN, G.: Pablo Picasso. Photos, Dokumente, Bibliographie. Zurich 1958. – TZÁRA, T.: Picasso et les chemins de la connaissance. Paris 1948. – TZÁRA, T.: Picasso et la poésie. Rome 1953. – UHDE, W.: Von Bismarck bis Picasso. Erinnerungen und Bekenntnisse. Zurich 1938. – VERDET, A.: Pablo Picasso. With Photographs by R. Hauert. Geneva 1956. – VOLLARD, A.: Recollections of a Picture Dealer. Boston (MA) 1936. – WEILL, B.: Pan! Dans l'œil! Ou trente ans dans les coulisses de la peinture contemporaine, 1900–1930. Paris 1933.

5. Biographies, monographs, analyses, illustrated volumes, studies:
AHLERS-HESTERMANN, F.: Pablo Picasso. Maler und Modell. Stuttgart 1956. – AMÓN, S.: Picasso. Madrid 1973. – APOLLINAIRE, G.: "La Femme assise". Paris 1948. – BARR, A.H.: Picasso. Forty Years of His Art. New York 1939, 1940. – BARR, A.H.: Picasso. Fifty Years of His Art. New York 1946, 1980. – BARR, A.H. and PENROSE, R.: Pablo Picasso. Geneva 1968. – BAUMANN, F.A.: Pablo Picasso. Leben und Werk. Stuttgart 1976. – BERGER, J.: The Success and Failure of Picasso. Harmondsworth and Baltimore (MD) 1965, New York 1989. – BERNADAC, M.-L. et P. DE BOUCHET: Picasso, le sage et le fou. Paris 1988. – BOECK, W. and J. SABARTÉS: Picasso. London and New York 1955. – BOUDAILLE, G. and R.-J. MOULIN: Picasso. Paris 1971. – BOUDAILLE, G., M.-L. BERNADAC and M.P. GAUTHIER: Picasso. Paris 1985. – CABANNE, P.: Pablo Picasso: His Life and Times. New York 1977. – CABANNE, P.: Picasso. Pour le centenaire de sa naissance. Neuchâtel 1981. – CARUSO, C.: Pablo mon amour. Rio de Janeiro 1986. – CASSOU, J.: Pablo Picasso. New York 1940. – CHAMPRIS, P. DE: Picasso, ombre et soleil. Paris 1960. – CHIARI, J.: Picasso: L'homme et son œuvre. Paris 1981. – COGNIAT, R.: Picasso. Munich and Vienna 1962. – CUENCA, C.F.: Picasso en el cine tambien. Madrid 1971. – DAIX, P.: Picasso. New York 1964, London 1965. – DAIX, P. and C. DURAND: La vie du peintre Pablo Picasso. Paris 1977. – DAIX, P.: Picasso 1982. – DAIX, P.: Picasso créateur. La vie intime et l'œuvre. Paris 1987. – DAIX, P. and E. QUINN: Picasso con Picasso. Barcelona 1987. – DAIX, P.: Picasso. Paris 1990. – DAMASE, J.: Pablo Picasso. New York 1965. – DESCARGUES, P.: Picasso, témoin du XXe siècle. Paris 1956. – DESCARGUES, P.: Picasso. New York 1974. – DEXEUS, V.C. (ed.): Estudios sobre Picasso. Barcelona 1981. – DIEHL, G.: Picasso. New York 1960, 1971. – DIMITRIEVA, N.A.: Picasso. Moscow 1971. – DUNCAN, D.D.: Picasso's Picassos: The Treasures of Californie. New York and London 1961. – ELGAR, F. and R. MAILLARD: Picasso: A Study of His Work. New York 1956, 1960 (Rev. ed.: New York 1972). – ELUARD, P.: Pablo Picasso. New York 1947. – ERBEN, W.: Picasso und die Schwermut. Eine andere Deutung. Heidelberg 1947. – FELS, F.: L'art vivant. De 1900 à nos jours. Geneva 1950. – FERMIGIER, A. and W.F. LEVAILLANT: Picasso. Paris 1969. – FOURNET, C.: Picasso. Terre – soleil. Paris 1985. – GAYA NUÑO, J.A.: Picasso. Barcelona 1957, Madrid 1975. – GEDO, M.M.: Picasso. Art as Autobiography. Chicago (IL) and London 1960, 1980. – GEDO, M.M.: Picasso's Self-Image: A Psycho-iconographic Study of the Artist's Life and Works. Ann Arbor (MI) 1986. – GIEURE, M.: Initiation à l'œuvre de Picasso. Paris 1951. – GIRAUDY, D.: Pablo Picasso. La mémoire du regard. Paris 1986. – GREENFIELD, H.: Pablo Picasso: An Introduction. Chicago (IL) 1971. – GUILLÉN, M.J.: Pablo Picasso. Madrid 1973. – GUSTAV, J.: Pablo Picasso. Gemälde und Graphik. Geneva 1972, Ramerding 1974. – HAGEBÖLLING, H.: Pablo Picasso in Documentary Films. Frankfurt am Main and Bern 1988. – HILTON, T.: Picasso. New York and London 1975. – HOFMANN, W.: Die Karikatur von Leonardo bis Picasso. Vienna 1956. – "Homage to Pablo Picasso". New York 1971. – INGOLD, F.P.: Picasso in Rußland. Materialien zur Wirkungsgeschichte 1913–1971. Zurich 1973. – JAFFÉ, H.L.: Pablo Picasso. New York 1964, London 1967. – KAY, H. and D.-H. KAHNWEILER: Picasso's World of Children. Garden City (NY) 1965. – LASSAIGNE, J.: Picasso. New York 1940. – LEIGHTEN, P.D.: Re-Ordering the Universe. Picasso and Anarchism, 1897–1917. Princeton 1989. – LEYMARIE, J.: Picasso: The Artist of the Century. London and New York 1972. – LIEBERMANN, W.S.: Picasso and the Ballet 1917–1945. New York 1946. – LIPTON, E.: Picasso Criticism 1901–1939. The Making of an Artist-Hero. Diss. New York and London 1975. – MAC, G.R.: Historien om Picasso. Copenhagen 1960. – MACGREGOR-HASTIE, R.: Picasso's Women. London 1988. – MAISON, K.E. and M. ARYTON: Bild und Abbild. Meisterwerke von Meistern kopiert und umgeschaffen. Munich and Zurich 1960. – MAYER, S.: Ancient Mediterranean Sources in the Works of Picasso, 1892–1937. Diss. Institute of Fine Arts, New York University, New York 1980. – MERLI, J.: Picasso: El artista y la obra de nuestro tiempo. Buenos Aires 1948. – MICHELI, M. DE: Picasso.

New York and London 1967. – NEIGEMONT, O.: Picasso. Munich 1966. – O'BRIAN, P.: Pablo Picasso: A Biography. New York and London 1976. – OLANO, A.D.: Picasso íntimo. Madrid 1971. – ORIOL ANGUERA, A.: Para entender a Picasso. Mexico City 1973. – OROZCO DIAZ, M.: Introducción a la estética de Picasso. Málaga 1959. – ORS Y ROVIRA, E. D': Pablo Picasso. New York 1930. – PAD'RTA, J. and J. COCTEAU: Picasso: The Early Years. New York and London 1960. – PALAU I FABRE, J.: Picasso por Picasso. Barcelona 1970. – PALAU I FABRE, J.: L'extraordinaria vida de Picasso. Barcelona 1971. – PALAU I FABRE, J.: Picasso. Mexico City 1945. – PAYRO, J.E.: Picasso y el ambiente artístico-social contemporaneo. Buenos Aires 1960. – PENROSE, R.: Picasso. His Life and Work. London 1958, Berkeley (CA) 1981. – PENROSE, R.: The Eye of Picasso. New York 1967. – PENROSE, R. and J. GOLDING (eds.): Picasso 1881–1973. London and New York 1973, 1980. – PERRY, J.: Yo Picasso. Paris 1982. – PETROVA, E.: Picasso. Prague 1981. – Picasso (Collection: Génies et réalités). Paris 1967. – PODOKSIK, A.: Picasso: La quête perpétuelle. Paris 1989. – POMPEY, F.: Picasso, su vida y sus obras. Madrid 1973. – PORZIO, D. and M. VALSECCHI: Understanding Picasso. New York 1974. – QUINTANILLA, F.M.: Proceso a Picasso. Barcelona 1972. – QUINTAVAILLE, A.C.: Picasso oggi. Parma 1968. – RAPHAEL, M.: Von Monet zu Picasso. Grundzüge einer Ästhetik und Entwicklung der modernen Malerei. Munich 1913. – RAYNAL, M.: Picasso. Munich 1921. – RAYNAL, M.: Picasso. A Biographical and Critical Study. Geneva 1953. – REVERDY, P.: Pablo Picasso. Paris 1924. – RICHARDSON, J.: A Life of Picasso. New York 1991 ff. 4 vols. (published to date: Vol. I: 1881–1906). – ROJAS, C.: El mundo mítico y mágico de Picasso. Barcelona 1984. – SCHIFF, G.: Picasso in Perspective. New York 1976. – SCHÜRER, O.: Pablo Picasso. Berlin and Leipzig 1927. – SCORTESCO: P.: Saint Picasso. Peignez pour nous ou les deux conformismes. Paris 1953. – SOBY, J.T.: After Picasso. New York 1935. – SPIES, W.: Kontinent Picasso. Ausgewählte Studien aus zwei Jahrzehnten. Munich 1988. – STASSINOPOULOS HUFFINGTON, A.: Picasso. Creator and Destroyer. London and New York 1988. – SUBIRANA TORRENT, R.M.: El Museo Picasso de Barcelona. Léon 1975. – SWEETMAN, D.: Picasso. London 1973. – THOMAS, D.: Picasso and His Art. New York 1975. – TZÁRA, T.: Pablo Picasso. Geneva 1948. – UHDE, W.: Picasso and the French Tradition. New York 1929. – VALLENTIN, A.: Pablo Picasso. New York and London 1963. – WALTER, G.: Picasso. Stuttgart 1949. – WALTHER, I.F.: Pablo Picasso 1881–1973. Genius of the Century. Cologne 1986. – WERTENBAKER, L.: The World of Picasso. New York 1967. – WIEGAND, W.: Pablo Picasso in Selbstzeugnissen und Bilddokumenten. Reinbek 1973. – ZENNSTROM, P.O.: Pablo Picasso. Stockholm 1948. – ZERVOS, C.: Picasso. Paris 1951.

6. Early works (1895–1900):
AGUILERA-RODRIGUEZ, C.: Picasso in Barcelona. New York 1975. – BLUNT, A.F. and P. POOL: Picasso. The Formative Years. A Study of His Sources. Greenwich (CT) and London 1962. – CIRICI-PELLICER, A.: Picasso avant Picasso. Paris 1950. – CIRLOT, J.E.: Pablo Picasso. Birth of a Genius. New York and London 1972. – COOPER, D. (ed.): Pablo Picasso. Carnet Catalan. Paris 1958. – GLAESEMER, J. (ed.): Der junge Picasso. Frühwerk und Blaue Periode (Cat.). Bern 1984. – LASARTE, J.A. DE (ed.): Carnet Picasso. La Coruña, 1894–1895. Barcelona 1971. – McCULLY, M.: Els Quatre Gats: Art in Barcelona around 1900. Princeton 1978. – PAD'RTA, J.: Picasso: The Early Years. New York 1960. – PALAU I FABRE, J.: Picasso in Catalonia. New York 1968.

7. Blue and Rose Periods (1900–1906):
CHEVALIER, D.: Picasso: The Blue and Rose Periods. New York 1969. – ELGAR, F.: Picasso: Blue and Pink Periods. New York 1956. – PONGE, F. and J. CHESSEX (eds.): Dessins de Pablo Picasso. Epoques bleue et rose. Lausanne 1960. – SABARTÉS, J.: Picasso. Les bleus de Barcelone. Paris 1963. – SUBIRANA, R.M. (ed.): Carnet Picasso: Paris 1900. Barcelona 1972.

8. Cubism (1907–1916):
APOLLINAIRE, G.: The Cubist Painters. The Documents of Modern Art. New York 1949. – AZNAR, J.C.: Picasso y el cubismo. Madrid 1956. – BANDMANN, G.: Pablo Picasso. Les Demoiselles d'Avignon. Stuttgart 1965. – BARR, A.H.: Cubism and Abstract Art. New York 1936, 1966. – BERTRAND, G.: L'Illustration de la poésie à l'époque du cubisme, 1909–1914. Paris 1971. – COOPER, D.: The Cubist Epoch. London 1970. – CUENCA, C.F.: Picasso en el cine tambien. Madrid 1971. – DAIX, P.: Le journal du cubisme. Geneva 1982. – ELGAR, F.: Picasso y Horta de Ebro. Tarragona 1981. – FRY, E.: Cubism. New York

1966, Oxford 1978. – GOLDING, J.: Cubism. A History and an Analysis 1907–1914. London 1959, 1968. – GÓMEZ DE LA SERNA, R.: Completa y verídica historia de Picasso y el cubismo. Torino 1945. – GRAY, C.: Cubist Aesthetic Theory. Baltimore (MD) 1953. – HABASQUE, G.: Kubismus. Geneva 1959. – HERDING, K.: Pablo Picasso. Desmoiselles d'Avignon. Frankfurt am Main 1992. – JUDKINS, W.O.: Fluctuant Representation in Synthetic Cubism. Picasso, Braque, Gris, 1910–1920. Diss. Harvard University 1954, New York and London 1976. – KAHNWEILER, D.-H.: The Rise of Cubism. New York 1949. – LEAL, B.: Picasso: "Les Demoiselles d'Avignon". Paris and London 1988. – LEIGHTEN, P.D.: Picasso: Anarchism and Art 1897–1914. Ann Arbor (MI) 1986. – MUNDINGER, H.: Die Landschaft im Kubismus bei Pablo Picasso und Georges Braque. Diss. Tübingen 1963. – PAULHAN, J.: La peinture cubiste. Paris 1971. – RAYNAL, M.: Pablo Picasso. Les maîtres du cubisme. Paris n.d. – ROSENBLUM, R.: Cubism and Twentieth Century Art. New York 1976. – RUBIN, W.: Picasso and Braque: Pioneering Cubism. New York 1989 (Cat.). – SCHWARTZ, P.: Cubism. New York 1971.

9. **Works 1917–1936:**
ALLEY, R.: Picasso. The Three Dancers. Newcastle 1967. – COOPER, D.: Picasso Theatre. New York and London 1968, New York 1987. – COSTELLO, A.C.: Picasso's "Vollard Suite". Diss. Bryn Mawr College 1978. New York and London 1979. – DANILOWITZ, B.M.A.: The Iconography of Picasso's Ballet Designs: 1917–1924. Diss. University of the Witwaterstrand, Johannesburg 1985 (Ms.). – GASSMANN, L.: Mystery, Magic and Love in Picasso 1925–1937. Diss. Columbia University, Ann Arbor (MI) 1981. – GLOZER, L.: Picasso und der Surrealismus. Cologne 1964, 1974. – GOEPPERT, S. and H.C. GOEPPERT-FRANK: Die Minotauromachie von Pablo Picasso. Geneva 1987. – LEIRIS, M.: Miroir de la tauromachie. Paris 1938. – MACMILLAN, J.D.: Picasso's Painting and Graphic Work from 1925–1937 with Special Reference to His Relations with Surrealism and the Influence of Its Ideas upon Him. Diss. Edinburgh 1966. – MAHAR, W.J.: Neo-classicism in the Twentieth Century. A Study of the Idea and Its Relationship to Selected Works of Stravinski and Picasso. Diss. Syracuse University. Ann Arbor (MI) 1972. – MARRERO SUAREZ, V.: Picasso and the Bull. Chicago (IL) 1956. – MENAKER-ROTHSCHILD, D.: Picasso's Parade. From Street to Stage. London 1991. – MUJICA GALLO, M.: Le minotauromaquia de Picasso o El ocaso de los toros. Madrid 1971. – Picasso at Vallauris. New York and London 1959. – RUBIN, W.: Dada and Surrealism. New York 1968. – RUNNQUIST, J.: Minotauros: En studie i forhallandet mellan ikonografi och form i Picassos konst, 1900–1937. Stockholm 1959.

10. **"Guernica" (1937):**
ARNHEIM, R.: Picasso's Guernica. The Genesis of a Painting. Berkeley (CA) 1962. – BERNADAC, M.L. (ed.): Pablo Picasso. Guernica. The Forty-two Sketches on Paper. New York 1990. – BLUNT, A.F.: Picasso's "Guernica". London and New York 1969. – CHIPP, H.B.: Picasso's Guernica. History, Transformation, Meanings. Berkeley (CA) 1988. – DANZ, L.: Personal Revolution and Picasso. New York and Toronto 1941, New York 1974. – FERRIER, J.L.: Picasso. Guernica – Anatomie d'un chef d'œuvre. Paris 1977. – FERRIER, J.L.: De Picasso à Guernica: Généalogie d'un tableau. Paris 1985. – FISCH, E.: Picasso – "Guernica". Freiburg 1983. – IMDAHL, M.: Picassos Guernica. Frankfurt am Main 1985. – KRAHL, I. and S. QUANDT: "Guernica". Überlegungen, Vorschläge, Materialien zum fächerübergreifenden Unterricht. Ratingen 1974. – LARREA, J.: Guernica. Pablo Picasso. New York 1947, 1969. – OPPLER, E.C. (ed.): Picasso's Guernica. New York 1988. – PALAU I FABRE, J.: El Guernica de Picasso. Barcelona 1979. – PUENTE, J. DE LA: Guernica. The Making of a Painting. Madrid 1983. – RUSSELL, F.D.: Picasso's Guernica – The Labyrinth of Narrative and Vision. London 1980. – SAURA, A.: Contre Guernica, Pamphlet. Paris 1985. – SCHAPIRO, M.: Guernica: Studies, Postscripts. New York 1978. – TANKARD, A.: Picasso's "Guernica". Revisited Through the Looking Glass of Rubens' "Horror of War". London 1984. – THOMAS, G. and M. MORGAN-WITTS: The Day Guernica Died. London 1975.

11. **Works 1938–1973:**
ALBERTI, R.: A Year of Picasso Paintings: 1969. New York 1972. – ALBERTI, R.: Picasso, le rayon interrompu. Paris 1974. – COOPER, D.: Picasso "Les Déjeuners": Variations on Edouard Manet's Masterwork. New York 1962. – DOR DE LA SOUCHÈRE, R.: Picasso in Antibes. New York and London 1960. – DUFOUR, P.: Picasso, 1950–1968. Biographical and Critical Study. Geneva 1969. – FORESTIER, S.: Pablo Picasso. Krieg und Frieden. Stuttgart 1991. – GALLWITZ, K. and

J. BERGAMÍN: Picasso at 90: The Late Work. New York and London 1971. – GALLWITZ, M.: Picasso. The Heroic Years. New York 1985. – GASSER M.: Pablo Picasso. Der Maler und sein Modell. Zurich 1972. – GIRAUDY, D.: Picasso à Antibes. Paris 1987. – GUILLAUD, J. and M.: Picasso. La pièce à musique de Mougins. Paris 1982 (Cat.). – JANIS, H.G. and S. JANIS: Picasso. The Recent Years, 1939–1946. Garden City (NY) 1946. – MARCHIORI, G.: L'ultimo Picasso. Venice 1949. – PALAU I FABRE, J.: El secret de Les Menines de Picasso. Barcelona 1981. – PARMELIN, H.: Intimate Secrets of a Studio. Vol. I: Picasso: Women, Cannes and Mougins, 1954–1963; Vol. II: Picasso: The Artist and His Model, and other Recent Works; Vol. III: Picasso: At Notre Dame de Vie. New York 1965–1967. – PARMELIN, H.: Voyage en Picasso. Paris 1980. – PICON, G.: Pablo Picasso. La "Chute d'Icare" au Palais de l'Unesco. Geneva 1971. – ROY, C.: La guerre et la paix. Paris 1952. – RUSSEL, J.: Picasso: Paintings 1939–1946. London 1946. – SABARTÉS, J.: Picasso's Variations on Velázquez' Painting "The Maids of Honor" and other Recent Works. New York 1959, London 1969. – SABARTÉS, J.: Picasso: Faune et flore d'Antibes. Greenwich (CT) 1960. – SABARTÉS, J.: "A los toros" avec Picasso. Monte Carlo 1961. – SPIES, W. (ed.): Pablo Picasso. Traum und Lüge Francos. Frankfurt am Main 1968.

12. **Drawings and graphic works:**
ADHÉMAR, J.: Picasso, Graveur. Paris 1955. – BOECK, W.: Pablo Picasso. Linoleum Cuts. London and New York 1963. – BOECK, W. et al.: Picasso. Zeichnungen. Cologne 1973. – BOLLIGER, H. and B. GEISER: Picasso. Fifty-five Years of His Graphic Work. London and New York 1955. – BOLLIGER, H.: Pablo Picasso for Vollard. New York and London 1956. – BOLLIGER, H. and K. LEONHARD: Picasso: Recent Etchings, Lithographs and Linoleum Cuts. New York 1967. – BOLLIGER, H. and K. LEONHARD: Picasso: Graphic Works. London 1967. – BOLLIGER, H.: Picasso's Vollard Suite. London 1977. – BOUDAILLE, G. (ed.): Picasso Sketchbook. New York 1960. – BOUDAILLE, G. and L. DOMINGUIN: Bulls and Bull Fighters. London and New York 1961. – BOUDAILLE, G.: The Drawings of Picasso. London 1988. – BRUNNER, S.: Recent Drawings, 1966–1968. New York 1969, London 1970. – CARLSON, V.: Drawings and Watercolors, 1899–1907, in the Collection of the Baltimore Museum of Art. Baltimore (MD) 1976. – Carnet de dessins de Picasso (1940–1942). Paris 1948. – CASSOU, J. and H. PETERS: Pablo Picasso. Plakate, Affiches, Posters. Düsseldorf 1963. – CHAR, R. and FELD, C.: Picasso Dessins. Paris 1969 (Cat.). – COCTEAU, J.: Picasso de 1916 à 1961. Lithographies. Monaco 1962. – COOPER, D.: Pablo Picasso: Pour Eugenia. Paris 1976. – ELUARD, P.: Picasso. Dessins. Paris 1926, 1952. – ELUARD, P.: Picasso: Le visage de la paix. Paris 1951. – FEINBLATT, E. et al. (eds.): Pablo Picasso. Sixty Years of Graphic Works. Greenwich (CT) 1966 (Cat.). – FERMIGIER, A.: Picasso. Paris 1969. – FOSTER, J.K.: The Posters of Picasso. New York 1957, 1964. – GEORGE, W.: Picasso, Dessins. Paris 1926. – HORODISCH, A.: Picasso as a Book Artist. Cleveland (OH) 1962. – JARDOT, M. (ed.): Pablo Picasso. Drawings. New York 1959. – JOUVET, J. (ed.): Pablo Picasso. Der Zeichner. 1893–1972. 3 vols. Zurich 1982, 1989. – KAHNWEILER, D.-H.: Picasso. Dessins 1893 à 1907. Paris 1954. – KNIRIM, H.: Tradition und individuelle Schaffensweise. Studien zum Werk Picassos unter besonderer Berücksichtigung der Druckgraphik. Diss. Frankfurt am Main 1980. – LAMBERT, J.-C.: Picasso. Dessins de Tauromachie. 1917–1960. Paris 1960. – LASARTE, J.A. DE: Carnet Picasso: La Coruña, 1894–1895. Barcelona 1971. – LEIRIS, M.: Picasso and the Human Comedy. A Suite of 180 Drawings by Picasso. New York 1954. – LEYMARIE, J.: Picasso. Drawings. Geneva 1967. – LIEBERMAN, W.S.: The Sculptor's Studio: Etchings by Picasso. The Museum of Modern Art, New York 1952 (Cat.). – LONGSTREET, S. (ed.): The Drawings of Picasso. Alhambra 1974. – MARCENAC, J. (ed.): Picasso. Le goût de bonheur: A Suite of Happy, Playful and Erotic Drawings. New York 1970. – MARCENAC, J. (ed.): Picasso. Les enfants et les toros de Vallauris. Paris 1970. – MATARASSO, H.: Bibliographie des livres illustrés par Pablo Picasso. Œuvres graphiques 1905–1956. Nice 1956. – MIGEL, P.: Pablo Picasso. Designs for the Three-Cornered Hat. New York 1978. – MILLIER, A.: The Drawings of Picasso. Los Angeles (CA) 1961. – OCAÑA, M.T. (Intr.): Picasso: Viatge a Paris. Barcelona 1979. – PALAU I FABRE, J.: Child and Caveman: Elements of Picasso's Creativity. New York 1977. – PALAU I FABRE, J.: Picasso. Dessins pour les enfants. Paris 1979. – PARMELIN, H.: Picasso. La flûte double. Saint-Paul-de-Vence 1971. – PASSERON, R.: Picasso. Maître de la gravure. Paris 1984. – PENROSE, R.: Drawings of Picasso. Homage to Picasso. London 1951. – PERUCCHI-PETRI, U.: Pablo Picasso. 156 graphische Blätter, 1970–1972. Kunsthaus Zürich, Zurich 1978 (Cat.). – Picasso: 347 gravures. 2 vols. New York 1970 (Cat.). – Picasso: 145 Dessins pour la presse et les organisations

démocratiques. Paris 1973. – Picasso: Dessins et gouaches 1899–1972. Galerie Louise Leiris, Paris 1981 (Cat.). – RAU, B.: Pablo Picasso. Das graphische Werk. Stuttgart 1974. – RICHARDSON, J.: Pablo Picasso. Watercolours and Gouaches. London 1964. – SABARTÉS, J. (ed.): Picasso: Toreros. New York 1961. – SALAS, X. DE (ed.): Carnet Picasso, Madrid 1898. – Serge Lifar et la danse. Dessins de Pablo Picasso. Paris 1971. – SERULLAZ, M. (ed.): Picasso's Private Drawings. New York 1969. – SPIES, W. (ed.): Pablo Picasso. Traum und Lüge Francos. Frankfurt am Main 1968. – TINTEROW, G. (ed.): Master Drawings by Picasso. Cambridge (MA) 1981 (Cat.). – "Verve", vol. VIII, No. 29–30 (1954; Suite of 180 Dessins de Picasso). – WEISNER, U. (ed.): Zeichnungen und Collagen des Kubismus. Bielefeld 1979 (Cat.). – WESCHER, H.: Picasso, Papiers collés. Paris 1960. – ZERVOS, C.: Picasso. Dessins 1892–1948. Paris 1949.

13. Sculptures:
ARGAN, G.C.: Scultura di Picasso. Venice 1953. – FAIRWEATHER, S.: Picasso's Concrete Sculptures. New York 1982. – JOHNSON, R.W.: The Early Sculpture of Picasso 1901–1914. New York and London 1975. – KAHNWEILER, D.-H.: The Sculptures of Picasso. London 1949. – LICHTENSTERN, C.: Picasso, "Tête de Femme". Zwischen Klassik und Surrealismus. Städelsches Kunstinstitut und Städtische Galerie, Frankfurt am Main 1980 (Cat.). – PENROSE, R.: Picasso: Modern Sculptors. London 1961. – PENROSE, R. and A. LEGG: The Sculpture of Picasso. The Museum of Modern Art, New York 1967 (Cat). – PENROSE, R.: Picasso. L'idée pour une sculpture. Thème et variation: peintures, dessins et la sculpture "Femme au chapeau". Galerie Rosengart, Lucerne 1979 (Cat.). – PIOT, C.: Décrire Picasso. Diss. Université de Paris, Paris 1981. – PRAMPOLINI, E.: Picasso scultore. Rome 1943. – ROSENBLUM, R.: The Sculpture of Picasso. New York 1982 (Cat.).

14. Ceramics:
BATIGNE, R.: Une visite à Vallauris: Guide illustré. Vallauris 1950. – BLOCH, G.: Pablo Picasso: Catalogue of the Printed Ceramics 1949–1971. Bern 1972. – KAHNWEILER, D.-H.: Picasso Keramik. Hanover 1957, 1970. – Picasso Céramiques (with an Essay by D.-H. Kahnweiler). Galerie Beyeler, Basle 1990 (Cat.). – Picasso Keramiek. s'-Hertogenbosch 1985 (Cat.). – RAMIÉ, G. and S.: Ceramics by Picasso. New York 1955, 1960. – RAMIÉ, G.: Picasso's Ceramics. New York 1976. – RAMIÉ, A.: Picasso. Catalogue of the Edited Ceramic Works. 1947–1971. Vallauris 1988. – VERDET, A.: Faunes et nymphes de Pablo Picasso. Geneva 1952.

15. Exhibitions (catalogues):
1900: Els Quatre Gats, Barcelona. – **1901:** Pablo Picasso y Ramon Casas. Sala Parés, Barcelona. – Galerie Ambroise Vollard, Paris. – **1902:** Picasso et Louis Bernard Lemaire. Galerie Berthe Weil, Paris. – **1911:** Photo-Secession Gallery, New York. – **1912:** Blue and Rose Period. Galería Dalmau, Barcelona. – Drawings by Picasso. Gallery Stafford, London. – **1913:** Galerie Thannhauser, Munich. – **1914:** Braque and Picasso. Photo-Secession Gallery, New York. – Galerie Miethke, Vienna. – **1916:** Les Demoiselles d'Avignon. Salon d'Antin, Paris. – **1918:** Matisse-Picasso. Galerie Guillaume, Paris. – **1919:** Picasso and Matisse. The Leicester Galleries, London. – **1921:** The Leicester Galleries, London. – Galerie Paul Rosenberg, Paris. – **1922:** Galerie Thannhauser, Munich. – **1923:** Arts Club of Chicago, Chicago (IL). – Galerie Thannhauser, Munich. – Gallery Paul Rosenberg-Wildenstein, New York. – **1924:** Galerie Paul Rosenberg, Paris. – **1925:** From Ingres to Picasso. Baltimore Museum of Art, Baltimore (MD). – **1926:** Galerie Paul Rosenberg, Paris. – **1927:** Zeichnungen, Aquarelle, Pastelle 1902–1927. Galerie Flechtheim, Berlin. – Wildenstein Gallery, New York. – **1930:** Arts Club of Chicago, Chicago (IL). – Gallery John Becker, New York. – Gallery Reinhardt, New York. – **1931:** Thirty Years of Pablo Picasso. Alex Reid and Lefevre Gallery, London. – Picasso's Abstraction. Valentine Gallery, New York. – Galerie Paul Rosenberg, Paris. – **1932:** Metamorphoses. Harvard Society for Contemporary Art, Cambridge (MA). – Schlemmer and Picasso. Kestner-Gesellschaft, Hanover. – Gallery Julien Levy, New York. – Galerie Georges Petit, Paris (Cat. by C. Vrancken). – Kunsthaus Zürich, Zurich. – **1933:** Valentine Gallery, New York. – **1934:** Museo de Arte Moderno, Buenos Aires. – Wadsworth Atheneum, Hartford (CT). – **1935:** Collages. Galerie Pierre, Paris. – **1936:** Amigos de las artes nuevas, Barcelona and Madrid. – Zwemmer Gallery, London. – Valentine Gallery, New York. – Galerie Paul Rosenberg, Paris. – **1937:** De Chirico and Picasso. Zwemmer Gallery, London. – 20 Years in the Evolution of Picasso 1903–1923. Gallery Seligmann, New York. – Valentine Gallery, New York. – **1938:** Picasso and Henri Matisse. Museum of Modern Art, Boston (MA). – Guernica. New Burlington Galleries, London. – Valentine Gallery,

New York. – **1939:** Arts Club of Chicago, Chicago (IL). – Picasso, Forty Years of His Art. The Museum of Modern Art, New York (Cat. by A. H. Barr Jr.). – Picasso. Natures mortes. Galerie Paul Rosenberg, Paris. – **1940:** Dessins. Galerie MAI, Paris. – **1941:** Bignou Gallery, New York. – Collection of Walter P. Chrysler Jr., Virginia Museum of Arts, Richmond (VA). – **1944:** Sociedad de Arte moderna, Mexico City. – Palais des Beaux-Arts, Paris. – **1945:** Picasso and Matisse. Victoria and Albert Museum, London. – **1946:** Picasso. Fifty Years of His Art. The Museum of Modern Art, New York (Cat. by A.H. Barr Jr.). – **1947:** Pablo Picasso: 43 Lithographies 1945–1947. Stedelijk Museum, Amsterdam. – Lithographs. Valentine Gallery, New York. – **1948:** Lithographs. Galería Layetanas, Barcelona. – Juan Gris, Georges Braque, Pablo Picasso. Kunsthalle Basel and Kunsthalle Bern, Basel and Bern. – 55 Lithographs 1945–1947. The Arts Council, London. – Picasso, Gris, Miró: Spanish Masters of Twentieth Century Painting. San Francisco Museum of Art, San Francisco (CA); Portland Art Museum, Portland (OR) (Cat. by R.B. Freeman et al.). – **1949:** Gallery Buchholz, New York. – Maison de la Pensée Française, Paris. – Art Gallery of Ontario, Toronto. – **1950:** La Réserve, Knokke-Le-Zoute. – Maison de la Pensée Française, Paris. – Van Fantin tot Picasso. Musem Boymans-van Beuningen, Rotterdam. – **1951:** Homage to Picasso on His 70th Birthday. Drawings and Watercolours since 1893. Institute of Contemporary Art, London (Cat. by R. Penrose and P. Eluard). – Le massacre de Corea. Salon de Mai, Paris. – **1953:** Picasso (1898–1936). Alex Reid and Lefevre Gallery, London. – Musée des Beaux-Arts, Lyon (Cat. by M. Rocher-Jauneau). – Palazzo Reale, Milan (Cat. by F. Russoli). – Galerie Louise Leiris, Paris. – Mostra di Pablo Picasso. Museo Nazionale d'Arte moderna, Rome (Cat. by L. Venturi, E. Battista and R. Ponente). – Museo del Arte Moderno, São Paulo. – **1954:** El Quatre Gats. Sala Páres, Barcelona. – Galerie Beyeler, Basel. – Tauromachies et œuvres récentes, lithographies, céramiques. Musée Municipale d'Art Moderne, Céret. – Picasso 1938–1953. Lefevre Gallery. London. – Picasso. Deux époques, 1900–1914, 1950–1954. Maison de la Pensée Française, Paris. – Das graphische Werk. Kunsthaus Zürich, Zurich (Cat. by B. Geiser). – **1955:** Cerámicas Picasso. Galería Syra, Barcelona. – Obra gráfica original de Braque-Chagall-Picasso. Sala Gaspara, Barcelona. – L'œuvre gravé de Pablo Picasso. Musée Rath, Geneva (Cat. by J. Cocteau, B. Geiser et al.). – Contemporary Arts Association, Houston (TX). – Picasso 1900–1955. Haus der Kunst, Munich; Rheinisches Museum, Cologne; Hamburger Kunsthalle, Hamburg (Cat. by M. Jardot). – 63 Drawings 1953–1954, 10 Bronzes 1945–1953. Marlborough Fine Arts Ltd., New York. – L'œuvre gravé. Bibliothèque National, Paris (Cat. by J. Adhémar and C. Perussaux). – Peintures, 1900–1955. Musée des Arts Décoratifs, Paris (Cat. by M. Jardot). – **1956:** Litografías originales de Pablo Picasso. Sala Gaspar, Barcelona. – Guernica (avec 60 études et variantes). Palais des Beaux-Arts, Brussels; Stedelijk Museum, Amsterdam (Cat. by D.-H. Kahnweiler). – Picasso chez Goya. Museo Goya, Castres. – Picasso Himself. Institute of Contemporary Arts, London. – Fifty Years of Graphic Art. The Arts Council, London (Cat. by P.B. James et al.). – Malmö Museum, Malmö. – Un demi-siècle de livres illustrés. Galerie Henri Matarasso, Nice. – Kunstnernes Hus, Oslo. – Guernica. Nationalmuseet, Stockholm. – **1957:** Dessins, gouaches, aquarels 1898–1957. Musée Réattu, Arles (Cat. by D. Cooper). – Picasso: Pintura, Escultura, Dibujo, Cerámica, Mosaico. Sala Gaspar, Barcelona. – Pablo Picasso. Das graphische Werk. Kupferstichkabinett der Staatlichen Museen zu Berlin, Berlin (Cat. by W. Timm and D.-H. Kahnweiler). – Picasso. 75th Anniversary Exhibition. The Museum of Modern Art, New York; The Art Institute of Chicago, Chicago (IL) (Cat. by A.H. Barr Jr.). – Paintings 1954–1956. Saidenberg Gallery, New York. – Peintures 1955–1956. Galerie Louise Leiris, Paris (Cat. by D.-H. Kahnweiler). – **1958:** Céramiques. Musée Municipal d'Art Moderne, Céret. – Cent cinquante céramiques originales. Maison de la Pensée Française, Paris. – Picasso. A Loan Exhibition. Philadelphia Museum of Art, Philadelphia (PA) (Cat. by H. Clifford and C. Zigrosser). – Charlottenburg, Copenhagen. – Musée de l'Art Wallon, Liège. – Saidenberg Gallery, New York. – **1959:** La Tauromaquia. Sala Gaspar, Barcelona. – Picasso from 1907 to 1909. Museum of Fine Arts, Boston (MA). – Picasso. Musée Cantini, Marseilles (Cat. by D. Cooper). – Picasso, Faces and Figures, 1900 to 1959. Saidenberg Gallery, New York. – Les Ménines 1957. Galerie Louise Leiris, Paris. – Gallery Svensk-Franska, Stockholm. – **1960:** Picasso. 30 cuadros inéditos 1917–1969. SALA GASPAR, BARCELONA. – PICASSO. THE TATE GALLERY, LONDON (CAT. by G. WHITE AND R. PENROSE). – THE GRAPHICS WORKS. MUSÉE DES BEAUX-ARTS, MULHOUSE. – PICASSO. HIS BLUE PERIOD (1900–1905). Sidney Janis Gallery, New York; O'Hana Gallery, London; Galerie Motte, Geneva (Cat. by J. O'Hanna). – Œuvre gravé. Galerie des Ponchettes, Nice. – Drawings. Palma de Mallorca. – 45 gravures sur linóleum. Galerie Louise Leiris,

Paris. – Dessins 1959–1960. Galerie Louise Leiris, Paris. – Picasso et ses amis. Musée des Beaux-Arts, Strasbourg. – **1961**: Dibujos, aguades, acuarelas. Sala Gaspar, Barcelona. – Druckgraphik, Gemälde, Handzeichnungen, Plastik. Kunsthalle Bremen, Bremen. – Linocuts. Museum of Art, Cincinnati. – La Tauromaquia. Kestner-Gesellschaft, Hanover. – Paintings. UCLA Art Gallery, Los Angeles (CA). – "Bonne Fête" Monsieur Picasso. University of Los Angeles Art Galleries, Los Angeles (CA) (Cat. by F.D. Murphy and D.-H. Kahn weiler). – Gemälde 1950–1960. Galerie Rosengart, Lucerne. – Obra gráfica. Museo Español de Arte Contemporáneo, Madrid. – Cerámicas. Club Urbis, Madrid. – Cerámicas. Museo de Bellas Artes, Málaga. – Obra gráfica. Musée des Beaux-Arts, Paris. – **1962**: Libros ilustrados. Galería Syra, Barcelona. – 44 linóleos originales de Picasso. Sala Gaspar, Barcelona. – Les déjeuners. Galerie Madoura, Cannes. – Gravures, céramiques. Musée des Beaux-Arts, Lyons. – Picasso. An American Tribute. The Public Education Association of the City of New York, Cordier-Warren Gallery, New York (Cat. by J. Richardson). – Peintures. Vauvenargues, 1959–1961. Galerie Louise Leiris, Paris (Cat. by J. Leymarie). – Le Déjeuner sur l'herbe, 1960–1961. Galerie Louise Leiris, Paris. – Tableaux de Picasso. Œuvres offertes par des artistes français et de divers pays. Maison de la Pensée Française, Paris. – Picasso. Les potiers. Vallauris. – Picasso. His Later Works, 1938–1961. Museum of Arts, Worcester (MA). – **1963**: Musée de l'Athénée, Geneva. – 50 gravures sur linoléum 1958–1963. Galerie Gérald Cramer, Geneva. – 54 Recent Colour Linocuts. Hanover Gallery, London. – Picasso. Deux époques: 1912–1927, 1952–1961. Galerie Rosengart, Lucerne. – 42 incisioni su linoleum 1962. Galleria il Segno, Rome. – Les potiers. Vallauris. – 28 linographies originales. Galerie Madoura, Vallauris. – **1964**: The Printing Plates of The Tauromaquia. Museu Picasso, Barcelona. – Keramik 1947–1961. Mosaiken 1956–1958. Linolschnitte seit 1961. Lithographien 1956–1961. Plakate 1948–1962. Museum für Kunst und Gewerbe, Hamburg. – Pablo Picasso: Radierungen, Lithographien; Henri Laurens: Skulpturen, Radierungen, Lithographien. Karlsruhe (Cat. by K. Gallwitz). – Chefs d'œuvres des collections suisses de Manet à Picasso. Palais de Beaulieu, Lausanne. – National Gallery, Ottawa. – Peintures, 1962–1963. Galerie Louise Leiris, Paris (Cat. by M. Leiris). – Linogravures en couleurs. Galerie Louise Leiris, Paris. – Lithographies. Galerie Cahiers d'Art, Paris. – Picasso: 60 ans de gravure. Galerie Berggruen, Paris. – Première époque 1881–1906. Paris. – Pablo Picasso. National Museum of Modern Art, Tokyo; National Museum of Modern Art, Kyoto; Prefectural Museum of Art, Nagoya (Cat. by D.-H. Kahnweiler, A.H. Barr and S. Segui). – Picasso and Man. The Art Gallery of Ontario, Toronto; The Montreal Museum of Fine Arts, Montreal (Cat. by J.S. Boggs, J. Golding et al). – Les potiers. Vallauris. – **1965**: Gouache en tekeningen 1959–1964. Galerie d'Eendt, Amsterdam. – Aguafuertes. Sala Gaspar, Barcelona. – Museu Picasso, Barcelona. – Picasso gravures. Galerie Beyeler, Basel. – Druckgraphik aus dem Besitz der Kunsthalle Bremen, Bremen (Cat. by H. Bock, Cat. by Heusinger and J.H. Müller). – 150 Handzeichnungen aus sieben Jahrzehnten. Frankfurter Kunstverein, Frankfurt am Main; Kunstverein Hamburg, Hamburg. (Cat. by E. Rathke). – Picasso y Kiruna. Kiruna. – Apollinaire et le cubisme. Musée des Beaux-Arts, Lille. – Picasso et le théâtre. Musée des Augustins, Toulouse (Cat. by D. Milhau and J. Cassou). – **1966**: Picasso (1900–1932). Galerie Beyeler, Basel. – Aguafuertes. Centro de Artes Visuales, Buenos Aires. – Pablo Picasso, le peintre et son modèle. 44 gravures originales 1963–1965. Galerie Gérald Cramer, Geneva. – Picasso 1959–1965. The Israel Museum, Jerusalem. – Casa Colón, Las Palma. – Picasso. Sixty Years of Graphic Works. Los Angeles County Museum of Art, Los Angeles (CA) (Cat. by D.-H. Kahnweiler, B. Geiser and E. Feinblatt). – Deux époques de peintures (1960–1965 et des années 1934, 1937, 1944). Galerie Rosengart, Lucerne. – Galería Biosca, Madrid. – Grafika Picasso. Pushkin-Museum, Moscow. – Hommage à Pablo Picasso. Peintures: Grand Palais. Dessins, sculptures, céramiques: Petit Palais. Gravures: Bibliothèque National, Paris (Cat. by J. Leymarie). – Gravures. Galerie Berggruen, Paris. – Cent dessins et aquarelles 1899–1965. Galerie Knoedler, Paris. – Galerie Lucie Weil, Paris. – Papiers collés 1910–1914. Galerie au Pont des Arts, Paris. – Picasso et le béton. Galerie Jeanne Bucher, Paris. – Picasso. 100 affiches. Bookshop Fischbacher, Paris. – Picasso zum 85. Geburtstag. Zeichnungen und Druckgraphik 1905–1965. Staatsgalerie Stuttgart, Stuttgart (Cat. by G. Thiem). – Picasso: 20 ans de céramiques chez Madoura, 1946–1966. Galerie Madoura, Vallauris. – Picasso Since 1945. Gallery of Modern Art, Washington (DC). – **1967**: Stedelijk Museum, Amsterdam. – Picasso. Werke 1932–1965. Galerie Beyeler, Basel. – Grafiken. Museum, Belgrade. – Œuvres récentes. Musée d'Unterlinden, Colmar. – Picasso. Two Concurrent Retrospective Exhibitions. Art Center Museum, Fort Worth (TX); Dallas Museum of Fine Arts, Dallas (TX) (Cat. by D. Cooper). –

Meistergraphik. Wallraf-Richartz-Museum, Cologne. – 70 gravures, 1905–1965. Musée des Beaux-Arts, Le Havre. – Sculpture, Ceramics, Graphic Work. Tate Gallery, London (Cat. by R. Penrose et al.). – The Sculpture of Picasso. The Museum of Modern Art, New York (Cat. by M. Wheeler). – Picasso 1966–1967. Saidenberg Gallery, New York. – **1968**: Graphik 1904–1966. Augsburg (Cat. by R. Biedermann). – Das Spätwerk. Malerei und Zeichnung seit 1944. Staatliche Kunsthalle Baden-Baden, Baden-Baden (Cat. by K. Gallwitz and D.-H. Kahnweiler). – Pinturas, dibujos, grabados. Sala Gaspar, Barcelona. – Las Meninas. Museu Picasso, Barcelona (Cat. by J.A. Lasarte). – 347 graphische Blätter aus dem Jahre 1968. Berlin, Hamburg, Cologne (Cat. by H.E. Killy). – Picasso in Chicago. The Art Institute of Chicago, Chicago (IL) (Cat. by J. Speyer et al.). – 347 Engravings, 16/3/68 – 5/10/68. The Art Institute of Chicago, Chicago (IL). – Museum Louisiana, Humlebæk – Donación Sabartés, de bibliografia y de obra gráfica de Picasso. Museo Provincial de Bellas Artes, Málaga. – I Picasso Atelie. Malmö Museum, Malmö. – Cranach und Picasso. Nuremberg (Cat. by H. Hutter, D.-H. Kahnweiler et al.). – Dessins 1966–1967. Galerie Louise Leiris, Paris. – 347 gravures. Galerie Louise Leiris, Paris. – Pablo Picasso. Österreichisches Museum für angewandte Kunst, Vienna (Cat. by H. Hutter). – Das graphische Werk. Kunsthaus Zürich, Zurich (Cat. by A. Baumann et al). – **1969**: Picasso d'aujourd'hui. Dessins, gravures, linóleums, livres illustrés, sculptures, céramiques. Musée Réattu, Arles. – Maler und Modell. Staatliche Kunsthalle Baden-Baden, Baden-Baden. – Museo de Arte Moderno, Barcelona. – 347 graphische Blätter aus dem Jahre 1968. Akademie der Künste, Berlin; Kunsthalle, Hamburg; Kunstverein, Cologne (Cat. by F. Ahlers-Hestermann, A. and P. Crommelynck and F.A. Baumann). – Figures peintes entre le 30 janvier et le 7 mai 1969. Galerie Cahiers d'Art, Paris. – Picasso aujourd'hui, œuvres recentes. Galerie Rosengart, Lucerne. – Graphik von 1904–1968. Haus der Kunst, Munich. – Dunkelmann Gallery, Toronto. – Gravures récentes. Galerie Madoura, Vallauris. – Pablo Picasso. 347 graphische Blätter vom 16.3.1968 bis 5.10.1968. Kunsthaus Zürich, Zurich. – **1970**: Pablo Picasso, 1969–1970. Palais des Papes, Avignon (Cat. by Y. Zervos). – 347 grabados 16.III.68/5.IX.68. Sala Gaspar, Barcelona. – Picasso Grafik. Kunsthalle Bielefeld, Bielefeld (Cat. by U. Weisner). – The Cubist Epoch. Los Angeles County Museum of Art, Los Angeles (CA); The Metropolitan Museum of Art, New York (Cat. by D. Cooper). – Four Americans in Paris: The Collections of Gertrude Stein and Her Family. The Museum of Modern Art, New York (Cat. by J.B. Hightower and M. Potter). – Picasso: Master Printmaker. The Museum of Modern Art, New York. – Saidenberg Gallery, New York. – Hommage à Christian et Yvonne Zervos. Grand Palais, Paris. – Picasso for Portland. Portland Art Museum, Portland (OR). – 347 x Picasso, graphische Blätter aus dem Jahre 1968. Württembergischer Kunstverein, Stuttgart. – 347 gravures. Maison de la Culture, Toulouse and Caen; Institute of Contemporary Arts, London; Kunstverein, Regensburg and Stuttgart; Palazzo dei Diamanti, Ferrara; The Art Institute of Chicago, Chicago (IL); Museum, Helsinki. – Gravures récentes. Galerie Madoura, Vallauris. – **1971**: Obras de Picasso de la Colección Hugué. Museu Picasso, Barcelona. – Pinturas y dibujos. Sala Gaspar, Barcelona. – 150 grabados. Museo de Bellas Artes, Caracas. – Gravures, dessins. Musée de l'Athénée, Geneva. – 25 œuvres, 25 années 1947–1971. Hommage à Pablo Picasso pour son 90 anniversaire. Galerie Rosengart, Lucerne. – Picasso: Olii, gouaches, pastelli, chine, disegni dal 1921 al 1971. Galleria Levi, Milan (Cat. by P. Chiari). – 172 Radierungen des Sommers 1968 ("Le thèâtre amoureux"). Museum Villa Stuck, Munich. – Homage to Picasso for His 90th Birthday. Marlborough Gallery and Saidenberg Gallery, New York (Cat. by J. Richardson). – Gertrude Stein, Picasso and Gris. National Gallery, Ottawa. – Picasso 90. Exposición-homenaje. Sala Pelaires, Palma de Mallorca. – Picasso dans les Musées soviétiques. Musée d'Art Moderne, Paris (Cat. by J. Leymarie). – Dessins en noir et en couleurs. Galerie Louise Leiris, Paris. – Galerie Knoedler, Paris. – Galerie Berggruen, Paris. – From Cézanne to Picasso. National Museum, Tokyo. – Women. Engravings, 1904–1968. Tokyo Art Gallery, Tokyo. – Zeichnungen und farbige Arbeiten. Kunstmuseum, Winterthur; Galerie Beyeler, Basel; Wallraf-Richartz-Museum, Cologne. – **1972**: Galerie Veranneman, Brussels. – 347 Engravings. The Waddington Galleries, London. – Œuvre gravée 1904–1968. Galerie Municipal, Montreuil. – Galerie Vercel, Paris. – 172 Dessins en noir et en couleurs. Galerie Louise Leiris, Paris. – Gravures 1946–1972. Musée d'Art et d'Histoire, Neuchâtel. – Picasso in the Collection of The Museum of Modern Art, New York (Cat. by W. Rubin, E.L. Johnson and R. Castleman). – **1973**: Hommage à Picasso. Musée Réattu, Arles. – Picasso, 1970–1972. Palais des Papes, Avignon (Cat. by R. Char). – Les estampes céramiques de Picasso. Avignon. – Aguafuertes. Sala Gaspar, Barcelona. – Druckgraphik und illustrierte Bücher. Kunstmuseum Basel, Basel. – Pablo Picasso 1881–1973.

Gedächtnisausstellung. Kunsthalle Bremen, Bremen (Cat. by J. Schultze and A.-M. Winther). – Picasso et la paix. Musée Municipal d'Art Moderne, Céret. – Homage to Picasso (1881–1973). R.S. Johnson International Gallery, Chicago (IL) (Cat. by D.-H. Kahnweiler et al.). – In Memoriam Pablo Picasso. Cleveland Museum of Art, Cleveland (OH). – Une collection Picasso. Galerie Jan Krugier, Geneva. – Picasso in Hannover. Gemälde, Zeichnungen, Keramik. Übersicht über das graphische Werk. Kunstverein, Hanover (Cat. by H.R. Leppien). – Homage à Picasso. Kestner-Gesellschaft, Hanover (Cat. by J. Merkert and W. Schmied). – Picasso. His Graphic Work in the Israel Museum Collection. Jerusalem. – Œuvre gravée, 1904–1968. Musée des Beaux-Arts, Metz. – Gravures de Picasso. Musée Fabre, Montpellier. – 156 gravures récentes. Galerie Louise Leiris, Paris. – Picasso 100 estampes originales 1900–1937. Galerie Guiot, Paris. – **1974**: Pablo Picasso: Das graphische Werk. Hamburg, Frankfurt am Main and Stuttgart (Cat. by B. Rau). – Henie-Onstad Kunstsenter, Hovikodden. – Picasso und die Antike. Badisches Landesmuseum, Karlsruhe; Städtische Galerie, Frankfurt am Main (Cat. by J. Thimme). – Contemporary Art Museum, Seoul. – Pablo Picasso. From the Blue Period to the Last Years. Fuji Television Gallery, Tokyo (Cat. by S. Shinichi et al.). – **1976**: Picasso aus dem Museum of Modern Art New York und Schweizer Sammlungen. Kunstmuseum Basel, Basel (Cat. by A. Straumann, F. Meyer, W. Rubin et al.). – Las Meninas. Museu Picasso, Barcelona. – **1977**: Fundación Juan March, Madrid; Museu Picasso, Barcelona. – City Museum, Tokyo; Central Museum of Architecture and Culture, Fukuoka; National Contemporary Art Museum, Kyoto. – **1978**: Acht Werke der letzten zwanzig Jahre seines Lebens. Haus am Rhyn, Lucerne. – 156 Gravures et leurs 87 états préparatoires. Centre culturel du Marais, Paris. – Picasso, sa collection personnelle. Musée du Louvre, Paris. – 156 graphische Blätter 1970–1972. Kunsthaus Zürich, Zurich. – **1979**: Picasso érotico. Museu Picasso, Barcelona. – Die letzten Werke (1964–1972). Kunstmuseum Basel, Basel. – Graphische Werke 1904–1972. Galerie Kornfeld, Bern. – Zeichnungen und Collagen des Kubismus. Picasso-Braque-Gris. Kunsthalle, Bielefeld (Cat. by U. Weisner). – Master Drawings by Picasso. Fogg Art Museum, Cambridge (MA). – His Last Etchings: A Selection (1969–1972). R.S. Johnson International, Chicago (IL). – Letzte graphische Blätter 1970–1972. Kestner-Gesellschaft, Hanover (Cat. by C.-A. Haenlein). – Donation Rosengart. Haus am Rhyn, Lucerne. – Œuvres reçues en paiement des droits de succession. Grand Palais, Paris (Cat. by D. Bozo). – **1980**: Darrers gravats de Picasso. Museu Picasso, Barcelona. – Picasso gravats – lithografias. Sala Gaspar, Barcelona. – Letzte graphische Blätter 1970–1972. Galerie der Hochschule für Graphik und Buchkunst, Leipzig. – Picasso's Picasso. An Exhibition from the Musée Picasso, Paris. Arts Council of Great Britain, London. – Picasso from the Musée Picasso, Paris. Minneapolis (MN). – Pablo Picasso. A Retrospective. The Museum of Modern Art, New York (Cat. by W.S. Rubin). – Peintures 1901–1971. Galerie Claude Bernard, Paris. – The Seibu Museum of Art. Tokyo. – Picasso, The Saltimbanques. National Gallery of Art, Washington (DC) (Cat. by E.A. Carmean Jr.). – **1981**: Picasso, tout l'œuvre linogravé. Museum Granet, Aix-en-Provence. – Picasso à Antibes. Musée Picasso, Antibes (Cat. by D. Giraudy). – Das Spätwerk. Themen 1964–1972. Kunstmuseum Basel, Basel (Cat. by C. Geelhaar, K. Levin, R. Häsli, F. Meyer, D. Koepplin). – Master Drawings by Picasso. Fogg Art Museum, Cambridge (MA) (cat. by G. Tinterow). – Die letzten graphischen Blätter, aus der Sammlung Ludwig, Aachen. Kupferstichkabinett der Staatlichen Kunstsammlungen, Dresden. – Picasso 347. Henie-Onstad Kunstsenter, Hovikodden. – Picasso fra Musée Picasso, Paris. Museum Louisiana, Humlebæk. – Picasso Graphics. Institut Français, London. – Guernica-Legado Picasso. Cason de Buen Retiro, Museo del Prado, Madrid. – Picasso y los toros. Museo de Bellas Artes, Málaga. – Pablo Picasso. Eine Ausstellung zum hundertsten Geburtstag. Werke aus der Sammlung Marina Picasso. Haus der Kunst, Munich (Cat. by W. Spies and al.). – Picasso Druckgraphik. Westfälisches Landesmuseum für Kunst und Kulturgeschichte, Münster. – The Avignon Paintings. The Pace Gallery, New York. – Dessins et gouaches 1899–1972. Galerie Louise Leiris, Paris. – Gouaches, lavis et dessins. Galerie Berggruen, Paris. – Pablo Picasso in der Staatsgalerie Stuttgart. Ausstellung zum 100. Geburtstag des Künstlers mit Leihgaben aus Sammlungen in Baden-Württemberg. Stuttgart (Cat. by D.-H. Kahnweiler, C. Lichtenstern, S. and H.C. Goeppert). – Opere da 1895 al 1971 dalla Collezione Marina Picasso. Palazzo Grassi, Venice (Cat. by G. Carandente). – Picasso in Wien. Bilder, Zeichnungen, Plastiken. Kulturamt der Stadt Wien, Rathaus Wien, Vienna. – **1982**: Rétrospective de l'œuvre gravé (1947–1968). Fondation Capa/Galerie Herbage, Cannes. – The Essential Cubism: Braque, Picasso & Their Friends, 1907–1920. The Tate Gallery, London (Cat. by D. Cooper and G. Tinterow). – Picasso y la Musica. Ministerio de cultura, Madrid (Cat. by F. Sopena-Ibanez). – Picasso,

347 immagini erotiche. Milan. – La pièce à musique de Mougins. Centre Culturel du Marais, Paris (Cat. by M. Guillaud). – **1983**: 117 gravats 1919–1968. Museu Picasso, Barcelona. – Plastiken. Nationalgalerie, Berlin; Kunsthalle, Düsseldorf (Cat. by W. Spies and C. Piot). – Picasso the Printmaker: Graphics from the Marina Picasso Collection. Dallas Museum of Art, Dallas (TX); The Detroit Institute of Art, Detroit (MI); The Denver Art Museum, Denver (Cat. by B. Baer). – Picasso. The Last Years, 1963–1973. The Solomon R. Guggenheim Museum, New York (Cat. by G. Schiff). – Picasso. Œuvres de la collection Jacqueline Picasso. Musée des Beaux-Arts, Nîmes. – Picasso. Masterpieces from the Marina Picasso Collection and from Museums in the USA and USSR. Tokyo and Kyoto. – Picasso, couleurs d'Espagne, couleurs de France, couleurs de vie. Toulouse. – **1984**: Der junge Picasso. Frühwerk und Blaue Periode. Kunstmuseum Bern, Bern (Cat. by J. Glaesemer and M. McCully). – Picasso. National Gallery of Victoria, Melbourne; Art Gallery of New South Wales, Sidney (Cat. by P. McCaughey, M. Plant, M. Holloway et al.). – Picasso, su ultima decada. Museo Rufino Tamayo, Mexico City. – The Last Years. Grey Art Gallery and Study Center, New York University, New York. – Donation Louise et Michel Leiris. Collection Kahnweiler-Leiris. Centre Georges Pompidou, Paris. – Picasso: 51 peintures 1904–1972. Galerie Louise Leiris, Paris (Cat. by M. Leiris). – L'œuvre gravé, 1899–1972. Musée des Arts Décoratifs, Paris. – **1985**: Sidste grafiska arbejder 1970–72. Nordjyllands Kunstmuseum, Aalborg. – Picasso Keramiek. s'-Hertogenbosch. – Picasso at Work at Home. Center for the Fine Art, Miami (FL). – Pablo Picasso. Rencontre à Montreal. Musée des Beaux-Arts. Montréal (Cat. by M. Jardot, J. Richardson, P. Théberge et al.). – Picasso Linoleum Cuts. The Metropolitan Museum of Art, New York (Cat. by W.S. Liebermann and L.D. McVinney). – **1986**: 60 originales. Sala Gaspar, Barcelona. – Picasso. Der Maler und seine Modelle. Galerie Beyeler, Basel. – Picasso. Druckgraphik, illustrierte Bücher, Zeichnungen, Collagen und Gemälde aus dem Sprengel Museum, Hanover (Cat. by M.M. Moeller). – Mon ami Picasso. Limoges. – Je suis le cahier. The Sketchbooks of Picasso. The Pace Gallery, New York; Academy of Arts, London. – Picasso en Madrid. Colección Jacqueline Picasso. Museo Español de Arte Contemporáneo, Madrid. – Picasso sculptures. Galerie Sapone, Nice. – Pastelle, Zeichnungen, Aquarelle. Kunsthalle, Tübingen; Kunstsammlung Nordrhein-Westfalen, Düsseldorf (Cat. by W. Spies). – **1987**: Picasso. Cubist Works from the Marina Picasso Collection. New York (Cat. by P. Daix). – Pablo Picasso. Gli ultimi anni 1968–1973. Rome (Cat. by B. Baer). – **1988**: Picasso. Linograveur. Antibes, Martigny and Barcelona (Cat. by D. Giraudy and D. Bourgeos). – Picasso's Klassizismus. Werke 1914–1934. Kunsthalle Bielefeld, Bielefeld (Cat. by U. Weisner). – Picasso im Zweiten Weltkrieg 1939–1945. Museum Ludwig, Cologne (Cat. by S. Gohr, B. Baer, P. Daix et al.). – Neue Galerie der Stadt Linz, Linz. – Von Matisse bis Picasso: Hommage an Siegfried Rosengart. Kunstmuseum Luzern, Lucerne (Cat. by M. Kunz, A. Rosengart, W. Schmalenbach et al.). – Picasso en Madrid: Colección Jacqueline Picasso. Museo Español de Arte Contemporáneo, Madrid (Cat. by M. de Zayas). – Le dernier Picasso 1953–1972. Musée National d'Art Moderne, Centre Georges Pompidou, Paris; Late Picasso: Paintings, Sculpture, Drawings, Prints 1953–1972. The Tate Gallery, London (Cat. by M. Leiris, J. Richardson, M.-L. Bernadac et al.). – Les Demoiselles d'Avignon. Musée Picasso, Paris (Cat., 2 vols., by H. Seckel, B. Leal, L. Steinberg, W. Rubin, P. Daix et al.). – Picasso. The Late Drawings. New York (Cat. by J. Hoffeld). – **1989**: The Artist Before Nature. Auckland City Art Gallery, Auckland. – Picasso linogravador. Museu Picasso, Barcelona. – Picasso and Braque: Pioneering Cubism. The Museum of Modern Art, New York; Kunstmuseum Basel, Basel (Cat. by W. Rubin). – Peintures et dessins 1932–1972. Galerie Louise Leiris, Paris. – Picasso. Dibujos 1898–1917. Valencia (Cat. by M.T. Ocana and P. Daix). – **1990**: De Pablo a Jacqueline. Pintures, dibuixos, escultures i obra gràfica 1954–1971. Museu Picasso, Barcelona. – Portraits. Prefectural Museum of Art, Okayama; Prefectural Museum of Art, Kumamoto; Prefectural Museum of Art, Shizvoka; Navio Museum of Art, Osaka; The Museum of Fine Arts, Gifu. – Picasso. Une nouvelle dation. Grand Palais, Paris; Musée Cantini, Marseilles; Galerie des Beaux-Arts, Bordeaux; Ancienne Douane, Strasbourg; Musée des Beaux-Arts, Calais; Musée de Picardie, Amiens. – **1991**: Picasso. La Provence et Jacqueline, Arles (Cat. by P. Daix). – Picasso Surrealismus. Werke 1925–1937. Kunsthalle Bielefeld, Bielefeld (Cat. by U. Weisner). – Picasso. Retratos de Jacqueline. Madrid. – Picasso in Italia. Verona.

Acknowledgements and Picture Credits

I would like to thank, also on the publisher's behalf, the museums and public collections, the galleries and private collectors, the archives and photographers and all others who have assisted me in the preparation of this monograph. In addition to the two museums with the largest Picasso collections, the Musée Picasso in Paris and the Museu Picasso in Barcelona, I am especially grateful to the galleries already mentioned in the preface, in particular Quentin Laurens, Galerie Louise Leiris, Paris, Galerie Beyeler, Basel, Galerie Rosengart, Lucerne, as well as to Jacqueline Picasso's daughter, Catherine Hutin-Blay, Paris. I also wish to thank the Service Photographique de la Réunion des Musées Nationaux, Paris, and Mme. Charton, Documentation Photographique des Collections du Musée National d'Art Moderne, Centre Georges Pompidou, Paris. The editor and publisher have made an intensive effort to obtain and provide compensation for the copyright to the photos on which the reproductions are based in accordance with legal provisions. Persons who may nevertheless have still claims are requested to contact the publisher. The owners of the works are noted in the captions unless they wished to remain anonymous or were not known to the editor. The editor would appreciate being made aware of any incomplete or incorrect information as well as of any changes which may have taken place in the meantime. The copyright for the photos of Picasso's private life is held as follows: page 2 and 696 br: Man Ray, © Juliet Man Ray; page 542: © Lucien Clergue, Arles; page 382: Robert Doisneau, © rapho, Paris; page 701 and 708 b: Brassaï, © Gilberte Brassaï, Paris; page 710 br: © Gjon Mili; page 711 b: Robert Capa, © Cornel Capa, New York; page 714 ar, 718f. and 721: © André Villers, Mougins, and Musée Réattu, Arles; page 715 ar: © Edward Quinn, Nice; page 715 ar and 716 r: © Roger Hauert; page 716 l: © Brian Brake; page 720 br, 724 and 725: © Catherine Hutin-Blay, Paris; page 726 b: © Elisabeth Atzinger, Saint Maximin La Ste. Bonne. I would like to take this opportunity to thank, in addition to the persons already mentioned in the imprint and preface, Uli Reißer, Antje Günther and Joachim Hellmuth, all in Munich, for their collaboration in the preparation of the book and at various stages of its creation. (Key to abbreviations: l = left, m = middle, a = above, r = right, b = bottom.)   I.F.W

ANTIBES, Photo Germain: 373, 349, 466 b.- ARLES, Lucien Clergue: 542.- Musée Réattu: 718/719, 721.- BARCELONE, Museu Picasso: 28, 29, 30 a, 31 a, 32 m, 34, 37 r, 40 r, 41, 44 b, 46, 47, 48, 49, 50/51, 52, 55 r, 90, 91, 543, 602.- BASEL, Öffentliche Kunstsammlung Basel, Kunstmuseum, (Colorphoto Hans Hinz, Allschwil): Frontispiece (Vol. I), 155 a, 201, 490/491.- Sammlung Beyeler, Galerie Beyeler and Archive Beyeler: 98, 142, 231 b, 310, 311, 334, 347, 351, 402, 428, 448 br, 470, 471, 475, 492–495, 498 b, 510, 511, 518, 557, 559 b, 560 a, 569, 600, 601, 649, 659.- ECUBLENS, Archive André Held: 95 l, 121, 145 r, 149, 165, 169 r, 187 ar, 191, 193 a, 196 a, 198/199, 213, 214, 241, 256 ar, 256 bl, 261 l, 264 b, 273 b, 277, 278 ar, 314 b, 315 a, 362 a, 364 a, 365, 366 r, 406 r, 417,

420 a, 429, 432 l, 433 ar, 464, 480 l, 481 r, 505.- FRANKFURT/MAIN, Richard Grübling: 26 b.- GRAZ, Akademische Druck- und Verlagsanstalt: 386, 391 (Repro. 15, 20, 21, 23), 393 (repro. 25, 29, 31), 395 (Repro. 36–42, 44).- HIROSHIMA, Hiroshima Museum of Art: 102 b.- LIEGE, Musée d'Art Moderne: 96/97.- LUCERNE, Collection Angela Rosengart, Galerie Rosengart and Archive Rosengart: 229, 284 a, 421, 424, 473, 483, 506 a, 507, 520, 530 a, 560 b, 572, 596, 639, 641, 646, 647, 650 r, 655, 661, 672.- MOSCOW, Pushkin Museum: 15 l, 60 b, 78, 84, 94 r, 126 a, 127 l, 128 a, 177 al, 184 a, 185 a, 208.- MUNICH, Bildarchiv Alexander Koch: 18 a, 42, 44 b, 45, 71, 355, 431, 503, 573, 580.-NEW YORK, Collection Mrs. Victor W. Ganz: 227 r, 285, 354.- Collection William A.M. Burden: 127 r.- NICE, Edward Quinn: 715 l.- PARIS, Archives d'UNESCO: 551.- Galerie Louise Leiris and Archives Photographiques Galerie Louise Leiris: 21, 108 b, 216, 263, 264 a, 316, 328, 330, 332, 422, 447, 450, 465, 472, 496, 512, 521 b, 526, 527, 529, 556 a, 597, 627, 632, 633, 634 b, 635, 636 a, 637, 638, 642, 643, 651, 656, 657, 658, 662, 663, 667 ar, 667 b, 668, 670, 671, 674–676, 679. - Catherine Hutin-Blay: 717 am, 717 b, 720 br, 724, 725.-Musée d'Art Moderne de la Ville de Paris: 87, 231.- Musée National d'Art Moderne, Centre Georges Pompidou: 2, 192, 217, 222, 223, 226, 230 a, 239, 254/255, 297, 313, 336, 533 a, 631, 701.- Musée Picasso (Photo: Service Photographique de la Réunion des Musées Nationaux): 11, 20 b, 35, 80, 86 a, 99, 132 l, 137, 145 l, 158 l, 205, 207, 209 a, 215, 218, 219, 220, 221, 225, 233 al, 236, 237, 240, 242, 244, 249, 262, 265, 269 a, 271, 275 b, 280, 281, 287, 302, 303, 304, 305, 309, 312, 313, 320 al, 320 b, 321 a, 321 br, 322, 323, 324, 325, 326 br, 329, 331, 333, 337 b, 338 a, 341, 342, 343, 344, 345, 358, 359, 360, 361, 364, 368, 369, 370, 375, 376 b, 378, 379, 404, 406 l, 409, 412, 413, 416 r, 425, 426/427, 432 l, 435, 437 b, 443, 444, 449 a, 455 r, 468 a, 469 b, 477 b, 478/479, 484–486, 488, 489, 499, 500/501, 502, 508 l, 516, 544/545, 558 a, 566, 567 l, 612, 648 a, 664–666, 667 al, 669, 677, 678.- Photographie Giraudon: 54 r, 268 b, 414, 423.- Rapho: 382.- PEISSENBERG, Artothek: 400/401.- PHILADELPHIA, Philadelphia Museum of Art: 155 b.- PRAGUE, Národni Galerie: 158 r, 194 r, 576 b.- SAINT MAXIMIN LA STE. BONNE, Elisabeth Atzinger: 726 b.- ST. PETERSBOURG, Ermitage: 15 r, 85, 93 a, 95 r, 106 ar, 131, 135 l, 166 a, 167 l, 168, 171, 172 a, 173 b, 174, 175 a, 175 br, 177 br, 180, 182 al, 183 ar, 190 b, 206, 212 r, 228, 233 b.- STUTTGART, Staatsgalerie Stuttgart: 197, 462 a, 538/539.- TOKYO, Bridgestone Museum of Art: 260, 289 ar.- Fuji Television Gallery: 8.- WASHINGTON, National Gallery of Art: 129.- Collection Eisenstein: 130 r.- Collection Mr. and Mrs. David Lloyd Kreeger: 238 b. Additional documents were received from the collections mentioned in the captions as well as the editor's Picasso archive, Alling, the archive of the former Walther & Walther publishing house, Alling, the archive of Benedikt Taschen publishing house, Cologne, and the archive of the author Carsten-Peter Warncke, Tübingen.

Index of names